THE PAPERS OF ULYSSES S. GRANT

THE PAPERS OF

ULYSSES S. GRANT

Volume 5: April 1– August 31, 1862

Edited by John Y. Simon

ASSISTANT EDITOR

Thomas G. Alexander

SOUTHERN ILLINOIS UNIVERSITY PRESS

CARBONDALE AND EDWARDSVILLE

FEFFER & SIMONS, INC.

LONDON AND AMSTERDAM

Library of Congress Cataloging in Publication Data

Grant, Ulysses Simpson, Pres. U.S., 1822–1885.
    The papers of Ulysses S. Grant.

    Prepared under the auspices of the Ulysses S. Grant Association.
Bibliographical footnotes.
    CONTENTS: v. 1. 1837–1861.—v. 2. April–September 1861.
—v. 3. October 1, 1861–January 7, 1862.—v. 4. January 8–March
31, 1861.—v. 5. April 1–August 31, 1862.
    1. Grant, Ulysses Simpson, Pres. U.S., 1822–1885. I. Simon,
John Y., ed.
E660.G74   973.8'2'0924 [B]   67–10725
ISBN 0-8093-0636-0 (v. 5)

To Allan Nevins (1890–1971)

Contents

Maps and Illustrations

=====

Introduction

===

O~N~ APRIL 1, 1862, Major General Ulysses S. Grant commanded an army of more than 44,000 men, stationed on the Tennessee River, ready to move against the Confederate railroad center of Corinth, Mississippi, as soon as Major General Don Carlos Buell arrived with his Army of the Ohio. Most of the army was stationed at Pittsburg Landing, Tenn., where Grant had formally established his headquarters, but Grant himself remained at Savannah, nine miles away, to arrange a meeting with Buell. From Pittsburg Landing on April 5, Brigadier General William T. Sherman wrote: "I do not apprehend anything like an attack on our position." Forwarding this message to his superior, Major General Henry W. Halleck, Grant added that he had "scarsely the faintest idea of an attack." As Grant wrote, a Confederate army of nearly equal size was making final preparations for an attack the next morning.

Thus Grant was not even on the field when the battle of Shiloh began. Surprised and disorganized, the U.S. troops fell back to the Tennessee River; yet the next day, aided by the first of Buell's troops to arrive, Grant pushed the Confederates from the field with heavy losses. Controversy soon hung over the field like battle-smoke, with Confederates claiming victory, Buell and his commanders claiming to have rescued Grant's defeated army, and much public opinion aroused about the great bloodshed of the two-day battle. Grant's detractors emphasized unpreparedness, while his defenders emphasized resilience.

A few days after the battle, Halleck arrived to take personal command of a mighty force composed of the armies of Grant, Buell, and Major General John Pope. For nearly three weeks Halleck organized his army; for one month he slowly advanced across the twenty miles separating Pittsburg Landing from Corinth. Gradually separated from active command while Halleck organized, then given the barren post of second-in-command during the advance on Corinth, Grant became increasingly dissatisfied, and finally resolved "to ask either full restoration to duty, according to my rank, or to be relieved entirely from further duty." Although Grant considered leaving the army, his respect for Halleck, the encouraging advice of Sherman, and the promise of an eventual separate command influenced him to remain.

Halleck's slow advance on Corinth was practically bloodless, and then Beauregard evacuated the city. With so little news from the western armies, newspapers continued to refight the battle of Shiloh. With his deep aversion to public controversy, Grant was appalled when Jesse Grant forwarded a private letter from his son to the *Cincinnati Commercial*. Grant was determined to maintain public silence, even though, as he told his wife, "I have been so shockingly abused that I sometimes think it almost time to defend myself." Undergoing one of the dramatic reversals of fortune so frequent in his life, Grant maintained his customary equanimity and composure, and could even be somewhat jaunty, as in writing home: "We are all well and me as sober as a deacon no matter what is said to the contrary."

On June 21, Grant left Corinth for his own command, in recently captured Memphis, where he found scope for his energies in governing a sullen city, supporting an expedition on the White River in Arkansas, and guarding miles of vulnerable railroad track against marauding Confederates. After less than three weeks in Memphis came another dramatic shift in fortune. Halleck was called to Washington as general-in-chief, and Grant inherited a vast domain of responsibility stretching from southern Illinois to northern Mississippi, from the Tennessee River to the Mississippi River.

This vast area represented a generous share of all Confederate territory then under U.S. control. Grant inherited the railroads Halleck had been so busily repairing along with the obligation to keep them open, and had to guard miles of lines against an enemy with every offensive advantage. Surveying Grant's position, Confederate General Braxton Bragg came to the conclusion that he could afford to take half his army east to oppose Buell's drive on Chattanooga. This hardly improved Grant's position, for his lines remained as long as ever, while his army was diminished by calls for more troops for Buell. Grant later recalled the defensive summer of 1862 as "the most anxious period of the war."

We are indebted to W. Neil Franklin, C. Percy Powell, and Karl L. Trever for searching the National Archives; to Barbara Long for maps; to Eleanore Schmeck, Harriet Simon, and Susan Stover for typing; to Stephen L. Bell, Janet Bridges, Margaret Dwight, Robert H. Forsyth, Jr., Dennis O'Connor, Dolly Springer, and Marcia Swider, graduate students at Southern Illinois University, for research assistance; and to Edgar F. Raines, Jr., graduate student at the University of Wisconsin, for research assistance.

Financial support for the Ulysses S. Grant Association for the period during which this volume was prepared came from Southern Illinois University and the National·Historical Publications Commission. The latter also provided the fellowship which brought Thomas G. Alexander from Brigham Young University to spend one year with the Grant Association as assistant editor.

JOHN Y. SIMON

October 2, 1972

Editorial Procedure

1. Editorial Insertions

A. Words or letters in roman type within brackets represent editorial reconstruction of parts of manuscripts torn, mutilated, or illegible.

B. [. . .] or [— — —] within brackets represent lost material which cannot be reconstructed. The number of dots represents the approximate number of lost letters; dashes represent lost words.

C. Words in *italic* type within brackets represent material such as dates which were not part of the original manuscript.

D. Other material crossed out is indicated by ~~cancelled type~~.

E. Material raised in manuscript, as "4th," has been brought in line, as "4th."

2. Symbols Used to Describe Manuscripts

AD	Autograph Document
ADS	Autograph Document Signed
ADf	Autograph Draft
ADfS	Autograph Draft Signed
AES	Autograph Endorsement Signed
AL	Autograph Letter
ALS	Autograph Letter Signed
D	Document
DS	Document Signed
Df	Draft
DfS	Draft Signed

ES   Endorsement Signed
LS   Letter Signed

3. Military Terms and Abbreviations

Act.	Acting
Adjt.	Adjutant
AG	Adjutant General
AGO	Adjutant General's Office
Art.	Artillery
Asst.	Assistant
Bvt.	Brevet
Brig.	Brigadier
Capt.	Captain
Cav.	Cavalry
Col.	Colonel
Co.	Company
C.S.A.	Confederate States of America
Dept.	Department
Gen.	General
Hd. Qrs.	Headquarters
Inf.	Infantry
Lt.	Lieutenant
Maj.	Major
Q. M.	Quartermaster
Regt.	Regiment or regimental
Sgt.	Sergeant
USMA	United States Military Academy, West Point, N.Y.
Vols.	Volunteers

4. Short Titles and Abbreviations

ABPC	*American Book-Prices Current* (New York, 1895–)
CG	*Congressional Globe* Numbers following represent the Congress, session, and page.
J. G. Cramer	Jesse Grant Cramer, ed., *Letters of Ulysses S. Grant to his Father and his Youngest Sister, 1857–78* (New York and London, 1912)
DAB	*Dictionary of American Biography* (New York, 1928–36)

Garland | Hamlin Garland, *Ulysses S. Grant: His Life and Character* (New York, 1898)

HED | *House Executive Documents*

HMD | *House Miscellaneous Documents*

HRC | *House Reports of Committees* Numbers following *HED, HMD,* or *HRC* represent the number of the Congress, the session, and the document.

Ill. AG Report | J. N. Reece, ed., *Report of the Adjutant General of the State of Illinois* (Springfield, 1900)

Lewis | Lloyd Lewis, *Captain Sam Grant* (Boston, 1950)

Lincoln, Works | Roy P. Basler, Marion Dolores Pratt, and Lloyd A. Dunlap, eds., *The Collected Works of Abraham Lincoln* (New Brunswick, 1953–55)

Memoirs | *Personal Memoirs of U. S. Grant* (New York, 1885–86)

O.R. | *The War of the Rebellion: A Compilation of the Official Records of the Union and Confederate Armies* (Washington, 1880–1901)

O.R. (Navy) | *Official Records of the Union and Confederate Navies in the War of the Rebellion* (Washington, 1894–1927) Roman numerals following *O. R.* or *O. R.* (Navy) represent the series and the volume.

PUSG | John Y. Simon, ed., *The Papers of Ulysses S. Grant* (Carbondale and Edwardsville, 1967—)

Richardson | Albert D. Richardson, *A Personal History of Ulysses S. Grant* (Hartford, Conn., 1868)

SED | *Senate Executive Documents*

SMD | *Senate Miscellaneous Documents*

SRC | *Senate Reports of Committees* Numbers following *SED, SMD,* or *SRC* represent the number of the Congress, the session, and the document.

USGA Newsletter | *Ulysses S. Grant Association Newsletter*

Young | John Russell Young, *Around the World with General Grant* (New York, 1879)

5. Location Symbols

CSmH | Henry E. Huntington Library, San Marino, Calif.

CU-B | Bancroft Library, University of California, Berkeley, Calif.

DLC	Library of Congress, Washington, D.C. Numbers following DLC–USG represent the series and volume of military records in the USG papers.
DNA	National Archives, Washington, D.C. Additional numbers identify record groups.
IaHA	Iowa State Department of History and Archives, Des Moines, Iowa
I-ar	Illinois State Archives, Springfield, Ill.
IC	Chicago Public Library, Chicago, Ill.
ICarbS	Southern Illinois University, Carbondale, Ill.
ICHi	Chicago Historical Society, Chicago, Ill.
ICN	Newberry Library, Chicago, Ill.
IHi	Illinois State Historical Library, Springfield, Ill.
In	Indiana State Library, Indianapolis, Ind.
InHi	Indiana Historical Society, Indianapolis, Ind.
InNd	University of Notre Dame, Notre Dame, Ind.
InU	Indiana University, Bloomington, Ind.
KHi	Kansas State Historical Society, Topeka, Kan.
MH	Harvard University, Cambridge, Mass.
MHi	Massachusetts Historical Society, Boston, Mass.
MiD	Detroit Public Library, Detroit, Mich.
MiU-C	William L. Clements Library, University of Michigan, Ann Arbor, Mich.
MoSHi	Missouri Historical Society, St. Louis, Mo.
NHi	New-York Historical Society, New York, N.Y.
NjP	Princeton University, Princeton, N.J.
NjR	Rutgers University, New Brunswick, N.J.
NN	New York Public Library, New York, N.Y.
OClWHi	Western Reserve Historical Society, Cleveland, Ohio
OFH	Rutherford B. Hayes Library, Fremont, Ohio
OHi	Ohio Historical Society, Columbus, Ohio
OrHi	Oregon Historical Society, Portland, Ore.
PHi	Historical Society of Pennsylvania, Philadelphia, Pa.
PPRF	Rosenbach Foundation, Philadelphia, Pa.
RPB	Brown University, Providence, R.I.
TxHR	Rice University, Houston, Tex.

USG 3	Maj. Gen. Ulysses S. Grant 3rd, Clinton, N.Y.
USMA	United States Military Academy Library, West Point, N.Y.
ViU	University of Virginia, Charlottesville, Va.
WHi	State Historical Society of Wisconsin, Madison, Wis.

Chronology

April 1.   USG sent a reconnaissance under Brig. Gen. William T. Sherman from Pittsburg Landing, Tenn., to Eastport, Miss., and Chickasaw, Ala., on the Tennessee River to destroy C.S.A. batteries, but the expedition found the sites abandoned.

April 3.   Advance elements of Maj. Gen. Don Carlos Buell's Army of the Ohio neared Savannah, Tenn.

April 3.   C.S.A. Army of the Miss., under Gen. Albert Sidney Johnston, began to advance from Corinth, Miss., to attack USG at Pittsburg Landing.

April 4.   Pickets skirmished near Pittsburg Landing.

April 5.   Despite continued skirmishing at Pittsburg Landing, USG remained at Savannah to await the arrival of Buell. USG had "scarsely the faintest idea of an attack," but C.S.A. forces were preparing to attack the following day.

April 5.   Maj. Gen. George B. McClellan established siege lines at Yorktown, Va.

April 6.   Johnston, with some 40,000 troops, attacked at Shiloh Church, near Pittsburg Landing. USG hurried to the field from Savannah. When Johnston was killed, Gen. P. G. T. Beauregard succeeded to command. By the end of the day, U.S. forces had lost considerable ground and casualties were heavy.

APRIL 7. Aided by reinforcements from the Army of the Ohio under Buell, USG drove C.S.A. forces from the field in the concluding day of the battle of Shiloh.

APRIL 7. C.S.A. forces at Island No. 10 in the Mississippi River surrendered to Maj. Gen. John Pope.

APRIL 8. A reconnaissance from Pittsburg Landing under Sherman returned after encountering C.S.A. cav.

APRIL 11. Maj. Gen. Henry W. Halleck assumed command at Pittsburg Landing.

APRIL 11. Fort Pulaski, near Savannah, Ga., surrendered to U.S. forces.

APRIL 13. An expedition sent by USG destroyed a railroad bridge at Bear Creek in Ala.

APRIL 25. Maj. Gen. Charles F. Smith died.

APRIL 25. U.S. forces occupied New Orleans, La.

APRIL 27. USG's fortieth birthday.

APRIL 29. Halleck began to advance slowly against Corinth.

APRIL 30. USG was assigned as second-in-command to Halleck.

MAY 3. C.S.A. forces evacuated Yorktown.

MAY 9. C.S.A. forces evacuated Norfolk, Va.

MAY 11. USG asked Halleck "to be relieved from duty entirely or to have my position so defined that there can be no mistaking it."

MAY 18. Flag Officer David G. Farragut arrived with his fleet at Vicksburg, Miss.

MAY 25. C.S.A. Maj. Gen. Thomas J. Jackson defeated Maj. Gen. Nathaniel P. Banks at Winchester, Va.

MAY 30. Evacuating Corinth, C.S.A. troops pulled back to Tupelo, Miss.

MAY 31–JUNE 1. Battle of Seven Pines near Richmond, Va.

JUNE 3. C.S.A. forces began to evacuate Fort Pillow, Tenn., completing their withdrawal on June 5.

JUNE 6. Following a naval battle, U.S. forces captured Memphis, Tenn.

JUNE 10. USG was restored to command of the Army of the Tenn.

JUNE 17. Gen. Braxton Bragg replaced Beauregard in command.

JUNE 21. USG left Corinth to establish hd. qrs. at Memphis.

JUNE 23. USG arrived at Memphis.

JUNE 25. C.S.A. cav. derailed and captured a train near Germantown, Tenn.

JUNE 25. Seven Days battles began near Richmond.

JUNE 26. USG sent two regts. to reinforce an expedition on the White River in Ark.

JUNE 27. Pope assumed command of the Army of Va.

JUNE 28. Farragut's fleet ran the batteries at Vicksburg.

JUNE 30. C.S.A. forces attacked a U.S. wagon train at Rising Sun, Tenn.

JULY 1. Under authority from USG, publication of the *Memphis Avalanche* was suspended.

JULY 3. USG issued orders that losses caused by guerrillas would be recouped by levies on rebel sympathizers.

JULY 3. C.S.A. Maj. Gen. Sterling Price assumed command of the Army of the West.

JULY 10. USG issued orders to expel the families of C.S.A. soldiers and officials from Memphis.

JULY 11. Halleck was appointed gen.-in-chief.

JULY 11. Halleck ordered USG to report to Corinth.

JULY 13. USG and his family reached Columbus, Ky.

JULY 15. USG arrived at Corinth.

JULY 15. USG was ordered to send troops from Memphis to Maj. Gen. Samuel R. Curtis in Ark.

JULY 16. USG was assigned to command the districts of Cairo and Miss., the Army of the Miss., and the Army of the Tenn., as well as the District of West Tenn.

JULY 16. Halleck left Corinth.

JULY 17. USG was ordered to send the division of Maj. Gen. George H. Thomas to Buell.

JULY 17. Second Confiscation Act signed.

JULY 20. Sherman assumed command at Memphis.

JULY 22. Bragg decided to move half of his army to Chattanooga, Tenn.

JULY 25. USG banned the payment of gold and silver for cotton. This order was countermanded in Washington.

AUG. 8. USG ordered the arrest of the Memphis correspondent of the *Chicago Times*.

AUG. 9. Battle at Cedar Mountain, Va.

AUG. 12. Buell requested two divisions from USG.

AUG. 14. USG sent two divisions to Buell.

Aug. 18. Col. Rodney Mason surrendered Clarksville, Tenn., to rebel guerrillas.

Aug. 18. Rebel guerrillas captured and burned two steamboats on the Tennessee River.

Aug. 25. Maj. Gen. John A. McClernand was ordered to Springfield, Ill.

Aug. 29. Second battle of Manassas or Bull Run, Va., began. At its conclusion the next day, Pope's army had been defeated.

Aug. 30. C.S.A. cav. under Act. Brig. Gen. Frank C. Armstrong skirmished with U.S. forces near Bolivar, Tenn.

Aug. 31. Steamboat *W. B. Terry* was captured by rebel guerrillas on the Tennessee River.

Aug. 31. Armstrong skirmished at Medon, Tenn., and near Toone's Station, Tenn.

The Papers of Ulysses S. Grant
April 1–August 31, 1862

To Capt. Nathaniel H. McLean

———

Head Quarters, Dist. of West Ten.
Savanna, April 3d 1862

Capt. N. H. McLean
A. A. Gen. Dept. of the Mississippi,
St. Louis, Mo.
Capt.

Enclosed herewith I send you report of Col. Webster, Chief of Staff, who accompanied the gunboats up the river with the view of determining the practicability of destroying the railroad East of Corinth, without special danger of bringing on an engagement.[1]

There will be no great difficulty in going any place with the army now concentrated here but a battle will necessarily ensue at any point on the rail-roads touched.

A dispatch from the telegraph opperator is just in. He states that Gen. Nelson has arrived in sight. The advance will arrive probably on Saturday.[2]

The dispatch received does not state the number of miles out the telegraph wire is laid.

Nothing is learned from Corinth very reliable. Deserters occationally come in but all that can be learned from them that is reliable is that the force there is large and increasing.[3] They do not discribe the feeling of the men as atall hopeful, on the contrary say that many would desert if they could.

I have been engaged for the last two days reviewing the troops of this command. I find the men in excellent condition and as a general thing well clothed. Some however are still in the grey uniform and owing to the bad quality of clothing on hand are reluctint to draw other to replace that on hand.

I have already twenty-one batteries here which looks to me quite enough for the other force but if atal consistent with the public interest, and more Artillery is to be sent, I would ask that the 1st Ill. Artillery be sent, Col. Webster, Col. of the regiment, being here with me.

> very respectfully
> your obt. svt.
> U. S. GRANT
> Maj. Gen.

ALS, DNA, RG 94, War Records Office, Union Battle Reports. *O.R.*, I, x, part 1, 84–85.

1. On April 3, 1862, Col. Joseph D. Webster wrote to USG. "In obedience to your order of yesterday eveing, I visited the vicinity of Eastport and Chickasaw this forenoon, on the gun-boat Taylor, Capt. Gwin. The abandonment by the enemy of their batteries in that neighborhood, heretofore reported, seems to be permanent. There is no apparent difficulty in making a landing at any point this side of the shoals above Chickasaw which form the present limit of navigation for our gun-boats. Is it desirable to make that landing with our forces, and attempt the destruction of the Memphis and Charleston R. Road at its nearest approach to the river? The shortness of the distance is in favor of the idea. The considerations on the other side arise chiefly from the broken character of the ground over which the march would have to be made. The road running out from Eastport is understood to be a good one so far as transportation along it is concerned. But it is understood that it passes along a hollow or ravine—the hills on each side of which are abrupt, and would probably afford numerous positions which could be readily defended by a small force. This would make the progress along the route necessarily slow—probably sufficiently so to offset the gain in distance, besides causing loss of life without achieving *decisive* results. I apprehend that these considerations apply, with greater or less force to *any* route from the river to the rail road, starting from any point above *Hamburg*. Information received today seems to confirm the accounts heretofore given, and deemed reliable, of the country over which these routes would pass. Besides this, if the river continues to fall, Hamburg will, in a few days, be the head of navigation for our gun boats, whose services would be necessary to cover the debarkation of the troops. The enemy can hardly be so improvident as not to keep in readiness a large train of cars in readiness to throw a force to any threatened point of the line of Railroad. Suppose they send by express riders from Hamburg to Corinth notice of our forces having gone up. This notice will be received at Corinth in little more than an hour from the time of our passing. Would be the work of but a few minuts, to fill a train of 100 or 150 cars with troops, and start them in time to reach the point of our attack before us.—to reinforce the troops already there. The country in the vicinity of Corinth is understood, from reliable information, to be comparatively level. The woods are open—very free from undergrowth. I apprehend that a large, if not the principal, part of the enemys artificial defences, will consist in the rude 'abattis' so much employed heretofore. To dislodge them from this,

what means can be more effectual than a large artillery force, with plenty of shrap-nel and canister? Do not the means exist in this Military Department of making such an attack almost *certainly overpowering and decisive?* It would afford me great pleasure if your views of duty should coincide with my wishes, which constantly lead me to hope that several batteries of the 1st Illinois Light Artillery now at St. Louis, may be ordered here in time to connect the name of that Regiment with a decisive victory." ALS, DNA, RG 94, War Records Office, Union Battle Reports. *O.R.*, I, x, part 1, 85–86.

    2. April 5.

    3. On April 3, Brig. Gen. William T. Sherman wrote to Capt. John A. Rawlins. "I enclose herewith report of Col Taylor of his scout last night, and send in charge of a Guard with one of my aids Capt Taylor the two prisoners, one private Lammon of the 1st Co. Alabama Cavalry and the other a Citizen Dr Parker. Col Taylor is a most inteligent officer and is fully impressed with General Grants views relative to the unjust arrest of citizens. My orders to him were to molest no citizen farmer or mechanic whom he found at home or engaged in his usual legitimate pursuit, but this Dr. Parker he found at a farm house on his way out, and after wards found him beyond with attending circumstances to show he had given warning to other pickets whom I expected near Greers. My plan was to post in ambush Col Smiths Regiment of Zouaves at Greers on Lick Creek. They started at 8 P M last night with two excellent guides. The Cavalry of Col Taylor was to take the Corinth road & turn towards Greers. He executed his orders capturing one of the enemys pickets whom I send forthwith for General Grant to question as he is pretty inteligent. The Dr. Parker I advise should also be held prisoner for having given important information to the enemy. I have yet no reports from Col Smith and expect him back momentarily, when I will com-municate the result of his 'scout.' " ALS, DNA, RG 393, District of West Tenn., Letters Received. *O.R.*, I, x, part 2, 90. The report of Col. William H. H. Taylor, 5th Ohio Cav., is *ibid.*, part 1, 86. On April 3, Sherman wrote to his wife. "We are constantly in the presence of the enemys pickets, but I am satisfied that they will await our coming at Corinth or some point of the Charleston Road." ALS, InNd. On April 4, Sherman wrote to Thomas Ewing, Jr. "We have now here about 60 000 men of Ohio, Indiana & Illinois—We now daily expect the arrival of a large force overland from Nashville, and then I suppose we move against Corinth 19 miles distant   I have been within 9 miles and have a good idea of the country. The Roads are narrow, and lined with wood & undergrowth, much like the hills down hocking, and the trees are beginning to leave, which will increase the ambush. The enemy are at Corinth with detachments at all the stations along the Railroad. Our Pickets are in constant contact, but little execution done. When we move forward the first collision will occur at Monterey or Pea Ridge and from there all the way to Corinth." ALS, *ibid.*

To Brig. Gen. William Nelson

———

Head Quarters, Dist of West. Tenn.
Savanna, April 3rd 1862.

Gen. Wm Nelson
Commdg. 4th Division
Buell's Army.

Your advance has arrived here. All difficulties in our neighborhood will be remedied before your arrival.

I am &c U. S. Grant,
Major Genl. Commdg.

Copies, DLC-USG, V, 1, 2, 3, 9, 86; DNA, RG 393, USG Letters Sent. *O.R.*, I, x, part 2, 89.

To Commanding Officer, Paducah, Ky.

———

Head Quarters, Dist of West. Tenn.
Savanna, April 3rd 1862.

Commdg Officer
Paducah, Ky.

We are entirely out of coal here. Please send some at once.

U. S. Grant.
Major. Genl.

Copies, DLC-USG, V, 1, 2, 3, 86; DNA, RG 393, USG Letters Sent. On April 3, 1862, Col. Joseph D. Webster wrote to the q. m. or master of transportation, Paducah. "Please forward at once to this place a supply of Coal, as the supply is exhausted, and the want is, or course urgent. Send at once as much as you can by one tow boat." Copies, DLC-USG, V, 1, 2, 86; DNA, RG 393, USG Letters Sent.

To Capt. Algernon S. Baxter

———

Head Quarters, Dist of West. Tenn.
Pittsburg, April 3rd 1862.

CAPT. A. S. BAXTER
CHIEF QR. MASTER OF THE DIST.

You will retain the Steamer "Iatan" as a Commissary Boat for the 6th Division, Brig. Gen. B. M. Prentiss, Commanding, unless there should be some good reason for not doing so.

U. S. GRANT.
Major. Gen. Commdg.

Copies, DLC-USG, V, 1, 2, 86; DNA, RG 393, USG Letters Sent.

To Julia Dent Grant

———

Savanna, April 3d 1862

DEAR JULIA,

Letters from you drop along occationally, generally two or three at a time; sometimes one will be three weeks old whilst another will come in as many days.

I have received three written from Louisville one of them by Charles Page.[1] I am very glad you are having a pleasant visit. I wish I could make a visit anywhere for a week or two. It would be a great relief not to have to think for a short time. Soon I hope to be permitted to move from here and when I do there will probably be the greatest battle fought of the War. I do not feel that there is the slightest doubt about the result and therefore, individually, feel as unconcerned about it as if nothing more than a review was to take place. Knowing however that a terrible sacrifice of life must take place I feel conserned for my army and their friends at home.

It will be impossible for you to join me at present. There are constantly ladies coming up here to see their husbands and consequencely destroying the efficiency of ~~their~~ the army until I have determined to publish an order entirely excluding females from our lines. This is ungallant but necessary.

Mr. & Miss Safford were up here and returned a few days ago. I sent my watch by him to be expressed to you. I want you to keep it and not leave it with anyone els. I sent for a plain silver watch for myself. There would be no great danger in keeping the other but if it should be lost I never could forgive myself. I want to preserve it to the last day of my life, and want my children to do the same thing, in remembrance of poor Simp. who carried it in his lifetime.

Kiss Jess & Buck for me, and your cousin also, I mean the young lady,[2] if you want.[3] Remember me kindly to Uncle & Aunt Page[4]

ULYS.

ALS, DLC-USG.

1. Charles A. Page of Louisville, Ky., the son of Samuel K. Page and Emily Wrenshall Page, was listed in the 1860 U. S. Census as thirty-seven years of age, no occupation given, with real estate valued at $40,000 and personal estate at $10,000.

2. The 1860 U. S. Census listed two young ladies, Ellen Page, age twenty, and Dellia Page, age eighteen, in the home of Samuel K. Page. Dellia apparently died in Dec., 1861. Letter of Samuel K. Page, July 18, 1862, to postmaster, New Hampton, N. H., copy, The Filson Club, Louisville, Ky.

3. Three lines crossed out and illegible.

4. Emily Wrenshall Page, then sixty-two years old, born in Pittsburgh, Pa., was the fourth of seven children born to John and Mary Wrenshall, who had come from England to Philadelphia in 1794. Her older sister, Ellen Bray Wrenshall Dent, was the mother of Julia Dent Grant. Josiah H. Shinn, "John Wrenshall, Julia Dent and Ulysses S. Grant," *New York Genealogical and Historical Record*, 34, 28 (April, 1903), 97–98. She married Samuel K. Page, of N. H., listed in the 1860 U. S. Census as a retired farmer living in Louisville, age sixty-two, with real estate valued at $81,000 and personal estate of $20,000. Page had been listed in Louisville city directories since 1836 with occupations including trader, builder, and farmer. Of the thirteen children born to the Pages, only three were still living in 1862: Charles, Edward (twenty-seven or twenty-eight years old), and Ellen. Information supplied by James R. Bentley, The Filson Club.

To Brig. Gen. William T. Sherman

———

> Head Quarters, Dist of West. Tenn.
> Pittsburg, April 4th 1862.

GEN. W. T. SHERMAN
COMMDG 5TH DIVISION
GEN:

Information just received would indicate that the enemy are sending ~~in~~ a force to Purdy, and it may be with a view to attack Gen. Wallace at Crumps Landing. I have directed Gen. W. H. L. Wallace, Commdg 2nd Division, temporarily, to reinforce Gen. L. Wallace in case of an attack with his entire Division, although, I look for nothing of the kind, but it is best to be prepared.

I would direct, therefore, that you advise your advance guards to keep a sharp look out for any movement in that direction, and should such a thing be attempted, give all the support of your Division, and Gen. Hurlbut's if necessary. I will return to Pittsburg at an early hour tomorrow, and will ride out to your camp.

> I am, Gen, Very Respectfully
> Your Obt Servant.
> U. S. GRANT.
> Major. Gen. Commdg

Copies, DLC-USG, V, 1, 2, 3, 86; DNA, RG 393, USG Letters Sent. *O.R.*, I, x, part 2, 91. On April 4, 1862, Maj. Gen. Lewis Wallace, Crump's Landing, wrote to Capt. John A. Rawlins. "The news of the reinforcement of the rebel troops at Purdy is confirmed. There are now eight Regts of Infantry, and twelve hundred Cavalry at that town, with an equal if not larger body at Bethel, four miles back of it. The object of the movement is not known, as a measure of precaution I would respectfully ask the General to hasten down to me the Batteries newly assigned to my Division to-wit: Stones & Margroffs. Be pleased also to send me such blanks of every description as you can conveniently spare." Copies, DLC-USG, V, 1, 2, 3, 86; DNA, RG 393, USG Letters Sent. *O.R.*, I, x, part 2, 90–91.

On the same day, Capt. John H. Hammond wrote to Rawlins. "About 5 o clock—intelligence arrived that the Rebel Cavalry had picked up 1 Lieut & 3 pickets   Fifty men were sent to examine into the matter   a Regiment supported them & finally the whole Brigade—Heavy firing was heard to the right of our front, & say 5 cannon shots—Genl Sherman has gone to investigate ~~the investi-~~

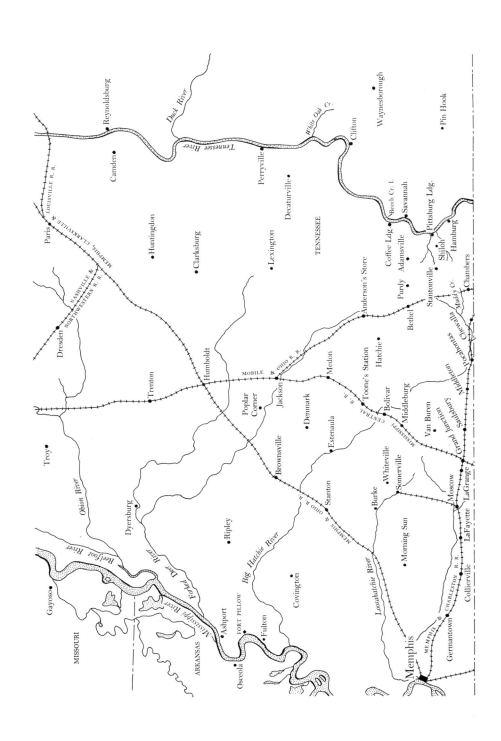

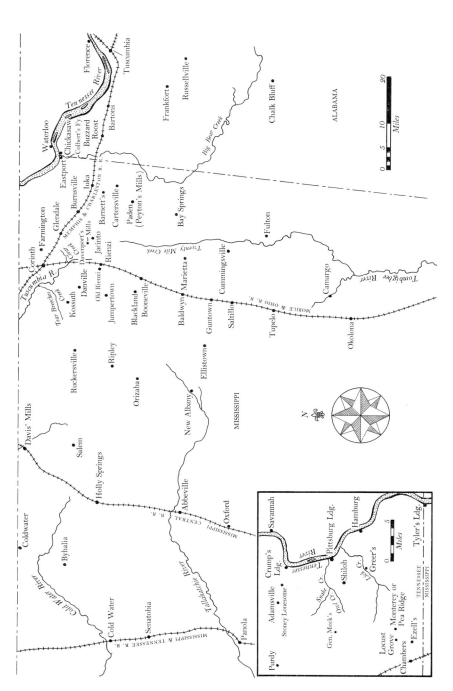

Grant's Area of Operations in middle 1862

gate the matter—Half an hour later, intelligence came that a considerable number of the enemy had appeared on our right at Meeks house, said to be 2000—I sent word to Genl Sherman & then to Genls McClernand & Prentiss—Orders have just arrived to do this, from Genl Sherman, & it being done—I have collected orderlies & await orders   No firing has been heard during the last half hour" Copy, DNA, RG 94, Generals' Papers and Books, William T. Sherman, Letters Sent.

To Brig. Gen. William H. L. Wallace

————

Head Quarters Dist of West. Tenn.
Pittsburg, April 4th 1862

BRIG. GEN. W. H. L WALLACE
COMMDG. 2ND DIVISION

Please send out order immediately to have Stones[1] and Magroffs batteries join Major Gen L. Wallace's command at Crump's Landing, at an early hour tomorrow.

These are new Batteries that have been sent up recently and I do not know where they have been temporarily assigned. It is believed that the enemy are reinforceing at Purdy, and it may be necessary to reinforce Gen. Wallace to avoid his being attacked by a superior force. Should you find danger of this sort, reinforce him, at once, with your entire Division.

I am, Genl, Very Respectfully
Your Obt Servant.
U. S. GRANT.
Major. Gen. Commdg.

Copies, DLC-USG, V, 1, 2, 3, 86; DNA, RG 393, USG Letters Sent. *O.R.*, I, x, part 2, 91.

1. Battery K, 1st Mo. Light Art., commanded by Capt. George H. Stone, arrived at Pittsburg Landing on March 16, 1862.

To Maj. Gen. Henry W. Halleck

———

Savanna April 5th 1862.

Maj Gen H W Halleck St Louis Mo

The Main force of the enemy is at Corinth, with troops at different points East ~~also at Bethel Jackson & Humbolt are~~ Small Garrisons are also at Bethel, Jackson and Humboldt. The numbers at these places seem to constantly change   The Number of the enemy at Corinth and within supporting distance of it cannot be far from 80.000 men. Information obtained through deserters place their force west at 200.000. One Division of Buell's column arrived yesterday. Gen Buell will be here himself to day. Some skirmishing took place ~~with~~ between our out Guards and enemy's, yesterday & day before

U S Grant
Maj Gen

Telegram, copies, DLC-USG, V, 4, 5, 7, 8, 9, 88; DNA, RG 393, USG Hd. Qrs. Correspondence. *O.R.*, I, x, part 2, 94.

To Maj. Gen. Henry W. Halleck

———

Head Quarters, Dist. of West Ten.
Savanna, April 5th 1862.

Maj. Gen. H. W. Halleck,
Comd.g Dept. of the Miss.
St. Louis, Mo.
Gen.

Just as my letter of yesterday to Capt. McLean, A. A. Gen. was finished notes from Gens. McClernand's & Sherman's A. A. Gens. were received stating that our outposts had been attacked by the enemy apparently in ~~in~~ conciderable force. I immediately went up but found all quiet. The enemy took two officers and four or five of our men prisoners and wounded four. We took eight prisoners and killed several. Number of the enemy wounded not know.

They had with them three pieces of Artillery and Cavalry and Infantry. How much cannot of course be estimated.

I have scarsely the faintest idea of an attack, (general one,) being made upon us but will be prepared should such a thing take place.

Gen. Nelsons Division has arrived. The other two of Gen. Buells Column will arrive to-morrow and next day.[1] It is my present intention to send them to Hamburg, some four miles above Pittsburg, when they all get here. From that point to Corinth the road is good and a junction can be formed with the troops from Pittsburg at almost any point.

Col. McPherson has gone with an escort to-day to examine the defensibility of the ground about Hamburg and to lay out the position of the Camps if advisable to occupy that place.

> I am Gen. very respectfully
> your obt. svt.
> U. S. Grant
> Maj. Gen.

ALS, DNA, RG 94, War Records Office, Union Battle Reports. *O.R.*, I, x, part 1, 89. USG enclosed a letter of April 5, 1862, in two parts from Brig. Gen. William T. Sherman. "All is quiet along my lines now. We are in the Act of exchanging Cavalry according to your order. The enemy has cavalry in our Front, and I think there are two Regts. of Infantry & 1 Battery of artillery about 6 miles out. I will send you in ten prisoners of War, and a Report of Last nights affair in a few minutes. Yr note is just read—I have no doubt that nothing will occur today more than some picket firing. The enemy is saucy, but got the worst of it yesterday, and will not press our pickets far—I will not be drawn out far unless with certainty of advantage, and I do not apprehend anything like an attack on our position" ALS, DNA, RG 94, War Records Office, Union Battle Reports. *O.R.*, I, x, part 2, 93–94. Also on April 5, Sherman wrote to Capt. John A. Rawlins. "I have the honor to report that yesterday about 3 P M, it was reported to me that the Lieut and 7 advance pickets had imprudently advanced from their posts & were captured. I ordered Maj Ricker of the 5 Ohio Cavalry to proceed rapidly to the Picket station, ascertain the truth & act according to circumstances. He reached the station found the picket had been captured as reported, and that a Company of Infantry sent by the Brigade Commander had gone forward in pursuit of some Cavalry. He rapidly advanced some two miles & found them engaged,

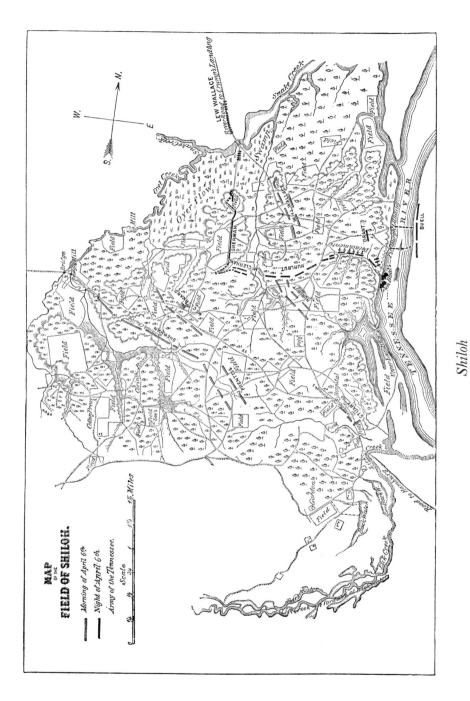

Shiloh

Reproduced from *Personal Memoirs of U. S. Grant* (New York, 1885–86), I, 341

charged the enemy & drove them along the Ridge Road till he met & received three discharges of artillery, When he very properly wheeled under Cover, and returned till he met me. As soon as I heard Artillery I advanced, with two Regts of Infantry and took position and remained until the scattered Companies of Infantry & Cavalry returned. This was after night. I infer that the enemy is in some considerable force at Pea Ridge, that yesterday morning they crossed a Brigade of two Regiments of Infantry, 1 Regiment of Cavalry, and 1 Battery of Field Artillery to the Ridge on which the Corinth Road lays. They halted the Infantry & artillery at a point about 5 miles in my front, and sent a detachment to the Lane of Gen Meeks on the North of Owl Creek, and the Cavalry down towards our Camp. This cavalry captured a part of our advance picket, and afterwards engaged the two companies of Colonel Bucklands Regiment as described by him in his Report herewith enclosed. Our Cavalry drove them back upon their Artillery & Infantry, Killing many and bringing off ten prisoners, all of the 1st Alabama Cavalry, Whom I send to you. We lost of the Picket 1. 1st Lt and seven men of the Ohio 70th Inf. List enclosed, taken prisoners   1 Major & 1 Lieut, 1 Sergt. & 1 private of the 72 Ohio Infy taken prisoners. 8 privates wounded. Names of all embraced in Report of Col Buckland enclosed herewith. We took ten prisoners, left two wounded, and many Killed on the Field." ALS, DNA, RG 94, War Records Office, Union Battle Reports. *O.R.*, I, x, part 1, 89–90.

1. On April 5, USG telegraphed to Maj. Gen. Henry W. Halleck the substance of the information above. "Gen Nelson of Buells column has just arrived The other two Divisions will arrive to-morrow and next day. Some skirmishing took place last night between our advance and the enemy resulting in four wounded & four or five men and two officer (of our side) taken prisoners. Enemy lost several killed and eight prisoners taken." Copies, DLC-USG, V, 4, 5, 7, 8, 88; DNA, RG 393, USG Hd. Qrs. Correspondence; *ibid.*, Dept. of the Mo., Telegrams Received. *O.R.*, I, x, part 2, 94.

To Maj. Gen. Don Carlos Buell

———

Savanna [*April*] 5th [*1862*]

GEN BUELL NEAR WAINSBORO TEN

Your dispatch just recd   I will be hear to meet you to morrow. The enemy at and near Corinth are probably from 60 to 80 thousand. Information not reliable. Have abundance of rations here and some forage. More arriving daily.

Pontoon bridge arrived to day.

U S GRANT
Maj Gen Comdg

Copies, DLC-USG, V, 1, 2, 3, 9, 88; DNA, RG 393, USG Letters Sent. *O.R.*, I, x, part 2, 93. On April 4, 1862, Maj. Gen. Don Carlos Buell, "Camp 3 Miles west of Wainsboro," wrote to USG. "I shall be in Savanna myself tomorrow with one perhaps two divisions. Can I meet you there; Have you any information for me that should affect my movements? what of your enemy, and your relative positions. What force at Florence or [*Corinth*.] we will require forage as soon as we arrive, and provisions in two or three days after. Has a Steamer arrived with a Bridge for me" Copies, DLC-USG, V, 1, 2, 3, 9, 88; DNA, RG 393, USG Letters Sent; *ibid.*, District of West Tenn., Letters Received. *O.R.*, I, x, part 2, 91–92.

To Maj. Gen. Don Carlos Buell

———

Savanna, April 6th 1862

Gen. D. C. Buell,

Heavy firing is heard up the[1] indicating plainly that an attack has been made upon our most advance positions. I have been looking for this but did not believe the attack could be made before Monday[2] or Teusday.

This necessitates my joining the forces up the river instead of meeting you to-day as I had contemplated.

I have directed Gen. Nelson to move to the river with his Division.[3] He can march to opposite Pittsburg.

Respectfully your obt. svt.
U. S. Grant
Maj. Gen Com

ALS, Colorado College, Colorado Springs, Colo. *O.R.*, I, lii, part I, 232. In a contemporary report, dated April 15, 1862, and in an article written twenty-three years later, Maj. Gen. Don Carlos Buell makes no mention of the receipt of this letter. Buell, like USG, learned of the battle of Shiloh by hearing it. In the report Buell implies that he had no contact with USG until he had traveled by steamboat from Savannah, Tenn., to Pittsburg Landing; in his article he states that while on the river he read USG's letter to "Commanding Officer, Advance Forces." *Ibid.*, I, x, part I, 292; Don Carlos Buell, "Shiloh Reviewed," *Battles and Leaders of the Civil War*, eds., Robert Underwood Johnson and Clarence Clough Buel (New York, 1887), I, 492. See following letter.

1. The word inadvertently omitted was probably "river."
2. April 7.

3. On April 6, Capt. John A. Rawlins wrote to Brig. Gen. William Nelson, Savannah. "An attack having been made on our forces you will move your entire command to the river opposite Pittsburgh. You can obtain a guide easily in the village." Copies, DLC-USG, V, 1, 2, 3, 9, 86; DNA, RG 393, USG Letters Sent. *O.R.*, I, x, part 2, 95. Later on the same day, 1st Lt. Clark B. Lagow wrote to Nelson. "I am directed by Major Gen. Grant to say to you that you will hurry up your command as fast as possible. The boats will be in readiness to transport all troops of your command across the river. All looks well, but it is necessary for you to push forward as fast as possible." Copies, DLC-USG, V, 1, 2, 3, 9, 86; DNA, RG 393, USG Letters Sent. *O.R.*, I, x, part 2, 95–96.

To Commanding Officer, Advance Forces

Pittsburg, April 6th 1862

COMD.G OFFICER
ADVANCE FORCES NEAR PITTSBURG, TEN.
GEN.

The attack on my forces has been very spirited from early this morning. The appearance of fresh troops on the field now would have a powerfu[l] effect both by inspiring our men and disheartining the enemy. If you will get upon the field leaving all your baggage on the East bank of the river it will be a move to our advantage and possibly save the day to us.

The rebel forces is estimated at over 100.000 men.[1]

My Hd Qrs. will be in the log building on top of the hill where you will be furnished a staff officer to guide you to your place on the field.

Respectfully &c
U. S. GRANT
Maj. Gen.

ALS, deCoppet Collection, NjP. *O.R.*, I, x, part 2, 95; *ibid.*, I, lii, part 1, 232–33. The officer addressed was in Maj. Gen. Don Carlos Buell's Army of the Ohio. On April 6, 1862, Capt. William S. Hillyer wrote to Brig. Gen. Thomas J. Wood, Army of the Ohio. "You will move your Command with the utmost dispatch to the river at this point, where Steamboats will be in waiting to transport you to Pittsburg." Copies, DLC-USG, V, 1, 2, 3, 9, 86; DNA, RG 393, USG Letters Sent. *O.R.*, I, x, part 2, 95. According to a letter to his wife, April 11, Hillyer had

The Battle of Shiloh. Charge and taking of a New Orleans Battery by the 14th Regt. Wisconsin Volunteers. Lithograph from a sketch by Alfred E. Mathews. *Courtesy Ohio Historical Society Library.*

Battle of Shiloh. The Gunboats Tylor [*sic*] and Lexington Supporting the National troops, by firing up the ravine back of Pittsburg Landing. Lithograph from a sketch by Alfred E. Mathews. *Courtesy Ohio Historical Society Library.*

Shiloh Church. Lithograph from a sketch by Alfred E. Mathews. *Courtesy Ohio Historical Society Library.*

Pittsburg Landing. Lithograph from a sketch by Alfred E. Mathews. *Courtesy Ohio Historical Society Library.*

carried USG's letter to "Comd.g Officer" to Savannah to deliver to Brig. Gen. Thomas L. Crittenden. Finding that the divisions of Brig. Gen. Alexander M. McCook and Wood were close at hand, Hillyer ordered them forward on USG's authority. *USGA Newsletter*, I, 2 (Jan., 1964), 11.

Under the pressure of battle 1st Lt. Clark B. Lagow also wrote important communications. On April 6, Lagow wrote to Maj. Isaac N. Cooke. "You are hereby directed to arrest every Commissioned Officer that shows himself on the Levee near Steamers unless sick or wounded, taking his sword, name, Regiment and Company and order him back to his quarters there to remain until he is regularly released." Copies, DLC-USG, V, 1, 2, 3, 86; DNA, RG 393, USG Letters Sent. On the same day, Lagow wrote to Capt. Algernon S. Baxter. "I am directed by Major Gen Grant to say to you that during the present press, Com. G. W. Graham will have complete control of Steamers." Copies, DLC-USG, V, 2, 86; DNA, RG 393, USG Letters Sent. On the same day, Lagow issued Special Orders No. 47. "Brig Gen McArthur Lt Col A S. Chetlain 12th Ills. Lt Col Morgan 25th Ind Col Reed (of Cruffs Brigade) & Col Gaddis 8th Iowa are hereby released from arrest & will resume their Swords and return to duty with their respective commands" Copies, DLC-USG, V, 15, 16, 82, 87, 89; DNA, RG 393, USG Special Orders.

1. Thomas L. Livermore estimated C. S. A. strength at Shiloh as 40,335 effectives. *Numbers & Losses in the Civil War in America: 1861–65* (Bloomington, Ind., 1957), p. 80.

To Maj. Gen. Henry W. Halleck

———

By Telegraph from Pittsburgh Tennessee 7th April *1862*

To Maj Gen Halleck

Yesterday the rebels attacked us here with an overwhelming force driving our troops in from their advanced position nearer to the landing—General Wallace was immy. ordered up from Crumps landing and in the evening one division of Buells Army and D C. Buell in person arrived, during the night one other division arrived, and still another today. This morning at the break of day I ordered an attack which resulted in a fight that continued until late this afternoon with a very heavy loss on both sides but a complete repulse of the enemy. I shall follow tomorrow far enough to see that no immediate renewal of attack is contemplated

U S Grant

Telegram received, DNA, RG 94, Generals' Papers and Books, Telegrams Received by Gen. Halleck; copies, *ibid.*, RG 393, USG Hd. Qrs. Correspondence; *ibid.*, Dept. of the Miss., Telegrams Received; DLC-USG, V, 4, 5, 7, 8, 9, 88. *O.R.*, I, x, part 1, 108. On April 9, 1862, Maj. Gen. Henry W. Halleck replied to USG. "Recd your dispatch of the 7th about battle of Pittsburgh last night. Dispatched a Hospital early this morning, will have more on the way to day. Preparations are making at Cincinnatti to accommodate 10.000 sick and wounded. I leave here to join you with considerable reinforcements. Avoid another battle if you can 'till all arrive, we shall then be able to beat them without fail" Copies, DLC-USG, V, 4, 5, 7, 8, 9, 88; DNA, RG 94, Generals' Papers and Books, Telegrams Sent in Cipher by Gen. Halleck; *ibid.*, RG 393, USG Hd. Qrs. Correspondence; *ibid.*, Dept. of the Miss., Telegrams Sent. *O.R.*, I, x, part 2, 99. On April 8, Halleck telegraphed to USG. "Gen Pope has crossed the River   Captured all enemy's works including Island No 10 which is now in our possession, and also the enemy's large floating (14) Gun Battery. Our victory is complete. No details yet received. I leave to join you tomorrow. Send this to Genl Buell." Copies, DLC-USG, V, 4, 5, 7, 8, 88; DNA, RG 94, Generals' Papers and Books, Telegrams Sent in Cipher by Gen. Halleck; *ibid.*, RG 393, USG Hd. Qrs. Correspondence; *ibid.*, Dept. of the Miss., Telegrams Sent. *O.R.*, I, x, part 2, 98.

To Maj. Gen. Don Carlos Buell

———

Head Quarters, Dist of West. Tenn.
Pittsburgh, April 7th 1862.

MAJOR GEN. D. C. BUELL
GENL:

When I left the field this evening my intention was to occupy the most advanced position possible for the night, with the Infantry engaged through the day and follow up our success with Cavalry and fresh troops expected to arrive during my last absence on the field. The great fatigue of our men, they having been engaged in two days fight, ~~to day~~ and subject to a march yesterday and fight to day, would preclude the idea of making any advance to night without the arrival of the expected reinforcements. My plan therefore will be to feel on in the morning with all the troops on the outer lines, until our Cavalry force can be organized (one Regiment of your Army will finish crossing soon) and a sufficient Artillery and Infantry support to follow them are ready, for a move.

Under the instructions which I have previously received and a dispatch also of to-day from Major Gen. Halleck[1] it will not then ~~to~~ do to advance beyond Pea Ridge, or some point which we can reach and return in a day. Gen. Halleck will probably be here himself tomorrow. Instructions have been sent to the different Division Commanders not included in your command to be ready in the morning either to find if an enemy was in front or to advance.

> Very Respectfully
> Your Obt. Servant
> U. S. GRANT
> Major. Genl. Commdg.

Copies, DLC-USG, V, 1, 2, 3, 9, 86; DNA, RG 393, USG Letters Sent; Eleanor Bullock, Wayne City, Ill. *O.R.*, I, x, part 2, 96–97; *ibid.*, I, lii, part 1, 233–34. The copy owned by Mrs. Bullock is in the same hand as the copies of 1862 correspondence now in the Buell Papers, TxHR.

1. This telegram has not been found.

General Orders No. 34

———

Head Quarters Dist of West Tennessee
Pittsburgh April 8th 1862.

GENL ORDERS No 34

The General commanding congratulates the Troops who so gallantry maintained their positions repulsed and routed a numerically superior force of the enemy composed of the flower of the southern army commanded by their ablest Generals and fought by them with all the desperation of despair.

In numbers engaged no such contest ever took place on this continent. In importance of result, but few such have taken place in the history of the world.

Whilst congratulating the brave and gallant soldiers it becomes the duty of the General Commanding to make special notice of the brave wounded and those killed upon the field. Whilst they leave friends and relatives to mourn their loss they have won a nations gratitude and undying laurels not to be forgotten by future generations who will enjoy the blessings of the best government the sun ever shone upon preserved by their Valor.

By Command of
Maj Genl U. S. Grant Comdg
JNO A RAWLINS
A. A. Genl—

DS, McClernand Papers, IHi; Buell Papers, TxHR; DNA, RG 393, District of West Tenn., Letters Received. *O.R.*, I, x, part 1, 111–12.

On April 8, 1862, Capt. John A. Rawlins issued Special Orders No. 48. "Division Commanders will make out and send to these Hd. Qrs without delay Consolidated Field Returns of their Commands   Reports of the part taken by each division in the Battle of Pittsburg are required at the earliest possible day. Notice must be taken of those officers & men especially the former who disgraced themselves by their Cowardice and charges brought against them." DS, McClernand Papers, IHi; copies, DLC-USG, V, 15, 16, 82, 87, 89; DNA, RG 393, USG Special Orders.

To Maj. Gen. Henry W. Halleck

BY TELEGRAPH FROM Pittsburg Tenn [*April 8*] *186*[*2*]

To MAJ. GENL. HALLECK
COMDG. DEPT.

Enemy badly routed & fleeing towards Corinth   Our Cavalry supported by Infy. are now pursuing him with instructions to pursue to the swampy grounds near Pea Ridge. I want transports sent here for our wounded.

U. S. GRANT

Telegram received, DNA, RG 94, Generals' Papers and Books, Telegrams Received by Gen. Halleck; copies, *ibid.*, War Records Office, Union Battle Reports; *ibid.*, RG 393, Dept. of the Miss., Telegrams Received. *O.R.*, I, x, part 1, 108. See telegram to Maj. Gen. Henry W. Halleck, April 7, 1862.

To Maj. Gen. Henry W. Halleck

By Telegraph from Pittsburg Tenn [*April*] 8 *1862*

To Gen Halleck

The cavalry supported by infantr[y] pursued the retreating foe today causing them to abandon a no. of wagons & other property   Boats are required to carry off the wounded   It will be several days before I can possibly get in reports to show my present strength   Among the killed in our possession are Gen A. Johnston[1] & Col Preston[2] [&] a number of officers of rank names not known   Provisional Governor Johnson of Ky[3] is a prisoner morta[lly] wounded.

U S Grant
Maj Genl

Telegram received, DNA, RG 94, Generals' Papers and Books, Telegrams Received by Gen. Halleck; copy, *ibid.*, RG 393, Dept. of the Miss., Telegrams Received.

1. Although Gen. Albert Sidney Johnston was killed on the afternoon of April 6, 1862, his body did not fall into U.S. hands. USG believed that the news of Johnston's death was encouraging to the U.S. forces, but the event did not otherwise affect the outcome of the battle. *Memoirs*, I, 360–63. The question is discussed in Charles P. Roland, *Albert Sidney Johnston: Soldier of Three Republics* (Austin, Tex., 1964), pp. 340–42.

2. Col. William Preston, who served on the staff of his brother-in-law, Gen. Albert Sidney Johnston, was neither killed nor captured at Shiloh. His report is in *O.R.*, I, x, part 1, 403–5. See *DAB*, XV, 205–6.

3. George W. Johnson of Scott County, Ky., who was appointed provisional governor of Ky. by a pro-secession convention in Nov., 1861, was mortally wounded at Shiloh fighting in the ranks of the 4th Ky.

To Maj. Gen. Don Carlos Buell

———

Head Quarters, Dist of West. Tenn.
Pittsburgh, April 8th 1862.

MAJOR GEN. D. C. BUELL.
GEN:

In making the reconnoisance ordered for this morning, none of the Cavalry, belonging to your command was directed to take part. I have directed that if the enemy are found retreating, information ~~will~~ be at once sent to Gens McClernand & Sherman who will immediately advance with a portion of their forces in support of the reconnoisance. It will not be practicable to move Artillery. If the enemy are retreating, and can be made to hasten across the low land between here and Pea Ridge, they will probably be forced to abandon their Artillery and Baggage. Will you be good enough to order your Cavalry to follow on the Corinth roads, and give two or three of your fresh Brigades to follow in support. P. S. Information has just reached me that the enemy have retreated.

U. S. GRANT.
Major Gen. Commdg.

Copies, DLC-USG, V, 1, 2, 3, 86; DNA, RG 393, USG Letters Sent. *O.R.*, I, x, part 2, 97–98.

To Maj. Gen. John A. McClernand

———

Pittsburg, April 8th 1862

MAJ. GEN. J. A. MCCLERNAND
COMD.G 1ST DIV.
GEN

I have instructed Taylor's Cavalry[1] to push out the road towards Corinth to ascertain if the enemy have retreated and if so to return the information to you and Gen. Sherman.

Should they be retreating I want all the Cavalry belonging to the entire command to follow them, supported by three or four ~~Divisions~~ Brigades of Infantry.

It will not, after the rain of last night, be practicable to move Artillery.

You will furnish one of the Brigades

Respectfully &c

U. S. Grant

Maj. Gen.

ALS, McClernand Papers, IHi. The same letter is entered as written by Capt. John A. Rawlins in DLC-USG, V, 1, 2, 3, 86; DNA, RG 393, USG Letters Sent. *O.R.*, I, x, part 2, 97. A similar letter of April 8, 1862, is entered as addressed by Rawlins to Brig. Gen. William T. Sherman. "I have instructed Taylor's Cavalry to push out on the road towards Corinth, to ascertain if the enemy have retreated, and if so return the information to yourself and Gen. McClernand, who would support him with sufficient Infantry (the roads will not be practicable for Artillery) to enable him to push the reconnoisance into the bad road between here & Corinth." Copies, DLC-USG, V, 1, 2, 3, 86; DNA, RG 393, USG Letters Sent. *O.R.*, I, x, part 2, 97. The use of the personal pronoun suggests that this letter also was originally written by USG. See following letter. On the same day, Sherman sent USG a lengthy report of his reconnaissance on the road toward Corinth which had been checked by C. S. A. cav. ALS, DNA, RG 94, War Records Office, Union Battle Reports. *O.R.*, I, x, part 1, 639–41.

1. William H. H. Taylor was commissioned col., 5th Ohio Cav., to rank from Aug. 26, 1861.

To Col. William H. H. Taylor

Head Quarters, Dist of West. Tenn.

Pittsburgh, April 8th, 1862.

Col. W H H Taylor
5th Ohio Cavalry,
Colonel:

Move out on the right hand Corinth road with the entire Cavalry at your command, and ascertain if the enemy are retreating. If you find they are retreating, return the information by some intelligent Officer to Genls. ~~Buell~~ Sherman & McClernand who will be instructed to support your further advance with Infantry.

> Very Respectfully,
> Your Obt Servant
> U S GRANT
> Major Gen. Comdg

Copies, DLC-USG, V, 1, 2, 3, 86; DNA, RG 393, USG Letters Sent. See preceding letter.

To Commanding Officer

———

> Head Quarters, Dist of West. Tenn.
> Pittsburgh, April 8th 1862.

COMMDG OFFICER OF TROOPS,
ON BOARD STEAMER PLANET.
SIR:

You will cause the debarkation of the troops of your command, and discharge of Steamer without delay.

The troops will be encamped for the night at the nearest suitable point to the landing and remain there, until their ground for encamping is designated to morrow.

> Respectfully,
> Your Obt. Servant.
> U. S. GRANT
> Major Gen. Commdg.

Copies, DLC-USG, V, 1, 2, 86; DNA, RG 393, USG Letters Sent.

To Julia Dent Grant

———

Pittsburg, Ten. April 8th 1862

Dear Julia,

Again another terrible battle has occured in which our arms have been victorious. For the number engaged and the tenacity with which both parties held on for two days, during an incessent fire of musketry and artillery, it has no equal on this continent. The best troops of the rebels were engaged to the number of 162 regiments[1] as stated by a deserter from their camp, and their ablest generals. Beaurigard commanded in person aided by A. S. Johnson, Bragg,[2] Breckenridge[3] and hosts of other generals of less note but possibly of quite as much merit. Gen. Johnson was killed and Bragg wounded. The loss on both sides was heavy probably not less than 20,000 killed and wounded altogether.[4] The greatest loss was sustained by the enemy. They suffered immensly by demoralization also many of their men leaving the field who will not again be of value on the field.

I got through all safe having but one shot which struck my sword but did not touch me.

I am detaining a steamer to carry this and must cut it short.

Give my love to all at home. Kiss the children for me. The same for yourself.

Good night dear Julia.

Ulys.

ALS, DLC-USG.

1. A list of C. S. A. regts. in Robert Underwood Johnson and Clarence Clough Buel, eds., *Battles and Leaders of the Civil War* (New York, 1887), I, 539, indicates that USG doubled the number present.
2. Braxton Bragg of N. C., USMA 1837, served in the U.S. Army until Jan. 3, 1856, when he resigned with the rank of bvt. lt. col. to operate a sugar plantation in La. Recognized as an able art. officer who won special distinction at the battle of Buena Vista, Bragg was also considered "naturally disputatious." *Memoirs*, II, 86. Confirmed as C. S. A. maj. gen. on Nov. 21, 1861, Bragg was both chief of staff and commander of the 2nd Corps at Shiloh, from which he emerged unwounded and with reputation so enhanced that he was promoted to

gen. on April 12, 1862. See Grady McWhiney, *Braxton Bragg and Confederate Defeat* (New York and London, 1969), I, chaps. x–xi.

3. John C. Breckinridge of Ky., educated at Centre College, the College of New Jersey, and Transylvania College, practiced law and won a reputation as an orator. He was elected as a Democrat to the U.S. House of Representatives in 1851, served as U.S. Vice President 1857–61, and was nominated for President by the Southern Democrats in 1860. When Ky. neutrality ended, Breckinridge left a seat in the U.S. Senate and was confirmed as C. S. A. brig. gen. on Nov. 21, 1861. After commanding the Reserve Corps at Shiloh, Breckinridge was confirmed as maj. gen. on April 18, 1862.

4. Thomas L. Livermore assessed U.S. casualties as 1,754 killed, 8,408 wounded, 2,885 missing. C. S. A. casualties were 1,723 killed, 8,012 wounded, 959 missing. *Numbers & Losses in the Civil War in America: 1861–65* (Bloomington, Ind., 1957), pp. 79–80. On April 8, information about battle losses was still incomplete. On that day, Maj. Gen. John A. McClernand wrote twice to Capt. John A. Rawlins, and Maj. Mason Brayman also wrote twice to Rawlins, reporting the discovery of additional wounded of both sides and the taking of prisoners. Copies, McClernand Papers, IHi. On April 9, McClernand wrote to USG to report the capture of three more prisoners. ADfS, *ibid*.

General Orders No. 35

———

Head Quarters Dist of West Tenn
Pittsburgh April 9th 1862

GEN ORDERS No 35.

I. All persons are prohibited from passing beyond the Pickets without special authority from these [Headqu]arters, or on duty as herinafter specially provided

II. Officers so offending will be arrested and charges prefered against them. Enlisted men will be confined and charged with desertion.

III. Citizens attempting to pass in or out without proper authority will be arrested and sent before the Provost Marshall, Col E Wood,[1] office near the landing.

IV. Pickets, or out guards, of Cavalry will be stationed on all the approaches to camp, under the supervision of Division commanders, each guarding their own front and one half of the space on each side.

V. A cavalry force will be sent out each day, from each

Division, for the purpose of executing paragraphs one, two, & three of this order.

VI. As soon as possible sanitary regulations will be made by different Division and Brigade commanders, and if necessary camps may be moved either to the front or rear but not to change the effectiveness of the present line.

VII. All firing by the troops is possitively prohibitited in camp. Where it is necessary to discharge fire arms it will be done [under] proper regulations made by Division Commanders, and such men as are to discharge their pieces will be marched in an orderly manner; to the front of the out guards for that purpose and back to their camps.

By Command of Maj Genl U. S. Grant Comdg.
JNO A RAWLINS
A. A. Genl—

DS, McClernand Papers, IHi; Buell Papers, TxHR; copies, DLC-USG, V, 12, 13, 14, 95; DNA, RG 94, 9th Ill., Letterbook; *ibid.*, RG 393, USG General Orders; *ibid.*, District of West Tenn., Letters Received; McClernand Papers, IHi. *O.R.*, I, x, part 2, 100.

1. On April 8, 1862, Capt. John A. Rawlins issued Special Orders No. 48. "Col   Wood of the 14th Regiment Wis Vols is hereby appointed Provost Marshal for this Camp   His regiment will form the Provost Guard and will be excused from all other details"   Copies, DLC-USG, V, 15, 16, 82, 87, 89; DNA, RG 393, USG Special Orders. On April 9, 1st Lt. Clark B. Lagow wrote to Col. David E. Wood. "You will see that there is a regular guard detailed from your Command to be and placed, on all Steamers leaving this Post for down the river for the purpose of keeping preventing Soldiers from leaving this post who have not having a passes approved at these Head Quarters. All Citizens applying for passes to you will be granted passes if you deem them worthy." Copies, DLC-USG, V, 1, 2, 86; DNA, RG 393, USG Letters Sent. On April 28, Rawlins issued General Orders No. 46. "Lt Col D C. Anthony of 23rd Ind Vols is hereby appointed Provost Marshall Genl of the Army of the Tenn, and will at once enter upon his duties as such and relieve Col Wood of the 14th Wis now acting." Copies, DLC-USG, V, 12, 13, 14, 95; DNA, RG 393, USG General Orders. *O.R.*, I, x, part 2, 139–40. Dated April 29 in DLC-USG, V, 13. On April 29, USG wrote to hd. qrs., Dept. of the Miss., "in relation to the retention of Col. Woods as Prov. Marshal & his Regt. as Prov. Guard." DNA, RG 393, Dept. of the Miss., Register of Letters Received.

To Gen. P. G. T. Beauregard

Head Quarters Army in the Field
Pittsburg Ten April 9th 1862

GEN G T BEAURIGARD
COMDG CONFEDERATE ARMY OF THE MISSISSIPPI
MONTEREY TEN
GEN

Your despatch of yesterday is just received. Oweing to the warmth of the weather I deemed it advisable to have all the dead, of both parties buried immediately. Heavy details were made for this purpose and it is now accomplished

There cannot therefore be any necessity of admitting within our lines the parties you desire to send, on the grounds asked

I shall always be glad to extend any courtesy consistent with duty and especially when dictated by humanity

I am Gen Very respectfully
Your Obt Servt
U. S. GRANT
Maj Gen.

LS, DNA, RG 109, Documents Printed in *O.R. O.R.*, I, x, part 1, 111. On April 8, 1862, Gen. P. G. T. Beauregard, Monterey, had written to USG. "At the close of the conflict of yesterday, my forces being exhausted by the extraordinary length of time during which they were engaged with yours on that and the preceding day, and it being apparent that you had received and were still receiving reinforcements, I felt it my duty to withdraw my troops from the immediate scene of conflict. Under these circumstances, in accordance with usages of war, I shall transmit this under a flag of truce, to ask permission to send a mounted party to the battle-field of Shiloh, for the purpose of giving decent interment to my dead. Certain gentlemen wishing to avail themselves of this opportunity to remove the remains of their sons and friends, I must request for them the privilege of accompanying the burial party; and in this connexion I deem it proper to say, I am asking only what I have extended to your own countrymen under similar circumstances." LS, DNA, RG 94, War Records Office, Union Battle Reports. *O.R.*, I, x, part 1, 111.

To Maj. Gen. Henry W. Halleck

Pittsburg Ten.
April 9th 1862

Maj. Gen. H. W. Halleck
St. Louis Mo.
Gen.

There is but little doubt but that the enemy intend concentrating upon the railroad at and near Corinth all the force possible leaving many points heretofore guarded entirely without troops. I learn this through Southern papers and from a Spy who was in Corinth after the rebel army left.

They have sent steamers up White river to bring down Van Dorn's[1] and Price's commands. They are also bringing forces from the East.—Prisoners also confirm this information.

I do not like to suggest but it appears to me that it would be demoralizing upon our troops here to be forced to retire upon the opposite bank of the river and unsafe to remain on this, many weeks, without large reinforcements.

The attack on Sunday was made, according to the best evidence I have, by one hundred & sixty-two regiments.[2] Of these many were lost by killed, wounded and desertion.

They are at present very badly crippled and cannot recover under two or three weeks. Of this matter you may be better able to judge than I am.

There was one act of the rebels on the battle field on Sunday which cannot be justified. I have the evidence of officers who say, and could not be deceived, that a Brigade dressed in black, and with the Union flag unfurled, passed through an open field in front of one of our batteries thereby securing a position that could not otherwise have been attained without loss of life.

I am Gen. very respectfully
your obt. svt.
U. S. Grant
Maj. Gen.

P. S. I enclose herewith invoice of ordnance and ordnance stores shipped from Fort Henry together with notes explaining the condition of it.

U. S. G.

ALS, deCoppet Collection, NjP. *O.R.*, I, x, part 2, 99–100.

1. Earl Van Dorn of Miss., USMA 1842, resigned as maj. from the U.S. Army on Jan. 31, 1861, and was confirmed as C. S. A. maj. gen. on Nov. 21. On Jan. 10, 1862, he was assigned command of the Trans-Mississippi District and on March 4 of the Army of the West. After his defeat at Pea Ridge, Van Dorn was ordered to move his command to Memphis on March 23, but when USG wrote, Van Dorn's troops still awaited steamboat transportation. *Ibid.*, p. 354; *ibid.*, I, xiii, 813.
2. See letter to Julia Dent Grant, April 8, 1862, note 1.

To Capt. Nathaniel H. McLean

Head Quarters Disct of West Tenn
Pittsburgh April 9th 1862

Capt N H McLean
A A Genl Dept of the Mississippi
Saint Louis. Mo.
Capt

It becomes my duty again to report another battle fought between two great armies, one contending for the maintainance of the best Government ever devised the other for its destruction. It is pleasant to record the success of the army contending for the former principle.

On Sunday morning our pickets were attacked and driven in by the enemy. Immediately the five Divisions stationed at this place were drawn up in line of battle ready to meet them. The battle soon waxed warm on the left and center, varying at times to all parts of the line.

The most continuous firing of musketry and artillery ever heard on this Continent was kept up until night fall, the enemy having forced the entire line to fall back nearly half way from their Camps to the Landing. At a late hour in the afternoon a desperate effort was made by the enemy to turn our left and get possession of the Landing, transports &c. This point was guarded by the Gun boats Tyler and Lexington, Capt's Gwinn & Shirk U S N[1] commanding Four 20 pounder Parrott guns and a battery of rifled guns. As there is a deep and impassable ravine for artillery or Cavalry and very difficult for Infantry at this point. No troops were stationed here except the neccessary Artillerists and a small Infantry force for their support   Just at this moment the advance of Maj Genl Buells Column (a part of the Division under Genl Nelson) arrived, the two Generals named both being present. An advance was immediately made upon the point of attack and the enemy soon driven back.

In this repulse much is due to the presence of the Gun boats Tyler and Lexington and their able Commanders Capt Gwinn and Shirk.

During the night the Divisions under Genl Crittenden[2] and McCook arrived. Genl Lew Wallace, at Crumps Landing six miles below, was ordered at an early hour in the morning to hold his Division in readiness to be moved in any direction to which it might be ordered. At about 11 oClock the order was delivered to move it up to Pittsburgh, but owing to its being led by a ~~highl~~ circuitous route did not arrive in time to take part in Sundays action.[3]

During the night all was quiet, and feeling that a great moral advantage would be gained by becoming the attacking party, an advance was ordered as soon as day dawned. The result was a gradual repulse of the enemy at all parts of the line from morning until probably 5 oClock in the afternoon when it became evident the enemy was retreating. Before the close of the action the advance of Genl T J Woods[4] Division arrived in time to take part in the action.

My force was too much fatigued from two days hard fighting and exposure in the open air to a drenching rain during the intervening night to pursue immediately.

Night closed in cloudy and with heavy rain making the roads impracticable for artillery by the next morning. Genl Sherman however followed the enemy find ng that the main part of the army had retreated in good order.

Hospitals of the enemies wour.ded were found all along the road as far as pursuit was made. Dead bodies of the enemy and many graves were also found.

I enclose herewith report of Genl Sherman which will explain more fully the result of this pursuit.[5]

Of the part taken by each seperate Command I cannot take special notice in this report, but wil. do so more fully when reports of Division Commanders are handed in.

Genl Buell, coming on the Field with a distinct army, long under his command, and which d d such efficient service, commanded by himself in person on the field, will be much better able to notice of those of his com nand who particularly distinguished themselves than I possibly can.[6]

I feel it a duty however to a gallant and able officer Brig Genl W T Sherman to make special mention. He not only was with his Command during the entire of the two days action, but displayed great judgment and skill in the management of his men. Altho severely wounded in the hand the first day, his place was never vacant. He was again wounded and had three horses killed under him.[7] In making this ment on of a gallant officer no disparagement is intended to the other Division Commanders Major Generals John A McClernand[8] and Lew Wallace,[9] and Brig Generals S A Hurlbut, B M. Prentiss[10] and W H L Wallace, all of whom maintained their places with credit to themselves and the cause   Genl Prentiss was taken prisoner in the first days action, and Genl W H L Wallace severely, probably mortally wounded.[11] His Ass Adj Genl Capt William McMichael is missing, probably taken prisoner.[12]

My personal Staff are all deserving of particular mention, they having been engaged during the entire two days in conveying orders to every part of the field. It consists of Col J D Webster, Chief of Staff, Lt Col J B McPherson Chief Engineer, assisted by Lieuts W L B Jenney[13] and William Kossack,[14] Capt J A Rawlins[15] A A Genl Capts W S Hillyer,[16] W R Rowley and C B Lagow aides-de-Camp Col G. G. Pride[17] Volunteer aide and Capt J P Hawkins Chief ~~Engineer~~ Commissary who accompanied me upon the field.

The Medical Department under the direction of Surgeon Hewitt Medical Director, showed great energy in providing for the wounded and in getting them from the field regardless of danger[18]

Col Webster was placed in special charge of all the artillery and was constantly upon the field. He displayed, as always heretofore, both skill and bravery. At least in one instance he was the means of placing an entire Regiment in a position of doing most valuable service, and where it would not have been but for his exertions.

Lt Col McPherson attached to my staff as Chief Engineer deserves more than a passing notice for his activity and courage. All the grounds beyond our Camps for miles have been reconnoitred by him, and plats carefully prepared under his supervision, give accurate information of the nature of approaches to our lines. During the two days battle he was constantly in the saddle leading troops as they arrived to points where their services were required. During the ~~day~~ engagement he had one horse shot under him.

The Country will have to mourn the loss of many brave men who fell at the battle of Pittsburgh, or Chilo more ~~probably~~perly. The exact loss in killed and wounded will be known in a day or two. At present I can only give it approximately at 1500 killed and 3500 wounded.

The loss of Artillery was great, many pieces being disabled by the enemies shots and some loosing all their horses and many men. There was probably not less than two hundred horses killed.

The loss of the enemy in killed and left upon the field was greater than ours. In wounded the estimate cannot be made as many of them must have been sent back to Corinth and other points.

The enemy suffered terribly from demorilization and desertion. A flag of Truce was sent in to day from Genl Beaurigard.
I enclose herewith a copy of the Correspondence.[19]

>   I am. Very Respectfully
>   Your Obt Servt
>   U. S. GRANT
>   Major General Comdg

LS, DNA, RG 94, War Records Office, Union Battle Reports. *O.R.*, I, x, part 1,
108–11. Because this report is similar in form, content, and length to USG's
report of Fort Donelson sent to Brig. Gen. George W. Cullum, Feb. 16, 1862,
and to other battle reports of USG, it is puzzling that he states in his *Memoirs*
(I, 370, 372) that he never made "a full official report" of Shiloh because he had
no access to the reports of Maj. Gen. Don Carlos Buell and his subordinates until
after they were published. Perhaps USG meant that after seeing the Buell reports
he intended to revise and amplify his own. See the fragmentary report, [*Aug.–
Sept.*, 1862?].

1. The report of Lt. William Gwin, commanding the gunboat *Tyler*, is in
O.R. (Navy), I, xxii, 762–64. The report of Lt. James W. Shirk, commanding
the gunboat *Lexington* since Jan. 1, 1862, is *ibid.*, pp. 764–65.
2. Thomas L. Crittenden of Ky., second son of U.S. Senator John J. Crittenden, was a lawyer who had served as aide to Maj. Gen. Zachary Taylor and as
lt. col., 3rd Ky., during the Mexican War. As maj. gen., Ky. State Guards, in
1861, he assumed command of all loyal to the U.S. when Ky. neutrality ended,
and was appointed U.S. brig. gen. on Sept. 27. Crittenden commanded the 5th
Division, Army of the Ohio, at Shiloh. See *O.R.*, I, x, part 1, 354–56.
3. See endorsement to Maj. Gen. Henry W. Halleck, April 25, 1862.
4. Thomas J. Wood of Ky., USMA 1845, was a capt., 1st Cav., on the eve
of the Civil War. Appointed brig. gen. on Oct. 11, 1861, he commanded the 6th
Division, Army of the Ohio, at Shiloh. See *O.R.*, I, x, part 1, 376–79.
5. See letter to Maj. Gen. John A. McClernand, April 8, 1862.
6. The report of Buell, April 15, 1862, is printed in *O.R.*, I, x, part 1, 291–96.
7. On April 10, Brig. Gen. William T. Sherman addressed a lengthy report
of Shiloh to Capt. John A. Rawlins. ADfS, Sherman Papers, InNd; LS, DNA,
RG 94, War Records Office, Union Battle Reports; *ibid.*, Generals' Papers and
Books, William T. Sherman, Letters Sent. *O.R.*, I, x, part 1, 248–54.
8. See letter to Capt. Andrew C. Kemper, April 28, 1862.
9. See endorsement to Maj. Gen. Henry W. Halleck, April 25, 1862.
10. Because of his capture, Brig. Gen. Benjamin M. Prentiss did not submit
his report of Shiloh until Nov. 17. *O.R.*, I, x, part 1, 277–80.
11. Brig. Gen. William H. L. Wallace, commanding the 2nd Division, was
mortally wounded on April 6 and died on April 10. On April 11, Rawlins issued
Special Orders No. 51, and, on April 12, Special Orders No. 52, both of which detailed officers to accompany Wallace's body to Ottawa, Ill. Copies, DLC-USG, V,
15, 16, 82, 87, 89; DNA, RG 393, USG Special Orders. On Aug. 8, Col. Edward
D. Townsend telegraphed to USG. "Please report to this office the precise date

of ~~the death of~~ Brigadier General William H. L. Wallace's death." Copies, *ibid.*, RG 107, Telegrams Collected (Unbound); *ibid.*, RG 94, Letters Sent; *ibid.*, RG 393, USG Hd. Qrs. Correspondence; DLC-USG, V, 7. On Aug. 9, USG telegraphed to Townsend. "Genl Wallace died eight 8. o'clock P. M. on the tenth 10th. of April." Telegram received, DNA, RG 94, Letters Received; *ibid.*, RG 107, Telegrams Received (Bound, Press); copies, *ibid.*, RG 393, USG Hd. Qrs. Correspondence; DLC-USG, V, 4, 5, 7, 8, 88.

12. Capt. William McMichael was captured at Shiloh. See Isabel Wallace, *Life & Letters of General W. H. L. Wallace* (Chicago, 1909), pp. 213–15.

13. William Le Baron Jenney of Mass., engineer and architect, was appointed capt. and aide-de-camp on Aug. 19, 1861, and assigned to work on the fortifications at Cairo.

14. William Kossak, born in Prussia, served as 1st lt., 5th Mo., until appointed capt. and aide-de-camp on Aug. 19, 1861.

15. On April 8, 1862, Rawlins described the battle of Shiloh in a letter to his mother. James Harrison Wilson, *The Life of John A. Rawlins* (New York, 1916), pp. 90–91.

16. On April 11, Capt. William S. Hillyer described his role at the battle of Shiloh in a letter to his wife. *USGA Newsletter*, I, 2 (Jan., 1964), 10–13.

17. George G. Pride served on USG's staff as vol. aide-de-camp for many months after Shiloh without holding a U.S. Army commission. See letter to Maj. Gen. Henry W. Halleck, Oct. 5, 1862. On Feb. 15, Pride wrote to Lt. Col. James Totten stating that since the governor of Mo. had appointed him a staff officer with permission to offer his services in the field, he wished to join the staff of Maj. Gen. Henry W. Halleck. "For past eight years my time has been fully occupied in Railroad Construction, principally Bridge Building in some of the Southern States—" ALS, DNA, RG 94, Staff Papers, George G. Pride.

18. Medical reports concerning Shiloh are in *The Medical and Surgical History of the War of the Rebellion* (Washington, 1870–88), I, part 1, appendix, 29–33, 37–44.

19. See letter to Gen. P. G. T. Beauregard, April 9, 1862.

To Maj. Gen. John A. McClernand

Head Quarters, Dist. of West Ten
Pittsburg, April 9th 1862

MAJ. GEN. J. A. McCLERNAND
COMD.G 1ST DIVISION
GEN.

Complaints are made of promiscuous firing by men of your Divi[sion] by which several men have already been sho[t.] My orders as well as your own Division orde[rs] forbid this.

I would advise very summary punishment for this offence and if it cannot be reached any other way arrest the regimental commanders who do not prevent it.

It is within the power of regimental Comd[rs] enforcing orders but not so easy with Div. Comdrs. without the cooperation of those under them.

> I am Gen very respectfully
> your obt. svt.
> U. S. GRANT
> Maj. Gen Com.

P. S. Four men have been wounded this morning in Gen. Shermans camp by firing from the 1st Div.

> U. S. G.

ALS, McClernand Papers, IHi. In an undated letter, Maj. Gen. John A. McClernand replied to USG. "The complaint made 'of promiscuous firing by men of your (my) Division by which several men have already been shot,' is without foundation. ~~I deny its correctness~~. On the contrary the men of my division, with the rarest exceptions, have fired under orders. I cannot say so much for all others. You are probably aware of the order I have published on this subject. I shall limit firing according to its terms, but to that extent it will be necessary to permit it— the men having no ball-screws, and firing being the only mode of preserving the efficiency of their guns. The men under my command will not take alarm at the proper and harmless discharge of arms, for the purpose I have named, and I trust that my neighbors will not suffer inconvenience from it. I repeat the denial that any have been thus killed by any of my men. I claim that my command has been exemplary in this respect, and expect them to remain so." ADf (in Maj. Mason Brayman's hand), *ibid.* This letter is erroneously entered as April 8, 1862, in McClernand's Register of Letters, *ibid.*

To Maj. Gen. Don Carlos Buell

> Head Quarters, Dist of West Tenn
> Pittsburgh, April 10th 1862.

MAJOR. GEN. D. C. BUELL,
PITTSBURGH, TENN.
GEN:

In the emergency of Sunday an order was sent to Gen. Thomas[1] of your command to leave his transportation to follow and move his effective force with dispatch to Savannah. Part of his command could not comply with the order, and as the emergency has passed it would be well to have the order of Sunday countermanded so far as they are concerned, so that the force now on the way ~~should~~ can move with transportation

> I am, Gen. Very Respectfully,
> Your Obt Servant.
> U. S. GRANT
> Major General.

Copies, DLC-USG, V, 1, 2, 3, 86; DNA, RG 393, USG Letters Sent. *O.R.*, I, x, part 2, 101. On April 7, 1862, Capt. William S. Hillyer wrote to Brig. Gen. George H. Thomas. "You will move your command with the utmost dispatch to the landing at Savannah, where steamboats will be in waiting to transport you to this place. Let your cavalry proceed overland to a point on the river opposite Pittsburg, and leave your transportation and baggage, &c., to follow you to Savannah." *Ibid.*, p. 96. According to the diary of Col. Jacob Ammen, 24th Ohio, Thomas's division arrived at Pittsburg Landing at 11:00 a.m., April 7. *Ibid.*, I, x, part 1, 336. Maj. Gen. Don Carlos Buell, however, reported that Thomas did not arrive in time to enter the battle. *Ibid.*, p. 296.

1. George H. Thomas of Va., USMA 1840, served continuously in the U.S. Army, ranking as maj., 2nd Cav., on the eve of the Civil War. Appointed brig. gen. as of Aug. 17, 1861, on Sept. 10 he was ordered to take command of Camp Dick Robinson, Ky. On Jan. 19, 1862, in command of the 1st Division, Army of the Ohio, he won a notable victory at Logan's Cross Roads, near Mill Springs, Ky.

To Gen. P. G. T. Beauregard

———

> Head Quarters, Army in the Field
> Pittsburg, April 12th 1862

GEN.

Herewith I send you a note from Col. Battle of the Confederate Army who has particularly requested that this might be done, and his exchange effected.

I am perfectly willing to release Col. Battle in exchange for an officer of equal rank taken at the battle of Shiloah.

Should you decide to make the exchange please state when, and at what point between here and Corinth, you would desire the transfer to take place.

> I am Gen. very respectfully
> your obt. svt.
> U. S. GRANT
> Maj. Gen.

To GEN. G. T. BEAURIGARD
COMD.G CONFED. FORCES
MONTEREY[1] TEN.

ALS, DNA, RG 109, Documents Printed in *O.R. O.R.*, II, iii, 446. USG enclosed a letter of April 11, 1862, from C. S. A. Col. Joel A. Battle, 20th Tenn., to Gen. Albert Sidney Johnston. "In consequence of injuries received from the fall of two horses shot under me in the engagements of sunday & monday last, I was unable to remain with my command & was captured by the Federal forces about noon on monday   The Federal officer in command at this place has consented to exchange me in accordance with an arrangement entered into by the contending parties, for an officer of equal rank, or officers of inferior rank, agreeing to the proposition without hesitation; I have confidence that the arrangement will be satisfactory, & speedily consumated, that I may be allowed to return to my Regt as early as possible . . . N. B. I have recovered from my injuries so as to be able to walk" ALS, DNA, RG 109, Documents Printed in *O.R. O.R.*, II, iii, 446–47.

On April 13, Gen. P. G. T. Beauregard wrote to USG. "Your communication of yesterday, by flag of truce, enclosing the application of Colonel Battle for exchange, has been received, and I hasten to answer as soon as my pressing engagements have permitted. Although Col Battle may be disabled for active service, I will nevertheless ~~send you in~~ exchange him for an officer of the same rank provided you will indicate one who did not command a Brigade in your expedition. But The prisoners of War, having been sent to the interior the Colonel you may desire to have in exchanging will have to be sent for ~~and when~~ and will be delivered at some point to be arranged hereafter   Meantime I hope you will feel authorized to permit Colonel Battle to be ~~discharged~~ released on his parole so that ~~he may~~ as soon as practicable he may have the benifit of the care of his family and friends in his injured condition. I have been induced to make the distinction in connexion with Colonels commanding brigades, because I have observed that nearly, if not all brigades in the United States service during this war are in command of Colonels, while in the Confederate Service most of our brigades are commanded by Brigadiers: Consequently, unless some such distinction shall be regarded, we may suffer materially in exchanges. I propose also in a few days either to permit the Medical Officers of your Army in my possession to return to your camp or to send them by the Mississippi River to General Pope" Copies, DNA, RG 109, Documents Printed in *O.R.*; DLC-P. G. T. Beauregard. *O.R.*, II, iii, 449–50. See letter to Maj. Gen. Henry W. Halleck, April 26, 1862.

1. Monterey, Tenn., about ten miles southwest of Pittsburg Landing.

To Capt. Nathaniel H. McLean

———

Head Qrs Dist W. Tenn—
Savanna April 12, 1862

CAPT N. H. MCLEAN
ASST ADJ GEN.—
SIR.

a union man living about three miles from the head of Colvert shoals[1] has just imparted to my aid Capt Hillyer the following information.—

He left home yesterday—on the day before he left his son in law heard a conversation between some prominent secessionists of the neighborhood in which one of them who pretended to be advised of the plans of the enemy stated that Beauregard was arranging to send thirty thousand men around across the Florence bridge and march them up to cut off our force at and near Savannah, seize our transports and then advance on us in front and rear—

The informant states that this same man stated on yesterday week the exact plan afterwards carried out in the attack of Sunday—

respectfully &c
U. S. GRANT
Maj. Gen.

LS, DNA, RG 393, Dept. of the Miss., Letters Received.

1. Colbert Creek joins the Tennessee River in Ala., about thirty-eight miles upriver from Pittsburg Landing.

To Brig. Gen. William T. Sherman

———

Head Quarters, Dist of West. Tenn.
Pittsburgh, April 12th, 1862.

GEN. W. T. SHERMAN

I am ~~just~~ instructed by Gen Halleck to detail two Regiments to go on board a Steamer this evening to proceed up the river to Florence and destroy a portion of the bridge there ~~and return~~, and if practicable cut the Bridge over Bear Creek.[1] The two Gun Boats will accompany. You can select Regiments from your Command to execute this work.

Very Respectfully
Your Obt Servant
U. S. GRANT
Major Genl.

Copies, DLC-USG, V, 1, 2, 3, 86; DNA, RG 393, USG Letters Sent. *O.R.*, I, x, part 2, 102. On April 14, 1862, Brig. Gen. William T. Sherman wrote to Capt. John A. Rawlins. "I have the honor to report, that in obedience to verbal orders from Gen'l Grant, ratified in person by Gen'l Halleck, I embarked on board the Transports, Tecumseh and White Cloud, during the evening of the 12th inst, one hundred men of the 4th Ills Cavalry, under command of Major S. M. Bowman, and the Brigade of General Fry, and escorted by the Gun boats Tyler and Lexington Commanders Gwinn and Shirk, proceeded up the Tennessee River to Chickasaw Landing, where all the troops were disembarked at 7 A. M. the 13th inst. By my orders Maj. Bowman proceeded rapidly on the road to Iuca, the enemy's pickets retreating before him, and destroying themselves by fire a Road bridge across Bear Creek, which I had ordered Gen'l Fry to destroy to secure the right flank of the movement on the Bear Creek Bridge. This Bridge about 7 miles from Chickasaw being destroyed, Major Bowman proceeded rapidly up the road 8 miles further, and on approaching the Railroad bridge across Bear Creek he ~~found~~ found it guarded by the enemy. He dismounted his men and advanced along the track with flankers in the swampy ground, and drove the enemy from the Bridge into the cut beyond, and from that to the West. Then with axes which had been provided he began the destruction of the trustle work to the ~~west~~ east of the Bridge, and with fire destroyed the Bridge itself. This latter consisted of two spans of 110 ft. each, which were burned and fell into the River. With axes and fire he destroyed three pieces of trustle work of an aggregate length of 500 feet, also tearing down about half a mile of telegraph wire rolling it up, and throwing it into the River. He gathered ties and other timber, made bon-fires and piled on them the Railroad Iron, so as to bend it and render it useless for future repairs. Whilst so employed the head of General Fry's column of Infantry arrived and assisted in this work of destruction. They jointly destroyed Bear Creek Bridge and five hundred feet of trustle work, that cannot be repaired in a month. Bear Creek is very bad in itself and the swampy bottom is impassable to wheeled vehicles, so that the breach is vital to the operations of an enemy. Having thus fulfilled well their orders, Major Bowman and Genl Fry returned to Chickasaw with their commands reaching the boats about 9 P. M., having marched about 30 miles   Having thus succeeded in the main purpose of the expedition I wanted to proceed twenty miles further up the Tennessee and there make another break, as well as to push on to Tuscumbia Landing and Florence. At Florence there is a very fine Bridge for a branch Railroad that connects Florence with Tuscumbia, with a Road Bridge underneath, but it was the unanimous opinion of all the pilots, that the Gun boats and even one of the transports could not pass Bee-tree Shoals or Colbert Shoals, both rock bottom, on which it would not do to risk the Gunboats. Having no personal knowledge on the subject, and bound to defer to the opinion of pilots who had navigated the Tennessee for thirty years, I was reluctantly compelled to abandon the latter part of [your] design, the destruction of the Florence Bridge. I am still ready to undertake it with boats of light draft, made secure by some field pieces and bales of hay; or to march by land from Waterloo, just above Chickasaw, to Florence   Our Cavalry under Major Bowman moved finely on this ocassion, and the Infantry column of Gen'l Fry sustained their well earned reputation for steadiness and discipline"   LS, DNA, RG 94, War Records Office, Union Battle Reports. *O.R.*, I, x, part 1, 644–45; *O.R.* (Navy), I, xxiii, 60–61. In an undated endorsement, USG forwarded this report to hd. qrs. of the army. ES, DNA, RG 94, War Records Office, Union Battle Reports. On April 14, Maj. Samuel M. Bowman, 4th Ill. Cav., reported his actions at Bear Creek Bridge to Sherman. ALS, *ibid.*, RG 393, District of West Tenn., Letters Received. *O.R.*, I, x, part 1, 646. Also on April 14, Sherman wrote to his wife, discussing this expedition. ALS, Sherman Papers, InNd.

1. The Memphis and Charleston Railroad crossed Bear Creek in Ala. almost at the state boundary with Miss.

To Brig. Gen. George H. Thomas

Headquarters District of West Tennessee,
Pittsburg, April 12, 1862.

[General Thomas:]
General:

I am directed by Major-General Halleck to organize a force for special service to-night. You will therefore report one brigade of your command on board the steamers White Cloud and Universe this evening with one day's rations. The lateness of the hour prevents sending this through Major-General Buell, commanding. You will please therefore notify him of this detail. No artillery and but one company of cavalry will be required. Instructions will be given after your troops are embarked.

I am, general, very respectfully, your obedient servant,

U. S. GRANT,
Major-General.

O.R., I, lii, part 1, 235. See preceding letter.

To Capt. Nathaniel H. McLean

————

Head Quarters Disct of W. Tenn
Pittsburgh, April 14, 1862

CAPT N. H. McLEAN
A. A GENL. DEPT OF THE MISS
CAPT
I would respectfully request that Genl Davis[1] be ordered to take Command of the 2nd Division, (Genl Smith and McArthur[2] of that Division being unable for service) without delay

I am Capt Very Respcty
Your Obt Servt
U. S. GRANT
Maj Genl

Copies, DLC-USG, V, 4, 5, 7, 8, 88; DNA, RG 393, USG Hd. Qrs. Correspondence. *O.R.*, I, lii, part 1, 236. On April 15, 1862, Capt. Nathaniel H. McLean endorsed this letter. "General Grant will assign General Davies to such command as he may deem best for the service." *Ibid.*, p. 237.

1. Thomas A. Davies of N. Y., USMA 1829, resigned from the U.S. Army on Oct. 31, 1831, and spent the following thirty years as an engineer working on the Croton Aqueduct and as a merchant in New York City. On May 15, 1861, he was appointed col., 16th N. Y., and on March 7, 1862, was confirmed as brig. gen. On April 14, Capt. John A. Rawlins issued Special Orders No. 54. "Brig Genl Thomas A Davies having reported for duty to Maj Genl Grant is hereby assigned to the Command of the 2nd Division of the Army in the Field." Copies,

DLC-USG, V, 15, 16, 82, 89; DNA, RG 393, USG Special Orders. *O.R.*, I, x, part 2, 106.

2. Brig. Gen. John McArthur was wounded on April 6 during the battle of Shiloh. *Ibid.*, I, x, part 1, 158. On April 16, McArthur sent a brief report of casualties to USG. *Ibid.*, p. 148. On April 25, USG endorsed this letter. "Respectfully referred to headquarters of the department. From the casualties occurring in the Second Division it is not probable that any further reports than those now sent will be received." *Ibid.*

To Brig. Gen. William T. Sherman

Head Quarters, Dist. of West Ten.
Pittsburg, April 15th 1862

GEN. W. T. SHERMAN
COMD.G 5TH DIV.
GEN.

Order the 71st Ohio vol. regiment to the landing ready to embark for Fort Donelson and Clarkesville to relieve the garrison at those two places.

They need not take any of their land transportation with them the supply of those garrisons being sufficient.

Instructions will be made out here for them.

I am Gen. very respectfully
your obt. svt.
U. S. GRANT
Maj. Gen. Com

ALS, Stephenson County Historical Society, Freeport, Ill. The same letter is entered as written by Maj. John A. Rawlins in DLC-USG, V, 2, 86; DNA, RG 393, USG Letters Sent. See following letter.

On April 16, 1862, Rawlins wrote to Col. Rodney Mason, 71st Ohio. "You will proceed with your Command to Fort. Donelson, Tenn. and relieve Col. Fouke and his Command of the Garrison duty of that place. In the Command of said place you will prevent all marauding and destroying of private property. The Citizens are not to be molested by our troops. Make severe examples of Company Commanders whose companies are guilty of such conduct. If necessary ~~ship~~ send them to Head Quarters with charges, and request they be mustered out of the service. You will make or cause to be made Requisitions upon the Qr. Master and Commissary at Paducah, Ky. for such supplies as you may need for your command, being careful to have at least 15 days rations, and 8 days forage on hand at all times. You will see that the telegraph line at Dover is properly guarded, and that all Public Property is taken care of. Col. Fouke will turn over to you ~~any~~ all instructions he may have received, relative to the duties of Post Commander, for your future guidance. And your particular attention is called to General Orders No 3 series 1861, from Head Quarters of the Dept. ~~No 3 of Series of 1861.~~ and to accompanying orders from these Head Quarters. All information you may obtain that in your judgment would be beneficial to be known at these Head Quarters, you will immediately forward. Six companies of your command will be stationed at Clarkesville for the purpose of Garrisoning that place to be governed by same instructions as above." Copies, DLC-USG, V, 1, 2, 3, 86; DNA, RG 393, USG Letters Sent. *O.R.*, I, x, part 2, 108–9.

Mason and his regt. had left the field during the battle of Shiloh. *Ibid.*, I, x, part 1, 259, 261–62. USG later recalled that Mason had come to him "with tears in his eyes and begged to be allowed to have another trial." *Memoirs*, I, 398–99. See letter to Julia Dent Grant, Aug. 22, 1862.

To Col. Philip B. Fouke

Head Quarters, Dist. of West. Tenn.
Pittsburgh, April 15th 1862.

COL. P. B. FOUKE
COMMDG U. S. FORCES
FORT. DONELSON, TENN.
COLONEL:

I send the 71st Ohio Vols. to relieve your command at Fort. Donelson & Clarkesville. Use all dispatch in getting here leaving your wagons at Clarkesville for the new Garrison, and four teams at Fort Donelson, ~~leaving every thing else~~.

I am Col, Respectfully &c.
U. S. GRANT.
Major Gen

Copies, DLC-USG, V, 1, 2, 3, 86; DNA, RG 393, USG Letters Sent. See preceding letter.

To Col. William W. Lowe

————

Head Quarters, Dist of West. Tenn.
Pittsburgh, April 15th 1862.

COL. W. W. LOWE
COMMDG FORT. HENRY.
COLONEL:

Send the 52nd Ind. Regt. to this place without delay. They will bring with them all their transportation, baggage &c.

Very Respectfully
Your Obt. Servant.
U. S. GRANT
Major. Genl.

Copies, DLC–USG, V, 1, 2, 86; DNA, RG 393, USG Letters Sent.

To Julia Dent Grant

————

Pittsburg Ten
April 15th 1862

DEAR JULIA,

I am now living in camp about half a mile from the river preparing my army for the field. Gen. Halleck is here in command of the whole, Buell & myself commanding our seperate armies.[1] I am looking for a speedy move, one more fight and then easy sailing to the close of the war. I really will feel glad when this thing is over. The battle at this place was the most desperate that has ever taken place on the Continant and I dont look for another like it. I suppose you have read a greatdeel about the battle in the papers and some quite contradictory? I will come in again for heaps of abuse from persons who were not here.

I sent you Simps watch and bought me a plain silver one.

Also sent my citizens clothing, all of which no doubt has been received.

I have just learned that a boat was going down the river to-day and Orly[2] is waiting to ~~th~~ take this. Orly is doing very well and saving his money. I sent you $205 00 by express the other day. Did you get it?

We have had the most incessent rains here ever known I expect. The roads are now almost impassable and until they improve we cannot move. Give my love to all at home. Kiss the children for me and accept the same for yourself.

ULYS.

ALS, DLC-USG.

1. Maj. Gen. Henry W. Halleck arrived at Pittsburg Landing on the evening of April 11, 1862. On April 14, he wrote to his wife. "The officers seemed very glad to see me, as according to all accounts and my own observations, this army is undisciplined and very much disorganized, the officers being utterly incapable of maintaining order. I have been very hard at work for the last three days endeavoring to straighten things out, and hope to succeed in time." James Grant Wilson, "Types and Traditions of the Old Army. II. General Halleck—A Memoir," *Journal of the Military Service Institution of the United States*, XXXVI, cxxxv (May–June, 1905), 556.

On April 13, Capt. Nathaniel H. McLean issued General Orders No. 16. "The Major Genl Comdg the Dept thanks Major Genl Grant and Major Genl Buell, and the officers and men of their respective commands for the bravery and endurance with which they sustained the general attacks of the enemy on the 6th and for the heroic manner in which on the 7th inst they defeated and routed the entire rebel army. The soldiers of the great West have added new laurels to those which they had already won on numerous fields. 2. While congratulating the troops on their glorious successes, the Comdg Genl desires to impress upon all officers as well as men, the necessity of greater discipline and order. These are as essential to the success as to the health of the army, and without them we cannot long expect to be victorious; but with them we can march forward to new fields of honor and glory, till this wicked rebellion is completely crushed out and peace restored to our country. 3 Major Genl's Grant and Buell will retain the immediate command of their respective armies in the Field" DS (certified by Capt. John A. Rawlins), McClernand Papers, IHi; copies, DNA, RG 94, 9th Ill., Letterbook; *ibid.*, 48th Ill., Letterbook; (printed), *ibid.*, Orders and Circulars, Dept. of the Miss.; DLC-USG, V, 83. *O.R.*, I, x, part 2, 105.

On April 14, Halleck wrote to USG. "Immediate and active measures must be taken to put your command in condition to resist another attack by the enemy. Fractions of batteries will be united temporarily under competent officers; supplied with ammunition, and placed in position for service. Divisions and Brigades should where necessary be reorganized and put in position; and all stragglers returned to their companies and regiments. Your army is not now in condition to resist an attack. It must be made so without delay. Staff officers must be sent out to obtain returns from Division Commanders, and to assist in supplying all deficiencies" Copies, DLC-USG, V, 4, 5, 7, 8, 9; DNA, RG 393, USG Hd. Qrs. Correspondence; *ibid.*, Dept. of the Miss., Letters Sent. *O.R.*, I, x, part 2, 105–6. On the same day, McLean wrote to USG. "The Major General Commanding desires that, you will again call the attention of your officers to the necessity of forwarding official communications through the proper military channel, to receive the remarks of intermediate commanders. Letters should relate to one matter only, and be properly folded and indorsed. Where the Regulations on this subject are not observed by officers, their communications to these Head Quarters will be returned." LS, DNA, RG 393, District of West Tenn., Letters Received.

On April 17, Maj. John A. Rawlins issued General Orders No. 39. "Constant Guards must be kept around the different Camps of this Command and no officer or soldier permitted to leave his Brigade grounds without the authority of Brigade Commanders, except on duty. Special pains will be taken to instruct sentinels in their duties. Officers will not be permitted to visit the Steamboat Landing except on duty. Most of the command being deficient in drill and discipline, Division Commanders will see that as many hours per day as is consistent with the health of the men be devoted to drill, and that Company Commanders excuse no soldier from any part of his duties" DS, McClernand Papers, IHi; copies, DLC-USG, V, 12, 13, 14, 95; DNA, RG 393, USG General Orders; *ibid.*, District of West Tenn., Letters Received. *O.R.*, I, x, part 2, 109.

Also on April 17, McLean issued Special Field Orders No. 12. "The commanding Generals of the armies of the Tennessee and of the Ohio will immediately establish a System of drills and inspections and prepare their respective forces for active operations. The arms and ammunition of all the Regiments and Batteries will be thoroughly examined and all deficiencies supplied. All defective arms and ammunition at and in the vicinity of the camps, will be collected and turned over to the Ordnance Department. For this purpose wagons and squads of men will be detailed from each camp. All troops will be immediately placed in line of battle, the Army of the Ohio, resting its left on Lick Creek, and the Army of Tennessee with its right on Owl Creek, the different Divisions and Brigades being arranged according to the nature of the ground. Guards of cavalry will be placed in rear of each Army to prevent all access to the landings except by authorized persons. All trains or wagons going to the landing must be under the charge of a commissioned officer, and each regimental train should be accompanied by a detail of men to assist in loading, and in assisting the wagons through the bad roads. Sufficient working parties will be detailed from each army and placed under commissioned officers to build bridges and repair roads from the several landings to the camp. These working parties will receive tools from the Quarter Master's Department, and will be placed under the General direction of Staff officers whose duty it shall be to see that the roads are immediately put in good order. Having repaired those leading to the landings, they will proceed to repair and open those in front of the camps. Where the working parties so detailed fail to do their duty properly, the officers in charge of them will be reported to the Commanding General of the Army to which they belong, who will have them arrested and punished. Provost Guards will be established in each army to patrol the roads and landings and examine all Boats, so as to arrest all Stragglers and place them in confinement. They will also see that the bars on all boats are closed and that no spiritous Liquors are sold on the Boats at the landings or in the camps. They will arrest and confine any one guilty of vending such Liquors. Strong pickets will be established in advance of each camp, and the Division Commanders in charge of the roads in front will see that they are well guarded. The Generals Commanding the Armies will immediately appoint Boards or Commissions to examine into the character and capacity of Volunteer officers in their respective commands, and more especially of all such as did not conduct themselves with military propriety in recent battles. In all cases of improper conduct the Boards will report whether the officer should simply be discharged from service, or whether he should be tried and punished for cowardice. No papers not requiring, under the law or Army Regulations, the action of the Commanding General of the Department will be sent to Department Head Quarters, but the Generals Commanding the Armies in the field will act upon them as they may deem proper. Every Regiment and corps should take pride in preparing itself, with the least possible delay, to again meet the enemy in battle and to agai[n] drive him from the field. These orders will be read at the head of each Regiment." DS (certified by Rawlins), McClernand Papers, IHi; copies, *ibid.*; DLC-USG, V, 83. In this document, Halleck referred to USG's command as the Army of the Tenn. Although ordering no formal reassignment of command, USG appears to have retained nominal command of the District of West Tenn. while commanding the Army of the Tenn. In reality, however, Halleck's presence brought a great diminution of USG's authority. See General Orders No. 50, May 1, 1862.

In accordance with section VI of Special Field Orders No. 12, on April 18, Rawlins issued General Orders No. 40 appointing a board of officers, headed by Brig. Gen. John A. Logan, "to examine the capacity, qualifications, propriety of conduct and efficiency of any commissioned officer who may be reported to the Board, and more especially of all such as did not conduct themselves with military propriety in the recent battles." Copies, DLC-USG, V, 12, 13, 14, 95; DNA, RG 94, 48th Ill., Letterbook; *ibid.*, RG 393, USG General Orders. On April 19, Rawlins wrote a letter to gen. officers. "A Board of Officers having been appointed by General Orders No 40 Current Series, from these Head Quarters, to convene at the Head Qrs of the 2nd Division Army of the Tenn, on monday the 21st inst, all commanders of Divisions, Brigades, Regiments, Detachments or Corps are directed to send in the name of such officers of their respective commands as they believe to be disqualified from any cause to fill the positions assigned them by their commissions; and especially the names of all such as did not conduct themselves with Military propriety in recent battles. The names of witnesses will also be sent in each case." LS, McClernand Papers, IHi; copies, DLC-USG, V, 1, 2, 86; DNA, RG 393, USG Letters Sent. On April 21, Brig. Gen. William T. Sherman forwarded to USG charges against Capt. John H. Blinn, 72nd Ohio (who resigned on Jan. 15, 1863); Capt. Joseph Clay, 55th Ill. (who was dismissed from U.S. service on Sept. 16, 1862); 2nd Lt. Jonas L. Buck, 55th Ill. (who was dismissed from U.S. service on Sept. 16, 1862); Col. Jesse J. Appler, 53rd Ohio (who was mustered out of U.S. service on April 18, 1862); and Maj. Silas B. Walker, 57th Ohio (who resigned on April 26, 1863). Copy, *ibid.*, RG 94, Generals' Papers and Books, William T. Sherman Letters Sent.

On April 23, 1862, Secretary of War Edwin M. Stanton telegraphed to Halleck. "The President desires to know [w]hy you have made no official report to this department respecting the late battles at Pittsburg landing. An[d] whether any neglect or misconduct of General Grant or any other officer contributed to

the sad casulties that befell our forces on Sunday." ALS (telegram sent), *ibid.*,
RG 107, Telegrams Collected (Bound). *O.R.*, I, x, part 1, 98–99. On April 24,
Halleck telegraphed to Stanton. "The said casualties of suday the sixth were due
in part to the bad conduct of officers who were utterly unfit for their places & in
part to [t]he numbers & bravery of the enemy   [I] prefer to express no opinion
in regard [to] the misconduct of individuals till [I] receive the reports of commanders of Division. A Great Battle cannot [b]e fought or a victory gained
without many casualties   in this instance the [e]nemy suffered more than we did"
Telegram received, DNA, RG 107, Telegrams Collected (Bound). *O.R.*, I, x,
part 1, 99.

On April 22, McLean issued Special Field Orders No. 21. "As the troops
advance their camps, care will be taken to exclude and keep outside of our lines
all unauthorized persons of whatsoever description. To this end the Provost
Marshals of the several Army Corps will cause each regimental camp to be
searched, and all who, are improperly retained or harbored in them excluded.
When fugitives slaves who have become free under the laws of Congress are hired
as servants, the officers so hireing them must give a certificate of the facts, stating
where the negro was captured or how and when he was made free. where such
fugitives are harbored or supported in reward for information given or services
rendered, they must be supplied with a certificate to that effect, approved by the
General commanding the army which harbors them. Complete lists of officers
servants and camp employees and retainers will will be filed at the Head Qrs. of
each regiment and copies furnished to the commanders of Divisions. All passes
and permits to enter our lines heretofore issued are hereby revoked untill the the
same are endorsed by the General commanding an army corps. Division Commanders will be held responsible that no unauthorized persons are permitted to
enter their lines. Transports will be permitted to convey citizens at their own
expense, from this place, but no Government transport will convey any citizen up
the Tennessee river to Savanna or above without the special authority of the
Secretary of War   Captains of transports and commanding officers of the troops
on board will be held responsible for the execution of this order. No sick will be
removed from this place or any field hospital, without the the authority of a
Medical Director. The forces, under the command of Maj General Pope will be
designated and known as the 'Army of the 'Mississippi' "   DS (certified by
Rawlins), McClernand Papers, IHi; copy, DLC-USG, V, 83.

On April 23, Capt. Andrew C. Kemper issued Special Field Orders No. 25.
"The attention of the commanding General of the Department has been called to
this slovenly and negligent manner in which guard duty is performed in various
Divisions, the sentinels often being seated or lying down on their posts, sometimes
even in the presence of their officers. If such negligence be permitted in lines, but
little reliance can be placed upon the vigilance of picket guards to prevent a surprise. Hereafter the Generals of Divisions and Brigades will visit their guards
daily and have every sentinel who neglects his duty properly punished. Every
officer of the guard who englects to enforce discipline and to properly instruct his
guard will be arrested and tried for neglect of duty   Staff officers will be sent
frequently to inspect the guard and to see that this this important duty is properly
performed. Commanders of Divisions and Brigades will see that their camps are
properly policed, and that sinks are constructed in sufficient numbers and at convenient places for the men. A culpable neglect of these sanitary measures has been
the cause of much sickness, for which the officers are justly chargeble   Where

working parties are detailed for the construction of bridges and the repair of roads, officers will always be sent in charge, and will be held responsible that the men do their duty properly. Where the men refuse or neglect to work, they will be punished, and where the officers in charge of such details fail to make them do their duty, he will be arrested and tried by Court Martial or be mustered out of service. Where a detail from a regiment persistently neglects its duty as a working party, the fact will be reported to these Head Quarters, when the staff officers of the regiment will be ordered out with a sufficient force to compel obedience to orders." DS (certified by Rawlins), McClernand Papers, IHi; copy, DLC-USG, V, 83.

2. Orlando H. Ross, cousin of USG. See letter to Julia Dent Grant, June 27, 1861, note 1.

To Maj. Gen. Henry W. Halleck

Pittsburgh Tennessee
April 16th 1862

MAJOR GENERAL H W. HALLECK
COMMANDING DEPT OF THE MISSISSIPPI
GENL

Immediately after the battle of Fort Donelson I addressed a communication to the War Department asking that Clark B Lagow and William S. Hillyer, now Aides-de-Camp to me, be made additional Aides with the rank of Colonel, in consideration of courage and good conduct displayed at the Battles of Belmont and Fort Donelson

The Communication was referred to the Adjutant General of the army who decided that it could not legally be done.[1]

I found on reference to the law that such appointments could only be made on the nomination of Maj Genls of the Regular Army

To the battles ~~of~~ above named I can now add that of Pittsburgh, or Shiloh, in which these two officers rendered most valuable services.

I would therefore respectfully ask that you ~~would~~ nominate them as additional Aides, with the rank of Colonel on your staff to be transferred to mine, when so commissioned.

> I am Genl Very Respcty
> Your Obt Servt
> U. S. GRANT

Copies, DLC-USG, V, 4, 5, 7, 8, 88; DNA, RG 393, USG Hd. Qrs. Correspondence. In accordance with USG's request, William S. Hillyer, Clark B. Lagow, and John Riggin, Jr., were all confirmed as col. on July 17, 1862, to rank from May 3 on the staff of Maj. Gen. Henry W. Halleck, though assigned to USG. On April 18, Brig. Gen. John A. Logan wrote to U.S. Representatives Elihu B. Washburne and James C. Robinson of Ill. "My *Christian* friends, enclosed you will find copy of letter from Genl Grant, which explains itself, these two Gentlemen are deserving officers and if you can aid in any way to have them promoted as desired it will be gratifying to their numerous friends here and elsewhere." ALS, DLC-Elihu B. Washburne. The USG letter is no longer attached, but was probably the letter about Hillyer and Lagow.

On May 6, Washburne wrote to USG. "I have the pleasure of enclosing you herewith the appointments of your aids Hillyer, Riggin and Lagow, with the rank of Colonel. The glorious victory you won at Pittsburgh Landing has evoking much criticism from the men who are never satisfied with anything, but who always keep out of harm's way, and from the cowardly scoundrels who fled from the field. I took occasion the other day in the House to ventilate the matter a little. I send you my remarks. But let 'em howl—'Truth is omnipotent and public justice certain.' I have just received your letter in regard to Dr. Simons, and as soon as the Sec'y of War returns from Yorktown I will see him on the subject. Regards to Rawlins and Rowley." ALS, CSmH. See letter to Edwin M. Stanton, April 20, 1862.

1. See letter to Julia Dent Grant, March 29, 1862, note 1.

To Capt. Nathaniel H. McLean

———

> Head Quarters Dist of West Tenn.
> Pittsburg, April 17, 1862.

CAPT. N. H. MCLEAN
A. A. GEN. DEPART OF THE MISS.
CAPT:

I have the honor to acknowledge the receipt of your communication, and in reply, to inform you, that the Regiments of

"Cruft's Brigade" under my command are the 17th Kentucky Volunteers, (which is a consolidation of the 17th and 25th Kentucky)[1] and the 31st and 44th Indiana Infantry

> I am, Captain
> Very Respectfully
> Your Obt. Serv't.
> U. S. GRANT
> Maj. Gen.

LS, DNA, RG 393, Dept. of the Miss., Letters Received. On April 17, 1862, Capt. Nathaniel H. McLean wrote to USG. "Will you please send me word by the Orderly what regiments of of *Crufts* brigade are now with your Army. Your return does not show what regiments compose your brigades." Copy, *ibid.*, Letters Sent. On the same day, McLean endorsed USG's letter. "The Major General Comdg desires to know in whose Brigade of Genl Hurlbuts Division these regiments are." AES, *ibid.*, Letters Received. Also on the same day, USG endorsed his own letter. "The Brigade formerly commanded by Col. Crufts is the third Brigade, 4th Division commanded by Brig. Gen. J. G. Lauman. It never was my intention that he should command that Brigade but having a number of Brig. Gens. to dispose of I assigned Gen. Lauman to Gen. Hurlbuts Division." AES, *ibid.* On April 18, McLean issued Special Field Orders No. 13. "The 17th Regt Ky Vols and the 31st & 44th Regts Ind Vols are hereby relieved from duty with Maj Genl Grants army, and will report for duty with the army of the Ohio. The Comdg Officers of these Regiments will at once report to Maj Genl Buell for his orders." Copy, DLC-USG, V, 83. *O.R.*, I, lii, part 1, 240.

1. On April 4, Special Orders No. 74, Dept. of the Miss., announced the consolidation of the 17th Ky. and 25th Ky. as the 17th Ky. Copy, DNA, RG 94, Dept. of the Miss., Special Orders. Beneath the orders, McLean added a note to USG. "Major Genl. Grant will cause this conso[li]dation to be effected at once, and report to these Head Qrs. the date on [w]hich it was made. Such will be the date on which the Officers not [c]ontinued in service and who do not resign, will be mustered out [of] service" LS, *ibid.* On April 11, Capt. John A. Rawlins added a note to a copy of Special Orders No. 74. "In pursuance of the foregoing order Col Jno H McHenry Jr will at once effect the consolidation, and the Officers of said Regts not therein named are respectfully requested to send in their resignations immediately and when said order of consolidation is effected Col John H McHenry will report the fact to these H'd Quarters." Copy, DLC-USG, V, 83.

To Brig. Gen. Stephen A. Hurlbut

———

> Head Quarters, Dist of West. Tenn.
> Pittsburgh, April 17th 1862.

Gen. S. A. Hurlbut
Commdg 4th Division
General—

There has been constant firing this morning by soldiers of your Division, in violation of orders.

Send out & have the Officers permitting it arrested, and ~~if possible~~ the men punished. if possible

> Very Respectfully
> Your Obt. Servant.
> U. S. Grant.
> Major Gen.

Copies, DLC-USG, V, 1, 2, 3, 86; DNA, RG 393, USG Letters Sent. On April 16, 1862, Capt. Nathaniel H. McLean wrote to USG. "I am directed by the Major General Commanding to call your attention to the unnecessary discharge of fire arms, which might cause unfounded alarm and endanger the life of our men. Hereafter, old guards, and all officers and men will draw the charges from their arms instead of discharging them." Copy, *ibid.*, Dept. of the Miss., Letters Sent. On the same day, Maj. John A. Rawlins issued General Orders No. 38. "Hereafter *Old Guards*, and all officers and men will draw the charge from their arms instead of discharging them; and it is made the special duty of all officers to see that this is ridgidly enforced." DS, McClernand Papers, IHi; copies, DLC-USG, V, 12, 13, 14, 95; DNA, RG 94, 9th Ill., Letterbook; *ibid.*, RG 393, USG General Orders. On April 19, Capt. William S. Hillyer wrote to Brig. Gen. Stephen A. Hurlbut. "I am instructed by Gen Grant to say to you that the order prohibiting firing is made by direction of Gen Halleck and cannot be suspended without his authority and must *be strictly enforced in all cases*—" ALS, *ibid.*, 16th Army Corps, Miscellaneous Papers. On the same day, Hurlbut wrote to Rawlins. "Col. Taylor 5th Ohio Cavalry desires leave to return all his Pistols as *worthless* (they are the Joslyn Pistol) & rely upon the Sabre. He also asks leave to fire off the Charges now in his pistols   I await directions from the Major General.—I am satisfied from personal inspection that the Pistols are useless—but think that videttes should have fire arms" ALS, *ibid*. On April 21, USG endorsed this letter. "Return the Pistols to Capt. Brinck, ordnance officer. Authority cannot be given, nor is it necessary, to fire them off." AES, *ibid*.

On April 26, Rawlins issued General Orders No. 43. "Division Commanders will detail Daily Ten mounted men, under command of Commissioned officers, to patrol the entire grounds within the limits of the Army of the Tenn, who will arrest personally ~~arrest~~ all officers and men, guilty of discharging fire arms, in violation of paragraph Second of General Orders No 38, current Series issued from these Head Quarters, and report them to their Division commanders, who will cause enlisted men to be punished, and officers to be tried before Courts Martial for such violations"   DS, McClernand Papers, IHi; copies, DLC-USG, V, 12, 13, 14, 95; DNA, RG 94, 9th Ill., Letterbook; *ibid.*, 48th Ill., Letterbook; *ibid.*, RG 393, USG General Orders. See letter to Maj. Gen. Henry W. Halleck, April 25, 1862.

To Brig. Gen. Thomas J. McKean

Head Quarters, Dist of West. Tenn
Pittsburgh, April 17th 1862.

BRIG. GEN. THOMAS MCKEAN.
COMMDG 6TH DIVISION
GENERAL:

Consolidate the 18th Ohio[1] Regiment into Eight or less Companies, and order a Field Officer from one of the other Regiments to command it, temporarily, until such time as the Governor may appoint a Field Officer ~~to~~ for the Regiment.

Where two Regiments are very much reduced in numbers and also reduced in Field Officers they may be attached, and the Senior Field Officer take Command as ~~if~~ one regiment.

Very Respectfully
Your Obt. Servant
U. S. GRANT
Major General.

Copies, DLC-USG, V, 1, 2, 3, 86; DNA, RG 393, USG Letters Sent. Thomas J. McKean of Pa., USMA 1831, resigned from the U.S. Army on March 31, 1834, but served as a vol. in both the Second Seminole War (1837–38) and the Mexican War (1846–48). He was a civil engineer and farmer in Iowa before his appointment as additional paymaster on June 1, 1861. Promoted to brig. gen. on Nov. 21, he was assigned to the Central District of Mo. On April 10, 1862, Capt. John A. Rawlins issued Special Orders No. 50 assigning McKean to command the 6th Division. Copies, DLC-USG, V, 15, 16, 82, 87, 89; DNA, RG 393, USG Special Orders. *O.R.*, I, x, part 2, 101.

1. The 18th Ohio at that time was at Huntsville, Ala., in the command of Maj. Gen. Ormsby M. Mitchel. USG probably meant some other regt., perhaps the 18th Mo., which was then under McKean.

To Capt. Nathaniel H. McLean

Head Quarters, Dist. of West Ten
Pittsburg, April 18th 1862

CAPT. N. H. MCLEAN
A. A. GEN. DEPT. OF THE MISS.
CAPT.

A detail has been standing in the rain at my Hd Qrs. since an early hour this morning awaiting the arrival of Capt. Sheridan[1] or some one to take charge of them.

In view of the heavy rain however I question whether much work can be done to-day and will therefore dismiss them to be assembled when called upon.

very respectfully
your obt. svt.
U. S. GRANT
Maj. Gen

ALS, DNA, RG 393, Dept. of the Miss., Letters Received. On April 18, 1862, Capt. Nathaniel H. McLean wrote to USG. "Capt Sheridan will take charge of the Repair of the Roads from the Main Landing to Your Head Qrs and, Col McKibben from the lower or forage landing to the Same point and, Col Cutts from that point to Shiloh Cross Roads   Col Thom will make examination for Roads in advance of Shiloh to your New Camping Grounds   These officers will report to you early to Morrow Morning for Working parties which will be detailed from the different divisions along the Roads   it is of the utmost importance that these Roads should be put in order without further delay. You will therefore see that working parties provided with Tools be ready to Commence operations to Morrow Morning   each Regmt Brigade & Division as it takes position in New Camps Will open proper Communication with the Main roads with proper care Your army can be Supplied far in advance of present position without additional Transportation"   Copies, DLC-USG, V, 4, 5, 7, 8, 9; DNA, RG 393, Dept. of the Miss., Letters Sent; *ibid.*, USG Hd. Qrs. Correspondence. *O.R.*, I, lii, part 1, 240.

1. Philip H. Sheridan of Ohio, USMA 1853, served in the U.S. Army continuously after graduation, spending the six years before the Civil War on the Pacific Coast with the rank of 1st lt. Promoted to capt. as of May 14, 1861, he served as q. m. and commissary of the Army of Southwest Mo. from Dec. 26, 1861, then purchased horses for army use, until reassigned as q. m. and commissary of the hd. qrs. of Maj. Gen. Henry W. Halleck. Sheridan later recalled that he first met USG in Sept., 1862. *Personal Memoirs of P. H. Sheridan* (New York, 1888), I, 181.

To Maj. Gen. Lewis Wallace

Head Quarters, Dist of West. Tenn.
Pittsburgh, April 18th 1862.

MAJOR GEN. LEW. WALLACE,
COMMDG 3RD DIVISION
GENL:

Notice has just been sent me from Gen Halleck's Head Quarters that the barge Ripley is laying at Crump's Landing with quite a number of sick and that some of the Rebel Cavalry are at Adamsville[1] with scattering men quite near in to the landing.

I have ~~just~~ ordered the Qr. Master to send a Steamer to tow the Ripley up to this place, and to bring away any other floating property that may be there.

You will please take immediate steps, to night, to have any troops or property you may have them brought away.

I am, Gen, Very Respectfully &c
U. S. GRANT
Maj Genl.

Copies, DLC-USG, V, 1, 2, 3, 86; DNA, RG 393, USG Letters Sent. On April 15, 1862, Maj. John A. Rawlins issued Special Orders No. 55. "Genl L. Wallace is hereby directed to move the forces of his Command now at Crumps Landing together with their Garrison & Camp Equipage to Pittsburgh, to rejoin their Division." Copies, DLC-USG, V, 15, 16, 82, 87, 89; DNA, RG 393, USG Special Orders. *O.R.*, I, x, part 2, 108. On April 18, USG wrote to Capt. Charles A. Reynolds. "Send a Steamer immediately to Crump's Landing and have the Barge Ripley towed up to Pittsburgh Landing. Should there be any other Craft there order them up also. Nothing is to be left at that point." Copies, DLC-USG, V, 1, 2, 86; DNA, RG 393, USG Letters Sent.

1. Adamsville, Tenn., about seven miles west of Crump's Landing, on the Purdy road about six miles east of Purdy.

To Brig. Gen. Stephen A. Hurlbut

———

Head Quarters, Dist of West. Tenn.
Pittsburg, April 18th 1862.

BRIG. GEN. S. A. HURLBUT,
COMMDG 4TH DIVISION.
GENL.

You will please hold your command in readiness to move tomorrow morning to a position in front of Gen. Wallace's Division.

A guide will be sent to indicate the point where you are to encamp. Immediately on getting your new position, you will have roads and all necessary bridges made to communicate freely with Pittsburgh Landing, and to the front ~~with~~ on the main Corinth road.

I am, Gen, Very Respectfully,
Your Obt Servant.
U. S. GRANT.
Maj. Genl.

Copies, DLC-USG, V, 1, 2, 3, 86; DNA, RG 393, USG Letters Sent. On April 19, 1862, Brig. Gen. Stephen A. Hurlbut wrote to Maj. John A. Rawlins. "In obedience to Orders by Letter from the Major Genl—My command will be ready to move to new position at ½ past 8 this morning. If it be deemed advisable to delay this movement on account of the Weather & roads will you advise me before that hour." ALS, *ibid.*, 16th Army Corps, Miscellaneous Papers. On the same day, Rawlins endorsed this letter. "You need not move to-day. The weather may be more favorable tomorrow" ES, *ibid.*

To Brig. Gen. Thomas J. McKean

———

Head Quarters, Dist of West. Tenn.
Pittsburgh, April 18th 1862.

BRIG. GEN. THOS. J. McKEAN,
COMMDG 6TH DIVISION
GENL:

You will please hold your command in readiness to move tomorrow morning to a position in front of that now occupied by Gen Wallace, and to the left of Genl Hurlbut's new position. A guide will be sent to point out the ground. Immediately on taking your new position, parties will be detailed to make roads and bridges to make your access easy to Pittsburgh Landing, and to the main Corinth roads

I am, Gen, Very Respectfully
Your Obt. Servant.
U. S. GRANT.
Major Genl.

Copies, DLC-USG, V, 1, 2, 3, 86; DNA, RG 393, USG Letters Sent.

To Edwin M. Stanton

———

Pittsburg Landing, Ten.
April 20th 1862

HON E. M. STANTON
SEC. OF WAR
WASHINGTON, D. C.

Learning through the press that two additional grades have been created in the Medical Corps of the Army I would respectfully call your attention to the name of Surgeon Jas. Simons.

Dr. Simons, though a Southern man, has ever been loyal to the cause of the Union, has rendered most efficient service in the West, and I think justly entitled to promotion. If he can be advanced to the highest position created under the new law I feel that the public service will be benefitted and a meritorious officer rewarded.

Dr. Simons was the Assistant Surgeon of the regiment to which I belonged more than sixteen years ago—therefore I speak of him knowingly.

> very respectfully
> your obt. svt.
> U. S. GRANT
> Maj Gen

ALS, Mrs. Walter Love, Flint, Mich. Surgeon James Simons was not promoted to lt. col. until June 26, 1876, though he received rank as bvt. lt. col. and bvt. col. as of March 13, 1865. See letter to Maj. Gen. Henry W. Halleck, April 16, 1862.

To Surgeon Henry S. Hewit

> Head Quarters, Dist. of W. Ten.
> Pittsburg, April 20th 1862.

SURGEON H. W. HEWITT
MEDICAL DIRECTOR.
DR.

It is with great regret that I learn, through the papers, that you have been relieved from your duties with this army. Your whole course was most satisfactory to me and certainly to all those who had simply the good of the sick and wounded at heart.—The influance brought to bear to cause your removal from this Military District, not being honest, can work you no ultimate harm.—You have my warmest approval for all your official course whilst under me and I can only hope that others filling the same position may do it just as you did.

> very respectfully
> your obt. svt.
> U. S. GRANT
> Maj. Gen.

ALS, DNA, RG 94, Letters Received. On March 31, 1862, Agate (Whitelaw Reid), Savannah, Tenn., wrote a bitter attack upon Surgeon Henry S. Hewit, accusing him of incompetence, arrogance, drunkenness, and disloyalty. *Cincinnati Gazette*, April 4, 1862. On April 4, G. W. Gans, Eaton, Ohio, sent a copy of the article to U.S. Senator Benjamin F. Wade, who in turn sent it to the War Dept. DNA, RG 107, Letters Received. On April 8, E. F. Riley, Leonardsburg, Ohio, sent a copy of the article to President Abraham Lincoln. *Ibid.*, RG 94, Letters Received. On April 11, Secretary of War Edwin M. Stanton telegraphed to the editor, *Cincinnati Gazette*, that Hewit had been suspended from duty. ALS (telegram sent), *ibid.*, RG 107, Telegrams Collected (Bound). See *Cincinnati Gazette*, April 12, 1862. A file of papers concerning Hewit, 477H, DNA, RG 94, Letters Received, includes letters of endorsement from Maj. Gens. Charles F. Smith and William T. Sherman. On Aug. 19, Surgeon Gen. William A. Hammond wrote to Stanton that charges against Hewit had been withdrawn and that he should be restored to duty.

To Maj. Gen. Henry W. Halleck

———

Pittsburg Landing, Ten.
April 21st 1862

MAJ. GEN. H. W. HALLECK
COMD.G DEPT. OF THE MISS.
GEN.

A Mr. Saunders of this state who has acted as guide for our troops and given all the information he could of the movements of the rebels has just come in and reports that the enemy have about 15,000 troops at Bethel. They have cut timber between Crumps Landing and Purdy but not on the road from here. It is said to be the intention of the enemy to take possession of Chalk Bluffs, six miles below Savanna, and interrupt the navigation of the river.

I give the information for what it is worth not thinking it unlikely however that some such movement might be made.

I am Gen. very respectfully
your obt. svt.
U. S. GRANT
Maj. Gen.

ALS, DNA, RG 109, Union Provost Marshals' File of Papers Relating to Individual Civilians.

To Capt. Nathaniel H. McLean

———

Head Quarters, Army of the Ten
Pittsburg Landing Apl 21st/62

CAPT. N. H. McLEAN
A. A. GEN. DEPT OF THE MISS.

I transmit herewith the report of the action of the 1st Division at the battle of Fort Donelson.

I have no special comments to make on it further than that the report is a little highly colored as to the conduct of the first Division, and I failed to hear the suggestions spoken of about the propriety of attacking the enemy all around the lines on Saturday.

No suggestions were made by Gen. McClernand at the time spoken of.[1]

U. S. GRANT
Maj. Gen.

ALS, DNA, RG 94, War Records Office, Union Battle Reports. *O.R.*, I, vii, 170. Maj. Gen. John A. McClernand's lengthy report of the battle of Fort Donelson is dated Feb. 28, 1862, though probably completed later. LS, DNA, RG 94, War Records Office, Union Battle Reports; DLC-Robert T. Lincoln. *O.R.*, I, vii, 170–82. On March 27, Capt. John A. Rawlins wrote to McClernand. "I am directed by Maj Genl U S. Grant Comd'g to request that you make out and foward to these Head Quarters, Copies of the Brigade Commanders reports of the Battle of Fort Donelson, made to you, to accompany your report." LS, McClernand Papers, IHi.

1. "In reply to my suggestion, urging a simultaneous assault, at all points, I was gratified to receive an order to that effect." LS, DNA, RG 94, War Records Office, Union Battle Reports; DLC-Robert T. Lincoln. *O.R.*, I, vii, 179.

To Maj. Gen. John A. McClernand

Head Quarters, Army of the Ten.
Pittsburg Landing, April 21st 1862

MAJ. GEN. J. A. MCCLERNAND
COMD.G 1ST DIV.
GEN.

It is reported to me that outside the Picketts of Gen. Garfields[1] Brigade there is a deserted camp of the rebels where some sixty Sibley tents[2] are still standing, besides other property.

I wish you would order some teams, with a Cavalry escort, after this property and have it taken up by your Quarter Master.

I am Gen. very respectfully
your obt. svt.
U. S. GRANT
Maj. Gen. Com

ALS, McClernand Papers, IHi. On April 22, 1862, Maj. Gen. John A. McClernand wrote to USG. "According to your direction, I sent forward a number of Waggons &c. under escort of 30 cavalry men, guided by the man reporting to me, under your order, for that purpose. The party returned last night bringing in two ammunition Chests and number of Artillery carriage wheels of little or no value. The party went as far as the guide would conduct them, and our pickets would let them go. The guide reports that he found the enemy's picket advanced some two miles nearer our lines, and this side of the 'Deserted Camp,' which I am inclined to doubt. Lt Jones waits upon you for direction in regard to the disposal of the property." Copies, *ibid.*

1. James A. Garfield, born in Ohio, attended the Western Reserve Eclectic Institute (later Hiram College) and graduated from Williams College, returned to the former to teach, then was elected to the Ohio Senate in 1859 as a Republican. On Aug. 21, 1861, he was commissioned lt. col., 42nd Ohio, was promoted to col. on Nov. 27, and to brig. gen. on Feb. 19, 1862, in recognition of his victory at Prestonburg (Middle Creek), Ky. On April 2, he was ordered to join Maj. Gen. Don Carlos Buell's advance to Savannah and was assigned command of the 20th Brigade, 6th Division, which arrived at Shiloh just at the end of the battle. Theodore Clarke Smith, *The Life and Letters of James Abram Garfield* (New Haven, 1925), I, 203–8; Frederick D. Williams, ed., *The Wild Life of the Army: Civil War Letters of James A. Garfield* ([East Lansing, Mich.], 1964), pp. 79–81.
2. A drawing and description of the Sibley tent, which resembled a tepee, is in Francis A. Lord, *Civil War Collector's Encyclopedia* (Harrisburg, Pa., 1963), pp. 279–80.

To Maj. Gen. John A. McClernand

———

> Head Quarters, Army of the Ten.
> Pittsburg, April 22d 1862

GEN. J. A. MCCLERNAND
COMD.G 1ST DIV.
GEN.

Your Division will take the position last agreed upon; that is two Brigades move forward of Gen. Wallace and the third move so as to guard Owl creek[1] crossing.

> I am Gen. very respectfully
> your obt. svt.
> U. S. GRANT
> Maj. Gen. Com

ALS, McClernand Papers, IHi.

1. Owl Creek runs north of Shiloh, then joins Snake Creek, which enters the Tennessee River north of Pittsburg Landing.

To Maj. Gen. John A. McClernand

———

> Head Quarters, Dist of West. Tenn.
> Pittsburgh, April 24th 1862.

MAJOR. GEN. J. A. MCCLERNAND,
COMMDG. 1ST DIVISION
GENL:

Detail two companies from your command to hold themselves in readiness, subject to the call of Col. McPherson tomorrow morning to build a bridge across Owl. Creek.

They will require axes and spades. Col. McPherson will leave here in the morning at 6 O'clock and determine the point where the bridge should be built and call for the detail by half past 7 O'clock.

> I am, Gen, Very Respectfully &c
> U. S. GRANT.
> Major Gen.

Copies, DLC-USG, V, 1, 2, 3, 86; DNA, RG 393, USG Letters Sent. On April 24, 1862, Maj. Gen. Henry W. Halleck wrote to USG. "Owl Creek opposite Genl Wallas position will be bridged and a strong reconnoittering party sent out on the Purdy road to feel the enemy and ascertain his position & force in that direction and especially on the Road to Crumps Landing"   Copies, DLC-USG, V, 4, 5, 7, 8, 9; DNA, RG 393, USG Hd. Qrs. Correspondence; *ibid.*, Dept. of the Miss., Letters Sent. *O.R.*, I, x, part 2, 121. On the same day, Capt. William S. Hillyer wrote to Maj. Gen. Lewis Wallace. "You will detail a sufficient fatigue party and have a bridge made over Owl Creek, opposite or above your position. You will also send as soon as possible a Regt. of Infantry and a section of Artillery out on the Purdy road to reconnoiter and feel the enemy and ascertain his position and force in that direction." Copies, DLC-USG, V, 1, 2, 3, 86; DNA, RG 393, USG Letters Sent. USG added a postscript to this letter. "P. S. I have just ordered Gen. Sherman to send you all the Cavalry at his disposal to join the reconnoitering party on the Purdy road. Upon a reperusal of Gen. Halleck's note I am satisfied that he desires only one reconnoisance and that on the Purdy road. He wishes to ascertain the position and force of the enemy in that direction and especially on the road to Crump's Landing. For the guidance of the Officer in charge I copy that part of Gen. Halleck's Order which refers to it." Copies, *ibid.* Also on the same day, Maj. John A. Rawlins wrote to Brig. Gen. William T. Sherman. "You will detail whatever available Cavalry you have, to report to Major Gen. Wallace for duty without delay." Copies, *ibid.*

On April 26, Halleck wrote to USG. "No report has been received of the reconnoitering party ordered to move on the Purdy road on the 24th. I have anxiously waited to hear from it. Send me a sketch showing the position of your troops." Copy, *ibid.*, Dept. of the Miss., Letters Sent. On the same day, Wallace wrote to his wife. "Yesterday I returned with my Division from a recconnoisance towards Purdy. We drove the enemy in and out of the town and returned— nobody hurt several of the rebels killed. The march was in a continual rain with mud everlastingly." ALS, Wallace Papers, InHi.

To Maj. Gen. Henry W. Halleck

Pittsburgh Landing, Tenn
April 25th 1862

MAJ GENL H W. HALLECK
COMMANDING DEPT OF THE MISS
GENL

I would be most happy to correct any abuses that take place within my command, if Genl Buell or any of his Division Commanders would call my attention to them, without refering these matters to General Head Quarters. In the case referred to to-day, and which is herewith returned endorsed, the same complaint was made to me against troops of Genl Buells command. The Communication of Genl Nelson does not seem to charge this violation upon my command, but simply that the violaters do not belong to his own Division. I have not a doubt but that every Division Commander here uses every exertion to prevent firing, and that all flatter themselves that so far as the order against it goes, it is implicitly obeyed within their respective Commands.

I am Genl Very Respectfully
Your Obt Servt
U. S. GRANT
Maj Genl

Copies, DLC-USG, V, 4, 5, 7, 8, 88; DNA, RG 393, USG Hd. Qrs. Correspondence. On April 25, 1862, Brig. Gen. William Nelson wrote to Col. James B. Fry, chief of staff for Maj. Gen. Don Carlos Buell. "A regular skirmishing fire is opened every morning in front of my line, and has now been going on for 30 minutes. It is utterly impossible for me to tell whether my pickets are attacked or not. The order relative to firing is wholly disregarded by the people who do this (they are not of my Division)— I have to say that this thing is simply intolerable, and I report it." Copies, DLC-USG, V, 88; DNA, RG 393, District of West Tenn., Letters Received. On the same day, Buell endorsed the letter. "Respectfully referred to Genl Head Quarters. The firing is by the troops belonging to General Grants force, encamped in the midst of mine." Copies, *ibid.* Also on the same day, USG endorsed the letter. "I have no troops encamped in the midst of Genl Buell. Genl McKean's Division haves moved to the position assigned them it, but a portion of the troops under Genl Buells have gone to the front and are now occupying most of the line from Owl to Lick Creeks making it impossible for me to encamp all of my force without occupying, with a portion of them, a position either in front or rear of some part of the other command. The A A. Genl to Genl McKean made a personal complaint to these Head Quarters to day that frequent firing was kept up, some of the balls having passed through their Camp, but it was not done by persons of this command. Further that violent and abusive language was used by the guilty parties when ordered to desist. As a correction it would be easy for Division Commanders to arrest and punish all violation of orders, no matter whether the offenders belong to their command or not." Copies, *ibid*. See letter to Brig. Gen. Stephen A. Hurlbut, April 17, 1862.

To Maj. Gen. Henry W. Halleck

———

Head Quarters, Army of the Ten
Pittsburg, April 25th 1862.

Respectfully forwarded to Head Quarters of the Dept. I directed this Division at about 8 O'Clock a. m. to be held in readiness to move at a moments warning in any direction it might be ordered. Certainly not later than 11 a. m. the order reached Gen. Wallace to march by a flank movement to Pittsburg Landing. Waiting until I thought he should be here I sent one of my staff to hurry him, and afterwards sent Col. McPherson and my A A. G. This report in some other particulars I do not fully endorse.

U. S. GRANT
Maj. Gen.

AES, DNA, RG 94, War Records Office, Union Battle Reports. *O.R.*, I, x, part 1, 174, 188–89. On April 12, 1862, Maj. Gen. Lewis Wallace sent a lengthy report of the battle of Shiloh to Capt. John A. Rawlins. The portion disputed by USG read: "Hearing heavy and continuous cannonading in the direction of Pittsburg Landing early Sunday morning, I inferred a general battle, and, in anticipation of an order from Gen. Grant to join him at that place, had the equipage of the several brigades loaded in wagons for instant removal to my first camp at the river. The First and Third Brigades were also ordered to concentrate at the camp of the Second, from which proceeded the nearest and most practicable road to the scene of battle. At 11:30 o'clock the anticipated order arrived, directing me to come up and take position on the right of the army, and forming my line of battle at a right angle with the river. As it also directed me to leave a force to prevent surprise at Crump's Landing, the 56th Ohio and 68th Ohio regiments were detached for that purpose, with one gun from Lt. Thurber's battery. Selecting a road that led directly to the right of the lines as they were established around Pittsburg Landing on Sunday morning, my column started immediately, the distance being about six miles. The cannonading, distinctly audable, quickened the steps of the men. Snake Creek, difficult of passage at all times on account of its steep banks and swampy bottom, ran between me and the point of junction. Shortway from it Captain Rowley, from General Grant, and attached to his Staff, overtook me. From him I learned that our lines had been beaten back; that the right, to which I was proceeding, was then fighting close to the river; and that the road pursued would take me me in the enemy's rear, where, in the unfortunate condition of the battle, my command was in danger of being entirely cut-off. It seemed, on his representation, most prudent to carry the column across to what is called the 'river road'; which, following the windings of the Tennessee bottom, crossed Snake creek by a good bridge close to Pittsburg Landing. This movement occasioned a countermarch, which delayed my junction with the main army until a little after nightfall. The information brought me by Capt. Rowley was confirmed by Col. McPherson and Capt. Rawlins, also of the General's staff, who came up while I was crossing to the river road. About 1 o'clock at night my brigades and batteries were disposed, forming the extreme right, and ready for battle." ALS, DNA, RG 94, War Records Office, Union Battle Reports. *O.R.*, I, x, part 1, 170.

On April 25, USG endorsed another report to Maj. Gen. Henry W. Halleck. "Respectfully forwarded to Head Quarters of the Dept. This is a fare candid report assuming none to much for officers or men of the Div." AES, DNA, RG 94, War Records Office, Union Battle Reports. *O.R.*, I, x, part 1, 208. Written on the report of the battle of Shiloh of Brig. Gen. Stephen A. Hurlbut, April 12, addressed to Rawlins. LS, DNA, RG 94, War Records Office, Union Battle Reports. *O.R.*, I, x, part 1, 203–8. On April 10, Hurlbut described his role at the battle of Shiloh in a letter to his wife. Stephen A. Hurlbut, *Between Peace & War* . . . (Charleston, S. C., 1953), pp. 17–21.

At approximately 8:00 a.m. on April 6, while on his way from Savannah to Pittsburg Landing, USG told Wallace to prepare his division at Crump's Landing to join the remainder of the army at Pittsburg Landing. After arriving on the battlefield of Shiloh, USG soon concluded that Wallace's men were much needed, and he sent verbal orders through Capt. Algernon S. Baxter for Wallace, which Baxter put in writing before he reached Wallace. USG believed that Wallace was ordered to follow "the road nearest the river." *Memoirs*, I, 336. See also *O.R.*, I, x, part 1, 181, 185. As Wallace remembered the paper he received, he was to "form junction with the right of the army. Form line of battle at right angle to the river, and be governed by circumstances." *Lew Wallace: An Autobiography* (New York and London, 1906), I, 463.

During the morning, Wallace had concentrated his force, strung out westward along the road from Crump's Landing to Adamsville, at the midpoint, Stoney Lonesome, and when he received orders, he advanced on the Shunpike Road, which ran in a southwesterly direction before turning south. USG sent several staff officers to Wallace to hurry him forward, but it was not until 3:30 p.m. that Rawlins and Lt. Col. James B. McPherson found Wallace on the Shunpike Road and persuaded him to countermarch to follow the river road. By the time Wallace's force reached the battlefield, the first day of battle was over. When Wallace discovered that USG was critical of his conduct on that day, he began a dispute which continued intermittently for the remainder of USG's life. A discussion which includes documents submitted by Wallace is "The March of Lew Wallace's Division to Shiloh," *Battles and Leaders of the Civil War*, eds.,

Robert Underwood Johnson and Clarence Clough Buel (New York, 1887), I, 607–10. Wallace began a letter to his wife on April 17 which he completed later. "The newspapers have several lies about me aside from the report of my death— some that do me no good in the public estimation, but which will eventually be put to rest. 1. They say I lost my way from Crump's Landing to the scene of battle, and got there too late. The fact is I recd the order to march at 11:30 in the forenoon, and started immediately, having six miles to go. The road I selected would have carried me exactly to the right of our army where I was ordered.— that is, the right as it was early Sunday morning. Every step was in hearing of the fight. After getting within two miles and a half of the place, I was overtaken by Capt. Rawlins, Gen. Grant's Ass't Adjt. Genl., who told me that our right had been beaten back clear to the river, and that if went on I would be landed two or three miles in rear of the enemy, and effectually cut off. This, you see, was official. Upon the strength of it, I countermarched and took another road close along the river bank, and this movement delayed me until nightfall. So I did not lose the road, nor make any mistake, as the liars say. 2. They also say I had 19000 men, one third of Grant's army. My whole force was nine regiments averaging about five hundred men, which, with my cavalry and artillery, made me near five thousand strong. With 19000 men I should have attacked the enemy's rear. 3. They also say that Gen Grant sent me a verbal order to come up, and that I refused to recognise it because it was not in writing. The truth is I started every- thing without any order at all. You can imagine how welcome anything having the semblance of an order would be. So the world goes—Lord how it is given to lying. Time will set everything right at last. It did so with the Donalson fight and will do so in this instance. I can afford to wait." ALS, Wallace Papers, InHi. In testimony before the Committee on the Conduct of the War, July 9, 1862, Wallace stated that he had received no orders at all from those staff officers who arrived after Baxter (though he left unclear why they had come to him), and was also indirectly critical of USG's conduct of the second day of fighting at Shiloh. *HRC*, 37–3–108, III, 340–42. For a summary of the controversy, see Harold Lew Wallace, "Lew Wallace's March to Shiloh Revisited," *Indiana Magazine of History*, LIX, 1 (March, 1963), 19–30. See letter to Col. John C. Kelton, April 13 1863.

To Capt. Nathaniel H. McLean

———

                                              Head Quarters Army of the Tennessee
                                                     Pittsburgh, April 25th 1862

Capt N. H. McLean
A A Genl Dept of the Miss
Capt

     A note from Maj Gen.l Halleck just received states that his order of the 23d[1] for troops of my command to move on yesterday, has only been complied with in part, and directing that a report be immediately made of those who failed to comply with the order, and and that they be arrested. There were but three Divisions to move, Genl Wallace having moved his before the last rain; Genl Sherman occupying the position thought best for him to retain, and Genl Davies being directed to remain where he is as a reserve and for the purpose of furnishing such details as may be required inside. Genl.s McClernand & Hurlbut moved yesterday I know, and supposed Genl McKean did also.

I will ascertain the facts and report again as soon as one of my Staff can visit the Division Commanders.

Very Respectfully
Your Obt Servt
U. S. GRANT
Maj Genl

Copies, DLC-USG, V, 4, 5, 7, 8, 9, 88; DNA, RG 393, USG Hd. Qrs. Correspondence. On April 25, 1862, Maj. Gen. Henry W. Halleck wrote to USG. "My order of the 23d that your Command move forward yesterday was only partially obeyed. You will immediately report thise reason of this neglect, and will arrest any commanding officer who failed to obey the order." Copies, DLC-USG, V, 83; DNA, RG 393, Dept. of the Miss., Letters Sent. USG endorsed this letter to Brig. Gen. Thomas J. McKean. "Forwarded to Brig Genl McKean Comdg 6th Division who is directed to report why his Division did not move on the 24th as directed" Copy, DLC-USG, V, 83. McKean also endorsed the letter. "Part of my Div moved as ordered, the balance having orders to follow as soon as their teams returned from the river where they had gone for supplies. The ground between Hurlbuts Division and Buell's Army was occupied last night by my Division" Copy, *ibid*.

1. On April 23, Halleck wrote to USG. "You will advance with Your Command to Morrow and take position on the right in front of Shiloh Church Your right resting on owl Creek. You will guard the Bridge and ford over this Creek and Send out Cavalry to reconoitre the road to Purdy Strong Guards will be kept up in front of your position." Copies, *ibid*., V, 4, 5, 7, 8, 9; DNA, RG 393, USG Hd. Qrs. Correspondence. *O.R.*, I, x, part 2, 117–18.
On April 23, Maj. Gen. John A. McClernand wrote to USG. "My Infantry Scouts have just come in from a reconnoisance towards Purdy, and report, upon what they accept as credible authority, that the Enemy have felled a stretch of trees, for a stretch of two miles—about six miles from here on what is called the 'Shun Pike Road.' I will send out another party—Cavalry—this evening to gather particulars." Copy, McClernand Papers, IHi. On April 24, McClernand wrote to USG. "My Cavalry returned last night and Lt Col McCullough commanding them, reports that he went forward eight miles on the road leading from Pittsburgh

to Purdy. At that point on the road he found that the bridge on the 'Shun Pike Road' had been broken and obstructed by trees felled by the enemy yesterday. Going a mile and a fourth further, he found that trees had been felled for a reach of half a mile along and across the road, and that the enemy had been foraging in that vicinity. It was reported that the party destroying the bridge and obstructing the road was from Purdy not Corinth. Col McCullough's party crossed Owl creek at the 'Ford' a short distance in front and to the right of my present camp"   Copy, *ibid.*

To Julia Dent Grant

———

Pittsburg Landing, Ten.
April 25th 1862

MY DEAR WIFE,

Again I write you from this place where I verily believe it has rained almost continuously since the begining of the year. No doubt we will leave here so soon as the roads become passable. I however am no longer boss. Gen. Halleck is here and I am truly glad of it. I hope the papers will let me alone in future. If the papers only knew how little ambition I have outside of putting down this rebellion and getting back once more to live quietly and unobtrusively with my family I think they would say less and have fewer falshoods to their account. I do not look much at the papers now consequently save myself much uncomfortable feeling.

I would have written you before but as I was writing to father I made that answer for one letter to you. I will enclose with this a letter from Gen. Smith who I fear will not live many days.[1] He was my old Commandant of whilst a Cadets and a better soldier or truer man does not live. I want the letter saved.

I am afraid the money you let White[2] have will be lost. Give yourself no trouble however over spilt milk.—I sent you $200 00 by express not yet acknowledged. Will send you some more soon. I also sent Simp's watch which is not yet acknowledged.

Kiss all the children for me. When you hear of me being on the Mississippi river you can join me leaving the children at home. Give my love to all at home.

Col. Riggin is not with me. All the rest of my Staff are however. Hillyer & Lagow will be Colonels.[3] Rawlins is a Maj. and
ought to be a Brig. Gen.

I have been writing here in my tent ever since breakfast, it is
now long after dinner, and have a pile yet before me that will
take until bed time.

Kisses for yourself dear Julia.

ULYS.

ALS, DLC-USG.

1. On April 25, 1862, Capt. Andrew C. Kemper issued General Orders
No. 21 announcing the death of Maj. Gen. Charles F. Smith and praising his
character and ability. In forwarding these orders, Maj. John A. Rawlins instructed
that they be read to each regt. Copy, DNA, RG 94, 48th Ill., Letterbook. See
letter to Mrs. Charles F. Smith, April 26, 1862.
2. See letter to Julia Dent Grant, May 10, 1861, note 11.
3. See letter to Maj. Gen. Henry W. Halleck, April 16, 1862.

To George P. Ihrie

Pittsburg Landing, Ten.
April 25th 1862

DEAR IHRIE,

Your letter of the 12th inst. has just reached me.

In reply I would state that I should be very glad if it was
possible to have you attached to my Staff as Inspector Gen. I have
however no power of appointing but if my recommendation will
do any good you shall have it most cheerfully.

There will be another movement here before this reaches you
which I hope will wind up the big battles. By the way the papers
are giving me fits for the last. This matter will all be understood
after a while, without any explanations from me, and will appear
much better than at present. It does not seem to be taken into
account that with a force ⫯of less than 35,000 men we kept at bay
all day Sunday over 80,000. As to the surprise spoken of we could
not have been better prepared had the enemy sent word three

days before when they would attack. Skirmishing had been going on for that time and I could have brought on the battle either Friday[1] or Saturday if I had chosen. My object was to keep it off, if possible, until Buell arrived.

Let me hear from you.

yours of old

U. S. GRANT

ALS, USG 3. George P. Ihrie of N. J. attended USMA (1845–47), was appointed 2nd lt. on June 18, 1855, was promoted to 1st lt. on Feb. 28, 1857, and resigned on Dec. 31, 1859. He was appointed lt. col., 3rd Calif., on Sept. 4, 1861, then resigned on Dec. 11. On April 21, 1877, Ihrie endorsed USG's letter. "Through the influence of U.S. Senator O. H. Browning, (my wife's Uncle,) subsequently Sec'y of the Interior under Presd't A. Johnson, Sec'y Stanton told me to 'select my General for staff duty; report to him at once for duty; and my Coms'n as Colonel & A. D. C. should follow me.' I selected Gen'l U. S. Grant, and reported to him on the 7th of May, one month after the Battle of Shiloh, but my Coms'n did not reach me till 27th of June." AES, *ibid.* On May 7, 1862, USG telegraphed to Secretary of War Edwin M. Stanton. "I would respectfully request that George. P. Ihrie of San Francisco be appointed Inspector General of Volunteers & be attached to my staff as such." Telegram received, DNA, RG 107, Telegrams Received. USG also wrote to Stanton on the same subject on May 9. *Ibid.*, Register of Letters Received. On May 23, Brig. Gen. Catharinus P. Buckingham wrote to USG. "The Secretary of War directs me to acknowledge the receipt of your letter of the 9th instant, asking that George P. Ihrie, late Lieutenant Colonel of the 3rd California Infantry be commissioned with suitable rank for Inspector General and appointed on your staff, and in reply to inform you that the appointment would have to be made on General Hallecks staff and the officer assigned to duty on your staff which the secretary of war will not do except on application of General Halleck   Your telegram was not received by the Secretary"   Copy, *ibid.*, Letters Sent, Military Affairs. On July 17, Ihrie was appointed col., additional aide-de-camp, to rank from May 7.

1. April 4.

To A. Lizzie Whipple

Pittsburg Landing, Ten.
April 25th 1862

MISS A. LIZZIE WHIPPLE
GALVA, HENRY CO. ILLINOIS,

Your beautifully expressed letter of the 15th instant come duly to hand and of course I shall take great pleasure in granting a request so easily complied with as the one you make.

True Illinois, and all the states, have lost many brave sons, fathers and brothers, but they have died to perpetuate homes and happiness to many generations.

Very truly yours

U. S. GRANT

Maj. Gen.

ALS, IHi. On April 8, 1862, President Abraham Lincoln sent his autograph and that of his wife to Lizzie A. Whipple. Lincoln, *Works*, VIII, 489.

To Maj. Gen. Henry W. Halleck

Head Quarters Army of the Tennessee

In the Field, Shiloh, April 26, 1862

MAJOR GENL H W HALLECK

COMMANDING THE DEPT OF THE MISS

GENERAL

Col Battel of the Confederate Army, now a prisoner, has just called on me to know what action has been taken in his case. I reported the conversation had with you this morning, and from that could give no assurance that any exchange could be made ~~except~~ unless an officer of corresponding rank should be brought so that the exchange might be made at once. The Col is now on the Steamer Hannibal and I would respectfully recommend that he be sent to join the other prisoners. If advised to do so however I will send another flag and see if the exchange can be effected.

I am Genl Very Respcty

Your Obt Servt

U. S. GRANT

Maj Genl

Copies, DLC-USG, V, 4, 5, 7, 8, 88; DNA, RG 393, USG Hd. Qrs. Correspondence. See letter to Gen. P. G. T. Beauregard, April 12, 1862. See also *O.R.*, II, iii, 576, 854.

To Maj. Gen. Henry W. Halleck

———

Head Quarters, Army of the Ten
Pittsburg, April 26th 1862

MAJ. GEN. H. W. HALLECK
COMD.G DEPT. OF THE MISS.
GEN

Mr. Cherry who writes the within is undoubtedly a Union man. His information no doubt can be relied upon.

Respectfully
U. S. GRANT
Maj. Gen.

ALS, DNA, RG 109, Union Provost Marshals' File of Papers Relating to Individual Civilians. On April 26, 1862, William H. Cherry, Savannah, wrote to USG. "Pardon me for troubling you   I have it from undoubted authority that a party of Rebel Cavalry were at Coffee Landing 4 Miles below here yesterday and Stated they intended coming in to my farm on the West side and burn everything they could find, they gave as their reason that I was exerting myself to aid the Federal officers & Army—The Citizens of that side are compelled to lie out from their homes. If any thing can be done to protect us it would certainly be gratefully recieved. Several of the Citizens have been to see me in a few days and say if they had arms they would organize & protect themselves—" ALS, *ibid*. See letter to Julia Dent Grant, March 22, 1862, note 1.

To Capt. Andrew C. Kemper

———

Head Quarters Army of the Tennessee
In Field, Shiloh April 26th 1862

CAPTAIN

I have the honor herewith to transmit to you the Official reports of the Division Commanders of the Army of the Tennessee, of their respective Divisions during the battle of Pittsburg, or Shiloh, on the 6th & 7th inst. together with the Brigade and Regimental Reports. The reports of the 2nd and 6th Divisions, Commanded by Brig Generals. Wallace and Prentiss are necessarily imperfect; the former having been mortally wounded the first day of the Battle (and General McArthur who succeeded in command being also wounded and unable to continue in the Field) and the latter taken prisoner on the afternoon of the 6th. As soon as Regimental and Brigade Reports are received they will be forwarded with Genl McClernand's whose report is not yet in

> I am Sir Very Respectfully
> Your Obt Servt
> U. S. GRANT
> Maj. Gen Com

To CAPTAIN AND C KEMPER

LS, DNA, RG 393, Dept. of the Miss., Letters Received. Andrew C. Kemper of Ohio was appointed capt. and asst. adjt. gen. on Nov. 16, 1861. Reports of the battle of Shiloh from officers of USG's command are printed in *O.R.*, I, x, part 1, 113–291; *ibid.*, I, lii, part 1, 21–26. See also *SED*, 37–2–66.

To Capt. Nathaniel H. McLean

———

> Head Quarters Army of Tennessee
> Pittsburgh, April 26, 1862

CAPT N H MCLEAN
A A. GENL DEPT OF THE MISS
CAPT

I would respectfully ask that Lt J Vestal,[1] 53rd Ind Vols, and the detail of men from the same Regiment be ordered to join their proper ~~companies~~ command at this place. Col Zam[2] of Genl Buells forces being senior to the Col of the 53rd Ind Regt[3] took command at Savanna, where he had been left and I ordered the latter up here. It seems that Col Zam refused to relieve Lt Vestal, and a detail of men on duty at the time, on the order I ~~had~~ sent.

> Very Respectfully
> Your Obt Servt
> U. S. GRANT
> Maj Genl

Copies, DLC-USG, V, 4, 5, 7, 8, 88; DNA, RG 393, USG Hd. Qrs. Correspondence.

1. 2nd Lt. John Vestal, 53rd Ind., resigned on Aug. 2, 1863.
2. Col. Lewis Zahm, 3rd Ohio Cav.
3. Col. Walter Q. Gresham, 53rd Ind.

To Jesse Root Grant

———

Pittsburg Landing, Tenn., April 26, 1862.

I will go on, and do my duty to the very best of my ability, without praise, and do all I can to bring this war to a speedy close. I am not an aspirant for any thing at the close of the war.

There is one thing I feel well assured of; that is, that I have the confidence of every brave man in my command. Those who showed the white feather will do all in their power to attract attention from themselves. I had perhaps a dozen officers arrested for cowardice in the first day's fight at this place. These men are necessarily my enemies.

As to the talk about a surprise here, nothing could be more false. If the enemy had sent us word when and where they would attack us, we could not have been better prepared. Skirmishing had been going on for two days between our reconnoitering parties and the enemy's advance. I did not believe, however, that they intended to make a determined attack, but simply that they were making a reconnoisance in force.

My headquarters were in Savannah, though I usually spent the day here. Troops were constantly arriving to be assigned to brigades and divisions, all ordered to report at Savannah, making it necessary to keep an office and some one there. I was also looking for Buell to arrive, and it was important that I should have every arrangement complete for his speedy transit to this side of the river.

U. S. Grant.

Cincinnati Commercial, May 2, 1862. The newspaper stated that the recipient was "a personal friend of Gen. Grant, in this city." That the letter was addressed to Jesse R. Grant is established by USG's letter to Julia Dent Grant, May, 11, 1862.

The elder Grant's decision to furnish his son's letter to the newspapers was probably provoked by newspaper criticism of USG's conduct at Shiloh. Such criticism was particularly strong in the *Cincinnati Gazette*, which printed White-law Reid's account of Shiloh, reported rumors that USG was under arrest, and editorialized that USG's report of Shiloh was "such an one as a General, conscious that he had sacrificed his army by his incompetency and neglect, and desirous to cover it up, would make." April 14, 17, 19, 1862. The printing of USG's letter to his father led only to more editorial criticism from newspapers unfriendly to USG. *Ibid.*, May 3, 7, 1862; *Chicago Times*, May 19, 1862.

Jesse R. Grant was almost certainly responsible for the release to the newspapers of a letter of April 21 from Capt. William S. Hillyer. "It must be a matter of great annoyance to you to read the unjust, untrue and unmanly criticisms and denunciations of our mutual friend Gen. Grant, with which some of the newspapers teem. I sometimes wonder, and I imagine he does, whether these reiterated slanders affect the confidence of those who have known and esteemed him long and well. What prompts this systematic defamation? In whose way is he? Whose sins has he to bear—whose shortcomings to cover? Remarkable as he has ever been for modesty, affability, generous appreciation of others' merit, never claiming any for himself—in discipline kind, but impartial, ever at his post and prompt in the discharge of duty, who can he have offended that he should be so belied? Is *success* a crime? Are the fairly and hardly earned laurels of victory to be withered because they were fairly and hardly earned? I can well understand why three or four thousand officers and men, ignominiously falling back at the first fire and fleeing to the river at Pittsburg Landing, should report themselves surprised and their comrades bayonetted in their tents. I can understand why they should attempt to divert the public attention from the naked deformity of their own base coward-ice, and screen themselves behind the pretence of bad generalship. But that men who ought to know better and *do* know better than to base their opinions upon such testimony, should give credence and currency to these miserable lies, is to me a matter of astonishment. There are two divisions of our army which are said to have been *surprised*—General Sherman's and General Prentiss's. These, with McClernand's, were in the advance, Sherman occupying the extreme front and Prentiss the left front. It was in one or both of these two divisions that 'our brave boys were bayonetted in their beds,' and 'to whom the first announcement of the enemy's approach was a volley of musketry.' Such are the statements. Now what are the *facts*. Gen Sherman, in his official report, states that *he had his division formed in line of battle two hours before he was attacked*. SURPRISED, and yet waiting two long hours for the enemy's attack? Not a regiment of Sherman's command was taken prisoners, and yet his men *'were bayonetted in their beds.'* Some of his officers and men sought refuge on the river bank, but they *never saw the enemy.* Sherman was indeed surprised—painfully surprised—but it was not by the enemy. Prentiss is not here to make his report; but the official report of an officer has been made, who states that early on Sunday morning General Prentiss sent him out on the Corinth road, with two companies of skirmishers, *to make reconnoisance of the enemy, who had been reported as approaching in force.* He met our pickets *one mile beyond our lines,* coming back to announce the enemy's approach. The fact was duly reported to General Prentiss, and his line of battle was immediately formed; and up to three o'clock on Sunday afternoon his line remained unbroken. No regiment of his command was captured until after three o'clock on Sunday, at which time he himself was taken prisoner, with part of his command. And this did not happen until after the capture of a portion of Smith's division, and probably never would have happened had it not been for that disaster. And now I will explain to you how a portion of Smith's division came to be captured. This was a reserve force located at the Landing. It was the division of Major-General C. F. Smith. General Smith being very sick, and unable to take the field, the division was led into action by Brigadier General Wallace. In the afternoon of Sunday, while in a severe engagement with the enemy, General Wallace fell mortally wounded. The command devolved upon Brigadier-General McArthur, who soon after was also wounded and carried from the field. At this time the enemy were pouring a murderous fire upon the division, and the Adjutant-General of Wallace, as soon as possible, announced to Colonel Tuttle, the ranking Colonel, the disasters to Wallace and McArthur, and that the command devolved upon him. This, however, caused a short interruption in the command of the division, during which the enemy were pushing on with overwhelming numbers. Before the command of Colonel Tuttle to fall back could reach the entire line, a portion of the command were flanked and captured. So much for the surprise. General Halleck says the talk of surprise is sheer nonsense. And I tell you what I know to be true—that the conduct and management of Grant in the capture of Fort Henry, Fort Donelson, and the battle of Pittsburg Landing has the unqualified approval of General Halleck; and yet it has been, I am told, currently reported in Chicago that General Halleck, since his arrival here, had *arrested* General Grant. There is no officer in his command in whom General Halleck has reposed so much confidence as in General Grant, and that confidence has been manifested in many ways since Halleck's arrival at Pittsburg. I need only instance his congratulatory order, made after his arrival here, and his having been made acquainted with all the main facts of the battle. There are other matters about which I will write you in another letter on this subject, but forbear for the present, with one additional remark on the 'bayonetting in camp' matter. After the battle it was found that *not a single man of our army had been either killed or wounded by the bayonet."* *Cincinnati Commercial,* May 6, 1862.

Jesse R. Grant also prepared for publication a statement containing extracts from two other letters written by Hillyer, one dated only April, the other April 25. "The inquiry as to the conduct of General Grant, ordered by the War Department, was solely with reference to matters subsequent to the capture of Fort Donelson. I send you herewith copies of correspondence between Adjutant General Thomas and General Halleck, which covers the whole ground of complaint, and pretty fully explains itself. It was Thomas's letter that was the foundation of the telegraphic dispatch to the Cincinnati papers, that the 'War Department had ordered

General Grant to be superseded for bad conduct at Fort Donelson and elsewhere.'
In further explanation I would state that immediately after the surrender of Fort
Donelson, General Grant issued the most stringent orders with reference to the
captured property. He had several officers arrested for their violation, one of
whom was the Provost Marshal of Clarksville. He did everything that a commander of an army to some extent demoralized by victory could do to enforce his
orders. He had one regiment detailed solely for that duty. But in spite of all, so
vast was the amount of plunder, and so great the eagerness of the soldiers and
citizens to procure trophies, that even officers of high rank were willing to risk
their commissions in their violation; and in spite of all precautions much of the
captured property was surreptitiously carried off. So much for that complaint."
"Here we are, advanced toward Corinth. Rain, rain, rain, is the daily chronicle of
the camps. Talk about Potomac mud! It is not to be compared to the Tennessee
mud. That awful road over which our brave troops marched from Fort Henry to
Fort Donelson, when General Grant marched to accomplish that victory which
was the death-blow to the rebellion, is the only one comparable to the road to
Corinth. With twenty-eight thousand troops he not only took that stronghold,
but at the same time took Bowling Green and Nashville, which one hundred
thousand troops, under the generalship of the brave Buell, had failed to accomplish. 'Did Buell cooperate in the taking of Fort Donelson?' Let us see. But first
let me remind you of Grant's celebrated—I should rather say notorious—'expedition against Columbus,' where twenty-five (?) thousand men 'marched up the
lane, and then marched down again.' You remember it well. Grant's friends had
high hopes at the promise and great disappointment at the result. That expedition
was made to divert the enemy and enable Buell to attack Bowling Green, which
he failed to do. How was it reciprocated? You remember an order of General
Halleck's, in which he thanked Major General Hunter for his aid and cooperation
in the capture of Fort Donelson. It meant to thank Hunter; but it meant much
more. You will appreciate that order better when I narrate a few facts which have
come into my possession. When Grant, with an army of less than twenty thousand
men, was about to march on Fort Donelson, General Halleck telegraphed to
General Buell: 'Grant is about to attack Fort Donelson. Can't you send him
reinforcements?' Buell's answer was, 'I have none to spare.' Soon after Halleck
telegraphed: 'The enemy are evacuating Bowling Green and reinforcing Fort
Donelson. Can't you attack Bowling Green?' Buell answered, 'I am not prepared.'
Halleck then telegraphed, 'Can't you make a demonstration?' Buell replied, 'I
never make demonstrations.' And so Grant was left with twenty-eight thousand
troops and the gunboats to strike the blow which drove the rebel army from
Kentucky and Tennessee and from their stronghold at Manassas. What has been
his reward? The *Cincinnati Gazette*, a paper making great pretensions to high-
toned morality and impartiality, uses such language as this concerning him: 'But
even in case of victory time should be taken to receive the full reports and find
out who it was that attacked, pursued, and captured the enemy and took intrench-
ments at the point of the bayonet, and who were tardy and inert while the battle
was going on. By a proper exercise of this moderation the government might
avoid the extraordinary predicament of promoting a commander to a major generalship one day and suspending him from command the next, and eventually
restoring him, chiefly to save its own consistency.' No baser paragraph was ever
published in the most venal press on earth. There is not a line in it that is not
pregnant with most malicious falsehood. The editor of that paper either delib-

erately stated as a fact what he knew to be false, or he stated as a fact something concerning the truth or falsity of which he was ignorant. In either case he has committed a grave crime. It is enough to assure you that every act and order of General Grant, in the investment and capture of Fort Donelson, met with the cordial indorsement and freely expressed approbation of the commanding general of the department. True, he was absent in the necessary discharge of duty at the gunboats at the time of the terrible conflict between McClernand's division and the enemy on our right on Saturday morning. But he had so disposed his forces as to enable McClernand, as he eventually did, to check and repulse the advance of the enemy there, and had sent a portion of his staff, with authority and instructions to represent him; while the brilliant and successful charges of General C. F. Smith on our left and Colonel Morgan L. Smith on our right, on Saturday afternoon, were made by the order and under the immediate supervision of General Grant in person. I shall not soon forget the reply of General Smith to a remark by General Buckner, on the morning of the surrender. It indicated the soldier and the gentleman. Immediately after General Smith came in and was saluted by General Buckner the latter remarked, 'You made a brilliant charge and terribly surprised us on our right yesterday afternoon General Smith. It decided the day against us.' 'I simply obeyed orders, nothing more, sir,' was General Smith's prompt reply. No complaint whatever was ever made by the President, or the War Department, or any other authority or any responsible man, for any action or want of action on the part of General Grant in the investment and capture of Fort Donelson. He has received no allusion to it by any authority above him, except unqualified praise. I speak what I know." M. J. Cramer, *Ulysses S. Grant: Conversations and Unpublished Letters* (New York and Cincinnati, 1897), pp. 184–92. This defense of USG was apparently not printed.

Instead, John S. Nixon of Covington, Ky., Jesse R. Grant's closest neighbor, prepared two letters for the *Cincinnati Gazette*, printed May 20, 23, 1862, over the initials "J. S. N." See John S. Nixon to Elihu B. Washburne, May 20, ALS, DLC-Elihu B. Washburne. The material presented obviously came from Jesse R. Grant; indeed, the style indicates that he may be the true author.

Jesse R. Grant continued to write private letters to assist his son. On May 16, he wrote to U.S. Representative Elihu B. Washburne to thank him for a speech in defense of USG, and on May 27 he furnished Washburne with biographical information on USG. ALS, *ibid*. On July 11, Grant wrote to Governor David Tod of Ohio. "I was at Ft Henry early in March when Ulysses recd your complimentary letter, and noticed what you said in a note about your humble servt, for which please accept my thanks. Since that time the Press aided by Demagogues have tried so hard to put him down that you may have droped him. I propose briefly to give you a few of the reasons which have caused such 'intense feelings against Gen Grant' as Lieut Gov Stanton says   In the first place he has refused to quarter Newspaper reporters on the army at the expence of the Government. That has caused the whole fraternity of scriblers to unite against him to put him down, & Editors who have Reporters in the field, misled by these lying Reporters, and to be revenged on him for not providing for their Reporters have also greatly abused him. Then there is Buell & his army have found it necesy to draw public attention from their short comings to unite with them. Then again there is the five thousand cowards who threw down their arms deserted the standard of their country & their Comrades in arms in the midst of danger, and sought safty under the banks of the Tennessee, & prayed for the rocks & hills to fall on them to hide them from the force of Beauregard, & his army, they too must have some excuse for conduct, hence the cry of 'surprise' than which nothing could be more absurd —You may have seen it stated that Gen Grant did not arive on the battle field till 10, 11, 12, & some say 2 o'clock when the truth is he started from savanna within ten minuets after he heared the first boom of the cannon & after stoping at Crumps landing to order Lew Walace he arrived at Pittsburg at 8, & at 20 minuets past was in his saddle, & at the head of his army. He found six Regts of his men panic stricken, & wholly demoralized, & more constantly breaking through the lines like frightened deer. By a masterly stroke of Generalship he stoped the panick in ten minuets, & there was not an other escaped during the day—His next move was to arest some 12 or 15 white feathered officers who were trying to demoraliz the rest of the army to hide their own cowardice   Then by the assistance of the gallant Sherman he reorganized his army, & by dint of strategy, good generalship able help, undanted bravery & hard fighting, he held the field for ten long bloody & doubtful hours, ~~he held the~~ against an army nearly three to his one, & they flushed with victory, & engaged in the last desperate struggle for victory—That night he lay on the ground with his soldiers, & as soon as day dawned he was lifted on his horse (for he had recd a hurt on friday night while reconnoitering which so crippled him he could not help himself) and moved up on the enemy strongly reinforced & after 20 hours more hard fighting, with but little apparant gain on either side, he headed a last desperate charge which send Beauregard & his hosts crawling to their strong hold at Corinth. And this is the Gen your subaltern would have shot while he would justify the five thousan scadadlers—Shame on such a Demagogue   I must close"   ALS, Warren A. Reeder, Hammond, Ind. Grant expressed similar ideas about his son in a letter of July 12 to Washburne. ALS, DLC-Elihu B. Washburne.

To Mrs. Charles F. Smith

Pittsburg Landing Tenn
April 26th 1862

Mrs C F Smith
No 191 East 4th St New York

It becomes my painful duty to announce to you the death of your lamented husband Major General Charles F Smith. He died at 4 Oclock P M yesterday at Savanna Tennessee

In his death the nation has lost one of its most gallant and most able defenders

It was my fortune to have gone through West Point with the Gen. (then Captain ~~as~~ & Commandant of Cadets) and to have served with him in all his battles in Mexico, And in this rebellion, And I can bear honest testimony ~~of~~ to his great worth as a soldier and friend. Where an entire nation condoles with you in your bereavement. ~~No~~ no one can do so with more heartfelt grief than myself

> Very Truly Yours
> U S GRANT
> Maj Genl.

Copies, DLC-USG, V, 1, 2, 3, 88; DNA, RG 393, USG Letters Sent. *O.R.*, I, x, part 2, 130.

To Maj. Gen. Henry W. Halleck

———

> Head Quarters, Army of the Ten.
> Pittsburg, April 27th 1862

MAJ. GEN. H. W. HALLECK
COMD.G THE DEPT. OF THE MISS.
GEN.

I would respectfully call your attention to the case of Capt. W. F. Brinck, Act. Ordnance officer of the Army of the Tennessee whose case I have before represented.

On taking command of the District of South East Missouri I found Capt. Brinck Acting Ordnance officer and very efficient in his duties. When the order was published to have mustered out of service all of Maj. Gen. Frémont's appointments, not otherwise recognized, I ascertained that Capt. Brinck, though not one of those appointments, had no regular legal appointment. He seems to have been placed in his position by Col. G. Waagner, then Chief of Artillery, and with a verbal promise from Maj. Gen. McClelland that he should retain the position.

I addressed several communications, unofficial, hoping to secure the commission for him feeling that his services were highly valuable to Government both on account of his business qualifications and experience in the Department.

I have never had an officer regularly belonging to the Department with whom to relieve Capt. Brinck nor one to appoint as Act. Ord. officer who I thought could fill the place.

I would respectfully ask that Capt. Brinck be nominated, and, if confirmed, transfered to the Army of the Tennessee.

> I am Gen. very respectfully
> your obt. svt.
> U. S. GRANT
> Maj. Gen. Com

P. S. Capt. Brinck has been Acting Ordnance officer since since the 6th of ~~September~~ August 1861.

> U. S. G.

ALS, DNA, RG 94, Generals' Papers and Books, Henry W. Halleck. On Dec. 30, 1861, Capt. Wilbur F. Brinck wrote to President Abraham Lincoln. "I have been attached to this Post, since the 29th of May, doing duty 'in the artillery' and in the Ordnance Department. I was promised immediately after entering the service 'the rank of Captain   And untill now have daily expected to receive my commission   I have never had time to leave my duties to give personal attention to the matter   On the seventh of September I was appointed Ordnance Officer to the command of Brig General U. S. Grant the duties of which position I have performed untill now   My Petition is that I may receive a captains commission and remain attatched to the command of Brig General U S Grant"   ALS, IHi. On the same day, USG endorsed this letter. "Capt. Brinck has most faithfully performed the duties of Ordnance officer to this command for the time specified and very much to the interest of the service. I do not see how his services can be dispensed with without being replaced by an officer of experience in the Ord. Dept. I therefore most heartily recommend the appointment of Capt. Brinck." AES, *ibid*. Both Brig. Gen. John A. McClernand and Maj. Mason Brayman added undated endorsements concurring with USG.

On Feb. 2, 1862, USG issued Special Orders No. 29. "Paymaster I. N. Cook will pay Capt. W. F. Brinck, Act. Ord. Officer. all pay due him to the 31st of December 1861. Pay will be given as Light Artillery without the extra allowance for Comd.g Company." ALS, Abraham Lincoln Book Shop, Chicago, Ill.

On Aug. 20, Maj. John A. Rawlins issued Special Orders No. 169. "The resignation of Capt. W. F. Brinck, Acting Ordnance Officer for the Dist of West. Tenn. is hereby accepted. Capt. Brinck will proceed to St Louis, Mo. to close up his accounts with Government reporting to the Commanding Officer of the United States Arsenal there, for such facilities as he may require for this purpose." DS, DNA, RG 94, Special Orders, District of West Tenn.; copies, *ibid*., RG 393, USG Special Orders; DLC-USG, V, 15, 16, 82, 87.

To Maj. Gen. Henry W. Halleck

———

Head Quarters, Army of the Ten.
Pittsburg, April 27th 1862

MAJ. GEN. H. W. HALLECK
COMD.G DEPT. OF THE MISS.
GEN.

Some of the Cavalry from Gen. McClernand's Division have just returned from a little beyond the pickets having captured two negroes found skulking about. One of them reports having heard his master state that the enemy at Corinth intended making an attack on our forces to-day.

This of course it will be impossible to do but it may fore-shadow an intention of attacking.

Shall I send for the negroes and forward them to you? I give all here that has been reported to me, officially, by Gen. McCler-nand.

I am Gen. very respectfully
your obt. svt.
U. S. GRANT
Maj. Gen.

ALS, DNA, RG 393, Dept. of the Miss., Letters Received. See following letter.

To Maj. Gen. John A. McClernand

———

Head Quarters, Army of the Ten.
Pittsburg, April 27th 1862

MAJ. GEN. J. A. McCLERNAND
COMD.G 1ST DIV.
GEN.

Your note accompanying the negroes brought in this morn-ing is just received.—I sent Gen. Halleck the substance of the report made by the officer who come to my Quarters whilst you was here and asked if I should send them to him to be questioned.

These negroes do not come under the class intended to be turned out of camp evidently and can therefore be retained by you until otherwise ordered at least.

> I am Gen very respectfully
> your obt. svt.
> U. S. GRANT
> Maj. Gen.

ALS, McClernand Papers, IHi. On April 27, 1862, Maj. Gen. John A. McClernand wrote to USG. "I send by the bearer the two Negroes brought from Picket lines this morning   I have heard their Statement. Their answers to questions concerning re-inforcements received by the enemy and their plan of attack from Corinth and Purdy at the same time are the most interesting—One of them says that his master has once or oftener had the Cavalry at Pea Ridge brought to his house and that he intimated that an attack would be made to day   I give the whole for what it may be worth . . . P S   Please send word as to the disposition to be made of the negroes—They might be useful in furnishing information in regard to the road in my vicinity as they live near my camp"   Copies, *ibid.* On the same day, McClernand again wrote to USG. "Upon returning from your Head Quarters, to day, in view of the information given by the negroes whom I sent you, I ordered a reconnoissance by my Cavalry, under Lt Col M'Cullough. He has just come in reporting that he went to Staunton eight miles from Pittsburgh and on the road from that place to Purdy. On his way from Staunton to Pea Ridge he captured one of the enemy's Cavalry scouts, who is now in my Camp. Upon arriving at Pea Ridge he encountered the enemy's pickets—killing three of them— and driving others back. He met with their pickets about five miles from my Camp. Two other negroes picked up by my mounted pickets report that they belong to a man named Johnson, who lives four miles from my camp. These negroes say that the enemy's pickets were formerly posted at their Masters. house, but are now about one mile beyond; and the enemy's camp about four miles beyond that. It was also discovered by my cavalry, that the roads over which they passed, from the Purdy to the Corinth road, was much cut up, probably by the Artillery of the enemy about the time of the battle of Shiloh"   Copies, *ibid.* *O.R.,* I, x, part 1, 652. See preceding letter.

On April 28, McClernand wrote to USG. "The bearer brings before you Mr H Neal, who lives about four miles in advance of my camp to the right of Owl creek   Two Negroes picked up by my scouts report that he was active in showing the enemy the road on the first day of the late battle, and that he has by himself and his agents, been corresponding, with the enemy at Pea Ridge and Corinth, since the battle. He denies all this, but I am not satified and, and therefore refer them to you"   Copies, McClernand Papers, IHi.

To Maj. Gen. Henry W. Halleck

———

Head Quarters Army of the Tenn
Pittsburgh April 28th 1862

MAJ GENL HALLECK
COMDG DEPT OF THE MISS
GENL.

The expedition ordered this morning from Genl Hd Qrs. to go out on the Purdy Road & destroy the Rail Road near Adams, has starte[d] with 3 days Rations in Haversacks. The expedition consists of Maj Genl Wallaces entire ~~Brigade~~ Division with the exception of Artillery. But one battery ~~is~~ was taken. All the cavalry belonging to my forces fit for duty and not otherwise employed accompanyied the expedition.

I am Genl Very Respecty &c.
U. S. GRANT
Maj Genl

Copies, DLC–USG, V, 4, 5, 7, 8, 9, 88; DNA, RG 393, USG Hd. Qrs. Correspondence. *O.R.*, I, x, part 2, 135.

To Maj. Gen. Henry W. Halleck

———

Head Quarters, Army of the Ten
Pittsburg, April 28th 1862

MAJ. GEN. H. W. HALLECK
COMD.G DEPT. OF THE MISS.
GEN.

The sketch called for was given Col. Thom[1] as soon as completed by Col. McPherson to have copies taken of it on tracing linnean. The original is now in the hands of Col. Thom's assistants.

It was made as promptly as possible after my troops had taken up their new position.

> I am Gen. very respectfully
> your obt. svt.
> U. S. GRANT
> Maj. Gen

ALS, DNA, RG 393, Dept. of the Miss., Letters Received. On April 28, 1862, Maj. Gen. Henry W. Halleck wrote to USG. "You will immediately send to these Head Qrs. a sketch showing the position of your troops as heretofore ordered. My orders to you are not obeyed with the promptness of the commanders of the other Army Corps." Copy, *ibid.*, Letters Sent.

1. George Thom of N. H., USMA 1839, served in the topographical engineers, holding the rank of capt. on the eve of the Civil War. Appointed col. and additional aide-de-camp on Nov. 16, 1861, he served as topographical engineer for the Dept. of the Mo., then for the Dept. of the Miss.

To Capt. Andrew C. Kemper

> Head Quarters, Army of the Ten
> Pittsburg, April 28th 1862

CAPT. A. C. KEMPER
A. A. GEN. DEPT. OF THE MISS.
SIR:

Herewith I forward the report of Maj. Gen. McClernand of the 1st Division which closes the reports of the Army of the Tennessee in the Battle of Shiloh on the 6th & 7th inst.

The report is faulty in two particulars; first, in giving the idea that Gen. Prentiss was surprised and taken prisoner in the morning, wheras he was not taken until a late hour in the afternoon[,] and, second, in reporting too much of other Divisions remote from ~~him~~ the 1st and from which reports are received conflicting somewhat from his statements.

> very respectfully
> U. S. GRANT
> Maj. Gen.

ALS, IHi. This letter is dated April 29, 1862, in copies, DLC-USG, V, 4, 5, 7, 8, 9, 88; DNA, RG 94, War Records Office, Union Battle Reports; *ibid.*, RG 393,

USG Hd. Qrs. Correspondence. *O.R.*, I, x, part 1, 114. Maj. Gen. John A. McClernand prepared a lengthy report of the battle of Shiloh, dated April 24, for USG. LS, DNA, RG 94, War Records Office, Union Battle Reports; copies, *ibid.*; McClernand Papers, IHi. *O.R.*, I, x, part 1, 114–23. On April 27, McClernand wrote to USG. "Herewith you will find my report of the part taken by my Division, at the Battle of Shiloh, Tennessee, on the 6th & 7th Inst. My engineer being wounded, I am unable to furnish drawings illustrative of the movements of my command during the Battle. The commanders of two of the three ~~of the~~ Brigades forming my division having changed as often as three times by the casualties of the ~~B~~battle, I am unable at present to send you such Brigade reports as would be desiriable" Copies, McClernand Papers, IHi. On May 1, USG wrote to Capt. John C. Kelton. "Herewith I enclose report of Maj Genl J A. McClernand which he wishes to substitue for the report forwarded two days ago. The remarks made on that report are applicable to this one also." Copies, DLC-USG, V, 4, 5, 7, 8, 88; DNA, RG 393, USG Hd. Qrs. Correspondence.

To Maj. Gen. John A. McClernand

———

Head Quarters, Army of the Tenn.
Pittsburgh, April 28th 1862.

MAJOR. GEN. J. A. McCLERNAND.
COMMDG 1ST DIVISION.
GENL:

Move your ~~camp~~ entire command tomorrow forward to the Point where Gen. Smith[1] had the skirmish on the 24th inst. You will recognize the place by a white frame house on the right of the Corinth road. This is a permanent move of your camp.

On arrival throw out guards on all the approaches, and as soon as possible repair the roads in front of you as far as practicable, and build bridges over the runs.

Leave orders for your Cavalry to follow as soon as they return. Take with you all the sick that can be moved. The remainder may be left with proper Medical attendance in Hospital where they are ~~with proper Medical attendance~~. Sherman's & Davies' Division will follow you.

I am, Gen, Very Respectfully,
Your Obt Servant.
U. S. GRANT.
Maj. Gen.

Copies, DLC-USG, V, 1, 2, 3, 86; DNA, RG 393, USG Letters Sent. *O.R.*, I, x, part 2, 136. On April 28, 1862, Maj. Gen. John A. McClernand wrote to USG. "The roads are desperate. I advanced to the White House—found a few rebel pickets—or rather found evidence that they had fled upon our approach, and have encamped for the night upon a creek in the rear of the White House about three-fourths of a mile. This creek being nearly impassible I will have to bridge it in the morning unless I can find a better crossing higher up. Shall I rest where I am until further orders? Genl Sherman is encamped to my right and rear." ALS, DNA, RG 393, District of West Tenn., Letters Received. On the same day, Capt. William S. Hillyer wrote to McClernand. "You will make no further advance until further orders. Camp where you are and bridge the creek there in pursuance of former orders." Copy, DLC-USG, V, 2.

1. Andrew J. Smith of Pa., USMA 1838, served in the 1st Dragoons until the beginning of the Civil War when he held the rank of capt. Appointed col., 2nd Calif. Cav. on Oct. 2, 1861, and brig. gen. on March 17, 1862, he served as chief of cav., Dept. of the Mo. and Dept. of the Miss.

To Brig. Gen. William T. Sherman

Head Quarters, Dist of West. Tenn
Pittsburgh, April 28th 1862.

Brig. Gen. W. T. Sherman,
Commdg 5th Division
Genl:

Move out in the morning on the Purdy road to Veatches or Stantonville[1] to the support of Gen. Wallace who left this afternoon for the purpose of destroying the Rail Road at or near Bethel.

Two Brigades and one Company of Artillery will be sufficient to take, and one days rations the men having breakfast before leaving.

I am, Gen, Very Respectfully. &c
U. S. Grant.
Maj. Gen.

Copies, DLC-USG, V, 1, 2, 3, 86; DNA, RG 393, USG Letters Sent. *O.R.*, I, x, part 2, 136. On April 28, 1862, Maj. Gen. Henry W. Halleck wrote to USG. "You will push forward one Division on the Purdy Road to Veals or Stantonville to hold the Cross Road to Monterey while the Cavalry pushes forward, and destroys the Rail Road near Bethel   the wing officers of the Division will be directed [*to protect*] his flank from any movement from the direction of Monterey the Movement should be made as soon as possible   I have a telegram from the Sect of War Confirming the Capture of New Orleans By Com Farragut"   Copies, DLC-USG, V, 4, 5, 7, 8, 9; DNA, RG 393, USG Hd. Qrs. Correspondence; *ibid.*, Dept. of the Miss., Letters Sent. *O.R.*, I, x, part 2, 134. On the same day, Capt. William S. Hillyer wrote to Brig. Gen. William T. Sherman. "You will move your entire command tomorrow morning, with 3 days rations and forage, to the point on the Corinth road where the skirmish occurred on the 15th inst. From that point Pickets will be thrown out upon every approach to prevent surprise. Heavy details will be made to repair the roads and bridge the streams. Not to exceed two tents to each Company will be taken along, nor more than one to the Field and Staff of each Regiment. Brigade and Division Commanders will be limited in proportion. You will see that 100 rounds of Cartridges per man are provided to all the Regiments and require your Acting Ordnance Officer to supply an equal amount more to follow, in wagons. You will be preceded by Gen. McClernand's Division which will occupy the position where Gen. A. J. Smith had a skirmish with the enemy of on the 24th, and you will be supported by the other Divisions of the Army of the Tenn. following with like instructions. Your Cavalry will join your command as soon as they return from the expedition toward Purdy." Copies, DLC-USG, V, 1, 2, 3, 86; DNA, RG 393, USG Letters Sent. *O.R.*, I, x, part 2, 137. On the same day, Hillyer sent instructions similarly worded to Brig. Gen. Stephen A. Hurlbut and to Brig. Gen. Thomas J. McKean. Copies, DLC-USG, V, 1, 2, 3, 86; DNA, RG 393, USG Letters Sent. *O.R.*, I, x, part 2, 135, 136.

1. Stantonville, Tenn., about seven miles west of Shiloh Church, midway on the road between Purdy and Monterey.

To Maj. Gen. Lewis Wallace

                                          Head Quarters, Army of the Tenn.
                                          Pittsburgh, April 28th 1862.

MAJOR. GEN. L. WALLACE
COMMDG 3RD DIVISION.
GENL:

Your note from Stantonville is just received 10 O'clock P. M. The object of the expidition being to cut off the Rail Road, and you being with the command to do it can tell better whether any change from the plan laid down should be made. If so you will be at liberty to do it so.

Cut the Road if possible but do not engage a force that you are not certain of success over, and if possible an engagement should be avoided altogether.

Very Respectfully
Your Obt. Servant.
U. S. GRANT.
Maj. Gen.

Copies, DLC-USG, V, 1, 2, 3, 86; DNA, RG 393, USG Letters Sent. *O.R.*, I, x, part 2, 135.

To Maj. Gen. Henry W. Halleck

———

Head Quarters Army of the Tennessee
In Field. Shiloh, April 29th 1862

MAJ GENL H W. HALLECK
COMMANDING DEPT OF THE MISS
GENL

I enclose herewith a note just received from Genl Wallace. I have ordered him foward with his entire Command, and ordere[d] Genl McKean to follow with all his Infantry and any Cavalry he may have, not on duty.

Very Respcty
Your Obt Servt
U. S. GRANT
Maj Genl

Copies, DLC-USG, V, 4, 5, 7, 8, 88; DNA, RG 393, USG Hd. Qrs. Correspondence. On April 28, 1862, Maj. Gen. Lewis Wallace wrote to Maj. John A. Rawlins. "I am only waiting for the Cavalry. Two Battalions of Ill have reported, which with three Comp's of our men are not enough. At Bethel there are two Regts of Infantry and one of Cavalry. Not knowing the extent of the Cavalry accompanying me I send you the above as a suggestion. Shall I look for more Cavalry, and if so who will command it?" Copies, DLC-USG, V, 88; DNA, RG 393, District of West Tenn., Letters Received. On the same day, USG endorsed the letter. "Your instructions are plain. You were not to await the arrival of Cavalry, but the Cavalry was to follow and report. Too often my orders and instructions are misunderstood or totally disregarded by you." Copies, DLC-USG, V, 1, 3, 88.

To Capt. Andrew C. Kemper

Head Quarters Army of the Tenn
In Field, Shiloh, April 29, 1862

CAPT A C. KEMPER,
A A. GENL
DEPT OF THE MISS
CAPT

I have just received reports from Genls McClernand & Sherman,[1] the former stating that he had halted short of the point to which he had been ordered by ¾ of a mile in consequence of a bad creek for crossing.[2] I know the place and think it about 2½ miles short. Genl Sherman was to follow McClernand, and consequently he and Genl Davies are still this side. In consequence of this I have sent orders for Genl Sherman to take the advance,[3] Genl Davies following,[4] and move foward as early as possible tomorrow morning. Genl McClernand to remain where he is for further orders.[5]

Very Respcty
Your Obt Servt
U. S. GRANT
Maj Genl

Copies, DLC-USG, V, 4, 5, 7, 8, 9, 88; DNA, RG 393, USG Hd. Qrs. Correspondence.

1. On April 29, 1862, Brig. Gen. William T. Sherman wrote to USG. "Gen McClernand has halted his Division on this East side of the branch of Lick Creek which empties into the main stream near Strattoon. The position indicated for me I understand to be on the Ridge beyond him though he has the advance. I have halted abreast of the Hospital & will encamp close to McClernand though I think he has not gone far enough in advance. If you have strategic reasons which I think likely, one advance should be as far as the Savanna & Corinth Road. You

had better see to it. McClernand says his orders are to go to the White house, but that there is no camping ground there. Please order my cavalry to come forward at once. Col Dickey & Maj Thielman—I left the 20 lb Parrott Guns because the horses cant pull them on easy ground, much less on broken. I bring such as we now have." ALS, *ibid.*, District of West Tenn., Letters Received.

2. On April 29, Maj. Gen. John A. McClernand wrote to USG. "The inconvenience and discomfort, which owing to the night's rain, would necessarily attend the breaking up and moving of my camp to-day, prompts me to inquire whether it would conflict with your wishes, for me to postpone moving until to-morrow?" LS, McClernand Papers, IHi. On the same day, Maj. John A. Rawlins endorsed the letter. "Orders for moving come from General Head Quarters, and will be obeyed, [unless] countermanded, from the same source." ES, *ibid.*

3. On April 29, Capt. William S. Hillyer wrote to Sherman. "You will move your column as soon as practicable in the morning beyond McClernand, and occupy the position assigned to him by yesterday's orders. Gen McClernand has been directed to remain where he is." Copies, DLC-USG, V, 1, 2, 3, 86; DNA, RG 393, USG Letters Sent. *O.R.*, I, x, part 2, 140. On April 30, Sherman wrote to Rawlins. "I have the honor to acknowledge the Receipt of your order this morning to advance my Division to the point designated in the order for Genl McClernand—I started at once and two of my brigades 1st & 4th are on the ground where Genl Smith had the cavalry engagement April 25th   A large open field is on the summit of the Hill   In this I will group the artillery—On the space Westward will place my 1st Brigade—On the space leading to Monterey the 4th Brigade—On the North line of the field the the the 3d Brigade—And on the road to the rear the 2nd Brigade—I have no cavalry as yet, and trust to you to order it forward as soon as it is able to rally from the hard ride to Purdy—No Enemy's pickets were seen on the road this morning, but Col McDowell reports that the pickets thrown forward from his Brigade have seen a few on the Road leading westward   From this point I can move on Monterey and by a road six miles west to a Road leading south to Corinth   We must use many Roads. If we attempt so much on a single Road—we will be jammed by scattered teams— McClernand or Hurlbut should move to the point indicated in your order for me —viz where the Ridge Road crosses the main Road from Savanna to Monterey— Known as the White house or Chamberlains—A kind of general center for Cross Roads"   Copy, DNA, RG 94, Generals' Papers and Books, William T. Sherman, Letters Sent. *O.R.*, I, x, part 2, 143–44.

4. On April 29, Hillyer wrote to Brig. Gen. Thomas A. Davies. "You will move on your column as soon as practicable in the morning passing beyond Gen. McClernand and encamping in the rear of Gen. Sherman." Copies, DLC-USG, V, 1, 2, 3, 86; DNA, RG 393, USG Letters Sent. *O.R.*, I, x, part 2, 141.

5. On April 29, Hillyer wrote to McClernand. "You will make no further advance until further orders. Camp where you are and bridge the creek there in pursuance of former orders." ALS, McClernand Papers, IHi.

To Capt. Andrew C. Kemper

> Head Quarters Army of the Tenn
> In Field, Shiloh, April 29, 1862

CAPT A C. KEMPER
A A. GENL &c
CAPT

Three Divisions of the force under my Command advanced
to day to the points indicated by the General Comdg in his order
of yesterday, a fourth is under orders to move in the morning,
and the two Divisions now out on the Purdy Road will advance
as soon as they return.

I will move my head quarters tomorrow to near the point
marked "B" if the weather is at all favorable & within a day or
two to the place indicated by the General Comdg ~~himself~~.

> Very Respcty
> Your Obt Servt
> U. S. GRANT
> Maj Genl

Copies, DLC-USG, V, 4, 5, 7, 8, 9, 88; DNA, RG 393, USG Hd. Qrs. Correspondence. On April 28, 1862, Maj. Gen. Henry W. Halleck wrote to USG. "You
will to-morrow morning move forward one division to the position marked "A"
in the accompanying sketch, and support it by the advance of your other divisions.
Guards & pickets will be pushed forward towards Montery, and fatigue parties
employed in making roads over the streams & marshes for an advance in full
force." ALS, James S. Schoff, New York, N. Y. *O.R.*, I, lii, part 1, 244.

To Maj. Gen. Lewis Wallace

————

Head Quarters, Army of the Tenn.
Pittsburgh, April 29th 1862.

MAJOR. GEN. L. WALLACE,
COMMDG 3RD DIVISION.
GENL:

Return to the Rail Road and do the work thoroughly. Gen. McKean is on the road to support you. Three Divisions of my forces, several of Gen. Buell's and some of Pope's have been advanced to near Pea Ridge.

You can be in but little danger of an attack from Monterey. The front is to be most guarded against.

Very Respectfully
Your Obt. Servant.
U. S. GRANT.
Maj. Gen

Copies, DLC-USG, V, 1, 2, 3, 86; DNA, RG 393, USG Letters Sent. *O.R.*, I, x, part 2, 140. On April 29, 1862, USG wrote to Maj. Gen. Lewis Wallace. "Push on with your forces. I will reinforce you with at least two Brigades of Infantry." Copies, DLC-USG, V, 1, 2, 3, 86; DNA, RG 393, USG Letters Sent. *O.R.*, I, x, part 2, 140. On the same day, Capt. William S. Hillyer wrote to Wallace. "The purpose of your expedition having been satisfactorily accomplished you will return with your command without delay." Copies, DLC-USG, V, 1, 2, 3, 86; DNA, RG 393, USG Letters Sent. Also on the same day, Hillyer wrote to Brig. Gen. Thomas J. McKean. "You will return with your command without delay. Similar orders are sent to Gen. Wallace." Copies, *ibid. O.R.*, I, x, part 2, 140.

To Brig. Gen. Stephen A. Hurlbut

————

Head Quarters, Army of the Tenn.
In Field, Shiloh, April 29th 1862.

BRIG. GEN. HURLBUT
COMMDG 4TH DIVISION
GEN:

Move your camp forward tomorrow taking ground in rear or to the right of 2nd Division, taking every thing including sick

if practicable. Such sick, however, as are not likely to be fit for
duty within the next ten days may be left in your present camp,
proper Medical attendance being left with them. Make immediate arrangements to have and to keep on hands at all times at
least 200 rounds of Cartriges per man including those with
Regiments

> Very Respectfully
> Your Obt. Servant.
> U. S. GRANT.
> Maj. Gen.

Copies, DLC-USG, V, 1, 2, 3, 86; DNA, RG 393, USG Letters Sent. The text
varies slightly, though not in substance, in *Charles Hamilton Auction No. 5*, Oct. 8,
1964, p. 17.

On April 30, 1862, Brig. Gen. Stephen A. Hurlbut wrote to Maj. John A.
Rawlins. "I desire to say to the General that if it is not positively required for me
to move Camp to day I would like the troops to remain until tomorrow for these
reasons. I am very busy perfecting exchanges of arms from the stock brought up
by Adj. Gen Fuller and of course this requires substitution of ordnance. Clothing
has just arrived & is reported ready to be delivered this morning   I shall of
course hold the troops ready at Noon—but would like the extention. Answer at
once as the teams are waiting. . . . P. S. *No Brigade Surgeon*" ALS, DNA,
RG 393, 16th Army Corps, Miscellaneous Papers. On the same day, Rawlins
endorsed this letter. "It is required that you move to-day. You can Start as late
in the afternoon, however, as you may see fit." ES, *ibid.*

To Capt. John C. Kelton

———

> Head Quarters Army of the Tennessee
> In Field, Shiloh, April 30th 1862

CAPT J C KELTON
A A. GENL

The troops sent on the Purdy road on the 28th inst have
returned. I have ordered them all to move to the advance with
the exception of 1st Brigade of the 3rd Division which is left
back to guard the Purdy roads.

They will be off tomorrow morning. All the balance of my forces are now moved.

Very Respcty
Your Obt Servt
U. S. GRANT
Maj Genl

Copies, DLC-USG, V, 4, 5, 7, 8, 9, 88; DNA, RG 393, USG Hd. Qrs. Correspondence.

To Capt. Andrew C. Kemper

Head Quarters, Army of the Ten.
Pittsburg, April 30th 1862

CAPT. A. C. KEMPER
A. A. GEN. DEPT. OF THE MISS.
CAPT.

Enclosed I forward an account similar to several that have been presented to me for approval, with my endorsement on it.

These accounts should be settled though my instructions given at Fort Donelson have not been complied with.

I would respectfully ask the Gen. Comd.g. what should be done with these accounts.

very respectfully
your obt. svt.
U. S. GRANT
Maj. Gen.

ALS, DNA, RG 393, District of West Tenn., Letters Received. On April 30, 1862, Capt. John C. Kelton endorsed this letter. "The Med. Director St Louis will be ordered to pay all such accounts and hold the Med Officer who recd the property strictly accountable for it." AES, *ibid.*

To Maj. Gen. Lewis Wallace

Head Quarters, Army of the Tenn.
In Field, Shiloh, April 30th 1862.

MAJOR GEN. L. WALLACE,
COMMDG 3RD DIVISION

Advance tomorrow with two Brigades of your Division on the Corinth Road beyond the creek where Gen. McClernand is now encamped, closing up on Gen Davies forces. You will keep to the right ~~to the right~~ of Gen. Buell's Corps-de-Armée, and avoid mixing in with them.

As soon as encamped make roads and bridge the ravines in front and rear of your position to the Corinth road and repair the latter thro' your limits.

Take all your Camp and Garrison Equipage. Make immediate requisition for ammunition sufficient for 200 rounds per man including that already on hand, and get it to your camp as soon as possible. Leave Col. M. L. Smith's Brigade and instruct him that he is to guard the two Purdy roads establishing pickets about where they have been stationed heretofore. All your Cavalry will be left with Col. Smith and one Battery.

Very Respectfully,
Your Obt Servant.
U. S. GRANT.
Maj. Gen.

Copies, DLC-USG, V, 1, 2, 3, 86; DNA, RG 393, USG Letters Sent. Later on April 30, 1862, USG wrote to Maj. Gen. Lewis Wallace. "You will remain where you now are and not move your command until further orders." Copies, *ibid*.

To Maj. Osborne Cross

———

Head Quarters, Army of the Tenn.
Pittsburgh, April 30th 1862.

MAJOR O. CROSS,
CHIEF Q. M. ARMY IN THE FIELD.
MAJOR:

I enclose herewith the report called for in your note of yesterday, complete except for one Brigade of one Division. I had called for a similar report from my command and have taken from that report for the delinquent Brigade and ordered the arrest of the Commander of it for non-compliance with orders.

Very Respectfully,
U. S. GRANT.
Maj. Genl.

Copies, DLC-USG, V, 1, 2, 3, 86; DNA, RG 393, USG Letters Sent. For Maj. Osborne Cross, see *PUSG*, I, 308–10. On April 13, 1862, Capt. Nathaniel H. McLean issued Special Field Orders No. 2 appointing Cross inspector and chief of the q. m. dept., Army of the Tenn. Copy, DLC-USG, V, 83. On April 16, McLean wrote to USG. "The Major General commanding desires that you will furnish Major O. Cross, Chief Quartermaster of the Army on the Tennessee at your earliest convenience, with a statement of the transportation of your army and its condition. Also an estimate of clothing, camp and garrison equipage that you may require for the next three months." Copies, *ibid.*, V, 4, 5, 7, 8, 9; DNA, RG 393, USG Hd. Qrs. Correspondence; *ibid.*, Dept. of the Miss., Letters Sent. On the same day, Maj. John A. Rawlins issued General Orders No. 38 embodying this request. DS, McClernand Papers, IHi; copies, DLC-USG, V, 12, 13, 14, 95; DNA, RG 94, 9th Ill., Letterbook; *ibid.*, RG 393, USG General Orders.

On April 30, Rawlins wrote to Maj. Gen. John A. McClernand. "I am instructed by Maj. Gen. U. S. Grant to say that in your Report of the Transportation of your Division, as required by General Orders No. 38. current Series. from these Head Quarters, you simply report the 3d Brigade of your Division is 'Not Reported.' This is no compliance with the orders, and disregard of them will not be tolerated. You will immediately arrest the Commander of the 3d Brigade, referred to, and keep him under arrest until a report of Transportation for his Brigade is furnished you, which must be done within 24 hours after the receipt of this order." LS, McClernand Papers, IHi. On May 1, McClernand wrote to Rawlins that the report had been compiled by Capt. James Dunlap based upon reports from the q. m. of each brigade; the report for the 3rd brigade, which had arrived late, had already been forwarded with the consolidated report. McClernand then asked if he should proceed with the arrest of Brig. Gen. Leonard F. Ross. ADf, *ibid*.

To Julia Dent Grant

Camp in the Field
Near Pittsburg Ten.
April 30th 1862

DEAR JULIA,

I move from here to-morrow. Before this reaches you probably another battle, and I think the last big one, will have taken place or be near at hand. I mean the last in the Mississippi Valley and this of course implies if we are successful which no doubt we will be. You need give yourself no trouble about newspaper reports. They will all be understood and me come out all right without a single contradiction. Most or all that you have seen has been written by persons who were not here and thos few items collected from persons nominally present, eye witnesses, was from those who disgraced themselvs and now want to draw off public attention. I am very sorry to say a greatdeel originates in jealousy. This is very far from applying however, I think, to our Chief, Halleck, who I look upon as one of the greatest men of the age. You enquire how I was hurt? For several days before the battle of Pittsburg our out Pickets were skirmishing with the enemies advance. I would remain up here all day and go back to Savanna in the evening where I was anxiously looking for the advance of Gen. Buell's column. My object was, if possible, to keep off an attack until Buell arrived otherwise I would have gone out and met the enemy on Friday before they could have got in position to use all their forces advantageously. Friday evening I went back to Savanna as usual and soon after dark a messenger arrived informing that we were attacked. I immediately returned here and started out onto the field on horseback, my staff with me. The night was intensely dark. I soon found that the firing had seased and started to go back to the river. Being very dark and in the woods we had to ride in a slow walk and at that got off the road. In geting back to it my horse's foot either cought or struck something and he fell flat on his side with my leg under him. Being wet and muddy I was not hurt much at the time but being in the saddle all of Sunday and Monday, and in the rain the intervening night without taking off boots or spurs my ancle swelled terribly and kept me on crutches for several days, unable to get on a boot. Col. Riggin is not with me. The rest of the gentlemen are. In addition I have Col. McPherson of the regular Army and one of the nicest gentleman you ever saw, Capt. Reynolds,[1] regular, Lieuts Bowers[2] & Rowley. We are all well and me as sober as a deacon no matter what is said to the contrary. Mrs. Turner[3] & Miss Hadley run on the steamer Memphis carrying sick soldiers to hospital. As I am out from the river and they are only here about one day in eight or ten I rarely see them. There are no inhabitants here atall

Kiss all the children for me. Tell Jess I have a five shooter pistol for him. When you hear of me being on the Mississippi river join me leaving all the children except Jess. Draw the hundred dollars you have as a matter of course. If I had an opportunity I would send you $200 00 now. Give my love to all at home. Kisses for yourself.

Good buy
ULYS.

ALS, DLC-USG.

1. Charles A. Reynolds of Md. served as a private in the Mexican War, and was appointed 2nd lt., 9th Inf., on March 3, 1855. He was confirmed as capt. and asst. q. m. on Feb. 3, 1862, to rank from Nov. 18, 1861.

2. Theodore S. Bowers of Pa., born in 1832, was a printer who edited and published the Mount Carmel, Ill., *Register*, 1852–61. Mustered in as a private, 48th Ill., on Oct. 25, 1861, he was promoted to 1st lt. on March 24, 1862. On April 26, Maj. John A. Rawlins issued General Orders No. 45 announcing Bowers's appointment as aide-de-camp to USG. DS, McClernand Papers, IHi; copies, DNA, RG 94, 9th Ill., Letterbook; *ibid.*, 48th Ill., Letterbook; *ibid.*, RG 393, USG General Orders; DLC-USG, V, 12, 13, 14, 95. A letter of June 13

from Bowers to his family is in the Ritzman Collection, Aurora College, Aurora, Ill. See Theodoe G. Risley, "Colonel Theodore S. Bowers," *Journal of the Illinois State Historical Society*, XII, 3 (Oct., 1919), 407–11.

3. Asst. Surgeon W. D. Turner, 1st Ill. Light Art., served on the hospital ship *City of Memphis*.

General Orders No. 50

Head Quarters Army of the Tennessee
Pittsburgh May 1. 1862

GENERAL ORDERS No 50

In compliance with Special Field Orders No 35, from General Head Quarters, the undersigned takes command of the Army of the Tennessee, including the Reserve, under Maj General John A McClernand.

All reports of the right wing and the reserve will be consolidated at the Head quarters of each respectively, and forwarded to these Head Quarters.

All orders heretofore in force will continue so, until otherwise directed.

By Command of Maj Gen U. S. Grant
JNO. A. RAWLINS
A. A. General.

DS, McClernand Papers, IHi. Letterbook copies indicate USG's signature. DNA, RG 94, 48th Ill., Letterbook; *ibid.*, RG 393, USG General Orders; DLC-USG, V, 12, 13, 14, 95. *O.R.*, I, x, part 2, 154. See letter to Julia Dent Grant, April 15, 1862, note 1.

On April 28, 1862, Capt. Andrew C. Kemper issued Special Field Orders No. 31. "The troops on the Tennessee River will retain their present organization of three distinct Army Corps, viz: the first of the Tennessee Commanded by Major Genl Grant, which will constitute the right wing; the second of the Ohio, commanded by Maj Genl Buell which will constitute the center, and the third of the Mississippi, commanded by Maj Genl Pope, which will constitute the left wing. The Reserve will be formed of detachments ordered from the several Army Corps. Each Genl Commanding ~~the~~ an army Corps will be charged with its organization, discipline, and preperation for service in the field, as well as police in camp. Having his own Staff, and Chiefs of administrative Corps, he will be held responsible that his troops are properly provided for thro the Quarter Master, Commissary,

Ordinance, and Medical Departments. The Commanding Genl will interfere in these matters only in cases of negligence or abuse." Copy, DLC-USG, V, 83. *O.R.*, I, x, part 2, 138–39.

On April 30, Capt. John C. Kelton issued Special Orders No. 35. "Maj Genl Thomas division is hereby transferred from the Army of the Ohio to the Army of the Tennessee and Genl Thomas will take command of the right wing which will consist of his own and the Divisions of Brig Genls W T Sherman, T W Sherman, S A. Hurlbut and T A Davies   The Divisions of Major Genl McClernand, Maj Genl Wallace, and one Division from Genl Buells Army corps to be designated by him, together with the heavy artillery, will constitute the Reserve, to be commanded by Maj Genl McClernand. . . . Major Genl Grant will retain the general command of the Disct of West Tennessee, including the Army Corps of the Tennessee, and reports will be made to him as heretofore, but in the present movement he will act as second in command under the Maj Genl Commanding the Dept." Copies, DLC-USG, V, 83; DLC-Elihu B. Washburne. *O.R.*, I, x, part 2, 144. On the same day, Maj. Gen. Henry W. Halleck wrote to USG. "The change of organization made by Special Field Order No 35, will render it necessary that your Head Qrs should be near mine. I shall move in a day or two to the vicinity of Grier's House, and whenever you change I think it should be in that direction. If Genl Buell's forces can cross Lick Creek I shall direct them to move south of Monterey, which will make the centre of the advance near Grier's. . . . P. S. McClernand's & Wallace's divisions should remain in position till further orders." ALS, James S. Schoff, New York, N. Y. *O.R.*, I, lii, part 1, 245.

On May 3, Kelton issued Special Field Orders No. 40. "The Staff of the Army of the Tenn. will at once report to, and be subject to the orders of, Maj Genl Thomas, Commanding the right Wing of the Army." Copy, DLC-USG, V, 83. On May 4, Rawlins wrote to Maj. Gen. George H. Thomas. "I am instructed by Major Gen. U. S. Grant. to inform you that the only Staff Officers embraced in Special Field Orders No 40. from General Head Quarters directed to report to you, are Surgeon Simons, Medical Director, Capt Reynolds, Senior Qr. Master, and Capt. Hinsdill, ~~Senior~~ Commissary of Subsistance. Surgeon Simons will report to-day. Capt. Reynolds is detained for duty by Chief Qr. Master Major Cross, and Capt. Hinsdill is on duty issuing to the Army." Copies, *ibid.*, V, 1, 2, 3, 86; DNA, RG 393, USG Letters Sent. On May 5, Rawlins again wrote to Thomas. "I am directed by Major Gen. Grant to say that Major Roper already on your Staff, being the Senior Commissary, he will remain in that position, in place of Capt. Hinsdill, who was only temporarily attached to ~~my~~ his Staff on account of Seniority"   Copies, *ibid*. On the same day, Rawlins issued General Orders No. 53. "In pursuance of Special Field Orders No 40. from General Head Quarters, Capt. Chas. A. Reynolds, A. Q. M. is transferred to the Staff of Major Gen. Thomas, Commdg Right Wing of the Army of the Tenn. The Medical Director, Surgeon J. Simons, will remain with Head Quarters of the Army of the Tenn. and all Certificates of Disability from the *Right Wing* and from the *Reserve* will be referred to him and discharges ordered from these Head Quarters"   Copies, DLC-USG, V, 12, 13, 14, 95; DNA, RG 393, USG General Orders; McClernand Papers, IHi.

To Capt. John C. Kelton

Head Quarters Army of the Tennessee.
In Field, Shiloh, Tenn. May 1, 1862

CAPT. J. C. KELTON
A. A. G. DEPART OF THE MISS:
CAPT:

I have the honor to report that the following orders received from Head Quarters Department of the Mississippi, have been obeyed and executed:

Of the 30 men ordered to be detailed by Special Orders No 32, twenty men reported on the 30th, and ten men to-day, as required by your note of this date.

Special Field Orders. No. 34, permanently detailing men for Hospital Boat "Louisiana." received, and the proper orders sent to the Commanding Officers of the Several Divisions to which the men belong

Special Field Orders No 35 has been complyed with, and Gen. McKean assigned to the command of a Brigade of 6th Division.

One Regiment of Gen. Wallace's Division has been ordered to guard the Crump's Landing ~~or Purdy~~ Road, leading from Pittsburg Landing, with directions for one company to camp at the Bridge, and the remainder of the Regiment near by.[1]

I am, Sir,
Verry Respectfully,
Your Obt Servt.
U. S. GRANT
Maj. Gen. Comd.g

LS, DNA, RG 393, Dept. of the Miss., Letters Received.

1. On May 1, 1862, Maj. John A. Rawlins wrote to Maj. Gen. Lewis Wallace. "You will send one Regiment of your command. to guard the Crump's Landing road near Gen. Hallecks Head Quarters. One Company will encamp at the bridge, and the remainder of the Regt. near by to remain on duty until further orders." Copies, DLC-USG, V, 1, 2, 3, 86; DNA, RG 393, USG Letters Sent.

To Col. William W. Lowe

Head Quarters, Dist of West Tenn.
Pittsburgh, May 1st 1862.

COL. W. W. LOWE
COMMDG FORTS HENRY & HEIMAN
COLONEL:

I have ordered some ambulances and Ambulance Teams from Fort. Donelson. As soon as they arrive ship them to the Care of Major O. Cross, A. Q. M. Pittsburg Landing, Ten

With respect to the man Bell against whom complaints are made, if they seem to be well founded, ship him North at your pleasure with orders not to return so long as the place is garrsoned by United States Troops. Should he return after such notification ship him to the Commanding Officer at St Louis, with a request that he be confined in the Military prison there, sending the charges against him

Very Respectfully
Your Obt. Servant.
U. S. GRANT.
Major General.

Copies, DLC-USG, V, 1, 2, 3, 86; DNA, RG 393, USG Letters Sent. On May 1, 1862, USG wrote to the commanding officer, Fort Donelson. "As soon as possible after the receipt of this send all Ambulances and Ambulance Teams at Fort Donelson to Fort Henry to be forwarded here. Fort Donelson and Clarkesville if garrisoned by the 71st Ohio Alone will be regarded as in the Dist of West. Tenn. and all reports will be made to these Head Quarters until further orders." Copies, *ibid.*

On May 22, Col. Rodney Mason, 71st Ohio, Clarksville, telegraphed to USG. "Your telegram of may 1st rcd today   I have ordered the ambulances to be sent   if not wanted please inform me. In absence of both ~~to~~ you & Genl. Dumont a squadron of Cavalry have orders to report to Genl Dumont & to receive no order except from him or an officer higher in rank than him" Telegram received, *ibid.*, Dept. of the Mo., Telegrams Received.

On May 5, USG wrote to Maj. Gen. John A. McClernand. "You will make requisition of Maj O Cross Chief Qr. Master, for such transportation and ambulances, as may need, he has plenty." Register of Letters, McClernand Papers, IHi.

To Maj. Gen. John A. McClernand

Head Quarters, Army of the Tenn
In Field, Shiloh, May 2nd 1862.

Gen. J. A. McClernand,
Commdg 4th Army Corps
Genl:

A note just received from Gen Halleck says that the enemy are moving towards Purdy to operate on our flank.[1]

Have all the approaches by way of Owl Creek well watched, and tomorrow early, or tonight if practicable send a strong reconnoitering party towards Purdy. Cavalry alone will answer for this reconnoisance. I will direct Gen Wallace to use extra vigilance on the two roads leading from here.

Very Respectfully,
Your Obt. Servant.
U. S. Grant.
Maj. Genl.

Copies, DLC-USG, V, 1, 2, 3, 86; DNA, RG 393, USG Letters Sent. *O.R.*, I, x, part 2, 157. On May 3, 1862, Maj. Gen. John A. McClernand wrote to USG. "Pursuant to your order, I dispatched all the available Cavalry of my command, this morning to reconnoitre towards Purdy, and to report the result   I will in due time, advise you of the result"   Copies, DNA, RG 393, Dept. of the Tenn., Letters Received from Reserve Corps, Jackson, Tenn.; McClernand Papers, IHi.

On May 3, McClernand wrote to USG. "I received the following order this morning, and have issued orders accordingly to the different Division Commanders. The order to move as you [*are*] aware from previous communications, finds a portion of my command without a sufficient supply of Haversacks, Knapsacks, canteens and camp equipage. . . . Leaving the guards previously detailed to protect the crossing of Snake & Owl creeks, you will tomorrow morning advance with four days cooked rations to Monterey, keeping in supporting distance of the right wing. Cavalry will be thrown out the right, to give notice of any flank movement of the enemy   You will give all possible assistance to the advance of the Heavy Artillery which will follow the corps to which it belongs   A regular organization of Artillery reserve will not be made till the army corps unite near Corinth—sgd—H. W. Halleck . . . As you will perceive I am instructed to keep in supporting distance of the right wing—Now I understand that Genl McKeans Division, a portion of the right wing does not move until to morrow, unless the right wing (understood to be Genl Thomas command moves rapidly it will delay my advance   If your Engineer could immediatly impart information as to the route of my advance and the ground I am to occupy at Monterey he would facilitate my advance   The bearer will wait for any instructions you may think proper to forward   I also hand you herewith a communication showing that the wants of men cannot be supplied at the Pittsburg Landing." LS (misdated May 2), DNA, RG 393, District of West Tenn., Letters Received; (dated May 3) *ibid.*, Dept. of the Tenn., Letters Received from Reserve Corps, Jackson, Tenn.

On May 3, McClernand wrote to USG. "You doubtless received this morning, the copy of a communication from Genl Halleck, instructing me to advance with my command—One of my orderlies bearing an order to Genl Van Cleve, in command of Crittenden's Division, to move accordingly, in the morning, has just returned informing me that Genl. Van Cleve is moving forward to Monterey, to-day. The presumption is, that Genl Van Cleve's movement is being made pursuant to an order from some other source—Besides this disarrangement, I am also in posession of a note from Genl Buell requesting me to send Sutermeister's heavy battery in compliance with a telegram from Dept Head Quarters—This request seemingly conflicts with the order of Genl Halleck to me, of this date, yet, in view of explanations made by one of Genl Buell's officers, I sent the battery forward—Such conflicting orders, and authority must necessarily lead to confusion, and make it [impracticable] for me to answer the expectations either of Genl Halleck or yourself—. . . P. S. At this moment Genl Buell sends an extract of Genl Hallecks order rescinding the order attaching Gen Crittendens Division to my army Corps—Will its place be supplied?" Copies, *ibid.*; McClernand Papers, IHi.

1. On May 2, Maj. Gen. Henry W. Halleck wrote to USG. "Reports just received that the enemy is Moving a considerable force from Corinth toward Purdy—to operate on our flank   Direct Genl McClernand to watch the Passes of owl Creek and to Send out a reconoitng party of Cavalry on the purdy Road" Copies, DLC-USG, V, 4, 5, 7, 8, 9; DNA, RG 393, USG Hd. Qrs. Correspondence; *ibid.*, Dept. of the Miss., Letters Sent. *O.R.*, I, lii, part 1, 246.

To Maj. Gen. Lewis Wallace

Head Quarters, Army of the Tenn.
In Field, Shiloh, May 2nd 1862.

MAJOR GEN. L. WALLACE,
COMMDG 3RD DIVISION
GENL:

It being reported that the enemy are moving a strong force from Corinth towards Purdy with a view of operating on our flank you will cause extra vigilance in that direction and increase the guards. I have informed Gen. McClernand that this order would be sent direct to save time. Send out all your Cavalry towards Purdy, to reconnotre the country in that direction.

Very Respectfully,
Your Obt. Servant
U. S. GRANT
Maj. Gen.

Copies, DLC-USG, V, 1, 2, 3, 86; DNA, RG 393, USG Letters Sent. *O.R.*, I, x, part 2, 157–58. See preceding letter. See also *O.R.*, I, x, part 2, 158–59.

To Julia Dent Grant

———

Monterey Ten.
May 4th 1862

DEAR JULIA,

Olando Ross[1] has just arrived bringing a letter for me from you and also one from father. The latter seems very anxious that I should contradict the statements made by the newspapers! Dont he know the best contradiction in the world is to pay no attention to them? I am in the best health in the world. I think I must be twenty pounds heavyer than when first arrived at Savanna. I was then much reduced however from Diareah. My weight now must be 150 pounds. Orley says that Missy is one of the smartest little girls to learn in Covington. I wrote to you that when you heard of my arrival any place on the Mississippi river you might join me. We now have our advance within three miles of Corinth. Every day our column moves up closer to the enemy. It is a big job however to get a large Army over country roads where it has been raining for the last five months. If we could go strung along the road where there was no enemy to meet it would be different. Here however the front must be kept compact and we do well to approach a few miles every day.

Yesterday Gen. Pope had quite a skirmish with the rebels in geting possession of the town of Farmington three miles of Corinth.² Pope lost two men killed & twelve wounded whilst the enemy left thirty dead on the field and lost quite a number taken prisoners. You will hear the result of the attack on Corinth, by telegraph, before this reaches you.—I sent you $250 00 by express the other day. Draw the $100 00 you got from Mr. Safford as a matter of course. I want you to let father have all you can for us to start on at the close of the war but dont stint yourself. I want you and the children to dress well. You can say to father that Nelsons troops made a good march on Saturday and were ordered that evening to march up the river to opposite Pittsburg Landing the next morning, which they did starting at an early hour. After the attack commenced orders were sent hurrying them up. But it is no small matter to march 10 000 men nine miles and cross a river with them when there are no ferry boats and but a small landing overcrouded with steamers.

The papers will get done with this thing after awhile and look upon the first days fight at Pittsburg Landing as one of the best resistances ever made. The enemy outnumbered us three to one that day and we held the field.

Kiss the children for me. Give my love to all at home. Did you get Simp's watch? I shall not want my citizens clothing until my return to the loyal states. I hope and feel that my return there is not going to be long defered. After one more big battle it certainly cannot be necessary to keep this large army to-gether and I am anxious to go either to Texas or on the coast someplace. Kisses for yourself.

ULYS.

The letter I sent you from Gen. Smith was probably the last he ever wrote. That was written by himself but seeing how badly it was done he had it copied and signed it himself. He was a gallant soldier and one whos esteem was worth having. In Gen. Sherman the country has an able and gallant defender and your husband a true friend.

U.

ALS, DLC-USG.

1. On May 8, 1862, Maj. John A. Rawlins issued Special Orders No. 75. "The Chief Quartermaster of the Army of the Tenn, will cause to be paid the account of O. H. Ross, Special Mail Agent, including actual expenses incurred by him whilst in the performance of his duties." Copies, *ibid.*, V, 15, 16, 82, 87, 89; DNA, RG 393, USG Special Orders.

2. See *O.R.*, I, x, part 1, 801–3.

To Maj. Gen. John A. McClernand

—————

Head Quarters—
Monterey May 6th 1862

If the regiment you spoke of this morning are already at Pittsburg Landing, leave them there. If the last have not gone however you need not send it as Genl. Halleck only contemplated leaving three regiments from the Reserve back.

The regiments stationed near Genl. Halleck's old Hd Quarters was all the support of Col. Woods. Capt Hawkins is Telegraphed to come up and make the necessary arrangements for fresh beef.

Copy, Register of Letters, McClernand Papers, IHi. On May 6, 1862, Maj. Gen John A. McClernand endorsed this letter. "Having brought the subject of the foregoing communication Genl. Grant with the request that he would bring it to the attention of Genl. Halleck he was pleased to do so, and with the result here shown. If the regiment ordered by me to be detached for service at the Purdy Bridge, near your late camp has been sent back, and the one called for by Col Wood's has not; then return the latter, and vice verse." Copy, *ibid.*

To Capt. John C. Kelton

Head Quarters Army of the Tennessee
In Field near Monterey Tenn May 8th 1862

CAPT J C. KELTON
A A G. DEPT OF THE MISS
COL

In reply to your letter of this date, I have the honor to say that the 10 boxes of Blanks were received; that Division Commanders were advised of the fact, and requested to send ~~orders~~ for such blanks as they needed, and that they were judiciously issued to the different Divisions of the Army of the Tenn, and receipts taken therefore.

A supply of blanks were issued to Maj Genl Thomas yesterday, and a similar requisition was filled for Genl Judah[1] to day. I have yet on hand a sufficient supply for present use, which will be issued as fast as called for.

I am Col Very Respcty
U. S. GRANT
Maj Gen

Copies, DLC-USG, V, 4, 5, 7, 8, 88; DNA, RG 393, USG Hd. Qrs. Correspondence. On May 8, 1862, Capt. John C. Kelton wrote to USG. "Regiments and Batteries in the Army of the Tennessee are continually applying to me for Blanks. —I have sent to your address a very large supply for distribution. Please advise me if they have reached their destination, that I may know whether to refer these applicants to you, or order more blanks.—Gen. Thomas' old Division, and one of the Brigades of the 2d Division are reported out of Blanks." LS, *ibid.*, District of West Tenn., Letters Received.

1. Henry M. Judah of N. Y., USMA 1843, was a classmate of USG and a fellow officer of the prewar 4th Inf. See *PUSG*, I, *passim*. Confirmed as brig. gen. on March 21, 1862, Judah served as inspector gen. of the Army of the Tenn. and commanded the 1st Division, Reserve Corps, during the Corinth campaign. On May 12, Maj. Gen. John A. McClernand wrote to USG. "Herewith you will find the Report of the Surgeon relative to Genl Judahs illness. upon that report I have forwarded the order, a copy whereof is herewith enclosed   The urgency of the case requires prompt action which was accordingly taken"   Copy, DNA, RG 393, Dept. of the Tenn., Letters Received from Reserve Corps, Jackson, Tenn. Apparently due to illness, Judah took a minor part in the Corinth campaign, and he began a formal sick leave of absence on June 16.

To Maj. Gen. Henry W. Halleck

——

Near Monterey, Ten.
May 11th 1862

MAJ. GEN. H. W. HALLECK
COMD.G DEPT. OF THE MISSISSIPPI,
GEN.

Since the publication of Special Field Orders No 35[1] relieving me from the immediate command of any portion of the *Army in the Field* I have felt my position as anomylous and determined to have it corrected, in some way, so soon as the present impending crisis should be brought to a close. I felt that sensure was implied but did not wish to call up the matter in the face of the enemy.

Now however as I believe it is generally understood through this army that my position differs but little from that of one in arrest, and as this opinion may be much strengthened from the fact that orders to the *Right Wing* and the *Reserve*, both nominally under my command, are transmitted direct from General Head Quarters, without going through me, I deem it due to myself to ask either full restoration to duty, according to my rank, or to be relieved entirely from further duty.

I cannot, do not, believe that there is any disposition on the part of yourself to do me any injustice, but ~~my~~ suspicions have been aroused that you may be acting under instructions, from higher authority, that I know nothing of.

That there has been a studied persistent opposition to me by persons outside of the army, and it may be by some in it, I am fully aware. This I care nothing for further than it is calculated to weaken confidance in me with those whom it becomes my duty to command.

In conclution then General I respectfully ask either to be relieved from duty entirely or to have my position so defined that there can be no mistaking it.

I address you direct instead of through the A. A. Gen. because this is more a private matter, and one in which I may possibly be wrong, than on official business.

> I am Gen. very respectfully
> your obt. svt.
> U. S. GRANT
> Maj. Gen.

ALS, DNA, RG 393, Dept. of the Miss., Letters Received. On May 12, 1862, Maj. Gen. Henry W. Halleck wrote to USG. "Your position as second in command of the entire forces here in the field rendered it proper that you should be relieved from the direct charge of either the right wing or the reserve, both of which are mainly composed of your forces   Orders for movements in the field will be sent direct from these Headquarters to commanders of army corps, division, brigades or even regiments, if deemed necessary, and you will have no more cause of complaint on that more than others have. I am very much surprised, General, that you should find any cause of complaint in the recent assignment of commands. You have precisely the position to which your rank entitles you. Had I given you the right wing or reserve only it would have been a reduction rather than an increase of command, and I would not give you both without placing you in the position you now occupy. You certainly will not suspect me of any intention to injure your feelings or reputation, or to do you any injustice. If so you will eventually change your mind on this subject   For the last three months I have done every thing in my power to ward off the attacks which were made upon you. If you believe me your friend, you will not require explanation; if not, explanation on my part would be of little avail." Copies, DLC-USG, V, 7; DNA, RG 393, USG Hd. Qrs. Correspondence; *ibid.*, Dept. of the Miss., Letters Sent. *O.R.*, I, x, part 2, 182–83.

1. See General Orders No. 50, May 1, 1862.

To Julia Dent Grant

> Camp Near Corinth, Miss.
> May 11th 1862

DEAR JULIA,

I write again and probably the last from this side of Corinth. A few days more will no doubt tell the tale and relieve further suspense.—We here of course do not feel the same feverish excitement that is felt by persons at a distance, but I begin to understand their anxiety to know the result of every move that is made on the checkerboard.—I am thinking seriously of going home, and to Washington, as soon as the present impending fight or footrace is decided. I have been so shockingly abused that I sometimes think it almost time to defend myself. But my record in this war will bear scrutiny without writing anything in reply to the many attacks made. Take only the orders and instructions issued to me and those written by myself for their execution and it will make all right. I have seen with pain two publications, one from Hillyer and the other from myself, to father bearing our respective names.[1] This should never have occured.

I have but little to write you about this country. People have mostly left and indeed there is not much to remain for. It is heavily wooded and looks much that on the Gravois.[2] People, what there are of them, Big river like.—Tell Jess I will take him his pistol before many weeks. I feel that the time cannot be long before I see you all either by my going home or being where you can join me. If the latter I would like very much to have Mary come with you.

I hope Fred & Buck are good boys and learn their lessons well! Missy I know learns hers and will soon be able to write me long letters. Kiss all of them for me. The same for yourself dear Julia.

ULYS.

ALS, DLC-USG.

1. See letter to Jesse Root Grant, April 26, 1862.
2. Gravois Creek, which ran near the Dent estate of White Haven in St. Louis County.

To Maj. Gen. Henry W. Halleck

BY TELEGRAPH FROM Near Corinth [*May 13*] 3 P M *1862*

TO MAJ GEN HALLECK

Telegraph complete. Head Quarters about two hundred (200) yards from Mr Lents

U S GRANT
Maj Genl

Telegram received, DNA, RG 94, Generals' Papers and Books, Telegrams Received by Gen. Halleck; copy, *ibid.*, RG 393, Dept. of the Miss., Hd. Qrs. in the Field, Telegrams Received. On May 13, 1862, Capt. John C. Kelton telegraphed to USG. "The Cavalry drove in the pickets—killed two and captured five. Went within a mile of their first Battery which was supported by a Brigade of Infantry—no casualities" ALS (telegram sent), *ibid.*, RG 108, Telegrams Sent.

To Julia Dent Grant

Camp Near Corinth, Miss
May 13th 1862

DEAR JULIA,

I have just received two letters from you one written on the 3d and the other on the 4th of this month both complaining of not receiving letters from me. I write usually twice a week and why in the world you do not get my letters I cant tell. You also ask if I wont send you a remittance soon! It is only a month since I sent you $205 00 and since that I have sent you $250 00 more and wrote to you to draw the $100 you got from Mr. Safford. I have also written two or three times to join me the moment you hear of me being on the Mississippi river. Since that however I have written to you that I expected to go home after the approaching battle. If I do not however and you hear of our arrival at Memphis join me at once. You may draw on Mr.

Safford for $200 00 if you like. I shall not probably be able to send any from here at the end of this month as I will use my pay for secret service funds to make up for the money I have of that kind with Mr. Safford and with the Sub Treasurer in New York City. I would just as leave you would draw all I have with Mr. Safford as not however. The amount is between three and four hundred dollars. We are now encamped in the state of Mississippi within hearing of the enemies drums at Corinth. Every day we have more or less skirmishing but nothing that could be magnified into a battle. As I have said before in several of my letters I regard this as the last great battle to be fought in the valley of the Mississippi. If the War is to be continued I am anxious to go to some other field. I have probably done more hard work than any other General officer and about as much fighting and although I will schrink from no duty I am perfectly willing that others should have every opportunity for distinguishing themselves. I have had my full share of abuse too but I think no harm will come from all that.

In my last letter I told you that it would probably be my last this side of Corinth. But we move slow Gen. Halleck being determined to make shure work. Then too, the roads have been so intolerable until within the last few days that it has been very difficult to get up supplies for the army.

Kiss all the children for me. Give my love to all at home. If you do not get letters dont blame me with it for I write every three or four days.

Kisses for yourself.

                                                        Ulys.

P. S. I never enjoyed better health in my life than for the last month. I must weigh ten or fifteen pounds more now than at any time since leaving Calafornia.

ALS, DLC-USG.

To Elihu B. Washburne

———

Camp Near Corinth, Miss.
May 14th 1862

HON. E. B. WASHBURN,
DEAR SIR:

The great number of attacks made upon me by the press of the country is my apology for not writing to you oftener, not desiring to give any contradiction to them myself.—You have interested yourself so much as my friend that should I say anything it would probably be made use of in my behalf. I would scorn being my own defender against such attacks except through the record which has been kept of all my official acts and which can be examined at Washington at any time.

To say that I have not been distressed at these attacks upon me would be false, for I have a father, mother, wife & children who read them and are distressed by them and I necessaryily share with them in it. Then too all subject to my orders read these charges and it is calculated to weaken their confidance in me and weaken my ability to render efficient service in our present cause. One thing I will assure you of however; I can not be driven from rendering the best service within my ability to suppress the present rebellion, and when it is over retiring to the same quiet it, the rebellion, found me enjoying.

Notoriety has no charms for me and could I render the same services that I hope it has been my fortune to render our just cause, without being known in the matter, it would be infinately prefferable to me.

Those people who expect a field of battle to be maintained, for a whole day, with about 30,000 troops, most of them entirely raw, against 70,000, as was the case at Pittsburg Landing, whilst waiting for reinforcements to come up, without loss of life, know little of War. To have left the field of Pittsburg for the enemy to occupy until our force was sufficient to have gained a bloodless victory would have been to left the Tennessee to become a second

Potomac.—There was nothing left for me but to occupy the West bank of the Tennessee and to hold it at all hazards. It would have set this war back six months to have failed and would have caused the necessity of raising, as it were, a new Army.

Looking back at the past I cannot see for the life of me any important point that could be corrected.—Many persons who have visited the different fields of battle may have gone away displeased because they were not permitted to carry off horses, fire arms, or other valuables as trophies. But they are no patriots who would base their enmity on such grounds. Such I assure you are the grounds of many bitter words that have been said against me by persons who at this day would not know me by sight yet profess to speak from a personal acquaintance.

I am sorry to write such a letter, infinately sorry that there should be grounds for it. My own justification does not demand it, but you, a friend, are entitled to know my feelings.

As a friend I would be pleased to give you a record, weekly at furthest, of all that transpires in that portion of the army that I am, or may be, connected with, but not to make public use of.

I am very truly Yours

U. S. GRANT.

ALS, IHi. On May 2, 1862, U.S. Representative Elihu B. Washburne defended USG's conduct at Shiloh in a speech in Congress. *CG*, 37–2, 1931–33. He received letters of thanks for this speech, both dated May 16, from Jesse R. Grant and Julia Dent Grant. Bruce Catton, *Grant Moves South* (Boston and Toronto, 1960), pp. 260–61. See letter to Jesse Root Grant, April 26, 1862. See also John Y. Simon, "From Galena to Appomattox: Grant and Washburne," *Journal of the Illinois State Historical Society*, LVIII, 2 (Summer, 1965), 175–76.

To Maj. Gen. George H. Thomas

_____

Head Quarters, Army of the Tenn.
Camp in the Field, May 15th 1862.
MAJOR. GEN. G. H. THOMAS,
COMMDG RIGHT WING.
GENERAL:

The two Divisions of the Reserve having an extended line to guard with Cavalry, and but about 350 men to do the duty, You will please designate two squadrons from your Command to report to Major Gen J. A. McClernand, Commdg Reserve, for duty temporarily.

Very Respectfully,
Your Obt. Servant.
U. S. GRANT.
Major Gen.

Copies, DLC-USG, V, 1, 2, 3, 86; DNA, RG 393, USG Letters Sent.

On May 14, 1862, Maj. Gen. John A. McClernand wrote to USG. "I am guarding a line of about three miles by a cavalry force of 255 men. Part of this line is in front and near the enemy's picket. The consequence is, that the Cavalry of the 1st Division (Genl. Logan) being continually on duty, is nearly worn out. Between the right of the picket line of the 1st Divn. and Genl Wallace's camp some five miles intervene. I desire to close this space, by an extension of the line of pickets. What has been said verifies Genl. Logan's inability to do it; while it is quite as much out of the power of Genl Wallace to do it. Genl Wallace, if possible is still worse off, in this respect, than Genl Logan. Two of his companies being detached on fatigue, at Pittsburgh, leaving him only 104 Cavalry men. As all the passes of Owl Creek are guarded, and as the two Cavalry Companies refered to are used (as I understand) only as an escort for teams, cannot they be remanded to their Division? It appears that the 5th Division of the army of the Tenn. has 10 Companies of Cavalry—the 4th Division 8 Comps.—the 2nd Divn. 7 Comps.—the 7th Division 12 Comps. and the 6th Division 8 Comps. I respectfully ask and urge a detachment from some one or more of these Divisions to increase the Cavalry force of the Reserves. The exhaustion and suffering of the small Cavalry force of the latter, as well as the good of the service, would plead for it. Genl. Wallace's Cavalry has not been relieved from duty for three days; while the same is true in a great measure, in regard to Genl. Logan's Division. Genl Wallace also informs me that he is in great need of an Engineer for his Division. Please bear with me in adding the further request that this want be early supplied." LS, _ibid._, District of West Tenn., Letters Received; DfS, _ibid._, Dept. of the Tenn., Letters Received from Reserve Corps, Jackson, Tenn.

On May 15, McClernand wrote to USG. "In compliance with your order, received this morning Lt. Col McCullough, and all the available cavalry of the 1st Divn. (Genl Logan) made a reconnoisance for some five miles, along the stage road, in the direction of the M. & C. R. R. and Purdy. He reports all to be quiet in that direction; but says that he was informed by negroes that the enemy were assembling in considerable force at the junction of the State line road with the Rail Road, about five miles nearly due west from Locust Hill and about two and a half miles from my picket line. The correctness of this information is corroborated by information said to be derived from a deserter, to day. I venture to call your attention again to the probability, and as I think certainty, that the enemy will make a strong demonstration against our extreme right, with the purpose of turning our flank, when we attack their centre on the direct road to Corinth. Neither the two squadrons of cavalry nor any part of it, ordered by you from Genl. Thomas, under instructions to report to me has come." DfS, *ibid.*; copy, McClernand Papers, IHi. See also *O.R.*, I, x, part 2, 192–93.

Also on May 15, McClernand again wrote to USG. "The order, organizing my command gave it the designation of 'Army Corps of the Reserve,' and limited its composition of Infantry, Cavalry, and Artillery, according to the import of the name. The Corps, in the first place, consisted of, Wallace's, Crittendens and my own Division—including Cavalry and Artillery attached, and two unattached Seige Batteries. Since the organization Crittenden's Division and one of the seige Batteries have been transferred to Buell's Army Corps, and Wallace's and my old Division have been subdivided into detachments, posted at intervals, from the Pittsburgh and Crumps Landing bridge to Ezell's—a distance of some sixteen miles   The disposition and use of these two remaining Divisions having divested them of the real character of a Reserve, I submit whether their numbers should not be increased by the addition of other forces—Infantry, Cavalry and Artillery —and their equipments and appointments conformed to their new character and service. To illustrate the expediency, if not necessity of doing this, let me cite the operations transpiring this morning   Receiving your order, this morning, to advance a Brigade from this Camp (Locust Grove) along the road to Ezells, I immediately dispatched Genl. Ross with the 2nd Brigade to take position at Ezell's, and, in some measure, to command the wide space left, a regiment of another Brigade to take position at the Camp occupied by Genl W. T. Sherman yesterday   These detachments needed the support of Artillery; and whence was it to come? Only from the 1st Divn. (Genl. Logans) which was the only one from which it could be obtained in time   Detaching 4 guns to go with Genl Ross and 2. to go with the regiment to be posted intermediately between him and Genl Logan, and 4 others, which have been posted for some days, at the crossing of Muddy Creek, only 10 are left here. If it should be the policy, or probable, that my command will continue to be thus divided, I submit whether it is not advisable to increase its strength in Artillery. I thank you for the addition to my Cavalry of which I am this moment advised by your communication on that subject. All that I have said is intended to illustrate this central and leading idea—viz 'that the organization and appointment of my Corps shall conform to the character assigned to it and the service required of it—whether it be the Character and service of a Reserve or an Advance.' . . . P. S. Since the completion of the foregoing communication I have been advised by Genl. Sherman that he will not remove from Izell's, today, therefore, I will halt Genl. Ross' brigade at Genl. Sherman's Camp of yesterday morning, and retain the regiment here, that I pro-

posed to send to the latter place." ALS, DNA, RG 393, District of West Tenn.,
Letters Received.

On May 17, McClernand wrote to Maj. John A. Rawlins. "In response to
my application for more Cavalry, I was informed that two Squadrons would report
to me. This morning Capt Curtis of Co "G" 5th O. Cav. reported with forty men
armed with thirteen Carbines, and fifteen revolvers, which Capt Curtis informs
me are worthless, and Capt Elwood Co. "I." 11th Ill. Cav. with forty six men
armed with defective revolvers and sabres." LS, *ibid.*, Dept. of the Tenn., Letters
Received from Reserve Corps, Jackson, Tenn. USG added an undated endorsement. "Before the receipt of this learning that Gen. Thomas had but few Cavalry
armed with carbines I directed a communication to Maj. Gen. Halleck stating the
necessity for more cavalry in the Reserve Corps and hope they will be ordered
from some other portion of the Army." AES, *ibid.*

On May 27, McClernand wrote to USG. "You will recollect that, some days
ago, I requested that the Cavalry force of this Division should be increased. In
response you were kind enough to order two Battalions to be sent from Genl.
Thomas' Corps under instructions to report to me. After some considerable delay
only two Companies came and they were small in numbers and almost totally
deficient in arms. Since that date the line occupied by my command has been
extended near three miles by ordering forward two Brigades—one of which
occupies the camp formerly occupied by Genl Sherman at Ezell's, and the other
a camp between that and the Locusts. The small Cavalry force now attached to
the 1st Division is inadequate to the service required of it, and General Judah
urgently appeals for an addition to it. Indeed the protection of the extended line
occupied by my command against surprise requires it." Copies, *ibid.*; McClernand
Papers, IHi.

To Julia Dent Grant

Camp Near Corinth Miss.
May 16th 1862

DEAR JULIA;

I do hope all suspense about the approaching conflict will be
ended before it is time for me to write you another letter. We
are moving slowly but in a way to insure success. I feel confidant
myself and believe the feeling is general among the troops.

What move next after the attack upon Corinth is hard to
predict. It must depend to a great extent upon the movements
of the enemy.

Jim Casey[1] is here. He arrived to-day. He is very anxious to
have you visit them and says that if you come down he will go

with you and Emma to St. Louis on a short visit. I have no objections to the arrangement. They also want Fred. to spend his vacation with them. All were very much pleased with Fred. for his modesty and good sense.—Your father sent ~~Casey~~ Emma a bill of sale for the negroes he gave her. To avoid a possibility of any of them being sold he ought to do the same with all the balance. I would not give anything for you to have any of them as it is not probable we will ever live in a slave state again but would not like to see them sold under the hammer.

Aunt Fanny is back in Mo. She says that Mo. is a better place than she thought it was until she tried Ohio again.

John Dent is going back to the country. Poor John! I pitty him. Dont tell him that I say so though   I am anxious to see you and the children once more.

I enjoy most excellent health and am capable of enduring any amount of fatigue. But I want to see this thing over. As I have before said I think the hard fighting in the West will end with the battle of Corinth, supposing all the time that we are successful. Of that, our success, I have no doubt. Kiss all the children for me. I know they are all good and well behaved. Does Jess find any one to fight now that I am away? Give my love to all at home. Write often but dont find fault if you do not receive my letters. I write often enough. Remember me to Mrs. Van Dyke and Mrs. Tweed.[2]

                                             ULYS.

Kiss ~~the child~~ for yourself

ALS, DLC-USG.

1. See letter to Julia Dent Grant, May 10, 1861, note 8.
2. On Jan. 14, 1870, USG wrote to Secretary of the Treasury George S. Boutwell introducing J. R. Tweed, "an old merchant of Cincinnati . . . our families have been intimate from my childhood." Conway Barker, List 709 [1971]. See letter to Julia Dent Grant, Aug. 22, 1862.

To Maj. Gen. John A. McClernand

———

Head Quarters, Army of the Tenn.
In Field, near Corinth, Miss, May 19th 1862.

MAJOR GEN. J. A. MCCLERNAND,
COMMDG RESERVE CORPS
GENL:

Reconnoiter the movements of the enemy and if you find that you are to be attacked by a superior force make the best possible disposition of the forces under your command. If your force is not deemed sufficient, inform me by telegraph, and also inform Division Commanders nearest you.

Respectfully U. S. GRANT. Maj. Gen.

Copies, DLC-USG, V, 1, 2, 86; DNA, RG 393, USG Letters Sent. Misdated May 29, 1862, in DLC-USG, V, 3. *O.R.*, I, x, part 2, 203. On May 19, Maj. Gen. John A. McClernand wrote three letters to USG. "Genl Sherman informs me that the movements of the enemy this morning indicate a purpose on their part to attack us in force to day. I write to say that I think the movements referred to import an apprehension on their part of a purpose of ours to turn their position on their left. This apprehension I think is tracable to the fact, that a Brigade of the 1st Division of the Reserve Army Corps attacked their guard at the Rail Road this morning killing two of them and chasing away the rest. Capt Felter of the 4th Cavalry having come in last from the expedition reports at the time he left the roads two trains coming from opposite directions were stopped by the break in the road, made by the brigade already mentioned   The trains immediately returned in opposite directions. Hence it follows that if the road had been cut nearer Corinth it must have been since repaired by the enemy." Copy, DNA, RG 393, Dept. of the Tenn., Letters Received from Reserve Corps, Jackson, Tenn. "The enemy are represented to be advancing in my right—It may be that reinforcements will be required—provided in the limited extent in my power for such a contingency   I have ordered Genl Wallaces Brigade from Cook's house and may have to call back Genl Ross from his present camp to this position" Copy, *ibid.*; McClernand Papers, IHi. "Your dispatch in answer to mine is received, and I hasten to reply in explanation. After the return of my forces from the rail road, this morning, Genl Sherman sent word, to me, that great commotion and a probable advance to attack our lines were observed in his front. As I am informed, the 6th Mo. Inf'ry, were thrown forward by Genl Sherman, to meet this contingency and were deployed in front and beyond the left of my picket line. These men were in their shirt sleeves and were mistaken for the enemy and were reported by my picket as his advance, to Genl Judah. This, togather with the further fact that one of my picket on my extreme right, was reported to have been shot. (which appears to be true) led Genl. Judah. to report to me the threatened attack of which I advised you. If any thing else should transpire giving color of truth to the report mentioned, I will hasten to advise you and, meantime, will be on the elert to repel and retaliate any hostile attack that may be made." LS, DNA, RG 393, District of West Tenn., Letters Received.

To Dr. H. Johnson

Camp Near Corinth, Miss.
May 19th 1862

Dr. H. Johnson, Esq
Dear Sir;

Yours of the 8th inst. is just received. I believe the bill refered to has not yet passed Congress. If it does pass it will afford me great pleasure to ~~afford~~ give you all the assistance in my power to procure one of the appointments.

You will see by my heading that Corinth is not yet taken. I hope it will be in a few days. If the rebels make a determined stand the battle will be a te[r]ific one. The enemy are in large force and well fortified. Our men are determined and believe themselvs invincible.

It is late at night and I am already fatigued writing. You must excuse, therefore a very short letter.

My wife and children were all well the last news from them. They are with my father in Covington Ky.—Mrs. Grant would be delighted to hear from Mrs. Johnson.

Remember me to Mrs. Johnson and children.

Your friend
U. S. Grant

ALS, Ralph F. Brandon, M. D., Short Hills, N. J.

To Julia Dent Grant

Camp Near Corinth, Miss.
May 20th 1862

DEAR JULIA,

Again I write you from this camp in the Oak woods near Corinth. It would be a beautiful place for a Picnic but not so pleasant to make home at. Since my last our troops have moved up some two miles nearer the scene of the next great conflict but Gen. Halleck and myself still remain. ~~Our~~ The lines are so long that it is about as convenient to visit them from here as from some nearer point.

When the great battle will come off is hard to predict. No pains will be spared to make our success certain and there is scarsely that man in our army who doubts the result. I write to you very often but it does not appear that you get all my letters. It becomes necessary therefore to repeat some things said before. First then I sent you $250 00 by Express the receipt of which you have not acknowledged. Next I authorized you to draw what is still remaining with Mr. Safford in Cairo, something over $300 00 I think. Our rent in Galena is still unpaid. Authorize the amount to be deducted from your next loan to the store.

I will send every dollar I can to you which will be about $400 00 per month. Get yourself everything of the very best, and the same for the children, but avoid extravigance. A few thousand saved now will be of great benefit after a while.

I want very much to see you and the children. When I will have that pleasure is hard to tell. If we get any place where we are likely to remain any time you can join me but the children must remain at school. Does Missie continue to learn as fast as she did? Is Jess a good boy and how often does he fight his Grandpa and Aunt Mary? You have never told me what he says about his five shooter that I am saving to take him. Jess must be about big enough now to leave his Ma and join me as Aid-de-Camp. Tell him that if he can ride a horse, wear a sword and fire his pistol to come on. It wont do for him to be a soldier though if he ever cries. He must try and go without showing such youthful weakness for a week before he starts.

Give my love to all at home. This is the third letter I have written since receiving one from you.

Kisses for yourself and children.

ULYS.

ALS, DLC-USG.

To Maj. Gen. John A. McClernand

Head Quarters, Army of the Ten.
In field Near Corinth, May 21st 1862

Report the names of absentees, how long absent and by what authority. The order for their discharge will come from Gen. Head Quarters. Those discharged under P II of the order refered to will be entitled to an honorable discharge and consequently their pay. Those discharged under Par IV being discharged as deserters necessarily forfeit all pay and allowances that is or may become due them.

U. S. GRANT
Maj. Gen. Com

AES, DNA, RG 393, Dept. of the Tenn., Letters Received from Reserve Corps, Jackson, Tenn. Written on a letter of May 20, 1862, from Maj. Gen. John A. McClernand to Maj. John A. Rawlins. "As there is some confusion in the understanding of the proper manner of carrying out Pars II & IV of General Order No 14 Head Quarters Department of the Mississippi April 2d 1862 I would respectfully ask for general information, instructions as follows   First, Par II. When the discharge is ~~ordered~~ made by a Special Order from Department Head Quarters, how is the discharge to be completed, that is, what final papers are to be given to the soldier & how certified to make them sufficient for him to draw his pay & allowances the same as other discharged soldiers? Second. Par IV. Should the men (list of names) be reported to Department Head Quarters for discharge, or, should they be reported on their company Rolls & returns as Deserters. (the remarks opposite their names explaining) the same as in case of other deserters?" LS, *ibid.*

To Maj. Gen. John A. McClernand

———

Head Quarters, Army of the Tenn.
In Field, near Corinth, Miss, May 24th 1862.

MAJOR. GEN. J. A. MCCLERNAND
COMMDG RESERVE CORPS.
GENERAL:

Twice now, portions of my ~~guard~~ escort have returned from Pittsburg Landing, arriving late at night, and both times without having their passes called for, or examined on the route.

This indicates neglect of duty on the part of some portion of Gen. Wallace's Command that should be rectified.

> I am, Gen, Very Respectfully,
> Your Obt Servant.
> U. S. GRANT.
> Maj. Gen.

Copies, DLC-USG, V, 1, 2, 3, 86; DNA, RG 393, USG Letters Sent. On May 25, 1862, Maj. Gen. John A. McClernand wrote to USG. "Gen Wallace reports in regard to the service performed by his command in policing the roads leading to the landing, that he has issued orders to his pickets stationed on the Corinth road (leading from Pittsburg Landing to Monterey) to stop all persons who have not passes signed by at least a Brigade Commander. Will this order suffice? If not will you please inform me what authority is needed to permit persons passing to and from the Landing. Inother words by whom must passes be signed?" Copy, *ibid.*, Dept. of the Tenn., Letters Received from Reserve Corps, Jackson, Tenn.

To Julia Dent Grant

———

Camp Near Corinth, Miss.
May 24th 1862

MY DEAR WIFE,

I have just received three letters from you one of them enclosing a letter from Fred. I wish you would make all the children write to me even if it is only a few lines they have to copy.

You must have received some of my letters before this but you make no reference to them which would indicate it.

I have written to you to join me whenever you hear of my being on the Mississippi river! I will now change that. You must join me as soon as possible but wait until you get a letter from me saying where.—It is hard to predict where I may be after the next great battle is fought.

If our success is complete I may [be s]tationed in some Southern state with [s]ome degree of perminancy or may be sent around on the coast to opperate there, or may get leave of absence to go home for a time.—I want no leave whilst there are active opperations but confess that a few weeks relaxation would be hailed with a degree of pleasure never experianced by me before.

My duties are now much lighter than they have been heretofore. Gen. Halleck being present relieves me of great responsibility and Rawlins has become thoroughly acquainted with the routine of the office and takes off my hands the examination of most all papers. I think he is one of the best men I ever knew and if another War should break out, or this one be protacted, he would make one of the best General officers to be found in the country. He unites talent with energy, and great honesty, which, I am sorry to say, is not universal in this war where patriotism alone, (and which cannot be jenuine unless strictly honest) governs.

I venture no prediction when Corinth will be taken but that it will be taken there is no doubt.—You may expect to hear from me every three or four days and to join me soon.—William Smith[1] arrived here this evening. He will probably remain a week.

Enclosed you will find receipt for the $250 00 sent some time ago.—I will probably be able to send $500 00 more at the end of the month. Love to all at home. Kiss the children for me. Same for yourself.

ULYS.

ALS, DLC-USG.

1. Fanny Fieldhouse Wrenshall, sister of Ellen Wrenshall Dent, USG's mother-in-law, married William Smith of Washington, Pa., and was the mother of William W. Smith. On May 3, 1862, USG wrote a pass. "Pass W. W. Smith and one friend to Pittsburg Landing Ten." ADS (facsimile), *ibid*. On May 23, USG telegraphed to Smith. "Pass W. W. Smith to Head Quarters." Telegram received (facsimile), *ibid*.

To Elihu B. Washburne

Near Corinth, Miss.,
May 24th, 1862.

HON. E. B. WASHBURN,
WASHINGTON, D. C.
DEAR SIR:

Permit me to introduce to your acquaintance Surgeon Brinton of the Army, a gentleman who has served on my Staff at Cairo and in the field. Dr. Brinton was with me at Belmont, Fort Henry and Fort Donelson, and as we have lived together most of the time for the last six months our acquaintance is more than transient, it has become intimate.

Any attention shown Dr. Brinton will be regarded as a personal favor to myself.

Yours truly,
U. S. GRANT.

Personal Memoirs of John H. Brinton (New York, 1914), p. 355. Surgeon John H. Brinton received orders on May 3, 1862, to report to Washington. Efforts were made in the Dept. of the Miss. to retain Brinton, but a peremptory telegram arrived from Washington on May 23. *Ibid*., p. 166. Brinton's new duties were to prepare a surgical history of the rebellion, to serve on a board to examine the qualifications of candidates for brigade surgeon, and to organize a medical museum. *Ibid*., pp. 169, 180.

To John H. Vincent

———

Camp Near Corinth, Miss.
May 25th 1862

Rev. J. H. Vincent,

Your letter of the 17th inst. is just at hand and I hasten to answer.—Since we last met, and since I had the pleasure of listening to your feeling discourses from the pulpit, much has transpired to make and unmake men. I felt that any who would say that this free and prosperous country of ours should be two, were traitors, deserving of instant punishment, and having been educated a soldier, at the expense of the nation, it was my clear duty to offer my services. I never asked for any position or any rank but entered with my whole soul in the cause of the Union, willing to sacrifice every thing in the cause, even my life if needs be, for its preservation. It has been my good fortune to render some service to the cause and my very bad luck to have attracted the attention of newspaper scriblers. It certainly never was my desire to attract public attention but has been my desire to do my whole duty in this just cause.

I was truly rejoiced at receiving a letter from you and hope it will not be the last. If you should make your expected trip to Palestine it would afford me the greatest pleasure to hear from you from that far off land and to reply punctually to your letters.

Although in general robust health I now write from a sick bed. For several days I have been quite unwell and very much fear a spell of sickness.

The papers keep you advised of our position, therefore it is not necessary for me to say anything on that subject. Two large armies however are menacing each other and it cannot be long before they come together.

Remember me to Mrs. Vincent,

Yours Truly
U. S. Grant

ALS (facsimile), John H. Vincent, "The Inner Life of Ulysses S. Grant," *The Chautauquan*, XXX, 6 (March, 1900), 636; typescript, Lloyd Lewis Notes, USGA. The facsimile contains the first paragraph except for the second and the first half of the third sentences. John H. Vincent, born in Ala., educated at Wesleyan Institute, N. J., pastor of the Methodist Episcopal church in Galena, first met USG in a Dubuque, Iowa, hotel in 1860, and afterwards claimed to have seen him frequently in church. See *DAB*, XIX, 277–79.

To Brig. Gen. Thomas W. Sherman

———

Head Quarters, Army of the Tenn.
In Field, near Corinth, May 28th 1862

GEN. SHERMAN,
COMMDG 7TH DIVISION
ARMY OF THE TENN.
GENERAL:

Should Gen. McCook be attacked in the morning, you will reinforce him with your Division, leaving nothing in your present Camp, except the necessary guard over public property.

I am, Gen, Very Respectfully.
Your Obt Servant.
U. S. GRANT.
Major. Gen.

Copies, DLC-USG, V, 1, 2, 3, 86; DNA, RG 393, USG Letters Sent. Thomas W. Sherman of R. I., USMA 1836, held the rank of bvt. maj. on the eve of the Civil War. Confirmed as brig. gen. on Aug. 3, 1861, Sherman took command of the land forces in the Port Royal, S. C., expedition. On April 30, 1862, by Special Field Orders No. 35, Dept. of the Miss., he was assigned to command a division of the Army of the Tenn. under Maj. Gen. George H. Thomas. *O.R.*, I, x, part 2, 144.

On May 28, Maj. Gen. Henry W. Halleck wrote to USG. "If Genl. McCook should be attacked to-morrow morning he must be reinforced by Genl. T. W. Sherman's Division, the remainder of McKean's Division being brought into line. W. T. Sherman and Hurlbut will probably be able to connect with McKean's right to-morrow, which will leave Davies in reserve. The enemy will probably attack our advance in the morning, McClernand and Wallace have been ordered up." Copies, DNA, RG 393, District of West Tenn., Letters Received; *ibid.*, Dept. of the Miss., Letters Sent; *ibid.*, USG Hd. Qrs. Correspondence; DLC-USG, V, 7, 8. *O.R.*, I, x, part 2, 222.

To Julia Dent Grant

———

Corinth Miss.
May 31st 1862

DEAR JULIA,

Corinth is now in our hands without much fighting. Yesterday we found the enemy had gone taking with them all their men, arms and most of their supplies. What they did not take was mostly burned, in flames as we entered. What the next move, or the part I am to take I do not know. But I shall apply to go home if there is not an early move and an important command assigned me. My rank is second in this Department and I shall expect the first seperate command and hope it will be to go to Memphis and make Head Quarters there. In that case I will write for you to join me leaving the three oldest children at school.—I will be writing you every few days and will give you notice when and where to come to me. If there is not to be an early move I will apply for a short leave and go home. In that case I may reach Covington as soon as this letter.

Some of our troops are following the enemy and to-day distant canonading has been heard.

Although but few prisoners have yet been taken many may yet be captured. I hope so at least. What the rebels plans were for evacuating I am unable to see. But they will turn up some where and have to be whipped yet.—The country through which we have passed so far is poor and desolated by the presence of two large armies. What the people are to do for the next year is hard to surmise but there must be a vast amount of suffering. I pity them and regret their folly which has brought about this unnatural war and their suffering.

Col. Hillyer will go home in a day or two for the purpose of taking his family to New Jersey. If they go by the way of Cincinnati they will stop and see you. Kiss all the children for me and tell me all about them. How they learn at school and how they bear themselvs among other children. I will not be able to send you any money this month as it will take all my savings to make up the amount I authorized you to draw from Mr. Safford.

Orly Ross paid me and I sent $40 00 a few days ago by Capt. Rowley to be placed to your credit. There is about $130 00 rent to be paid in Galena which will have to be deducted out of the deposites made. I have written to Orvil on that point.

Give my love to all at home. Write often to your long absent husband.

ULYS.

ALS, DLC-USG.

To Edwin M. Stanton

Head Quarters, Army of the Ten.
Camp Near Corinth, Miss.
June 1st 1862

HON. E. M. STANTON
SEC. OF WAR
WASHINGTON D. C.
SIR;

It is with great pleasure that I recommend to the War Department 1st Lieut. Wm. G. Pinckard of the 9th Ill. Vol. Infantry for the appointment of Assistant Quartermaster.

Lieut. Pinckard is now performing the duties of Assistant Quartermaster, and has for several months, under orders first given, assigning him to those duties, by the late Maj. Gen. C. F. Smith.

It is with increased solicitude that I make this recommendation knowing that it was the earnest desire of Gen. Smith that Mr. Pinckard should receive the appointment now asked.

I am Sir, very [re]spectfully
your obt. svt.
U. S. GRANT
Maj. Gen.

ALS, DNA, RG 94, Letters Received. William G. Pinckard, Jr., of Edwardsville, Ill., was appointed 1st lt. and q. m., 9th Ill., on Aug. 21, 1861, and promoted to asst. q. m. of vols. on June 30, 1862. USG's recommendation was supported by a copy of a letter of Maj. Gen. Charles F. Smith and an endorsement by U.S. Senator Lyman Trumbull.

To Elihu B. Washburne

———

Camp Near Corinth Miss.
June 1st 1862

HON. E. B. WASHBURN
WASHINGTON D. C.
DEAR SIR;

Enclosed I send a letter addressed to the Hon. E. M. Stanton, Sec. of War which I would be pleased if you would cause to be delivered with any recommendation that you may deem proper.

Lieut. Dickey[1] is the son of Col. Dickey of the 4th Ill. Cavalry, and brother-in-law of the late Gen. W. H. L. Wallace who fell at the battle of Shiloh.

Although Lt. Dickey has served under my command almost from his first enterance into service I can not answer from personal knowledge as to his qualifications but Gen. Judah, who recommends him, is an experianced officer and fully qualified to judge of his merits.

The siege of Corinth has ~~atlast~~ last terminated. On Friday[2] morning it was found that the last rebel had left during the preseding night. On entering the enemies entrenchments it was found that they had succeeded in taking off or destroying nearly everything of value. Gen. Pope is now in full pursuit of the retreating foe and I think will succeed in capturing and dispersing many of them.

There will be much unjust criticism of this affair but future effects will prove it a great victory. Not being in command howe[v]er I will not give a history of the battle in advance of official reports.

I leave here in a day or two for Covington Ky. on a short leave of absence.[3] I may write you again from there if I do not visit Washington in person.

Yours Truly

U. S. GRANT

ALS, IHi.

1. Both 2nd Lt. Charles H. Dickey, 4th Ill. Cav., and 1st Lt. Cyrus E. Dickey, 11th Ill., fit USG's description, but the latter was more likely meant, since he was promoted to capt. and asst. adjt. gen. as of May 1, 1863.
2. May 30, 1862.
3. See following letter.

To Julia Dent Grant

———

Camp Near Corinth, Miss.

June 3d 1862

DEAR JULIA,

So confidant was I that I should be starting home by to-morrow or next day, with all my staff, that I let Col. Lagow start last evening[1] with W. W. Smith, your cousin. Necessity how-ever changes my plans, or the public service does, and I must yeald.—In a few weeks I hope to be so stationed that you can join me. Where is hard to say. May be Memphis. I wish Mary would come with you if the latter place should be my destiny and bring all the children to remain until after their vacation. ~~They~~ She could then return with the three oldest and let them go to school. As soon as I know definately you will be informed when, where and how to join me. Wm Smith will call to see you on his way to Washington Pa and will deliver Jess' pistol. Tell Jess he must hurt nobody with it but all the little boys may look at it.

I will move up to-mor[r]ow into Corinth   Corinth is a new town of but about three years growth, neatly built and probably contained about 1500 inhabitants. Now it is desolate the families all having fled long before we got possession, windows broken

furniture broken and destroyed, and no doubt the former occupants destitute and among friends but little better off than themselvs. Soldiers who fight battles do not experience half their
horrors. All the hardships come upon the weak, I cannot say
innofensive, women and children. I believe these latter are wors
rebels than the soldiers who fight against us. The latter mostly
are heartily tired of the war. This is the evidence of prisoners
and deserters who come in at least.

It is no[w] pretty certain that we will take near 10.000 prisoners, 20,000 stand of arms and now doubt a greater number of
men have deserted and will be lost to the rebel army than the
whole number taken.

Give my love to all at home. Kiss the children for me and
accept the same to yourself.

ULYS.

ALS, DLC-USG.

1. On June 2, 1862, Maj. John A. Rawlins issued Special Orders No. 98.
"Leave of Absence, is hereby granted to Col. C. B. Lagow, of Gen. Grants Staff,
to report upon the receipt of orders by telegraph or otherwise." Copies, *ibid.*,
V, 15, 16, 82, 87; DNA, RG 393, USG Special Orders.

To Abraham Lincoln

———

Corinth, Mississippi,
June 7th 1862

HON. A. LINCOLN
PRESIDENT OF THE UNITED STATES
WASHINGTON D. C.
SIR:

I would most respectfully recommend the name of Major I. N.
Cook, paymaster U. S. Army, to be transfered from the Volunteer
to the regular service.—To Major Cook more than any one else
are the Western troops indebted for the promptness with which

they have been paid. ~~And~~ I could cite instances where but for his energy and persiverance some suffering of familie[s] and much discontent would have been encountered with a less prompt man in his office.

I will take it as a personal favor if this transfer can be made.

I am very respectfully
your obt. svt.
U. S. GRANT
Maj. Gen

ALS, ICarbS. This letter was unsuccessful; Maj. Isaac N. Cooke soon left the U.S. Army.

To David Tod

Corinth, Mississippi,
June 7th 1862

HON. D. TODD,
GOV. OF OHIO
COLUMBUS OHIO,
GOVERNOR:

I would most earnestly recommend to your favorable conciederation the name of Doulas Putnam Jr. of Ohio for an appointment to a field office in an Ohio regiment if you should have such an appointment at your disposal.

Mr. Putnam is an Ohioan and now Clerk with Paymaster I. N. Cook of the same state.—I have known Mr. P. for a number of months and can vouch for him being steady, capable and trustworthy. His courage also I will vouch for he having been with me at the battle of Shiloh without showing the slightest sign of discomfature.

I am sir, very respectfully
your obt. svt.
U. S. GRANT
Maj. Gen.

ALS, DLC-USG. David Tod of Youngstown, unsuccessful Democratic candidate for governor of Ohio in 1844 and 1846, prosperous in coal and iron in the 1850's, was elected governor by the Union Party in 1861. Jesse R. Grant, who had once lived with Tod's parents, maintained a friendship with the family. *Memoirs*, I, 19–20; *Richardson*, pp. 42–44; *New York Times*, Sept. 7, 1868. On March 22, 1863, Douglas Putnam, Jr., was appointed lt. col., 92nd Ohio. His account of experiences at Shiloh with USG is in T. M. Hurst, "Battle of Shiloh," *American Historical Magazine*, VII, 1 (Jan., 1902), 27–28; Douglas Putnam, Jr., "Reminiscences of the Battle of Shiloh," *Sketches of War History 1861–1865* (Cincinnati, 1890), III, 197–211.

To Julia Dent Grant

Corinth Mississippi,
June 9th 1862

MY DEAR JULIA,

I expected by this time to be at home, but fate is against it. — You need not now look for me atal but you may look for a letter soon where to join me. I do not know where myself but in all probability it will be in West Tennessee.

Privately I say to you that when I talked of going home and leaving my command here there was quite a feeling among the troops, at least so epressed by Gen. officers below me, against my going.[1] I will have to stay. It is bearly possible that I may be able to leave long enough to go after you and bring you on. If so I will do it. — It would afford me the greatest pleasure to be relieved from active duty for even a short time. People in civil life have no idea of the immense labor devolving on a commander in the field. If they had they never would envy them. Rawlins has become so perfectly posted in the duties of the office that I am relieved entirely from the routine. ~~of the office~~ Cols. Hillyer & Lagow are also familiar with the duties and Aid me out of doors materially.

Although Gen. Sherman has been made a Maj. Gen. by the battle of Shiloh I have never done half justice by him. With green troops he was my standby during that trying day of Sunday,

(there has been nothing like it on this continent,⧸ nor in history.)
He kept his Division in place all day, and aided materially in
keeping those to his right and left in place—He saw me frequently and received, and obeyed, my directions during that day,
but some others, I will say only one other, may have forgotten
them. In writing this last sentence it would leave an inference
against a commander on Sunday. I would imply nothing of the
sort, but against one of my commanders on Monday.[2]

Give my love to all at home. Kiss the children for me and
accept the same for your self. Has Jess got his pistol yet.—I sent
it by Wm Smith.

Goodbuy
ULYS.

ALS, DLC-USG.

1. On June 6, 1862, Maj. Gen. William T. Sherman, Chewalla, Tenn., wrote
to USG. "I have just received your note, and am rejoiced at your conclusion to
remain. For yourself, you could not be quiet at home for a week, when armies
were moving, and rest could not relieve your mind of the gnawing sensation that
injustice has been done you. There is a power in our land, irresponsible, corrupt
and malicious, 'the press,' which has created the intense feelings of hostility that
has arrayed the two parts of our country against each other, which must be curbed
and brought within the just limits of reason and law, before we can have peace in
America. War cannot cease as long as any flippant fool of an editor may stir up
the passions of the multitude, arraign with impunity the motives of the most
honorable, and howl on their gang of bloody hounds to hunt down any man who
despises their order. We can deal with armies who have a visible and tangible
existence, but it will require tact and skill and courage to clip the wings of this
public enemy, and I hope you have sufficiently felt the force of what I say to join
in their just punishment before we resign our power and pass into the humble
rank of citizens. The moment you obtained a just celebrity at Donelson, by a
stroke of war more rich in consequences than was the battle of Saratoga, envious
rivals and malicious men set their pack of hounds at you, to pull you from the
pinnacle which you had richly attained. By patience and silence we can quiet their
noise, and in due time make them feel that in defaming others, they have destroyed
themselves. Already is their power of mischief on the wane, and as soon as a few
I could name, drop the dirty minions of a corrupt press, they will drop back into
the abyss of infamy they deserve. Of course I only asked for your escort, when I
believed you had resolved to leave us, and assure you that I rejoice to learn of
your change of purpose. I wish you would see that the other three companies of
the 4th Illinois Cavalry ordered to me are made so by the order. I instantly
relieved Thielemanns Cavalry and sent it to where you assigned it, but the companies ordered to me in their place have not yet come, nor do I hear of them. I
would account it a favor if you would remind McClernand of the importance of

seeing such orders of transfer obeyed promptly. I need this cavalry as I have to picket forward and to the right strongly, and should have in reserve a pretty large cavalry force to send on special scouts. My Cavalry is sadly reduced in strength by sickness, and even with the addition of the other three companies, I doubt if I shall be able out of the eleven companies of the 4th Illinois Cavalry to get three hundred men in the saddle." Copies, InNd; DNA, RG 94, Generals' Papers and Books, William T. Sherman, Letters Sent; (2) DLC-William T. Sherman. See *Memoirs*, I, 385; *Personal Memoirs of Gen. W. T. Sherman* (3rd ed., New York, 1890), I, 283.

2. USG probably meant Brig. Gen. Alexander M. McCook, whom he criticized in 1884 as complaining on April 7, 1862, that his troops were too tired to pursue the enemy. "The Battle of Shiloh," *Battles and Leaders of the Civil War*, eds., Robert Underwood Johnson and Clarence Clough Buel (New York, 1887), I, 479. In a letter of June 21, 1885, USG retracted this charge. *Ibid.*, I, 479*n*; *Memoirs*, I, 354*n*–55*n*. In this letter, USG also assumed responsibility for the same criticism in Adam Badeau, *Military History of Ulysses S. Grant* (New York, 1868–81), I, 91. There, however, McCook is represented as being joined in his complaints by Brig. Gen. Thomas L. Crittenden.

To Julia Dent Grant

———

Corinth Miss.
June 12th 1862

DEAR JULIA

It is bright and early (before the morning mail leaves) and I thought to write you that in a few days, Monday the 16th probably, I would leave here. I hope to be off on Monday for Memphis[1] and if so want you to join me there. I will write again however just before starting and it may be will have arranged to go after you instead of you coming by yourself.—I would love most dearly to get away from care for a week or two.

I am very well. This is apparently an exceedingly fine climate and one to enjoy health in.—Citizens are begining to return to Corinth and seem to think the Yankees a much less bloody, revengeful and to be dreaded people, than they had been led to think.

In my mind there is no question but that this war could be ended at once if the whole Southern people could express their unbiased feeling untramelled by by leaders. The feeling is kept up however by crying out Abolitionest against us and this is unfortunately sustained by the acts of a very few among us.— There has been instances of negro stealing, persons going to the houses of farmers who have remained at home, being inclined to Union sentiments, and before their eyes perswaid their blacks to mount up behind them and go off. Of course I can trace such conduct to no individual but believe the guilty parties have never heard the whistle of a single bullet nor intentionally never will.

Give my love to all at home. Kisses for yourself and children.

Your husband
ULYS.

ALS, DLC-USG.

1. USG left Corinth for Memphis a few days later than Monday, June 16, 1862. On June 10, Capt. John C. Kelton issued Special Field Orders No. 90. "The order dividing the army near 'corinth' into right wing, Center, left wing and reserve, is hereby revoked. Major Generals Grant, Buell; and Pope will resume the command of their seperate army corps, except the division of Major General Thomas which will, till further orders be stationed in Corinth as a part of the army of the Tennessee. General Thomas will resume the immediate command of his former division on its arrival at Corinth and Brigr General T. W. Sherman will report to Major General Buell for duty with the army of the Ohio" Copy, *ibid.*, V, 83. *O.R.*, I, x, part 2, 288. About this time, 1st Lt. Theodore S. Bowers wrote to Capt. William R. Rowley. "The General received an order from Depart Head Quarters this evening, restoring him to full and complete command of his old army with the addition thereto of Thomas' Division. There is every probability that within a week the General and his command will go to Memphis and occupy that city. Commissary Stores are already being sent there by river." ALS, Rowley Papers, IHi. On June 19, Maj. John A. Rawlins issued General Orders No. 55. "Hereafter, until further notice, Head Quarters of this District will be at Memphis, Tenn. All communications for Head Quarters will be addressed accordingly." Copies, DLC-USG, V, 12, 13, 14, 95; DNA, RG 393, USG General Orders; *ibid.*, District of West Tenn., Letters Received.

To Julia Dent Grant

———

Corinth, Mississippi,
June 16th 1862

My Dear Julia,

I hope this will be my last letter but one from this place. The next will likely inform you of the day I shall leave for Memphis and how you are to join me. If atal practicable I will go after you and spend a few days at home, if not will provide means, and ways, for you to join me.

I have just received your letter enclosing Nellie's card of merit. It is very pretty and shows that she is a good girl and learns well at school. I think after vacation we will have to send Jess back to go to school and see if he cannot get some cards for good behavior.

That was quite a mistake made in the announcement of my arrival at home.[1] I wish it could have been true. It would be a great relief to get away for a few days if and if there is no likelyhood of active service soon I must try and go.

This is a dreary and desolated country. I went North to Jackson on Friday[2] and returned on Saturday and found the country looking much more prosperous however. Some of my troops are occupying that place, and guard all the road from here there, from there to Grand Junction,[3] and also a portion of the road from Humboldt to Memphis. You will have to look at the map to see where these places are.—My command at present embraces all Tennessee West of the Tennessee river and Forts Henry and Donelson East of it and I can choose any point within this District for Head Quarters. It is proper though that a point within easy communication of all other points and Department Head Quarters should be selected. Memphis will be connected by rail and telegraph with all, and near Arkansas where, if necessary a portion of my troops might be required in case of an imergency. —Give my love to all at home.—Do not write any more after the receipt of this unless you receive directions from me. I would like to have Mary come with us, or you as the case may be, to spend the vacation of the children.

Kisses to all and good night.

Ulys.

ALS, DLC-USG.

1. On June 7, 1862, the *Cincinnati Gazette* reported that USG was expected to reach Covington, Ky., that day to visit his family and friends.

2. June 13.

3. Grand Junction, Tenn., about fifty miles east of Memphis at the intersection of the Memphis and Charleston and the Mississippi Central railroads.

To Elihu B. Washburne

———

Corinth Miss,
June 19th 1862

Hon. E. B. Washburn
Washington D. C.
Dear Sir:

Your letter of the 8th inst. addressed to me at Covington Ky. has just reached.—At the time the one was written to which it ~~was~~ is an answer I had leave to go home, or to Covington, ~~for a few days~~, but Gen. Halleck requested me to remain for a few days. Afterwards when I spoke of going he asked that I should remain a little longer if my business was not of pressing importance. As I really had no business, and had not asked leave on such grounds, I told him so and that if my services were required I would not go atal. This settled my leave for the present, and for the war, so long as my services are required I do not wish to leave.

I am exceedingly obliged to you for for the interest you have taken in the appointment recommended by me and also ~~th~~ for the assurances that the Sec. of War receives them with such favor. I will endeavor never to make a recommendation unsafe to accede to.

I shall leave here on the 21st for Memphis where my Head Quarters will be located for the time being.—Fast Western Tennessee is being reduced to working order and I think with the introduction of the Mails, trade, and the assurance that we can hold it, ~~they~~ it will become loyal, or at least law abiding. It will not do however for our arms to meet with any great reverse and still expect this result. The masses this day are more disloyal in the South, from fear of what might befall them, in case of defeat to the Union cause than from any dislike to the Government. One week to them (after giving in their adhesion to our laws) would be worse under the so called Confederate Government than a year of Martial Law administered by this army.

It is hard to say what would be the most wise policy to pursue towards these people but for a soldier his duties are plain. He is to obey the orders of all those placed over him and whip the enemy wherever he meets him. "If he can" should only be thought of ~~in case of~~ after an unavoidable defeat.

If you are acquainted with Senitor Collamer,[1] of Vermont, I would be pleased if you would say to him that there is a young Colonel in the 11th Ill. regiment, a native of his state, that I have taken a great interest in for his gallantry and worth. I mean Col. Ransom.[2] He has now been wounded ~~in~~ three times, in seperate engagements, but never showed a willingness to relinquish his command until the day was decided and always declines a leave to recover from his wounds lest something should transpire in his absence.

I will endeavor to write you again soon after arriving at Memphis.

> Yours Truly
> U. S. GRANT

ALS, IHi.

1. U.S. Senator Jacob Collamer of Vt. had served as asst. judge of the supreme court of Vt. (1833–42, 1850–54), as U.S. Representative (1843–49), as U.S. postmaster-general (1849–50), and as U.S. Senator since 1855.

2. On June 7, 1862, Col. Thomas E. G. Ransom, 11th Ill., wrote to Brig. Gen. Grenville M. Dodge. "My freinds are making an effort to get me promoted. Genl Grant & Genl McClernand have both written letters in the last few days,

urging my appointment. They wrote to Judge Collamer of Vt. to be used in the Senate—As the Judge is an old friend of my family, and as my freinds ~~for~~ in Vermont have requested him to assist me, I am of the opinion that he will urge my appointment." ALS, Dodge Papers, IaHA. See also Ransom to Dodge, June 12, *ibid*. Ransom was appointed brig. gen. on Nov. 29, 1862. Ransom's father had been president of Norwich University, Norwich, Vt., and col., 9th Inf., in the Mexican War. After graduating from Norwich, Ransom came to Ill. as an engineer, but his interest shifted to real estate.

To Maj. Gen. Henry W. Halleck

Memphis June 23rd 1862

MAJ GENL H W HALLECK

I have just arrived, tired and dusty, having made the entire distance on horseback. Will ascertain the facts and answer your telegram of this date as soon as possible.[1] Col Fitc[h][2] dispatches from St Charles,[3] June 21, that considerable bodies of Light troops are collecting in his neighborhood. Will make enquiries and do what may seem neccessary.

Very Respcty &c
U. S. GRANT

Copies, DLC-USG, V, 4, 5, 7, 8, 9, 88; DNA, RG 393, USG Hd. Qrs. Correspondence; *ibid*., Dept. of the Miss., Hd. Qrs. in the Field, Letters Received. On June 22, 1862, USG, La Grange, Tenn., telegraphed to Maj. Gen. Henry W. Halleck. "I leave here today & go to Memphis tomorrow." Telegram received, *ibid*., RG 94, Generals' Papers and Books, Telegrams Received by Gen. Halleck; copy, *ibid*., RG 393, Dept. of the Miss., Hd. Qrs. in the Field, Telegrams Received.

1. On June 23, Halleck telegraphed to USG. "Ascertain the condition of R R from Memphis west towards Little Rock also the means of sending supplies & reinforcements to Genl Curtis—Reports heretofore received from Memphis are entirely unsatisfactory Let me know about the supplies & means of transportation from that place" Telegram received, *ibid*., Dept. of the Mo., Telegrams Received; copies, *ibid*., Dept. of the Miss., Telegrams Sent; *ibid*., USG Hd. Qrs. Correspondence; DLC-USG, V, 7. *O.R.*, I, xvii, part 2, 26.

2. Graham N. Fitch, born in Genessee County, N. Y., in 1809, attended Geneva College and the College of Physicians and Surgeons, then began to practice medicine at Logansport, Ind., in 1834. Active as a Democrat, he was elected to the Ind. House of Representatives (1836–1839), to the U.S. House of Representatives (1849–1853), and to the U.S. Senate (1857–1861). Appointed col.,

46th Ind., on Nov. 1, 1861, he served until forced to resign by wounds on Aug. 5, 1862.

3. St. Charles, Ark., on the White River about eighty miles southwest of Memphis. General orientation is available in Edwin C. Bearss, "The White River Expedition June 10–July 15, 1862," *Arkansas Historical Quarterly*, XXI, 4 (Winter, 1962), 305–62.

To Maj. Gen. Henry W. Halleck

By Telegraph from Memphis [*June*] 24 186[2]

To Maj. Gen H W Halleck
Gen.

The R. R. to Madison, Ark.[1] has not been injured by the rebels—the high water however has so destroyed the first ten miles west that would require a weeks work for ten men to get a locomotive over: to work upon this would require a guard placed over the St. Francis bridge to prevent rebels from destroying it when the work commenced. Col. Fitch has returned to the mouth of white River with his forces. I will get the particulars of the Mound City disaster[2] & forward it to you by first train— There is here of Col. Stacks[3] command of effective men 1943 Infy., 418 Cav. & one battery 115 men. There are 4 steamers here that could carry troops through, partially loaded with freight. I have waited 2 hours to get the strength of Genl. Wallace's command at present here, but have not yet recd. it.[4]

U. S. Grant
Maj. Genl.

Telegram received, DNA, RG 94, Generals' Papers and Books, Telegrams Received by Gen. Halleck; copy, *ibid.*, RG 393, Dept. of the Miss., Hd. Qrs. in the Field, Telegrams Received.

1. The Memphis and Little Rock Railroad had then laid approximately forty miles of track from a point opposite Memphis to Madison, Ark., on the west side of the St. Francis River.

2. On June 17, 1862, the gunboats *Mound City, St. Louis, Conestoga*, and *Lexington* attacked C. S. A. batteries at St. Charles, Ark., on the White River.

During the engagement, a shell penetrated and exploded the steam drum of the *Mound City*. Of 175 men on board, 110 were killed and 37 wounded. *O.R.* (Navy), I, xxiii, 180–81.

3. James R. Slack was born in Pa. in 1818. As a lawyer at Huntington, Ind., he served nine years as county auditor and seven terms in the state senate. On Dec. 13, 1861, he was appointed col., 47th Ind., and on June 13, 1862, assumed command of Memphis.

On June 24, Maj. Gen. Henry W. Halleck telegraphed to USG. "What forces has Col Slack at Memphis? Is there transportation to send troops to reinforce Col Fitch?" ALS (telegram sent), DNA, RG 108, Telegrams Sent; telegram received, *ibid.*, RG 393, Dept. of the Mo., Telegrams Received. Slack drafted a reply with the figures USG sent at the foot of Halleck's telegram. DfS, *ibid.*; copies, *ibid.*, USG Hd. Qrs. Correspondence; DLC-USG, V, 7.

4. On June 25, USG telegraphed to Halleck. "The effective strength of Wallace's command present here—3,800. I have ordered two of the Regts. left at Bolivar & one left at Jackson to come here. This will leave at Bolivar one Regt of Infy., 2 co.s of Cav. & one of artilly." Telegram received, DNA, RG 94, Generals' Papers and Books, Telegrams Received by Gen. Halleck; copies, *ibid.*, USG Hd. Qrs. Correspondence; *ibid.*, Dept. of the Miss., Hd. Qrs. in the Field, Telegrams Received; DLC-USG, V, 4, 5, 7, 8, 9, 88. Misdated June 28 in *O.R.*, I, xvii, part 2, 43. See telegram to Maj. Gen. John A. McClernand, June 29, 1862.

To Maj. Gen. Henry W. Halleck

―――――

Memphis Tenn. June 24th 1862

MAJ GENL H. W. HALLECK
COMDG DEPT OF THE MISS
CORINTH
GENL

I arrived here yesterday afternoon after a warm ride of three days, coming through from "Le Grange"[1] with an escort of twelve men. The entire road is ~~in good order, and~~ a very fine one and in good order.

Affairs in this city seem to be in rather bad order, secessionists governing much in their own way.[2] I have appointed Col Webster commander of the Post. Lt Col Anthony, of the 23rd Ind Vols. Provost Marshall. for the City, and Col Hillyer Provost Marshal General.[3] In a few days I expect to have everything in good order.[4]

I enclose you herewith report of J A Double of Gun Boat "Conestoga" relative to the disaster to the Mound City.[5] The prisoners spoken of are now here, and such disposition will be made of them as you may direct. I have not been here long enough to determine the practicability of furnishing Genl Curtis by the way of White river, but on consultation with Capt Phelps, of the Navy, I think it can be done by preparing two light draft Steamers so that the boilers would be proff against musketry, and arming them with two Howitzers on the bows. An Infantry escort would have to accompany each boat ready to take the shore and march past threatened points.[6]

On my arrival, Genl Wallace[7] applied for a leave of absence. I granted it to the extent of my authority the command being left with Genl Hovey[8] who is fully quallified to fill the place of the former commander.

I am Genl Very Respcty
Your Obt Servt
U. S. GRANT
Maj Genl

Copies, DLC-USG, V, 4, 5, 7, 8, 9, 88; DNA, RG 393, USG Hd. Qrs. Correspondence. *O.R.*, I, xvii, part 2, 29–30.

1. La Grange, Tenn., about fifty miles east of Memphis.
2. On June 24, 1862, Maj. John A. Rawlins wrote to the provost marshal, Memphis. "I am directed by Major Gen. U. S. Grant to say that he has been informed that a Major Polk of the Confederate Army, is on Parole, and permitted to go at large in the City. You will please ascertain by whom he was paroled and by what authority he is permitted to run at large and report the same to these Head Quarters, immediately. You will arrest said person at once, and keep him in custody until further orders." Copies, DLC-USG, V, 1, 2, 86; DNA, RG 393, USG Letters Sent. On the same day, Col. William S. Hillyer wrote to Brig. Gen. Stephen A. Hurlbut. "I am directed by Major Gen. Grant to say to you that you can compel all Clergyman within your lines to omit from their church services any portion you may deem *treasonable*, but you will not compel the insertion or substitution of any thing" LS, *ibid.*, 16th Army Corps, Miscellaneous Papers. *O.R.*, I, xvii, part 2, 30.
3. On June 24, Rawlins issued Special Orders No. 118. "For the guidance and control of this City, the following orders are published. Col. J. D. Webster, Chief of Artillery and Chief of Staff, is appointed Commander of the Post. All needful rules and regulations for the Government of the City will be made by him, subject to the approval of the General Commanding. Col. Wm. S. Hillyer, Aid-

de-Camp, is appointed Provost Marshal General for the District. All local Provosts will report to him weekly, and will receive instructions from him. Lt. Col. D. C. Anthony 23d Ind. Vol is appointed Provost Marshal for the city of Memphis. He will report to the Provost Marshal General for instructions, and assume his duties without delay. The 34th, 43rd & 47th Regts. Ind. Vols. Col. J. R. Slack, Commanding, will form the Garrison of Memphis and will encamp East of the town. Company "A," 4th Ills. Cavalry, Capt. Osband, Commdg. is specially assigned to assist the Provost Marshal in the performance of his duties. All the troops in Memphis, not enumerated above, will immediately go into Camp outside of the City on the line of the Rail Road to Grenada, Miss. They will ~~also~~ Picket all the roads leading to the City from the South-East quarters and enforce such orders as have been, or may hereafter be published." Copies, DLC-USG, V, 15, 16, 82, 87; DNA, RG 393, USG Special Orders. *O.R.*, I, xvii, part 2, 30–31. On June 25, Col. William L. Sanderson, 23rd Ind., Bolivar, Tenn., telegraphed to USG. "Col Anthony not yet arrived"   Telegram received, DNA, RG 393, Dept. of the Mo., Telegrams Received.

4. On June 24, Rawlins issued General Orders No. 56. "Complaints of recent irregularities, brought to the attention of the General Commanding, render necessary the publication of the following Orders: Officers, non-commissioned officers and soldiers, and persons in the service of the United States, are forbidden to trespass upon the orchards, gardens or private grounds of any person or persons, or in any manner whatever to interfere with the same, without proper written authority so to do. Marauding, pilfering and unauthorized and unnecessary seizure or destruction of private property is prohibited by General Orders of the Department No's 8 and 13, series of 1861, and will be punished with the extreme penalty imposed by the laws of war, which is death. Commissioned officers of companies will not pass their camp lines without written permission of their District, Brigade or regimental Commanders, an[d] then only on official business or other urgent and satisfactory reasons, to be given in the letters of permission. Non-commissioned officers and soldiers are prohibited from leaving camp at any time, except when detailed on duty or on the written permission of the regimental commanders, who may grant such permission to not more than three men at any one time from each company, to be absent under charge of a non-commissioned officer, who will be held responsible for their good conduct. The pickets and guard relief will remain at the immediate picket or guard stations, unless in the discharge of proper military duty, and will not straggle therefrom, under penalty of being arrested and severely and summarily dealt with. No commissioned officer, non-commissioned officer or soldier, will be permitted to be absent from camp after 'Retreat.' The military police, patrols and picket guards will arrest all persons found violating any of the provisions of this order, either by trespassing upon the gardens, orchards and grounds herein mentioned, or seizure or destruction of private property or being outside of camp lines, or straggling from their guard stations, without proper authority; commissioned officers to be reported to District, Division or Brigade Headquarters, and non-commissioned officers and soldiers to be taken before the Provost Marshal   Officers of regiments, detachments and companies, and officers of the day, and of police, are enjoined to use their utmost diligence in making known and enforcing all orders necessary for the safety of the command." Copies, DLC-USG, V, 12, 13; DNA, RG 393, USG Special Orders; (printed) *ibid.*, RG 94, Dept. of the Tenn., Orders.

USG also had other orders issued in the interest of "good order" in Memphis.

On June 28, Rawlins issued Special Orders No. 122 specifying that passes out of Memphis would not cover "goods, letters or packages." Copies, DLC-USG, V, 15, 16, 82, 87; DNA, RG 393, USG Special Orders. On June 29, Rawlins issued Special Orders No. 123 which declared that persons who made charges against other citizens, then failed to provide evidence, would be "confined or banished." Copies, *ibid*. *O.R.*, I, xvii, part 2, 51. On June 29, Rawlins issued General Orders No. 59 limiting the hours when USG would receive citizens. Copies, DLC-USG, V, 12, 13, 14, 95; DNA, RG 393, USG General Orders.

5. On June 17, 1st Master John A. Duble, *Conestoga*, was ordered to take command of the *Mound City* after Commander Augustus H. Kilty was scalded. See preceding telegram, note 2. Duble's report of June 18, addressed to Flag Officer Charles H. Davis, is in *O.R.* (Navy), I, xxiii, 168–71. The *Mound City* brought to Memphis twenty prisoners taken with the battery at St. Charles, Ark. *Ibid.*, p. 170.

6. On June 24, USG telegraphed to Maj. Gen. Henry W. Halleck. "Two or three light steamers might be fitted up with howitzers in front to clear the banks of White River, sending Infy. to march along the banks, which they can do as fast as a steamer can run around the bends & thus supply Curtis Army. The boilers should be protected from musket balls with sheet Iron. I do not know the state of Genl Curtis supplies or how supplied but make this suggestion, thinking it probable they can better be obtained from here than elsewhere." Telegram received, DNA, RG 94, Generals' Papers and Books, Telegrams Received by Gen. Halleck; copies, *ibid*., RG 393, USG Hd. Qrs. Correspondence; *ibid*., Dept. of the Miss., Hd. Qrs. in the Field, Telegrams Received; DLC-USG, V, 4, 5, 7, 8, 9, 88.

7. Maj. Gen. Lewis Wallace later explained that he requested leave to settle the business of his law partnership. He also considered himself "superseded in command" by USG's arrival at Memphis. *Lew Wallace: An Autobiography* (New York and London, 1906), II, 588. Before his leave expired, he states, Halleck forced him to give up field command for recruiting duty. *Ibid.*, II, 590. But on Aug. 4, Wallace, Indianapolis, telegraphed to Rawlins. "Govonor Morton is enjoining me to canvass the state for Enlistments. He has obtained Maj Genl Hallecks permission for that purpose   Has Genl Grant any immediate need for me   answer"   Telegram received, DNA, RG 393, Dept. of the Mo., Telegrams Received. On July 31, Halleck had telegraphed to Governor Oliver P. Morton of Ind. granting permission for Wallace to aid in recruiting. ALS (telegram sent), *ibid*., RG 107, Telegrams Collected (Bound). On the same day, Halleck telegraphed substantially the same message to Wallace. ALS (telegram sent), *ibid*. On June 24, Rawlins issued Special Orders No. 118. "Leave of Absence is hereby granted Major Gen. Lewis Wallace, Commdg 4th 3d Division, Army of the Tenn, for twenty days, with authority to take with him his personal Staff, and, Asst. Adjt. Genl." Copies, DLC-USG, V, 15, 16, 82, 87; DNA, RG 393, USG Special Orders.

8. Alvin P. Hovey, born in Ind., had served as 1st lt. in the Mexican War, and was a prominent Ind. Democratic lawyer-politician until he switched to the Republican Party in 1858. Appointed col., 24th Ind., on July 31, 1861, he was promoted to brig. gen. on April 28, 1862.

To Maj. Gen. John A. McClernand

———

Head Quarters, Dist of West. Tenn.
Memphis, Tenn, June 24th 1862.

Major Gen. McClernand
Jackson, Tenn.

An order just published changes your command and takes out of it most of Wallace's Division.[1]

Sherman and Hurlbut both remain at or near Grand Junction, or at least opposed to any movement from the South.

U. S. Grant.
Major. Gen.

Copies, DLC–USG, V, 1, 2, 3, 86; DNA, RG 393, USG Letters Sent. On June 24, 1862, Maj. Gen. John A. McClernand wrote to USG. "The unsettled and hostile state of the Country between the rivers will induce me, with your approbation, to concentrate Genl. Wallace's Division at and near Bolivar,—including Grand Junction, if Genl. Sherman should go further south. ~~Ans. by telegraph~~ ~~Please answer~~" ADfS, *ibid.*, Dept. of the Tenn., Letters Received from Reserve Corps, Jackson, Tenn.; copies, *ibid.*; McClernand Papers, IHi.

On June 25, USG telegraphed to McClernand. "Send the troops of Genl. Wallace's division now with you to this place without delay" Copies, *ibid.* On the same day, McClernand wrote to USG. "But one of Gen Wallaces Regts here   shall I send it & if so on foot if Engineer refuses cars—Rest of Gen W s Div at & between Bolivar & Memphis   What military functions if any are expected of me in future" Telegram received, DNA, RG 393, Dept. of the Mo., Telegrams Received; ADfS, *ibid.*, Dept. of the Tenn., Letters Received from Reserve Corps, Jackson, Tenn.; copies, McClernand Papers, IHi.

1. On June 24, Maj. John A. Rawlins issued Special Orders No. 118. "The Corps heretofore known as the 'Reserve Corps' of the Army of the Tenn. is hereby ~~dissolved~~ broken up and Maj Gen McClernand and Maj Gen. Wallace will each resume command of their respective Divisions. Major Gen. J. A. McClernand will have immediate command of all troops occupying the country south of Union City, and north of the Memphis and Charleston road; and on the line of the rail roads. He will make all needful rules for the protection of the different lines of road, and for the preservation of order, within the District commanded by him. Tri-monthly Returns will be required as heretofore. The 3rd Division will drop from their reports the command at Bolivar, and it will be taken up by Gen. McClernand." Copies, DLC–USG, V, 15, 16, 82, 87; DNA, RG 393, USG Special Orders. *O.R.*, I, xvii, part 2, 31. On June 28, USG telegraphed to McClernand. "Orders have been sent you changing and defining your command.

If they do not reach you by the 30th Telegraph and duplicates will be sent."
Copy, McClernand Papers, IHi. On June 29, McClernand telegraphed to USG.
"The order has not been received   I am very anxious to see you personally &
will avail myself of the first ~~poss~~ favorable opportunity with your permission to
do so   is the Rail Road open through to Memphis"   Telegram received, DNA,
RG 393, Dept. of the Mo., Telegrams Received; copies, *ibid.*, Dept. of the Tenn.,
Letters Received from Reserve Corps, Jackson, Tenn.; McClernand Papers, IHi.
On the same day, McClernand again telegraphed to USG. "The order changing
& defining my command is not received   please send duplicate by Telegraph—
I have no control over the Reenforcements sent to Grand Junction"   Telegram
received, DNA, RG 393, Dept. of the Mo., Telegrams Received; copies, *ibid.*,
Dept. of the Tenn., Letters Received from Reserve Corps, Jackson, Tenn.;
McClernand Papers, IHi. McClernand's records show he did not receive Special
Orders No. 118 until July 2. Summary of orders received, *ibid.* On July 3, Col.
John C. Kelton issued Special Orders No. 140. "The commanding officer at
Columbus is charged with guarding the railroad from that place to Humboldt,
inclusive; the commanding officer at Jackson, from that place to Grand Junction
and Bethel, inclusive; the commanding officer of Memphis, from that place to
Grand Junction; the commanding officer at Corinth, to Bethel, Iuka, and south
and west as far as the roads are opened, except where they come within the limits
of other commands; and the commanding officer at Tuscumbia, from Decatur to
Iuka, inclusive. Such officers will be under the general orders of their superiors
in brigades, divisions, districts, and sub-districts." *O.R.*, I, xvii, part 2, 68–69.
The remainder of the orders concerned railroad administration. McClernand received Maj. Gen. Henry W. Halleck's orders on July 3. Summary of orders
received, McClernand Papers, IHi. On the same day, McClernand telegraphed
to USG. "Genl Halleck suspends your order   My state of incertitude is most
embarassing   I will ask to be relieved unless my official relations & responsibility shall be defined"   Telegram received, DNA, RG 393, Dept. of the Mo.,
Telegrams Received; copies, *ibid.*, Dept. of the Tenn., Letters Received from
Reserve Corps, Jackson, Tenn.; McClernand Papers, IHi. Also on the same day,
USG telegraphed to McClernand. "I have no control over the matter, Genl.
Halleck telegraphs me as follows. 'Please rescind your orders about districting' "
Copy, *ibid.* On the same day, Halleck telegraphed to McClernand. "Bolivar should
be occupied, but cannot speak of Brownsville as it is not on my maps.—do not
think it safe to abandon Bethel. Genl. Grants Districting of West Tenn will not
be carried into effect at present, no warehouse will be erected at Grand Junction."
Copy, *ibid.* On July 7, McClernand telegraphed to USG. "I have taken the liberty
to send herewith copies of Genl. Halleck's order subdistricting your district, and
of orders predicated thereon, and published by me. You will perceive that I have
assigned every portion of my command to the performance of an amount of duty
equal to its capabilities. The order prescribing the mode of recruiting to fill up
deficiencies in regiments will be fruitless of all valuable results. If the Governors
had been left to obtain the recruits, or if the Officers of Regiments or Brigades
had been allowed to do so, something would be done. I wish to see the Governor
of Illinois upon this and many other subjects connected with the consolidation,
reorganization and commissioning of different arms of my command. Will you
place me under an order to see the Governor upon these and such other subjects
as you may choose to designate, leaving it to me to adopt such time for doing so
as may not interfere with my duties and the good of the service here. I attach

much importance to an interview with the Governor upon these points. Indeed it is essential to the effeciency of my command and the good of the service that I or some one else should do so. Please let me hear from you by Dr Williams." Copies, *ibid.*

To Maj. Gen. Henry W. Halleck

———

Memphis June 25th 1862

MAJ GENL H W HALLECK
COMMANDING DEPT OF THE MISS
CORINTH
GENL

I will with your approval, send such of the boats now loaded with supplies for General Curtis as can ascend the White river, and reinforcing Col Fitch with two Regiments from here.[1]

There are two Gun Boats at the mouth of White river, but they cannot ascend over 60 miles ~~from~~ with the present stage of water.

I would recommend ~~on~~ after consultation with Capt Phelps, that two or three light draught Steamers be fitted up to keep open the communication with Genl Curtis.

I am informed that a body of rebel troops are now trying to get in North of Gen. Curtis : also learn that Bragg is occupying the line from Vicksburg to Jackson, Tenn.—intended to make that their line : this seems to have come from a rebel soldier writing to his friends here. I give it as received for what it is worth.

U. S. GRANT
Maj. Genl.

Telegram received (incomplete), DNA, RG 94, Generals' Papers and Books, Telegrams Received by Gen. Halleck; copies, *ibid.*, RG 393, USG Hd. Qrs. Correspondence; DLC-USG, V, 4, 5, 7, 8, 9, 88. *O.R.*, I, xiii, 117–18.

1. On June 25, 1862, Maj. Gen. Henry W. Halleck telegraphed to USG. "If your information from Arkansas is such as to render it safe for the expedition to ascend White river, send all of Col Slack's force to reinforce Col Fitch & open

a communication with Genl Curtis. If the boats cannot get up the river we must repair the Rail Road. Have we no gunboat in White River?" ALS (telegram sent), DNA, RG 108, Telegrams Sent; telegram received, *ibid.*, RG 393, Dept. of the Mo., Telegrams Received. *O.R.*, I, xiii, 117. On the same day, Maj. John A. Rawlins wrote to Capt. Henry S. Fitch. "You will please report to these Head Quarters whether the Transports now ladened with stores for Gen. Curtis are of such light draught as to enable them, to proceed up White river. If not you will discharge them at once." Copies, DLC-USG, V, 1, 2, 3, 86; DNA, RG 393, USG Letters Sent. Also on June 25, Rawlins issued Special Orders No. 119. "The 34th and 43rd Indiana Regiments will proceed at once, with fifteen days rations aboard the Steamers 'Meteor', 'John Bell', 'Emma', 'Ella' and 'Clide,' and accompany them up white river. On forming a junction with Col. Fitch he will take charge of the entire expedition, and return to his present position as soon as possible after discharging the boats. These Regiments will not take with them their Camp Equipage nor land transportation." Copies, DLC-USG, V, 15, 16, 82, 87; DNA, RG 393, USG Special Orders.

To Maj. Gen. Henry W. Halleck

Memphis Tennessee June 25, 1862

MAJ GENL H W HALLECK
COMMANDING DEPT OF THE MISS
CORINTH
GENERAL

Is there an order requiring Nolemans & Barrells Company's of Cavalry to be sent to Saint Louis to be mustered out of service? These companies are now here.

Very Respcty
Your Obt Servt
U. S. GRANT
Maj Genl

Telegram, copies, DLC-USG, V, 4, 5, 7, 8, 88; DNA, RG 393, USG Hd. Qrs. Correspondence. On June 28, 1862, Col. John C. Kelton telegraphed to USG. "There has been no order issued from this office to send Nolemans & Burells Companies to St Louis   there was an order given to Muster out of service the disorganized Companies [of] [t]he first Illinois Cavalry in Missouri" Telegram received, *ibid.*, Dept. of the Mo., Telegrams Received; copies, *ibid.*, USG Hd. Qrs. Correspondence; DLC-USG, V, 7.

Most of the 1st Ill. Cav. was captured at Lexington, Mo., on Sept. 20, 1861, paroled, and exchanged in Dec. After exchange, dissatisfaction with some newly appointed officers reached such proportions that the entire regt. was disbanded. Co. H, commanded by Capt. Robert D. Noleman of Centralia, and Co. I, commanded by Capt. Orlando Burrell of Alton (organized in White County with the intention of serving with the 18th Ill.), had been under USG's command when the rest of the regt. was captured and not involved in the organizational disputes. They were, however, mustered out with the remainder of the regt. on July 5, 1862. *Ill. AG Report*, VII, 485.

To Col. Benjamin H. Grierson

Head Quarters, Dist of West. Tenn.
Memphis, Tenn, June 25th 1862.

Genl B H Grierson
Commdg Officer
6th Ills. Cavalry.

Get all your available force in readiness to march immediately with the wagon train now about leaving going East. Rations and forage for one day will be taken.

Encamp with the train to-night and return tomorrow. If in your judgment it should prove advisable you may accompany the train a few miles, or as far as necessary tomorrow.

Very Respectfully
Your Obt Servant,
U. S. Grant.
Major. Gen.

Copies, DLC-USG, V, 1, 2, 3, 86; DNA, RG 393, USG Letters Sent. Benjamin H. Grierson, born in Pittsburgh, Pa., in 1826, taught music in Youngstown, Ohio, and Jacksonville, Ill., and was a merchant at Meredosia, Ill. He was appointed maj., 6th Ill. Cav., on Oct. 24, 1861, and col. on April 12, 1862.

To Maj. Gen. Henry W. Halleck

BY TELEGRAPH FROM Memphis [*June*] 26th 186[2]

TO GEN HALLECK

There is a reported cut in R. R. west Germantown.[1] Wires now down for two days with small bodies of rebel Cavalry through the Country, burning Cotton & cutting wire as fast as ~~possible~~ filled up.[2] Additional Cavalry troops would enable me to partially clear the Country of these men: there are five Cos. 6th Ill Cav. at Humboldt & some here. Can they all come here? Steamers for White River start this morning taking 2 Regts to reinforce Col. Fitch who will convey them to Gen. Curtis.

U. S. GRANT
Maj. Genl

Telegram received, DNA, RG 94, Generals' Papers and Books, Telegrams Received by Gen. Halleck; copies, *ibid.*, RG 393, USG Hd. Qrs. Correspondence; *ibid.*, Dept. of the Miss., Hd. Qrs. in the Field, Telegrams Received; DLC-USG, V, 4, 5, 7, 8, 9, 88. *O.R.*, I, xvii, part 2, 36. On June 25, 1862, Col. George G. Pride, "Gen Shermans Head Quarters," wrote to USG. "On reaching a point three miles west of Germantown, our Engine was thrown off the track and turned completely over disabling it—The cars remained on the track, but some of the men were thrown off, and a few injured although not seriously—Three Rails had been removed or probably displaced just enough to throw us off—The Wire of the Telegraph was also cut—Col Kinney was on the train and about 25 muskets —I left him in charge of the train, and went up ½ a mile to farmers houses, and Secured two wagons, and put the knapsacks of the men in one of them, with instructions to the men to come on following us—Three or four of us came on here to report Facts to Gen Sherman, but he has but few cavalry and could not send any down there—He moves in the morning to Moscow, supporting Gen Hurlburt—The Railroad Regiment will go down towards Germantown in the morning, with instructions to repair and defend the road—One of the men left at the break in the road has just come in, says the party that were left to guard were attacked, but from his account, I am inclined to think that it is incorrect, as it was an hour and a half after the accident before I left—Still it may be so—Major Main of the R. Rd Regiment (52nd Indiana) will write you particulars—I sent a man on horseback to you with a hurried pencil account, and asking you to send some cavalry there if possible—It is neccessary to have a patrol up and down the road all the time—Shall go on to La Grange and try and get a train on from that direction—" ALS, DNA, RG 393, District of West Tenn., Letters Received. Attached was an undated letter from Maj. Gen. William T. Sherman. "Genl Halleck's Dispatch to me is, Reinforce Genl Hurlbut if necessary. If so call on

Genl Grant to assist you. I send to Germantown the R R Regt—Maj Main which with the 56 Ohio should be enough. I leave a Regiment & Section of Artillery here. I have no doubt of the gathering of a force at Holly Springs which must be attacked and driven off before we can attempt to use this Road. If we could effect the Junction of about 15000 men we should quickly do so and attack Holly Springs. I will at Moscow be at a good point for attack. I dont think they contemplate attacking Hurlbut, but they will fill the country with cavalry & endanger our trains" ALS, *ibid*. Beneath this letter, Pride wrote an undated endorsement. "I shall not attempt to start a Train to Memphis for some time; at least until we hear from you—" AES, *ibid*. See *O.R.*, I, xvii, part 1, 10–12.

    1. Germantown, Tenn., on the Memphis and Charleston Railroad about fifteen miles southeast of Memphis.
    2. On June 26, Duncan T. Bacon, manager of the military telegraph office at Memphis, wrote to USG. "Our line is not yet in operation nor have we heard anything from the repairers sent out. If it is not in order by noon I would respectfully suggest that a small force should be sent out to ascertain the trouble" ALS, DNA, RG 393, Dept. of the Mo., Telegrams Received. On June 30, Bacon wrote to USG. "We close the Telegraph Line at 11 oclock P M. Genl Hallecks office is already closed & ~~wou~~ we could not get any despatches from him. tonight Genl Shermans office is closed also." ALS, *ibid*.

To Maj. Gen. Henry W. Halleck

Memphis Tennessee
June 26th 1862

MAJ GENL H W HALLECK
COMDG DEPT OF THE MISS
GENL

    News ~~has just reached me or~~ reached me during ~~the~~ last night that Jackson's forces[1] come in on the Railroad near Germantown yesterday, and captured the train with all on board, and also the waggon train loaded with supplies for Genl Shermans Division, ~~also~~ and cut the Road.

    Day before yesterday I heard of Jackson being 20 miles south-east from here, intending to make a raid upon this wagon train with a view of destroying it at their camping place for last night. I immediately issued orders for the Cavalry here to accompany this train to their Camp Ground for last night, and if deemed advisable, accompany them this morning to beyond danger.

The wagon train left the evening this order was published, going out of the city to encamp. The additional escort followed in the morning and with the usual cavalry stupidity took the wrong road thus leaving the train protected ~~by~~ only with the escort furnished by Genl Sherman. As this last force followed on after the Capture it is not at all improbable that they too have been taken. My information is all from citizens who come in last night, and may not be strictly reliable.

Accompanying the Rail Road train was a letter to yourself and one to Genl Sherman which I am very sorry to have (these letters, particularly the former) fall into the hands of the rebels. Col Gierson commander of the Cavalry sent from here, has just returned from Germantown and discredits the reports of the capture of our trains. He says that Jackson's men have been hovering along the line of the Railroad in squads, burning cotton   That cotton was burned yesterday at three or four places visited by him.

An impression seems to prevail here that a force is collecting 35 miles south East ~~from~~ of here for the purpose of making an attack on this place and burning it. My force now here is small, having sent two Regts to reinforce Col Fitch and to protect 5 Steamers loaded with supplies for Genl Curtis ~~Army~~ command. These steamers are now ready to start. I had precautionary measures taken to protect the Pilots from musketry.

I reported to you the effective strength of this command but you may not have received it. As my Office and Qrs ~~are~~ have been moved to the suburbs of the City, and all the records are there I cannot now give you the exact strength   I believe the entire effective force left after reinforcing Col Fitch is about 4000.

It seems to me that one of the Div's of the Army of the Tenn now at Corinth should move West so as to strengthen this point. ~~by another Division~~   This would enable me to hold Hernando or some suitable point on the railroad to Grenada.[2]

Very Respcty
Your Obt Servt
U. S. GRANT
Maj Gen'l

Copies, DLC-USG, V, 4, 5, 7, 8, 9, 88; DNA, RG 393, USG Hd. Qrs. Correspondence. *O.R.*, I, xvii, part 2, 36–37.

1. William H. Jackson of Tenn., USMA 1856, served in Tex. and N. M. as a 2nd lt., then resigned his commission on May 16, 1861. First appointed a C. S. A. capt. of art., he was successively col., 7th Tenn. Cav. and 1st Miss. Cav. On June 25, 1862, he raided and destroyed a train near Germantown, Tenn. *Ibid.*, I, xvii, part 1, 10–12.

2. Hernando, Miss., on the Mississippi and Tennessee Railroad about twenty-four miles south of Memphis; Grenada, Miss., about ninety-five miles south of Memphis at the junction of the Mississippi Central and the Mississippi and Tennessee railroads.

To Flag Officer Charles H. Davis

————

Memphis Ten.
June 26th 1862

FLAG OFFICER DAVIS
COMD.G WESTERN FLOTILLA,
SIR:

It is my desire to dispatch the five steamers now laying here loaded with supplies for Gen. Curtis' Army at as early an hour to-day as practicable. I submit to you whether they should not be convoyed at least to the mouth of White river by one or more of the gun boats?

I am Flag officer, very respectfully your obt. svt.
U. S. GRANT
Maj. Gen.

ALS, ICarbS. Charles H. Davis of Mass. was appointed a midshipman on Aug. 12, 1823, and remained in the U.S. Navy throughout his life, though achieving more fame as a scientist than as an officer. Promoted to capt. on Nov. 15, 1861, he relieved temporarily Flag Officer Andrew H. Foote in command of the Mississippi Flotilla on May 9, 1862, and was himself advanced to flag officer on June 17. On June 26, Davis wrote to USG. "I have had the pleasure to receive your note of to day. The gun-boat Conestoga is ready at any moment to convoy the steamers to the mouth of White river. I will direct Capt. Winslow the commander of the Naval detachment at that place to give them convoy as far up the river as may be practicable." Copy, DNA, RG 45, Letterbook of Charles H. Davis. *O.R.* (Navy), I, xxiii, 182.

To Col. Graham N. Fitch

———

Head Quarters Army of the Tenn.
Memphis June 26th 1862.

Col. G. N. Fitch
Comdg Expedition On White River.
Sir,

I send Five Steamers loaded with supplies for Genl. Curtis Army. As they necessarily pass through a hostile country great caution will have to be exersized to prevent these supplies from falling into the hands of the enemy. Or from being destroyed.

I have selected you as commander of the expedition and reinforce you with two additional regiments, as you will procure from Special Orders Accompanying this.

It would be impossible to give full Special instructions for the management of this Expedition. Much must necessarily be left to the discretion of the Officer in command. I would suggest however that two pices of Artillery be placed on the bow of the boat intended to lead. That all of them be kept well togather. When you tie up for the night, strong Guards be thrown out upon the shore, and that troops be landed and required to march and clear out all points suspected of concealing Foe.

It is desirable those supplies should reach Genl. Curtis, as early as possible. As soon as the Boats can possibly be discharged Return them bringing Your entire command to St. Charles—or to where you now are.

It is not intended that you shall reach, Genl. Curtis, against all obsticles, but it is highly desirable that he should be Reached.

I am Col. Very Respectfully
Your Obt. Serv't.
U. S. Grant.
Major Genl. Com'dg.

Copy, Curtis Papers, IaHA. *O.R.*, I, xiii, 118. On June 27, 1862, Col. Graham N. Fitch, Montgomery's Point, Ark., wrote to USG. "You are probably aware by this time that owing to the rapid fall of White River, the iron-clad Gun Boats, considering it unsafe to remain longer as high up as St. Charles descended to the Mississippi? Having but one regiment with me which was entirely insufficient to protect both sides from the attacks of Guerrillas & hold the town & ensure safety to the transport 'White Cloud' laden with stores for Gen. Curtis' command. The Regt. & transports accompanied the Gun Boats to the Mouth of White River to await farther orders. At this place your letter of instructions of 26th inst. was handed me, and in obedience thereto and to former instructions, this command will proceed again up White river, and I beg that you will send without delay another transport with 200 or 300 Cavalry,—which are indispensable in scouring the country & protecting the Infantry from the annoyance of Guerrillas. They can join this command at St. Charles or above. The excessive heat & character of the country render the assistance of Cavalry highly necessary, indeed almost indispensable. The route from St. Charles a few miles back of that town is through a prairie country, through which rove mounted rangers in addition to foot guerrillas. In my dispatch to Major. Gen. Wallace which you may have seen I stated that he undoubtedly could have passed Duvall's Bluff which was then only partially fortified without much difficulty if the gun boats could have been prevailed upon to proceed up the river but that the Bluff would be strengthened as soon as the enemy discovered we had returned down the river. I am *now* advised that there are 2 or 3 heavy guns mounted there, with a considerable force of Infantry.—It will be necessary to successfully attack that place for an additional force of Infantry besides the Cavalry to be sent, as I fully stated to Genl. Wallace & if it is absolutely necessary to open communication with Gen. Curtis I would respectfully ask that you send the reinforcements of Infantry and Cavalry as soon as possible in light transports with rations for the troops, the transports can be used if necessary to lighten the boats now freighted for Genl. Curtiss.— Upon a consultation just had with the commanders of the Gunboat fleet I fear that they will refuse to escort the troops & transports any farther than St. Charles and thus for the third time compel the expedition to return. Above Duval's we could proceed without aid of Gun boats, as we could indeed from St. Charles with a force of 4000 Infantry & a corresponding number of Cavalry & guns.—'' ALS, DNA, RG 393, Dept. of the Mo., Letters Received.

To Maj. Gen. Henry W. Halleck

By Telegraph from Memphis [*June*] 27th *186*[*2*]

To MAJ. GEN.L HALLECK

I have sent one Regt. of Infy. & 5 Co.s of Cav. beyond Germantown in hopes of opening the R. R. & telegraph[1] with the aid of one Division from Corinth I think it practicable to occupy Holly Springs,[2] Hernando & an intermediate point between these places to intercept Jeff Thompson[3] & Jackson's Cotton burners. I would also like to have the 11th Cavalry sent.

U. S. GRANT

Maj. Genl

Telegram received, DNA, RG 94, Generals' Papers and Books, Telegrams Received by Gen. Halleck; copies, *ibid.*, RG 393, USG Hd. Qrs. Correspondence; *ibid.*, Dept. of the Miss., Hd. Qrs. in the Field, Telegrams Received; DLC-USG, V, 4, 5, 7, 8, 9, 88. *O.R.*, I, xvii, part 2, 41.

    1. On June 27, 1862, Maj. John A. Rawlins issued Special Orders No. 121. "One Regiment of Infantry and Col. Greerson's Cavalry will proceed with three days forage on the Germantown road to the point where there is a break in the Memphis and Charleston road. The regiment of Infantry will be designated by Brig. Gen. Hovey and will be in readines to move at 3 Oclock P. M. today. The Officer Commanding will call on the Genl. Commdg for instructions." Copies, DLC-USG, V, 15, 16, 82, 87; DNA, RG 393, USG Special Orders.

    2. Holly Springs, Miss., on the Mississippi Central Railroad about forty-three miles southeast of Memphis. On June 28, Maj. Gen. William T. Sherman, Moscow, Tenn., telegraphed to USG. "Your letter by Gould received this A M telegraphed its contents to Halleck   I sent the Rail Road Regt to Germantown intending it to make a Junction before starting with the 56 Ohio but the latter did not wait for it   I hope both Regts are at Germantown   I can hear nothing definite from Holly Springs   No spy can get in & out since Gould went   I dont like to risk him too much   he has already exposed his life some half dozen times   I want to move with our forces on Holly springs for as long as an enemy occupies that point there can be no safety in running cars on this road   I am sending a messenger to La grange to find out if there is any news of Rosecrans who is moving on Holly Springs from Corinth via Ripley   I dont know the strength of his forces but we should act in concert   Hallecks reiterated orders to me are move not a mile west unless it be absolutely necessary"   Telegram received, *ibid.*, Dept. of the Mo., Telegrams Received; copies, *ibid.*, RG 94, Generals' Papers and Books, William T. Sherman, Letters Sent; DLC-William T. Sherman. *O.R.*, I, xvii, part 2, 44. On the same day, Sherman telegraphed to Maj. Gen. Henry W. Halleck concerning an expedition to Holly Springs. *Ibid.*

    3. After failing in his defense of Memphis, on June 6, Brig. Gen. M. Jeff Thompson moved his force to Grenada, Miss. In late June, his units were operating between the Mississippi and Tennessee and the Memphis and Charleston railroads. Jay Monaghan, *Swamp Fox of the Confederacy: The Life and Military Services of M. Jeff Thompson* (Tuscaloosa, 1956), p. 55; *O.R.*, I, xvii, part 2, 619–20.

To Maj. Gen. Henry W. Halleck

Head Quarters Disct of West Tennessee
Memphis June 27th 1862

MAJ GENL H W HALLECK
COMDG DEPT OF THE MISS.
GENL

Between Jackson's and Jeff Thomson's forces, with the weak force here, I fear that it will be impossible for me to keep the Railroad open from here to Grand Junction, and at the same time keep the City in subjection. There is great disloyalty manifested by the citizens of this place and undoubtedly spies and members of the southern army are constantly finding their way in and out of the city in spite of all vigilance.

There is every probability that an attempt will be made to burn the City, and no doubt from the extent to be guarded it will prove partially successful. This however is a matter which will operate more against the rebels than against ourselves. The Regiment sent from here to repair the Railroad has just returned. I ordered it to remain as a guard to the road until further orders were received, but as this order was carried by the Col of the Regt and he being taken prisoner before reaching his command[1] it returned here in obedience to previous orders. I have to-day sent out to Germantown, or to the point where the Railroad is broken, ~~to day~~ a regiment of Infantry and five companies of cavalry. They go with three days rations, but as some cars and locomotives have just arrived I will keep these troops there if practicable until troops from Bollivar[2] can relieve them. I will make the effort to keep the road and Telegraph open. As I am without instructions I am a little in doubt as to my authority to license and limit trade, punish offences committed by citizens, and in restricting civil authority. I now have two citizens prisoners for murder who I shall have tried by a military commission and submit the findings and sentence to you.

All communication is prevented south of our lines as far as

our guards can prevent it. There is a Board of Trade established to regulate what goods are authorized to be received and who are authorized to sell.

I think it will be neccessary also to establish some sort of court to settle private claims. When a direct channel for mails is opened I will submit to you a copy of all orders published for the government of the City.

I would again urge the importance of having here one division of the army of the Tenn, ordered from Corinth.

> I am Genl Very Respct.y
> Your Obt Servt
> U. S. GRANT

Copies, DLC-USG, V, 4, 5, 7, 8, 9, 88; DNA, RG 393, USG Hd. Qrs. Correspondence. *O.R.*, I, xvii, part 2, 41–42.

1. Col. Peter Kinney, 56th Ohio, was captured near Germantown, Tenn., when C. S. A. cav. raided a disabled railroad train. *Ibid.*, I, xvii, part 1, 11. See telegrams to Maj. Gen. Henry W. Halleck, June 26, 30, 1862.
2. Bolivar, Tenn., on the Mississippi Central Railroad about fifty-seven miles east of Memphis.

To Maj. Gen. Henry W. Halleck

Memphis June 28th 1862

MAJOR GENL H W HALLECK.
CORINTH, MISS

News has just been received from Commodore Farragut.[1] Gun Boats have left here to co-operate in the attack on Vicksburgh. A land force of 13,000 is said to be up from New Orleans. One if not two Gun boats will be here in the morning from mouth of White river. I have sent a force from here and thus again opened ~~again~~ telegraph communication. Will endeavor to keep it so. I have written and telegraphed via Columbus, Ky.

> Very Respcty
> Your Obt Servt
> U. S. GRANT
> Maj Genl.

Telegram, copies, DLC-USG, V, 4, 5, 7, 8, 9, 88; DNA, RG 393, USG Hd. Qrs. Correspondence; *ibid.*, Dept. of the Miss., Hd. Qrs. in the Field, Telegrams Received. *O.R.*, I, xvii, part 2, 43; *O.R.* (Navy), I, xxiii, 233.

On July 9, 1862, Brig. Gen. Thomas Williams, "below Vicksburg," wrote to USG. "I'm here with 4 regiments & two batteries co-operating against Vicksburg with the fleets of flag-officers Farragut & Davis. We need a greater land force here. The place cannot be taken by a naval force. A portion of flag-officer Farragut's fleet passed Vicksburg in the morning of June 28, without silencing the batteries. We assisted them with eight rifled field guns from Burney's point. The batteries & town will have to be taken by a land force. Lovell, Van Dorn, Smith, & some *three* other Generals are at Vicksburg & in its near vicinity. Their force is reported to be from 20 to 30,000. If I had 10,000 additional to my present 2500, I think the place could be taken. Can't you come yourself? My hopes, at present, center in a Canal cut-off. Its nearly ready for the water. If it does not turn the course of of the river, I shall, I think, take a turn at the enemy's batteries anyhow, & try, at least, to spike their guns. Let me hear from you at your earliest leisure, & meanwhile, accept my grateful appreciation of your great success." ALS, DNA, RG 393, District of West Tenn., Letters Received.

1. Born in 1801, David G. Farragut entered the U.S. Navy as midshipman in 1810, and served for nearly sixty years. Ranking as capt. since Sept. 14, 1855, he was assigned to command the West Gulf Blockading Squadron on Jan. 9, 1862. On April 24, he ran his ships past Fort Jackson and Fort St. Philip at the mouth of the Mississippi River, forced the surrender of New Orleans, then ascended the Mississippi to Vicksburg.

To Maj. Gen. Henry W. Halleck

By TELEGRAPH FROM Memphis [*June*] 29th 186[*2*]

To MAJ. GEN. HALLECK

A man thro' from Okolona[1] reports that there are but 3000 at that place, Columbus[2] is being strongly fortified—30,000 men said to be at *Abbeyville*,[3] intending to march on Lagrange so soon as the Tallahatchee bridge is repaired—this I telegraphed via Columbus, Ky. while the direct line was down.

U. S. GRANT
Maj Genl.

Telegram received, DNA, RG 94, Generals' Papers and Books, Telegrams Received by Gen. Halleck; copies, *ibid.*, RG 393, USG Hd. Qrs. Correspondence;

ibid., Dept. of the Miss., Hd. Qrs. in the Field, Telegrams Received; DLC–USG, V, 4, 5, 7, 8, 9, 88. *O.R.*, I, xvii, part 2, 46. On June 29, 1862, Maj. Gen. Henry W. Halleck telegraphed to USG. "You say thirty thousand rebels at Shelbyville to attack La Grange. Where is Shelbyville? I cant find it on any map. Dont believe a word about an attack in large force on La Grange or Memphis. Why not sent out strong reconnaissance & ascertain *facts*? It looks very much like a mere stampede. Floating rumors are never to be received as facts. Order an investigation of the loss of the train & capture of our men by a paltry force of the enemy, & report the facts. I mean to make somebody responsible for so gross a negligence." ALS (telegram sent), DNA, RG 108, Telegrams Sent; telegram received, DLC–USG, V, 9. *O.R.*, I, xvii, part 2, 46. See following telegram.

1. Okolona, Miss., on the Mobile and Ohio Railroad about sixty-five miles south of Corinth.
2. Columbus, Miss., close to the Ala. state line about ninety-five miles south of Corinth.
3. Abbeville, Miss., on the Mississippi Central Railroad just south of the Tallahatchie River and about thirty-eight miles south of La Grange, Tenn.

To Maj. Gen. Henry W. Halleck

By Telegraph from Memphis [*June*] 29th 186[*2*]

To Maj. Gen. Halleck

I did not say 30,000 troops at Shelbyville but at Abbeyville which is South of Holly Springs, on the road to Grenada. I made a report of all I knew of the capture of the train & sent by way of Columbus, Ky. I have kept my Cavalry force on the road from here to Germantown, most of the time since my arrival in Memphis. The balance of the Cavalry force here are ordered to make daily reconnoisance to the South East from here. I heed as little of the ~~rum~~ floating rumors about the City as any one—only gave you the statement of a man from Okolona who has fled from there with no intention of returning until he can go under the Federal Flag. I do not credit his reports as to exact numbers but believe the Tallahatchee Bridge is being repaired & that a considerable rebel force is at Abbeyville. I know that from rumors that Jeff Thompson & Jackson are both to the South East of us. I have applied for the 11th Ill. Cav. now at Corinth that I might do effectually what you now ask why I have not done. Stampeding is not my weakness—on the contrary I will always execute any order to the best of my ability with the means at hand. Immediately on taking command here I ordered troops of my command from Jackson and Bolivar where they could be spared, that I might have the force to guard effectually the Road from here to where guarded by Gen. Sherman. Your orders have countermanded mine. It will be very difficult however to prevent the occasional taking out of a rail & cutting of a wire as my troops of my command passed the scene of the late catastrophe before it occurred & after on the same day. I do not see that there was any more culpable neglect than was shown by Beauregard in permitting the road from Corinth to Bethel to be cut by my forces or the Road south of him by Col. Elliott[1]   as the disposition of [the] forces of the Army of the Tenn. have been made without my orders & in many cases without my being informed of the changes & as the running of the cars are expressly placed under the control of Gen. McPherson[2] who had his Agt here & as I have never been directed to place any troops on the Road no blame can be attached to me.

Very Respectfy.
U. S. GRANT
Maj. Genl.

Telegram received, DNA, RG 94, Generals' Papers and Books, Telegrams Received by Gen. Halleck; copies, *ibid.*, RG 393, USG Hd. Qrs. Correspondence; *ibid.*, Dept. of the Miss., Hd. Qrs. in the Field, Telegrams Received; DLC-USG, V, 4, 5, 7, 8, 9, 88. *O.R.*, I, xvii, part 2, 46–47.

On June 29, 1862, Maj. Gen. Henry W. Halleck telegraphed to USG. "The part of Wallace's division at Bolivar was ordered to Grand Junction. There is no danger of an attack in force on Memphis; it is a mere stampede. The great object now is to protect the rail roads against marauders. There was culpable neglect in sending out the train from Memphis till the road was properly guarded. You will report by whose neglect the accidents to the train & the capture of telegraph repairers occurred." ALS (telegram sent), DNA, RG 108, Telegrams Sent; telegram received, DLC-USG, V, 9. *O.R.*, I, xvii, part 2, 46.

On July 3, Halleck wrote to USG. "Other pressing business has prevented me from giving an earlier answer to your telegram of the 29th ult. In asking you to report by whose negligence the train which was destroyed by the enemy had been sent over the road before it was properly guarded, I made no insinuation that there had been the slightest neglect on *your* part. Indeed I supposed the whole thing had been done before you assumed the immediate command at Memphis. What I wanted to know was the facts of the case—who sent it out, and why it was exposed to destruction. This I directed you to investigate and report, and you take offence at the order, as intended to reflect upon you Nor did I suppose for a moment that *you* were *stampeded*; for I know that is not in your nature; but I believed there was a stampede about the enemy threatening our line to Memphis with thirty thousand men, and I now have good evidence that he did not have one tenth of that number. Again, you complain that troops belonging to your general command received orders direct from me. While present with the army here, I shall, whenever occasion requires it, exercise the right of issuing orders direct to any detached command, or any undetached command if I deem it necessary. On moving your Head Quarters to Memphis where there was only a very small part of the troops of this army, with communications difficult and precarious, you could hardly suppose that I would send orders which required immediate execution, through you, who were more than a hundred miles away, when my direct orders would reach them in a few minutes. Moreover I had information of the enemy which you could not possibly have had. I will further add, that, from your position at Memphis, it is impossible for you to exercise the immediate command in this direction. I must confess that I was very much surprised at the tone of your dispatch, and the ill feeling manifested in it, so contrary to your usual style, and especially towards one who has so often befriended you when you were attacked by others." LS, DNA, RG 393, Dept. of the Mo., Telegrams Received; *ibid.*, Letters Sent (Press). *O.R.*, I, xvii, part 2, 67–68.

1. Washington L. Elliott of Pa., who attended USMA 1841–44 but did not graduate, was appointed 2nd lt., U.S. Mounted Riflemen, on May 27, 1846. He served in the U.S. Army continuously thereafter, until appointed col., 2nd Iowa Cav., on Sept. 14, 1861. On May 30, 1862, while commanding a brigade under orders of Maj. Gen. John Pope, Elliott cut the Mobile and Ohio Railroad near Booneville, Miss., about twenty miles south of Corinth, doing much damage to C. S. A. supplies and taking many prisoners. *Ibid.*, I, x, part 1, 861–67.

2. On June 4, Capt. John C. Kelton issued Special Field Orders No. 86 appointing Brig. Gen. James B. McPherson superintendent of military railroads. *Ibid.*, I, lii, part 1, 253. On July 3, Kelton issued Special Field Orders No. 140 clarifying the position of officers assigned to guard tracks and trains, who were not to interfere with the running of the trains under orders of McPherson. *Ibid.*, I, xvii, part 2, 69. On July 1, McPherson, Corinth, telegraphed to USG. "The work of opening the Memphis & Ohio Road will be discontinued for the present" Telegram received, DNA, RG 393, Dept. of the Mo., Telegrams Received.

To Maj. Gen. John A. McClernand

———

Memphis June 29 1862

The Rail road is not running through   as all my orders for the change of troops so far have been countermanded, I shall decline giving further orders to, for the present except for those immediately under my here. Although I have the right to permit you to visit m[e] here: in view of all circumstances I would prefer you should ~~not~~ telegrah Genl. Halleck for the authority

U S GRANT

Telegram, copy, McClernand Papers, IHi. On June 26, 1862, Maj. Gen. John A. McClernand telegraphed to USG. "In compliance with orders received last evening from Genl Halleck as many troops as the cars can carry including the 78 Ohio of Wallaces Div will go forward to reinforce Genl Hurlburt at Grand Junction & Moscow where that Regt will be halted subject to your further orders" Telegram received, DNA, RG 393, Dept. of the Mo., Telegrams Received; copies, *ibid.*, Dept. of the Tenn., Letters Received from Reserve Corps, Jackson, Tenn.; McClernand Papers, IHi. On the same day, McClernand telegraphed to both Maj. Gen. Henry W. Halleck and USG. "I am sending 3 Regts from here & 3 from Bolivar to support Genl Hurlbut" Copies, DNA, RG 393, 16th Army Corps, Letters Sent; McClernand Papers, IHi. On June 27, McClernand telegraphed to USG. "Asking the approbation of Gen Halleck to send the 78 Ohio now at Grand Junction to Memphis he declines & says on the contrary he expects to reinforce Sherman from Memphis" Telegram received, DNA, RG 393, Dept. of the Mo., Telegrams Received; copies, *ibid.*, Dept. of the Tenn., Letters Received from Reserve Corps, Jackson, Tenn.; McClernand Papers, IHi. On June 28, Col. William L. Sanderson, Bolivar, Tenn., telegraphed to USG. "The twentieth and sixtieth eighth Ohio have been sent to Grand Junction to reinforce General Hurlburt by order of General McClernand   will send them on to Memphis as soon as they return unless otherwise ordered" Telegram received, DNA, RG 393, Dept. of the Mo., Telegrams Received. USG wrote a note on the reverse of this telegram. "Immediately on my taking command here I ordered troops of my command, not needed where they then were, to guard the very road" AE, *ibid.* On June 29, McClernand telegraphed to Sanderson. "I send the following Telegram from Genl. Halleck to me as the answer to your inquires. 'Corinth June 29, 1862. Col. Sanderson will obey the order given him through you. Genl. Grant was notified not to order him to Memphis but probably did not receive my communication. H W HALLECK, Maj Genl'" Copy, McClernand Papers, IHi. On June 30, Sanderson telegraphed to USG. "There is but forty effective cavalry men here   the rest have gone to Grand Junction by order of Genl McClernand—Have sent copy of your despatch to comdg officer at Grand Junction" Telegram received, DNA, RG 393, Dept. of the Mo., Telegrams Received.

To Maj. Gen. Henry W. Halleck

———

By Telegraph from Memphis [*June*] 30th 186[2]

To Genl. Halleck

The beef drovers who were captured on their return from Lafayette[1] have got back—one of them has reported to me that they were carried about ten miles south of Holly Springs. The force at that point was Jackson's Cavalry & one Regt. besides: he heard determination expressed not [*to*] permit the cars to run or Supplies be carried over the Road. I have re-inforced Col. Fitch with 3 Infy. Regts. & sent one Regt. of Cavalry & five Cos. of Cav. to guard the Road   an escort of 150 are now via Rolla[2] with beef Cattle for Sherman's command: my present effective force here is 5 Infy. Regts., about 190 Cavalry & four batteries. From this 2 Cos. of Infy. & one of Cav. are escorting a wagon train to Germantown—one Co. guarding a barge to the mouth of White River: the 150 guarding beef cattle.

U. S. Grant

Maj. Genl.

Telegram received, DNA, RG 94, Generals' Papers and Books, Telegrams Received by Gen. Halleck; copies, *ibid.*, RG 393, USG Hd. Qrs. Correspondence; *ibid.*, Dept. of the Miss., Hd. Qrs. in the Field, Telegrams Received; DLC-USG, V, 4, 5, 7, 8, 9, 88. *O.R.*, I, xvii, part 2, 55.

1. La Fayette, Tenn., on the Memphis and Charleston Railroad about thirty miles east of Memphis.
2. Rolla, Mo., about forty-five miles southwest of St. Louis. On June 30, 1862, Maj. John A. Rawlins issued Special Orders No. 124. "Brig. Gen. A. P. Hovey, Commdg 3rd Division Army of the Tenn. will send 150 men as an escort with Beef Cattle via Rolla to Moscow, the men to return as soon as they meet an escort from Gen. Sherman's command. They should take four days rations, and sufficient ammunition." Copies, DLC-USG, V, 15, 16, 82, 87; DNA, RG 393, USG Special Orders.

To Maj. Gen. Henry W. Halleck

By Telegraph from Memphis [*June*] 30th *186*[*2*]

To Maj. Gen Halleck
Gen.

Col Kinney who was captured with the train at Germantown has been paroled & permitted to return to Memphis on condition that he would return & give himself up within 60 days or effect an exchange for Col. Alex. Brown of a Tenn. Regt. captured at Island No 10—No. Regt. not given. Col Brown supposed to be at Columbus, O. or Boston, Mass. Col. Kinney says Jackson has 2 large Regts *his own & a Miss. Regt*

U. S. Grant.
Maj. Genl

Telegram received, DNA, RG 94, Generals' Papers and Books, Telegrams Received by Gen. Halleck; copies, *ibid.*, RG 393, USG Hd. Qrs. Correspondence; *ibid.*, Dept. of the Miss., Hd. Qrs. in the Field, Telegrams Received; DLC-USG, V, 4, 5, 7, 8, 9, 88. For the capture of Col. Peter Kinney, 56th Ohio, see telegrams to Maj. Gen. Henry W. Halleck, June 27, July 2, 1862. On July 3, 1862, Maj. John A. Rawlins issued Special Orders No. 127. "In pursuance of directions from Major Gen. Halleck, Commanding Dept. of the Miss., Col. Peter Kinney will report to Col. Hoffman, Superintendent of Prisoners of War, to effect his exchange." Copies, DLC-USG, V, 15, 16, 82, 87; DNA, RG 393, USG Special Orders. On July 24, Kinney wrote to USG. "Since writing you from Paducah I understand my regiment has been ordered to Helena, Ark. I now repeat the substance I wrote you, for fear you would not get my first letter. I was taken prisoner the 25th of June and promised if I could to get exchanged for Col. Alexander J. Brown, of a Tennessee regiment, who was taken prisoner at Island No. 10, and supposed to be at Columbus, Ohio, or at Boston, all of which I stated to you on my arrival at your headquarters. You immediately wrote on the subject, as I supposed from the inquiries made at the time. If it becomes necessary for me to go to Washington to effect the exchange I will do so by your permission. You will please in that event to send me a pass. My honor is at stake on this subject to surrender myself a prisoner or procure the exchange. I hope you will write me at Memphis soon, as I will remain there and wait your answer." *O.R.*, II, iv, 276–77. In writing to Secretary of War Edwin M. Stanton on Aug. 1, Kinney, then at Columbus, Ohio, stated that he had written to USG twice about his exchange, but had received no reply. *Ibid.*, p. 323. Kinney was finally exchanged on Sept. 25 for Col. William A. Quarles, 42nd Tenn. In the meantime, Col. Alexander J. Brown, 55th Tenn., brother-in-law of Col. William H. Jackson who had captured Kinney, had been exchanged for another officer. *Ibid.*, pp. 437, 556.

To Maj. Gen. Henry W. Halleck

By Telegraph from Memphis [*June*] 30th *186*[*2*]

To Maj. Gen. Halleck

There is not transportation here for the removal of troops—
orders to me were to reinforce Fitch with all of Slack's command:
this would have left nothing but a part of Wallace's Div. here;
if retained Col. Slacks Regt. here however, & sent in lieu another
Regt. to reinforce Col. Fitch: this I done to avoid superseding
Col. Fitch in the command & because Slack & his Regt. had been
employed in maintaining order in the City & could not well be
relieved—transportation can be had in a day or two.

U. S. Grant
Maj. Genl.

Telegram received, DNA, RG 94, Generals' Papers and Books, Telegrams
Received by Gen. Halleck; copies, *ibid.*, RG 393, USG Hd. Qrs. Correspondence;
ibid., Dept. of the Miss., Hd. Qrs. in the Field, Telegrams Received; DLC–USG,
V, 4, 5, 7, 8, 9, 88.

To Maj. Gen. Henry W. Halleck

Memphis, Tenn. June 30, 1862

Maj Genl H W Halleck
Corinth, Miss.
Genl

A gentleman from Arkansas who has just made his escape
from there and come up on one of our Gunboats says that Genl
Curtis has lost several foraging parties. The Texas Rangers[1]
take no prisoners. Thinks the rebel force on White river cannot
be less than 5 or 6000.[2] It is estimated by citizens at more than
double that number. The troops from Little Rock have all been
brought over to the White River.

There are some Louisiana troops, between one ~~or~~ & two thousand ~~from~~ Missouri, four or five regiments of Texas Rangers and a large number of Arkansas Conscripts. The number of the latter is estimated very large and is increasing daily.

I seriously doubt the force under Col Fitch (2200) being sufficient to effect a junction with Genl Curtis.

He cannot be reinforced from here without the troops coming from elswhere. Bands of Cotton burners are now within twelve or fifteen miles of here, destroying every thing and arresting citizens favorable to the Union. I keep the little Cavalry at my command constantly engaged but they are not sufficient for the task. My instructions to Col Fitch are such that he should not permit himself to be cut off, but he may fail in affording relief to Genl Curtis[3]

I do not doubt the entire sincerity of my informant, but I never ~~estimate~~ believe numbers to be equal to ~~that~~ what they are reported.

Same informant also says that he saw letters from men of Pikes command which said they had been ordered into Fort Smith.[4]

Very Respcty
Your Obt Servt
U. S. GRANT

Telegram, copies, DLC-USG, V, 4, 5, 7, 8, 9, 88; DNA, RG 393, USG Hd. Qrs. Correspondence; *ibid.*, Dept. of the Miss., Hd. Qrs. in the Field, Telegrams Received. *O.R.*, I, xvii, part 2, 54–55.

1. The well-known Tex. Rangers did not fight as a body in the Civil War. Several C. S. A. units attracted some of their men and several appropriated their name. Walter Prescott Webb, *The Texas Rangers* (Boston and New York, 1935), p. 219; *O.R.*, I, xiii, 71; *ibid.*, I, xvii, part 2, 835.

2. C. S. A. Maj. Gen. Thomas C. Hindman reported that his peak force for the defense of the White River had been 2,000; at the time USG wrote, however, 1,500 men had been detached to oppose the advance of Maj. Gen. Samuel R. Curtis. *Ibid.*, I, xiii, 37.

3. See letter to Col. Graham N. Fitch, June 26, 1862.

4. Albert Pike, born in Mass. in 1809, settled in Ark. as a young man and embarked upon a varied career as schoolteacher, newspaper editor, lawyer, soldier, poet, and politician. Sent as a commissioner to negotiate with the tribes of Indian Territory, he was later assigned to command the territory as brig. gen. When

ordered to Fort Smith, Ark., on July 8, 1862, Pike complained that this violated
a pledge not to remove his troops from Indian Territory, and he began a quarrel
with his superiors which terminated in his resignation. *DAB*, XIV, 593–94;
O.R., I, xiii, 856–58.

To Maj. Gen. Henry W. Halleck

———

Memphis [*June*] 30th [*1862*]

MAJ. GENL. HALLECK

I have no Engineer Officer to locate or direct the work of
fortifying the City as directed. Can't you send one?

U. S. GRANT
Maj Gen

Telegram received, DNA, RG 94, Generals' Papers and Books, Telegrams
Received by Gen. Halleck; copies, *ibid.*, RG 393, USG Hd. Qrs. Correspondence;
DLC-USG, V, 4, 5, 7, 8, 9, 88. See telegram to Maj. Gen. Henry W. Halleck,
July 2, 1862.

To Maj. Gen. Henry W. Halleck

———

BY TELEGRAPH FROM Memphis [*June*] 30th 186[*2*]

TO MAJ. GEN. HALLECK

There are 7 boats here that are ready & *could be got in so in
a few hours capable.* The Q. M.s reports of carrying 5000 men:
my force here is four Regts. of I[n]fy. numbering 1,879 men four
batteries of Artillery 322 men: seven Cos. of Cav. 260 men:
there is one Regt. of Infy. 429 men & 5 Cos. of Cav. 382 men at
Germantown, 1 Regt. of Infy. of 525 men, 1 Compy. of Cav. [45]
men at Bolivar—at Grand Junction, 3 Regts. of Infy. 1700 belonging to Wallaces Div—the only remaining Regts here would
be Col. Slacks Regt. 699 men. Col. Fitch has hardly left the

mouth of White River or cannot be far up: if the troops from Germantown can march in 6 hours, those from Grand Junction with cars can come safely by running a hand car in advance of train. There is also here the 24th Indiana Regt., 536 men strong, just starting for white River—this is a Regt. ordered yesterday & not got off. A part of the Cav. put down as here is out of the city on duty but could be got back as early as the troops from Germantown: of the Infy. one Compy. has gone down the River to give safe conduct to a barge & a detail of 150 men to guard beef cattle for Sherman's command. They have gone via Rolla.

U. S. GRANT

Maj Genl

Telegram received, DNA, RG 94, Generals' Papers and Books, Telegrams Received by Gen. Halleck; copies, *ibid.*, RG 393, USG Hd. Qrs. Correspondence; *ibid.*, Dept. of the Miss., Hd. Qrs. in the Field, Telegrams Received; DLC-USG, V, 4, 5, 7, 8, 9, 88. *O.R.*, I, xvii, part 2, 56. On June 30, 1862, Maj. Gen. Henry W. Halleck twice telegraphed to USG. "Have you steamers at Memphis to transport ~~the part of~~ Wallace's division, except the part at Grand Junction, to Cairo or St Louis?" ALS (telegram sent), DNA, RG 108, Telegrams Sent; telegram received, *ibid.*, RG 393, Dept. of the Mo., Telegrams Received. *O.R.*, I, xvii, part 2, 55. "Report immediately the effective force under your command at Memphis & vicinity, exclusive of Sherman's & Hurlbut's divisions. Also, the parts of Wallace's division which can be concentrated at Memphis. I dont want comments, but facts. The defeat of McClellan at Richmond has created a stampede at Washington, & I want facts as to position of troops & how they can be concentrated in order to enable me to answer questions & carry out orders. State precisely how many troops you have transportation to Cairo from Memphis for —I want exact facts." ALS (telegram sent), DNA, RG 108, Telegrams Sent; telegram received, *ibid.*, RG 393, Dept. of the Mo., Telegrams Received. *O.R.*, I, xvii, part 2, 55.

On June 30, Halleck received a garbled telegram from Secretary of War Edwin M. Stanton requesting that 25,000 troops be sent to Washington if operations in Tenn. would not be harmed. Halleck immediately began to arrange to send the troops of Maj. Gen. John A. McClernand and Maj. Gen. Lewis Wallace, while protesting that Tenn. might be lost. After receiving clarifying telegrams from Stanton and President Abraham Lincoln the next day, Halleck cancelled all plans to send troops. *Ibid.*, pp. 42–61 *passim*; Lincoln, *Works*, V, 295, 300–1, 305.

To Col. John C. Kelton

————

Corinth June 30/62

Col. J. C. Kelton A. D. C.

Will you be kind enough to telegraph me ~~accurately~~ occasional[ly] the latest news from Richmond & from other points where Military operations going on.

U. S. Grant
Maj. Gen.

Telegram received, DNA, RG 94, Generals' Papers and Books, Telegrams Received by Gen. Halleck; copy, *ibid.*, RG 393, Dept. of the Miss., Hd. Qrs. in the Field, Telegrams Received.

To Maj. Gen. Henry W. Halleck

————

By Telegraph from Memphis [*July*] 1st 1862

To Maj Genl Halleck

My particular anxiety has been to get cavalry to capture & drive off Jackson[1] Forrest[2] & Jeff Thompson bands that are depredating so much[3]   the only danger I fear is a raid being made into the city & burning part of it[4]   Breckenridge is said to be south east of here but I do not know this to be so & do not credit his being nearer than abbeyville[5]   the wagon train sent in by Gen'l Sherman was attacked yesterday afternoon at Rising Sun[6]   a stampede among the mules ensued & eight of the wagons were broken to pieces & the mules run into the woods & were not recovered   the rebels were whipped off with a loss of 13 killed & wounded picked up on the field & twelve (12) wounded men reported to have been carried to a neighboring House but were not seen by our men   loss on our side three wounded & eight teamsters & one wagon master missing   I telegraphed this to Gen'l Sherman on the statement of a wagon master who came through   his statement only differs from the Col Comdg escort not knowing much about the rebel loss[7]   I have detailed at River a Reg't of Wallaces Division ordered to reinforce Col Fitch   expecting an answer to my Telegraph of last night

U S GRANT

Maj Genl

Telegram received, DNA, RG 94, Generals' Papers and Books, Telegrams Received by Gen. Halleck; copies, *ibid.*, War Records Office, Union Battle Reports; *ibid.*, RG 393, Dept. of the Miss., Hd. Qrs. in the Field, Telegrams Received; *ibid.*, USG Hd. Qrs. Correspondence; DLC-USG, V, 4, 5, 7, 8, 9, 88. *O.R.*, I, xvii, part 1, 14. See letter to Officer Commanding Detachment, 58th Ohio, July 1, 1862.

1. See letter to Maj. Gen. Henry W. Halleck, June 26, 1862. On July 1, 1862, Maj. Gen. William T. Sherman, Coldwater, Miss., telegraphed to USG. "Arrived this morning   no infantry at Holly springs   about 800 cavalry who retreated south   large forces reported at Tallahatchee 18 miles south   I hope the escort with my wagon train protected against Jackson cavalry   am much troubled about supplies   I have asked Halleck to let me march toward Memphis & take post in front of Germantown   that is the place of mischief   I think Jackson as soon as he learned we had come in this direction must have started south toward Hernando or Tallahatchie   He could not have had more than 600 men with him" Telegram received, DNA, RG 393, Dept. of the Mo., Telegrams Received.

2. Born in humble circumstances in middle Tenn., Nathan B. Forrest rose to a position of wealth through investments in land and slaves. After serving in the city government of Memphis, Forrest enlisted as a private in June, 1861, in the 7th Tenn. Cav., and was later elected col., 3rd Tenn. Cav. On June 9, 1862, shortly after recovering from a severe wound received at the battle of Shiloh, he was ordered to assume command of cav. in north Ala. and middle Tenn. *O.R.*, I, x, part 2, 602; John Allen Wyeth, *That Devil Forrest: The Life of General Nathan Bedford Forrest* (New York, Evanston, and London, 1959), pp. 67–68.

3. USG had exhibited previous concern about the absence of cav. in his command. See telegrams to Maj. Gen. Henry W. Halleck, June 26, 27, 30, 1862. On July 1, Halleck telegraphed to USG. "All accounts confirm the belief that no large force of the enemy has moved west towards Memphis: on the contrary they are concentrating east of the Tombigbee and opening roads to Marietta. I have very little doubt that they are preparing to attack us somewhere between here & Decatur. You will percieve the absurdity under these circumstances of moving more of our troops west." ALS (telegram sent), DNA, RG 108, Telegrams Sent; copies, *ibid.*, RG 393, Dept. of the Mo., Telegrams Sent; *ibid.*, USG Hd. Qrs. Correspondence; *ibid.*, Dept. of the Mo., Telegrams Received; DLC-USG, V, 4, 5, 7, 8, 9. *O.R.*, I, xvii, part 2, 60.

4. Some time in July, Maj. John A. Rawlins wrote to Col. John M. Thayer, 1st Neb., Memphis. "I am instructed by Maj.-Gen. U. S. Grant to say that it is reported there is a fire in the North part of the city. You will ascertain if such is the fact, and if so, have your forces of all arms in readiness to quell any outbreak that may occur." *The Collector*, LVIII, 4 (June–July, 1945), 123.

5. Maj. Gen. John C. Breckinridge commanded the Reserve Corps, Army of the Miss. Reports received by Brig. Gen. William S. Rosecrans placed Breckinridge on the way to Holly Springs on June 27. *O.R.*, I, xvii, part 1, 13.

6. Morning Sun, Tenn., about twenty-five miles northeast of Memphis.

7. On June 30, an escort under Col. William Mungen, 57th Ohio, skirmished with cav. under the command of C. S. A. Maj. William L. Duckworth. On July 1, USG forwarded a preliminary account of the skirmish to Halleck which Capt. J. Condit Smith, Moscow, Tenn., had telegraphed to Sherman. "The following dispatch just received   Maj Gen Sherman. Your train has arrived with a loss of eight teams & drivers & one wagon master. They were attacked at a place called Sunset about four oclock yesterday   the teams that were lost run off breakin[g] everything to pieces & the mules run into woods   The Infantry escor[t] killed & wounded a few of the guerrallas & got some guns   four horses were also lost on our side   I will not let this train go back until a sufficient escort can be sent with them   Inform Gen'l Halleck"   Telegram received, DNA, RG 94, Generals' Papers and Books, Telegrams Received by Gen. Halleck; copy, *ibid.*, War Records Office, Union Battle Reports. On July 5, Smith telegraphed to USG, in answer to an inquiry by Rawlins, that Mungen had arrived safely with his train at Germantown, Tenn. Telegram received, *ibid.*, RG 393, Dept. of the Mo., Telegrams Received. On July 22, USG forwarded Mungen's report, dated July 5, together with Sherman's endorsement, dated July 9, to hd. qrs., Dept. of the Miss. AES, *ibid.*, RG 94, War Records Office, Union Battle Reports. *O.R.*, I, xvii, part 1, 14–17. On July 5, Col. Thomas Jordan issued General Orders No. 93 for Gen. Braxton Bragg. "On the 30th ultimo another detachment, under the command of Major Duckworth, in the same vicinity, dashed upon the enemy's pickets and killed 6 and captured 8, with slight casualty to his own command." *Ibid.*, p. 12.

To Maj. Gen. Henry W. Halleck

By Telegraph from Memphis [*July*] 1st *1862*

To Maj Gen'l Halleck

I will locate the points to be fortified immediately & as soon as authorized to draw in my Cavalry now outside the city[1]   will impress negroes to work on them   there are but few negroes men in the city[2]

U S Grant
Maj Genl

Telegram received, DNA, RG 94, Generals' Papers and Books, Telegrams Received by Gen. Halleck; copies, *ibid.*, RG 393, Dept. of the Miss., Hd. Qrs. in the Field, Telegrams Received; *ibid.*, USG Hd. Qrs. Correspondence; DLC–USG,

V, 4, 5, 7, 8, 9, 88. *O.R.*, I, xvii, part 2, 60. On June 30, 1862, Maj. Gen. Henry W. Halleck had telegraphed to USG. "Secure the land side of Memphis by entrenchments & batteries as rapidly as possible. You can impress negroes for that purpose." ALS (telegram sent), DNA, RG 108, Telegrams Sent; copies, *ibid.*, RG 393, Dept. of the Mo., Telegrams Sent; *ibid.*, Telegrams Received; *ibid.*, USG Hd. Qrs. Correspondence; DLC-USG, V, 4, 5, 7, 8, 9. *O.R.*, I, xvii, part 2, 56. See telegrams to Maj. Gen. Henry W. Halleck, June 27, 30, 1862.

1. USG had placed much of his cav. force on the Memphis and Charleston Railroad between Memphis and Germantown. See telegrams to Maj. Gen. Henry W. Halleck, June 29, 30, July 1, 1862.

2. It may be that the reason for the absence of Negroes in Memphis at this time was the policy followed by Col. James R. Slack, commander at Memphis before USG, of returning Negroes who escaped from their masters to Memphis. *Chicago Tribune*, June 24, 1862; Gerald M. Capers, Jr., *The Biography of a River Town: Memphis, Its Heroic Age* (Chapel Hill, 1939), p. 159. It may also be that some of the Negroes Flag Officer David G. Farragut had put to work digging a canal across the peninsula of land opposite Vicksburg had come from near Memphis, although most appear to have come from plantations along the lower Mississippi. *New York Herald*, July 9, 1862. On July 6, U.S. troops captured a large number of Negroes near Memphis, who belonged to southerners engaged in burning cotton, and set them to work on the fortifications. *Chicago Tribune*, July 9, 1862.

To Col. William S. Hillyer

Memphis, July 1, 1862.

The AVALANCHE can continue, by the withdrawal of the author of the obnoxious article under the caption of "Mischief Makers," and the editorial allusion to the same.

U. S. Grant, Maj. General.

Memphis Avalanche, July 2, 1862. The clash between USG and the *Memphis Avalanche* began with an editorial, "The Cup of Aloes," which condemned "unconscientious satraps" of both North and South for mistreating civilians. *Ibid.*, June 27, 1862. On June 28, 1862, Col. William S. Hillyer wrote to the editors of the *Memphis Avalanche*. "The editorial in your paper this morning entitled 'The Cup of Aloes,' is exceedingly objectionable. No criticism of the acts of the military authorities of the United States will be permitted in the press of Memphis. Every officer and private of the army is responsible to his military superiors for his official acts, and not to the press or people of Memphis. To these superiors, all complaints of improper or illegal acts can be made, and such complaints will receive respectful consideration and a just adjudication. But it is not the purpose of the military authorities to have their movements guided by the opinions of men, to say the least, of *inexperienced* loyalty. You will not repeat the offense." *Ibid.*, June 28, 1862.

The article "Mischief Makers" appeared in the form of an anonymous letter. "Men whose courage and zeal have reached a red heat only after the Federal occupation of our city, can well afford to restrain the present exhibition of a furious temper, since an exemplary prudence comports so well with that patient self-control which has hitherto kept them from joining the army. . . . In common with all cities, we have here not a few who would fatten on the public calamities, and who are capable of embracing a time of distress to satiate their malice towards individuals. Like the incendiary who applies the torch to combustible materials for the purpose of plunder, some of these men are now seeking to approach the military authorities with the intent of satifying grudges which, in times past, they had not the manhood to redress. . . . We have nearly all spoken, and written, and labored, against the United States Government. Most of us have given our money, and our influence—ay, and our property too, with our own sons and brothers to aid the Confederate cause. We did it because we chose to do it, and the man who should shrink from the honest confession before any tribunal, would render himself infamous. . . . No man out of the army deserves to live, who is base enough to act the part of a *spy* and *informer*, in this hour, and such men may well beware! Whatever may be their impunity now, there may be a day of reckoning with those they would oppress. The wheel of fortune may turn over—and what then will be the fruits of this system of crimination and recrimination, and cowardly vengeance, inaugurated by the false and traitorous informer?" *Ibid.*, June 30, 1862. The article was supported by an editorial advising the provost marshal to require that all information leading to arrests be put in writing, be sworn to and signed. *Ibid.* On July 1, Hillyer wrote to the *Memphis Avalanche*. "You will suspend the further publication of your paper. The spirit with which it is conducted is regarded as both incendiary and treasonable, and its issue cannot longer be tolerated. This order will be strictly observed from the time of its reception." *Ibid.*, July 2, 1862. In response to the orders of USG and Hillyer, Wills, Bingham and Co. sold the newspaper to B. D. Nabers and R. Hough, who changed the name to *Memphis Bulletin* and announced their intention to comply with Hillyer's Special Orders No. 10, July 3. "No newspaper will be permitted to be published within this district, unless the editors and proprietors thereof shall first take an oath that they will bear true allegiance to the Government of the United States of America, and that they will support the Constitution and laws thereof, and disclaim or renounce all allegiance to the so-called Confederate States. Local Provost Marshals will see that this order is strictly enforced." *Memphis Bulletin*, July 4, 1862.

To Officer Commanding Detachment, 58th Ohio

Head Quarters, Dist. of West Ten.
Memphis, July 1st 1862

OFFICER COMD.G
DETACHMENT 58TH OHIO [.].A VOLS
MEMPHIS TEN.

You will take all the well men of your command except suffi-cient to care for the sick, all the transportation of the regiment here and the camp & Garrison equipage of the regiment, and hold yourself in readiness to accompany the train leaving here on the 3d and join your regiment at Germantown.

Should there be more teams than are required to convey the camp & Garrison equipage you will load the balance with forage. Such rations as are now on hand will be taken and if not enough for five days sufficient will be drawn to make that amount.

Each team must take also five days forage of grain should there be no wagons exclusively for that purpose.

respectfully
U. S. GRANT
Maj. Gen. Com

P. S. Lieut. J. B. Wilson[1] will instruct what hour the train will leave and where you will meet.

U. S. GRANT

ALS, Concordia Historical Society, St. Louis, Mo. The commander of the 58th Ohio at this time was Lt. Col. Ferdinand F. Rempel, but the detachment com-mander is not known.

1. 1st Lt. Jesse B. Wilson, Harrisburg, Ill., Co. K, 6th Ill. Cav., was mus-tered in on Jan. 9, 1862.

To Henry Wilson

————

Memphis, July 1st 1862

Hon. H. Wilson
U. S. Senator
Washington D. C.
Sir:

Excuse the liberty I take in addressing you, a stranger to me except through your public acts, on a subject of no interest to my self but of some importance to the public service. It is relative to the confirmation of some of the nominations for the appointment of Brigadier Generals.

As commanding officer in some of the important engagements in the West my opportunities have been good for judging of the merits of at least Division & Brigade Commanders. With a full knowledge of their merits as military men I most earnestly recommend the confirmation of Brig. Gens. Morgan L. Smith,[1] J. M. Thayer[2] and Calvin C. Marsh.[3]

All these officers have commanded Brigades, in action, and have farely won the promotion.

I do not ask this as a personal favor to myself but that the public good may be subserved and honest merit rewarded.

There are no doubt many Colonels fully deserving of like promotion but these have come directly under my observation and have been nominated.

I might add that the two first mentioned commanded Brigades at Fort Donelson and continuously ever since.

I am sir, very respectfully
your obt. svt.
U. S. Grant
Maj. Gen.

ALS, RPB. Henry Wilson, born in poverty at Farmington, N. H., worked as a laborer, artisan, and teacher until he amassed enough capital to finance his own shoe factory. An early opponent of slavery, he was active in Mass. politics as a Whig and Free Soiler. He began serving in the U.S. Senate in 1855, and, at the time USG wrote to him, was chairman of the Committee on Military Affairs and the Militia.

    1. Col. Morgan L. Smith, 8th Mo., led a brigade in the campaigns of Fort Donelson, Shiloh, and the siege of Corinth. For his report of operations near Corinth, see *O.R.*, I, x, part 1, 841–42, 855–56. His appointment as brig. gen. was confirmed on July 16, 1862. See letter to Edwin M. Stanton, March 14, 1862.

    2. Col. John M. Thayer, 1st Neb., led a brigade at the battles of Fort Donelson and Shiloh. For his report of Shiloh, see *O.R.*, I, x, part 1, 193–95. His appointment as brig. gen. was introduced on May 17, 1862, tabled on July 16, reintroduced, and approved on March 13, 1863. *Senate Executive Journal*, XII, 299, 418; XIII, 309–10.

    3. Col. C. Carroll Marsh, 20th Ill. For his report of Shiloh, see *O.R.*, I, x, part 1, 133–37. Marsh was nominated on Jan. 19, but resigned on April 22, 1863, without having been confirmed as brig. gen. *Senate Executive Journal*, XIII, 93, 128.

To Maj. Gen. Henry W. Halleck

——————

Memphis [*July*] 2d [*1862*]

Maj Gen Halleck

    It seems that supplies for the Army from here to Lagrange must go from this place.   to render the trains secure a larger Cav. force than I now have is required. At present it is necessary to use Infy. for this duty.

U. S. Grant
Maj. Gen

Telegram received, DNA, RG 94, Generals' Papers and Books, Telegrams Received by Gen. Halleck; copies, *ibid.*, RG 393, USG Hd. Qrs. Correspondence; *ibid.*, Dept. of the Miss., Hd. Qrs. in the Field, Telegrams Received; DLC-USG, V, 4, 5, 7, 8, 9, 88. On July 1, 1862, Maj. Gen. Henry W. Halleck telegraphed to USG. "Passes to go south, except for military purposes, must come from Washington. No forces can be sent you from here. On the contrary it may be necessary to withdraw Hurlbut or Sherman & abandon the line between here & Memphis. Col Keeny will be ordered to report to Col Hoffman Supt of Prisoners of war to effect the exchange. I have no engineer officer to send you at present. It is evident that Wallace's division cannot be removed from Memphis till Sherman's or Hurlbut's is sent to that vicinity, & one is insufficient to defend the road. It is possible that we shall be obliged to abandon the rail road entirely. I will wait ~~to hear~~ for further orders from Washington. Perhaps the Secty of war may be induced to revoke his order." ALS (telegram sent), DNA, RG 108, Telegrams Sent; telegram received, *ibid.*, RG 393, Dept. of the Mo., Telegrams Received. *O.R.*, I, xvii, part 2, 60.

To Maj. Gen. Henry W. Halleck

By Telegraph from Memphis [*July*] 2d 186[2]

To Maj Gen. Halleck

Where shall I send prisoners? There are now some thirty of the White River prisoners[1] & others taken by our Cavalry.

Maj Gen U. S. Grant

Telegram received, DNA, RG 94, Generals' Papers and Books, Telegrams Received by Gen. Halleck; copies, *ibid.*, RG 393, Dept. of the Miss., Hd. Qrs. in the Field, Telegrams Received; *ibid.*, USG Hd. Qrs. Correspondence; DLC-USG, V, 4, 5, 7, 8, 88. *O.R.*, II, iv, 115. On July 3, 1862, Maj. Gen. Henry W. Halleck telegraphed to USG. "Deliver to enemy's line all your prisioners (not officers), except those guilty of barbarously treating our men, on parole not to serve till exchanged. As already stated no more troops can be sent to Memphis at present. The enemy attacked Boonville yesterday, but was driven back with considerable loss. Please rescind your [or]der about districts. They [can]not be formed yet. As order to send troops to Washington is suspended, do all in your power to reinforce Curtis. It is very possible that he has moved to Madison to open communication with Memphis; if not, he is going down east side of White River. We have no telegraphic communication with him, & can only guess where he is. Do all you can to ascertain." ALS (telegram sent), DNA, RG 108, Telegrams Sent; telegram received, *ibid.*, RG 393, Dept. of the Mo., Telegrams Received. *O.R.*, I, xvii, part 2, 67; (incomplete) *ibid.*, II, iv, 118. On July 5, Maj. John A. Rawlins issued Special Orders No. 129. "Brig. Gen. Hovey will detail at once from his command an intelligent Officer with six mounted Soldiers to report to Col. T. Lyle. Dickey, Commander of Post at Post Head Quarters for orders, touching the sending of certain paroled prisoners of War to the lines of the enemy." Copies, DLC-USG, V, 15, 16, 82, 87; DNA, RG 393, USG Special Orders.

1. The White River prisoners were taken by Col. Graham N. Fitch on the White River expedition. See *O.R.*, I, xiii, 103–19; *Chicago Tribune*, June 22, 23, 25, 29, 1862; telegrams to Maj. Gen. Henry W. Halleck, June 24, 25, 26, 30, 1862.

To Flag Officer Charles H. Davis

———

Head Quarters, Dist. of West Tenn.,
Memphis, July 2, 1862.

Flag Officer C. H. Davis,
Comdg. Western Flotilla,
Off Vicksburg, Miss.
Sir:

Yours, also letter from Flag Officer Farragut, is just received. The latter I will telegraph immediately to Gen. Halleck.

Troops I know cannot be sent from here immediately, certainly not until they can be brought from points further east. If the cheering news just arrived however should prove true I do not doubt but that sufficient forces could be spared from La Grange and Corinth to possess and hold Vicksburg. The information is that McClellan has taken Richmond with 50,000 prisoners.[1]

I am, very respectfully
Your obt. svt.
U. S. Grant,
Maj. Gen.

Copy, DNA, RG 45, Area 5, Letters Supplied by Capt. Charles H. Davis, May 14, 1902. On June 30, 1862, Flag Officer Charles H. Davis wrote to USG. "I have received a communication from Commodore Farragut, saying that it will be absolutely necessary to have additional troops to occupy Vicksburgh, after the batteries are silenced. May I request you to communicate this to General Halleck." Copy, *ibid.*, Letterbook of Charles H. Davis. *O.R.* (Navy), I, xxiii, 232–33; *ibid.*, I, xviii, 593. On July 3, Maj. Gen. Henry W. Halleck answered in a telegram to Flag Officer David G. Farragut. "The scattered & weakened Condition of my forces renders it impossible for me at the present to detach any troops to cooperate with you on Vicksburg   probably I shall be able to do so as soon as I can get my troops more concentrated. this may delay the clearing of the River but its accomplishment will be certain in a few weeks—Allow me to congratulate you on your great success"   Telegram received, DNA, RG 45, Area 5, Letters Supplied by Capt. Charles H. Davis, May 14, 1902.

1. On July 2, USG received a message from telegraph operator Duncan T. Bacon "that Richmond is ours with 50000 prisoners   McClellan cut his way through the swamps before Richmond"   Telegram received, *ibid.*, RG 393,

Dept. of the Mo., Telegrams Received. See telegram to Col. John C. Kelton, June 30, 1862. On July 4, Brig. Gen. M. Jeff Thompson wrote to USG. "I send this letter by George Allen, a private of Compy B, 24th Indianna Vol. U. S. A., who was picked up by one of my Missourians near the Mississippi River on Tuesday last—I have paroled him until exchanged, and hope you will send some one of our men for him, and believe that even if you pick out the poorest in the lot—that I will cheat you in the trade—We have neither Whiskey nor Ice to have a very gay celebration to day, neither have we powder to waste—but the news from Richmond makes us jovial enough—" ALS, DNA, RG 393, District of West Tenn., Letters Received. *O.R.*, II, iv, 124.

To Col. Benjamin H. Grierson

———

Head Quarters, Dist. of West Ten.
Memphis, July 2d 1862

Col. B. H. Grierson
Comd.g U. S. Forces
Germantown, Ten.
Col.

It will be necessary to retain your command where they are for the present. The troops at LaFayette and Moscow[1] will be geting their supplies from here for the present and it will be the duty of your command to give them all the protection possible on both sides of Germantown.[2]

Try to keep yourself posted as to the position of the rebel cavalry and the time trains will be passing. When necessary move your forces to strengthen the escorts accompanying them.[3]

Send your wagons with the first train coming this way for your camp equipage and supplies.[4]

Peacibly disposed citizens are not to be annoyed but those undoubtedly giving information to the enemy may be arrested and sent here with the charges against them stated. In cases of arrest take no private property from the prisoner except fire arms.

Respectfully &c
U. S. Grant
Maj. Gen. Com

ALS, deCoppet Collection, NjP. See letter to Maj. Gen. John A. McClernand, June 24, 1862, note 1.

1. Moscow, Tenn., on the Memphis and Charleston Railroad about thirty-eight miles east of Memphis.

2. Col. Thomas Worthington, 46th Ohio, commanded at La Fayette, and Col. Ralph P. Buckland, 72nd Ohio, commanded at Moscow. On July 1, 1862, Buckland telegraphed to USG. "I have 60 Teams belonging to Gen Hurbuts Div with an escort of 10 cavalry & 150 Infantry   the state line road at this end is clea[r]   if you consider it safe I will send it as far as Germantown tomorrow" Telegram received, DNA, RG 393, Dept. of the Mo., Telegrams Received. On July 1, Buckland again telegraphed to USG. "Genl Sherman left for Holly Springs at two P M yesterday under orders from Genl Halleck to act in concert with Genl Rosecrans going from Corinth via Ripley   One Regiment left here   Train of sixty wagons with one Regiment of Infantry left for Memphis at 4 a m   heard nothing from it   Suppose it safe as Oakland is only five miles from the road   the train   Rebel cavalry attacked Col Worthington at Lafayette last evening   all queit this morning   Genl Sherman will reach Holly Springs this morning" Telegram received, *ibid.*

3. On July 2, Maj. Gen. William T. Sherman, in whose district both La Fayette and Moscow were located, telegraphed to USG. "I have positive knowledge that Jacksons Cavalry have passed to the South of the Talahatchie where there is an Infantry force   Nothing at Holly Springs   have not yet yet heard from Hamiltons Division which ought to have been here from Corinth since yesterday Have heard of the attack on my train   ~~They~~ am satisfied with the result—They wont try it again at this point   I cover nearly the whole road east of Germantown I will take in the country enough Mules to make good the loss by the Stampede It is going to cost much to supply us & it might be better for a time to reoccupy Lagrange and Moscow but Hallecks orders were for me to Cooperate with Hamilton   would be at Holly Springs Tuesday morning"   Telegram received, *ibid. O.R.*, I, xvii, part 2, 66.

4. On July 2, Capt. J. Condit Smith, q. m. at Moscow, telegraphed to USG. "I will send forward Hurlbuts train this P M with 350 infantry & 110 cavalry will get in Memphis tomorrow night   We must have Provisions at once & we have no resources except the Train now in Memphis   Also please send the Beef cattle with the Train" Telegram received, DNA, RG 393, Dept. of the Mo., Telegrams Received. Shortly thereafter, the telegraph operator telegraphed to USG. "Make message from Capt Smith read 210 Infantry & 135 cavalry"   Telegram received, *ibid.*

General Orders No. 60

———

Head Quarters, Dist of West. Tenn.
Memphis, July 3rd 1862.

GENERAL ORDERS NO 60.

The system of Guerilla warfare now being prosecuted by some troops organized under authority of the so called Southern Confederacy, and others without such authority, being so pernicious to the welfare of the community where it is carried on, and it being within the power of communities to suppress this system, it is ordered that wherever loss is sustained by the Government collections shall be made, of personal property, from persons in the immediate neighborhood, sympathizing with the rebellion, sufficient to remunerate the Government all loss and expense of collection.

Persons acting as Guerillas without organization, and without uniform to distinguish them from private citizens, are not entitled to the treatment of prisoners of War, when caught, and will not receive such treatment.

By order of Maj Gen U. S. Grant
JNO. A. RAWLINS
a. a. Genl.

Copies, DLC-USG, V, 12, 13, 14, 95; DNA, RG 393, USG General Orders. *O.R.*, I, xvii, part 2, 69. On July 5, 1862, Maj. Gen. Henry W. Halleck telegraphed to President Abraham Lincoln that the uneasiness among U.S. commanders and pro-Union Tennesseeans caused by the organization of guerrilla units made inadvisable the detachment of troops to reinforce the Army of the Potomac. *Ibid.*, pp. 71–72. On July 16, George R. Merritt, Senatobia, Miss., wrote to USG. "We have seen your infamous and fiendish proclamation. It is characteristic of your infernal policy. We had hoped that this war would be conducted upon principles recognized by civilized nations. But you have seen fit to ignore all the rules of civilized warfare, and resort to means which ought to, and would, make half-civilized nations blush. If you attempt to carry out your threat against the property of citizens, we will make you rue the day you issued your dastardly proclamation. If we can't act upon the principle of *lex talionis* in regard to private property, we will visit summary vengeance upon your men. You call us guerrillas, which you know is false. We are recognized by our government, and it was us who attacked your wagon-train at Morning Sun. We have twenty-three men of yours, and as soon as you carry out your threat against the citizens of the vicinity

of Morning Sun, your Hessians shall pay for it. You shall conduct this war upon proper principles. We intend to force you to do it. If you intend to make this a war of extermination, you will please inform us of it at the earliest convenience. We are ready, and more than willing, to raise the 'black flag.' There are two thousand partisans who have sworn to retaliate. If you do not retract your proclamation, you may expect to have scenes of the most bloody character. We all remember the manner in which your vandal soldiers put to death Mr. Owens, of Missouri. Henceforth our motto shall be, Blood for blood, and blood for property. We intend, by the help of God, to hang on the outskirts of your rabble, like lightning around the edge of a cloud. We don't intend this as a threat, but simply as a warning of what we intend to do, in case you pursue your disgraceful and nefarious policy toward our citizens, as marked out in your threat of recent date."
P. C. Headley, *The Life and Campaigns of General U. S. Grant* (New York, 1868), pp. 167–68.

To Maj. Gen. Henry W. Halleck

By Telegraph from Memphis [*July*] 3 1862

To Maj Gen'l H. W. Halleck
Gen'l—

There are many families who have their entire means of support south & who have been caught here by federal occupation of the City   these persons wish to go to their plantation to remain during present difficulties   Cannot discretion be left with commanding officers to let such persons return   I would resp'y refer this to the war Dep't

U S Grant
Maj Gen'l

Telegram received, DNA, RG 94, Generals' Papers and Books, Telegrams Received by Gen. Halleck; copies, *ibid.*, RG 393, USG Hd. Qrs. Correspondence; DLC-USG, V, 4, 5, 7, 8, 9, 88. On June 30, 1862, USG had telegraphed to Maj. Gen. Henry W. Halleck. "Is there any discretion left now with the Commandg. officers on the borders about passing Citizens South?   there are cases where families have been caught here, whilst their means of support are south & it would seem that they should be allowed to go home." Telegram received, DNA, RG 94, Generals' Papers and Books, Telegrams Received by Gen. Halleck; copies, *ibid.*, RG 393, USG Hd. Qrs. Correspondence; *ibid.*, Dept. of the Miss., Hd. Qrs. in the Field, Telegrams Received; DLC-USG, V, 4, 5, 7, 8, 88. On July 5, Halleck telegraphed to USG. "If you have persons in Memphis which from any motive be sent south, you can place them beyond our lines, but no passes or safeguards will be given in such cases. Such papers are often used for improper purposes, and should not be permitted in the hands of any one outside of our lines." ALS (telegram sent), DNA, RG 108, Telegrams Sent; telegram received, *ibid.*, RG 393, Dept. of the Mo., Telegrams Received.

On July 8, Maj. John A. Rawlins issued Special Orders No. 132. "All crossing of the river in skiffs or private boats is positively prohibited. Private boats crossing either way will be seized and turned into the Quartermaster's Department; owners or passengers arrested and required to take the oath of allegiance, or be placed on the Arkansas shore, and admonished not to be caught within the Federal lines again on pain of being dealt with as spies. The Navy is requested to cooperate with the Military, in the enforcement of this order." Copies, DLC-USG, V, 15, 16, 82, 87; DNA, RG 393, USG Special Orders. On July 9, Col. William S. Hillyer issued Special Orders No. 13 prohibiting the issuing of passes to persons who had not taken an oath of allegiance. *Memphis Bulletin*, July 10, 1862.

On July 10, USG telegraphed to Halleck. "There are a great many families of Officers in the rebel army here who are very violent. Will you approve of sending them all south of our lines?" Copies, DLC-USG, V, 4, 5, 7, 8, 88; DNA, RG 393, USG Hd. Qrs. Correspondence. *O.R.*, I, xvii, part 2, 88. On the same day, Halleck telegraphed to USG. "Yes if you deem it expedient" Telegram received, DNA, RG 393, Dept. of the Mo., Telegrams Received; copies, *ibid.*, Telegrams Sent; *ibid.*, USG Hd. Qrs. Correspondence; DLC-USG, V, 4, 5, 7, 8, 88. *O.R.*, I, xvii, part 2, 88. Also on July 10, Hillyer issued Special Orders No. 14. "The constant communication between the so called Confederate army and their friends and sympathizers in the city of Memphis, despite the orders heretofore issued and the efforts to enforce them, has induced the issuing of the following order: The families now residing in the city of Memphis of the following persons are required to move South beyond our lines within five days from the date hereof: FIRST. All persons holding commissions in the so-called Confederate army, or who have voluntarily enlisted in said army, or who accompany and are connected with the same. SECOND. All persons holding office under or in the employ of the so-called Confederate Government. THIRD. All persons holding State, county, or municipal offices, who claim allegiance to said so-called Confederate Government and who have abandoned their families and gone South. Safe conduct will be given to the parties hereby required to leave, upon application to the Provost Marshal of Memphis." *Memphis Bulletin*, July 11, 1862. On July 12, Hillyer issued Special Orders No. 15. "In order that innocent, peaceable, and well disposed persons may not suffer for the bad conduct of the guilty parties coming within the purview of Special Order No. 14, dated July 10, 1862, can be relieved from the operation of said order No. 14, by signing the following parole, and producing to the Provost Marshal General or the Provost Marshal of Memphis, satisfactory guarantees that they will keep the pledge therein made: PAROLE. FIRST. I have not since the occupation of the city of Memphis by the Federal army given any aid to the so-called Confederate army, nor given or sent any information of the movements, strength or position of the Federal army to any one connected with said Confederate army. SECOND I will not during the occupancy of Memphis by the Federal army and my residing therein, oppose or conspire against the civil or military authority of the United States, and that I will not give aid, comfort, information, or encouragement to the so-called Confederate army, nor to any person cooperating therewith. All of which I state and pledge upon my sacred honor." *Ibid.*, July 12, 1862. On July 12, the *Memphis Bulletin* commented on the orders. "We direct attention to special order No. 15, published in another column. No person innocent of the offense intended to be suppressed by special order No. 14 will hesitate to subscribe their names to the prescribed parole. We understand that many innocent and helpless families are greatly excited by these orders, but we assure them that all such fears are groundless. Improper correspondence with the Confederate army must be stopped. We know the ladies think it hard that any restrictions should be imposed upon them, but they must remember that civil war is very inconvenient business, and we venture to advise them to yield gracefully to the manifold hardships incidental to the present state of affairs." *Ibid.*

On July 14, Brig. Gen. M. Jeff Thompson wrote to USG from Senatobia, Miss. "Upon my return from Grenada this day, I find a copy of your Special Order No 14—of July 10th ordering the families of certain parties therein named to leave your lines within five days. If, General you intend to carry this order into effect, which we, of course, presume you will, the cause of humanity will require that you make some arrangement with us, by which the helpless women and children who will thus be turned out of doors, can be provided for: for you must well know, by this time, that nine tenths of the people of Memphis come under your ban, for there is scarcely a respectable family in that city, who have not a Father, Husband or Brother in our Army, or are the Widows and orphans of those who have fallen bravely fighting for our cause—The present terminus of the Mississippi & Tennessee Rail Road is at Cold Water Station, which is thirty four miles from Memphis and our regular lines are on the stream of the same name, near the station. We do not know where your regular lines are, and therefore ask that you will please define some point, in a Southerly direction from Memphis, to which the Fathers, Husband[s,] Brothers, Sons, or friends of the exiles can go in safety to meet them, or that you will extend the time for leaving, as it is not possible that the number covered by your order can get transportation to Cold Water, within the time granted—and I would not for an instant suppose that you propose that the little feet that will thus be driven from their homes, and birthspots should plod the weary distance of thirty miles   At the same time, General, that I make this appeal to you, I feel it my duty to remark, that you must not, for a moment suppose, that the thousands who will be utterly unable to leave, and the many who will thus be forced to take the hateful oath of allegiance to a despised Government, are to be thus converted into loyal citizens of the United States or weaned from their affection for our glorious young Confederacy—and while to 'threaten' were unsoldierly, yet to '*warn*' is kindness and therefore, General, I would tell you to beware of the curses and oaths of vengence, which the Fifty Thousand brave Tennesseeans, who are still in our Army, will register in Heaven, against the persecutor of helpless old men, women, and children, and the *General who cannot guard his own lines*   The bearer of the Flag, and of this letter Capt Edward E. Porter C. S. A. is authorized to agree with you upon the point asked in the foregoing." ALS, DNA, RG 393, Dept. of Kan., Unentered Letters Received. *O.R.*, I, xvii, part 2, 98–99. On July 15, Brig. Gen. Alvin P. Hovey, then in command at Memphis, forwarded the letter to USG, explaining that he had taken "the liberty of opening it and sending a reply." ALS, DNA, RG 393, Dept. of Kan., Unentered Letters Received. *O.R.*, I, xvii, part 2, 98. On July 16, Hovey wrote to Thompson. "I have yours of the 14th. inst in relation to Special Order No. 14, heretofore issued by Major Genl. Grant.

I herewith send you Special Order No. 15, which considerably modifies the order to which you allude.—You will permit me to say that your sympathetics are entirely out of place, as truth and history must record the fact that the Southern people residing in localities where both of our Armies have been camped, prefer the continuity of the 'Northern invaders' to the protection of the Southern Chivalry—You are too well versed in the science of War, to be ignorant of the fact that these orders are far more mild than could have been expected after the treatment that helpless Union families have received at the hands of rebels in this city. —Add to this the fact that a large part of all the information received by you, can be traced directly through the families excluded by these orders, and your application for sympathy in their behalf is somewhat amusing.—The great error that the Federal Officers have committed during this war has been their over kindness to a vindictive and insulting foe. Your threats and intimations of personal danger to Genl Grant are in bad taste and should be carefully revised before publication; whether he 'can guard his own lines' the history of the battles of Shiloh and Donelson will fully show;—Should any families embraced within the orders above alluded to, be obstinate and refuse to comply with order 15, they shall be escorted to the distance of ten miles from this City to such points as they may request." LS, DNA, RG 393, Dept. of Kan., Unentered Letters Received. *O.R.*, I, xvii, part 2, 99. On July 15, Thompson wrote a letter to the editors of the *Memphis Appeal*, then published in Grenada, Miss., enclosing a copy of his letter of July 14 to USG. "Knowing the great anxiety which will prevail among the citizens of Memphis who are now in our army, when they see the order of Gen. Grant, it may be well to let them know that the matter is being attended to, and if the order is carried out, (which I now doubt, as no one has yet arrived here who left Memphis upon the order,) that all that human energy can do to relieve the exiles shall be done. Mr. Howard, of Memphis, has tendered me a thousand dollars as his quota, if necessary, to provide for them, and there are doubtless other patriots near at hand to tender sufficient means to alleviate their wants. Let the brave Memphians and Tennesseeans stand firm at their posts, wherever they are—Northern Mississippi is filled with their friends, who will see that no evil befall their loved ones, if mortal power can avert it. I have sent into Memphis a flag of truce with the following letter, by Capt. Ed. E. Porter, C. S. A., and hope that satisfactory arrangements will be made." *Memphis Appeal*, July 16, 1862.

To Maj. Gen. Henry W. Halleck

Memphis July 3rd 1862

MAJ GENL H W HALLECK
CORINTH, MISS
GENL.

So well satisfied am I from information received, and which I telegraph herewith, that I deem it my duty in the absence of instructions to dispatch to Col Fitch to take no risks in reaching Genl Curtis

It is impossible to sufficiently reinforce him from here ~~sufficiently~~ to insure the success of the expedition.

Very Respcty
U. S. Grant

Telegram, copies, DLC-USG, V, 4, 5, 7, 8, 9, 88; DNA, RG 393, USG Hd. Qrs. Correspondence. *O.R.*, I, xiii, 118–19. See following telegram.

To Maj. Gen. Henry W. Halleck

By Telegraph from Memphis [*July*] 4th *186*[*2*]

To Maj Gen. Halleck
Gen.

I have completed arrangements by which I think information may be got from Gen Curtis & which will be reliable if successful   in conversation with the gentleman who brought the information, telegraphed yesterday,[1] I find there is a good wagon road from opposite here to Batesville by the way of the Military Road 13 miles thence by Berry's Ferry over the St Francis, on to Jacksonport & Batesville:[2] my impression would be in favor of this Route rather than Steamers up White River to Supply Gen Curtis. In the City one or two teams per Reg.t could supply troops using the balance as a supply train for Curtis Army. I am not prepared to say how many teams this would give but will ascertain immediately.

U. S. Grant
Maj. Gen.l

Telegram received, DNA, RG 94, Generals' Papers and Books, Telegrams Received by Gen. Halleck; copies, *ibid.*, RG 393, Dept. of the Miss., Hd. Qrs. in the Field, Telegrams Received; *ibid.*, USG Hd. Qrs. Correspondence; DLC-USG, V, 4, 5, 7, 8, 9, 88.

1. On July 3, 1862, USG telegraphed to Maj. Gen. Henry W. Halleck. "The following dispatch was left by a gentleman that can be vouched for, and who has just returned from Arkansas." Copy, *ibid.*, V, 88.

2. The road went west from a point directly across the Mississippi River from Memphis to a point on the St. Francis River, about thirty-five miles west of Memphis. About five miles west of the St. Francis River approximately five miles north of the town of St. Francis, a second road curved in a northwesterly direction. From the crossroads to Jacksonport on the White River and on across the Black River to Batesville, also on the White River, was a distance of about seventy-five miles. The total distance from Memphis to Batesville by this route would have been about 115 miles. USG apparently selected this route because the White River had fallen so rapidly that the movement of steamboats up the river was impractical. See letters to Col. Graham N. Fitch, to Maj. Gen. Henry W. Halleck, and to Flag Officer Charles H. Davis, June 26, 1862.

To Maj. Gen. Henry W. Halleck

Memphis, July 5th 1862

Maj Genl H W Halleck
Corinth, Miss

Constant applications are made for permits to allow boats to go to different points ~~to~~ south of here after Cotton. I do not feel authorized to grant any such permits, but would ask the question if they can be given under restrictions to carry nothing from here.

Very Respcty
Your Obt Servt
U. S. Grant
Maj Genl

Telegram, copies, DLC-USG, V, 4, 5, 7, 8, 9, 88; DNA, RG 393, USG Hd. Qrs. Correspondence. On July 5, 1862, Maj. Gen. Henry W. Halleck telegraphed to USG. "Permits to trade come from the Treasury Dept   The Military will not interfere except to prevent trade in Articles which are contraband"   Telegram received, *ibid.*, Dept. of the Mo., Telegrams Received; copies, *ibid.*, Telegrams Sent; *ibid.*, USG Hd. Qrs. Correspondence; DLC-USG, V, 7, 9. On July 4, Capt. Henry S. Fitch, asst. q. m. and master of transportation, issued an order for USG. "All boats, immediately upon landing at this port, will report at this office with a copy of manifest   No boat will be permitted to go down the river, without a permit from this office." *Memphis Bulletin*, July 6, 1862. On the same day, Maj. John A. Rawlins issued Special Orders No. 128. "The Post Quartermaster will immediately seize the Steamer 'Saline,' with all the freight aboard, and hold the same subject to future orders, the 'Saline' having been engaged in unlawful trade with the states in rebellion." Copies, DLC-USG, V, 15, 16, 82, 87; DNA, RG 393, USG Special Orders.

To Maj. Gen. Henry W. Halleck

———

Memphis July 6th 1862

MAJ GENL H. W. HALLECK
CORINTH, MISS

A message is just here from Col Fitch. He reached Clarenden[1] with nine casualities from Gurrilla firing, three fatal, when the Gun boats declined proceeding further. This is below "Balls Bluff"[2] the point of greatest danger. Col Fitch has despatched two messingers to Genl Curtis informing him of his position. I will instruct him to remain where he now is, (he has dropped back to St Charles) a reasonable time to hear from Genl Curtis and if ~~the latter~~ Curtis is not making his way to Fitch, the latter to return here. ~~in~~ In the mean time I have two Separate messengers on their way to Gen. Curtis. Col Fitch says that it will be impossible to reach Jacksonport without Cavalry & Artillery & a very considerably increased superior force from what he now has. I have neither the Infy. or Cav.—the Artillery might be spared.[3] I will forward by mail Col. Fitch's dispatches.

U. S. GRANT.
Maj. Gen

Telegram received (incomplete), DNA, RG 94, Generals' Papers and Books, Telegrams Received by Gen. Halleck; copies, *ibid.*, RG 393, Dept. of the Miss., Hd. Qrs. in the Field, Telegrams Received; *ibid.*, USG Hd. Qrs. Correspondence; DLC-USG, V, 4, 5, 7, 8, 9, 88. *O.R.*, I, xiii, 119. On July 3, 1862, Col. Graham N. Fitch wrote to USG. "While at Clarenden I Started, two messengers to communicate with Genl Curtis. One left our lines at 11 A. M of 1st inst the other at Sundown Same day   Neither had any knowledge of the others absence or intentions   Only one carried any papers. They were mounted and directed to communicate with him, with all dispatch, consistent with thier own safety, So far as the latter could be consulted   They were told to notify Genl Curtis, of our presence, and that any communication would reach me at or near St Charles. That if he felt ablee and it was consistant with his duty, to aproach Duvalls Bluff's from above on any given day, as early as the 8th or 10th of this month, and would notify me of the day. I would make a demonstration with my command, from below against the Same place. in view of the fact that the country is full of the Enemys Scouts, and Guerrilla Band's the undertaking of the messenger's is extremely Hazardous Thier names Shall be given you hereafter, and for obvious reasons—I make no ~~Mention~~ allusion to them or thier errand in my dispatch." Copy, DNA, RG 393, Dept. of the Mo., Letters Received. On July 9, Fitch again wrote to USG. "In accordance with the intention expressed in my report of yesterday, the troops was formed at 6 P. M. of that day, on the river bank for the march up the Cache when a transport was reported ascending the river. The troops were held in readiness but the expedition delayed for the arrival of the transport. Upon its arival your dispatch of 6th was immediately placed in my hand, in which you state 'I have not the troops here if I were to send all I have got to reinforce you sufficiently to insure the success of the expedition up White River' 'Genl. Halleck positively refuses to send me more,' and in which you directed me to 'remain at St. Charles, awaiting a certain congency' of course the expedition up the Cache was abandoned. I deeming it useless to bring on an engagement with the enemy's troops on this side of the river with no adequate force to cross it or tho follow up any advantage to open the communication with Genl. Curtis. Your direction to remain at St. Charles I presume would not preclude my remaaining here instead of that point the length of time you indicate but in the absence of any probability of aid to follow up the expedition and in view of the low and falling water (the Gun-Boats and transports having dragged upon the bar a Mile below this place in ascending.) We will decend again to St. Charles from whence there is good water to the mouth of the river and await the time you indicate. The most remote period to which in my message to Genl. Curtis our ability to remain with the heavy transports in the river on account of the water was the 14th inst. soon after that time therefore if nothing is heard from him or any additional dispatch received from you, we shall probably leave the river for Memphis." ALS, Curtis Papers, IaHA. Between the time that USG wrote on July 6 and Fitch received his letter on July 9, Fitch had written two more letters to USG explaining his situation and outlining possible future troop movements. July 6, copies, *ibid.*; DNA, RG 393, Dept. of the Mo., Letters Received. July 8, copy, *ibid.*, RG 94, War Records Office, Dept. of the Mo.

1. Clarendon, Ark., on the White River, about fifty-three miles east of Little Rock.

2. Devall's Bluff, Ark., on the White River, about forty-five miles east of Little Rock.

3. On July 6, Maj. John A. Rawlins issued Special Orders No. 130. "Brig. Gen. A. P. Hovey, Commdg 3rd Division, Army of the Tenn. will send one Howitzer in charge of a Commissioned Officers, with a sufficient detail from the same company to man it, to report at once to Capt. H. S. Fitch, Post. Quarter-master, to proceed on Steamer up White river. They will take with them seven days rations and sufficient ammunition." Copies, DLC-USG, V, 15, 16, 82, 87; DNA, RG 393, USG Special Orders. On July 7, Rawlins issued Special Orders No. 131. "Brig. Gen. J. M. Thayer will detail a detachment of eight men in charge of a non-commissioned officer, with guns of a long range, to report at once, to Capt. H. S. Fitch, A. Q. M. to embark on Steamer to proceed up White river, in the capacity of Sharp Shooters. They will take with them seven days rations." Copies, *ibid.*

To Maj. Gen. Henry W. Halleck

Memphis Tenn July 8 [7]/62

Maj Gen Halleck

I commenced gathering contrabands last Saturday[1] to work on fortifications   They are now at work. On account of the limited force here we are only fortifying south end of city to protect stores & our own troops.[2] Col Webster has been too unwell to push this matter & I have no other engineer.[3]

Secessionists here have news from Richmond by the South which makes them jubilant. I would like to hear the truth[4]

U S. Grant
Maj Gen

Telegram received (misdated July 8, 1862), DNA, RG 94, Generals' Papers and Books, Telegrams Received by Gen. Halleck; copies, *ibid.*, RG 393, USG Hd. Qrs. Correspondence; (misdated) *ibid.*, Dept. of the Miss., Hd. Qrs. in the Field, Telegrams Received; DLC-USG, V, 4, 5, 7, 8, 9. *O.R.*, I, xvii, part 2, 82.

1. July 5.
2. On July 10, Brig. Gen. Alvin P. Hovey wrote to Maj. John A. Rawlins. "There are now in the city about 200 runaway negros in the negro yards at Memphis—These men have attempted to reach our works but the 'loyal police' for the hope of reward have stopped them—Many of the negros no doubt are from rank rebels in the army and are coming in here in hopes that thier masters Treason will liberate them—Have them sent out under the Escort of the Cavalry and we will give them work on the fortifications . . . P. S. The negroe yard is on Adams Street, A & N Delap—" ALS, DNA, RG 393, District of West Tenn., Letters Received. On July 12, Col. Benjamin H. Grierson, Germantown, Tenn., wrote to USG. "I hereby report to you Ninety four Negros, which I have taken in pursuance of your instructions, received yesterday. Enclosed you will find a list of owners, and the number of negroes taken opposite their names." LS, *ibid.* See telegram to Maj. Gen. Henry W. Halleck, July 1, 1862.
3. See telegram to Maj. Gen. Henry W. Halleck, July 2, 1862. Apparently, no special orders were issued assigning Col. Joseph D. Webster to superintend the construction of fortifications and placing Col. T. Lyle Dickey in command of the post of Memphis. Special Orders No. 124, June 30, indicated that Webster was still post commander, but Special Orders No. 129, July 5, showed that Dickey had replaced him. The *Memphis Bulletin* said that Webster had been detached to take charge of constructing the fortifications. July 8, 1862.
4. On July 8, Maj. Gen. Henry W. Halleck telegraphed to USG. "McClellan has suffered severe losses, but holds his own. He is being largely reinforced. Whether troops go from this Dept is not yet positively determined. You will

therefore make no changes in the disposition of troops for the present, unless it may be to assist Genl Curtis." ALS (telegram sent), DNA, RG 108, Telegrams Sent; telegram received, *ibid.*, RG 393, Dept. of the Mo., Telegrams Received. *O.R.*, I, xvii, part 2, 82. On July 7, USG telegraphed to Halleck. "The following is the substance of a dispatch just recd. from Genl. Sherman. 'Returned to Moscow—think Cold Water the line to hold for possession of the R. R.—want McClernand to hold Grand Junction, Humboldt, Moscow and Lafayette, and Sherman's Div. to move to Germantown and Colyerville.' Shall I make the order for this disposition?" Copies, DNA, RG 393, Dept. of the Miss., Hd. Qrs. in the Field, Telegrams Received; *ibid.*, USG Hd. Qrs. Correspondence; DLC-USG, V, 4, 5, 7, 8, 9. *O.R.*, I, xvii, part 2, 79. Other copies of the telegram read "Hurlbut" instead of "Humboldt." Maj. Gen. William T. Sherman to USG, July 7, telegram received, DNA, RG 393, Dept. of the Mo., Telegrams Received; copy, *ibid.*, RG 94, Generals' Papers and Books, William T. Sherman, Telegrams Sent. *O.R.*, I, xvii, part 2, 79.

To Ellen Ewing Sherman

Memphis Ten.
July 7th 1862

Mrs. Maj. Gen. Sherman
Lancaster Ohio;
My Dear Madam,

Your letter of the 2d inst. is just this moment received.

Two weeks ago to-day on my way from Corinth Miss. to this place I passed the place where your husband was then in camp with his command. Knowing that he had been quite unwell for some time,[1] and knowing too his indefatigable zeal and energy in whatever it is his duty to do, I proposed giving him a leave then. He would not listen to it then saying that he was improving and would take good care of himself; and further that his services could not be spared at this time I felt the truth of the latter objection knowing that Gen. Shermans place would be hard to fill.

I will telegraph to the Gen. and if he will consent to a leave will have it obtained for him.[2]

Just as the above was pened a dispatch was handed me from the Gen. of this date.[3] No mention is made of his health however.

Having known Gen. Sherman for a great many years, and so favorably too, there is nothing he, or his friends for him, could ask that I would not do if it were in my power. It is to him and some other brave men like himself that I have gained the little credit awarded me, and that our cause has triumphed to the extent it has.

> very truly
> your friend
> U. S. GRANT

ALS, DLC-William T. Sherman. Ellen (Eleanor) Ewing Sherman, the daughter of Thomas Ewing, William T. Sherman's guardian, was born in Lancaster, Ohio, and grew up with the advantages of education and position which came from being the daughter of a U.S. Senator and cabinet member. She married in 1850. Concerned about the career and reputation of her husband as well as his health, during the months of June and July, 1862, she wrote to various newspapers and influential officials such as Secretary of War Edwin M. Stanton in her husband's behalf. Ellen E. Sherman to Maj. Gen. William T. Sherman, June 17, 20, 26, July 3, 1862, Sherman Family Papers, InNd. See Anna McAllister, *Ellen Ewing: Wife of General Sherman* (New York, Cincinnati, Chicago, San Francisco, 1936).

1. After the capture of Corinth, Sherman was ordered to inspect the Memphis and Charleston Railroad to Grand Junction. He found a number of locomotives, cars, and supplies which had been abandoned in the swamps west of Chewalla. Working in the swamps in hot June weather to salvage the materiel, Sherman "got a touch of malarial fever." *Memoirs of Gen. W. T. Sherman, Written By Himself* (4th ed.: New York, 1891), I, 284. On July 27, Sherman wrote to his wife. "I have been very sick, bilious from terrible head ache, pains & lassitude. for the first time in my life on a March I found myself unable to ride and had to use an ambulance—I attribute my attack to a small military cap I wore. I now have two straw hats from Memphis." ALS, Sherman Family Papers, InNd. See also Sherman to his wife, June 6, 22, 1862, *ibid.*

2. On July 7, Sherman telegraphed to USG. "Dispatch received. I am opposed to any body leaving on account of Sickness. I see the danger of loosing our whole force by this process, and prefer even to haul my sick in wagons to letting them go home. Tis so hard to come back from home. Halleck thinks the Columbus & LaGrange R. R. can supply us with Provisions   I have sent to recall my train. I have two weeks supply in camp. Memphis should be fortified. If the Report be true that McClellan is badly defeated we will have hard fighting for the Mississippi—Memphis should be secure beyond all hazards." Copy, DNA, RG 94, Generals' Papers and Books, William T. Sherman, Letters Sent. On July 9, Ellen E. Sherman wrote to her husband that she was sending a box to him and that she had written to USG on July 8 asking him to forward it. ALS, Sherman Family Papers, InNd.

3. See telegram to Maj. Gen. Henry W. Halleck, July 7, 1862, note 4.

To Maj. Gen. Henry W. Halleck

By Telegraph from Memphis [*July*] 8th 186[2]

To Maj. Gen. Halleck

I have just learned from a respectable refugee from Ark., &
who is vouched for, that a skirmish took place on Wed. or thur.[1]
between Curtis advance & some rebels in ambush between Jacksonport & Augusta.[2] On Saturday, the telegraph battery was
removed from Madison to Des Arc[3]—Such disposition was
shown in getting this off, that Curtis must have been near that
line.—the wire from Madison to Helena[4] has also been removed.
All rebel troops East of White River have been ordered to White
River returning thro' Mo. I learn that the Army at Tupello[5] is
leaving, some are going probably to cross over to Vicksburg &
a column marching northwest on the Mobile & Memphis direct
road:[6] there are said to be large No. of Missourians returning
to their homes thro' Ark. Would it not be well to destroy all
means of crossing south of here.

U. S. Grant
Maj. Gen.

Telegram received, DNA, RG 94, Generals' Papers and Books, Telegrams
Received by Gen. Halleck; copies, *ibid.*, RG 393, Dept. of the Miss., Hd. Qrs.
in the Field, Telegrams Received; *ibid.*, Dept. of the Mo., Telegrams Received;
ibid., USG Hd. Qrs. Correspondence; DLC-USG, V, 4, 5, 7, 8, 88.

    1. July 2 or 3, 1862.
    2. Augusta, Ark., on the White River near the confluence of the White and
Black rivers, about seventy-six miles northwest of Memphis; Jacksonport, Ark.,
about twenty-five miles north of Augusta on the White River. On June 17,
C. S. A. Maj. Gen. Thomas C. Hindman, Little Rock, Ark., issued General
Orders No. 17 calling upon citizens to organize guerrilla units to fight against
the U.S. Army. *Nashville Daily Union*, July 18, 1862. It is not known to which
skirmish USG's informant referred. On June 30, Maj. Gen. Samuel R. Curtis
was in Batesville preparing to move his troops to Jacksonport. *O.R.*, I, xiii, 457.
    3. Des Arc, Ark., about twenty-three miles southwest of Augusta.
    4. Helena, Ark., on the Mississippi River, about fifty-five miles southwest
of Memphis.
    5. Tupelo, Miss., on the Mobile and Ohio Railroad, about fifty miles south
of Corinth.

6. On July 5, a correspondent at Corinth reported that a former employee of the Memphis and Ohio Railroad had informed him that Gen. Braxton Bragg was in command at Tupelo with 40,000 to 50,000 troops, Maj. Gen. John C. Breckinridge had left with 30,000 troops, and all soldiers were short of clothing and provisions. *New York Herald*, July 6, 1862. On July 12, Bragg reported that he had detached 12,000 troops "to support Vicksburg and Chattanooga." This left him with only 40,000 troops. He had poor transportation, though his cav. had been able to inflict losses on the U.S. Army "in the region between Memphis, Grand Junction, and the Tallahatchie River." *O.R.*, I, xvii, part 2, 645.

To Maj. Gen. Henry W. Halleck

BY TELEGRAPH FROM Memphis [*July 9*] 186[2]

To MAJ GENL. HALLECK

I understand the Hospital at Mound City is being broken up. Cannot a portion of the furniture be ordered here?

U. S. GRANT

Maj. Genl.

Telegram received, DNA, RG 94, Generals' Papers and Books, Telegrams Received by Gen. Halleck; copies, *ibid.*, RG 393, Dept. of the Miss., Hd. Qrs. in the Field, Telegrams Received; *ibid.*, USG Hd. Qrs. Correspondence; DLC-USG, V, 4, 5, 7, 8, 88. On July 7, 1862, Brig. Gen. William K. Strong, Cairo, and the members of the Cairo Commission, George S. Boutwell, Charles A. Dana, Shelby M. Cullom, and Thomas Means, wrote to Secretary of War Edwin M. Stanton protesting the proposed closing of the Mound City hospital on the grounds that the cost of erecting a similar facility would be $100,000, while the Mound City hospital cost the government only $2,000 per year in rent. Copy, DNA, RG 107, Letters Received. On July 11, Maj. Gen. Henry W. Halleck telegraphed to USG. "Hospital at Mound City *not* to be broken up. Orders of Surgeon Genl countermanded by Secty of War." ALS (telegram sent), *ibid.*, RG 108, Telegrams Sent; telegram received, *ibid.*, RG 393, Dept. of the Mo., Telegrams Received.

To Maj. Gen. Henry W. Halleck

Memphis July 8th [9] 1862

MAJ GEN HALLECK,

A citizen of this place reliably vouched for has just returned from Mobile via Marion[1] Jackson[2] & Grenada, paying Columbus a visit. He left Mobile on the 3d inst. He says there is no large force on the Mobile & Ohio road. The largest is at Marion. At Jackson there is a large force. Between Coldwater[3] & Hernando they are collecting many troops, mostly conscripts. The whole state of Mississippi capable of bearing arms seem to be entering the army[4]

U S GRANT
Maj Gen

Telegram received, DNA, RG 94, Generals' Papers and Books, Telegrams Received in Cipher by Gen. Halleck; copies, *ibid.*, RG 393, Dept. of the Miss., Hd. Qrs. in the Field, Telegrams Received; *ibid.*, USG Hd. Qrs. Correspondence; DLC-USG, V, 4, 5, 7, 8, 88. *O.R.*, I, xvii, part 2, 87. All of USG's copies are dated July 9, 1862.

1. The word "Marion" at this point and in the fourth sentence was corrected to "Meridian" in the copy in DLC-USG, V, 88, to indicate Meridian, Miss., on the Southern Mississippi Railroad, about eighty-five miles east of Jackson.
2. Jackson, Miss., on the Southern Mississippi Railroad, about forty miles east of Vicksburg.
3. Coldwater is located about ten miles south of Hernando. It should not be confused with Maj. Gen. William T. Sherman's camp on the Coldwater River. On July 8, Sherman wrote to Maj. John A. Rawlins. "I would much prefer the concentration of our whole force on Cold Water, near where the Memphis & Holly Springs crosses, and leave but small detachments along the Road itself." ALS, DNA, RG 393, District of West Tenn., Letters Received. *O.R.*, I, xvii, part 2, 84–86.
4. On April 16, the C. S. A. Congress had passed a conscription act which covered all men between the ages of eighteen and thirty-five. Five days later, it exempted all government officials, persons employed in transportation and communication, some industrial workers, and a number of professional people. Conscripts or their substitutes were sent from local induction centers to camps of instruction, then into service. USG's assertion about the effectiveness of the act is not borne out by contemporary reports from the state. By June 14, Miss. still had no camps for conscripts in operation. As late as Aug. 18, there was some question as to whether Governor John J. Pettus would allow Miss. state troops to be used as replacements in C. S. A. armies. In fact the military activity which

made Miss. look like an armed camp was probably due to the guerrillas or partisan rangers rather than to the conscripts. Albert Burton Moore, *Conscription and Conflict in the Confederacy* (Reprint ed.: New York, 1963), pp. 13, 27, 52–53, 115–16; John K. Bettersworth, *Confederate Mississippi: The People and Policies of a Cotton State in Wartime* (Baton Rouge, 1943), pp. 64–65; *O.R.*, IV, 1, 1153.

To Maj. Gen. Henry W. Halleck

Memphis July 10th/62

MAJ. GENL. HALLECK.

I would respectfully suggest the propriety of sending to this place some seige guns for the fortifications now being built, 4 eight inch howitzers and about 6 others, say 24 pound howitzers could be advantageously located.

McAllister's Battery now at Jackson, would answer for the latter.

U S. GRANT Maj. Genl.

Telegram, copies, DNA, RG 393, Dept. of the Miss., Hd. Qrs. in the Field, Telegrams Received; *ibid.*, USG Hd. Qrs. Correspondence; DLC-USG, V, 4, 5, 7, 8, 9, 88. On July 11, 1862, Maj. Gen. Henry W. Halleck telegraphed to USG. "Capt Prime, corps of engrs. has gone to Memphis. Consult him about siege guns. They can be taken from Fort Pillow, or the Kentucky batteries near Island No 10." ALS (telegram sent), DNA, RG 108, Telegrams Sent; telegram received, *ibid.*, RG 393, Dept. of the Mo., Telegrams Received. See telegrams to Maj. Gen. Henry W. Halleck, July 1, 7, 1862.

To Brig. Gen. Alvin P. Hovey

———

Head Quarters, Dist. of West Ten.
Memphis, July 11th 1862

BRIG. GEN. A. P. HOVEY
COMD.G U. S. FORCES
MEMPHIS TEN.
GEN.

Having just this moment received a dispatch from Gen. Halleck to report forthwith to his Head Quarters you are directed to assume the command of this city including the troops at Germantown.

If convenient I would be pleased to see you this evening.

I am Gen. very respectfully
your obt. svt.
U. S. GRANT
Maj. Gen. Com

ALS, Hovey Papers, InU. On July 13, 1862, Maj. Gen. Henry W. Halleck wrote to his wife. "Two messengers were sent to me, one from the President and one from McClellan, inviting me to go to Washington and the President and Secretary of War both telegraphed me to the same effect, but I declined the invitation, knowing that the object was to involve me in the quarrel between Stanton and McClellan. One of the messengers said that I was the only man in the United States who could reconcile the present difficulties. I replied that if that was the case I was probably the only person in the United States who would have nothing to do with these Cabinet quarrels, and that I would not go to Washington if I could help it! When lo and behold, the President issues a mandate making me general-in-chief, and *ordering* me to Washington to assume command of McClellan and all the other generals of the army! In fact, putting me in General Scott's place. This is certainly a very high compliment, but I doubt very much whether I shall accept the promotion. I fear it may bring me in conflict with McClellan's friends. Everybody who knows me, knows that I have uniformly supported him, and I do not wish to be placed in a false position. Nevertheless, I must obey my orders and shall start for Washington some time next week." The two messengers were Asst. Secretary of War John Tucker and Governor William Sprague of R. I. James Grant Wilson, "Types and Traditions of the Old Army: II. General Halleck—A Memoir," *Journal of the Military Service Institution of the United States,* XXXVI, cxxxv (May–June, 1905), 556–57. See also Lincoln, *Works,* V, 308, 312–13; dispatch from Corinth, July 11, 1862, in *Missouri Republican,* July 17, 1862; telegram of Secretary of War Edwin M. Stanton to Halleck,

July 11, copy, DNA, RG 107, Telegrams Collected (Bound); *O.R.*, I, xvii, part 2, 90; *ibid.*, I, xi, part 3, 281, 293.

On July 11, Halleck telegraphed to President Abraham Lincoln. "Your orders of this date are this moment received. Genl Grant next in command is at Memphis I have telegraphed to him to immediately repair to this place—I will start for Washington the moment I can have a personal interview with Genl Grant" Telegram received, DLC-Robert T. Lincoln. *O.R.*, I, xvii, part 2, 90. On July 11, Halleck telegraphed to USG. "You will immediately repair to this place [— — —] report to these Head Qrs." ALS (telegram sent), DNA, RG 108, Telegrams Sent; telegram received, *ibid.*, RG 393, Dept. of the Mo., Telegrams Received. *O.R.*, I, xvii, part 2, 90. On July 11, USG telegraphed to Halleck. "Your telegraph just rec.d   Am I to repair alone or take my Staff?" Telegram received, DNA, RG 94, Generals' Papers and Books, Telegrams Received by Gen. Halleck; copies, *ibid.*, RG 393, Dept. of the Miss., Hd. Qrs. in the Field, Telegrams Received; *ibid.*, USG Hd. Qrs. Correspondence; DLC-USG, V, 4, 5, 7, 8, 9, 88. On July 11, Halleck replied by telegraph to USG. "This place will be your Head Quarters. You can judge for yourself" LS (telegram sent), DNA, RG 108, Telegrams Sent; telegram received, *ibid.*, RG 393, Dept. of the Mo., Telegrams Received. On the same day, USG answered Halleck by telegraph. "I leave here at 10 o'c this evening: go by Columbus." Telegram received, *ibid.*, RG 94, Generals' Papers and Books, Telegrams Received by Gen. Halleck; copy, *ibid.*, RG 393, Dept. of the Miss., Hd. Qrs. in the Field, Telegrams Received.

A newspaper report from Cairo on July 14 said that USG and his family arrived in Columbus on July 13 by steamboat. *Chicago Tribune*, July 15, 1862. USG's family, escorted by Col. Clark B. Lagow, had arrived in Memphis on July 1. *Memphis Bulletin*, July 4, 1862. On July 13, USG telegraphed to Halleck from Columbus. "Arrived here at six AM   The cars left at five." Telegram received, DNA, RG 94, Generals' Papers and Books, Telegrams Received by Gen. Halleck; copy, *ibid.*, RG 393, Dept. of the Miss., Hd. Qrs. in the Field. On July 15, Halleck telegraphed to Lincoln. "Genl Grant has just arrived from Memphis   I am in communication with Genl Buell and Gov Johnson in Tennessee   Hope to finally arrange disposition of troops and to reinforce Curtis by tomorrow, and to leave Thursday morning the seventeenth—" Telegram received, DLC-Robert T. Lincoln; copy, DNA, RG 107, Telegrams Received (Bound). See General Orders No. 62, July 17, 1862.

To Elihu B. Washburne

———

Memphis Tennessee
July 11th, 1862

Hon. E. B. Washburne
Washington City.
Sir:

Permit me to introduce to you, Mr. F. S. Richards, a citizen of Memphis, who visits Washington for the purpose of securing the position of Collector for this Port.

Mr. Richards is one of the few citizens of Memphis, who have held firm for the Union, throughout all its trials.

I feel that this class of our brethern are entitled to considerations, and most heartily recommend him to the authorities of Washington.

Very respectfully
your obt. svt.
U. S. Grant

Copy, DLC-Andrew Johnson. On July 8, 1862, James S. Wilkins and twelve other citizens of Memphis petitioned President Abraham Lincoln to appoint F. S. Richards surveyor of the port of Memphis. On July 11, USG endorsed this petition. "Mr F. S Richards. has been represented to me by the best men of this city of Union proclivities, as one who has sustained the Federal Government in all its trials and as being a man of fine business qualifications and integrity." Copy, *ibid*. On Aug. 29, Richards wrote to Governor Andrew Johnson asking for his support as applicant for the position of postmaster at Memphis. ALS, *ibid*. On Sept. 22, he wrote to Postmaster Gen. Montgomery Blair applying for the position of postmaster at Memphis. ALS, *ibid*.

To Brig. Gen. Alvin P. Hovey

———

By Telegraph from Columbus [*July*] 13 1862

To Brig Gen A P Hovey

Should information be received from Curtis telegraph it to me at Corinth   I sent two 2 Couriers to Try & reach him who should be back about this time & Col Fitch also sent from Clarendon

U S GRANT
Maj Genl

Telegram received, Hovey Papers, InU. See telegrams to Brig. Gen. Alvin P. Hovey, July 11, 18, 1862.

In his capacity as commander at Memphis, Brig. Gen. Alvin P. Hovey informed USG of the movements of enemy troops. On July 16, 1862, Hovey telegraphed to USG. "Evidence accumulates that the rebels are concentrating near us. 2000 Cavalry with some artillery are reported within 18 miles on the Horn Lake road   this comes from several sources. Rebel women are anxious to leave, & are leaving City. I shall burn the bridges on the Horn Lake & Hernando roads unless you forbid it." Telegram received, DNA, RG 393, Dept. of the Mo., Telegrams Received. On July 17, Hovey telegraphed to USG the substance of an article in the *Grenada Appeal*, July 16, which reported the encounter of the C. S. A. gunboat *Arkansas* with U.S. gunboats near Vicksburg. Telegram received, *ibid.*

To Maj. Gen. John A. McClernand

[*July 16, 1862*]

The Divisions of Sherman & Hurlbut have been ordered to Memphis.[1] The Hatchie[2] will be made the line of defence from Bolivar[3] to Bethel, this policy renders it necessary to with draw the troops from Grand Junction to Bolivar & the Hatchie. If you deem it expedient the force at Bolivar may be further increased from Jackson.

Copy, Register of Letters, McClernand Papers, IHi. On July 15, 1862, Capt. Nathaniel H. McLean issued Special Field Orders No. 160. "Major Gen. Grant will order the divisions of Generals Sherman and Hurlbut to Memphis. Major Gen. Sherman will be placed in command of that Post and vicinity. The troops at Grand Junction will be withdrawn to Bolivar or the Hatchie river, which will be made the main point of defence from Memphis to Bethel." Copies, DLC-USG, V, 83; DLC-William T. Sherman. *O.R.*, I, xvii, part 2, 99–100. On July 16, Maj. Gen. John A. McClernand telegraphed to USG. "I will start a Brigade to Bolivar in the morning. Place the forces north of me under my command & I can act with much better effect." Telegram received, DNA, RG 393, Dept. of the Mo., Telegrams Received; copy, McClernand Papers, IHi. On July 16, McClernand again telegraphed to USG. "The unmasking my front from Corinth to Memphis makes it necessary that I should withdraw a regiment of Infantry and most of my cavalry now at Booneville; I deem it now vital that the troops North of me to Union City should be under my command so that in common with those now under my command they might be handled so as to meet emergencies. Six companies of cavalry now at Humbolt are not needed there. Col. Leggett remains temporarily at Grand Junction." Copy, *ibid*. See telegram to Maj. Gen. John A. McClernand, July 17, 1862.

1. On July 16, Maj. Gen. William T. Sherman telegraphed to USG from Moscow, Tenn. "Your despatch rec.d   Gen. Hurlbut will move in the morning & I will take up the line of March as soon as he reaches Moscow." Telegram received, DNA, RG 393, Dept. of the Mo., Telegrams Received.
2. The Hatchie River flows in a generally northwesterly direction from creeks having their sources generally north and west of Corinth. It crosses the Tennessee and Ohio Railroad at Bolivar, the Memphis and Ohio Railroad about five miles southwest of Brownsville, Tenn., swings in a long loop, passes about five miles north of Covington, Tenn., and flows into the Mississippi River at Randolph, Tenn.
3. Bolivar, Tenn., on the Tennessee and Ohio Railroad, about thirty-seven miles northwest of Corinth.

General Orders No. 62

———

Head Quarters, Dist of West. Tenn.
Corinth, Miss July 17, 1862

GENERAL ORDERS No 62.

In compliance with Special Field Orders No 161. from Head Quarters, Dept of the Miss, Corinth, Miss. July 16, 1862: the undersigned takes the command of all the troops embraced in the Army of the Tenn, the Army of the Miss, and Districts of Miss and Cairo.

All reports and returns required by Army Regulations, and existing orders will be made to the Dist Head Quarters, Corinth, Miss.

U. S. GRANT
Maj Gen. U. S. Vols.

Copies, DLC-USG, V, 12, 13, 14, 95; DNA, RG 393, USG General Orders; *ibid.*, RG 94, 21st Ill., Order Book; (printed) *ibid.*, Special Orders, District of West Tenn. *O.R.*, I, xvii, part 2, 102. On July 16, 1862, Capt. Nathaniel H. McLean issued Special Field Orders No. 161. "The District of West Tennessee, Major-General Grant commanding, will include the Districts of Cairo and Mississippi; that part of the State of Mississippi occupied by our troops, and that part of Alabama which may be occupied by the troops of his particular command, including the forces heretofore known as the Army of the Mississippi." *Ibid.*, p. 101.

To Maj. Gen. John A. McClernand

[*July 17, 1862*]
By Telegraph from Corinth.

Hold Grand Junction with your present force until otherwise directed   I will make Grand Junction a cavalry out post with light transportation enabling them to move back rapidly to Bolivar should it prove a necessary contingency, which I do not expect.

Copy, Register of Letters, McClernand Papers, IHi. On July 13, 1862, Maj. Gen. John A. McClernand telegraphed to USG. "The enemy are reported, by one of Col. Leggetts scouts, who has been in their camp, to be in some force with cavalry, Infantry and Artillery at and in the vicinity of Salem, under instructions, cut off supply Trains, destroy the Rail road and attack Grand Junction, now protected by the forces under Col. Leggett. Genl. Thayer refuses to forward from Memphis the mail to the troops at Grand Junction. will you please order it forward"   Copies, *ibid.* On July 12, McClernand had written details of the same operation to Col. John C. Kelton. LS, DNA, RG 393, District of West Tenn., Letters Received. On July 16, Maj. Gen. William T. Sherman telegraphed to USG. "Gen. Hurlbut's & my Divisions are ready to move, but Col. Leggett declines to move his command from the Junction without McClernand's orders— my orders to Hurlbut are to see Col. Leggett with all his stores at the Junction fairly off for Bolivar, before evacuating Lagrange & marching west. I shall give him another day to move: he got my written orders sent by express yesterday & if he dont move I will then put in motion my column by first, bringing Hurlbut up to Moscow & then marching west taking up our detachments by the way." Telegram received, *ibid.*, Dept. of the Mo., Telegrams Received; copies, *ibid.*, RG 94, Generals' Papers and Books, William T. Sherman, Telegrams Sent; DLC-William T. Sherman.

On the same day, McClernand telegraphed to USG. "Your telegram enables me to act intelligently. It is hard to evacuate Grand Junction to the Enemy— leaves loyal men & their property a prey to rebel bandits. Give me another

Brigade & I will maintain it, or if you say so I will detach from here & Bethel & try & do it. Meantime I will proceed to execute the order of removal to Bolivar. Save me the mortification of falling back if you can consistently." Telegram received, DNA, RG 393, Dept. of the Mo., Telegrams Received; copy, McClernand Papers, IHi. Col. Mortimer D. Leggett, commanding at Grand Junction, telegraphed to USG the same day. "I hope you will concede Gen. McClernand's request & allow me to hold Grand Junction. By moving forw.d one Brigade to Bolivar, part of one to Middleburg & two Co.s of Cav. to my command, I can hold this position against any force that there is any probability of being brought against us. The Union sentiment is being rapidly developed in the Country around. A large No. of Citizens have voluntarily taken oath of allegiance. They are now bringing in their Cotton at rates of 200 bales a day. 700 bales now here to be destroyed as soon as we leave & by the order we must leave in a few hours. With my present force, I am perfectly safe for several days yet. I shall be off very soon unless ordered to remain." Telegram received, DNA, RG 393, Dept. of the Mo., Telegrams Received. On the same day, McClernand telegraphed to USG. "There are said to be 500 bales of Cotton at Grand Junction. I have instructed Col. Leggett not to leave there, until the public property is secured. I suppose Genls. Sherman's & Hurlbut will observe the same course. Col. Leggett says he will maintain the Junction, with some re-inforcement." Telegram received, *ibid.*; copy, McClernand Papers, IHi. McClernand telegraphed the substance of the preceding telegram to Maj. Gen. Henry W. Halleck. Telegram received, DNA, RG 393, Dept. of the Mo., Telegrams Received; copy, McClernand Papers, IHi. Halleck endorsed the telegram to USG. "If in the opinion of Genl Grant & Genl McClernand an out post can be safely kept up for the present at Grand Junction, in order to remove the cotton, they will so order." AE, DNA, RG 393, Dept. of the Mo., Telegrams Received. On July 17, McClernand telegraphed to USG. "I am rejoiced that you have determined to hold Grand Junction. What would be the opinion if we should give it up to the enemy I will not answer   A brigade started from here by day light for Bolivar   Genl Ross will command the forces there and at Grand Junction. My plan was for Genl Ross to march towards the Junction 6 or 7 miles before Col Leggett should leave for Bolivar. Your order to hold the place will be obeyed"   Telegram received, *ibid.* See also Sherman to Maj. John A. Rawlins, July 25, copy, *ibid.*, RG 94, Generals' Papers and Books, William T. Sherman, Letters Sent. *O.R.*, I, xvii, part 2, 121–23.

To Brig. Gen. William S. Rosecrans

Corinth July 17th 1862

GENL. ROSECRANS

Morgans[1] division will not move until monday.[2] Should the Clothing spoken of in your dispatch, arrive after that time, it can be sent immediately to them by Rail. Supplies will have to be sent in that way. I will be out to see you tomorrow, and will have with me, the distribution to be made of the troops going to relieve Genl. Thomas

U. S. Grant

Maj Genl

Telegram, copy, DNA, RG 393, Army of the Miss., Telegrams Received. William S. Rosecrans of Ohio, USMA 1842, served in the U.S. Army as an asst. professor at USMA (1843–47) and as an engineer officer on several Atlantic Coast projects before his resignation as 1st lt. on April 1, 1854. An oil refiner of Cincinnati on the eve of the Civil War, he joined Maj. Gen. George B. McClellan as vol. aide, and was confirmed as brig. gen. on Aug. 3, 1861, to rank from May 16. Following successes in campaigns in what is now W. Va., he was transferred to the Dept. of the Miss., arriving at Pittsburg Landing on May 23, 1862. Although his promotion to maj. gen. dated from March 21, he was not nominated until later in the year and not confirmed until March 10, 1863. William M. Lamers, *The Edge of Glory: A Biography of General William S. Rosecrans, U. S. A.* (New York, 1961).

1. Brig. Gen. James D. Morgan had served as a brigade commander with Maj. Gen. John Pope's Army of the Miss. in the battles at Island No. 10 and New Madrid, Mo. He served under Pope in the capture of Corinth, and was promoted to brig. gen. on July 17, 1862. On July 15, Capt. Nathaniel H. McLean issued Special Field Orders No. 160. "A division will be ordered by Gen. Grant. to replace the division of Gen. Thomas on the road from Iuka to Decatur as soon as the latter is ready to move across the Tenn. river to join Gen. Buell." Copies, DLC-USG, V, 83; DLC-William T. Sherman. *O.R.*, I, xvii, part 2, 99–100. On July 16, Maj. John A. Rawlins issued Special Orders No. 136. "Brig. Gen. Morgan's Division of the Army of the Miss will hold themselves in readiness to move to the East, on the line of the Memphis & Charleston road to relieve the command of Maj Gen. Thomas, when directed to do so. All supplies that may be left at Eastport by Gen. Thomas will be taken charge of and issued to the troops. For further supplies this place will be looked to. All the points now occupied by the troops of Major Gen. Thomas' Command will be taken possession of by the troops relieving him. Brig Gen. Morgan's Division of the Army of the Miss. will move at an early hour on Monday the 21st inst. to the East on the Memphis & Charleston road and relieve the command of Major Gen. Thomas now on duty guarding said road. The A. Q. M. & Com of Sub. of the Staff of Gen. Morgan's Division will proceed to Iuka & Eastport, and relieve the A. Q. M. & C. S. of Gen. Thomas' Division. Brig. Gen. Rosecrans will detach his largest Regt. of Cavalry to proceed with Gen. Morgan." Copies, DLC-USG, V, 15, 16, 82, 87; DNA, RG 393, USG Special Orders. *O.R.*, I, xvii, part 2, 102. On July 16, Rosecrans telegraphed to USG. "Your dispatch ~~requiring~~ directing Morgans division to prepare for to occupying Iuka—has been received and its directions complied with but is very desirable that the division should get its clothing & equipments before leaving   They are on the way from St Louis"   Telegram received, DNA, RG 393, Dept. of the Mo., Telegrams Received; copy, *ibid.*, Army of the Miss., Telegrams Sent.

2. July 21.

To Brig. Gen. Alvin P. Hovey

By Telegraph from Corinth [*July*] 18 *1862*

To Brig Genl A P Hovey
Gen—

Upon the arrival of Maj Gen Sherman all the Infantry under your command at Memphis will proceed to reinforce Genl Curtis at Helena Ark   Take with you camp and Garrison Equipage of the twenty fourth Indiana Vols   when you arrive there it will be under your command   Gen Sherman has the orders for you—

U. S. Grant
Maj Genl

Telegram received, Hovey Papers, InU. On July 15, 1862, Capt. Nathaniel H. McLean issued Special Field Orders No. 160. "A division of Infantry will be sent from Memphis to Helena to reenforce Gen. Curtis. Gen. Grant will make the necessary changes and assignments for carrying out these orders." Copies, DLC-USG, V, 83; DLC-William T. Sherman. *O.R.*, I, xvii, part 2, 99–100. On July 17, Brig. Gen. Alvin P. Hovey, Memphis, telegraphed to USG. "My old regiment twenty fourth (24th) Indiana is at Helena without tents teams or baggage of officers having left them here   I would regard it as personal favor if that regiment could be again placed under my command if the exigencies of the services will admit   what shall be done" Telegram received, DNA, RG 393, Dept. of the Mo., Telegrams Received. On June 27, Hovey had written to Secretary of War Edwin M. Stanton asking for a leave of absence of twenty days to take care of personal business. LS, *ibid.*, RG 94, Letters Received. On July 1, USG approved and forwarded Hovey's request to hd. qrs., Dept. of the Miss. AES, *ibid.* On July 19, AGO Special Orders No. 166 granted Hovey twenty days leave. Copy, DLC-USG, V, 93. On July 19, Hovey telegraphed to USG. "Genl Sherman has not yet arrived. Shall I open his dispatch" Telegram received, DNA, RG 393, Dept. of the Mo., Telegrams Received. On July 20, Hovey telegraphed to USG. "Your telegram to me commands me to take all the infantry in Memphis and join Genl Curtis—Genl Shermans despatches says all of Wallaces ~~Division~~ command   Wallaces command is scattered along the line as you are aware and 2 Regts of Genl Quinbys Infantry were here when you left—shall I take them with me—" Telegram received, *ibid.* On July 20, Maj. Gen. William T. Sherman, Memphis, telegraphed to USG. "Arrived this morning   left my troops at a good camp nine miles out   came in to select good camp   will dispatch Genl Hoveys Infantry force to Helena and enforce your orders about rent of stores   also will communicate your request to the senior commander of the navy as to destruction of all boats from the north line of Tenn to Vicksburg" Telegram received, *ibid.* *O.R.*, I, xvii, part 2, 109. On July 25, Sherman sent a full report of the movement to Maj. John A. Rawlins. Copy, DNA, RG 94, Generals' Papers and Books, William T. Sherman, Letters Sent. *O.R.*, I, xvii, part 2, 121–23.

On July 15, Hovey telegraphed to USG. "Is the despatch to Col. Fitch of sufficient importance to have it sent by Steamer? The operator refuses to send me Copy under the plea it would be in violation of his instructions; this I think cannot be the case. The Commandant of a Post ought to be fully informed of all important facts that pass over the lines, that may affect the Service in his locality." Telegram received, DNA, RG 393, Dept. of the Mo., Telegrams Received. On the same day, Hovey telegraphed that Col. Graham N. Fitch had not yet returned. Telegram received, *ibid*. On July 16, Hovey telegraphed to USG. "Col Fitch has ordered about 400 of an effective force from here to join him at Helena. Under existing circumstances would it not be better for them to remain." Telegram received, *ibid*. On July 10, Fitch, St. Charles, Ark., wrote to USG. "We arrived here last evening. The report prevails here among the few so called 'Union Men' (a part of whom claim our protection and propose remaining with us) that Genl. Curtis is on the Cache river endeavoring to reach or communicate with us. We will remain here the time indicated in yesterday's despatch and if no reinforcements or further orders arrive and no *positive* intelligence from Genl. Curtis, will greable to your orders proceed to Memphis. My regrets at this necssity (if it accures) becouse of its probable effect upon Genl. Curtis' Command has been heretofore expressed. With even 100 Cavalry—a battery—and 1000 More Infantry I would attempt communication with him up Cache. The attempt with caution I believe would be successful. At all events there need be no risk of disaster." Copy, Curtis Papers, IaHA. *O.R.*, I, xiii, 112–13. On July 14, Fitch wrote to USG. "My dispatches to you of 8th from Clarendon, and 10th from St. Charles, apprised You that circomstantial evidence, sufficient in my mind, to justify a movement of the command in that direction, was obtained that Genl. Curtis, was at or near Cotton plant—on Cache River, in the former dispatch you were advised that that an expedition, was fitted out and on the point of starting, but was abandoned in conequence of reciept of yours of 6th Inst. and that the fleet left Clarendon that evening—Soon after it arrived at St. Charles, on the evening of the 11th a scouting party brought in a prisoner, whos statement was positive that Genl. Curtis had been but two or three days previous to that, at Cotten plant seeking to make his way to Clarendon, where he was expected to arive that evening (11th). Immediately two Transports with Howitzers and six Companies of Troops under Major Grill of 24th Ind. were ordered to return to Clarendon, with dispatch and assertain the truth of the statement and communicate with him if possible. On arriving at that place, 2. P. M. of the 12th Major Grill ascertained that Genl. Curtis had been there the evening of the 9th and that his rear guard cavalry had left on the road to Helena only two hours previous. The Howitzers on the Transports fired signals all the afternoon. Hearing no response they returned to St. Charles, reaching there about 1. A. M. of the 13th A strong scouting party was immediately ordered, led by myself, with a view of reaching that road and intersecting his line of march.—The party left Camp at 3 A.M. and after a laborious march of 18 miles finding he had passed the point where we reached the Helena road, Eight hours, it was deemed useless for Infantry, the only troops at my Command, to attempt, especially during the extreme heat which prevailed, to overtake him, and not absolutely essential it should be done, as it was presumed that his army could not be more than 20 or 30 miles from Helena and his advance perhaps already there—The party therefore returned to the transports, and they were ordered to leave forthwith for Helena. On the morning of the 9th soon after our attack of the night previous upon a camp of the enemy, 7 miles from Duvals bluff, that place was avacuated, the enemy taking his guns and munitions to Little Rock tearing up the Rail Road Track behind him and he appears to be concentrating all his troops at that place." Copy, Curtis Papers, IaHA. *O.R.*, I, xiii, 113. On July 15, Fitch again wrote to USG. DLC-USG, V, 10; DNA, RG 393, USG Register of Letters Received.

On July 19, Maj. Gen. Henry W. Halleck, St. Louis, wrote to Maj. Gen. Samuel R. Curtis, Helena, Ark., that he had heard that Fitch had joined Curtis and that he had ordered "all the infantry" from the division of Maj. Gen. Lewis Wallace to join him at Helena. ALS, Curtis Papers, IaHA. *O.R.*, I, xiii, 477. On July 22, Fitch wrote to Curtis. "As this Brigade constituting the late 'White River Expedition' was operating in you District and now constitutes a part of your command I forward you herewith copies of of my verious reports wile upon the expedition and which compose its record." Copy, Curtis Papers, IaHA. See also letters of Halleck to Curtis, and of Stanton to Halleck, July 13, *O.R.*, I, xiii, 469–70.

To Brig. Gen. William S. Rosecrans

Corinth July 18th 1862

Brig Genl. Rosecrans
Comdg Army of Miss

I will not be out to see you to day, for information of Genl Morgan who is relieve Genl. Thomas' Command, as to the location of his troops on the road, I send you the following dispatch of Maj Genl Thomas   Genl. Morgans troops will be stationed as there in indicated

U. S. Grant
Maj Genl

Telegram, copy, DNA, RG 393, Army of the Miss., Telegrams Received. On July 17, 1862, Maj. Gen. George H. Thomas, Tuscumbia, Ala., telegraphed to USG. "I shall be ready to commence moving my Division on Monday next. Please start the Division to relieve mine on that day. I would suggest that it be posted as follows:—. . .The remainder of the Division should be posted at this place, and if one extra Brigade could be spared, it would be well to post it at Courtland, with a Battery of Artillery in place of the Regiment above mentioned, which Regiment could then be posted at Decatur. It is important to send one of your best and largest Regiments of Cavalry, as the country south of the Railroad for twenty miles should be kept thoroughly examined every other day by cavalry.

I wish you to send an officer of the Qr. Master's Dept. and one of the Commissary Dept. to relieve my Qr. Master and Commissary at Iuka and Eastport. Please answer if you can commence moving a Division on Monday." Copies, *ibid.*, Dept. of the Cumberland, 1st Division, District of the Ohio, Letters Sent; *ibid.*, Army of the Miss., Telegrams Received. *O.R.*, I, xvi, part 2, 174. On July 15, Maj. Gen. Henry W. Halleck, Corinth, telegraphed to Maj. Gen. Don Carlos Buell, Huntsville, Ala. "I am ordered to Washington, and shall leave to-day after to-morrow Thursday. Very sorry for it   can be of more use here than there. As soon as Gen. Thomas can get up his supplies he will cross at Decatur to reinforce you and be replaced by one of Grants divisions. I abandon the road to Memphis and will keep that open to Decatur as long as you deem it essential. Our lines must be shortened. What more can I do for you." Copy, Buell Papers, TxHR. *O.R.*, I, xvi, part 2, 151. On July 16, Halleck telegraphed to Buell giving supplementary instructions on Thomas's movement. Copy, Buell Papers, TxHR. *O.R.*, I, xvi, part 2, 160.

On July 18, Brig. Gen. William S. Rosecrans telegraphed to USG. "I have just telegraphed Thomas inquiring if there are not points south of the road where out troops massed could cover the front preserve discipline or damage the rebel bands who come up on search of adventures and mischief   I am fully satisfied that with a strong nuclius at Tupelo waiting attack or opportunity for mischief they have left considerable forces to Vicksburg with an intermediate point above Grenada and detached strong column towards Mobile and Richmond, while another under Price has gone towards Chattanooga or Rome. They cover their front by Cavalry and guerrillas. They have a desert Country of dry ravines and rough ridges on their front below us and can move much better towards Fulton, or West ward by their front"   Telegram received (incomplete), DNA, RG 393, Dept. of the Mo., Telegrams Received; copy, *ibid.*, Army of the Miss., Telegrams Sent. *O.R.*, I, xvii, part 2, 103. On July 19, Thomas telegraphed to Rosecrans. "Telegram received. have telegraphed Maj Genl Grant, all the points where your troops will be posted. Can give you maps and detail here, which cannot be telegraphed. Have telegraphed this morning to Genl Grant to send four Companies by Rail Road to relieve the Provost Guard here. There is a fine field opened here for your disciplined troops and Cavalry Brigades to operate against, roving bands of Rebels. Russleville and Courtland probably Courtland is the best position for Cavalry. Russleville, Frankfort, &C. are important points leading South towards Tupello &C. Send your division with as little delay as possible." Copy, DNA, RG 393, Army of the Miss., Telegrams Received. *O.R.*, I, xvi, part 2, 185. See telegram to Brig. Gen. William S. Rosecrans, July 19, 1862.

To Brig. Gen. William S. Rosecrans

Corinth July 18th 1862

GENL. ROSECRANS

GENL:

Morgans Division will be under your Command as before. It will be impossible to furnish other Cavalry than that attached to the old Army of the Mississippi, for the present   all points of the district are calling for more Cavalry and as I know from personal observations the wants of all parts, except that to be occupied by Genl. Morgan, I will soon be able to make the proper distribution

U. S. GRANT
Maj Genl

Telegram, copy, DNA, RG 393, Army of the Miss., Telegrams Received. On July 18, 1862, Brig. Gen. William S. Rosecrans telegraphed to USG. "I take it for granted that Genl Morgans division while preforming the duties assigned will remain under my command   Should that be the intention please Telegraph Genl Thomas to send down the best map or sketch of the Country he can. I will try to send a cavalry brigade but this demand on our already over taxed cavalry is a grave matter   cant some of Thomas cavalry be left"   Telegram received, *ibid.*, Dept. of the Mo., Telegrams Received; copy, *ibid.*, Army of the Miss., Telegrams Sent.

To Maj. Gen. Henry W. Halleck

Head Quarters Dist of West. Tenn.
Corinth, Miss July 19th 1862.

MAJOR GEN. H. W. HALLECK.

ST LOUIS MO.

Mr. Whitfield,[1] a prisoner declining to take the oath has a number of negro women and children here that he desires to send to his cousins living south of our lines. Have I authority to let them go?

U. S. GRANT
Major General.

Telegram, copies, DLC-USG, V, 4, 5, 7, 8, 88; DNA, RG 393, USG Hd. Qrs. Correspondence. On July 19, 1862, Maj. Gen. Henry W. Halleck telegraphed to USG. "If you want the help of Negro Slaves use it   if not let them go when they please if unless there is a Military reason for detaining them"   Telegram received, *ibid.*, Dept. of the Mo., Telegrams Received; copies, *ibid.*, USG Hd. Qrs. Correspondence; *ibid.*, Dept. of the Mo., Telegrams Sent; DLC-USG, V, 7.

1. On July 17, Maj. John A. Rawlins issued Special Orders No. 137. "John D. Chadwick and Francis E. Whitfield of the County of Tischmingo and State of Mississippi having been guilty of holding treasonable and forbidden communication with the enemy, it is ordered that they each be confined as Prisoners in the Penitentiary at Alton, Madison County, Illinois, where persons guilty of such offences are kept. Col. Clark. B. Lagow, Aid-de-Camp will proceed with them at once to said Prison, and deliver them into the custody of the Officer in command of the same. The Asst. Quartermaster U. S. Army at this place will furnish the necessary transportation for said prisoners." DS, DNA, RG 249, Records of Prisoners Confined at Alton; copies, *ibid.*, RG 393, USG Special Orders; DLC-USG, V, 15, 16, 82, 87. *O.R.*, II, iv, 238.

On Aug. 1, John D. Chadwick, Alton, wrote to the provost marshal, St. Louis, stating that his imprisonment had come about as a result of a misunderstanding. "On the morning of the 7th of July, I visited a neighbor, Mr. Reed, whose house was near your pickets and ½ mile from my home. While there I met with Dr. J. Stout a practicing physician who lived beyond your lines and was going to Corinth. He handed me a letter addressed to Mr. F. E. Whitefield, who lived on the farm adjoining my father-in-law's and not on his route to town, asking me to deliver it. I thought nothing of the letter, did not ask where it came from, and during the day delivered it to Mr. Whitefield; while in his presence he opened the letter and glancing over it said it was not for him, but for Mrs. March a widow lady living on his farm. As far as the letter was read it contained no army news, though it was from the son of the lady who was in the army." James W. Milgram, "Grant Frees a Prisoner," *S. P. A.* [*Society of Philatelic Americans*] *Journal* (Feb., 1964), 423–24. On Aug. 2, Brig. Gen. John M. Schofield referred the letter to USG. *Ibid.* On Aug. 13, USG endorsed the letter. "I have no objection to the release of Mr. Chadwick but not to return to Corinth." AES (facsimile), *ibid.*, p. 425.

USG occupied Francis E. Whitfield's house in Corinth. See letter to Jesse Root Grant, Aug. 3, 1862. Whitfield described himself as "an original Union Man" in a petition of Aug. 21, 1865, to President Andrew Johnson requesting amnesty. ALS, DNA, RG 94, Amnesty Oaths, Miss. In 1886, Whitfield filed a claim for compensation for the use of his store building and cotton shed in Memphis during the war, asserting his loyalty to the U.S. at that time. The case continued for many years, complicated by the existence of four vouchers (now *ibid.*, RG 109, Citizens File) showing that Whitfield furnished goods and services to the C.S. Army, a letter of Whitfield to the C.S. secretary of war recommending a prospective officer, the service of Whitfield's four sons in the C.S. Army, and Whitfield's arrest by USG. *Ibid.*, RG 123, Case No. 12,584; *HMD*, 50–2, 20.

In a letter written in 1885, Whitfield claimed that he held a receipt from USG for his property in Corinth. "Your property will not be destroyed or carried off, except for benefit of the United States government. In the latter case an accurate account will be kept, so that should you prove entitled to it you will have recourse upon the government, which you are charged with attempting to subvert. Knowing my own duty, I can allow no interference on the part of persons who cannot give evidence of loyalty." *Corinth Herald*, Dec. 15, 1903. All movable property was destroyed or stolen while Whitfield was imprisoned, he asserted, including fourteen wagonloads of furniture shipped to Springfield, Ill., where, he believed, Mrs. Grant lived. *Ibid.*

In a letter printed in the Corinth, Miss., *Subsoiler and Democrat*, Nov. 16, 1894, Louise Gay Whitfield stated that her father, Francis E. Whitfield, "one of the hottest Rebels around here," had been arrested by U.S. Army officers after he protested their use of his carriage. Her long account, filled with noble southerners, nasty Yankees, and loyal slaves, does not accord with any available contemporary documentation, and does not mention either the alleged receipt or the stolen furniture.

USG later wrote that: "I do not recollect having arrested and confined a citizen (not a soldier) during the entire rebellion. I am aware that a great many were sent to northern prisons, particularly to Joliet, Illinois, by some of my subordinates with the statement that it was my order. I had all such released the moment I learned of their arrest; and finally sent a staff officer north to release every prisoner who was said to be confined by my order." *Memoirs*, I, 398. See letters to Col. Jesse Hildebrand, Oct. 3, 30, 1862. Obviously USG took a more active role in arresting civilians, including Whitfield, than he later recollected, but accounts by Whitfield and his family are filled with too many errors, contradictions, and implausibilities to be acceptable. The alleged receipt of USG, available only in Whitfield's letter, must be viewed with suspicion.

In 1868, Gen. Nathan B. Forrest stated that he had investigated and disproved the story that USG had carried off furniture from Corinth. Stanley F. Horn, *Invisible Empire: The Story of the Ku Klux Klan 1866–1871* (Boston, 1939), pp. 415–16.

To Brig. Gen. William S. Rosecrans

Corinth July 19th 1862

GENL. ROSECRANS

Send four Companies of Morgans Division immediately to Tuscumbia[1] to relieve the Provost Guard there. I would like you to visit this Division, soon after its removal to see in person, that the locations are well chosen. I have no inspector or other Staff Officers to entrust this matter to. You may send Col Tinkham[2] as proposed. Send by Rail with rations

U. S. GRANT
Maj Genl

Telegram, copy, DNA, RG 393, Army of the Miss., Telegrams Received. On July 19, 1862, Maj. Gen. George H. Thomas, Tuscumbia, Ala., telegraphed to USG. "Please send up four companies at once by rail to relieve the provost guard stationed at this place" Telegram received, *ibid.*, Dept. of the Mo., Telegrams Received; copy, *ibid.*, Dept. of the Cumberland, 1st Division, District of the Ohio, Letters Sent. On the same day, Brig. Gen. William S. Rosecrans telegraphed to USG. "I directed Capt Taylor to telegraph for transportation for the four companies you ordered to be sent to Tuscumbia & have received the following reply. 'We cannot send out trains by orders from the Quartermasters. It must be from Military Authority' James C M McCibbon Col please give the required orders" Telegram received, *ibid.*, Dept. of the Mo., Telegrams Received; copy, *ibid.*, Army of the Miss., 16th Army Corps, Telegrams Sent. Rosecrans's copy reads, "Please give the requisite orders" On the same day, USG telegraphed to Rosecrans. "The object of sending Genl Morgan, East of here, is to protect the road and Telegraph, within the district assigned to him, the best method of scouring this End be adopted." Copy, *ibid.*, Army of the Miss., Telegrams Received. On July 20, Brig. Gen. James B. McPherson telegraphed to Rosecrans that there was still some confusion about the disposition of troops. Copy, *ibid.*

1. Tuscumbia, Ala., on the Memphis and Charleston Railroad, about fifty miles southeast of Corinth.
2. Lt. Col. Charles J. Tinkham of Homer, Ill., 26th Ill., was commissioned Aug. 29, 1861. On July 19, 1862, Rosecrans telegraphed to USG. "May [I orde]r Lt Col Tinkh[am 2]6th Ill Vols to Springfield Ills to confer with Supt of recruiting service as to bringing to the Ills regts the absentees" Telegram received, *ibid.*, Dept. of the Mo., Telegrams Received; copy, *ibid.*, Army of the Miss., Telegrams Sent.

To Maj. Gen. Don Carlos Buell

Corinth July 20th 1862

Maj. Genl. Buell

The following information is received here and seems to be reliable Bragg left Tupolo on the 7th with a large force and marched east probably towards Chatanooga There has also been a movement towards this place but I think nothing forminable

Genl. U. S. Grant

Telegram, copy, DNA, RG 393, Dept. of the Ohio and Cumberland, Telegrams Received. *O.R.*, I, xvi, part 2, 188. On July 20, 1862, Brig. Gen. William S. Rosecrans telegraphed to USG. "From a gentleman whom I know who was imprisoned by the rebels and escaped after two unsuccessful attempts bringing with him the irons with which he was manacled at Tupello and I learn the following important facts—Bragg with a large force left Tupello on the 7th the date of his flag of truce letter to Genl Halleck, for the East marching by Peakeville toward Chatanoogo—a small force left Tupello for Mobile July 1st there has been additional forces sent from Tupello to Saltillo—Bradfutes cavalry is at Fulton—Thos Jordan commands at Saltillo—Price is at Priceville six miles east of Tupello a brigade is half west of Tupello no troops any further west— total force in that vicinity will not exceed 20 000 no troops were seen by him north of New Albany except a fiew strooling cavalry" Telegram received, DNA, RG 393, Dept. of the Mo., Telegrams Received; copy, *ibid.*, Army of the Miss., 16th Army Corps, Telegrams Sent. *O.R.*, I, xvii, part 2, 107. On the same day, Rosecrans telegraphed to USG. "Two (2) dispatches from Genl Davis of the 4th disision at Jacinto give contradictory reports—The former that the enemy were moving from Jacinto to Saltillo the other that they were concentrating at Big Spring factory 15 miles south east of Jacinto and 25 miles south from Iuka that they imagine we are reduced in numbers and intend to attack Jacinto and Corinth. They say our guards about about Corinth are badly posted and their spies go where they please. While I do not credit the report of their intended attack on Jacinto I have given Davis orders to be prepared to fight or fall back sending his baggage before him on this position I have also given Morgan notice of the report—His Division will be in Bainsville tomorrow and at Iuka next day and evening. I venture to suggest Davis division requires caution as to its guard duty" Telegram received, DNA, RG 393, District of West Tenn., Letters Received; copy, *ibid.*, Army of the Miss., 16th Army Corps, Telegrams Sent. *O.R.*, I, xvii, part 2, 108. See letter to Maj Gen. Henry W. Halleck, July 23, 1862.

To Brig. Gen. Lorenzo Thomas

Corinth [*July*] 21. [*1862*]

ADJT GENL OF THE ARMY,

Has Brig Genl J B S Todd been confirmed If not he wishes to be relieved as soon as possible.

U. S. GRANT.
Maj Genl

Telegram received, DNA, RG 107, Telegrams Received (Press). On July 22, 1862, Brig. Gen. Lorenzo Thomas telegraphed to USG. "Brigadier General J. B. S. Todd has not been confirmed." Copies, *ibid.*, Telegrams Collected (Unbound); *ibid.*, RG 94, Letters Sent. On July 24, Maj. John A. Rawlins issued Special Orders No. 143. "Brig. Gen. J. B. S. Todd is, at his own request, is hereby relieved from duty with this Army. He will report in person or by letter to the Adjt. Genl of the Army. The ~~next~~ Officer next in rank in his Division will immediately take command." Copies, DLC-USG, V, 15, 16, 82, 87; DNA, RG 393, USG Special Orders. *O.R.*, I, xvii, part 2, 117.

John B. S. Todd of Ky., USMA 1837, moved with his parents to Ill., served in the U.S. Army until he resigned as capt. on Sept. 16, 1856, then spent the next five years as sutler at Fort Randall, Dakota Territory. Elected delegate from Dakota in 1861, he received a recess appointment as brig. gen. of vols. on Sept. 19, and his appointment expired July 17, 1862, because Congress failed to act on it.

To Brig. Gen. William S. Rosecrans

Corinth July 22nd 1862

BRIG GENL ROSECRANS

I have made the order, requested in your telegram of yesterday, and ordered the force at Hamburg[1] to join their Regt as soon as relieved.

U. S. GRANT
Maj Genl

Telegram, copy, DNA, RG 393, Army of the Miss., Telegrams Received. On July 21, 1862, Brig. Gen. William S. Rosecrans telegraphed to Maj. John A. Rawlins. "Ask the Maj Genl. Comdg to please order the regt. at Pittsburg Landing to send a battalion to releive three (3) companies of the 80th Ohio, I have at Hamburgh landing—Reasons the Maj Comdg is ~~sufficient~~ inefficient. The troops are demoralized & some of the officers have been stealing. The regt at Pittsburg Landing is a good one & both posts will be under our commander Please answer" Telegram received, *ibid.*, Dept. of the Mo., Telegrams Received; copy, *ibid.*, Army of the Miss., 16th Army Corps, Telegrams Sent.

1. Hamburg, Tenn., on the Tennessee River, about five miles above Pittsburg Landing.

To Brig. Gen. William S. Rosecrans

Corinth July 22d 1862

GENL. ROSECRANS

I will send the Ripley[1] man to you to morrow   he is now in the village. I will direct Genl. Todd to hold in readiness the Cavalry that can be spared from his division

U. S. GRANT
Maj Genl

Telegram, copy, DNA, RG 393, Army of the Miss., Telegrams Received. On July 22, 1862, Brig. Gen. William S. Rosecrans telegraphed to USG. "Have consulted with Grainger   we have one (1) brigade cavalry gone to Tuscumbia the other can muster about 650 or 700 but they are so distributed down on the front towards Booneville and Blackland and Marulla that they could not be assembled in time for a night march before tomorrow night   a day march would defeat our purpose—seven hundred cavalry can be got ready for a march tomorrow night by stripping our front for the time being—should you deem this expedient under the circumstances it will be desirable to know from the guide if there be a road by which we can come in below Ripley and avoid the Hatchie crossing where they unquestionably have a Picket and as I was yesterday informed had burned the bridges   please send over the guide from whom we may get some valuable local information" Telegram received, *ibid.*, Dept. of the Mo., Telegrams Received; copy, *ibid.*, Army of the Miss., 16th Army Corps, Telegrams Sent. *O.R.*, I, xvii, part 2, 111. On July 22, USG endorsed a letter of Rosecrans to Maj. Gen. Henry W. Halleck. "Respectfully forwarded to Maj. Gen. H. W. Halleck with the request that the within suggestions receive early attention. The proper arming of the Cavalry in this Department is of vital importance and demands prompt action." AES, DNA, RG 108, Letters Received. *O.R.*, I, xvii, part 2, 108. Rosecrans's letter of July 20 emphasized the necessity of arming the cav. and filling cav. units. ALS, DNA, RG 108, Letters Received. *O.R.*, I, xvii, part 2, 108.

On July 23, Rosecrans telegraphed to USG. "Campbell does not know enough of the country south of Ripley to make sure work of it. Please order private Moses Parker 11th Ill Cavalry at Bethel to report to me. He was formerly county surveyor & county assessor of Teppa county & we can get the very information we require to do our and other future work effectually. I will attend to the cases of some of these men soon" Telegram received, DNA, RG 393, Dept. of the Mo., Telegrams Received; copy, *ibid.*, Army of the Miss., 16th Army Corps, Telegrams Sent. On July 23, Rosecrans again telegraphed to USG. "Your despatch about Genl Ord is received   Did you order that man from the 11th Ill to come down & report here as requested. Please answer" Telegram received, *ibid.*, Dept. of the Mo., Telegrams Received; copy, *ibid.*, Army of the Miss., 16th Army Corps, Telegrams Sent. On the same day, USG telegraphed to Rosecrans. "I ordered the man referred to in your dispatch, to come down to night, and to report to you at once" Copy, *ibid.*, Army of the Miss., Telegrams Received. See also letter of Col. Philip H. Sheridan to Brig. Gen. Gordon Granger, July 22, 1862, *O.R.*, I, xvii, part 2, 111–12.

1. USG probably meant a guide from Ripley, Miss., about twenty-seven miles southwest of Corinth.

To Elihu B. Washburne

Corinth Mississippi
July 22d 1862

Hon. E. B. Washburn
Galena Ill.
Dear Sir:

Your letter of the 15th enclosing copy of a statement of the character and standing of Capt. Henry S. Fitch Assistant Quartermaster[1] is just received. It seems to be supposed that I made or had something to do with the appointment of Capt F.

Such is not the case. Capt. Fitch was among the first appointments made by the President, in his Dept. after the breaking out of the War.

On my taking command at Memphis I found him on duty in his there. If disposed I could not have removed him without charges and I knew of none against him.

I am not responsible for the acts of Capt. Fitch further than the accounts of his that I may be called on to approve, and the general duty to guard the public interest, in every particular, devolving upon me as commander.

I am glad you called my attention to this matter. I never knew Capt. F. either personally or by reputation until I met him in Memphis.

You will see by this letter that I am back again to this place. I was in hopes of another field, probably the taking of Vicksburg, but the call of Gen. Halleck to Washington made my recall necessary.

I do not know the object of calling Gen. H. to Washington but if it is to make him Sec. of War, or Commander-in-Chief, Head Quarters at Washington, a better selection could not be made. He is a man of gigantic intellect and well studied in the profession of arms. He and I have had several little spats but I like and respect him nevertheless.

I would have written you from Memphis but was kept very busy and knew you were also, and besides I had nothing special to write about.

All my staff are well.—Hoping to hear from you frequently I remain

Truly your friend
U. S. Grant

ALS, IHi. On July 25, 1862, U.S. Representative Elihu B. Washburne, South Livermore, Me., wrote to USG. "I am here on a brief visit to my father before returning west. Before leaving Boston I learned with great pleasure that you had been placed in command of the western army. I think the country will hail it as the precursor of more active and vigorous operations. It is scarcely possible for you to imagine the impatience of the public at the manner in which the war is being conducted   They want to see more immediate moving upon the 'enemy's works.' In fact they want to see *war*. This matter of guarding rebel property, of protecting secessionists and of enforcing 'order No. 3.' is 'played out' in public estimation. Your order in regard to the secessionists of Memphis taking the oath or leaving, has been accepted as an earnest of vigorous and decided action on your part. In fact, General, no military commander ever had a nobler field of operations before him than you have. No longer hampered in your operations by a superior officer in your department, holding the second most important command in the field in the army, I have no doubt the confidence of your friends will be realized. The cloud of obloquy that was temporarily raised by the fugitives and cowards at Pittsburgh Landing has passed away, even sooner than I thought, and I am no less surprised than gratified in finding the estimate in which you are everywhere held as a soldier. I believe I can say that a different policy is now to prevail. The administration has come up to what the people have long demanded—a vigorous prosecution of the war by all the means known to civilized warfare. The negroes must now be made our auxiliaries in every possible way they can be, whether by working or fighting. That General who takes the most decided step in this respect will be held in the highest estimation by the loyal and true men in the country. The idea that a man can be in the rebel army, leaving his negroes and property behind him to be protected by our troops, is to me shocking. The time is now come when we must adopt and act upon the principle that 'war must maintain war.' If the constitution or slavery must perish, let slavery go to the wall. My brother has been confirmed as brigadier general. The last I heard from him he had reached Helena. I hope he may be under your command somewhere. I am satisfied you will find him an officer upon whom you can rely. I shall be in Galena in about 10 days. If you have time I should like to have a word from you.—When the weather shall get a little cooler, I intend to visit you." ALS, USG 3.

1. Henry S. Fitch, son of Col. Graham N. Fitch, was born in N. Y., and eventually moved to Chicago, where he practiced law and was appointed U. S. attorney for the northern district of Ill. in 1858. In 1860, a question arose about his accounts, but an audit failed to reveal any wrongdoing on his part. A political associate of both President Abraham Lincoln and U.S. Senator Orville H. Browning, Fitch, a War Democrat, offered his resignation to Lincoln and applied for a commission as asst. adjt. gen. in 1861. Lincoln nominated him as asst. q. m. and capt. in July, 1861, and he was serving in Memphis when USG arrived. Fitch to Lincoln, Jan. 7, 1859, Jan. 30, 1861, DLC-Robert T. Lincoln; Fitch to Browning, June 26, 1861, DNA, RG 94, Letters Received; Fitch to Secretary of War Edwin M. Stanton, Dec. 27, 1862, *ibid.*; Fitch to Brig. Gen. Lorenzo Thomas, Sept. 10, 1861, *ibid.*; *HED*, 36–1–53.

To Maj. Gen. Henry W. Halleck

Head Quarters, Dist. of West Ten.
Corinth, July 23d 1862

MAJ. GEN. H. W. HALLECK
COMD.G DEPT. OF THE MISS.
WASHINGTON CITY.
GEN.

Since you left here the greatest vigilance has been kept up by our Cavalry to the front but nothing absolutely certain of the movements of the enemy have been learned.[1] It is certain however that a movement has taken place from Tupello. In what direction or for what purpose is not so certain. Deserters and escaped prisoners concur in this statement but all concuring so nearly I doubt whether they have not been misled with the view of having the information reach us. It would seem from these statements that a large force moved on the 7th of this month towards Chatanooga. That Price was at Tupello on the 17th and made a speech to his command promising to take them back to Mo. through Ky. That his ordnance and provision train had moved Westward with seventeen days rations and he has likely followed ere this.[2]

I do not regard this information of special value except as to giving an idea of points to watch and see if these statements are verified.

The changes directed by you before leaving here have all been made. Morgan's Div. has relieved Thomas.[3] Sherman & Hurlbut have reached ~~Columbus~~ Memphis[4] and the entire Memphis & Charleston road is abandoned by us West of here except at Chewalla[5] and a force yet retained at Grand Junction.[6]

Should anything occur within this District of a startling or important nature I will inform you by telegraph.

> I am Gen very respectfully
> your obt. svt.
> U. S. GRANT
> Maj. Gen.

ALS, IHi. *O.R.*, I, xvii, part 2, 114.

1. On July 16, 1862, Maj. Gen. John A. McClernand endorsed and forwarded to USG a report of July 13 from Maj. Martin R. M. Wallace, 4th Ill. Cav., to Brig. Gen. John A. Logan concerning patrols in the area around Jackson, Tenn. ALS, DNA, RG 393, District of West Tenn., Letters Received. On July 22, McClernand reported to Maj. John A. Rawlins a second cav. expedition of Wallace. ALS, *ibid.* On July 21, Brig. Gen. Isaac F. Quinby telegraphed to USG. "We have in this district 7 Companies of the 2nd & 5th five (5) Companies of the sixth (6th) Ill Cav. Also three (3) Companies of the Curtis horse. Having for duty respectively four hundred & ninety eight, two hundred & sixty eight & one hundred & twenty six. Genl Dodge commanding at Trenton reports Guerrillas troublesome   I send by mail a copy of his report. We cannot do much in chasing & breaking up such parties without Cavalry. I will at once order such force of Cavalry to Bolivar as you may designate"   Telegram received, *ibid.*, Dept. of the Mo., Telegrams Received. On July 23, Maj. Gen. Edward O. C. Ord, Corinth, wrote to Rawlins of sending out a cav. expedition to stop rebels interfering with the railroad. Copy, *ibid.*, 16th Army Corps, Post of Corinth, Letters Sent.
2. See telegram to Maj. Gen. Don Carlos Buell, July 20, 1862. On July 19, McClernand telegraphed to USG. "T. M. Phelps Rail Road Machinest who says he saw you at Shiloh was in Mobile on*e* sunday Grenada tuesday Talahatchee thursday Holly Springs last night. Jackson with four hundred Cavalry was reported under orders to move yesterday for Tupolo. Chalmers with a Brigade probably from Ripley for the same place. He speaks of it as a fact that Bragg moved his army eight days ago from Tupolo & has reached Baldwin sending on a division towards Iuka & repairing bridge between Baldwin & Booneville in his advance upon Corinth   He said Milton Brown said to him in Mobile that the Rebel army would be here in four weeks. That the second (2nd) Kentucky regiment had been mounted and were to make a morgan raid in this direction. Only four four thousand troops at Tallahatche"   Telegram received, DNA, RG 393, Dept.

of the Mo., Telegrams Received; copy, McClernand Papers, IHi. On July 22, Brig. Gen. William S. Rosecrans telegraphed to USG suggesting that C. S. A. movements had been made toward Chattanooga or Rome. Telegram received (incomplete), DNA, RG 393, Dept. of the Mo., Telegrams Received. On July 22, Col. John D. Stevenson, commanding at Pittsburg Landing, telegraphed to USG. "A messenger yesterday also one to-day from below on river near Decatur represents a body of rebel cavalry from direction of Murrfriesboro two hundred (200) strong laying waste country seizing union men. people ask assistance" Telegram received, *ibid*. On the same day, 1st Master Jason Goudy, Pittsburg Landing, of the gunboat *Alfred Robb*, telegraphed to USG. "I have just returned from East Perryville. The country around there is invested with a band guerrillas They made a decent on the town & robbed the Union men there of their property & money & taking some prisoners they withdrew about 20 miles back of the town & I could do nothing against them with my boat. They number about eighty. There is a man here now named Little who wants to guide a party of cavalry to them. He thinks with a body of cavalry of about a hundred & fifty he can take the whole party. I can vouch for his integrity & knowledge of the country Please answer immy." Telegram received, *ibid*. On July 23, Rosecrans telegraphed to USG. "A discharged Arkansas rebel is in. He has been well tested as to his honesty. He heard Price address their troops last Thursday in Tupello. Promised to take them to Missouri soon, by Kentucky he understood. Knows Price's ord. train passed from his Camp, east of the R. R. westward about the 14th that in brigade had 17 days rations, and marching orders to leave day before yesterday. Knows Bragg was at Tupello last Thursday That old Peck [*Polk*] was west the R. R. towards Saltillo, and will send details. The man is from Arkansas, and had better be sent to McClernand" Copy, *ibid*., Army of the Miss., 16th Army Corps, Telegrams Sent. On the same day, Rosecrans gave the same information in greater detail in a letter to Rawlins. ALS, *ibid*., District of West Tenn., Letters Received.

On July 23, McClernand telegraphed to USG. "Several Gentlemen arriving here last night and today report some six hundred (600) rebel cavalry opposite Perryvill on the Burreses [*Tennessee*] river who having burned Mr Howards dwellings & outhouses are threatening to cross the river—I have ordered a Detachment of cavalry and Infantry in that direction" Telegram received, *ibid*., Dept. of the Mo., Telegrams Received; copy, McClernand Papers, IHi. On the same day, McClernand telegraphed to USG. "Col Leggett reports four thousand (4000) of Braggs command this side of Holly Springs and that Jacksons cavalry are crossing the Rail Road near moscow in squads of six and seven concentrating above Somerville ought not Sherman and Hurlbut to protect the country west of the Hatchie with a smaller force I am protecting up to this time not only the country east of the Hatchie but our front Col Leggett will leave Grand Junction to night or tomorrow" Telegram received, DNA, RG 393, Dept. of the Mo., Telegrams Received; copy, McClernand Papers, IHi. For the moves which were actually contemplated by the C. S. A., see Special Orders No. 123, Dept. No. 2, Tupelo, Miss., July 17, *O.R.*, I, xvii, part 2, 648–49.

After the breakup of Maj. Gen. Henry W. Halleck's grand army, C. S. A. Gen. Braxton Bragg had decided that he ought to move on the offensive. In spite of the threat which USG's army posed to Vicksburg, Bragg believed that Maj. Gen. Don Carlos Buell posed a more immediate danger by his move toward Chattanooga. Bragg had sent a division to Chattanooga on June 27, and on July 23, additional troops began the move. In all, Bragg ordered about 30,000 troops to Chattanooga. He left Maj. Gen. Sterling Price at Tupelo with 16,000 men and Maj. Gen. Earl Van Dorn at Vicksburg with 16,000. These were in addition to the guerrilla and independent cav. units operating in northern Miss., Tenn., and Ky. against USG's army. Grady McWhiney, *Braxton Bragg and Confederate Defeat* (New York and London, 1969), I, 266–69.

On July 21, USG telegraphed to Maj. Gen. William T. Sherman asking for returns. Telegram received, DNA, RG 393, 16th Army Corps, 4th Division, Letters and Telegrams Received. On the same day, he telegraphed to Rosecrans to the same effect. Copy, *ibid.*, Army of the Miss., Telegrams Received. On the same day, Rosecrans telegraphed to Rawlins that he would secure the returns as soon as possible. Telegram received, *ibid.*, Dept. of the Mo., Telegrams Received. On July 29, Capt. Marcellus G. V. Strong, asst. adjt. gen. at Cairo, telegraphed returns to USG. Telegram received, *ibid.* The abstract of monthly returns for the District of West Tenn. for July 31 showed a total aggregate present of 78,870 officers and men. Of these, 9,706 served in the 1st Division, McClernand commanding, hd. qrs. at Jackson, Tenn.; 11,850 served under Ord, hd. qrs. at Corinth; 7,026 served in the 4th Division, Brig. Gen. Stephen A. Hurlbut commanding, hd. qrs. at Memphis; 8,949 served in the 5th Division, Sherman commanding, hd. qrs. at Memphis; 5,941 served in the District of the Miss., Quinby commanding, hd. qrs. at Columbus, Ky.; 1,533 served in the District of Cairo, Brig. Gen. William K. Strong commanding, hd. qrs. at Cairo; 31,542 served in the Army of the Miss., Rosecrans commanding, hd. qrs. at Camp Clear Creek near Corinth; and 2,312 served in detached commands. *O.R.*, I, xvii, part 2, 143–44. William M. Lamers, *The Edge of Glory: A Biography of General William S. Rosecrans, U. S. A.* (New York, 1961), pp. 92, 94.

3. See telegrams to Brig. Gen. William S. Rosecrans, July 17, 18, 19, 1862.

4. See telegrams to Maj. Gen. John A. McClernand, July 16, 17, and to Brig. Gen. Alvin P. Hovey, July 18, 1862.

5. Chewalla, Tenn., on the Memphis and Charleston Railroad, about ten miles northwest of Corinth.

6. See telegram to Maj. Gen. John A. McClernand, July 17, 1862. On July 18, McClernand telegraphed to USG. "How or when will any cavalry be sent to Grand Junction—I will send Maj Stewart to select camp if you will advise me in time—Genl Halleck said he would send surplus cavalry north down this way" Telegram received, DNA, RG 393, Dept. of the Mo., Telegrams Received; copy, McClernand Papers, IHi. On July 21, McClernand wrote to USG suggesting that the district which USG had originally assigned to McClernand, and which Halleck had altered, ought to be reassigned in view of the change in conditions since Halleck had left. ALS, DNA, RG 393, District of West Tenn., Letters Received; copy, McClernand Papers, IHi. See letter to Maj. Gen. John A. McClernand, June 24, 1862. On July 21, McClernand telegraphed to USG. "Col Leggett having telegraphed that Jacksons cavalry are within six miles of Grand Junction and Chalmers with cavalry and infantry at Burks springs fifteen miles threaten to attack G Junction I have telegraphed Genl Ross in command both at Grand Junction and Bolivar as follows—one of two things remain either to advance the force at Bolivar to Grand Junction for which I have no authority or for the force at Grand Junction to fall back on Bolivar   if you think there is real danger of an attack by superior numbers it is best that the force at Grand Junction should fall back on Bolivar—In that event it would probably be advisable for you

to advance a detachment so as to meet and support the retiring force from Grand Junction" Telegram received, DNA, RG 393, Dept. of the Mo., Telegrams Received; copy, McClernand Papers, IHi. On July 22, McClernand wrote to USG giving the results of a reconnaissance on the Memphis and Ohio Railroad from Memphis to Paris, Tenn., and estimating the cost of repairing damages to structures on the line. Copy, *ibid.* On July 22, McClernand telegraphed to USG. "Grand Junction is still in our possession   will the cavalry be sent   if not cant you send three or four regiments of infantry from points north" Telegram received, DNA, RG 393, Dept. of the Mo., Telegrams Received; copy, McClernand Papers, IHi.

To Brig. Gen. William S. Rosecrans

Corinth July 23rd 1862

W. S. Rosecrans
Brig Genl

When you want the Cavalry of Genl. Orders[1] command inform him where, and to whom to report. The Genl is directed to hold him subject to your call by telegraph

U. S. Grant
Maj Genl

Telegram, copy, DNA, RG 393, Army of the Miss., Telegrams Received. On July 22, 1862, Maj. John A. Rawlins issued Special Orders No. 141. "Maj Gen. Ord, Commdg U. S. Forces at Corinth Miss will have all the Cavalry in his command in readiness to march tomorrow evening, with three days rations and one days forage. He will report to these Head Quarters as early as practicable the number of such Cavalry as are available." Copies, DLC-USG, V, 15, 16, 82, 87; DNA, RG 393, USG Special Orders. *O.R.*, I, xvii, part 2, 112. On July 23, Rawlins issued Special Orders No. 142. "Col. T. Lyle Dickey, Chief of Cavalry will make an tour of inspection of the Cavalry stationed at the various points on the line of the rail road between Corinth and Columbus, and at Paducah, Ky. He will report upon their condition as to health, police of Camps, kind and condition of Arms, discipline, serviceableness of horses, clothing, Camp and Garrison Equipage and all other points that may suggest themselves to make the inspection thorough. The amount and kind of duty required of the Cavalry, and the apparent necessity of it should be particularly looked into." Copies, DLC-USG, V, 15, 16, 82, 87; DNA, RG 393, USG Special Orders. On July 18, Col. T. Lyle Dickey, Jackson, Tenn., telegraphed to USG. "Just arrived from Lagrange   Mrs Grant and Children here well   what orders have you for me." Telegram received, *ibid.*, Dept. of the Mo., Telegrams Received.

1. This should read "Genl. Ord." Edward O. C. Ord of Md., USMA 1839, served continuously in the army, and held the rank of capt., 3rd Art., on the eve of the Civil War. Appointed brig. gen. on Sept. 14, 1861, he served in the Army of the Potomac; then as maj. gen. as of May 2, 1862, he was assigned command of the 2nd Division, Army of the Tenn., at Corinth on June 22.

To Maj. Gen. William T. Sherman

———

By Telegraph from Corinth [*July*] 24th 1862

To Maj Genl. W. T. Sherman
Memphis.
Genl—
Inform Col. Fitch that his command will remain under Genl. Curtiss with the exception of the artillery taken from Memphis —that will be returned. I telegraphed this to Col. Fitch but suppose from communications just received that he never got my despatch. Send all the men, transportation, and such baggage to the Col as he may wish to have with him

U. S. Grant
Maj. Genl.

Telegram, copies, DNA, RG 393, District of Eastern Ark., Letters Received; Curtis Papers, IaHA. See telegrams to Brig. Gen. Alvin P. Hovey, July 13, 18, 1862.

To Brig. Gen. Lorenzo Thomas

Head Quarters Disct of W. Tenn
Corinth, July 25, 1862

Brig Genl L Thomas
Adjt Genl of the Army
Washington, D. C.
Genl

I have just been shown a letter of Capt J P. Hawkins C. S, to Col Haines, which, with the endorsement of the latter was sent to the Commissary General, and has caused an order for the discharge of Capt W W Leland from the service.

Capt Leland has served under my command for the last seven or eight months, and I feel it a duty to him to relieve him from such suspicions as I know, or believe, to be unjust.

In the first place Capt Leland seems to have been mustered out of service on charges of suspicions against his administration of affairs in his Department, without an opportunity to vindicate himself, and without the charges being sent through any Commanding Officer. Matters are alluded to that occurred back at Cairo, and which I had investigated; the investigation resulting entirely in the exculpation of Capt L. So much was said at the time as to prejudice me very much against the Captain. These charges were, being a partner in a baking contract given by himself,[1] crediting to his own account the full amount of wastage that can be covered under the regulations &c   The investigation showed conclusively that there was no bribery or corruption in the bread contract whatever, and the other charges could not be traced to a single person who knew anything about them except from hearsay. I refer you in this connection, to a letter addressed by me at the time to Capt Leland

I am not prepared to vindicate Capt Leland against all charges, but am ready to state that investigations heretofore have proven his entire innocence of a part, and failed to show guilt in any particular. I think the only cause of complaint that could be well founded in the start was lack of experience.

Capt Lelands administration of affairs in his Department have ever been prompt and satisfactory, and I hope he will be reinstated at least to give him an opportunity for a fair trial.

> I am Genl. Very Respcty
> Your Obt Servt
> U. S. GRANT
> Maj Genl

LS, Lincoln Papers, IHi. On June 10, 1862, Capt. John P. Hawkins, commissary of subsistence, Corinth, wrote to Col. Thomas J. Haines, chief commissary of subsistence, St. Louis. "A special Order from Genl Hallecks Head Quarters, of this date, directs that Captain W. W. Leland C. S. Vol shall at the expiration of his twenty days leave of Absence report for Orders to the Commissary General Captain Lelands services are no longer required with the Army in the field or any other place where I may have charge of Affairs. Captains Lelands Administration of the Subsistence Department is such as to beget suspicions in the minds of those who may notice him that it is not done honestly, and whether this suspicion is just or not, I think it would be better for the public service that he be not put on duty again in this or any other geographical department. I would respectfully request that you please forward this with your endorsement without delay to the Commissary General" ALS, DNA, RG 94, Letters Received. On June 17, Haines forwarded Hawkins's letter to Col. Joseph P. Taylor, commissary gen. of subsistence, with the recommendation that Capt. William W. Leland not be restored to duty. AES, *ibid.* On June 21, Taylor referred Hawkins's letter to Secretary of War Edwin M. Stanton with the recommendation "that he be mustered out of Service." ES, *ibid.* On June 21, Stanton approved the recommendation. ES, *ibid.* Leland was honorably discharged on June 24. USG and a number of others had supported Leland for promotion to maj. See letter to Edwin M. Stanton, Feb. 18, 1862.

1. On July 26, Maj. Gen. John A. McClernand wrote "To whom it may concern: In the matter of the charge brought by the Jew Lazar, at Cairo, about a bread contract, at Cairo, about which Capt Haines took some cognizance, I have to say that it appeared upon investigation that there was no foundation for it, except the cupidity of Lazar, who, not withstanding criminal short comings as a previous contracter, I regret to hear has again become a bread contractor. In all other matters affecting the official conduct of Capt Leland, he has, to the extent of my observation, displayed exemplary and commendable acuity and energy. This recommendation by honest and distinguished public men for promotion is a testimonial in his favor. To blast a man's character without giving him a hearing is an extreme measure inimical to fundamental principles. Justice and fair dealing prompt me to say that I think Capt L. is entitled to a hearing, and a revival of the order dismissing him from the service and disgracing him" Copy, DNA, RG 94, Letters Received. See letters to Capt. Thomas J. Haines, Dec. 17, 1861, and to Capt. William W. Leland, Dec. 17, 1861, Jan. 1, 1862. A question was also raised during Leland's tenure regarding his purchase of tobacco for the

Mississippi Flotilla, but USG had approved the purchase and this did not apparently come into question during the investigation. On April 30 and Aug. 10, Leland wrote to Taylor explaining the purchase. LS, DNA, RG 192, Letters Received.

To Brig. Gen. William S. Rosecrans

—————

Corinth July 25th [*1862*]

Genl. Rosecrans

I have just seen the Quarter Master who tells me that the wagons required by Genl. Morgan cannot be furnished unless details can be made from Regimental trains to keep up the present number now hauling, between here and Pittsburg Landing. I will see what can be done from Ords Command. In this way, will Morgans force be sufficient to defend the long line given him? It seems to me it will not

U. S Grant
Maj Genl

Telegram, copy, DNA, RG 393, Army of the Miss., Telegrams Received. On July 25, 1862, Brig. Gen. William S. Rosecrans telegraphed to USG. "Genl. Morgan has reached Tuscumbia, and halts there, demanding 100 wagons in addition to his present train before proceeding beyond that point. Genl. McPherson says he can transport 50 tons per day along that road : if it be loaded and unloaded promptly, and the road protected. But a train was cut off last night from returning, by the destruction of a bridge east of Tuscumbia and a party of Infantry, probably Thomas' attacked and probably captured by 500 Rebel Cavalry at Courtland" Copy, *ibid.*, 16th Army Corps, Telegrams Sent. *O.R.*, I, xvii, part 2, 120.

On July 24, Rosecrans telegraphed to Brig. Gen. James B. McPherson. "by Major Cross seizing supplies procured for this army, be cause not through him, on arrival, at Pittsburg Landing, we, and our persistent obedience to Department orders. We are now fifty days behind time, and some of our men are actually shoeless, shirtless and some cuslottes   Our supplies are at Columbus, but not coming up, because a heap of Sutler, and other freight arrived before ours is coming forward in the same order. Please give orders that our clothing shall come forward, and I will send an officer to take charge of it"   Copy, DNA, RG 393, Army of the Miss., 16th Army Corps, Telegrams Sent. On the same day, Brig. Gen. Isaac F. Quinby telegraphed to USG. "Special order No 135 is countermanded   please send me ~~certificate~~ definate instructions as to my duties connected with shipment of goods public and private over the Rail Road   you will understand my embarrasment"   Telegram received, *ibid.*, Dept. of the Mo.,

Telegrams Received. On July 26, Rosecrans telegraphed to USG. "Genl McPherson says he can supply Morgan on conditions stated. I have telegraphed Morgan that if he cannot protect the R.R. train he cannot protect wagon train beyond Tuscumbia   that therefore he should halt at that point up to which he can so cover his line until such disposition's as are needed can be made—There is no object in pushing his troop's beyond the point where he can protect the RR yet known to me   on the ~~country~~ contrary as soon as I hear from him will telegraph you." Telegram received, *ibid.*; copy, *ibid.*, Army of the Miss., 16th Army Corps, Telegrams Sent. *O.R.*, I, xvii, part 2, 120.

To Andrew Johnson

———

By Telegraph from Corinth [*July*] 25 1862

To Brig Genl A Johnson

   Mr J. W. Tarkington[1] a union man of Henderson Co reports that he has now five 5 companies already organized & five 5 more partially that ~~will~~ will be filled soon   He wishes to be commissioned as Col of the Regt raised in Henderson Haden Carroll & McNary counties[2] & Filan Huritt[3] to be Commissioned as Lt. Col   Huritt has been a refugee from his home & has acted as guide & scout for the army until our forces rendered it safe for him to return   this Regt if accepted will want arms orders of locating   Allow me to suggest Perryville until fully prepared to move   Dispatches sent to me will reach Col Tarkington   Col Tarkington has been petitioned by the union men of his county to organize a Regiment

                                                            U S Grant
                                                            Maj Genl

Telegram received, DLC-Andrew Johnson. On July 22, 1862, Col. J. W. Tarkington and Lt. Col. Fielding Hurst had telegraphed to Governor Andrew Johnson. "Have you sent our commissions   secessionists have taken two Union men thirty miles below here robbed one of three thousand dollars   are getting very bold here some of whom have taken the oath   citizens here are apprehensive of an attack on this place"   Telegram received, *ibid.* On July 23, Maj. Gen. John A. McClernand telegraphed to USG. "Is there no way by which you can furnish Loyal men arms & ammunition. As for myself I would hesitate at no responsibility. Our Cavalry are now out making fruitless expeditions to catch guerrillas who disperse & disappear before the approach of our army" Telegram received, DNA, RG 393, Dept. of the Mo., Telegrams Received; copy, McClernand Papers, IHi. On July 24, McClernand telegraphed to USG. "I started a Regt of Infantry and fifty mounted men this morning in the direction of Perrysville on the Tenn six miles above Decaturville" Telegram received, DNA, RG 393, Dept. of the Mo., Telegrams Received; copy, McClernand Papers, IHi. On July 25, McClernand telegraphed to Johnson about the possibility of raising a home guard to assist in occupying western Tenn. Telegram received, DLC-Andrew Johnson. On July 26, Johnson telegraphed to McClernand about ways to accomplish this. ALS (telegram sent), *ibid.*

On Aug. 9, McClernand telegraphed to USG. "Respecting the Cavalry being raised at and in the vicinity of Huntingdon, the following is Govr Johnson's despatch, giving directions to have them mustered into the U S service. 'Nashville Aug 5 1862. Maj Genl. McClernand—Please muster them into service I will commission them or have it done by the War Dept. What will they do for arms & horse's for the present? Have they ~~have~~ any they can use for the present? are they organized for service in the vicinity or will they come here, where we are organizing cavalry & receiving equipments &c we have sufficient for 1000, which we will soon raise & more ordered. ANDREW JOHNSON. Mily Govr.' of the 4 Comps. raising at that point, one has 90 men, who wish to mustered into the U S service and for that purpose, please detail Capt J Morris Young Co "C" 5th Iowa Cavalry (Curtis Horse) & at the request of Mr Hawkins on behalf of these men, to take charge & drill them." Copy, McClernand Papers, IHi. On Aug. 9, McClernand telegraphed to Johnson, urging the raising of a brigade in west Tenn., saying he was "satisfied that if you do so the Loyal men of this part of the state will guard it against any bands that can be raised here" Telegram received, DLC-Andrew Johnson; copy, McClernand Papers, IHi.

1. The 1860 U.S. Census lists J. W. Tarkington of Shady Hill, Henderson County, Tenn., as a fifty-three-year-old farmer.

2. The four Tenn. counties of McNairy, Hardin, Henderson, and Carroll run successively in a line northward from the Miss. border above Corinth.

3. Though his name was garbled in transmission, this was Fielding Hurst of Chester County, Tenn., a staunch unionist, who had served as guide for Maj. Gen. Lewis Wallace in April, and was attached to USG's command in May for the same purpose. Shortly after this time, Hurst became col., 6th Tenn. Cav. (originally known as the 1st West Tenn. Cav.). Capt. Nathaniel H. McLean to USG, April 19, 1862, DNA, RG 393, Dept. of the Miss., Letters Sent. USG Special Orders No. 71, May 2, 1862, copies, DLC-USG, V, 15, 16, 82, 87, 89; DNA, RG 393, USG Special Orders. McClernand to USG, and 1st Lt. Theodore S. Bowers to McClernand, May 18, 1862, ALS, *ibid.*, Dept. of the Tenn., Letters Received from the Reserve Corps, Jackson, Tenn.

On Aug. 10, McClernand telegraphed to USG. "Genl Ross reports great activity among the Rebels in Fayette 'Cos' & that they will probably raise a force of (500) men unless prevented He also says that he could probably raise Several 'Cos' of mounted men if he could ensure them of arms. It is deplorable that the Union are not armed in their own defense & placed under command of Officers who would see that the arms do not pass into the hands of Rebels. Will not the Department authorize you, me or some on to act in this respect. I ~~a~~ ask that you will forward this dispatch to the Secy. of War." Telegram received, *ibid.*, Dept.

of the Mo., Telegrams Received; copies, McClernand Papers, IHi. On Aug. 12, Johnson telegraphed to McClernand informing him of the appointment of Hurst as col., 1st West Tenn. Cav., and asking for support in equipping the unit. ALS (telegram sent), DLC-Andrew Johnson. On Sept. 13, Col. Isham N. Haynie, Bethel, telegraphed to USG. "I have applied to Comd'ant at Jackson for instructions authorzing me to issue forage & subsistence to the companys of Tenn sate guards   col Hurst now in camp here   No instructions have came—will you advise & instruct me whether to do it or not"   Telegram received, DNA, RG 393, Dept. of the Tenn., Telegrams Received.

On Sept. 28, Haynie telegraphed to Maj. John A. Rawlins. "The charges are that the dwellings & property of a citizen who had a safe guard was burned by Col Hurst's men, by his order—that he has evidently to destroy Gen Meeks property if Gen Meek refuses to pay him money demanded—that he has theratend his men shall destroy their mens residence—that he has liscenced his men to plunder & depridate in violation of Genl Grants orders—yesterday there was evidently an effort to stir up mutiny here   that is why I think it best he be away —but I can & will master the whol thing   I ask Gen Grants permission to visit his Head Quarters tomorrow to see him on this matter"   Telegram received, *ibid.*, Miscellaneous Letters Received.

To Brig. Gen. Isaac F. Quinby

U. S. Military Telegraph,
Corinth, July 26 [*1862*]

To Brig Gen J. T Quimby, Columbus, Ky.
General—

Examine the baggage of all speculators coming South, and, when they have specie, turn them back. If medicine and other contraband articles, arrest them and confiscate the contraband articles. Jews should receive special attention.

U. S. Grant, Maj. Gen.

Chicago Times, Aug. 4, 1862; *New York Times*, Aug. 7, 1862; P. C. Headley, *The Life and Campaigns of General U. S. Grant* (New York, 1868), p. 164. Isaac F. Quinby was professor of mathematics at the University of Rochester 1852–61. See letter of Aug. 20, 1859. He served as col., 13th N. Y., from May until Aug., 1861, when he resigned to return to the University of Rochester. On March 17, 1862, he was appointed brig. gen. and placed in command of the District of the Miss., Columbus, Ky., on April 10.

On July 25, Maj. John A. Rawlins issued General Orders No. 64. "The attention of the Major General Commdg, having been called to the fact of persons within this District, sympathizing with the Rebellion, who have Cotton for sale, refusing to receive U. S. Treasury notes in payment therefor, or any thing other than Gold and Silver, which is paid them by Speculators whose love of gain is greater than their love of Country, and the Gold and Silver thus paid, indirectly affording aid and comfort to the enemy, renders necessary the publication of the following orders: From and after the 1st day of August, 1862 Gold and Silver will not be paid within this Dist. by Speculators for the products of the Rebel States. U. S. Treasury notes are a legal tender in all cases, and when refused, the parties refusing them will be arrested, and such of their crops as are not actually required for the subsistence of their families, stock, &c. may be seized and sold by the nearest Quarter Master for the benefit of whom it may concern. Money so received will be accounted for by the Officer receiving it, on his next account current, and used for the benefit of the Govenment, only to be paid to the owners of the crops sold, on orders from authority above that of Dist. Commanders. Any Speculator paying out Gold and Silver in violation of this order will be arrested and sent North, and the property so purchased seized and turned over to the proper Dept. for the benefit of the Government. A strict enforcement of this order is enjoined upon all officers in this Dist." Copies, DLC-USG, V, 12, 13, 14, 95; DNA, RG 393, USG General Orders; *ibid.*, RG 94, 21st Ill., Order Book. *O.R.*, I, xvii, part 2, 123. On July 16, Col. William S. Hillyer had telegraphed to USG. "Parties who have purchased Cotton in the Country are asking permission to send armed Citizens to escort it to Memphis. Shall it be allowed?" Telegram received, DNA, RG 393, Dept. of the Mo., Telegrams Received. On July 17, Hillyer had telegraphed to Rawlins. "Ask the General to issue an order to me similar to the one issued by Gen Halleck to Provost Marshal Gen at Corinth to seize cotton and turn over to Quarter Master   Many persons in this vicinity would like to have their cotton seized and sold for their benefit   Some afraid to sell while others refuse to sell to the Yankees—Attend to this immediately"   Telegram received, *ibid.* On July 26, Quinby telegraphed to USG. "I have just received the following: TRENTON, *July* 26. General QUINBY: The gold paid out here by cotton buyers finds its way to the Southern army immediately. Hundreds have left for that army in the counties around here lately, carrying every dollar of gold paid for cotton. The circulation of gold should be stopped. G. M. DODGE, *Brigadier-General.* You will pardon me for again bringing this matter before you." *O.R.*, I, xvii, part 2, 123.

On July 26, Maj. Gen. John A. McClernand wrote to USG. "Your telegram concerning cotton dealers and currency is received. Our views probably accord as to both. Some days since, I recommended to the Treasury, through its agent Mr Mellon, the prohibition of payments in coin for cotton in the insurrectionary States—nay; more that the holders of cotton in such States should be required to sell it at the Market price, or a price to be fixed by the Treasury from time to time and receive for it Treasury notes. If you say so I will make an order covering both points, though, both more properly appertain to the Treasury Department. But you will pardon me for saying that this is one subject, and the safety of our communications another. It was of the latter I spoke in my telegram sent last night. If the fury of bandits and organized foes stopped at cotton burning there would be some apology for saying: 'let them burn'; but as it covets something more important—the safety of our communications and our army, we must guard against them. If we do not we will be held culpable. What is going on? Yesterday a considerable detachment of rebel cavalry was chased away from Denmark—

eight miles from here. Last night I ran the guantlet between here and Bolivar to secure the rail road from threatened attack—reinforcing Toon's Station, ten miles from Bolivar, for that purpose; and just before day-break this morning, my Infantry guard drove back a party of mounted rebels who were approaching to destroy the first bridge on the rail road north of this place. I need and again ask for reinforcements—protesting against any disposition which leaves my front for more than forty miles between Memphis and Corinth and my right flank for at least as great distance, parallel with the Hatchie river, exposed to attacks, which my small and exhausted command will not enable me everywhere certainly and successfully to meet. I will do all, at whatever peril, that may be done by a force no larger and as much worn as mine, but, if in dispite of their best efforts, our communications should be cut and the whole army disturbed the responsibility will not justly attach to me. I have so far preserved all the roads in my District intact and undisturbed. The trains have run as regularly as may be reasonably expected under their present management. I am desirous that no change for the worse should take place. If I shall be furnished with adequate means none shall. That is all I can say." ALS, DNA, RG 393, District of West Tenn., Letters Received. On July 26, McClernand telegraphed to USG the substance of his letter. Copies, McClernand Papers, IHi.

On July 30, Maj. Gen. William T. Sherman wrote to Rawlins. "I have been very busy in answering the innumerable questions of Citizens, and hope they are now about through. I found so many Jews & Speculators here trading in cotton and secessionists had become so open in refusing any thing but Gold that I have felt myself bound to stop it. This Gold has but one use, the purchase of arms & ammunition, which can always be had for Gold either at Nassau New Providence or Cincinati. All the Guards we may establish cannot stop it. Of course I have respected all permits by yourself or the Secretary of the Treasury, but in these new cases, (swarms of Jews) I have stopped it. In like manner so great was the demand for salt to make Bacon, that many succeeded in getting loads of salt out for cotton. Salt is as much contraband of war as Powder. All the Boards of Trade above are shipping salt south, and I cannot permit it to pass into the Interior. I hope you will at once write & telegraph to the rightful parties that money & salt will not be permitted to go into the Interior until you declare a district open to Trade. If we permit money & salt to go into the Interior, it will not take long for Bragg & Van Dorn to supply their armies with all they need to move. Without money, Gold Silver & Treasury notes, they cannot get arms & ammunition of the English Colonies, & without salt they can not make Bacon & Salt Beef. We cannot carry on war & trade with a people at the same time." ALS, DNA, RG 393, District of West Tenn., Letters Received. *O.R.*, I, xvii, part 2, 140–41.

On Aug. 4, Col. William W. Lowe, Fort Henry, telegraphed to Rawlins. "I would respectfully suggest that to enable Commanders to carry out the provisions of general order number sixty four (64) some such plan as the following be adopted—In all cases of purchase of cotton require the purchaser of cotton to report to the nearest military Commander make oath as to the quantity purchased the name and locality of the person from whom bought and the ~~person~~ Kind of funds paid   This would enable the Commander to discover any case of attempt to evade the order"   Telegram received, DNA, RG 393, Dept. of the Mo., Telegrams Received. See letters to Maj. Gen. Henry W. Halleck, July 28, to Salmon P. Chase, July 31, and General Orders No. 11, Dec. 17, 1862.

On Aug. 11, Rawlins telegraphed to Brig. Gen. William S. Rosecrans. "In pursuance of orders from Hd Qrs of the Army at Washington, all the restrictions upon the sale of cotton and prohibiting of the payment of gold therefore are hereby annulled. Every faculty possible will be afforded for getting cotton into market'' Copy, DNA, RG 393, Army of the Miss., Telegrams Received. On the same day, Rawlins sent a similar telegram to Sherman. *Memphis Bulletin*, Aug. 15, 1862. On the same day, Sherman telegraphed to USG. "Cotton order ~~will be enforced~~ of Hd Qrs of the Army encouraging trade in cotton is received and must be respected. But I will move Heaven & Earth for its repeal, as I believe it will be fatal to our success. If we provide our enemies with money we enable them to buy, all they stand in need of. Money is as much contraband of war as powder. All well here.'' ALS (telegram sent), DNA, RG 393, District of West Tenn., Letters Received; telegram received, *ibid.*, Dept. of the Mo., Telegrams Received. *O.R.*, III, ii, 350. On the same day, Sherman sent different telegrams to Brig. Gen. Lorenzo Thomas and Secretary of the Treasury Salmon P. Chase asking that the order be revoked. ALS (telegrams sent), DNA, RG 393, District of West Tenn., Letters Received. *O.R.*, III, ii, 349–50. Quinby endorsed Sherman's telegram to Chase. *Ibid.*, p. 350. On Aug. 12, the *Nashville Union* printed a dispatch from the Memphis correspondent of the *Philadelphia Press* echoing Sherman's sentiments. *Nashville Union*, Aug. 12, 1862.

On Aug. 14, Sherman wrote to Rawlins. "I have published Genl Grant order based on the one from Hd. Qrs. of the Army, annulling all restrictions on the purchases of cotton & paymt of Gold therefore. I cannot see how Genl Halleck can allow Gold which is universally contraband thus to pass into possession of an enemy, but I hope his reasons as are usual based on a far seeing Policy. I shall of course obey the order and facilitate the trade in cotton & its Shipment but it seems against the grain. . . ." Copy, DNA, RG 393, District of West Tenn., Letters Received. *O.R.*, I, xvii, part 2, 169–71.

On Aug. 14, R. W. Birch, Jackson, Tenn., telegraphed to USG. "Genl Quimby refuses to let gold pass his lines   please Send a permit to pass gold'' Telegram received, DNA, RG 393, Dept. of the Mo., Telegrams Received. On the same day, Maj. Gen. Henry W. Halleck telegraphed to Sherman advising him of the need to permit specie to be paid for cotton. ALS (telegram sent), *ibid.*, RG 107, Telegrams Collected (Bound). *O.R.*, III, ii, 382. On Aug. 16, Brig. Gen. James M. Tuttle, Cairo, telegraphed to USG. "A man here with gold going South to buy Cotton. Does your late order No 72 allow that'' Telegram received, DNA, RG 393, Dept. of the Mo., Telegrams Received. See telegram to Brig. Gen. William S. Rosecrans, Aug. 7, 1862.

To Brig. Gen. Lorenzo Thomas

———

F ROM Corinth [*July*] 27. [*1862*]

To L. T HOMAS. A. G.

G ENL

There are 3 or 4 officers of rank to whom a short leave seems indispensable   May I grant them?

U S G RANT

M G

Telegram received, DNA, RG 94, Letters Received; copy, *ibid.*, RG 107, Telegrams Received (Bound, Press). On July 29, 1862, Brig. Gen. Lorenzo Thomas telegraphed to USG. "Your request of the 28th inst, in regard to certain leaves of absence, is approved." Copies, *ibid.*, Telegrams Collected (Unbound); DLC-USG, V, 93.

On July 24, Col. Thomas F. Perley, medical inspector gen., wrote to USG that through a misunderstanding of AGO General Orders No. 61, officers who needed leave for health reasons had been forced to remain with the army, and that refusal to grant furloughs to soldiers endangered their health and caused overcrowding of hospitals. ALS, DNA, RG 393, District of West Tenn., Letters Received. On the same day, Perley submitted a report of conditions among recently arrived sick troops, whom he considered neglected. ADS (2), *ibid.* By AGO General Orders No. 61, June 7, only the secretary of war could grant leaves of absence to officers except when "necessary to save life, or prevent *permanent* disability." On July 24, Maj. Gen. Edward O. C. Ord wrote to USG complaining that since Medical Director Charles McDougall had refused to attend to the examination of disabled soldiers, they could not be granted passes. Copy, *ibid.*, 16th Army Corps, Post of Corinth, Letters Sent.

On July 30, USG telegraphed to Brig. Gen. William S. Rosecrans. "I have authority from Washington to give Genl Stanley, the ten days leave he wants, when you think his services can be spared" Copy, *ibid.*, Army of the Miss., Telegrams Received. On the same day, Rosecrans telegraphed to USG. "I think it best to spare Genl Stanley at once—I think his purpose is Executed will be benificial to the service" Telegram received, *ibid.*, Dept. of the Mo., Telegrams Received. *O.R.*, I, xvii, part 2, 139.

On July 30, Maj. John A. Rawlins issued Special Orders No. 148 granting leave to four officers, including Brig. Gen. David S. Stanley. Copies, DLC-USG, V, 15, 16, 82, 87; DNA, RG 393, USG Special Orders.

To Maj. Gen. Henry W. Halleck

———

Head Quarters, Dist. of West Ten.
Corinth, July 28th 1862

Maj. Gen. H. W. Halleck
Washington City, D. C.
Gen.

A report received late last night from Gen. Morgan states that three companies of Cavalry under Maj. Moyes[1] went out southeast from Tuscumbia to attack a party of rebel Cavalry which had surprised and captured two companies of Gen. Thomas' command and burnt the bridge near Courtland.[2] They found the enemy about two hundred strong and made the attack loosing twenty-tree killed, wounded & missing. Does not state whether the enemy were repulsed with loss or not and gives no dates.

Gen. Ross at Bolivar is threatened by a strong force, possibly Prices. I have had him reinforced as much as possible from Jackson and have sent six regiments of Infantry and one Battery from here. There was some skirmishing yesterday at the crossing of the Hatchee Northwest of Bolivar about eight miles distant.

This change of troops is only intended to be temporary but the necessity may arise to keep a larger force on the line of the Hatchee than we have had.[3]

There is an evident disposition on the part of many of the citizens to join the Guerrillas on their approach. I am decidedly in favor of turning all discontented citizens within our lines out South.[4]

Col. Sheridan has gone with all the available Cavalry belonging here to attack and drive out a body of rebel Cavalry that are pressing or conscripting men in that neighborhood.[5] I will probably hear from there to-morrow.

I am Gen. very respectfully
your obt. svt.
U. S. Grant
Maj. Gen.

ALS, DNA, RG 94, War Records Office, Union Battle Reports. *O.R.*, I, xvi, part 1, 830. On Aug. 2, 1862, Maj. Gen. Henry W. Halleck wrote to USG. "Your letter of July 28th is just received. It is very desirable that you should clean out West Tennessee and North Mississippi of all organized enemies. If necessary, take up all active sympathizers and either hold them as prisoners or put them beyond our lines. Handle that class without gloves and take their property for public use. As soon as the corn gets fit for forage, you get all the supplies you can from the rebels in Miss. It is time they should begin to feel the pressure of war on our side. Bolivar and the Hatchie river should be well defended in order to secure our R.R. communications. See that all possible facilities are afforded for getting out cotton. It is deemed important to get as much as we can into market. I see it stated in the newspapers that General Sherman has *forbidden* the payment of gold for cotton, while General Butler *advises* the payment of gold in order to induce the planters to bring it to market. I have called the attention of the Secty. of War to this difference, and he directs me to say that the payment of gold should not be prohibited. Instruct Genl. Sherman accordingly." Copies, DNA, RG 108, Letters Sent; *ibid.*, RG 393, USG Hd. Qrs. Correspondence; DLC-USG, V, 7. *O.R.*, I, xvii, part 2, 150.

On July 26, Maj. Gen. Don Carlos Buell, Huntsville, Ala., telegraphed to Brig. Gen. James D. Morgan informing him that several bridges west of Decatur, Ala., had been destroyed due to the carelessness of the guards, and urging him to communicate with USG with a view to keeping lines open. Copy, DNA, RG 393, Army of the Miss., Telegrams Received. *O.R.*, I, xvi, part 2, 214–15. On July 26, Buell telegraphed a similar message to Halleck. Telegram received, DNA, RG 107, Telegrams Collected (Bound); copy, Buell Papers, TxHR. On July 27, Brig. Gen. William S. Rosecrans telegraphed to USG. "It was three companies Our cavalry who had the skirmish ~~more~~ near Jannings south east of Tuscumbia   they went out to sercch for the rebel cavalry which had burnt the bridges near Courtland and surprised & captured two (2) companies of Thomas infantry—Maj Moyers reports the rebel cavalry force he skirmished with 200 strong"   Telegram received, DNA, RG 393, Dept. of the Mo., Telegrams Received; copy, *ibid.*, Army of the Miss., 16th Army Corps, Telegrams Sent.

1. Maj. Gilbert Moyers, 3rd Battalion, 3rd Mich. Cav., had served in the siege of Corinth. Moyers's report of action near Spangler's Mill, Ala., is in *O.R.*, I, xvi, part 1, 830–31. A summary of the battle by Gen. Braxton Bragg, claiming a victory for the C. S. A., is *ibid.*, p. 832.

2. Courtland, Ala., about eighty-three miles southeast of Corinth.

3. On July 24, Maj. Gen. John A. McClernand, Jackson, Tenn., telegraphed to USG. "It is vital that the bridges on the wagon road between this and Bolivar should be repaired at once. Shall I not require Bissell's Regiment of mechanics, under military protection, to repair them, they are here doing nothing, and ought to be made useful." Copies, McClernand Papers, IHi. On July 25, McClernand telegraphed to USG. "Col Leggett after seeing that the cotton and Govt stores at Grand Junction had been removed to Bolivar arrived there with his command this morning   He held the whole front until he was closely menaced by both Infantry & cavalry—I sent yesterday a Regt of Infantry and some cavalry to Lexington and this morning all of my available cavalry here and at Bolivar to prevent our communication between Humbolt and Bolivar from being cut   let the 3 companies of cavalry to be sent me be from the second Illinois one company

of which is at Humbolt and five at Trenton are well armed and mounted. I have tried them." Telegram received, DNA, RG 393, Dept. of the Mo., Telegrams Received; copy, McClernand Papers, IHi. On the same day, McClernand telegraphed to USG. "One hundred Cavalry crossed the Hatchie at Estanola between Bolivar & Brownsville wednesday night & were within twelve miles of this place last night but returning to day to Brownsville Wallace & Dollins are after them are after them them but I feer their numbers are not sufficient. I would respectfully urge that the Cavalry at Humboldt be ordered to move tonight in the direction of Brownsville to cooperate with Wallace I do not know that I am able to avoid a catastrophe unless you reinforce me. I am just returned from Bolivar. Considerable quantity of Cotton burned to day at Brownsville & Hickory Valley" Telegram received, DNA, RG 393, Dept. of the Mo., Telegrams Received; copies, McClernand Papers, IHi. On July 26, McClernand telegraphed to USG. "Genl Ross reports a large Rebel cavalry force passing by Middleburg eight miles south of Bolivar northwest I have ordered him to surprise and attack them if possible—" Telegram received, DNA, RG 393, Dept. of the Mo., Telegrams Received; copies, McClernand Papers, IHi. McClernand also telegraphed to Brig. Gen. Leonard F. Ross, Bolivar, asking him to "surprise and attack" the Confederates if possible. Copies, *ibid*. On July 26, McClernand telegraphed to USG. "Cotton burners are all around us. If I had more cavalry I could operate against them successfully." Copy, *ibid*. On July 26, McClernand, in a telegram to USG, suggested the need of repairing bridges between Jackson and Bolivar. Copies, *ibid*. On July 27, Rosecrans telegraphed to USG. "Your dispatch received Can that be Prices movement? You remember his cannons went west of Tupello." Copy, DNA, RG 393, Army of the Miss., 16th Army Corps, Telegrams Sent.

On July 27, McClernand sent eight telegrams to USG. "Your dispatch concerning Ripley & Price is received. Ross' pickets have been attacked but at present all quiet. Please hasten the two brigades over to him as rapidly as possible, by rail if possible. He says he can hold Bolivar with the reinforcements I am sending, until the brigades arrive." "Genl Ross telegraphs as follows—I am surrounded by a large force two thousand (2000) strong said to be advance guard. Were at Lagrange yesterday morning. Cavalry said to be on all sides said to be five thousand 5.000 strong. They have plenty of artilery and troops here so that I can send troops to Bolivar from here to Bolivar. Please place at my disposal the trains from Bethel to this place & from here to Bolivar. It would be best to send troops by Rail if you decide to reinforce this place" "I am just starting three regiments on train. Will send both on foot & by rail as rapidly as possible and follow them with Camp equipage. You will bear in mind that when I have sent the force from here the roads are left unprotected. Your dispatch instructing me to recall Dollings is received. I have ordered a concentration of cavalry there to hold the pass at Estinola & other places as long as possible & if absolutely neccessary to fall back and report. I will let this order stand until I hear from you beleiving it to be judicious. Send the two regiments through to Bolivar, with sufficient force I will hold all" "I have sent all cavalry and infantry from here except five pieces of regiments one of which is at Lexington but is returning—two others of which are guarding the R. R. & picketing high ways & the remaining two of which are are a reserve guarding the town & public property deeming it scarcely wise to send more away I will never not do so until the Reg. returns from Lexington unless actually exigincy requires in which case I can send further reinforcements by Rail or march them across in a few hours there are strong indications that the country around is disposed to rise in cooperation with the enemy" "I have just started Lawlers Brigade part on the cars part on foot also a batery to Bolivar   I have also started all of my available Cavalry to the aid of Dollins & have telegraphed to Col Bryant at Humboldt that he will send his Cavalry to join mine the whole to form a flying force to protect the line of the Hatchie. The two brigades gives a new face to affairs. With them I think I ~~can~~ will not only ~~keep~~ hold what we have but drive & keep the enemy at a distance   Dollins fight was about five miles from ~~Tonons~~ Toons station & ten (10) miles this side of Bolivar I have ordered the ~~fourth (4th)~~ train to drop one hundred ~~(100)~~ ~~armed men there~~ (100) armed men there" "Dolling whom I sent to try to destroy the ferry at ~~East~~ Estinaula between Brownsville & Hatchie telegraphs me through Genl Ross that he was repulsed in his attempt to destroy the ferry and asks for reinforcements. Ross cant furnish any and Logan is sending all that can possibly be spared from here to Ross. If you will give me force enough & promptly I will hold all at every hazard. What may I rely on" "Cant you send a train immy. to Bethel to bring a regiment from there to replace in part the troops I am sending from here to Bolivar. I must have some control over the trains or I can do nothing" "The Capt of the battery has the complement of one hundred & twenty (120) rounds but I wish more to meet contingencies. I will not send the regiment from Bethel hoping the two (2) regiments from Corinth will soon ~~arrive~~ come passing to Bethel on the cars. I have made every preparation that time and my limited means enabled"   Telegrams received, *ibid.*, Dept. of the Mo., Telegrams Received; copies, McClernand Papers, IHi.

On July 28, McClernand telegraphed to USG. "Have the two Brigades left for Bolivar—if so when & how far do you suppose they have gone. What will be their route. It comes through a citizen that Bragg is hesitating whether to make Bolivar the main point of attack or maneuver there for the purpose of diverting us & make a push against Nashville   having completed arrangements to meet eventualities at Bolivar I will leave to day for that place. When I am leaving I will telegraph you"   Telegram received, DNA, RG 393, Dept. of the Mo., Telegrams Received; copies, McClernand Papers, IHi. On the same day, McClernand telegraphed to USG. "Upon special enquiry Genl Ross reports the canonading to be north west of Bolivar"   Telegram received, DNA, RG 393, Dept. of the Mo., Telegrams Received; copies, McClernand Papers, IHi. On July 28, McClernand telegraphed to USG. "I am inclined to suspect that Genl. Tuttle has surprised a hostile force crossing the Rail-road east of Grand Junction and moving North. This may explain the cannonading." Copy, *ibid.* On July 28, McClernand telegraphed again to USG. "Dollins lost one man killed brought off one wounded killed several of the enemy & took nine prisoners when he fell back to Toons station in consequence of the enemy being reinforced. If my cavalry force was larger I would certainly drive the enemy across the Hatchie. I am trying to do it any how"   Telegram received, DNA, RG 107, Telegrams Collected (Unbound); copies, McClernand Papers, IHi. On the same day, McClernand telegraphed again, amplifying his other message. Telegram received, DNA, RG 393, Dept. of the Mo., Telegrams Received; copies, McClernand Papers, IHi.

4. On July 19, Col. William W. Lowe, 5th Iowa Cav., commanding at Fort Henry, telegraphed to Maj. Nathaniel H. McLean, who referred the telegram to USG. "Hearing of the organization of Guerrilla Bands in the vicinity of Huntington and this side I shall in a day or two unless otherwise ordered hunt them up—can the three detached companies of my Regiment be ordered here   they are needed   my command is very small"   Telegram received, DNA, RG 393,

Dept. of the Mo., Telegrams Received. On July 23, Brig. Gen. William K. Strong, Cairo, reported the arrest of a C. S. A. lt. recruiting in the area. ALS, *ibid.*, District of West Tenn., Letters Received. On July 24, Brig. Gen. Isaac F. Quinby, Columbus, Ky., telegraphed to USG. "The Curtis horse have been sent out after Orgies guerrilla band Genl Dodge reports that it may take several days to get them back" Telegram received, *ibid.*, Dept. of the Mo., Telegrams Received. On the same day, Col. George E. Bryant, 12th Wis., Humboldt, sent a similar message to USG. Telegram received, *ibid.* On July 25, Bryant telegraphed to USG. "I am instructed by Brig Genl Dodge to ask you if I shall send after Curtis Horse absent scouting as I telegraphed you last night If I shall send after them or if I shall send them to Jackson when they return" Telegram received, *ibid.* On July 28, Maj. John A. Rawlins issued General Orders No. 65. "Hereafter no Passes will be given to Citizens of States in Rebellion, to pass into our lines at any of the stations from Tuscumbia to Memphis; including Bolivar, except to persons employed on secret service, and to these only by Generals Commdg. Divisions. Deserters from the Rebel Army, or those claiming to be such, presenting themselves to the outer guards, will be taken as prisoners, and sent under guard to the nearest Commdg Officer, who will give them a thorough examination, and will only release them on their taking the oath of allegiance and his conviction that the persons so released take the oath in good faith, and with the intention of going north. Goods will not be permitted to pass out in any direction where they may be carried south of our lines, nor persons, except when employed in secret service, and then only on permits from Division Commanders." Copies, DLC-USG, V, 12, 13, 14, 95; DNA, RG 393, USG General Orders. *O.R.*, I, xvii, part 2, 130.

On Aug. 8, McClernand telegraphed to USG. "Is it intended that General Order No 65 shall exclude citizens living near our different posts and camps or only those offering to cross our lines between Memphis & Corinth our advance line the exclusion of Loyal men residing in the neighborhood of our Post & camps will deny us of much valuable information Please answer immidiately" Telegram received, DNA, RG 393, Dept. of the Mo., Telegrams Received; copy, McClernand Papers, IHi.

5. On July 27, Rosecrans telegraphed to USG. "How strong do you suppose them to be and can Sheridan do anything for that affair at present" Copy, DNA, RG 393, Army of the Miss., 16th Army Corps, Telegrams Sent. On the same day, Rosecrans telegraphed again to USG. "Col Sheridan sends to night one Regt. of Cavalry to Hatchee Crossing, to dash into Ripley at daylight, and then strike the Ripley and Fulton road 12 miles south of Ripley. The third with the battery and 2 Cos. of Infantry goes to Black land, and the Cavalry advance on the rebel pickets, towards Carrolville, and Ellistown, while Ords Cavalry goes via Kossuth and Ruckersville, On the Ripley and Pocahontas Road, and attack Ripley from the north. The whole Ripley force then moves south and joines Sheridan at Blackland. Nothing especial from Morgan except a terribly grumbling letter at the misbehavior of Thomas' troops at Courtland. Three Cos of our Cavalry had a skirmish, with rebel Cavalry south West of Courtland, in which we lost twenty three killed wounded and missing. No further particulars, except all safe" Copy, *ibid. O.R.*, I, xvii, part 2, 124. On the same day, Rosecrans again telegraphed to USG about Col. Philip H. Sheridan's plans. Telegram received, DNA, RG 393, Dept. of the Mo., Telegrams Received; copy, *ibid.*, Army of the Miss., 16th Army Corps, Telegrams Sent. *O.R.*, I, xvii, part 2, 124.

To Brig. Gen. John A. Logan

—————

July 28 1862
By Tel. from Corinth.

To GENL LOGAN,

What was extent of damage done the road? How far North of Jackson, what force was supposed to be engaged? Did we loose any men and what number? Was the rebel loss anything or did our men leave without firing? Had the train from Columbus passed.

U S GRANT
Maj Genl Comdg

Telegram, copy, DNA, RG 393, 16th Army Corps, Post of Jackson, Telegrams. *O.R.*, I, xvii, part 2, 129. On July 28, 1862, Brig. Gen. John A. Logan, Jackson, Tenn., telegraphed to USG. "My forces have all been sent to Bolivar, against my protest save two small Regts not enough to do Piqut duty   My Cavalry including orderlies been sent also. This morning the road has been attacked this side of Humbolt, & the bridges burned. I am sending all the force I have to repair & hold it. What will become of this place you can imagine. I shall hold it or be buried in its ashes"   ALS (telegram sent), Ira Batterton Papers, Mrs. John L. Probasco, Rockford, Ill.; copy, DNA, RG 393, 16th Army Corps, Post of Jackson, Telegrams. *O.R.*, I, xvii, part 2, 128. On the same day, John C. Holdredge, telegraph operator at Humboldt, Tenn., telegraphed to USG. "We have been expecting an attack here all day—Rebels burnt trestle work 5 miles below here at 11 Oclock this morning. forces in line of battle here   Col Bryant gone out with reinforcements of cavalry from Trenton to find enemy   Engagement this morning   enemy drove in our cavalry on march to Jackson—" Telegram received, DNA, RG 393, Dept. of the Mo., Telegrams Received. *O.R.*, I, xvii, part 2, 128. On the same day, W. S. Hewitt, asst. superintendent of the military telegraph, Humboldt, telegraphed to USG. "We have just arrived here   repaired line at the burnt bridge seven miles south of this. Col Bissell is here & desired me to say to you that Bridge would be ready to cross in morning. Train just arrived from Columbus, Col Logan on board"   Telegram received, DNA, RG 393, Dept. of the Mo., Telegrams Received. On the same day, Logan telegraphed to USG. "The extent of damage I do not know. The courier left while trestle was burning. Distance from Jackson 14 miles   Force supposed to be some 300 Cavalry. Our loss was said to be som[e] four or five wounded. I did not learn that any were killed. Rebel loss four killed and five prisoners. The train from Columbus had no[t] passed down. I learn that a large cavalry force, with perhaps two hundred infantry crossed Hatchie last night almost 18 mile[s] from here. This may be the force." Copy, *ibid.*, 16th Army Corps, Post of Jackson, Telegrams. *O.R.*, I, xvii, part 2, 129. On the same day, USG telegraphed to Logan. "Have we any force now at the Burning Bridge? Keep a sharp look out for rebel forces and if they are needed, I will send you from here at once. I will have all the cars here in readiness to send troops should they be needed." Copy, DNA, RG 393, 16th Army Corps, Post of Jackson, Telegrams. *O.R.*, I, xvii, part 2, 129. On the same day, Logan telegraphed to USG. "We have 50 infantry at Burnt bridge. The Engineer regiment 300 strong armed and equipped have gone." Copy, DNA, RG 393, 16th Army Corps, Post of Jackson, Telegrams. *O.R.*, I, xvii, part 2, 129. On the same day, USG telegraphed to Logan and to Maj. Gen. John A. McClernand. "Return a portion of the forces to Jackson as soon as possible. The two Brigades which will reach Bolivar in the morning, will enable you to do this. Answer if this is is not so." Copy, DNA, RG 393, 16th Army Corps, Post of Jackson, Telegrams. *O.R.*, I, xvii, part 2, 130. McClernand had gone to Bolivar. Capt. Charles T. Hotchkiss to USG, July 28, telegram received, DNA, RG 393, Dept. of the Mo., Telegrams Received. On July 29, Brig. Gen. Grenville M. Dodge wrote to USG. "The man who guided the rebels to the bridge that was burned was hung to-day. He had taken the oath. The houses of four others who aided have been burned to the ground." P. C. Headley, *The Life and Campaigns of General U. S. Grant* (New York, 1868), p. 165.

To Gideon Welles

Corinth, Mississippi
July 28th 1862

Hon. G. Wells
Sec. of the Navy.
Sir:

Understanding that promotions are to be made in the Navy, for meritorious conduct, permit me to recommend Capt. Henry Walke who has served on the Western Waters with distinction since the begining of our present troubles.

Capt. Walke has shown himself ever ready for any service the vessel commanded by him might be called for, and, if a landesman may judge, has shown both skill and personal bravery in all cases.

He served in guarding our frontier all the time I commanded at Cairo, (frontier of loyalty) protected our debarcation & re-imbarcation at Belmont besides doing good service in repelling the attack made upon our troops while embarking on that occa-tion, commanded a gunboat at the capture of Forts Henry & Donelson, and was the commander selected to run the gauntlet of the rebel batteries at Island No 10 which resulted in such advantages to our arms.

In every instance Capt. Walke has proven himself worthy of the confidance bestowed upon him and I hope will receive the reward of his merit.

I am sir, very respectfully
your obt. svt.
U. S. GRANT
Maj. Gen.

ALS, DNA, RG 45, Miscellaneous Letters Received. *O.R.* (Navy), I, xxiii, 269. Born in 1802 in Glastonbury, Conn., educated at Norwich University, and trained in law, Gideon Welles was an active Democrat during the administrations of Presidents Andrew Jackson and Martin Van Buren; but opposition to slavery later led him to join the fledgling Republican Party. After running unsuccessfully for governor of Conn. in 1856, he served as a member of the Republican National Committee and chairman of the Conn. delegation to the Chicago convention which nominated Abraham Lincoln for President. Searching for a New Englander and ex-Democrat for inclusion in his cabinet, Lincoln selected Welles as secretary of the navy.

On Dec. 1, 1862, Lincoln nominated Henry Walke for promotion to capt. The nomination was confirmed on Feb. 21, 1863. *Senate Executive Journal*, XIII, 2, 159.

To Maj. Gen. Henry W. Halleck

———

Corinth Mississippi July 29th [*1862*]

MAJOR GENERAL H. W. HALLECK
WASHINGTON D C

Information just in from Col Sheridan who attacked & drove six hundred Rebels from Ripley[1] this morning says large force leaving Saltilla[2] for Chattanooga by Rail, Wagons moved across the country. Genl. Cheatham (?)[3] with division had gone west; Withers[4] to follow with Division. The Hatchee north-west of Bolivar is now occupied by Rebels. McClernand is there with about six thousand men[5]

U. S. GRANT
Maj. Genl.

Telegram received, DNA, RG 94, Generals' Papers and Books, Telegrams Received by Gen. Halleck; copies, *ibid.*, RG 107, Telegrams Collected (Bound); DLC-Philip H. Sheridan. *O.R.*, I, xvii, part 2, 130–31. On July 31, 1862, Maj. Gen. Henry W. Halleck telegraphed to USG. "Cant you move on the flank & rear of the rebels on the Hatchie & cut them off? At any rate drive them out of West Tennessee & carefully guard the R. R. from Columbus to Decatur." ALS (telegram sent), DNA, RG 107, Telegrams Collected (Bound); copies, *ibid.*, RG 393, USG Hd. Qrs. Correspondence; DLC-USG, V, 4, 5, 7, 8, 88. *O.R.*, I, xvii, part 2, 142. On July 28, Brig. Gen. William S. Rosecrans telegraphed to USG. "Sheridan has returned from the front. Has captured a capt of Cavalry & some 30 letters on a private mail carrier. They show the enemy moving in large force on Chattanooga. Has sent the letters up. They had nineteen miles to come will dispatch you when they arrive" Telegram received, DNA, RG 393, Dept. of the Mo., Telegrams Received; copy, *ibid.*, Army of the Miss., 16th Army Corps, Telegrams Sent. *O.R.*, I, xvii, part 2, 130. On July 29, USG forwarded the following telegram to Maj. Gen. Don Carlos Buell. Copy, DNA, RG 393, Dept. of the Ohio, Telegrams Received. *O.R.*, I, xvi, part 2, 231. On July 29, Rosecrans telegraphed to USG. "From perusal of a large number of letters written by members of the 26th Ala. and a few others from Richmond captured by Sheridan it is clear that there is very considerable ~~number~~ movement of Troops from Satilla & Vicinage Via R.R. to to Chattanooga. Two or three of them Say —thence to Huntsville & all Speak of a movement in northern Alabama of expelling the Yankees from northern Alabama   one Says a considerable force will be left at Sattilla Supposed to be enough to meet the Emergency—Two (2) days cooked rations and the R.R. Via Mobile is in—Nearly all of them to leave tomorrow morning   two or three talk of going from chattanooga to Huntsville. Unfortunately they are all of the 26th Alabama, but the impression abroad among them that with Bragg on the East & Price in the center as they Say the Yankees will be *made to Skeddadle*" Telegram received, DNA, RG 393, Dept. of the Mo., Telegrams Received; copy, *ibid.*, Army of the Miss., 16th Army Corps, Telegrams Sent. On July 29, Rosecrans forwarded telegrams to USG from Col. Philip H. Sheridan about C. S. A. movements. *O.R.*, I, xvii, part 2, 131–32.

1. See *ibid.*, I, xvii, part 1, 25–26.

2. Saltillo, Miss., about forty miles south of Corinth on the Mobile and Ohio Railroad.

3. Maj. Gen. Benjamin F. Cheatham commanded the 2nd Division, 1st Corps, C. S. A. Army of the Miss. On July 21, Brig. Gen. Thomas Jordan issued Special Orders No. 4, ordering the Army of the Miss. to move to Chattanooga, "with the least delay practicable." Cheatham's division and that of Brig. Gen. Jones M. Withers were dispatched by rail via Mobile. *Ibid.*, I, xvii, part 2, 656–57.

4. Jones M. Withers of Ala., USMA 1835, studied law, served during the Creek uprising of 1836, and became private secretary to the governor of Ala. He served in the Ala. legislature and as mayor of Mobile, entered C. S. A. service as a col., commanded a division as brig. gen. at Shiloh, and was promoted to maj. gen. as of April 6, 1862. On June 30, he assumed command of the Reserve Corps, Army of the Miss.

5. On July 29, Maj. Gen. John A. McClernand, Bolivar, Tenn., telegraphed to USG. "Major Stewart has had a hard fight with rebel cavalry. Has taken a number of prisoners and reports that he is pursuing his advantage" Telegram

received, DNA, RG 107, Telegrams Collected (Unbound); copy, McClernand
Papers, IHi. *O.R.*, I, xvii, part 2, 135. On July 29, Brig. Gen. John A. Logan
telegraphed to USG, reporting Maj. Warren Stewart's cav. battle on the Hatchie
River. Copy, DNA, RG 94, War Records Office, Union Battle Reports. *O.R.*,
I, xvii, part 1, 27. On July 30, Logan telegraphed to USG. "Yesterday evening
Major Sewart and Cavalry were defeated, having met a large force near Denmark, some ~~fifteen~~ 15 miles from here. Our loss considerable in killed, wounded
and prisoners. He thinks the force was about ~~four hundred~~ 400 My information
is that Jackson has crossed the greater part of his regiment over the Hatchie on
this side, having crossed in squads for several days." Copy, DNA, RG 94, War
Records Office, Union Battle Reports. *O.R.*, I, xvii, part 1, 27. On July 30, Logan
telegraphed again to USG. "I have quite a number of prisoners here   what shall
I do with them   can I send them north tomorrow?" Telegram received, DNA,
RG 393, Dept. of the Mo., Telegrams Received; copy, *ibid.*, 16th Army Corps,
Post of Jackson, Telegrams.

On July 29, McClernand telegraphed to USG. "I Sent train and Strong
guard and party to restore wires and road to Jackson which were broken yesterday eveg   So Soon as I believe Gen Tuttle to be Striking distance I will Send
Lawler with three Regiments from here to Scour the East Side of Hatchee & to
establish a camp at, or near Estonola with Some cavalry in addition   He ought
to protect Rail Road from Humboldt to this place. The Enemys advance at least
is falling back. We are pretty well fortified at Ripley. Doubtless Genl Logan is
mistaken as to the danger of Jackson" Telegram received, *ibid.*, Dept. of the
Mo., Telegrams Received; copies, McClernand Papers, IHi. On July 30, McClernand telegraphed to USG. "I sent Courriers near Pocahantas last night. heard
nothing of Tuttle   have sent this morning on the Purdy road—Has he been
recalled. important movements await his arrival. Answer immediately" Telegram received, DNA, RG 393, Dept. of the Mo., Telegrams Received; copies,
McClernand Papers, IHi. On the same day, McClernand telegraphed to USG.
"The reinforcement ordered to Jackson will be very useful—Our cavalry from
Jackson engaged a Superior force of Rebel cavalry last evening near Denmark.
I have ordered the concentration of all the cavalry at Jackson including Hagg   I
think there is no other than cavalry force & that not very large now threatening
Jackson" Telegram received, DNA, RG 393, Dept. of the Mo., Telegrams
Received; copies, McClernand Papers, IHi. On July 31, McClernand telegraphed
to USG. "My wish is upon hearing from Genl Tuttle to pass from the defensive
to the offensive   having heard from him I have ordered Col Lawlers brigade to
make a force march tonight along the north bank of the Hatchie to Seize the
crossing and cut off the escape of the enemy all that side   I also hope to cut off
the escape and drive away other Rebel detachments below this place on the south
side of the Hatchie   to make this place tenable under all circumstances I am using
forced negro labor to fortify it   Genl Logan is protecting the Railroad in the
vicinity of Jackson" Telegram received, DNA, RG 393, Dept. of the Mo.,
Telegrams Received; copies (dated July 30), McClernand Papers, IHi. On
July 31, McClernand telegraphed again to USG. "Genl Tuttle arrived here
about noon   Col Leggitt left early this morning with detachment for Whitesville
on the Summerville road to intercept rebel Cavalry north of that place." Telegram received, DNA, RG 393, Dept. of the Mo., Telegrams Received; copies,
McClernand Papers, IHi. For further correspondence relating to movements
between Jackson and Bolivar, along the Hatchie River, see *O.R.*, I, xvii, part 2,

133–42. For a report by C. S. A. Col. Joseph Wheeler of his cav. expedition of about 1,000 in late July, which threatened both Jackson and Bolivar, see *ibid.*, I, xvii, part 1, 23–25.

To Maj. Gen. Henry W. Halleck

Corinth [*July*] 30th 5 P M [*1862*]

MAJ GENL HALLECK

Constant complaints are coming to me of Steamer coming up the Tennessee, landing large quantities of Freight at different points on the River, much of which, undoubtedly goes into States South of us. Salt is a leading article

U S GRANT
Maj Gen

Telegram received, DNA, RG 94, Generals' Papers and Books, Telegrams Received by Gen. Halleck; copies, *ibid.*, RG 107, Telegrams Collected (Bound); *ibid.*, RG 393, USG Hd. Qrs. Correspondence; DLC-USG, V, 4, 5, 7, 8, 9, 88. On July 24, 1862, Capt. Robert R. Townes, Jackson, Tenn., adjt. for Brig. Gen. John A. Logan, telegraphed to Maj. John A. Rawlins. "Leroy Carpenter states, 1st., 'That Mr. Wells lives 5 or 6 miles South of Corinth Miss hauling salt, flour, and coffee and tells that he has bought ten thousand pounds of Coffee, five hundred barrels of salt and five hundred barrels of flour at Hamburg. 2nd That he is hauling the same to the South by way of Youngs Station on Memphis and Charleston Rail Road; Crosses on Smith's Bridge on Tustubia river through Kossuth. 3rd That he does not wish his name to be known to the persons informed on, as they may do him a great injury.' " Copy, DNA, RG 393, 16th Army Corps, Post of Jackson, Telegrams. On July 26, O. W. Paxson, military telegraph operator at Henderson, Ky., telegraphed to USG. "The stmr, Fisher will arrive at Saltillo Landing Tenn. River tonight or in morning with large lot of salt which is evidently intended for use of Rebels. It comes from Norton & Bros Paducah Ky, I think, can tell positive in morning" Telegram received, *ibid.*, Dept. of the Mo., Telegrams Received. On the same day, Col. William W. Lowe, Fort Henry, telegraphed to USG complaining that the steamboat *Fisher* was carrying 1,256 barrels of salt. Telegram received, *ibid.* On July 28, Lowe telegraphed to USG. "Fisher was allowed to pass up because she had custom house permits for her entire cargo signed at Evansville & Paducah. Since she passed up learn that portions of the cargo were not put out at places named in manifest" Telegram received, *ibid.* On July 30, Lowe telegraphed to Rawlins that although the steamboat *Fisher* had properly signed manifests, "Something ought to be done to prevent Such quantities from going up." Telegram received, *ibid.*

On July 28, Maj. William S. Oliver, 7th Mo., provost marshal at Hamburg,

Tenn., telegraphed to USG. "Have just recd at Hamburg a lot of goods belonging to Champion & Cobb they having brandy which they sold put up in peach cans. They have been doing a very large business selling to Citizens. Have over a hundred bbls salt flour & altogether a large lot of goods. Have placed a sentinel over goods & await your orders to know what to do with them   Have they permit to sell to all citizens. They claim to be sutlers of the 27th Ohio Regt. The steamer Fisher had but twelve bbls salt when she arrived consigned to a sutler here   She put off salt all along the river   I detain her awaiting your orders"   Telegram received, *ibid.* On July 30, Oliver telegraphed to USG complaining that the steamboat *Evansville* had been selling liquor, salt, and other stores to disloyal people, and asking if such activities were proper. Telegram received, *ibid.*

On July 29, Brig. Gen. William S. Rosecrans telegraphed to USG. "Under whose authority does the Provost Marshall at Hamburg act." Telegram received, *ibid.*; copy, *ibid.*, Army of the Miss., 16th Army Corps, Telegrams Sent. On the same day, USG telegraphed to Rosecrans. "The Provost Marshal at Hamburg acts under the Authority of the Commanding officer at that place" Copy, *ibid.*, Army of the Miss., Telegrams Received. On July 31, Rawlins issued Special Orders No. 149 relieving Oliver from duty and ordering the commanding officer at Hamburg to appoint a successor. Copies, DLC-USG, V, 15, 16, 82, 87; DNA, RG 393, USG Special Orders.

On Aug. 11, Rosecrans telegraphed to USG. "I am credibly informed that there is great quantities of salt 4,000 to 5,000 barrels on the landings between Pittsburg Landg & the mouth of the Tenn. I am making a clean sweep at & above Eastport. Would it not be well to seize that salt" Telegram received, *ibid.*, Dept. of the Mo., Telegrams Received; copy, *ibid.*, Army of the Miss., Telegrams Sent.

To Maj. Gen. Henry W. Halleck

Corinth [*July*] 30th [*1862*]

Maj Genl H. W. Halleck
General

Information obtained by Col Sheridan who has been far to the front & right for several days shows that Bragg has made Head Quarters at Rome[1]   most of the Troops from Saltilla & Tupello have gone to Chattanooga by Rail   Wagons move across the Country to Rome   Cheatham & Wither has gone west. Price is in Command in Mississippi Head Quarters at Holly Springs with Force at Grand Junction.[2] Had I not better move Ords entire Command to Bolivar one Division of Rosecranz to

Corinth & drive the force in front South, they cannot number to exceed ten thousand (10,000)

U. S. GRANT
Maj Genl

Telegram received, DNA, RG 94, Generals' Papers and Books, Telegrams Received by Gen. Halleck; copies, *ibid.*, RG 107, Telegrams Collected (Bound); *ibid.*, RG 393, USG Hd. Qrs. Correspondence; DLC-USG, V, 4, 5, 7, 8, 9, 88; DLC-Philip H. Sheridan. *O.R.*, I, xvii, part 2, 136. On July 30, 1862, USG drafted a telegram to Maj. Gen. Henry W. Halleck, covering the latter part of the above message, which was not sent. Copy, DLC-USG, V, 88. On July 31, Halleck telegraphed to USG. "You must judge for yourself the best use to be made of your troops. Be careful not to scatter them too much; also to hold them in readiness to reinforce Buell at Chatanooga, if necessary." ALS (telegram sent), DNA, RG 107, Telegrams Collected (Bound); copies, *ibid.*, RG 393, USG Hd. Qrs. Correspondence; *ibid.*, Military Division of the Miss., Letters Received; DLC-USG, V, 4, 5, 7, 8, 9, 88. *O.R.*, I, xvii, part 2, 142. On the same day, Halleck wrote to Maj. Gen. Don Carlos Buell. "I have directed Maj. Gen. Grant to be prepared to reinforce you if you should find the enemy too strong at Chattanooga." Copy, Buell Papers, TxHR. *O.R.*, I, xvi, part 2, 236.

1. Rome, Ga., about fifty-five miles south of Chattanooga, Tenn.
2. On July 30, Brig. Gen. William S. Rosecrans telegraphed to USG. "A batch of captured letters th just in throws a flash of light on the rebel movements Bragg has gone to north Alabama Head Quarters at Rome. Price commands at in Mississippi line extends from Tupelo Via Ripley & Salem to Holly Springs Villepigue with seven regiments is ten miles below Grand Junction say they could take Corinth when they please Expect will leave and they will soon occupy the Mobile & Ohio RR &c&c When I have finished will send them to you" Telegram received, DNA, RG 393, Dept. of the Mo., Telegrams Received; copy, *ibid.*, Army of the Miss., 16th Army Corps, Telegrams Sent. *O.R.*, I, xvii, part 2, 139.

To Salmon P. Chase

Head Qrs Disct of West Tenn
Corinth, Miss. July 31, 1862

To HON S P CHASE
SECRETARY OF THE TREASURY
WASHINGTON, D. C.
SIR

Large quantities of salt flour, liquors and other articles of use and luxury are being shipped by the way of the Tennessee river and other lines of communication, to different points within our lines. It is presumed that these come under authority of regular permits from agents of the Treasury Department, and that the trade is so far legitimate. The collateral smuggling that goes on undoubtedly to a large extent is another matter not now under notice. It is however a very grave question in my mind whether this policy of "letting trade follow the flag" is not working injuriously to the Union Cause. Practically and really I think it is benefitting almost exclusively, first, a class of greedy traders whose first and only desire is gain, and to whom it would be idle to attribute the least patriotism, and secondly our enemies south of our lines. The quantities in which these goods are shipped clearly intimate that they are intended to be worked off into the enemys country thus administering to him the most essential "aid and comfort." Our lines are so extended that it is impossible for any military surveillance to contend successfully with the cunning of the traders, aided by the local knowledge and eager interest of the residents along the border. The enemy are thus receiving supplies of most neccessary and useful articles which relieve their sufferings and strengthens them for resistance to our authority; while we are sure that the benefits thus conferred, tend in no degree to abate their rancorous hostility to our flag and Government. If any hopes have been entertained that a liberal commercial policy might have a conciliatory effect, I fear they will not be realized. The method of correcting the evil which first suggests itself is restriction of the quantity of these articles which may be allowed to be shipped under one invoice, together with more careful investigation of the loyalty of persons permitted to trade. Very limited amounts will be sufficient to supply the wants of the truly loyal men of the Districts within our lines, for unfortunately they are not numerous, and outside (south) of our lines, I fear it is little better than a unanimous rebellion. The evil is a great and growing one, and needs immediate attention.

I am sir, your obt. svt

U. S. GRANT

Maj. Gen. Com

LS, DNA, RG *56*; Letters Received from Executive Officers. See General Orders No. 11, Dec. 17, 1862.

To Maj. Gen. Henry W. Halleck

Corinth Aug 1. [*1862*]

MAJ GEN. H W HALLECK

It is now almost an absolute certainty that there is but a small force in front of us most having gone Eastward   Bolivar seems to be the most important point to guard & retain troops here to reinforce Buell if necessary—I would suggest driving the rebels towards Columbus[1] as far as Possible as preparation to leave Corinth with a small garrison

U. S. GRANT
M. G.

Telegram received, DNA, RG 94, Generals' Papers and Books, Telegrams Received by Gen. Halleck; copies, *ibid.*, RG 107, Telegrams Collected (Bound); *ibid.*, RG 393, USG Hd. Qrs. Correspondence; DLC-USG, V, 4, 5, 7, 8, 9, 88. *O.R.*, I, xvii, part 2, 148.
    On Aug. 1, 1862, Brig. Gen. William S. Rosecrans telegraphed to USG. "Dispatch from Buell believes not more than two (2) Regiments of Infantry—brigade of Cavalry and Battery at Moulton. Thinks garrison of Decatur unsafe, would be made so by a Brigade at Courtland   Gives no reasons for holding that road   Morgan has no reliable information but reports continue to indicate considerable force at Moulton—says commandant at Courtland is informed by Cavalry of a force seven (7) miles from there   strength and kind of troops not stated   Lightening prevents using wires to get answer about this. Granger telegraphed last night from Rienzi   All Troops have left Tupello except Price with twenty thousand (20000). men gone East by Rail. Baggage and Artillery by Tuscaloosa to-wards Rome   Means heavy attack on Buell or Richmond" Telegram received, DNA, RG 393, Dept. of the Mo., Telegrams Received; copy, *ibid.*, Army of the Miss., 16th Army Corps, Telegrams Sent. *O.R.*, I, xvii, part 2, 148. A copy of the telegram of July 31 from Maj. Gen. Don Carlos Buell to Rosecrans is in DNA, RG 393, Army of the Miss., Telegrams Received.

    1. Columbus, Miss., about 100 miles south of Corinth.

To Brig. Gen. William S. Rosecrans

———

Corinth Aug 1st 1862

GENL ROSECRANS

A dispatch from Genl Halleck to day says for me to judge for myself the location of troops but to keep them on hand to reinforce Buell if necessary.[1] Under this state of facts Gen Morgan should be made strong enough to hold the road east of Buell. If reinforced from here the road will have to be used to take our supplies. I will be back to the telegraph office in an hour. I have telegraphed Genl. Halleck to authorize sending a force to drive out the Rebels from Saltillo and Tupello,[2] and compel them to cut the road as far south as possible

U. S. GRANT
Maj Genl

Telegram, copy, DNA, RG 393, Army of the Miss., Telegrams Received. On Aug. 3, 1862, Brig. Gen. William S. Rosecrans telegraphed to USG. "I have ordered Davis to send Mitchells Brigade to Iuka to relieve Morgans command thence to Bear Creek Bridge—Morgans troops go to Tuscumbia Davis to be ready to follow him with the remainder so soon as the news from Granger shall show what dispositions are advisable at the front. I have doubts if any operation in force will require support given to Morgan east from the nature of the Country south of Morgans line which is generally hilly & poor. It is probable that Column was a reconoitering covering & designed to cutt off the Union men from those hilly regions who were flocking to join us" Telegram received, *ibid.*, Dept. of the Mo., Telegrams Received; copies, *ibid.*, Army of the Miss., Telegrams Sent; *ibid.*, 16th Army Corps, Telegrams Sent. *O.R.*, I, xvii, part 2, 151–52. See also *ibid.*, I, xvii, part 1, 28–29.

1. See telegram to Maj. Gen. Henry W. Halleck, July 30, 1862.
2. See preceding telegram.

To Maj. Gen. Henry W. Halleck

Corinth Miss
Aug 2d 1862

MAJ GEN H W HALLECK
GEN IN CHIEF

I will try and hold the road to Decatur   Think it can be done without much difficulty.[1]

Anticipate no serious trouble on the Hatchie   Nothing more than an occasional raid from mounted men.

U S GRANT
Maj Genl

Telegram received, DNA, RG 94, Generals' Papers and Books, Telegrams Received by Gen. Halleck; copies, *ibid.*, RG 107, Telegrams Collected (Bound); *ibid.*, RG 393, USG Hd. Qrs. Correspondence; DLC-USG, V, 4, 5, 7, 8, 9, 88. *O.R.*, I, xvii, part 2, 150. On Aug. 2, 1862, Maj. Gen. John A. McClernand telegraphed to USG. "I have swept both sides of the Hatchie from Bolivar to Brownsville on the road to Somerville   the enemy fled precipitately & ~~encamped~~ escaped capture—The force I have on the Hatchie together with those you are sending and the three regiments here exclusive of the eleventh secures things in these Quarter for the present   I will send the eleventh the first opportunity. I have some three hundred negroes at work on the fortifications at Bolivar   I will probably return them on Monday   the twenty four hundred ammunition has not come"   Telegram received, DNA, RG 107, Telegrams Collected (Bound); copy, McClernand Papers, IHi. On the same day, McClernand telegraphed again to USG. "Can their be obtained at Corinth ammunition for 24 pounder Howitzer, Six (6) pounder Guns & small arms ammunition of the following calibre, fifty eight (58) fifty four (54) Sharps carbine & Colts Revolver Cartridges and to what extent. Can we procure to the extent of (500) five hundred stands of Arms & accoutrements for my command—The ordnance officer from Bolivar is waiting for a reply." Copies, *ibid.* On Aug. 5, McClernand telegraphed to USG. "I learn from unofficial Source that Lieut Col Hogg with his Cavalry has been ordered back to Trenton   did you intend they Should be withdrawn from the line of the Hatchie   I have not other Cavalry fit for duty"   Telegram received, DNA, RG 393, Dept. of the Mo., Telegrams Received; copies, McClernand Papers, IHi.

1. See telegram to Maj. Gen. Henry W. Halleck, July 29, 1862.

To Brig. Gen. William S. Rosecrans

———

> Head Quarters, Dist. of West Ten.
> Corinth, August 2d 1862

BRIG. GEN. W. S. ROSECRANS,
COMD.G ARMY OF THE MISS.
GEN.

The enclosed is *one* bill of damages against the 7th & 8th Kansas regiments,[1] or that portion of them that were stationed in Trenton Ten.[2] for a short time in the early part of June.

The owners of this property give some evidence of loyalty to the Government, but whether loyal or not the act of these troops is illegal and must be punished by a stopage of the amount of this bill, either for the benefit of Government or the owners on proof of loyalty.

I would suggest that these regiment[s] be not allowed to receive their pay until this amount is collected for the benefit of whom it may concern.

> very respectfully
> your obt. svt.
> U. S. GRANT
> Maj. Gen. Com

ALS, IHi. On July 7, 1862, Maj. Gen. Henry W. Halleck, Corinth, wrote to Secretary of War Edwin M. Stanton that the march of Kan. troops through the Dept. of the Miss. had "been marked by robbery, theft, pillage & outrages upon the peaceful inhabitants." ALS, DNA, RG 94, Letters Received. *O.R.*, I, xvii, part 2, 77. On June 26, Col. George M. Dietzler, 1st Kan., Trenton, Tenn., wrote to Brig. Gen. Isaac F. Quinby of bitter complaints from the people of the area against units of the brigade of Brig. Gen. Robert B. Mitchell for stealing horses and Negroes "from union and disloyal citizens indiscriminately." Copy, DNA, RG 94, Letters Received. *O.R.*, I, xvii, part 2, 34–35. See also *ibid.*, pp. 53–54, 66–67; DNA, RG 109, Union Provost Marshals' Files Relating to Two or More Civilians, 1585, 1589, 1590. On Aug. 21, Brig. Gen. William S. Rosecrans telegraphed to USG. "I have read Genl Mitchell's statement about the complicity of the 7th & 8th Kansas in taking the tobacco & sugar at Trenton Tenn   I think it plain, he has informed me that they ought to be exempted from the operation of the order & allowed to receive their pay & that the 2d Ill Cavalry ought to suffer for it   if you approve please order paymaster to pay those troops" Telegram received, *ibid.*, RG 393, Dept. of the Mo., Telegrams Received. The men of the 7th Kan. Cav. refused to cooperate in the stoppage of their pay, eventually carried their point and for some time resented USG. Simeon M. Fox, "The Story of the Seventh Kansas," *Transactions of the Kansas State Historical Society, 1903–1904* (Topeka, 1904), 31–32.

1. The 8th Kan. Inf., Lt. Col. John A. Martin commanding, was serving in the 1st Brigade, 4th Division, Army of the Miss., Mitchell commanding, near Jacinto, Miss. The 7th Kan. Cav., Col. Albert L. Lee commanding, was serving in the 4th Division, Army of the Miss., Brig. Gen. Gordon Granger commanding.

2. Trenton, Tenn., on the Mobile and Ohio Railroad, about twenty-seven miles north of Jackson, Tenn.

To Maj. Gen. Henry W. Halleck

Corinth, Aug. 3rd [*1862*]

H. W. HALLECK,
MAJ. GENL

Cadwallader[1] has reported for duty here. Order directs him to report to you. Where shall he be assigned   The efficiency of this army is weakened by making Commands for so many Officers of high rank

U. GRANT
Maj Genl

Telegram received, DNA, RG 94, Generals' Papers and Books, Telegrams Received by Gen. Halleck; copies, *ibid.*, RG 107, Telegrams Collected (Bound); *ibid.*, RG 393, USG Hd. Qrs. Correspondence; DLC-USG, V, 4, 5, 7, 8, 88. *O.R.*, I, xvii, part 2, 151. On Aug. 5, 1862, Maj. John A. Rawlins issued Special Orders No. 154. "Major Gen. E. O. C. Ord is hereby relieved temporarily from command of the 2nd Division, Army of the Tenn and of the town of Corinth. Major Gen. George Cadwalader is assigned to the command of the forces constituting the Garrison of Corinth, and will relieve Major Gen. E. O. C. Ord." DS, DNA, RG 94, Special Orders, District of West Tenn.; copies, *ibid.*, RG 393, USG Special Orders; DLC-USG, V, 15, 16, 82, 87. *O.R.*, I, xvii, part 2, 153. On Aug. 13, Maj. Gen. Henry W. Halleck telegraphed to USG. "Order Genl Cadwallader to report here." ALS (telegram sent), DNA, RG 107, Telegrams Collected (Bound); telegram received, *ibid.*, RG 393, Dept. of the Tenn., Telegrams Received. On Aug. 13, Rawlins issued Special Orders No. 162. "In accordance with directions from Head Quarters of the Army, Major Gen. George Cadwallader, is hereby relieved from duty in this District, and will report, in person, without delay to Major Genl. H. W. Halleck, General-in-chief of the Army, at Washington, D. C. Major Gen. E. O. C. Ord is hereby assigned to the command of the Post and Garrison of Corinth, Miss. and will relieve Major Genl. Cadwallader." DS, *ibid.*, RG 94, Special Orders, District of West Tenn.; copies, *ibid.*, RG 393, USG Special Orders; DLC-USG, V, 15, 16, 82, 87. *O.R.*, I, xvii, part 2, 167.

1. George Cadwalader was born in Philadelphia in 1804, where he attended school, read law, and was admitted to the bar. He served in the Mexican War, was discharged as bvt. maj. gen., and in April, 1861, again entered the service as maj. gen. of Pa. Vols. After commanding at Baltimore and serving in the Winchester expedition, he was confirmed as maj. gen. of vols. on April 25, 1862.

To Brig. Gen. John A. Logan

Corinth Mississippi
August 3d 1862

BRIG. GENL. J. A. LOGAN
JACKSON, TENN

Your Note of yesterday asking Me to appoint Cap't Carroll on My Staff and assign him to yours is received   I would be most happy to do so if it was in My power, But it is only on the Staff of Major General of the regular Army, Commanding Departments that this can be done   I am Neither in the regular service Nor am I commanding a Department.

Your course to pursue is to apply directly to the President to have Cap't Carroll appointed on the Staff of one of the regular Major Generals, Wool[1] for instance and assigned to you to take date from the time the Captain entered upon his duties so as to give him the pay.

As you say, I can testify to the Efficiency and credit due to Captain Carroll and will be pleased to see him receive the appointment saught.

Very respectifully
Your Obedient Sv't
U. S. GRANT
Maj. Genl.

Copies, DNA, RG 110, Recommendations for Appointments, Ill., 13th District; *ibid.*, RG 56, Collector of Customs Applications, Tex., Corpus Christi. On Oct. 9, 1862, President Abraham Lincoln endorsed this letter. "Submitted to the Secretary of War—If the appointment can be lawfully made as suggested by Genl. Grant let it be done" Copies, *ibid.* No appointment resulted. For William C. Carroll, newspaper correspondent, staff officer of Brig. Gen. John A. Logan, and, possibly, vol. aide to USG during the battle of Shiloh, see "William C. Carroll in the Civil War," *USGA Newsletter*, X, 2 (Jan., 1973), 7–16.

1. Maj. Gen. John E. Wool of N. Y., then commanding the 8th Army Corps, Middle Dept.

To Jesse Root Grant

——————

Corinth, Mississippi
August 3d 1862

Dear Father,

Your letter of the 25th of July is just received. I do not remember of receiving the letters however of which you speak. One come from Mary speaking of the secessionest Holt who was said to be employed in the Memphis post. office. I at once wrote to Gen Sherman who is in command there about it and he is no doubt turned out before this.

You must not expect me to write in my own defence nor to permit it from any one about me. I know that the feeling of the troops under my command is favorable to me and so long as I continue to do my duty faithfully it will remain so.[1] Your uneasiness about the influences surrounding the children here is unnecessary. On the contrary it is good. They are not running around camp among all sorts of people, but we are keeping house, on the property of a truly loyal secessionist who has been furnished free lodging and board at Alton, Illinois;[2] here the children see nothing but the greatest propriety.

They will not, however, remain here long. Julia will probably pay her father a short visit and then go to Galena or Covington in time to have the children commence school in September.

I expect General Hitchcock[3] to command the Department of the West. Have no fears of General Pope or any one junior to me being sent.

I do not expect nor want the support of the Cincinnati press on my side. Their course has been so remarkable from the beginning that should I be endorsed by them I should fear that the public would mistrust my patriotism. I am sure that I have but one desire in this war, and that is to put down the rebellion. I have no hobby of my own with regard to the negro, either to effect his freedom or to continue his bondage. If Congress pass any law and the President approves, I am willing to execute it. Laws are certainly as binding on the minority as the majority. I do not believe even in the discussion of the propriety of laws and official orders by the army. One enemy at a time is enough and when he is subdued it will be time enough to settle personal differences.

I do not want to command a department because I believe I can do better service in the field. I do not expect to be overslaughed by a junior and should feel exceedingly mortified should such a thing occur, but would keep quiet as I have ever done heretofore.

I have just received a letter from Captain Foley[4] about this same Holt said to be in the Memphis post office. You may say that I shall refer it to General Sherman with the direction to expel him if it is not already done.

Julia and the children are well. I do not expect to remain here long but when I will go I can't say now.

U. S. GRANT.

ALS (facsimile), Josiah H. Benton sale, American Art Association, March 12, 1920, No. 338. *J. G. Cramer*, pp. 84–86.

1. At this point the facsimile ends.
2. See telegram to Maj. Gen. Henry W. Halleck, July 19, 1862. Alton, Ill., was the site of a military prison.
3. See letters to Maj. Gen. Henry W. Halleck, Feb. 12, and to Julia Dent Grant, Feb. 22, 1862.
4. This was probably James Foley, son of Mayor Bushrod Foley of Covington, Ky.

To Andrew Johnson

BY TELEGRAPH FROM Corinth [*Aug. 3*] *1861* [*1862*]

TO GEN A JOHNSON GOVR
GOVERNOR

Lieut J M Jones[1] who is recruiting a company tore up his instructions to prevent them falling into the hands of Guerrillas   wants new ones supplied here

U S GRANT
Maj Gnl

Telegram received, DLC-Andrew Johnson. On Aug. 9, 1862, Governor Andrew Johnson telegraphed to USG. "Lieut J. M. Jones has authority to recruit a company for the first Tenn. Regt. governors guards & to bring them to this place. Please give him what facilityes you can" Telegram received, DNA, RG 393, Dept. of the Mo., Telegrams Received. On Aug. 17, Johnson telegraphed to USG. "Please direct Lt Jones to bring his recruits to Nashville without delay also please give them transportation to Louisville   I thank you for your kind offer of Cooperation" Telegram received, *ibid.*; copy, DLC-Andrew Johnson.

1. Probably 1st Lt. James M. Jones, 10th Tenn.

To Brig. Gen. Lorenzo Thomas

Corinth Aug 6th [*1862*]

GEN L THOMAS A.G.

Govrs of states are sending permits for soldiers to raise companies. Can furloughs be given in such cases?   while I would approve of promotion of soldiers to new companies I disapprove of further measures to deplete our thinned ranks.

U. S. GRANT
Maj Genl

Telegram received, DNA, RG 107, Telegrams Collected (Bound); copies, *ibid.*, Telegrams Received (Press); (dated Aug. 7, 1862) *ibid.*, RG 393, USG Hd.

Qrs. Correspondence; DLC-USG, V, 4, 5, 7, 8, 88. On Aug. 9, Col. Edward D. Townsend telegraphed to USG. "No Furloughs or discharges, can be given on permit of Governors of States except by Special orders from this Dept. by order." Telegram received, DNA, RG 393, Dept. of the Tenn., Telegrams Received; copies, *ibid.*, RG 107, Telegrams Collected (Unbound); *ibid.*, RG 94, Letters Sent; *ibid.*, RG 393, USG Hd. Qrs. Correspondence; DLC-USG, V, 4, 5, 7, 8, 88.

To Brig. Gen. William S. Rosecrans

Corinth Aug 6th 1862

GENL. ROSECRANS

Let nothing go south either with or without pass.[1]

I gave the Commanding officer at Hamburg special instructions, how to regulate trade, & complaints still coming from there I sent one of my Staff officers, who is now there to regulate this matter, and to go to Eastport[2]

U. S. GRANT
Maj Genl

Telegram, copy, DNA, RG 393, Army of the Miss., Telegrams Received. On Aug. 6, 1862, Brig. Gen. William S. Rosecrans telegraphed to USG. "The commander of the 2d has just arrested Three boys with a barrell of salt—Three bbls flour having pass from Provost Marshall at Hamburg—wishing to go through our lines   would it not be well to infuse a little more rigor there, also there must be a more vigilant secretary of passes. none should be held good that are not printed with our mark on them Beyond the possibility of Mistake"   Telegram received, *ibid.*, Dept. of the Mo., Telegrams Received; copy, *ibid.*, Army of the Miss., Telegrams Sent. On Aug. 1, Col. William W. Lowe, Fort Henry, telegraphed to USG. "Steamer Colonna heavily loaded with salt & Bacon has just arrived. She has permits for Every thing but believing the interest of the Country must suffer by such lattitudes in this business I have caused her detention & await the Generals orders. Answer at once"   Telegram received, *ibid.*, Dept. of the Mo., Telegrams Received. On the same day, Brig. Gen. Jefferson C. Davis wrote to USG. "For the information of the General commanding I have the honor to report that contraband goods and stores are being sold to rebel citizens by merchants, sutlers &c in the neighborhood of Corinth, and especially at the river landings. I have not a list of contraband articles in my possession but am satisfied trade of this kind is being carried on to a considerable extent. I arrested yesterday a Sutler of my command who had been selling cards for manufacturing cotton. He informed me as did others, that many of these articles were being sold all over the country. They bring fabulous prices. Salt is also an article which is being sold at the river landing. I have taken in custody some twelve barrels which the owners say they purchased there—from whom they could not tell. They were not asked any questions about their loyalty, or for what purpose the salt was obtained. It has been reported to me that salt is purchased at the different landings on the river and taken back into the country, where it falls into rebel hands. In fact I am satisfied much contraband trade is being carried on all around us." Copy, deCoppet Collection, NjP. On Aug. 2, USG forwarded the letter to hd. qrs., Washington, D.C. AES, *ibid.* On Aug. 18, Maj. Gen. Henry W. Halleck telegraphed to USG. "Letter of Genl Davis of the 1st inst is just recieved you will take stringent measures to prevent all articles deemed contraband of war from reaching the enemy. Arrest and exclude from your lines every suttler or trader engaged in unlawful traffic." ALS (telegram sent), DNA, RG 107, Telegrams Collected (Bound); telegram received, *ibid.*, RG 393, Dept. of the Tenn., Telegrams Received. *O.R.*, I, xvii, part 2, 179.

On Aug. 2, Rosecrans telegraphed to USG. "No report from the front Genl Morgan reports the Town Creek Bridge safe and the command returned there Genl Davis reports a brisk trade in salt and other contraband goods going on from Pittsburg south through the region east of him. He has seized twelve (12) Bbls in transit It seems to me the Provost Marshal & Commanding Officers at Pittsburg & Hamburg Landings should be held responsible for it. Patrols will be necessary to prevent unprincipled Sutlers Clerks and discharged Soldiers from selling whatever they please of contraband" Telegram received, DNA, RG 393, Dept. of the Mo., Telegrams Received; copy, *ibid.*, Army of the Miss., 16th Army Corps, Telegrams Sent. *O.R.*, I, xvii, part 2, 151. On Aug. 16, in an endorsement to a letter which Rosecrans also endorsed, USG authorized the sale of seized cotton. American Art Association, Anderson Galleries, Sale No. 4292, Jan. 20–21, 1937, No. 286.

On Aug. 6, Maj. Gen. John A. McClernand telegraphed to USG. "Wagon loads of salt are constantly passing from the Tennisee & Mississippi River & points south & West. My Pickets Seized all that come in ~~from~~ reach. from a driver from whome we took five Barrels yesterday I learn that he bought it at Saltillo on the Tennisee & that he met several wagons loaded with salt coming this way. One Boat landed between Paducah & Pittsburg twelve hundred (1200) Barrels last week—would it not be well to send boat and seize all the salt on the river togather with the owners & authorized sales only at Military Posts." Telegram received, DNA, RG 393, Dept. of the Mo., Telegrams Received; copies, McClernand Papers, IHi.

On Aug. 18, Brig. Gen. Isaac F. Quinby, Columbus, Ky., wrote to USG. "All persons who bring undoubted proof of loyalty have been permitted to take specie and other money South over the railroad. I do not permit the express company to take packages, except to officers of the army, without a permit. I will not allow my private judgment, however strongly it may condemn unrestricted traffic with the South, to interfere with orders unofficially. I cannot discourage it." *O.R.*, I, xvii, part 2, 179–80. On Aug. 23, Rosecrans telegraphed to USG. "I have Recd the following from the Provost Marshall here—Iuka 23 Steamer Goodin landed salt & flour 2 miles above Savannah on the Tenn River their goods were landed on the 20th" Telegram received, DNA, RG 393, Dept. of the Mo., Telegrams Received.

On Aug. 26, Maj. Gen. William T. Sherman wrote to USG. "We occasionally make hauls of Clothing, Gold Lace, buttons &c but I am satisfied that salt and arms are got to the interior somehow. I have addressed the Board of

Trade a letter on this point, that will enable us to control this better." Copies, *ibid.*, RG 94, Generals' Papers and Books, William T. Sherman, Letters Sent; DLC-William T. Sherman. *O.R.*, I, xvii, part 2, 187–88. On Aug. 27, Col. Josiah W. Bissell, Columbus, Ky., telegraphed to USG. "I have just arrived here for barges to load at points on the river with confiscated corn for Memphis have captured some Guerrillas & have them in irons sent out the 52d Indiana to break up band in Tipton county forming to occupy Pillow. delivered the second lot of guns & five hundred (500) tons projectiles to Genl Sherman am loading the third. full report by mail" Telegram received, DNA, RG 393, Dept. of the Mo., Telegrams Received.

1. On Aug. 6, Maj. John A. Rawlins issued General Orders No. 69. "Hereafter no Coin will be permitted to pass South of Cairo or Columbus, except such as is carried by Government Agents and for Government use. The same restriction will be observed at Fort Henry and Fort Donelson. Neither Coin, Treasury Notes or Goods will be permitted to pass South of Memphis, except, for the use of the Army. The payment of cash or any article of use in aid of the Rebellion, for Southern products, will be discouraged in every way possible. All Cotton and other articles coming from points below Memphis will be seized and sold for the benefit of whom it may concern, the proceeds being used by the Quarter Master until directed by proper authority to turn them over to other parties, unless the same has been passed by special permit from the Treasury Department." Copies, DLC-USG, V, 12, 13, 14, 95; DNA, RG 393, USG General Orders. *O.R.*, I, xvii, part 2, 155.

2. On July 10, Rawlins issued Special Orders No. 134 appointing Col. Clark B. Lagow act. inspector gen., District of West Tenn., and ordering him on a tour of inspection. Copies, DLC-USG, V, 15, 16, 82, 87; DNA, RG 393, USG Special Orders. On Aug. 5, Rawlins issued Special Orders No. 154. "Colonel C. B. Lagow Aid-de-Camp and Acting Inspector General, will proceed to Hamburg, Tenn., and Eastport, Miss., and examine into abuses said to exist in the manner of carrying on trade with citizens. Colonel Lagow will correct such abuses as he may discover, and report to these Headquarters, his action." DS, *ibid.*, RG 94, Special Orders, District of West Tenn.; copies, *ibid.*, RG 393, USG Special Orders; DLC-USG, V, 15, 16, 82, 87. On Aug. 6, Lagow, Hamburg, telegraphed to USG. "In case a person will take the oath of allegiance here will he be permitted to buy a barrell of salt" Telegram received, DNA, RG 393, Dept. of the Mo., Telegrams Received.

To Brig. Gen. Lorenzo Thomas

———

Corinth 1 a m. [*Aug.*] 7th [*1862*]

ADJT GENL OF THE ARMY.

SIR.

News from the front continue to indicate movement of the rebels towards Chattanoga, my opinion is that the best troops are being sent to Richmond, & conscripts with a little leaven from the more disciplined are left to hold the Western Army in check[1]—

U. S. GRANT
Major Genl.

Telegram received, DNA, RG 94, Generals' Papers and Books, Telegrams Received by Gen. Halleck; copies, *ibid.*, RG 107, Telegrams Received (Press); *ibid.*, RG 393, USG Hd. Qrs. Correspondence; DLC-USG, V, 4, 5, 7, 8, 9, 88. *O.R.*, I, xvii, part 2, 155. On July 31, 1862, Maj. Gen. William T. Sherman wrote to Maj. John A. Rawlins. "A scouting party returned last night from Collierville & beyond captured some officers & Guerillas, also intercepted several letters from Tupello, from which it appears that whole army was on the point of starting for Nashville via Chattanooga. I take it for granted you are advised of this and I merely repeat it as confirmatory. I enclose one of the letters. All quiet here and hereabouts. I have supplied Gen Curtis my extra ammunition. Will you please order the ordnance officer at Saint Louis to fill my Requisitions for ammunition and ordnance to arm the fortifications now under construction here. Either drawing from Pittsburg or one of the Forts above." ALS, DNA, RG 393, District of West Tenn., Letters Received. *O.R.*, I, xvii, part 2, 141. On Aug. 5, Sherman telegraphed to USG. "Col Daniels was here some days ago   called to see me but I was out on the lines   he has disappeared & I have no means of knowing where his reg't or he is—Col Bissell arrived today with Twelve (12) Guns   he will go to Columbus for as many more—work progressing pretty well   I have scouted out but there is nothing near me but guerrillas of which the whole country is full—another intercepted mail confirms the account of bragg on Chattenooga and nashville"   Telegram received, DNA, RG 393, Dept. of the Mo., Telegrams Received; copies, *ibid.*, RG 94, Generals' Papers and Books, William T. Sherman, Telegrams Sent; DLC-William T. Sherman. On Aug. 6, Brig. Gen. Isaac F. Quinby telegraphed to USG the substance of a letter which he forwarded from Sherman, written by a C. S. A. officer, which indicated a movement on Nashville via Chattanooga. *O.R.*, I, xvii, part 2, 153. See telegram to Maj. Gen. Henry W. Halleck, July 30, 1862.

1. On Aug. 6, Maj. Gen. John A. McClernand wrote to USG. "Gentlemen are here from Benton County who report that on Saturday one hundred and twenty rebels had organized themselves as guerillas and that they are drilling daily—their rendezvous is East of Huntonting at a place called Chaseville in Benton County   they also speak of a rumour that a guerilla company is forming on the East Side of Tennessee River near White Oak Creek—and that it is rumered that these guerillas are getting arms from a sunken Boat not far from Reynoldsburg. the speak with confidence as to the organization near Chaseville which is nearly due East from Trenton and Huntington   I would suggest that Genl Dodge establish a tempory camp at or near Camdon or that a force be sent by water from Paducah to Wagners Landing near Camdon   the latter movement is preferable because it would take the enemy in reverse and probably surprise— either move would be a Tempory arrangement and would answer untill the Road between Brownsville and Paris should be opened which I should recommend as

a means of affording occasional communication by rail along this line, but little injury as I am informed is done to this portion of the Rail Road" ALS, DNA, RG 393, District of West Tenn., Letters Received. On the same day, McClernand telegraphed the substance of this letter to USG. Telegram received, *ibid.*, Dept. of the Mo., Telegrams Received; copies, McClernand Papers, IHi.

To Maj. Gen. Samuel R. Curtis

By Telegraph from Corinth [*Aug. 7*] 186[*2*]

To Maj Gen S R Curtis Cairo
Gen.

Telegraph Gen Halleck yet nominally commanding the Department for authority to move seige guns to Helena   I do not like to authorize the removal of siege guns to that point not knowing his views about fortifying it & my own approving it

U S Grant
Maj Genl

Telegram received, DNA, RG 393, Dept. of the Mo., Army of the Southwest, Telegrams Received. On Aug. 6, 1862, Maj. Gen. Samuel R. Curtis, Cairo, telegraphed to USG. "There are Eight (8) Siged guns at Birds Point and Seventeen (17) light Quincy two pounders at Paducah which you have ordered to be mooved   I would like to have them for use in my command if you do not need them   I think Genl Shermans guns have gone down." Telegram received, *ibid.*, Dept. of the Mo., Telegrams Received; copies, *ibid.*, Dept. of the Mo., Army of the Southwest, Letters Sent; Curtis Papers, IaHA.
   On Aug. 5, Brig. Gen. William K. Strong, Cairo, telegraphed to USG. "There are eight 32 pounder seige Guns at Bird's point that ought to be removed please direct me to what point to send them" Telegram received, DNA, RG 393, Dept. of the Mo., Telegrams Received. On Aug. 6, Maj. Gen. John A. McClernand telegraphed to USG. "There are twenty three 23 pieces of woodruffs small Cannon at Paducah   The same belonged to the Sixth Ills Cavalry. if you say so I will send for them or part of them." Telegram received, *ibid.*; copies, McClernand Papers, IHi. On Aug. 6, Strong telegraphed to USG. "Steamers and men have been dispatched to bring Goverment property from Paducah   Maj Gen Curtiss is here from Helena. Says he is going to fortify Helena & would be glad to have four or six of the 32 Pounders cannon sent him from Birds Point if Genl Sherman does not want them all at Memphis   We have at Paducah seventeen mounted eight battery peices about 2 Pounders capital for scouts & reconnoisance in rough countries. three or four men can haul them anywhere rapidly if need be. Genl Curtiss wants you to spare him seven of them   Shall I send them to him"

Telegram received, DNA, RG 393, Dept. of the Mo., Telegrams Received. On Aug. 7, Brig. Gen. Isaac F. Quinby telegraphed to USG. "The Crescent City has just returned from Memphis Having '*taking*' there from New Madrid in all 12 Guns & gun Carriages   Genl Sherman wishes 10 more   They can all be furnished from New Madrid & Fort Pillow if you so direct   I am informed by Col Bessell that there is a large amt of Ord & Ordnance stores at Fort Pillow   You know without doubt that that post is guarded only by a Gunboat"   Telegram received, *ibid*. On Aug. 8, Maj. Gen. Henry W. Halleck telegraphed to Curtis. "It is decided that no land forces will be moved on Vicksburg at present. The fortification of Helena is approved. You can obtain guns at Birds Point, Columbus, or Fort Pillow. Use the negroes for that purpose so far as you can advantageously." ALS (telegram sent), *ibid*., RG 107, Telegrams Collected (Bound).

To Brig. Gen. William S. Rosecrans

Corinth Aug 7th 1862

GENL ROSECRANS

Appoint a Provost Marshall at Eastport and confiscate all goods impropriety, taking them and the boats carrying them, where a case can be made out. Make prisoner of all persons engaged in an illicit trade, and particularly of Northern men

U. S GRANT
Maj Genl

Telegram, copy, DNA, RG 393, Army of the Miss., Telegrams Received. On Aug. 7, 1862, Brig. Gen. William S. Rosecrans telegraphed to USG. "I am informed that there is an illicit trade carried on between Eastport and Florence by boats towards the south   with your approval, I will direct that a discreet Officer be appointed Provost Marshall at Eastport with instructions to search all Boats or persons & confiscate all contraband goods" Telegram received, *ibid*., Dept. of the Mo., Telegrams Received; copy, *ibid*., Army of the Miss., Telegrams Sent.

To Brig. Gen. William S. Rosecrans

Corinth Aug 7th 1862

GENL ROSECRANS

If you have supplies, Contrabands, send up fifty to go forward to Columbus to work there as stevadores.[1] Sheridan can send them if they are none now on hand.

U. S. GRANT
Maj Genl

Telegram, copy, DNA, RG 393, Army of the Miss., Telegrams Received. On Aug. 8, 1862, USG telegraphed again to Brig. Gen. William S. Rosecrans. "In addition to the fifty negroes to go to Columbus called for yesterday, thirty more are wanted here for teamsters. It will save a detail of that number of men from the ranks, If you have the refugees or can get them from men confessing allegiance to the Southern Confederacy" Copy, *ibid.*

On Aug. 7, Maj. Gen. John A. McClernand wrote to USG. "The enclosed communication having been forwarded to me I respectfully forward it to you, for your decision. I have only to state that I allow no negroes except those brought from the North or employed in Government service to travel on the Rail-roads through my District." Copy, McClernand Papers, IHi. On Aug. 10, Capt. Levi W. Vaughn, provost marshal at Hamburg, telegraphed to USG asking for instructions on the employment, payment, and subsistence of Negroes. Telegram received, DNA, RG 393, Dept. of the Mo., Telegrams Received.

On Aug. 14, Maj. Gen. William T. Sherman, Memphis, wrote to Maj. John A. Rawlins. "I found about 600 Negroes employed here, and daily others come into our works. I have knowledge that a Law had passed the Congress for using the Labor of such Negroes, approved by the President and sanctioned by General Halleck. No instructions had come or could come to guide me, and I was forced to lay down certain Rules for my own guidance. Masters and Mistresses so thronged my tent as to absorb my whole time, and necessity compelled me to adopt some clearly defined Rules, ~~for~~ and I did so. I think them legal, and just. Under this order I must assume to clothe and feed those Negroes, but you will observe I make no provisions for any; save laboring men.—The women and families take refuge here, but I cannot provide for them, but I allow no form or under pursuasion in any case. . . . I finally enclose a copy of letter from Genl. Pillow addressed to S. P. Walker Esqr of this city and designed for Genl Grant & my self. It did not come under a flag of truce, but by one of the secret mails which I have not yet succeeded in breaking up. I also enclose a copy of my answer which I will hand to Mr Walker & allow him to send as he best may. I do not consider my answer as strictly official as the matters enquired about are as to the situation of his private property." Copy, *ibid.*, District of West Tenn., Letters Received. *O.R.*, I, xvii, part 2, 169–71. On Aug. 2, C. S. A. Brig. Gen. Gideon J. Pillow had written to Samuel P. Walker asking the status of Negroes from his plantation near Helena, Ark., and asking that the letter be transmitted either to

Sherman or USG. Copy, DNA, RG 393, District of West Tenn., Letters Received. *O.R.*, I, xvii, part 2, 171. On Aug. 14, Sherman wrote to Pillow saying that the slaves had not been taken except where proof existed that the slaves had been used by the C. S. A. Copy, DNA, RG 393, District of West Tenn., Letters Received. *O.R.*, I, xvii, part 2, 172.

On Aug. 16, McClernand telegraphed to USG. "Please inform me whether in supposing that all requisitions for forced negro labor within my ~~lines~~ district must be made or approved by me I misconstrue orders" Telegram received, DNA, RG 393, Dept. of the Mo., Telegrams Received; copies, McClernand Papers, IHi. On Aug. 20, Capt. Charles A. Reynolds, Corinth, telegraphed to Rawlins. "Contrabands for teamsters & laborers are much needed can none be had" Telegram received, DNA, RG 393, Dept. of the Mo., Telegrams Received. On Aug. 22, Col. William W. Lowe, Fort Henry, telegraphed to Rawlins. "Can A A Q M ~~we~~ buy or issue clothing to such negroes as may be employed under the provision of your order I have the names of 16 prominent citizens who joined Col Woodward in taking Clarkesville—" Telegram received, *ibid.* On Aug. 26, Capt. Frederick E. Prime, Corinth, telegraphed to USG. "Will you please have (150) negroes sent here (40) for Genl McPherson & balance for Engineer Dep't I understand that a large number are coming into Iuka today & would like to have above number—if possible—" Telegram received, *ibid.*, Dept. of the Tenn., Telegrams Received. On Aug. 28, F. M. Pheps, Jackson, telegraphed to USG. "I have contract to complete the Rail Road from Paducah to Uion City can I use contrabands by paying them please reply" Telegram received, *ibid.*, Dept. of the Mo., Telegrams Received. On the same day, USG answered Pheps. "I have nothing to do with employment of contrabands as you propose" Copy, *ibid.*

1. USG's shift in policy from strict enforcement of Maj. Gen. Henry W. Halleck's General Orders No. 3, excluding fugitive slaves from U.S. Army camps, to active use of fugitives to further military purposes reflected changing U.S. government policy. On Aug. 11, Rawlins issued General Orders No. 72. "Recent Acts of Congress prohibit the Army from returning fugitives from labor to their claimants, and authorize the employment of such persons in the service of the Government. The following orders are therefore, published for the guidance of the Army in this Military District, in this matter. All fugitives thus employed must be registered, the names of the fugitives and claimants given, and must be borne upon the Morning Reports of the command in which they are kept, showing how they are employed. Fugitive Slaves may be employed as laborers in the Quartermaster's Dept. Subsistence and Engineers Depts. and wherever by such employment a Soldier may be saved to the ranks. They may be employed as Teamsters, as Company Cooks, (not exceeding four to a Company) or as Hospital attendants and nurses. Officers may employ them as private servants, in which latter case the fugitive will not be paid or rationed by the Government. Negroes not thus employed will be deemed unauthorized persons, and must be excluded from the camps. Officers and Soldiers are positively prohibited from enticing Slaves to leave their masters. When it becomes necessary to employ this kind of labor, Commanding Officers of Posts or troops, must send details, (always under the charge of a suitable Commissioned Officer,) to press into service the slaves of disloyal persons to the number required. Citizens within reach of any Military Station, known to be disloyal and dangerous, may be ordered away or arrested,

and their crops and stock taken, for the benefit of the Government, or the use of the Army. All property taken from rebel owners, must be duly reported and use for the benefit of the Government, and be issued to the troops through the proper Depts, and when practicable the act of taking should be avowed by the written certificate of the Officer taking, to the owner or agent of such property. It is enjoined on all Commanders to see that this order is executed strictly under their own directions. The demoralization of troops consequent upon being left to execute laws in their own way without a proper head, must be avoided." Copies, DLC-USG, V, 12, 13, 14, 95; (printed) DNA, RG 393, USG General Orders; *ibid.*, RG 94, 48th Ill., Letterbook; *ibid.*, 21st Ill., Order Book.

To Maj. Gen. William T. Sherman

Head Quarters, Dist. of West Ten.
Corinth, August 8th 1862

MAJ. GEN. W. T. SHERMAN
COMD.G U. S. FORCES
MEMPHIS TEN.
GEN.

Herewith I send you an article credited to the Memphis correspondent of the Chicago Times[1] which is both false in fact and mischievous in character. You will have the author arrested and sent to Alton Penitentiary under proper escort for confinement until the close of the war unless sooner discharged by competant authority.

I am Gen. very respectfully
your obt. svt.
U. S. GRANT
Maj. Gen. Com

ALS, IC. On Aug. 14, 1862, Maj. Gen. William T. Sherman endorsed USG's letter. "Do you know the man   Find him out and arrest him." AES, *ibid.* First published in 1955 as part of the reminiscences of *Chicago Times* correspondent Sylvanus Cadwallader, the authenticity of this letter came under attack by Kenneth P. Williams and Ulysses S. Grant, 3rd. The editor of Cadwallader's memoirs, Benjamin P. Thomas, was unable to locate the original letter at the time. Benjamin P. Thomas, ed., *Three Years with Grant as Recalled by War Correspondent Sylvanus Cadwallader* (New York, 1955), p. 3; Bruce Catton, "Reading, Writing and History," *American Heritage*, VII, 5 (Aug., 1956), 106–11; Kenneth P. Williams,

Lincoln Finds a General: A Military Study of the Civil War (New York, 1956), IV, 440–41; Ulysses S. Grant, III, "Civil War Fact and Fiction," *Civil War History*, II, 2 (June, 1956), 33–34.

On Aug. 17, 1862, Sherman wrote to USG. "A letter from you of August 4, asking me to write more freely and fully on all matters of public interest, did not reach me till yesterday. I think since the date of that letter you have received from me official Reports & Copies of orders telling almost every thing of interest hereabouts; but I will with pleasure take every occasion to advise you of everything that occurs here. Your order of arrest of the newspaper correspondent is executed, and he will be sent to Alton by the first opportunity. He sends you by mail today a long appeal, and has asked me to stay proceedings till you can be heard from. I have informed him, I would not do so; that persons writing over false names were always suspected by honorable men, and that all I could hold out to him was, that you might release him, if the dishonest Editor who had substituted his newspaper name to the protection of another, would place himself in prison in his place. I regard all these newspaper harpies as spies, and think they could be punished as such." In his lengthy letter, Sherman went on to discuss trade with the enemy, guerrilla activities, C. S. A. plans, and other matters. Copies, DLC-William T. Sherman; DNA, RG 94, Generals' Papers and Books, William T. Sherman, Letters Sent. *O.R.*, I, xvii, part 2, 178–79.

On July 28, under the pseudonym "Shiloh," Warren P. Isham, correspondent of the *Chicago Times*, sent a dispatch from Memphis. "Late advices from the South by rebel sources are somewhat important. Ten iron-clad gunboats, built in England, and fully equipped, have arrived off Mobile harbor, and signaled Fort Morgan. Three more are on the way. These constitute the fleet ordered by the Southern Confederacy to be purchased in Europe. They mount from ten to thirty guns each, and are said to be mailed with six-inch iron, being regular war steamers in every sense of the word. Gen. Bragg has been telegraphed to furnish 350 seamen to man them with, and orders are being dispatched over the whole Confederacy for supplies and munitions to furnish them equipment. The Commanders will be selected from officers of the old United States Navy who joined the Confederate service, and have been idle for want of a fleet. Their armament consists of the most approved modern artillery, and each boat is constructed with a view to ram service. The blockade was run openly by dint of superior strength and weight of metal, and Mobile is considered to be open to the world, with the support of her newly acquired power. The remaining vessels will be on soon. The above is from an authentic source, and is entitled to belief." *Chicago Times*, July 31, 1862.

The dispatch, though entirely false, reportedly caused considerable concern in Washington. "There was a hurrying and bustling about the Navy Department when the news came, and Mr. Gideon Welles is reported to have been considerably flurried—but had sufficient presence of mind to turn to an Assistant and inquire—'how long before the first new Monitor would be finished,'—and 'how thick was her mail to be?' When he heard the quick and short reply of his intelligent supernumerary—'the first of September, and five inches,'—he inclined down considerably, and remarked—'where in thunder did them gunboats come from?' " *Ibid.*, Aug. 7, 1862.

The *Chicago Times* of Aug. 19 reported Isham's arrest, and said that it regretted "that Gen. Grant should have found anything in any letter from our special correspondent at Memphis to provoke his displeasure, because he is one of the last men in the world whom we would knowingly permit to be unjustly treated in these columns, and because we are confident our correspondent has not intentionally treated him unjustly." *Ibid.*, Aug. 19, 1862.

1. After a background of journalism in Mich., Wilbur F. Storey became editor and publisher of the *Chicago Times* in June, 1861. Sensational stories and Democratic partisanship often put the newspaper in the center of controversy. Storey's pro-Copperhead editorializing led Maj. Gen. Ambrose E. Burnside to order the *Times* suppressed in June, 1863, whereupon President Abraham Lincoln revoked the suspension. A veteran newspaperman, Warren P. Isham had served as an employee and associate of his brother-in-law, Storey, since 1850. Generally considered an able reporter, Isham went south shortly after the outbreak of the war, where he had several run-ins with U.S. authorities. Isham's arrest led to his incarceration at Alton, Ill., until USG had him released on Nov. 12, 1862.

Isham's colleague, Thomas M. Cook, then at Cairo and writing under the pseudonym "K," also found himself in trouble. On Aug. 8, Col. Thomas E. G. Ransom, 11th Ill., Cairo, telegraphed to USG. "In persuiance of your telegraphic order to Genl Strong, I have ordered all news Reports to be Submitted to these Head Quarters for approval before being transmitted over the lines" Telegram received, DNA, RG 393, Dept. of the Mo., Telegrams Received. On Aug. 21, the *Chicago Times* published a dispatch dated Aug. 19, over the signature of Cook and approved by Brig. Gen. James M. Tuttle, in which Cook confessed to having made "misstatements" about Brig. Gen. William K. Strong and the provost marshal at Cairo. Justin E. Walsh, *To Print the News and Raise Hell!: A Biography of Wilbur F. Storey* (Chapel Hill, 1968), pp. 35, 116–17, 177–79.

To Austin Blair

———

Corinth Mississippi
August 8th 1862

HON. A. BLAIR,
GOVERNOR OF MICHIGAN, LANSING.
SIR:

Your letter of the 1st inst. relative to the resignation of Col. F. Quinn[1] is just received.

The resignation refered to passed through these Head Quarters on the 1st, the day your letter was written, and was endorsed and immediately forwarded to Head Quarters of the Department, St. Louis.

As Gen. Halleck has not been relieved from the Command of the Department, and is absent from it, there may be some delay. I will forward your letter to insure the acceptance of Col. Quinns resignation when a successor to Gen. Halleck is named.

> very respectfully, your obt svt.
> U. S. GRANT
> Maj. Gen.

ALS, Burton Historical Collection, MiD. Born in N. Y. in 1818, educated at Hamilton and Union colleges, Austin Blair was admitted to the N.Y. bar in 1841. He moved to Mich., was active in the Whig Party, and proposed Negro suffrage while serving as a state legislator. In 1854, he participated in the organization of the Republican Party, and was elected governor in 1860.

1. Col. Francis Quinn, 12th Mich., fought at Shiloh under Brig. Gen. Benjamin M. Prentiss. Quinn was accused of cowardice at Shiloh by many in his regt., but formal court-martial charges, signed by seventeen officers of the 12th Mich., were not filed until after Quinn's resignation. Joseph Ruff, "Civil War Experiences of a German Immigrant as Told by the Late Joseph Ruff of Albion," *Michigan History Magazine*, XXVII (Spring, Summer, 1943), 271–301, 442–48; *Detroit Free Press*, April 29, 1862; information supplied by John Gillette, Berrien Springs, Mich., Aug., 1971. On Aug. 27, 1862, Maj. Gen. John A. McClernand telegraphed to USG that Quinn had withdrawn his resignation. Copies, McClernand Papers, IHi. On Aug. 31, however, Capt. Simon M. Preston issued Special Orders No. 311, Dept. of the Miss., accepting the resignation. Copy, DNA, RG 94, Dept. of the Miss., Special Orders.

To Maj. Gen. Henry W. Halleck

> Head Quarters, Dist. of West Ten.
> Corinth, August 9th 1862

MAJ. GEN. H. W. HALLECK,
GEN. IN CHIEF OF THE ARMY
WASHINGTON D. C.
GEN.

I address you direct no order yet being received announcing your staff and not feeling certain that you should be addressed through the Adjutant General of the Army.

All is quiet now North of the Memphis and Charleston road there being no organized force nearer our line than Holly Springs in the center and Saltillo on the left.[1] There is abundant evidence that many citizens who appear to be quiet ~~citizens~~ non combattants in the presence of our forces are regularly enrolled and avail themselvs of every safe opportunity of depridating upon Union men and annoying our troops where in small bodies.

The Guerrillas have been driven entirely South of the Hatchee and I hope to be able to keep them there. I think of sending the remainder of the 6th Division of the Army of the Tennessee to Bolivar which will give a force there sufficient for this purpose.

I am anxious to keep the whole of the Army of the Mississippi together, and under the command of Brig. Gen. Rosecrans, ready for any imergency, either to move upon any force that may threaten my front, or to reinforce Gen. Buell. Having so many Maj. Generals to provide commands for, this may be difficult.[2] I regret that Gen. Rosecrans has not got rank equal to his merit to make this easy.

I have communicated to Gen. Buell several times such information as I had of interest to him, but have never received any acknowledgement. I do not know where he is.

I have sent an additional Brigade to hold the line East to Decatur and ordered another. In accordance with your instructions I will try to hold the communication with Gen. Buell and be in readiness to reinforce him if it should become necessary.[3]

All intercepted letters from rebel troops shows that most of the forces that were in front of us have gone to Chatanooga. I informed you by telegraph that I believe the enemy had no intention of attacking this line, in force, but only desire to hold Buell and myself in check whilst the mass of their disciplined troops are being sent to Richmond.[4] I have no positive evidence of this but the conviction is strong with me. I give this however for what it is worth.

All stores have been removed from Pittsburg Landing and the regiment that was stationed there I have sent to Jackson[5]

The 63d Ill. regiment has been brought from Cairo to Jackson and relieved by the 11th Ill. a very much reduced regiment. The 71st Ill. a new regiment, has also joined and has been assigned to duty at Columbus.[6] This embraces all the changes made in the position of troops since your departure except those previously reported.

Recent orders are bringing back great numbers of absentees.[7]

> I am Gen. very respectfully
> your obt. svt.
> U. S. Grant
> Maj. Gen.

ALS, IHi. *O.R.*, I, xvii, part 2, 160.

1. On Aug. 9, 1862, Maj. Gen. John A. McClernand telegraphed to USG. "A Mr N McKesy from Holly springs has just arrived at Bolivar making his way north out of reach of the conscript act   He reports great activity in enforcing the law   he also reports that in the state of Mississippi the entire militia is called out & are concentrating at Oxford   No troops this side of Holly springs that he knows of"   Telegram received, DNA, RG 393, Dept. of the Mo., Telegrams Received; copy, McClernand Papers, IHi.

2. See telegram to Maj. Gen. Henry W. Halleck, Aug. 3, 1862.

3. See telegram to Maj. Gen. Don Carlos Buell, Aug. 11, 1862.

4. See telegram to Brig. Gen. Lorenzo Thomas, Aug. 7, 1862.

5. See telegram to Brig. Gen. William S. Rosecrans, Aug. 6, 1862.

6. On July 17, Brig. Gen. Lorenzo Thomas issued AGO Special Orders No. 164 granting Brig. Gen. William K. Strong leave of absence for sixty days beginning Aug. 1. Copy, DLC-USG, V, 83. Strong requested the leave in order to bring his family home from Europe. *Chicago Tribune*, Aug. 7, 1862. On Aug. 24, Strong telegraphed to USG questioning whether he ought to leave so soon, and indicating he would discuss the matter with USG in person. Telegram received, DNA, RG 393, Dept. of the Mo., Telegrams Received. On July 29, Maj. John A. Rawlins issued Special Orders No. 147. "The 63rd Ills. Vols. at Cairo will immediately proceed via Columbus to Jackson, Tenn. and report to Maj Gen. John A. McClernand, Commanding, 1st Division Army of the Tennessee. Upon the arrival of the 63rd at Jackson, the 11th Ills. Regiment will proceed to Cairo and garrison that post, Col. T. E. G. Ransom relieving Brig Gen W. K. Strong in the command of the District of Cairo." Copies, DLC-USG, V, 15, 16, 82, 87; DNA, RG 393, USG Special Orders.

On Aug. 1, Strong telegraphed to USG. "Part of sixty third 63rd were out in Missouri. Returned this afternoon. Col. Ransom has ten (10) days yet unexpired of his leave of absence. The pay master has just arrived from Chicago to pay off this Regiment. But will not be ready to do so before Monday noon   if you know no objection I will have them paid & sent off to Jackson tuesday or Wednesday next. That will get the Eleventh (11th) here about time Col Ransom gets here   I shall not leave until Every thing is in good shape if I stay here ten days. please reply" Telegram received, *ibid.*, Dept. of the Mo., Telegrams Received. On Aug. 3, McClernand telegraphed to USG. "The 11th Regt has left for Cairo" Telegram received, *ibid.* On Aug. 4, Brig. Gen. Isaac F. Quinby telegraphed to USG. "The 71st Ills Vols arrived here last evening—It is a raw Regiment. I retain it & send 13th Wisconsin to No (10)   I am informed that the (35th) Indiana Vols. is at Nashville   the 63rd Ills. Vols will be sent to Jackson by morning train   it is five hundred fifty (550) strong" Telegram received, *ibid.*

On Aug. 5, Quinby telegraphed to USG. "Shall I await the arrival of Co. "B" 2nd Ills Cavalry before I send Co "I" to Jackson. It is the only Cavalry Company at this post. Genl Dodge is ordered to send another company from Trenton—The two Companies 15th Wisonsin at No "10" shall be sent to Corinth so soon as transportation can be procured to take down the 13th Wisconsin to relieve them" Telegram received, *ibid.* On Aug. 1, Rawlins issued Special Orders No. 150 ordering Co. B, 2nd Ill. Cav., from Bolivar, Tenn., to Columbus, Ky., and Co. I, 2nd Ill. Cav., and one other co. from Quinby's command to Jackson. DS, *ibid.*, RG 94, Special Orders, District of West Tenn.; copies, *ibid.*, RG 393, USG Special Orders; DLC-USG, V, 15, 16, 82, 87. On Aug. 8, Quinby telegraphed to USG. "Four (4) companies of the 71st Illinois Vols are retained in the state for some reason.   will they be sent me. I donot like to send the 13th Wisconsin to Island No (10) until the whole of the 71st which is very raw is here." Telegram received, DNA, RG 393, Dept. of the Mo., Telegrams Received. On Aug. 15, Quinby telegraphed to Rawlins. "Is Genl Robt Allen Chief Quarter master now at Corinth—Company I 2d Ills Cavalry will leave for Jackson on monday next   Company I 5th Mo vols will also start for Corinth the same day unless Countermanding orders are recd." Telegram received, *ibid.*

On Aug. 8, Brig. Gen. James M. Tuttle, Bolivar, telegraphed to USG. "Your telegram recd. Your proposition will suit that is take Cairo Command for present & return to the field when able. I hope in a month or two Col. Crockett succeed me in Command" Telegram received, *ibid.* On Aug. 11, Col. Thomas E. G. Ransom telegraphed to USG. "In persuiance of your general order no 148 I releived Genl Strong in Command of this District on the Seventh (7th) 'Inst.' " Telegram received, *ibid.* On Aug. 12, Tuttle telegraphed to USG. "I am here waiting orders   Have they been sent   if you recollect you gave me no authority to take command. Answer." Telegram received, *ibid.* On Aug. 12, Rawlins issued Special Orders No. 161. "Brig. Gen. J. M. Tuttle, is hereby relieved from duty at Bolivar, Tenn. and is assigned to the command of the District of Cairo." DS, *ibid.*, RG 94, Special Orders, District of West Tenn.; copies, *ibid.*, RG 393, USG Special Orders; DLC-USG, V, 15, 16, 82, 87. *O.R.*, I, xvii, part 2, 166. On Aug. 14, Tuttle, Cairo, telegraphed to Rawlins. "Orders received   I am now in command of this district" Telegram received, DNA, RG 393, Dept. of the Mo., Telegrams Received.

7. On July 24, Brig. Gen. Stephen A. Hurlbut wrote to Maj. John H. Hammond, asst. adjt. gen. for Maj. Gen. William T. Sherman, stating that several officers who had been absent and reported as deserters had reported for duty. LS, *ibid.*, Dept. of the Tenn., Miscellaneous Letters Received. On Aug. 6, Rawlins endorsed the letter. "See General Order No 68 from these Head Quarters." AES, *ibid.* On Aug. 5, Rawlins issued General Orders No. 68. "All Officers and Soldiers who have or may rejoin their Regiments from absence without leave prior to the 13th day of August, inst. will be restored to duty at once; but the

next muster roll will show the time absent without authority, and pay will be forfeited to the Government for such period. Officers or Soldiers who object to this method of punishing their offence, will be arrested and tried as deserter."
Copies, DLC-USG, V, 12, 13, 14, 95; DNA, RG 393, USG General Orders.

To Maj. Nathaniel H. McLean

Head Quarters Disct West Tenn
Corinth, Augt 10th 1862

MAJ N H MCLEAN
A. A. GENL. DEPT OF THE MISS.
SAINT LOUIS, MO
SIR

Enclosed herewith find some documents which are intended to bear on the recommendation of Genl Davies ~~that~~ in the cases of Col Crafts J Wright, Lt Col B P Wright[1] & 1st Lt W. Bradford[2] 22nd Ohio Vols. I fully endorse the recommendation of Genl Davies. From the day Col Wright first reported to me for duty, to the present time, he has been the cause of more complaints from his immediate commanders than any six officers of this Command. He has constantly raised the question of rank with those immediately over him; (this has even occured on the battle fields,) and he is constantly raising points and occupying the time of his superior officers with a correspondence, useless to the service and to some extent insubordinate.

Very Respcty
Your Obt Servt
U. S. GRANT
Maj Genl

Copies, DLC-USG, V, 4, 5, 7, 8, 88; DNA, RG 393, USG Hd. Qrs. Correspondence. On April 10, 1862, 1st Lt. Clark B. Lagow wrote to Brig. Gen. John McArthur. "I am directed by Major Gen. Grant Commdg. to say to you that you will have Col. Crafts J. Wright Commdg the 13th Mo. Regt. Vols. placed in arrest, and that the Senior Officer of the Regt. assume command." Copies, DLC-USG, V, 1, 2, 86; DNA, RG 393, USG Letters Sent. Two reports written on April 10 condemned Col. Crafts J. Wright and the 13th Mo. (later renamed 22 Ohio). Col. James M. Tuttle reported to McArthur that Wright had refused to obey orders to pursue the enemy on April 8. *O.R.*, I, x, part 1, 149. Col. C. Carroll Marsh reported to Maj. Mason Brayman that Wright had refused to obey orders to stop the retreat of his regt. on April 6 until threatened with arrest. *Ibid.*, p. 134. On the other hand, Brig. Gen. William T. Sherman added a favorable endorsement to Wright's undated report. *Ibid.*, p. 160. On Sept. 9, 1st Lt. Theodore S. Bowers issued Special Orders No. 189. "The resignation of Col. Crafts J. Wright, 22nd Regt Ohio Vol. Infy, is hereby accepted to take effect this day. The resignation of Lieut. Col. Benjamin F. Wright, 22nd Regt Ohio Vol. Infy, is hereby accepted to take effect this day." DS, DNA, RG 94, Special Orders, District of West Tenn.; copies, *ibid.*, RG 393, USG Special Orders; DLC-USG, V, 15, 16, 82, 87.

On Aug. 29, USG wrote to Brig. Gen. Lorenzo Thomas. "I herewith transmit Proceedings of Board of Examination, in cases of Col C. J. Wright and Lt Col Benj F Wright 22nd Ohio Infty" Copies, *ibid.*, V, 4, 5, 7, 8, 88; DNA, RG 393, USG Hd. Qrs. Correspondence. On Oct. 1, Thomas telegraphed to USG. "Have you accepted the resignation of Col Crafts J. Wright or Lt Col B F. Wright 22d Ohio Vols—& if so when." Telegram received, *ibid.*, Dept. of the Tenn., Miscellaneous Letters Received; copies, *ibid.*, RG 94, Letters Sent; *ibid.*, RG 393, USG Hd. Qrs. Correspondence; DLC-USG, V, 4, 5, 7, 8, 88. On Oct. 2, USG telegraphed to Thomas. "The resignations of Col Crafts J Wright & Lt Col F B Wright twenty secd Ohio Vols were accepted Sept 9th & Copy of Order & original Resignation forwarded to you" Telegram received, DNA, RG 107, Telegrams Received (Bound, Press); copies, *ibid.*, RG 393, USG Hd. Qrs. Correspondence; DLC-USG, V, 4, 5, 7, 8, 88. On Oct. 3, Col. Edward D. Townsend issued AGO Special Orders No. 275 revoking previous orders which had dismissed the Wrights from the service. Copy, DLC-USG, V, 93.

1. Benjamin T. Wright, 22nd Ohio, was appointed drill master with the rank of capt. on Aug. 20, 1861. He served in the battle of Shiloh; was commissioned lt. col. on Aug. 5, 1862, to date from May 1, 1861; and was serving in the 2nd Division, Army of the Tenn., under Brig. Gen. Richard J. Oglesby at the time of his resignation. *O.R.*, I, iii, 514; *ibid.*, I, x, part 1, 160; *ibid.*, I, xvii, part 2, 145.

2. 1st Lt. William Bradford, 22nd Ohio, was commissioned on Aug. 5, 1862, to date from Aug. 20, 1861. He was discharged on Oct. 6, 1862.

To Brig. Gen. William S. Rosecrans

———

Corinth Aug 10th 1862

GENL ROSECRANS

Yesterday instructions were given to allow Col Delworth,[1] and two other Citizens to protect their homes, even to the extent

of allowing them to keep arms. This was authorized on repre-
sentations which I now believe to be false   I would now say,
give them no protection and if they don't like the assertion advise
them to quit   I favor turning out of our lines all suspicious persons, and the use of their property for public purposes. This is
in accordance with instructions just received from Washington.[2]

U S GRANT
Maj. Genl

Telegram, copy, DNA, RG 393, Army of the Miss., Telegrams Received. On
Aug. 9, 1862, Col. Joseph D. Webster wrote to Brig. Gen. William S. Rosecrans.
"Messrs. A. B. Dilworth, J. B. Tanant, and Joseph Stout citizens, the first named
of whom is on parole, and has a safeguard, and the others have taken the oath of
allegiance to the United States, have made complaint at these Head Quarters,
that depredations are committed upon their property, at night, by negroes whom
they see, but against whom they are deterred from defending them selves, by
threats of some of our soldiers. These citizens are to be allowed all necessary
means and liberty of defence against these depredations, even to the possession,
and use of arms, if necessary. You will therefore, after due inquiry, see that the
rights of these citizens to self defence against such lawless acts are not interfered
with by any solders of your command." ALS, *ibid.*, RG 109, Union Provost
Marshals' File of Papers Relating to Individual Civilians. On Aug. 9, Maj.
George M. Van Hosen wrote to Maj. John A. Rawlins. "Col. A B Dilworth,
who hands you this letter has long been known to me as a [s]uspicious person.
He is known & in everybody's mouth, as leading secessionist. He declines to take
the oath of allegiance, and I refuse to give him a pass. He wishes to appeal from
me to Gen Grant, and, as the case must eventually come before the General if I
determine to detain ~~Dilworth~~ him, I refer him at once to Head Quarters." ALS,
ibid. On the same day, Webster endorsed Van Hosen's letter. "Respectfully
referred to Brig Gen. Rosecrans. This paper was handed in by Mr. Dilworth after
the order in reference to him & two others had been written. It furnishes additional reason for care in the inquiry as to the character of these parties before
according them any peculiar privileges within our lines." AES, *ibid.*

1. Andrew B. Dilworth, an early settler of Tishomingo County, Miss.,
active in Democratic Party politics, served as secretary of state of Miss. 1855–
1860. He ran unsuccessfully as a pro-secession candidate for the state convention
held at Jackson, Miss., Jan. 7, 1861. In 1861, he assisted in securing an emergency loan for the C. S. A. state government; and in April, 1862, he was active
in efforts to secure the parole of prisoners held at Camp Douglas Military Prison,
Ill. Dunbar Rowland, *History of Mississippi: The Heart of the South* (Chicago and
Jackson, Miss., 1925), II, 839; Mary Floyd Sumners, "Politics in Tishomingo
County, 1836–1860," *Journal of Mississippi History*, XXVIII, 2 (May, 1966),
140, 150; *O.R.*, IV, ii, 924; *ibid.*, II, iii, 859.
2. See letter to Maj. Gen. Henry W. Halleck, July 28, 1862.

To Abraham Lincoln

———

Corinth Mississippi
August 11th 1862

To his Excellency
A Lincoln
President of the U. S.
Sir :

Permit me in view of the great increase now being made to our army, and the consequent increase in General officers, to suggest the names of two Colonels from the state of Illinois who, to the natural capacity for a higher position which they have, have had experience in the field during our present struggles, and have proven their worthiness on the *battle field* and in the *Camp of instruction*. I allude to Isham N. Haynie[1] and John E. Smith,[2] Colonels of the 48th & 45th Illinois Infantry respectively.

Col. Haynie is from the extreme Southern part of the state and Col. Smith from the Northern part.

These promotions I am certain you would never have reason to regret nor would the troops over whom they might be called to command.

I am, very respectfully
your obt. svt.
U. S. Grant
Maj. Gen.

ALS, DNA, RG 94, ACP G658 CB 1863. On Oct. 11, 1862, U.S. Representative Elihu B. Washburne sent a copy of USG's letter to President Abraham Lincoln. "Please read this letter. The enclosed is a copy of a recommendation sent to you last August which has been overlooked. If there be any two men in the army who deserve the appointments these are the men. Will you read this letter of Haynie. I saw him the other day in Tennessee and he is with us heart and soul, and Jack Logan is all right also." ALS, DLC-Robert T. Lincoln.

1. Isham N. Haynie of Cairo, Ill., received a recess appointment as brig. gen. on Nov. 29, which expired on March 4, 1863, when the Senate refused to confirm. *Senate Executive Journal*, XIII, 128.

2. John E. Smith of Galena, Ill., received a recess appointment as brig. gen. which the Senate refused to confirm. The nomination was resubmitted, and Smith was confirmed on March 11, 1863, to rank from Nov. 29, 1862. *Ibid.*, pp. 214, 281.

To Maj. Gen. Don Carlos Buell

BY TELEGRAPH FROM Corinth [*Aug. 11*] *1862*

TO GENL BUELL

I will direct troops to remain at Clarkesville   Genl Rosecrans informs me that you had written or dispatched to me some days ago   I recd nothing from you

U S GRANT
Maj Genl

Telegram received, DNA, RG 94, Generals' Papers and Books, Telegrams Received by Gen. Buell. On Aug. 8, 1862, Maj. Gen. Don Carlos Buell, Huntsville, Ala., telegraphed to USG. "Cant you leave your Regiment at Clarksville for the present. It is very difficult for me to replace it"   Telegram received (misdated Aug. 10), *ibid.*, RG 393, Dept. of the Mo., Telegrams Received; copy, *ibid.*, Telegrams Received; copy, *ibid.*, Dept. of the Ohio, Telegrams Sent. On Aug. 12, Buell telegraphed to USG. "The Dispatches were recd by your operator night before last. please see them as soon as possible"   Telegram received, *ibid.*, Dept. of the Mo., Telegrams Received; copy, *ibid.*, Dept. of the Ohio, Telegrams Sent. *O.R.*, I, xvi, part 2, 316.

On Aug. 8, Buell telegraphed to USG. "General Halleck informs me you will answer my requisition for two (2) Divisions if necessary—Whose will they be and where?"   Copy, DNA, RG 393, Dept. of the Ohio, Telegrams Sent. *O.R.*, I, xvi, part 2, 286. This telegram may never have reached USG. See telegram to Maj. Gen. Don Carlos Buell, Aug. 12, 1862.

To Brig. Gen. William S. Rosecrans

Corinth Aug 11th 1862

GENL ROSECRANS

I have information that from 800 to 1000 men mostly new levies are now infesting the country about Ripley, and north of it. That a part or most of this force will be in the neighborhood of Pocahontas[1] today or tomorrow to burn cotton and impress men. Cant you send a few hundred men in that direction   Mounted men to remain for two or three days. Let them impress all the teams they want, and bring in all the cotton they can lay their hands on. Union men being permitted to come along and sell theirs. Oppressive secessionists may be arrested, and their horses, and mules, & whatever else they have of service to the Government taken. There is a strong union sentiment about Pocahontas, so their will be no difficulty about getting all the information required.

I will send an Infantry regt from here to remain a few days at Pocahontas

U. S. GRANT

Maj Genl

Telegram, copy, DNA, RG 393, Army of the Miss., Telegrams Received. On Aug. 11, 1862, Brig. Gen. William S. Rosecrans telegraphed to USG. "I sent word to Granger to Enquire into that matter Our Cavalry were over there on Saturday & Captured twenty five (25) conscripts Our spies from there agree in saying there are only (150) of those fellows who rendezvous 8 miles below Ripley. A spy who went to the Grand prairie & thence to Grenada thence back via Ripley at Grenada (50) conscripts & the sick Infantry Brigade formerly there gone south to west landing thirty nine miles lower down on the R.R. Brecken-ridge gone south to Baton Rogue no forces Except Cavalry north of Granada. Prices force said to be 12000 to 15000 above Tapelo" Telegram received, *ibid.,* Dept. of the Mo., Telegrams Received; copy, *ibid.,* Army of the Miss., Telegrams Sent. *O.R.,* I, xvii, part 2, 162–63. On the same day, USG telegraphed to Rosecrans. "I can send you guides if required. Well acquainted about Pocahontas." Copy, DNA, RG 393, Army of the Miss., Telegrams Received. Later the same day, Rosecrans telegraphed to USG. "I have just recd. the following from Genl Granger in reply to my dispatch predecated an yours of today I have already captured the Guerrillas party refered to. You have probably recd. as I forwarded to you with a free pass to alton—It consisted of (17) instead of (800) —In reply to my advice he says '*Sharpe is our Name game & practice*'—It seems so." Telegram received, *ibid.,* Dept. of the Mo., Telegrams Received; copy, *ibid.,* Army of the Miss., Telegrams Sent. *O.R.,* I, xvii, part 2, 163.

1. Pocahontas, Tenn., on the Memphis and Charleston Railroad, about twenty miles northwest of Corinth. On Aug. 10, Brig. Gen. Leonard F. Ross telegraphed to Maj. Gen. John A. McClernand. "General Grant telegraphs me to destroy the bridges and ferries on the Hatchie, except such as we can guard." *Ibid.,* p. 161. On Aug. 10, McClernand telegraphed to USG. "All the Bridges on the Hatchie except one at Bolivar & two (2) near Pocahontas have some time since been distroyed Would it not be better to destroy one of bridges at Pocahontas & guard the other by troops from Corinth it being nearer than Bolivar" Telegram received, DNA, RG 393, Dept. of the Mo., Telegrams Received; copies, McClernand Papers, IHi. On Aug. 11, McClernand telegraphed to USG. "Genl Ross sent force at four Oclock this morning to destroy all the bridges & Boats for sixteen miles up the Hatchee. The two bridges near Pocahontas could

be most easily destroyed by troops from Corinth. But you will decide in view of a despatch from me tonight whether you had not better hold those bridges for the present. Ross also sent a detachment today to Sutsburg to break up guerrillas & to capture horses mules & arms." Telegram received, DNA, RG 393, Dept. of the Mo., Telegrams Received; copies, McClernand Papers, IHi. On Aug. 11, McClernand wrote to USG. "Genl. Ross' Scout has just returned from Somerville, Legrange and the enemy's camp twelve miles below Holly Springs. He reports a force of 18000 rebels at under Genl. Villipigue—of which 1900 are cavalry. Twenty-four pieces of Artillery are in their possession—6 pieces of which are twenty-four pdrs. The He, also, reports that they are rapidly advancing and that they expected to be at Holly Springs today, and that they are being strengthened by soldiers recruited along the road. Furthermore, that the population along the road are expecting an important event. Assuming these facts to be true it is probable; nay, almost certain that the enemy intend to attack us; and as I think —at Bolivar. There are at Bolivar only 5224 effective Infantry men and say 16 pieces of artillery. Two plans of meeting the enemy occur to me—for our forces at Memphis to fall upon the enemy's rear while he is advancing toward Bolivar, and for the force at Bolivar to attack him at the same time: This combination may not be practicable for want of time. Again, for you to concentrate at Bolivar a sufficient force to meet and defeat the enemy. The latter appears to me to be the more practicable plan. I think all possible activity should be used." ALS, DNA, RG 393, District of West Tenn., Letters Received.

To Brig. Gen. Lorenzo Thomas

———

Corinth Aug 12th 1862

Genl Thomas—

Where Commissions are sent to officers or men for new Regts being raised can I accept resignations in case of Commissioned officers or discharge of soldiers.

U. S. Grant
Maj. Genl

Telegram received, DNA, RG 108, Telegrams Received by Lorenzo Thomas; copies, *ibid.*, RG 107, Telegrams Received (Bound, Press); *ibid.*, RG 393, USG Hd. Qrs. Correspondence; DLC-USG, V, 4, 5, 7, 8, 9, 88. On Aug. 15, 1862, Col. Edward D. Townsend, asst. adjt. gen., wrote to USG. "In reply to your despatch of the 12th inst, I have respectfully to inform you that you are not authorized to discharge officers or men to accept new commissions." ALS, DNA, RG 393, District of West Tenn., Letters Received. On Aug. 16, Townsend telegraphed a similar message to USG. Telegram received, *ibid.*, Dept. of the Tenn.,

Telegrams Received; copies, *ibid.*, USG Hd. Qrs. Correspondence; *ibid.*, RG 107, Telegrams Collected (Bound); *ibid.*, RG 94, Letters Sent; DLC-USG, V, 4, *5*, 7, 8, 9, 88.

To Maj. Gen. Don Carlos Buell

Corinth Aug. 12th [*1862*]

GEN BUELL

The letter referred to in your dispatch is not received   could not be interpreted as telegraphed   I cannot send all the troops called for in your dispatch on account of having been weakened by sending one ~~diversion~~ division to Curtis and the necessity ~~some~~ of having to send from here ~~have~~ some infantry regiments to Bolivar which can yet scarsely be regarded as secure   I will place an entire ~~diversion~~ division at Tuscumbia pains and another on the road from Iuka[1] to Tuscumbia   what is the necessity of guarding the road from Tuscumbia Eastward   do you not think it possible that the enemy are covering a movement of a large portion of their forces Eastward to Richmond   I will have the Tenn river guarded so that none of our steamers can possibly fall into their hands except by gross neglect of our troops   I will keep you well posted of the movements of the enemy and spare you all the force that can possibly be disposed with and you may require

GEN GRANT

Telegram received, DNA, RG 94, Generals' Papers and Books, Telegrams Received by Gen. Buell; copy, *ibid.*, RG 393, Dept. of the Ohio, Telegrams Received. *O.R.*, I, xvi, part 2, 316. On Aug. 12, 1862, Maj. Gen. Don Carlos Buell telegraphed to USG. "I think it plain that a mass of information derived from Tenn indicates that the main force of the enemy in the west is concentrating in Tenn & that no time should be lost in prepairing to meet him, please therefore dispatch at once the two divisions Genl Halleck authorised me to call for. They should cross under support at Eastport, I wish them to march up the Tenn, on the north side to about Rodgersville thence to Pulaski, where they will receive further orders. I take it forgranted they will have a complete organisation of twelve regiments of Infantry, three batteries of Artillery and two regiments of Cavalry at least, to each Division. Please order them to march promptly (& by good &)   they should carry ten days provisions & five days forrage for the rest get their forrage in the country leaving formal receipts in every case" Telegram received, DNA, RG 393, Dept. of the Mo., Telegrams Received; copy, *ibid.*, Dept. of the Ohio, Telegrams Sent. *O.R.*, I, xvi, part 2, 315–16.

1. Iuka, Miss., on the Memphis and Charleston Railroad, about twenty miles southeast of Corinth.

To Maj. Gen. Don Carlos Buell

Corinth Aug 12th 1862.

GENL BUELL

From the best information I can get there is but about twenty thousand 20.000 men including new levies or conscripts in front of my left—The main body having gone to Chattanooga—The rail road books at Mobile show that fifty six thousand men 56.000 have passed by rail from Tupelo and vicinity to Chattanooga; the same person who gives me this information and I believe him ~~to~~ reliable says the whole rebel force at Chattanooga and belonging to that command is estimated at One hundred and eight thousand—108.000—Price is at Tupelo   information is that he intends to demonstrate against this place to cover a flank movement on the rail road and Tenne east from here—This came in last night just as I had finished reading your dispatch and seems to confirm your information   I will telegraph you again during the day and inform you what I have done for your support in case of need—

U. S. GRANT

Telegram, copies, DNA, RG 393, Dept. of the Ohio, Telegrams Received; Buell Papers, TxHR. *O.R.*, I, xvi, part 2, 315. On Aug. 10, 1862, Maj. Gen. Don Carlos Buell telegraphed to USG. "The informant seems to be certain of the plans of the enemy to make a formidable advance upon Middle Tenn, But it is not so clear what route they will take, if it were not for the information contained in the accompanying letter, which was found yesterday, I should certainly expect the main advance to come from East Tenn, & I think the plan stated in the letter must have been suddenly changed, for Bragg has certainly been at Chattanooga since the evening of the 28th, & there is no doubt of the collection of a large force there from the Corinth army. You have better means of knowing what force is still at Tupelo. The passage of a large army at the point indicated can only be effected by surprising us completely & seizing some of our Steamers. I do not believe it will be attempted, but I hope you will see that the Steamers are not exposed to surprise, & that preparations are made to fire them instantly if it should be attempted. Under no sircumstan[ce] should the steamer lie at Florence, still I am pretty well satisfied that the plan was suddenly changed & that the attack will come from East Tenn, indeed there are already indications that it is about to be attempted, I apprehend that I shall have to call on you very soon for the two Divisions, Genl Halleck informed me you would put them at my disposal. Whose are they & where? Eastport would be the best point for them to cross & they should be prepaired to move at any hour's notice, & *rapidly*. I suppose they are organized with Cavalry & Artillery, I am guarding five hundred miles of Rail Road, which is swarming with regular & irregular cavalry of the enemy, there has been much trouble with the road beyond Decatur   it can be kept open against any force, if the bridges are protected with a stockade & guard, & not otherwise. I think it is well worth it for both of us, please peserve secrecy in regard to the letter. Answer by telegraph in Cypher"   Telegram received, DNA, RG 393, Dept. of the Mo., Telegrams Received; *ibid.*, Dept. of the Ohio, Telegrams Sent. *O.R.*, I, xvi, part 2, 302–3.

To Maj. Gen. Don Carlos Buell

Corinth Aug 13th 1862

GENL BUELL

My divisions are composed of ten Infy Regts—three 3 Batteries and about two 2 Battalions of Cavy.[1]   to send two divisions of my force beyond my control would be to leave this place an easy prey to the forces that are known to be at Saltillo Tupilo and points from which they could be concentrated[2]—in addition to troops now ordered to Tuscumbia intended to co-operate with you I will see what force I can send to Eastport as you suggest— and inform you. you have not informed me of the necessity of attempting to hold the Rail Road east of Tuscumbia—if I do not learn reasons not now in my possessions I will abandon all points east of that place[3]

U. S. GRANT

Telegram, copies, DNA, RG 393, Dept. of the Ohio, Telegrams Received; *ibid.*, Army of the Miss., Telegrams Received. *O.R.*, I, xvi, part 2, 325. On Aug. 13, 1862, Maj. Gen. Don Carlos Buell telegraphed to USG. "Please inform me of your action upon my dispatch of yesterday, I have no doubt of the necessity of sending the troops at once. your estimate of the force in east Tenn is substantially confirmed by information from Lambere & other sources. The supposition that they are moving to Virginia is hardly consistant with the fact that they are bringing troops from Va. It is undoubetedly true that they deem it of vital importance, not only to hold east Tenn, but regain what they have lost, & that is said to be their present plan. The road from Decatur is important as a chain of Outposts & a channel of communication." Telegram received, DNA, RG 393, Dept. of the Mo., Telegrams Received; copy, *ibid.*, Dept. of the Ohio, Telegrams Sent. *O.R.*, I, xvi, part 2, 325. On Aug. 13, Buell telegraphed again to USG. "Troops two hundred 200 miles away at least and on the other side of a river which with the means they have cannot be crossed in less than two 2 days are not in a position to Support me in any emergency—Tuscumbia is not a safe point for troops to cross in the presence of even an inferior force—The railroad is useful as a line of out-posts and to protect our Telegraphic communication—The latter cannot otherwise be kept open—but of course you can judge whether you have the means—Your small posts are certainly not safe there unless they fortify with Stoccades—with them they are perfectly so unless attacked by Artillery—It is best that I should know at once exactly what to depend on in the way of re-inforcements—" Copy, DNA, RG 393, Dept. of the Ohio, Telegrams Sent. *O.R.*, I, xvi, part 2, 325. See also telegram from Buell to Maj. Gen. Henry W. Halleck; Aug. 13, *ibid.*, pp. 324–25.

1. On Aug. 12, Maj. Gen. Henry W. Halleck telegraphed to USG. "Please telegraph the present position of the several divisions under your command." ALS (telegram sent), DNA, RG 107, Telegrams Collected (Bound); copies, *ibid.*, RG 393, USG Hd. Qrs. Correspondence; DLC-USG, V, 4, 5, 7, 8, 9, 88. *O.R.*, I, xvii, part 2, 164. On Aug. 13, USG telegraphed to Halleck. "Two Divisions Shermans and Hurlburt with the Fifty second Indiana Engineer Regt Five Cos 6th Ills Cavalry Rogers Battery one section Degoliers Battery and the cavalry and Artillery belonging to Genl Wallaces Division Except one Battery at Memphis Tenn   McClernand Battery Four Regts and one Battery of Wallaces Third Division six Regts and one Battery of Genl McArthurs sixth Division Seventh Regt Mo Infantry One Co Cav Fifty Third Ills and Capt Foster Fourth Independent Cavalry at Bolivar and Jackson   Genl Davies second Division and the sixth Divn excepting what is at Bolivar At Corinth   Division of the Army of the Miss are stationed as follows   Genl Baines First Division with an additional cavalry Regiment at Tuscumbia Genl Davies Fourth Division on line of roads between Tuscumbia and Corinth   Genl Stanlys Second Division at Camp Clear Creek Genl Hamilton Third Division at Jacinto   The Fifth Division at Rienzi   The several regiments of cavalry Division are distributed at the several Stations with the Infantry Division   Genl Quinbys command remains same as when you were here   The fourteenth Regt new Volunteer at Hamburg"   Telegram received (dated Aug. 14), DNA, RG 94, Generals' Papers and Books, Telegrams Received by Gen. Halleck; copies, *ibid.*, RG 393, USG Hd. Qrs. Correspondence; DLC-USG, V, 4, 5, 7, 8, 9, 88. *O.R.*, I, xvii, part 2, 168.

2. On Aug. 12, Brig. Gen. William S. Rosecrans telegraphed to Maj. John A. Rawlins. "The following has been recd. from Brig Genl Granger—Reinzi Aug 12th   Lt Col Kennt Chf of Staff.—A deserter from Saltillo belonging to one of the Mo. Regts. reports as follows   left there yesterday at about Eleven (11)

oclock—Genl Price in command. Head Quarters at Gun Town—Every thing has left below except Prices division which he reports is about (12000) strong— The movement has been by Brigades. The last Brigade under Genl Jackson moved moved about one week ago Infantry & Artilery going by Cars. Their horses by land towards Chattanooga. One (1) Division is to return and increase Prices force to (30.000) & that this Division is the first one that moved—Some four (4) or five (5) weeks ago & is under command of Genl Polk. After which the troops on this line are ~~for~~ to be attacked—I give this for what it is worth. The deserters is an Intelligent one—I send the above for the information of the Genl comdg." Telegram received, DNA, RG 393, Dept. of the Mo., Telegrams Received; copy, *ibid.*, Army of the Miss., Telegrams Sent. *O.R.*, I, xvii, part 2, 164–65.

3. On Aug. 13, Rosecrans telegraphed to USG. "Your dispatch & the coppy from Buell recd—If the Rebels will go into Tennesee let them do it. let the genl in front if he cannot successfully fight them draw them in & destroy the crops as he goes   Let the Government study Bear hunting ~~Even~~ Mean while & learn how even a Dog hanging on to the haunches of a Bear keeps time from morning till the hunter comes and kills him. Let us fortify & provision needful points so as to be foot & hand free   your reply to D. C. is good"   Telegram received, DNA, RG 393, Dept. of the Mo., Telegrams Received; copy, *ibid.*, Army of the Miss., Telegrams Sent. *O.R.*, I, xvii, part 2, 166.

To Maj. Gen. Henry W. Halleck

Corinth Miss
Aug 14 1862

MAJ GENL HALLECK
GENL IN CHIEF

Telegram received   I have ordered two more Divisions East   Those on the road to move to Decatur.[1] Information received last night shows that Prices forces have advanced to Guntown.[2] He was expecting yesterday the arrival of fifteen thousand reinforcements from Georgia probably From[3]   the best information I can get indicates that a feint only is intended here for the purpose to hold our troops, but sending so many troops away, may it not be turned into a real attack

U S GRANT
Maj Genl

Telegram received, DNA, RG 94, Generals' Papers and Books, Telegrams Received by Gen. Halleck; copies, *ibid.*, RG 107, Telegrams Collected (Bound); *ibid.*, RG 393, USG Hd. Qrs. Correspondence; DLC-USG, V, 4, 5, 7, 8, 9, 88.

O.R., I, xvi, part 2, 333. The dispatch was repeated by USG for Brig. Gen. William S. Rosecrans. Copy, DNA, RG 393, Army of the Miss., Telegrams Received. On Aug. 14, 1862, Maj. Gen. Henry W. Halleck telegraphed to USG. "Genl Buell has made requisition for your two divisions near Decatur. Replace them by two others." ALS (telegram sent), *ibid.*, RG 107, Telegrams Collected (Bound); telegram received, *ibid.*, RG 393, Dept. of the Tenn., Telegrams Received; copies, *ibid.*, USG Hd. Qrs. Correspondence; DLC-USG, V, 4, 5, 7, 8, 9, 88. *O.R.*, I, xvi, part 2, 333.

    1. On Aug. 14, Maj. John A. Rawlins issued Special Orders No. 163. "The two Divisions of the Army of the Miss. now guarding railroad East of Corinth, will proceed with all dispatch to Decatur, Ala. as soon as relieved by troops to be designated by Brig. Gen. Rosecrans. Gen. Rosecrans will designate, and order forward, sufficient forces to hold the points now held by these two Divisions, with as little delay as practicable. The troops advancing will carry with them all their Camp and garrison Equipage, Transportation, Ammunition, and if practicable, ten days. rations. At Decatur they will receive supplies from Corinth so long as they remain a part of the command of the Dist of West. Tenn. Should orders be received by these two Divisions from Major Gen. D. C. Buell they will be obeyed and supplies thereafter by such means as he may direct." DS, DNA, RG 94, Special Orders, District of West Tenn.; copies, *ibid.*, RG 393, USG Special Orders; DLC-USG, V, 15, 16, 82, 87. *O.R.*, I, xvii, part 2, 173.
    2. Guntown, Miss., about thirty-five miles south of Corinth.
    3. USG's copies read Rome.

To Brig. Gen. William S. Rosecrans

Corinth Aug 14th 1862

GENL ROSECRANS

    a man sent by me to Tupello confirm statement before received   was with Price sometime. Heard him read a dispatch to Baxter[1] the Guerrilla that Jackson had attacked Pope, and driven him back taking several hundred prisoners, including twenty six officers one of them a Brig General.[2] Says most of the force has moved to Gun Town, 15000 reenforcements were to arrive at Tupello yesterday from Georgia, thinks from Rome Price spoke confidently of taking this place. Brough with him Mobile papers of the Seventh (7) Eighth (8) & Ninth (9) confirm the loss of the Arkansas[3]

U S GRANT
Maj Genl

Telegram, copy, DNA, RG 393, Army of the Miss., Telegrams Received.

1. Probably Capt. George L. Baxter, who earlier in Aug. suggested a plan for the capture of USG. *O.R.*, I, xvii, part 2, 667.

2. Thomas J. Jackson of Va., USMA 1846, served in the Mexican War, and held the rank of 1st lt. and bvt. maj. at the time of his resignation in 1852. USG, who knew him at West Point, said that Jackson "governed his life by a discipline so stern that he steadily worked his way along and rose far above others who had more advantages. . . ." He was also, USG averred, "a religious man then, and some of us regarded him as a fanatic." *Young*, II, 210. A professor at Virginia Military Institute at the time of Va.'s entry into the war, he was commissioned col. and ordered to Harper's Ferry. He distinguished himself as a brig. gen. in the battle of Bull Run and as a maj. gen. in the Shenandoah Valley. The battle to which USG probably referred took place on Aug. 9, 1862, at Cedar Mountain, Va. Hailed at first as a victory by both North and South, it was, in fact, rather indecisive. Jackson retreated from a superior position held by Maj. Gen. Nathaniel P. Banks after losing 229 killed (one of them Brig. Gen. Charles S. Winder) and 1,047 wounded. Union losses included 314 killed, 1,445 wounded, and 622 captured or missing—including Brig. Gen. Henry Prince. Lenoir Chambers, *Stonewall Jackson* (New York, 1959), II, 106–18; Frank E. Vandiver, *Mighty Stonewall* (New York, Toronto, and London, 1957), pp. 338–45; *O.R.*, I, xii, part 2, 137, 178, 180.

3. On July 15, the ironclad C. S. S. *Arkansas* attacked the U.S. fleet near Vicksburg, causing considerable damage. On Aug. 6, at Baton Rouge, La., when the engines of the *Arkansas* failed during an attack, the ship was abandoned and blown up.

To Maj. Gen. Don Carlos Buell

———

Corinth, August 15, 1862.

GENERAL BUELL:

I have ordered the divisions of Paine and Davis to Decatur subject to your order and two more divisions to hold the road to that point. I have directed the engineer officer to locate and plan fortifications and block-houses for the defense of the road. Another will expedite the forwarding of troops all he can. I will inform you of progress made in forwarding these troops from day to day.

GRANT.

O.R., I, xvi, part 2, 337. On Aug. 14, 1862, Maj. Gen. Don Carlos Buell telegraphed to USG. "Please let me know exactly what force you place at my disposal, & where it is to cross the river. I dont understand from your dispatch of today, the report of troops marching from chattanooga or Rome to Tupelo   seems to me altogether improbable" Telegram received, DNA, RG 393, Dept. of the Mo., Telegrams Received; copy, *ibid.*, Dept. of the Ohio, Telegrams Sent. *O.R.*, I, xvi, part 2, 333. On Aug. 14, Capt. W. Willard Smith telegraphed to USG. "There was a number of bulls in the letter telegraphed from Buell   as soon as I can get it repeated I will forward to you." Telegram received, DNA, RG 393, Dept. of the Mo., Telegram Received.

To Richard Yates

———

Corinth Mississippi
August 15th 1862

HIS EXCELLENCY
HON. RICHARD YATES
GOV. OF ILLINOIS.
DEAR SIR,

In the large increase of forces now being put in the field allow me to recommend Capt. H. C. Freeman,[1] Aid to Gen. McClernan and Engineer officer to his command, as a suitable person for an appointment to a Field officer.

The regiment that gets him will be fortunate in having the services of an able and efficient officer of one years valuable and conspicuous service against this rebellion.

I recommend Capt. Freeman, a citizen of Southern Illinois, without fear of his future course disappointing me, or yourself, should you act favorably on this recommendation.

I am Governor very respectfully
your obt. svt.
U. S. GRANT
Maj. Gen

ALS (facsimile), Yates Papers, IHi.

1. For Capt. Henry C. Freeman, see endorsement to Maj. Gen. Henry W. Halleck, Jan. 29, 1862. Freeman had served as acting aide-de-camp to Maj. Gen. John A. McClernand during the battle of Shiloh. During the siege of Corinth, he served as engineering officer. *O.R.*, I, x, part 1, 117, 754.

To Maj. Gen. Henry W. Halleck

Corinth Aug 16th 1862, 1 20 P.M

MAJ GEN H W HALLECK

The Rebels have Bridge across the Tallahatchie completed & run cars to within eight (8) miles of Grand Junction.[1] If Gen Curtis could move on Panola[2] from Helena Rebels could be cleared out of Northwest Miss—I could send Genl Sherman at the same time on Oxford[3]—Four Divisions of the Army of the Miss are now moving to occupy the road to Decatur & to reinforce Gen Buell. Reconnoissance far to the front shows the country to be so dry that an attack on this place is hardly to be apprehended[4]

U S GRANT
Maj Genl

Telegram received, DNA, RG 94, Generals' Papers and Books, Telegrams Received by Gen. Halleck; *ibid.*, RG 107, Telegrams Collected (Bound); copies, *ibid.*, RG 393, USG Hd. Qrs. Correspondence; DLC-USG, V, 4, 5, 7, 8, 9, 88. *O.R.*, I, xvii, part 2, 175. On Aug. 13, 1862, Maj. Gen. William T. Sherman, Memphis, telegraphed to USG. "I hear from Grenada often & have no Idea that there is any movement towards Bolivar or Memphis   I had a letter a few days Since from Villipague at Abberville Station South of Tallahatchie that bridge is done & Cars now run to Davis Mills Eight (8) miles from Grand Junction   if Curtiss were to move on Panola from Helena all this country would be abandoned save by Geurrillas. I have three (3) parties of Cavalry out tonight & will know if there is any movement from the South towards Bolivar But I dont beleive it— The Enemy wants to keep Curtiss, myself & McClernand occupied with reports whilst they mass their forces on Chattanooga & Nashville. We ought to attack their Rail Roads. Curtiss & my troops moving from Helena and here striking them near Panola & Oxford"   Telegram received, DNA, RG 393, Dept. of the Mo., Telegrams Received; copy, *ibid.*, RG 94, Generals' Papers and Books, William T. Sherman, Letters Sent. *O.R.*, I, xvii, part 2, 166. Sherman discussed his plan in greater detail in a letter of Aug. 17 to USG. Copies, DNA, RG 94, Generals' Papers and Books, William T. Sherman, Letters Sent; DLC-William T. Sherman. *O.R.*, I, xvii, part 2, 179.

1. The Tallahatchie River crosses the Mississippi Central Railroad about three miles north of Abbeville, Miss. The railroad then continues on to Grand Junction, Tenn., where it connects with the Tennessee and Ohio and the Memphis and Charleston railroads.

2. Panola, Miss., about sixty miles south of Memphis, on the Mississippi and Tennessee Railroad.

3. Oxford, Miss., on the Mississippi Central Railroad, about fifty miles southwest of Grand Junction.

4. On Aug. 14, Brig. Gen. William S. Rosecrans telegraphed to USG. "Col Sheridan with three regiments of Cavalry went down last night with orders to take Ellistown & Baldwin burn the Depot at the latter place, feel of the Rebels & get information generally.—The work was to have been began at day light this morning" Telegram received, DNA, RG 393, Dept. of the Mo., Telegrams Received; copy, *ibid.*, Army of the Miss., Telegrams Sent. *O.R.*, I, xvii, part 2, 169. Later the same day, Rosecrans telegraphed to USG. "The following dispatch has been recd. by Genl Granger from Rienzi   14th Aug   Col Sheridan has returned   Captured four Secesh also 300 head of mules horses and Cattle on 20 Mile Creek in vicinity of Carrolsville   20 Mile Creek is dry   our horses had no water from the time they left camp till they returned   had great trouble to get water for the men and owing to its scarcity he was obliged to come home during the heat of the day—" Telegram received, DNA, RG 393, Dept. of the Mo., Telegrams Received; copy, *ibid.*, Army of the Miss., Telegrams Sent. *O.R.*, I, xvii, part 2, 169.

To Maj. Gen. Don Carlos Buell

Corinth, August 16, 1862—5 p.m.

General Buell:

I answered your dispatch of 14th. Two divisions under Paine and Davis go to Decatur and are subject to your orders when they reach there. Two other divisions are moving to take their places on the road. I have given orders to fortify Iuka and Tuscumbia and will do the same thing at Decatur. Also have ordered block-houses to be built at principal bridges.

Grant.

O.R., I, xvi, part 2, 344. On Aug. 16, 1862, Maj. Gen. Don Carlos Buell telegraphed to USG. "Please answer my inquiry of the 14th in regard to the exact force you place at my disposal & where it will cross." Telegram received, DNA, RG 393, Dept. of the Mo., Telegrams Received; copies, *ibid.*, Dept. of the Ohio, Telegrams Sent; Buell Papers, TxHR. *O.R.*, I, xvi, part 2, 344. Later on Aug. 16, Buell telegraphed to USG. "The troops can cross in less than half the time at Eastport, & time is of the utmost importance, please order them to cross there, unless they have passed that point, & if so, then at Tuscumbia, there is no time to lose. Kirby Smith is advancing on Kentucky or Nashville, & other offensive movements of the enemy may from their strength and dispositions fairly be expected." Telegram received, DNA, RG 393, Dept. of the Mo., Telegrams Received; copies, *ibid.*, Dept. of the Ohio, Telegrams Sent; Buell Papers, TxHR. *O.R.*, I, xvi, part 2, 344.

To Brig. Gen. James B. McPherson

———

Head Quarters, Dist. of West Ten.
Corinth, August 16th 1862

BRIG. GEN. McPHERSON
SUPT. OF R. ROADS.
GEN.

The bearer of this Mr. Hughes who has been superintending repairs in the machine shop in Memphis is an acquaintance of Hillyers and is vouched for by him in the strongest terms both as a friend to his country and for integrity and general worth.

Mr. Hughes is a man of experience in rail-road matters particularly in construction. If you need the services of such you could not do better than to retain Mr. Hughes who was put in charge in Memphis by Col. Pride.

Respectfully &c
U. S. GRANT
Maj. Gen.

ALS, USMA. On June 4, 1862, Capt. John C. Kelton issued Special Field Orders No. 86, Dept. of the Miss., assigning Brig. Gen. James B. McPherson as commander of an engineer brigade and appointing him general superintendent of military railroads. *O.R.*, I, lii, part 1, 253.

To Maj. Gen. Don Carlos Buell

———

Corinth, August 17, 1862.

GENERAL BUELL:

I sent troops by way of Decatur by General Halleck's order. As I must endeavor to keep the road open to that point I will ascertain the present position of the advance troops and change their route. If they are not too far advanced, by substituting another division for Paine's, which is in advance, the route may be changed. The command has no wagon train except the regimental teams of thirteen wagons to a regiment.

U. S. Grant.

O.R., I, xvi, part 2, 355. On Aug. 16, 1862, Maj. Gen. Don Carlos Buell telegraphed to USG. "I apprehend that I have not strongly enough urged upon you the importance of the immediate presence of the troops that are to come here, & in as great force as possible, they will not be to soon if they come by forced marches, they should by all means not cross at Decatur, but at Eastport except those that may already be near Tuscumbia. please let me know where & when they will cross. I hope you will press this matter." Telegram received, DNA, RG 393, Dept. of the Mo., Telegrams Received; copy, *ibid.*, Dept. of the Ohio, Telegrams Sent. O.R., I, xvi, part 2, 345. On Aug. 17, Buell telegraphed to USG. "My Dispatches to you have two or three times been delayed over night because operators beyond Decatur could not be raised" Telegram received, DNA, RG 393, Dept. of the Mo., Telegrams Received; copy, *ibid.*, Dept. of the Ohio, Telegrams Sent. O.R., I, xvi, part 2, 355. On Aug. 17, Mark D. Crain, telegraph operator at Corinth, wrote to USG. "We have only two operators here that are capable of doing work at present. we are both on all day & have been closing the office at 12 oclock at night. I am always on hand at 4 in the morning our new supt will be here tonight & also another operator" ALS, DNA, RG 393, Dept. of the Mo., Telegrams Received. On Aug. 17, Buell again telegraphed to USG. "When will the Divisions be at the points designated to cross and where will they cross?" Copy, *ibid.*, Dept. of the Ohio, Telegrams Sent. O.R., I, xvi, part 2, 355. On Aug. 17, Buell telegraphed to USG. "If Paines Division has passed Tuscumbia, please let it come on & cross at Decatur otherwise let it cross at Tuscumbia I should like particularly to have that Division, it may be here in good time." Telegram received, DNA, RG 393, Dept. of the Mo., Telegrams Received; copy, *ibid.*, Dept. of the Ohio, Telegrams Sent. O.R., I, xvi, part 2, 356.

To Maj. Gen. John A. McClernand

Head Quarters, Dist. of West Ten.
Corinth, August 17th 1862

Maj. Gen. J. A. McClernand
Comd.g at Jackson Ten.
Gen.

I have just had an interview with Dr. Crittenden[1] who has been sent here by your order. He seems to be a man of that class denominated dangerous, and should not be allowed to enter any of our camps, and by no means should he ever have been permitted to pass over our lines of communication.

I cannot find that your communication in this case has ever

reached me. If it did however the probabilities are that it has been endorsed, and refered to Gen. Dodge[2] whos troops, it seems, took the property now claimed.

There is one thing General in which your views seem to conflict with mine. It is in this; giving geographical limits to your command within which other commanders have no right to send their troops.[3]—My view of this matter is, and it will have to govern until higher authority decides against me, that I command all the troops that are within, or that may come within, certain limits. All ~~other~~ commanders under me command troops and not territory except such as may be covered by their troops and guards. With certain troops you are given certain lines of communications to hold and protect. When it becomes necessary for this purpose to send troops out through the country you can do so, and the troops do not sease to be under your command, nor do you sease to be responsible for their conduct, because they cross certain limits.

Gen. Quinby in the same way has to guard ~~the li~~ our lines of communication within certain limits and is responsible for the acts of all his troops wherever he may send them for this purpose.

In case of an attack upon any point of the roads to be protected by our troops, by a force superior to that convenient to be sent by the commander of the troops at the place where the attack is threatened, it is the duty of commanders convenient to send such reinforcements as may be required, and he can spare, reporting the fact to District Head Quarters. In this case, for the time being, troops pass from one commander to another.

Whenever I concieve that good order can be better maintained by Sub Districting my command I believe that I have the right to do so. I have not yet however done so.

This letter is a full answer to the case of Mrs. Witherspoon just refered to me since writing the above.

> I am Gen. very respectfully
> your obt. svt.
> U. S. GRANT
> Maj. Gen Com

ALS, DLC-USG. On Aug. 18, 1862, Maj. Gen. John A. McClernand wrote to USG. "Your letter of the 17th inst. is recd. and I hasten to answer it. Dr Crittenden called at my Head Quarters, yesterday, to ascertain whether you had answered Mrs Lea's petition. I told him I had not heard from you in regard to it —that I could do nothing; and that if he would invoke your action, he had better see you. Accordingly, he went to Corinth. His authority for coming here and going to Corinth rests, primarily, upon a pass given him at Humbolt, to continue in force until otherwise ordered, and reciting that he had taken the oath of allegiance. The petition referred to, sets forth that a party of cavalry from Humbolt had taken two or three Stallions, worth some three or four thousand dollars, the property of Mrs. Lea. And having no jurisdiction of the matter: was it not proper for me to have it referred it to you; either, that the horses might be returned; otherwise turned over and accounted for as public property? I thought so, then and think so, now. You speak of a conflict of views. I have never claimed to command a district of fixed and definite limits, though, I am free to confess, that the order proposed by you some weeks ago, assigning me to the command of such a district, indicated the true policy in regard to Subordinate commanders, in your district. I have claimed, however, that the assignment of the rail roads from Humbolt to Bethel and Bolivar vested me with authority over the contiguous and dependent country, and made me responsible for its good government. Hence, I immediately sub-divided these roads into sections or districts, assigning a commander to each, and disposed my troops accordingly—making each Sub-district commander, directly, responsible for the quiet and well-being of his district. This, as a matter of internal regulation, I had a right to do. Genl. Halleck was advised of it by means of the orders under which it was accomplished, which were duly reported. Genl. Logan having been assigned to the district including the road between here and Humbolt, and having repeatedly complained of unauthorized and lawless depredations committed by roving parties from Humbolt within his supposed district, I have sometimes reported the alleged facts to you; sometimes to Col. Bryant at Humbolt, and sometimes to his Commander, Genl. Dodge, at Trenton. And Genl. Dodge answering in the same spirit, has said punish all such offenders. More than that, at his instance I have proposed a boundary line between his supposed district and mine. In this way only have I claimed to command a district territorially. I have striven to prevent disorder, violence and every wrong from what source soever. I have never pretended that it was not right and proper for the different district commanders to reinforce and co-operate with each other, when occaision required it. Nor am I aware that I ever afforded any ground for such a supposition. On the contrary, in common with others I have frequently acted upon a different idea. You add upon the question of territorial jurisdiction. 'My view of this matter is, and it will have to govern until higher authority decides against me, that I command all the troops that are within, or that may come within certain limits' Pardon me for saying, that this is a boast of authority uncalled for by anything I have said or done. Whether sub-districted or not, your authority would be the same and superior throughout your district. In no instance have I gainsayed your authority. If any have told you otherwise, it is probably those who would lay their own sins at my door. Whosoever told you so falsifies the truth. My actions disprove the charge—My actions which have lent lustre to your authority, and which should, at least, bespeak for me the need of common justice. Respecting Mrs. Witherspoon, I have to say that her agent having preferred a complaint which I had no jurisdiction to hear, I referred it to you as the proper officer—endorsing, if I mistake not on the paper containing the complaint, that I did not desire to have anything to do with it. If in this I have offended, I plead guilty, and am willing to accept the consequences. Intending only, by these hasty lines to vindicate my conduct in a respectful but manly manner, I conclude by renewing the assurance, that I will continue to try to merit your approbation, whatever may be my success." LS, DNA, RG 393, District of West Tenn., Letters Received.

1. This was probably H. S. Crittenden of Madison County, Tenn., who on March 7, 1864, wrote to Brig. Gen. Augustus L. Chetlain, Memphis, that he was caring for his plantation and that of his mother-in-law, Mrs. F. A. Lea. The property had been subjected to repeated depredations by U.S. troops, and Crittenden wanted an official safeguard for his property. ALS, *ibid.*, RG 109, Union Provost Marshals' File of Papers Relating to Individual Civilians.

2. Grenville M. Dodge, born in Mass. in 1831, graduated from Norwich University as a civil engineer, then followed this profession in Ill. and Iowa. Appointed col., 4th Iowa, on July 6, 1861, then promoted to brig. gen. as of March 21, 1862, he was assigned to duty in the Dept. of the Miss. on May 22, 1862.

3. On Aug. 13, McClernand telegraphed to USG. "The following is a coppy of a telegram just sent by me to Genl Ross Bolivar   I understand Genl Ord is at Bolivar in the Exercise of some military function   as he has not advised me of the object I ~~would~~ wish to know by what authority"   Telegram received, *ibid.*, RG 393, Dept. of the Mo., Telegrams Received; copies (dated Aug. 12), McClernand Papers, IHi. See letter to Maj. Gen. John A. McClernand, June 24, 1862.

To Brig. Gen. William S. Rosecrans

Corinth Aug 17th 1862

GENL ROSECRANS

Buell telegraphs that crossing can be effected in half the time at East Port or Tuscumbia, that it can at Decatur, and that time is of the utmost importance to him, That Kirby Smith[1] is moving on Ky or Nashville, besides other offensive movements, which the Enemy from their strength may be expected to make.[2] He requests that this change of rule be adopted, as we have to attemp[t] to hold the line to Decatur. Cannot another Division be substituted for Payne's and let the troops take one of the routes indicated by Buell

U. S. GRANT
Maj Genl

Telegram, copy, DNA, RG 393, Army of the Miss., Telegrams Received. On Aug. 17, 1862, Brig. Gen. William S. Rosecrans telegraphed to USG. "Have instructed Paine & Mitchell to examine & prepare for crossing the former at Florence Courtland & Decatur. The latter at Eastport to observe the utmost secrecy & report to me fully without delay—In my instructions do you wish me to say they are detached from this army & will report from Athens to Genl Buell or that they will continue a part of this army on detached service & render reports as usual to these Head Quarters Granger reports the arrival of (15) Rebel Regiments 6.000 men at Guntown within the last two (2) days will the troops I asked for be sent him and will Danville be occupied by a Regiment from Davies command." Telegram received, *ibid.*, Dept. of the Mo., Telegrams Received; copy, *ibid.*, Army of the Miss., Telegrams Sent. *O.R.*, I, xvii, part 2, 177. On Aug. 17, Rosecrans telegraphed again to USG. "Under the last instructions from you I shall direct Stanly to occupy at Tuscumbia & Iuka Paine to cross at Tuscumbia Courtland and Decatur Mitchell to cross at Eastport—This will detach the first & 4th Division of the Army of the Mississippi at Farmington & this place Will require the troops I spoke of at Danville. This army will then extend from Rienzi to Tuscumbia a distance of fifty (50) miles front while your entire Corps will extend a distance of thirty (30) miles north. westward A small army covering a front of eighty (80) miles parallel The enemys front A speedy remedy must be applied or a bad result must be expected" Telegram received, DNA, RG 393, Dept. of the Mo., Telegrams Received; copy, *ibid.*, Army of the Miss., Telegrams Sent. *O.R.*, I, xvii, part 2, 177. On Aug. 18, Rosecrans telegraphed to USG. "My dispatch late last evening informed of the orders I have given Payne. I have very little doubt but that we can pass over the 1st Brigade at Decatur and Courtland, by day after tomorrow morning" Copy, DNA, RG 393, Army of the Miss., Telegrams Sent. On Aug. 18, USG forwarded a telegram from Maj. Gen. Don Carlos Buell to Rosecrans. "The following dispatch was received from Buell in the night If Payne's division has passed Tuscumbia, please let it come in and cross at Decatur otherwise let it cross at Tuscumbia. I should like particularly to have that division. It may be here in good time If any time is to be saved by their going on to Decatur let them go" Copy, *ibid.*, Telegrams Received. On Aug. 18, Rosecrans telegraphed to USG. "Found your orders on my return from Danville. The troops have not arrived at Either place the Union Brigade guards Danville until relieved. I have given them such a handing that I am disposed to let them try & send the two Regts to Granger. Your orders about the troops to Buell will be promptly attended" Telegram received, *ibid.*, Dept. of the Mo., Telegrams Received; copy, *ibid.*, Army of the Miss., Telegrams Sent. On Aug. 22, Rosecrans telegraphed to USG. "Paine say he must cross at Decatur he is sick will either Join his command or resign—must cross at Decatur no means elswhere. I will try to get the stemboat from east here up to florence—mitchell crossed his division today we ought to own some light draught boats properly protected and armed to patrol the river & cross our troops—This is of prieme importance whether we occupy this or the other side of the river fourteen (14) bales of cotton brought in last evening in bad order it must be sold here—where we find cotton of the country liable to confistication but find it unprotected to bring it in can I sell at a fair price to be taken at the purchasers risk—" Telegram received, *ibid.*, Dept. of the Mo., Telegrams Received; copy, *ibid.*, Army of the Miss., Telegrams Sent.

On July 28, Governor Richard Yates of Ill. wrote to USG. "Brig. Gen.

Paine of your army is still unable from continued illness to join his command. He is however I am glad to hear, improving and ~~will be~~ expects to be fit for duty by the 1st Sept. In the mean time, if you can extend his leave of absence, he will be of much benefit to the service here in aiding the organization of our new Regiments." ALS, *ibid.*, RG 94, Generals' Papers and Books, Eleazer A. Paine.

1. Edmund Kirby Smith of Fla., USMA 1845, after fighting in the Mexican War, served at Jefferson Barracks, as asst. professor of mathematics at USMA, and as commander of the escort and botanist for the Mexican Boundary Commission, 1854–55. A maj. at the time of the secession of Fla., he became col. of cav.; and on March 9, 1862, as a C. S. A. maj. gen., assumed command of the Dept. of East Tenn. In mid-Aug. he was moving between Knoxville, Tenn., and Barboursville in southeastern Ky.; but units of his command led by Col. John H. Morgan were operating between Nashville and Louisville. *DAB*, X, 424–25; *O.R.*, I, x, part 2, 307; *ibid.*, I, xvi, part 2, 759, 766–67.

2. On Aug. 19, Rosecrans telegraphed to USG. "Mobile Advertiser of 15th here   Breckenridge was whipped at Vicksburg   Genl Clark & two (2) Col's killed   they lost 250 men & say our troops acknowledge loss of (1000)   they mention 17 regts cavalry being in the fight, say these numbered (3500) men when they started but (500) dropped sick by rain & heat on the way—B. H. Hill was knocked over contused by their running Cavalry—Capt Todd Mrs Lincolns brother was killed. Grangers spies say movements Eastward—Two Sutlers' clerks & a soldier of the 59th Ills taken prisoners last Sunday week returned today liberated. they learned or were told that the Rebels intended to have Corinth at all cost that they were getting out timber to repair bridges on the R. R. & that conscripts were constantly coming in   they had already (25,000) men—Genl Hayne has a drover from the south who says that Van Dorn's command except that with Breckenridge is at Jackson & that Bragg is at Chattanooga with (40,000) men   he says he will march to Nashville or fight for it. Granger has sent out a cavalry reg't to attack Marietta at Day light tomorrow morning—" Telegram received, DNA, RG 393, Dept. of the Mo., Telegrams Received. *O.R.*, I, xvii, part 2, 181. The battle described by Rosecrans occurred Aug. 5 at Baton Rouge, La., and was largely inconclusive. On Aug. 16, Maj. Gen. John A. McClernand telegraphed to USG. "I send you coppy of Dispatches just recd from Genl ~~Ross~~ L. F. Ross Bolivar Aug 16th To Maj Genl McClernand   I have just been conversing with a reliable Union man from Summerville   he read in Grenada Appeal Genl Breckenridges official report of his attack on Baton Roage   He acknowledges a repulse & that he has lost three hundred (300) men—He fell back five miles & encamped but intended to renew the attack—" Telegram received, DNA, RG 393, Dept. of the Mo., Telegrams Received.

To Brig. Gen. William S. Rosecrans

Corinth Aug 17th 1862

GENL ROSECRANS

The order from Genl Halleck is imperative to send to divisions to Buell, and that after being telegraphed the position of all my forces, I have asked him to allow me to draw in, making Tuscumbia my Eastern terminus,[1] also to allow Curtiss to cross the river on Panola whilst I send Sherman to Oxford.[2] This would compel the enemy to cut this road at Granada, if they did not do it we would do it for them. I could then withdraw one Division from Memphis and a brigade from Bolivar　as it now is we will have to draw in our horns a little for the present, and spread again when we can. Your front had better be brought in about where your Hd Qrs now are.

U. S. GRANT
Maj Genl

Telegram, copy, DNA, RG 393, Army of the Miss., Telegrams Received. On Aug. 17, 1862, Brig. Gen. William S. Rosecrans telegraphed to USG. "The mackeral—I mean Union brigade reported to Genl Granger 520.—: 300 for duty advanced as far as Dansville where they bivoacked for the night. They attacked the Pigs of Danville deploying skirmishers for that purpose from the flanks of their column who open a sharp ~~fire~~ & brought Eight of the hairy rascals to the ground before Col Fenkham Commanding ~~Danville~~ 27th Stationed at Danville arrived & informed the commander of the brigade that these natives were noncombatants. As loyal as possible considering their limited information —The brigade awaits orders there　Genl Granger by our move looses Regts & Battery. Danville covers the crossing of the Tuscumbia in front of Oglesbys Camp —It seems to me General it would be best to order Granger another Regt. & direct Davies moreover to occupy Danville which protects the Bridge crossing both of the common and Rail Road—Moreover covers the larger opening on the M & C.H. RR left by vacating our Camp—Please give the necessary orders" Telegram received, *ibid.*, Dept. of the Mo., Telegrams Received; copy, *ibid.*, Army of the Miss., Telegrams Sent. *O.R.*, I, xvii, part 2, 177. On the same day, Rosecrans telegraphed to USG. "Do you understand that two (2) of our Divisions are to be sent to Buell & that we are more over to try & hold the line through to Decatur　If so the troops at Danville or other places must go to Iuka　If we cross at Eastport & Tuscumbia Stanleys Division will go to Iuka & Tuscumbia —Mitchell will cross at Eastport & Paine at Florence—Stanley will try to Cover the road till more troops can be got, but we must be careful"　Telegram received,

DNA, RG 393, Dept. of the Mo., Telegrams Received; copy, *ibid.*, Army of the Miss., Telegrams Sent. *O.R.*, I, xvii, part 2, 176.

1. On Aug. 17, USG telegraphed to Maj. Gen. Henry W. Halleck. "Now that two Divisions are on their way to Gen Buell would it not be well to abandon Railroad from Tuscumbia to Decatur" Telegram received, DNA, RG 94, Generals' Papers and Books, Telegrams Received by Gen. Halleck; *ibid.*, RG 107, Telegrams Received in Cipher; *ibid.*, Telegrams Collected (Bound); copies, *ibid.*, RG 393, USG Hd. Qrs. Correspondence; DLC-USG, V, 4, 5, 7, 8, 9, 88. *O.R.*, I, xvii, part 2, 176. On Aug. 18, Halleck telegraphed to USG. "As General Buell's communications in Tennessee and Kentucky are seriously threatened your communication with him should be kept open if possible." *Ibid.*, p. 179.

2. See telegram to Maj. Gen. Henry W. Halleck, Aug. 16, 1862.

To Brig. Gen. William S. Rosecrans

Corinth Aug 18th 1862

GENL ROSECRANS

The two Regiments ordered to Old Rienzi[1] and Danville,[2] will be subject to the orders of Genl Granger[3] whilst they remain there   Tell me what more you require from here and I will order them at once. You have been over the ground and can dispose of them better than I can

U. S. GRANT
Maj Genl

Telegram, copy, DNA, RG 393, Army of the Miss., Telegrams Received. On Aug. 18, 1862, Brig. Gen. William S. Rosecrans telegraphed to USG. "Will Genl Granger have protem the regiments called for & reported you in my last my telegrams of 16th 17th & 18th—The order takes the 47th Ills from Rinzi the 26th Ill from Danville while the order for the second (2d) Missouri took that from Rinzi   He says the union brigade would do better under there former Commander—I thin[k] he should take them & a regiment at Rienzi and a regt from Davies should hold Danville until we have finished the moves we are making" Telegram received, *ibid.*, Dept. of the Mo., Telegrams Received; copy, *ibid.*, Army of the Miss., Telegrams Sent. On the same day, Rosecrans telegraphed to USG. "Davies should send a Regt. to Danville   let it report to Granger to occupy that place and guard the Rail Road & ~~send~~ road bridges in that vicinity   I did not understand that the union brigade as it is termed was two (2) regiments they only report about 520 present of whom only about 350 are for duty" Telegram received, *ibid.*, Dept. of the Mo., Telegrams Received; copy, *ibid.*, Army of the Miss., Telegrams Sent. On the same day, USG telegraphed to Rosecrans. "I am going up to Genl Ords to order a Regiment immediately out   I did not suppose either that the Union Brigade had been sent, as the misrepresentation of two Regiments   It is rather a bad representation of anything at present"   Copy, *ibid.*, Telegrams Received.

1. Rienzi, Miss., about thirteen miles south of Corinth on the Mobile and Ohio Railroad.
2. Danville, Miss., about nine miles southwest of Corinth.
3. Gordon Granger of N. Y., USMA 1845, served in the Mexican War and in Indian campaigns on the western frontier before the Civil War. In Sept., 1861, he was appointed col., 2nd Mich. Cav., and served in the campaigns against New Madrid, Mo., and Island No. 10. He was promoted to brig. gen. on March 26, 1862; served in the siege of Corinth; and in Aug. was in command of the 5th Division, Army of the Miss. *O.R.*, I, xvii, part 2, 148.

To Brig. Gen. William S. Rosecrans

Corinth Aug 18th 1862

GENL. ROSECRANS

The two divisions goin[g] to Buell will be returned as on detatched service but of course will be subject to Buells Orders for the time being. Instruc[t] them to report to Buell as soon as possible after crossing the River

I ordered a regiment from Dav[ies] Division to occupy Danville, and one to occupy Old Rienzi. If they have not done it, inform and I will have them go at once   I am going to the Telegraph office and will be there for an hour or two

U. S. GRANT
Maj Genl

Telegram, copy, DNA, RG 393, Army of the Miss., Telegrams Received.

To Julia Dent Grant

———

Corinth August 18th 1862

DEAR JULIA,

I suppose you are this evening quietly at your fathers enjoying a social talk! I wish I could be there or any place els where I could be quiet and free from annoyance for a few weeks.

From present indications you only left here in time. Lively opperations are now threatened and you need not be surprised to hear at any time of fighting going on in Grants Army. I hope we will be let alone however for a short time.

We all miss you and the children very much. Without Jess to stauk through the office it seems as if something is missing— Col. Dickey[1] has not yet returned nor Hillyer[2] nor Ihrie[3] arrived. Riggin being absent and Rawlins confined to his bed makes our family small. Rowley[4] absent too. Rawlins was obliged to have a serious surgical opperation performed to prevent his biles, or carbuncle, from turning into Fistula. He will probably be ten days laid up.

No letters have come to you or none from home since you left.

As I cannot write of Military operations my letters to you, although they will be frequent, will not be long nor very interesting.—Since you left there has been several little skirmishes within my District resulting in the killing and capturing of quite a number of Guerrillas with but a small loss on our side.[5]

How did you find your pa Aunt Fanny[6] and the rest of the folks at home? Give my love to all of them.

Try and collect your money from Mr. White.[7] If that is not paid I will have to close on him which I do not wish to do during the continuance of the War.—Do any of the neighbors call to see you?

Good night dear Julia. Kiss the children for me and kisses for yourself. I will write again in a few days so that you will probably receive another letter by the same mail that takes this. You ought to write to Nelly[8] to come down now as you may have no other opportunity of seeing her unless you and Mrs. Hillyer should keep house together. I expect Mr. H. will be at home by the time you get this.

ULYS.

ALS, DLC-USG.

1. On July 23, 1862, Col. T. Lyle Dickey, chief of cav., had been sent on an inspection trip. See telegram to Brig. Gen. William S. Rosecrans, July 23, 1862. On Aug. 11, Dickey reported the results of the inspection to USG. ALS, DNA, RG 393, District of West Tenn., Letters Received. In a letter to his daughters on Aug. 27, Dickey said that he had been making various inspection trips. ALS, Wallace-Dickey Papers, IHi.

2. On Aug. 4, Col. William S. Hillyer telegraphed to USG from Columbus, Ky., that he was enroute to Corinth. Telegram received, DNA, RG 393, Dept. of the Mo., Telegrams Received. On Aug. 12, the *Memphis Bulletin* reported that Hillyer had returned to Memphis. *Memphis Bulletin*, Aug. 12, 1862.

3. On July 4, Col. George P. Ihrie, New York, had written to U.S. Representative Elihu B. Washburne asking whether USG would be called to Washington, D.C., and emphasizing that such a *"fighting* General" should not be shelved. ALS, DLC-Elihu B. Washburne. On Aug. 19, Ihrie, Columbus, Ky., telegraphed to USG. "Been stuck two days on a bar and missed connection today. Will reach you tomorrow the lord willing. Can I bring anything for you   Genl McClellan and his entire army are leaving front of Richmond & coming down James River"   Telegram received, DNA, RG 393, Dept. of the Mo., Telegrams Received.

4. On Aug. 11, Maj. John A. Rawlins issued Special Orders No. 160 directing Capt. William R. Rowley to conduct "all prisoners" at Corinth to Alton, Ill. DS, *ibid.*, RG 94, Special Orders, District of West Tenn.; copies, *ibid.*, RG 393, USG Special Orders; DLC-USG, V, 15, 16, 82, 87.

5. See telegram to Maj. Gen. Henry W. Halleck, Aug. 20, 1862.

6. Probably Frances Dent Gwinn. See letter to Julia Dent Grant, May 10, 1861.

7. Joseph W. White. See letter to Julia Dent Grant, May 10, 1861.

8. Ellen Dent Sharp, sister-in-law of USG.

To Maj. Gen. John A. McClernand

By TELEGRAPH FROM U. S. Grants Head Q.R.s. [*Aug. 19*] 186[2]

To GEN MACLERNAND

if you can spare the services of Capt Prime[1] Chief Engineer would like to have the Services of Capt Frendman[2] for a short

time to superintend the fortifications at Tuscumbia   if he can
come conviently let him report to Capt Prime as soon as possible

U S GRANT
Maj Genl

Telegram received, McClernand Papers, IHi.

    1. Frederick E. Prime of N.Y., USMA 1850, served as engineer at various
forts until 1861 and attained the rank of capt. Arrested at Pensacola, Fla., by
insurgents in Jan., 1861, he later served as engineer in and around Washington,
D.C., and as chief engineer, Dept. of the Ky., Dept. of the Cumberland, and
Dept. of the Ohio. Wounded and captured in Dec., he was exchanged on March
18, 1862, and served in Washington, D.C., until his appointment on May 22 as
asst. engineer, Dept. of the Miss. On July 18, he was appointed chief of engineers
on USG's staff.
    2. Probably Capt. Henry C. Freeman. See endorsement to Maj. Gen.
Henry W. Halleck, Jan. 29, 1862, and letter to Richard Yates, Aug. 15, 1862.

To Mary Grant

———

Corinth Mississippi
August 19th 1862.

DEAR SISTER,

    Julia and the children left here on Saturday[1] last for St. Louis
where they will remain on a visit until about the last of the month.
At the end of that time they must be some place where the children can go to school.—Mrs. Hillyer has a nice house in the city
and is all alone whilst her husband is on my Staff and it may be
that she and Julia will keep house together. If they do she would
be very much pleased to have you make her a long visit. Julia
says that she is satisfied that the best place for the children is in
Covington. But there are so many of them that she sometimes
feels as if they were not wanted. Their visit down here in Dixie
was very pleasant and they were very lothe to leave. Things however began to look so threatning that I thought it was best for
them to leave. I am now in a situation where it is impossible for
me to do more than to protect my long lines of defence. I have

the Mississippi to Memphis, the rail-road from Columbus to Corinth, from Jackson to Bolivar, from Corinth to Decatur and the Tennessee & Cumberland rivers to keep open. Guerrillas are hovering around in every direction geting whipped every day some place by some of my command but keeping us busy. The war is evidently growing oppressive to the Southern people. Their *institution* are begining to have ideas of their own and every time an expedition goes out more or less of them follow in the wake of the army and come into camp. I am using them as teamsters, Hospital attendants, company cooks &c. thus saving soldiers to carry the musket. I dont know what is to become of these poor people in the end but it weakning the enemy to take them from them. If the new levies are sent in soon the rebels will have a good time geting in their crops this Fall.

I have abandoned all hope of being able to make a visit home 'till the close of the war. A few weeks recreation would be very greatful however. It is one constant strain now and has been for a year. If I do get through I think I will take a few months of pure and undefiled rest. I stand it well however having gained some fifteen pounds in weight since leaving Cairo. Give my love to all at home.

ULYS.

ALS, PPRF.

1. Aug. 16, 1862.

To Brig. Gen. Lorenzo Thomas

———

U. S. Grants Head Quarters
August 20, *1862*

GENL L. THOMAS

I have the right to act on resignations of Commissioned officers under existing restrictions as to when they will be accepted.

U. S. GRANT
Major General

Telegram received, DNA, RG 94, Vol. Service Branch, Letters Received; copy, *ibid.*, RG 107, Telegrams Received (Press). On Aug. 21, 1862, Maj. Thomas M. Vincent telegraphed to USG. "For resignation of Vols see page sixteen forty seven 1647 Army Regulations" Telegram received, *ibid.*, RG 393, Dept. of the Mo., Telegrams Received; copies, *ibid.*, RG 94, Vol. Service Branch, Letters Sent; *ibid.*, Letters Received; *ibid.*, RG 107, Telegrams Collected (Bound). "Officers of the volunteer service tendering their resignations, will forward them through the intermediate commanders to the officer commanding the department or *corps d'armee* in which they may be serving, who is authorized to grant them honorable discharges. This commander will immediately report his action to the Adjutant-General of the Army, who will communicate the same to the Governor of the State to which the officer belongs. A clear statement of the cause will accompany every resignation." *Revised Regulations for the Army of the United States, 1861* (Philadelphia, 1861), p. 497.

To Maj. Gen. Henry W. Halleck

———

Corinth Miss 3.45 P.M
Aug 20th 1862—

MAJ GEN H. W. HALLECK
GEN IN CHIEF

The Guerillas are becoming so active in West Tennessee that a large mounted force is required to suppress them.[1] Cannot a portion of Gen Curtis cavalry be sent to me

U S. GRANT
Maj Genl

Telegram received, DNA, RG 94, Generals' Papers and Books, Telegrams Received by Gen. Halleck; *ibid.*, RG 107, Telegrams Collected (Bound); copies, *ibid.*, Telegrams Received in Cipher; *ibid.*, RG 393, USG Hd. Qrs. Correspondence; DLC-USG, V, 4, 5, 7, 8, 9, 88. *O.R.*, I, xvii, part 2, 182. On Aug. 21, 1862, Maj. Gen. Henry W. Halleck telegraphed to USG. "Genl curtis' cavalry is fully employed in Arkansas. Gov. Johnson of Tenn was requested some weeks ago to raise some cavalry regts to act against Guerrilla bands. I will send you more cavalry as soon as we can get it. You have charge of everything in your District, but no one has yet been designated to command the old Dept. It will probably be divided" ALS (telegram sent), DNA, RG 107, Telegrams Collected (Bound); copies, *ibid.*, RG 393, USG Hd. Qrs. Correspondence; DLC-USG, V, 4, 5, 7, 8, 9, 88. *O.R.*, I, xvii, part 2, 182.

1. On Aug. 10, Brig. Gen. Grenville M. Dodge telegraphed to USG about a skirmish with C. S. A. cav. at Wood Springs near Dyersburg, Tenn. Copies, DNA, RG 94, War Records Office, Union Battle Reports; *ibid.*, RG 393, Hd. Qrs., Central Division, District of the Miss., Letters and Telegrams Sent. *O.R.*, I, xvii, part 1, 30. On Aug. 11, Brig. Gen. Isaac F. Quinby telegraphed to USG that guerrillas were organizing in Trigg County, Ky. Telegram received, DNA, RG 393, Dept. of the Mo., Telegrams Received. On Aug. 18, Quinby telegraphed to USG. "Two Companies of Infantry & a Section of in a few moments for Smithland Ky orders to commanding officer are to occupy the place & protect public property, break up Guerrilla organizations arrest Disloyal & those engaged directly or indirectly in enlisting for the Rebel service & also all already enlisted. We are much in need of Cavalry." Telegram received, *ibid.*

On Aug. 14, Maj. Gen. John A. McClernand telegraphed to USG reporting skirmishing between Tenn. militia units and guerrillas near Jackson, Tenn. Telegram received, *ibid.*; copies, McClernand Papers, IHi. On Aug. 16, McClernand reported action in the same general vicinity and the movement of Ky. secessionists near the line of the Mobile and Ohio Railroad between Purdy and Humboldt, Tenn. Telegram received, DNA, RG 393, Dept. of the Mo., Telegrams Received; copies, McClernand Papers, IHi. On the same day, McClernand reported disturbances at Saulsbury, Tenn., on the Memphis and Charleston Railroad, to which he had sent Brig. Gen. Leonard F. Ross. Telegram received, DNA, RG 393, Dept. of the Mo., Telegrams Received; copies, McClernand Papers, IHi. On Aug. 18, McClernand reported that Col. Isham N. Haynie had captured seventeen rebels near Bethel, Tenn. Telegram received, DNA, RG 107, Telegrams Collected (Bound); copies, McClernand Papers, IHi.

On Aug. 17, USG telegraphed to Halleck. "The following dispatch just recd from Head quarters Central Division dist of the Mississippi. 'Trenton Tenn to Maj Genl Grant.' Col Harris of the fifty fourth Ills infantry with Capt Fullertons Co of second Illinois cavalry attacked a Rebel force from Kentucky one hundred fifty strong at Merriweathers ferry in Dyer county completely routing them & driving them into the river. The fight lasted thirty minutes & Capt Fullertons officers & men fought with great gallantry & bravery. His force was only sixty. The enemys loss was large in killed wounded & drowned. We took ten prisoners, forty horses, A large number of arms ammunition &c. Our loss Lieut Terry & Goodheart & one private killed & six wounded. Several companies cavalry from Kentucky are trying to push through south. This was the first that crossed the line. They are well armed & fought desperately. signed G. M. DODGE Br Genl."

Telegram received, DNA, RG 94, Generals' Papers and Books, Telegrams Received by Gen. Halleck; copies, *ibid.*, RG 107, Telegrams Collected (Bound); *ibid.*, RG 393, USG Hd. Qrs. Correspondence; DLC-USG, V, 4, 5, 7, 8, 9, 88. *O.R.*, I, xvii, part 1, 31. On the same day, Brig. Gen. James M. Tuttle reported a large force advancing between Caseyville, Ky., on the Ohio River and the Cumberland River, which was threatening Smithland and Paducah. Telegram received, DNA, RG 393, Dept. of the Mo., Telegrams Received. On Aug. 18, Dodge telegraphed to USG. "Capt Lynch of Sixth (6th) Ills Cavalry attacked a Small band of Rebels this morning on the Obion River six miles from Dyersburg taking all their horses Arms & amunition   they abandoned every thing   No report of killed & wounded   Large numbers of Rebels are flocking into this country from Missouri and Kentucky—All armed & forming bands under leaders from Jacksons & Morgans Cavalry. The Draft drives them over"   Telegram received, *ibid.*; copies, *ibid.*, Hd. Qrs., Central Division, District of the Miss., Letters and Telegrams Sent; *ibid.*, RG 94, War Records Office, Union Battle Reports. *O.R.*, I, xvii, part 1, 34–35.

On Aug. 18, Col. William W. Lowe wrote to Maj. John A. Rawlins. "I have the honor to report that I have just returned from an expedition to and beyond Paris, Tennessee, having left this Post on the 10th: instant. The object in view was two fold: First to be at Paris, to protect Hon Emerson Etheridge against mob violence during the delivery of an address to the people of that place. Second: To make a thorough search for Guerlla parties said to be organizing in Henry Co: It will be remembered that last year when Mr. Etheridge attempted to make a union speach in Paris, he was mobbed, and some two or three persons were shot. Hence the presence of a military was deemed necessary on this occasion. Henry County is famed for the bitter Secession proclivities: or as Mr Etheridge expresses it, 'it is the vilest district in North America,' and the presence of a small military force at short intervals is essential to the maintenance of peace and good order. No armed parties were discovered, though it is a well assertained fact that guerilla bands are in process of organization in various parts of the country especially in Benton County. The great difficulty in dealing with them or the fact that they are not uniformed, and in the presence of a military force would almost invariably be found guilty, working on their farms. I propose to make a scout through Benton county in a few days"   LS, DNA, RG 393, District of West Tenn., Letters Received.

On Aug. 19, McClernand telegraphed to USG. "Genl Ross reports that the detachment Sent by him to ~~guard~~ grand Junction returned last night. No Enemy at 'G—J—'   His Scouts who went Still below report Villepigues forces twelve (12) miles & below Holly Springs   More in detail by dispatch this Evening" Telegram received, *ibid.*, Dept. of the Mo., Telegrams Received; copies, McClernand Papers, IHi. On Aug. 19, Ross telegraphed to USG. "I have information that there is to be a meeting of conscripts at Ripley tomorrow for the purpose of organization. A portion of Fulkens cavalry will be there also—" Telegram received, DNA, RG 393, Dept. of the Mo., Telegrams Received. On Aug. 20, McClernand telegraphed to USG. "Genl Ross sent a detachment of Infantry & cavalry to Somerville last night to attack a party of Rebels first reported at 400. since magnified to over a thousand   he thinks he will capture ~~the enemy~~ or route the Enemy. It was reported yesterday that rebel cavalry were crossing the Hatchee now down. I have ordered a force to reconnoiter as far as Brownsville" Telegram received, *ibid.*; copies (one dated Aug. 21), McClernand Papers, IHi. On

Aug. 21, McClernand wrote to USG elaborating on the telegram and telling of the arrest of citizens and the confiscation of Negroes, "mules and horses, belonging to seditious and obnoxious citizens." ALS, DNA, RG 393, District of West Tenn., Letters Received. On Aug. 22, McClernand, Jackson, telegraphed to USG. "I will leave this morning for Bolivar—will be back day after to-morrow." Copy, McClernand Papers, IHi. On Aug. 24, McClernand telegraphed to USG. "The cavalry started for Memphis yesterday supported by one (1) Reg't of Infantry Expect to meet cavalry from Memphis at Sommerville & move the force to their respective destination via Covington hoping to cut off & capture Rebel cavalry as they retreat before cavalry from Trenton & Humboldt—" Telegram received, DNA, RG 393, Dept. of the Mo., Telegrams Received; copies, McClernand Papers, IHi. On Aug. 26, McClernand telegraphed to USG. "Col Chambers & reg't has returned to Bolivar from Somerville where it went to support the Cavalry on their transit to & from Memphis to prevent the Enemy from doing it any harm—He brought with him a considerable number of negroes horses & mules also 24 bales cotton being the property of Rebels in the Army or their sympathizers. I will leave here on Thursday morning" Telegram received, DNA, RG 393, Dept. of the Mo., Telegrams Received; copy, McClernand Papers, IHi. On Aug. 27, McClernand wrote to USG of a cav. reconnaissance down the Hatchie River which resulted in the destruction of two ferries used by rebels. Copies, *ibid.*

To Maj. Nathaniel H. McLean

Head Quarters District of West Tenn
Corinth, Miss. Aug. 20, 1862.

Maj. N. H. McLean,
Asst. Adjut General
Department of the Miss.
Saint Louis, Mo.
Major:

I have the honor to acknowledge the receipt of your Communication of date Augt. 15th, and to say in reply, that a number of packages of Orders from the A. G. O. have arrived at Corinth for the Commander of the Department, and these have been forwarded by Express to you at Saint Louis.

General Orders from the A. G. O. to include No 90, have been received at these Head Quarters, sent to my my address, and these have been properly distributed to the troops within the District of West Tennessee.

> Very Respectfully
> Your Obt Sev't
> U. S. GRANT
> Maj. Genl.

LS, DNA, RG 393, Dept. of the Mo., Letters Received. On Aug. 15, 1862, Maj. Nathaniel H. McLean, St. Louis, wrote to USG. "The following is a copy of an endorsement upon letter addressed to the Adjutant General of the Army asking for 1,000 copies all Genl. Orders A. G. O. 1862, subsequent to No. 72: 'Respectfully referred to Major N. H. McLean who is informed that the orders within referred to have been sent to the Commander of the Dept. of the Mississippi at Corinth, Miss. and, it is presumed, have been distributed to the troops, and the surplus copies can no doubt be obtained from the staff officer who received them at that place. Hereafter, however, orders will be sent to Saint Louis for distribution.'. . . Please inform these Headquarters if the above mentioned orders have been received at Corinth, and what troops have been furnished with copies. Also please forward all surplus copies to these Head Quarters that the troops in the South West &c. may be supplied" LS, *ibid.*, District of West Tenn., Letters Received; *ibid.*, Dept. of the Mo., Letters Sent (Press); copies, *ibid.*, Dept. of the Miss., Letters Sent; *ibid.*, USG Hd. Qrs. Correspondence; DLC-USG, V, 7, 8. On Aug. 20, USG telegraphed to Maj. Gen. Henry W. Halleck. "I am constantly receiving official communications from Washn. Directed to me as commander of the department I have assumed no such command nor seen any authority for it—" Telegram received, DNA, RG 94, Generals' Papers and Books, Telegrams Received by Gen. Halleck; *ibid.*, RG 107, Telegrams Collected (Bound). See preceding telegram.

To Maj. Gen. Henry W. Halleck

Head Quartes Genl Grant [*Aug.*] 21st [*1862*]

GENL HALLECK
GENL

There was a general muster through this district on the Eighteenth, 18th   as soon as the order for it appeared in the newspapers I ordered it

> U. S. GRANT

Telegram received, DNA, RG 94, Generals' Papers and Books, Telegrams Received by Gen. Halleck; copies, *ibid.*, RG 107, Telegrams Collected (Bound); *ibid.*, RG 393, USG Hd. Qrs. Correspondence; DLC-USG, V, 4, 5, 7, 8, 9, 88. On Aug. 20, 1862, Maj. Gen. Henry W. Halleck telegraphed to USG. "You will report whether the Genl muster ordered to be made on the 18th inst. was so made, & if not, you will cause it to be made immediately." ALS (telegram sent), DNA, RG 107, Telegrams Collected (Bound); telegram received, *ibid.*, RG 393, Dept. of the Tenn., Telegrams Received.

On Aug. 8, Maj. John A. Rawlins had issued General Orders No. 71 directing a general muster. Copies, DLC-USG, V, 12, 13, 14, 95; DNA, RG 393, USG General Orders; *ibid.*, RG 94, 21st Ill., Order Book. On Aug. 28, Brig. Gen. Isaac F. Quinby telegraphed to USG asking how many copies of the muster USG required. Telegram received, *ibid.*, RG 393, Dept. of the Mo., Telegrams Received. On Sept. 4, 1st Lt. Theodore S. Bowers issued General Orders No. 80. "Division Commanders throughout this Military District will at once appoint and cause to be organized and convened within their respective Divisions, Courts of Inquiry, as Provided by Section three of General Orders, No 92, A.G.O. War Department, and all applications made by officers who were reported absent without lawful cause at the General Muster on the 18th day of August 1862, to be restored to rank and Pay in the service; shall be heard and passed upon and reported without delay, through the proper military channels to the Head Quarters of the Army at Washington." Copies, DLC-USG, V, 12, 13, 14, 95; DNA, RG 393, USG General Orders. On Sept. 10, Brig. Gen. Leonard F. Ross telegraphed to USG. "Troops returned on the 18th of Aug absent without leave if they dont return by the thirty first Aug how should they be stricken from the Rolls—" Telegram received, *ibid.*, Dept. of the Mo., Telegrams Received.

On Sept. 22, a court of inquiry at Columbus, Ky., found that 1st Lt. George H. Tracy, 15th U.S. Inf., reported absent at the muster of Aug. 18, held a valid medical pass at the time. On Sept. 26, USG endorsed the report. "Respectfully forwarded to Headquarters of the Army, Washington D. C. for approval of the proper authorities" ES, *ibid.*, RG 94, Letters Received.

To Maj. Gen. Henry W. Halleck

Corinth Miss
Aug 21st 2. P M 1862

MAJ GEN H. W. HALLECK
GEN IN CHIEF.

Two Steamers are said to have been captured by Guerrillas on the Tennessee on the 18th. Steamer Terry has gone down armed with four 4 guns & a company of Sharp Shooters[1] General Tuttle informed me that three 3 new Regiments were to

leave Springfield for Cairo yesterday & today—I have directed
one of them & the 11th Illinois to occupy Paducha & Smithland
—one to be sent to Columbus & the other to remain at Cairo[2]
There is such a demand for Cavalry that I will have to mount
Infantry making Secessionists furnish horses & Forage[3]—
Should there not be two 2 or three 3 light draft Steamers bought
& fitted up proof against Minnie balls & armed with two guns
each to carry Government freight on the Tennessee from here[4]

U. T. GRANT
Maj Genl

Telegram received, DNA, RG 94, Generals' Papers and Books, Telegrams
Received by Gen. Halleck; copies, *ibid.*, RG 107, Telegrams Collected (Bound);
ibid., Telegrams Received in Cipher; (dated Aug. 20, 1862) *ibid.*, RG 393, USG
Hd. Qrs. Correspondence; DLC-USG, V, 4, 5, 7, 8, 9, 88. Dated Aug. 21 in
O.R., I, xvii, part 2, 182.

1. On Aug. 19, Brig. Gen. James M. Tuttle telegraphed to USG. "The
following telegram rec'd this P M—Paduch to Brig Gen Tuttle, Cairo   I have
just rec'd the following dispatch from Fort Henry to Stillman. We have rec'd
information of the following (2) boats the skylark & Callie were burned last
night by the Guerillas at the mouth of Duck River 50 miles above here   the
steamer W B Terry is reported lost   she cut her barges loose which were picked
up by the steamer Lancaster No 4 which has just come down the River—great
Excitement here   signed THOMPSON Tel Opr—GEO STILLMAN Govt Tel Opr
Have sent Col Ransom up to Smithland with (150) of the 11th Ills   he will take
command at Paducah—Gov Yates will send one (1) Reg't here tomorrow & two
(2) next day   will put one (1) at Birds point & the 11th & one (1) new one (1)
at Paducah & Smithland until stores are brought from Smithland which I am having done—" Telegram received, DNA, RG 393, Dept. of the Mo., Telegrams
Received. On the same day, Lt. Col. Lyman M. Ward, Hamburg, Tenn., telegraphed to USG. "The Steamboat Terry just arrived was fired on at Duck River
two & half miles below. cut away two (2) barges of hay & come through. The
Skylark from St Louis with Commisary Stores & the Callie with Cotton from
Hamburg both in possession of Guerillas about one thousand (1000) in number"
Telegram received, *ibid*. On Aug. 21, Brig. Gen. Grenville M. Dodge, Trenton,
Tenn., telegraphed to USG. "Capt Dougherty Capt Gilliam & Capt Napier with
about five hundred (500) rebels were on the Tenn River in Benton county on
Monday night last   they captured & burnt (2) steamboats & attacked another
but failed to get it   this occurred between Waggoners & Walkers landing   there
was a force on the opposite side of the river but could get no information as to
their number" Telegram received, *ibid.*; copy, *ibid.*, RG 94, War Records
Office, Union Battle Reports. *O.R.*, I, xvii, part 1, 34.
On Aug. 24, 1st Master Jason Goudy, Hamburg, commanding gunboat
Alfred Robb, telegraphed to USG. "I have returned from Duck River. The two
(2) boats Caller & Sky Lark was burned before I got there   I got several shots
at them   they run in the woods & I had not force to follow them   I found a lot

of stock on the bank which I could not fetch away on account of Shoal water—" Telegram received, DNA, RG 393, Dept. of the Mo., Telegrams Received. A dispatch to the *Chicago Times* from Cairo, Aug. 20, indicated that the steamers *Sky Lark* and *Callie* had been burned by a band of thirty guerrillas on Aug. 18 near the mouth of Duck River, about fifty miles above Fort Henry. The *Sky Lark* was captured while aground on a sand bar. "The Callie came down to the assistance of the Sky Lark. Both boats were captured, their furniture removed, and then burned. The pilot on the Callie was wounded, also the fireman on the Sky Lark." *Chicago Times*, Aug. 21, 1862.

2. On Aug. 21, Tuttle telegraphed to USG. "None of the new reg'ts have arrived here yet   had telegram from Gov Yates last night that he had ordered (3) three here. I have not sent Col Ransom to Paducah yet for reason I have no others here for guard   the new regts are to be equipped here   they will come here without any kinds of equipments—will comply with your order as soon as I have the troops   they are slow sending them. shall I prevent transportation boats from going up Tennessee river—" Telegram received, DNA, RG 393, Dept. of the Mo., Telegrams Received. On Aug. 22, Tuttle telegraphed to USG. "No new troops have arrived—I am constanly urging Gov Yates to send them forward. I will advise you as soon as they arrive and before I send them any where— They were to be here Nineteenth (19th)   I Telegraph now to Gov Yates— Will inform you of his answer as soon as recd—" Telegram received, *ibid*. On the same day, Tuttle telegraphed to USG that he had heard from Springfield, Ill., that the troops were being sent as rapidly as possible, but that some of the new troops had problems in moving. Telegram received, *ibid*. On Aug. 25, Col. Joseph D. Webster, Cairo, telegraphed to USG. "Am here here with four 4 companies of 13th Wisconsin from Columbus   will go up to Paducah at once where I will get a battery & the 11th Infantry. Gen Tuttle will send new regts to Ft Henry. Board of Trade Reg't is here without arms"   Telegram received, *ibid*. On the same day, Brig. Gen. Isaac F. Quinby telegraphed to USG. "I trust the fact that the board of trade Reg't Col Tarrany not having arms will not be ~~the~~ a reason for keeping it at Cairo   we can give it some kind of arms here until it is furnished with good ones—" Telegram received, *ibid*. On Aug. 26, Tuttle telegraphed to USG. "Col Webster telegraphs me that they are fighting at Donelson today—want reinforcements   have sent Col Ransom with his reg't 72d Ills is all I have in district & they are without arms   76th also arrived today & sent to Genl Quinby   also without arms   have made requistion on Col Camdon at St Louis for arms but he dont send them   dont know why   suppose they will be here soon   would send him some more men if I had arms"   Telegram received, *ibid*.

3. On Aug. 20, Brig. Gen. William S. Rosecrans, Iuka, Miss., telegraphed three times to USG. "Arrived here at 11 a.m. Head Quarters established here—" "There is a company of cavalry here owning their own horses and not their saddles   the paymaster does not know what to do about paying them for the use of their horses because they do not own their horse equipments   please give instructions"   "Genl Mitchell says there is 5 Regts of Cavalry in Kansas   cant we get a couple of these   ask Gen Halleck for the 2   tell him we have nearly two companies here already   would it not be well to urge H once more to send you some of Curtis cavalry—'Cavalry' 'Cavalry must be our cry—" Telegrams received, *ibid*.

4. On Aug. 19, Goudy, Hamburg, telegraphed to USG. "The Robb could

not move the Freight more than two (2) or three miles from the River & unless I have land force to co'operate with me I am afraid I cant accomplish much—" Telegram received, *ibid.* On the same day, Ward telegraphed to USG. "The Capt of the Gun Boats wants one hundred & fifty 150 men to go with him to duck river suck tonight   owing to demonstrations near this point I do not consider it prudent to weaken the force here   I shall not send any men unless ordered to do so by you"   Telegram received, *ibid.* On the same day, Ward telegraphed again to USG. "I have sent the troy with four (4) guns twenty (20) artillery men & thirty 30 sharpshooters   the Robb draws too much water to do any good—" Telegram received, *ibid.* On Aug. 20. Rosecrans telegraphed to USG. "There should in my opinion be no delay in ordering a couple or three (3) light draught Gun Boats armed with a couple of 12 pounders Howitsers & a few Sharp shooters   would it not be well to direct for the present that Guard be placed on each commissary Steamboat—say a first rate Lieut & 30 men well armed & vigilant   the pilot house ought to be made shot proof with thick plank & boiler iron   it will be a great reason for us to own the Boats we use in the Tennessee river or have them fitted up as suggested. this is my experience on the Kanawa river where I had the thing fully tested   the saving is immense—" Telegram received, *ibid.* On Aug. 30, Rosecrans telegraphed to USG. "Two 2 Barges loaded with hay were burned at the Point where those boats were burned—It appears probable they had no guards Lt   Yet orderes should be given to send small seach guard of 20 to 30 men armed with rifled muskets on each transport—The pilot house ought to be protected by three inch plank & boiler plate or no 8 iron & the boilers by 3 plank—" Telegram received, *ibid.*; copy (dated Aug. 29), *ibid.*, Army of the Miss., Telegrams Sent.

To Maj. Nathaniel H. McLean

Corinth Aug 21st 1862

MAJ N H McLEAN
A A GENL SAINT LOUIS

Notify the 13 Regt Infty to hold themselves in readiness to move to Memphis   I will order a Regiment from there to relieve them at once

U. S. GRANT
Maj Genl

Telegram, copies, DLC-USG, V, 4, 5, 7, 8, 9, 88; DNA, RG 393, USG Hd. Qrs. Correspondence. On July 31, 1862, Maj. Gen. William T. Sherman wrote to Maj. John A. Rawlins asking that the 13th U.S. Inf., Alton, Ill., be transferred to Memphis. Maj. Gen. Henry W. Halleck had promised to make the change because the unit was Sherman's regular U.S. Army command. ALS, *ibid.*, RG 108,

Letters Received. On Aug. 5, USG endorsed the letter to hd. qrs., Dept. of the Miss. "Respectfully forwarded to Head Quarters of the Dept. and urgently recommended. If there is any difficulty about finding troops with which to releive this battalion there are in this command a number of Illinois regiments that have been so reduced in numbers by battles and diseas that, by being sent to Alton, would be near home where they could fill up their thined ranks, and could proffitably be spared for this purpose." AES, *ibid.* On Aug. 20, Maj. Nathaniel H. McLean telegraphed to USG. "On three occasions General Halleck has ordered the eight organized companies of the 13th Infantry at Alton, Illinois, to be relieved and sent into the field. He now directs that you do it immediately." Copy, *ibid.*, RG 393, Dept. of the Mo., Telegrams Sent. On Aug. 23, McLean issued Special Orders No. 308 ordering USG to send a suitable regt. or battalion to Alton to relieve the 13th U.S. Inf., whereupon the 13th U.S. Inf. was to proceed to Memphis. Copies, *ibid.*, RG 94, Orders and Circulars, Dept. of the Miss.; *ibid.*, RG 393, USG Hd. Qrs. Correspondence. On Aug. 29, Sherman received orders from USG to carry out Special Orders No. 308, Dept. of the Miss. *Ibid.*, Records of the 15th Army Corps, Register of Letters Received. On Aug. 27, Sherman telegraphed to USG. "Five 5 compains of cavalry in from Bolivar encountered nothing on the road   all very well here   seventy seven 77th Ohio ordered to Alton to releive the 13th Infantry—" Telegram received, *ibid.*, Dept. of the Mo., Telegrams Received.

On Sept. 6, Sherman telegraphed to USG. "Dispatch of Aug first about a battalion 13th Infty was duly rec'd   I sent the 77th Ohio to Alton & expect hourly the battallion of 13th Infty   I had not heard from it although by the Newspapers I know the 77th had reached Alton   I am this moment in receipt of a dispatch from Genl Boyle Louisville—Genl in Chief has ordered Genl Grangers division here. Where is it! How will it come? will light draft boats be needed can you hurry it up. forces much needed   will you please answer—GENL BOYLE" Telegram received, *ibid.*

To Maj. Gen. Henry W. Halleck

Head Qrs General Grant 9.15 a m [*Aug.*] 22d [*1862*]

MAJ GENL HALLECK.
GENL,

Colonel Mason with portion of the 71st Ohio surrendered Clarksville to the Guerillas. Prisoners were parolled & sent down the River. I ordered them to Benton Barracks[1]   I have put forts Donelson & Henry under Command of Col Lowe & have ordered Six (6) Companies of Infantry to reinforce him[2]

U. S. GRANT
Maj Genl

Telegram received, DNA, RG 94, Generals' Papers and Books, Telegrams Received by Gen. Halleck; *ibid.*, RG 107, Telegrams Collected (Bound); copies, *ibid.*, RG 94, War Records Office, Union Battle Reports; *ibid.*, RG 393, USG Hd. Qrs. Correspondence; DLC-USG, V, 4, 5, 7, 8, 9, 88. *O.R.*, I, xvi, part 1, 862; (dated Aug. 25, 1862) *ibid.*, I, xvii, part 2, 186. On Aug. 22, Maj. Gen. Henry W. Halleck telegraphed to USG. "You will take all possible measures to put down the Guerrilla operations on the Tenn and Cumberland rivers. Act wherever you can without regard to District lines. Clarksville should be retaken and occupied as soon as possible. It is believed that most of the enemy's forces have left your front." Copies, DLC-USG, V, 4, 5, 7, 8, 9, 88; DNA, RG 393, USG Hd. Qrs. Correspondence. *O.R.*, I, xvii, part 2, 182–83.

1. On Aug. 5, Col. William W. Lowe, Fort Henry, telegraphed to Maj. John A. Rawlins. "Have just received a dispatch from Clarksville the substance of which is that the place is in great danger from Guerrillas & asking for help. I can give none   Three of my Companies scouting & all of them been at it for a week past   Were I to go over there would be nothing left here"   Telegram received, DNA, RG 393, Dept. of the Mo., Telegrams Received. On Aug. 20, Col. Rodney Mason, 71st Ohio, Paducah, Ky., telegraphed to USG. "I report my detachment being the garrison at Clarksville as paroled prisoners. I applied to Buell for reinforcements in vain—With the support of Artillery we were attacked on monday by a force of cavalry & Infantry (800) Eight hundred strong with a battery of six (6) & twelve (12) pounders under command of Col S Johnson & Woodward   they were immediately joined by large numbers of armed citizens   my little force was reduced by details on Telegraph & river to one hundred & fifty (150) effective men in camp   it was thought best to surrender. I refused to give my parole but otherwise would do it—I then gave it for 30 days when I am to surrender myself at Hopkinsville Ky—Where shall I take my men —other forces are organizing to attack Donelson & Henry—Donelson is very weak & will I think be overwhelmed unless immediate relief is given. The enemy will be able to overun this country again   they can any day bring over two thousand (2000) armed men to Donelson—" Telegram received, *ibid.*; copy, *ibid.*, RG 94, War Records Office, Union Battle Reports. *O.R.*, I, xvi, part 1, 862–63. On the same day, Brig. Gen. Isaac F. Quinby telegraphed to USG informing him of the capture of Clarksville and warning him of the activities of guerrillas in western Ky. and Tenn. Dated July 20, *ibid.*, I, xvii, part 2, 107.

On Aug. 27, Mason wrote a full report of the incident to USG. ALS, DNA, RG 94, War Records Office, Union Battle Reports. *O.R.*, I, xvi, part 1, 863–65. USG forwarded the report to hd. qrs. of the army. ES, DNA, RG 94, War Records Office, Union Battle Reports. On Aug. 22, Col. Edward D. Townsend issued AGO General Orders No. 115 cashiering Mason "for repeated acts of cowardice in the face of the enemy." *O.R.*, I, xvi, part 1, 865. Twelve officers of the 71st Ohio wrote an undated statement regarding the capture, pointing out that they had received insufficient support at Clarksville. At the time of the capture, they estimated the number of men fit for duty had been only two hundred. Mason had repeatedly asked for reinforcements, but his requests went unheeded. They were faced by a force estimated at between 800 and 1,000, reinforced by two batteries (when they had only one damaged piece), and the officers unanimously advised Mason to surrender. *Ibid.*, pp. 867–68. On Aug. 25, Mason wrote to the editor, *Ohio State Journal*, in defense of the surrender. *New York Times*,

Aug. 31, 1862. On March 22, 1866, Townsend issued AGO Special Orders No. 130, revoking AGO General Orders No. 115, 1862, and mustering Mason out of the service as of Aug. 22, 1862. Copy, DNA, RG 94, War Records Office, Union Battle Reports. *O.R.*, I, xvi, part 1, 865.

In a report to Maj. Gen. Don Carlos Buell, Aug. 20, 1862, Maj. William H. Sidell estimated that the C. S. A. force which attacked Clarksville had numbered only 300, all cav. with no art. *Ibid.*, pp. 869–70.

2. On Aug. 22, USG telegraphed to Halleck. "I gave orders yesterday for Col Lowe to take command of Donnelson in addition to Henry and Herman that I would reinforce him & he must retake ~~Clarksburg~~ Clarksville Col Webster goes tomorrow with my instructions" Telegram received, DNA, RG 94, Generals' Papers and Books, Telegrams Received by Gen. Halleck; copies, *ibid.*, RG 107, Telegrams Collected (Bound); *ibid.*, Telegrams Received in Cipher; *ibid.*, RG 393, USG Hd. Qrs. Correspondence; DLC-USG, V, 4, 5, 7, 8, 9, 88. *O.R.*, I, xvii, part 2, 183. On Aug. 22, Lowe telegraphed to Rawlins. "Have I a right to go to Clarksville I think I can retake it—" Telegram received, DNA, RG 393, Dept. of the Mo., Telegrams Received. On the same day, Maj. James H. Hart, 71st Ohio, Fort Donelson, telegraphed to USG asking for reinforcements. *O.R.*, I, xvii, part 2, 183. On Aug. 24, Lowe telegraphed to USG. "Yesterday a Seargt & 12 men had a skirmish with rebels killed 2 wounded (1) Rebels numbered 200 now after them." Telegram received, DNA, RG 393, Dept. of the Mo., Telegrams Received. On the same day, Lowe telegraphed to USG that the rebels had fled toward Clarksville. Telegram received, *ibid.* On Aug. 25, from Paducah, and on Aug. 26 from Fort Henry, Col. Joseph D. Webster telegraphed to USG about a skirmish near Fort Donelson. Telegrams received, *ibid.*, RG 107, Telegrams Collected (Unbound). This skirmish is described in *O.R.*, I, xvii, part 1, 37–38. Lowe pursued the attackers to the Cumberland Iron Works, where another skirmish followed. *Ibid.*, pp. 38–39. On Aug. 28, Webster, Cairo, telegraphed to USG that he had just received a dispatch from Lowe which indicated that Clarksville had been reinforced and that it was doubtful that Lowe could retake it with his small force. Telegram received, DNA, RG 393, Dept. of the Mo., Telegrams Received. On Aug. 29, Lowe telegraphed to Rawlins. "I would respectfully ask the genl comdg to telegraph at once to washington for arms for my Reg't they have never been half armed & it is certainly cruel to take them into action so poorly prepared I have repeatedly made the proper requistion & am now told there are no cavalry arms in this dept—" Telegram received, *ibid.* On the same day, Hart telegraphed to USG. "We have now here 4 Co's of 13th Wisconsin under command of Lt Col Chapman 4 Co's of same at Columbus 1 at Hickman & 1 at Smithland under Maj Bigney Why can they not be at once united at this point. I am here with my 4 Co's of 71st Ohio—Will you be kind enough Genl to advise me where the paroled soldiers of our reg't are. What hope is there of ever being reorganized the officers & men under my command will fight. they would take a new organization can we not have it. Why not let us that is the 4 Co's A. B. G & H only fragmentry now go up to Camp Dennison or chase or some point in ohio & form a new Reg't" Telegram received, *ibid.* On Sept. 18, Hart telegraphed to USG. "We have for duty at Ft. Donelson 214 enlisted men seventeen officers of these 21 men & two officers are sick these ~~20~~ 214 men compose cos A B H & G of the 71st O vols I.   there are paroled by ~~clar~~ clarksville surrender 301 if they could be attached we would have 515 men & 19 officers my opinion is that when exchanged they ought to be ~~sent~~

sent here to fill our companies   if this cannot be done why may I not take my men to Ohio as a nuclus to a new rgt by another number that might be formed   I submit this matter for your consideration   we are not disposed to avoid ~~but~~ fight but we do desire to be placed in a condition where our number & organization will give us respectibility   Be kind enogh to give me your views upon the matters suggested   I express the united sentiments of all my commissioned officers   we are in great need of clothing'' Telegram received, *ibid.*

On Sept. 10, Lowe reported to Rawlins that he had left Fort Donelson on Sept. 5 with about 1,030 men. After driving off troops under Col. Thomas G. Woodward, he had occupied Clarksville on the night of Sept. 7. While there, Lowe destroyed hay and commissary stores, and required citizens of the town to furnish rations for his command. *O.R.*, I, xvi, part 1, 955–56. On Sept. 15, a group of citizens of Clarksville wrote to USG outlining events through Sept. 7, and complaining of the actions of Lowe's troops. "Then commenced a series of outrages, robberies and insults upon the citizens without regard to sex or condition, which we believe to be without parallel, except in the case of Athens, Ala., in the present war and unknown to the civilized warfare of modern times. . . . The country along the line of march was utterly devastated for thirty miles on both sides of the road. Cattle were shot, hogs killed and stolen. The residences of the city were indiscriminately visited by inflamed and drunken soldiery. Horses were stolen and negroes did not escape the general spoilation. Everything indicated that the city was in the hands of brutal, indecent, and unprincipled band of thieves, from whose unbridled license no moderation or gentlemanly treatment could be expected. The citizens were preemptorily required to furnish subsistence upon pain of having their houses fired by the incendiaries' torches. Stores were broken open and thousands of dollars worth of goods destroyed. From Sunday noon until Monday noon, a reign of terror, kept alive by every species of outrage, was established in this city. . . ." In conclusion, they asked USG for redress. Ursula Smith Beach, *Along the Warioto or a History of Montgomery County, Tennessee* (n.p., 1964), p. 364. Apparently receiving no satisfaction from USG, the citizens complained to Jefferson Davis about the situation. *O.R.*, I, xvii, part 2, 730–32.

To Maj. Gen. Henry W. Halleck

Head Quarters, Dist. of West. Tenn
Corinth, Miss. Aug. 22nd 1862

Major Gen. H. W. Halleck
Commander in Chief
Washington, D. C.
General.

I have the honor to acknowledge the receipt of your telegram, dated Aug. 21st in relation to the case of Lieut. Col. Thomas. H.

Burgess of the 18th Regiment Illinois Volunteers.[1] Previous to the receipt of the papers referred to me by your order for investigation and report, I had received duplicates of same, sent direct by Col. Burgess, and upon which I made the following endorsement:

> "Head Quarters, Dist. of West Ten.
> Corinth, July 21st 1862
>
> Respectfully refered to Gen. Head Quarters, with the recommendation that Col. Burgess be released from arrest, and restored to duty with his regiment.
>
> In this case charges were forwarded to Dept. Hd Qrs. but returned to Dist. Hd Qrs. owing to the absence of a newspaper an article in which was made a part of the specification. This deficiency was supplied and all returned to Department Head Quarters since which no action has been taken. The enclosed would show that the attempt has been made to communicate with these Head Quarters, through the proper channel, but unsuccessfully.
>
> U. S. Grant
> Maj. Gen."[2]

and after the same had been forwarded to Dept. Hd. Qrs. those referred to by you were received, upon which I placed endorsement referring to the one made on those received from Col. Burgess. In a few days those containing my first were returned to me, with the following endorsement of Brig. Gen. W. Scott Ketchum A. Inspector General:

> "Although this officer pledges his word he will tender his resignation—neither resignation nor charges are filed in this office   neither is there any record of a trial filed here
>
> W. Scott Ketchum
> Brig Genl
> A I Genl"[3]

About the same time I received a communication signed by the officers of the 18th Regiment, asking that Col. Burgess be relieved from arrest, and stating his willingness to resign as a condition of release.[4]

Thereupon, I released Col. Burgess from arrest and ordered him to rejoin his Regiment, at Jackson, Tenn. (which he has done) a copy of which order and accompanying letter are herewith enclosed.[5]

> I am, General
> Very Respectfully
> Your Obt. Servt.
> U. S. GRANT
> Major General.

LS, DNA, RG 94, Vol. Service Branch, Letters Received; copies, *ibid.*, RG 393, USG Hd. Qrs. Correspondence; DLC-USG, V, 4, 5, 7, 8, 88.

1. On Aug. 21, 1862, Maj. Gen. Henry W. Halleck telegraphed to USG. "No report from you in the case of Lt Col Thos. H. Burgess 18th Ill. vols on file. Send a duplicate" ALS (telegram sent), DNA, RG 107, Telegrams Collected (Bound). Lt. Col. Thomas H. Burgess, 18th Ill., was arrested in Dec., 1861. See letters to Capt. John C. Kelton and to Brig. Gen. John A. McClernand, Dec. 24, 1861. On June 22, 1862, David T. Linegar, postmaster at Cairo, wrote to U.S. Senator Lyman Trumbull. "Enclosed I send you the petition of Thos H Burgess Lieut Col of the 18th Ills Reg. . . . You will see that his letter demanding a copy of the charges was not sent to Gen Grant as it should have been, but Col Burgess notified that the charges were forwarded to Gen Grant and that no copy had been retained. The letter of Major Eaton was properly started but was turned back by Gen McClernand. Now as I under stand the Army regulation all communications pass up throug the different grades of the comand untill it reaches the proper department   Col Burgess has addressed Gen Grant direct and has been notified that it must come throug Gen McClernand. Now that being the case when will Col Burgess get a hearing. If he addresses Gen McClernand it is turned back on the grond that the matter belongs to Gen Grant   If he addresses Gen Grant he can not recogenize it because it does not come to him according to regulations The order restricting his limits to the city and camps of Cairo was isued just two days before the Army marched for Tenn—And was no doubt issued to deprive him and ~~Col~~ Major Eaton of the poor privlage of ~~following~~ following their Reg— as prisoners. Major Eaton was releised a few days before the battle at Shiloh and fell mortaly wounded in that hard fought engagement—If you can I hope you will urge the Secretary of War until he will movve in this matter" ALS, DLC-Lyman Trumbull. On July 2, Trumbull referred to Secretary of War Edwin M. Stanton a petition asking for a speedy trial for Burgess. DNA, RG 107, Register of Letters Received. On July 17, Burgess wrote to Maj. John A. Rawlins. "I beg leave to inform you that I Still at Cairo under arrest upon certain charges and specifications preferred against me on 24th Dec last   I would again most respetfully ask that I may be furnished with a copy of the charges and that a trial be granted me with out delay if not incompatible with the good of the Service or that I be released from arrest and permitted to join my regiment   Should the Commanding General deem my continuance in arrest for the good of the Service I

request that my limits be changed so that I may be in DuQuoin Perry County Ills—that being my residence and having there the means of living while deprived of my pay as an officer" ALS, *ibid.*, RG 94, Carded Records, Vol. Organizations, Civil War, 18th Ill., Thomas H. Burgess. Burgess enclosed a letter addressed to USG reviewing his efforts to be tried or released. Copy, *ibid.*

2. The text of USG's endorsement has been inserted from the original. AES, *ibid.*

3. The text of this endorsement has been inserted from the original. AES, *ibid.* William S. Ketchum of Conn., USMA 1834, held the rank of maj., 4th Inf., on the eve of the Civil War. He was confirmed as brig. gen. on Feb. 3, 1862, while serving as act. inspector-gen., Dept. of the Mo.

4. On July 16, Maj. Gen. John A. McClernand referred to USG a petition of twenty-three officers of the 18th Ill. asking the release of Burgess, who had promised to resign if released. DS, *ibid.*

5. On Aug. 1, Rawlins wrote to Burgess informing him that he was released from arrest "with no view of having you withdraw from the service." Copy, *ibid.*, Vol. Service Branch, Letters Received. On the same day, Rawlins issued Special Orders No. 150 ordering Burgess's release and instructing him to return to his regt. at Jackson, Tenn. DS, *ibid.*, District of West Tenn., Special Orders; copies, *ibid.*, Vol. Service Branch, Letters Received; *ibid.*, RG 393, USG Special Orders; DLC-USG, V, 15, 16, 82, 87. Burgess tendered his resignation on Aug. 14. ALS, DNA, RG 94, Carded Records, Vol. Organizations, Civil War, 18th Ill., Thomas H. Burgess. On Aug. 16, USG endorsed this letter. "Respectfully forwarded to Head Quarters of the Department." ES, *ibid.* The resignation was accepted on Sept. 3.

To Julia Dent Grant

Corinth, August 22d 1862

DEAR JULIA,

Since my letter of three or four days ago I have but little news to write about. You have probably seen that Col. Mason of the 71st Ohio, the man who was sent away on account of bad conduct at Shiloh,[1] surrendered Clarkesville without firing a gun,[2] also that the Guerrillas captured two steamers on the Tennessee.[3]—About sixty of our troops had a fight with a party of about three times their numbers of Kentucky recruits trying to join the rebels and drove them into the Tennessee killing 37 and taking 14 prisoners besides all their arms and many of their horses.[4]

We have had several little figh[ts] since you left resulting favorabl[y] to our troops and one night alarm, [h]ere.

Rawlins is confined to his bed and is likely to be so for so long a time that I have ordered him home until he is able to take the field again.[5] Bowers will have to take his place during his absence.

I have just received three letters from home one from father, one from Mary and one to you from Alice Tweed[6] which I enclose with this. From fathers letter they are very anxious to have Jess. He asks in all earnestness to let Jess. go to Covington to stay altogether. He says tell him that he will give him a house and lot in the City if he will go

Remember me to your Pa, and all at home. Kisses for yourself and the children.

Ulys.

ALS, DLC-USG.

1. See letter to Brig. Gen. William T. Sherman, April 15, 1862.
2. See telegram to Maj. Gen. Henry W. Halleck, Aug. 22, 1862.
3. See telegram to Maj. Gen. Henry W. Halleck, Aug. 21, 1862.
4. See telegram to Maj. Gen. Henry W. Halleck, Aug. 20, 1862.
5. On Aug. 22, 1862, Maj. John A. Rawlins issued Special Orders No. 171. "In pursuance of Special authority from Adjutant General's Office, Washington, D. C. dated July 28th, 1862, leave of absence for twenty days, is hereby granted to Major John A Rawlins, Asst. Adjt. Genl, District of West. Tenn. of which he is now permitted to take the benefit." DS, DNA, RG 94, Special Orders, District of West Tenn.; copies, *ibid.*, RG 393, USG Special Orders; DLC-USG, V, 15, 16, 82, 87. On Aug. 29, at a dinner held at Galena, Ill., Rawlins delivered an hour-long speech in defense of USG. *Galena Daily Advertiser*, Aug. 30, 1862.
6. See letter to Julia Dent Grant, May 16, 1862, note 2.

To Col. Robert Allen

By Telegraph from Grants Hd Qrs. [*Aug.*] 23 186[2]

To Gen'l Robt Allen
Chief Q M

At present the Tennessee is not reliable for sending up supplies   They railroad is abundantly able to do it. I will have the Tennessee open in a few days & the Cumberland as far as

Clarksville   I wish I was able to order you to prepare three 3 light draft steamers made proof against musketry & two how-itzers each to navigate the rivers   I have not guard to be spared from Cairo or Paducah to accompany boats   hope to have in a few days   I will instruct Comdg officer at Paducah always to furnish them

U. S GRANT,
Maj Genl

Telegram received, Lewis B. Parsons Papers, IHi. On Aug. 23, 1862, Col. Robert Allen, St. Louis, telegraphed to USG. "The steamer Lake City loaded with army stores bound for Eastport is detained at Paducah   the steamer Lacon left here last night & will be delayed at Cairo   cant these boats go up the Tenn' River with a suitable guard   Please give orders to the Q M at Paducah & Cairo. in future can we rely on the Rail Road to keep your army supplied"   Telegram received, DNA, RG 393, Dept. of the Mo., Telegrams Received; copies, *ibid.*, USG Hd. Qrs. Correspondence; DLC-USG, V, 7. On Aug. 24, Brig. Gen. James M. Tuttle, Cairo, telegraphed to USG. "Steamer Lacon here with Gov't F'rt   I have orders from Gen Halleck through Maj McClean A A G to send her on to Hamburg with guard   I have no men here or in district that can go. Guerrillas all around crossed river last night above Mound City are threatning Smithland have sent all troops away from this place   Col Ransom in command at Paducah. What shall I do with Boat"   Telegram received, DNA, RG 393, Dept. of the Mo., Telegrams Received.

To Maj. Gen. Henry W. Halleck

─────────

Gen Grants Hd Qrs [*Aug.*] 25th [*1862*]

MAJ GEN H. W. HALLECK
GEN IN CHIEF—

Scouts in from the front report all quiet—Rebels are getting out Timber to build Bridges—Think the main force has gone east & have not stopped short of Virginia. One Division sent word is on forced march to Nashville—The other is pushing on to Decherd.[1]

U S GRANT
Maj Genl

Telegram received, DNA, RG 94, Generals' Papers and Books, Telegrams
Received by Gen. Halleck; *ibid.*, RG 107, Telegrams Collected (Bound); copy,
ibid., Telegrams Received in Cipher. *O.R.*, I, xvii, part 2, 186. On Aug. 25, 1862,
Brig. Gen. William S. Rosecrans, Iuka, telegraphed to USG. "Granger's scouts
in   all quiet at front—Very small cavalry forces formed at Marietta and bay
springs   Scouts from Below only say the same as before—Pickets come up to
guntown   rebels say they are getting out timber to build bridges—one or two
captives left Tupello after months of imprisonment says they are mostly moved
away from Tuppillo that there are three 3 divisions at Guntown & saltillo   did
not see them   did see a field filled with graves in a very short time—Says thier
soldiers look thin   nothing but guerrillas on our Alabama front under a con-
fedate major named Roddy   they are plunderers from the valley where property
must be confisticated   Telegram from Bull head quarters at Dechurd forwarded
by courier from Jonesboro orders mitchells division by forced marches to Nashville & paines to Decherd   dispatch four days old—Mitchell left florence this
morning—Paine is crossing   Have scouts out towards columbus—I am strongly
impressed with the belief they are all gone east and bull will be badly fooled
man—" Telegram received, DNA, RG 393, Dept. of the Mo., Telegrams
Received; copy, *ibid.*, Army of the Miss., Telegrams Sent. On Aug. 23, Brig.
Gen. Gordon Granger, Rienzi, telegraphed to USG. "Scouts returned yesterday
from Marietta & Bay springs & today from near Ripley by 2 routes obtained no
information of the Enemy—last news rec'd was that Price was advancing slowly,
to Saltillo   I beleive there is nothing worth noticing in our front   the country
is suffering greatly from drouth—" Telegram received, *ibid.*, Dept. of the Mo.,
Telegrams Received.

1. On Aug. 25, hd. qrs. of Maj. Gen. Don Carlos Buell were at Decherd,
Tenn., about seventy-eight miles southeast of Nashville. *O.R.*, I, xvi, part 2,
416–17.

To Maj. Gen. John A. McClernand

By Telegraph from Corinth [*Aug. 25*] 186[*2*]

To Maj Gen McClernand
    by directions just received from Maj. Gen Halleck you will
report Springfield Ills, and assist, Govnor Yates in the organaza-
ton of volunteers, turn over your command to Brig Gen J A
Logan if he has not left   if he has to Gen Ross[1]

                                    U S Grant
                                    Maj Gen Comdg

Telegram received, McClernand Papers, IHi. On July 9, 1862, Maj. Gen. John A. McClernand wrote to U.S. Representative Elihu B. Washburne asking to be sent to Richmond with the 1st and 2nd divisions, Army of the Tenn. ALS, DLC-Elihu B. Washburne. He included a petition of the same date to the Senate and House of Representatives asking to be sent to reinforce Maj. Gen. George B. McClellan. DS, *ibid.* On Aug. 19, Governor Richard Yates of Ill. wrote to McClernand that he had requested the War Dept. to detail McClernand for duty in Ill. ALS, McClernand Papers, IHi. On Aug. 20, Maj. Gen. Henry W. Halleck wrote to McClernand. "Your application of the 12th inst to the President for a leave of absence has been referred to me. The War Dept has directed that under existing circumstances no leaves of absence be granted except in extraordinary cases. Since this order was issued I have refused leaves to all applications from officers in Genl Grant's army & I cannot make your case an exception. Permit me, Genl, to call your attention to the fact that in sending this application directly to the President, instead of transmitting it through the prescribed channels, you have violated the Army Regulations. This is not the first instance of the kind, for I remember to have reminded you of this Regulation some months ago. Unless officers observe the Regulations themselves how can they enforce their observ-a[nce] upon others? A young officer was a few weeks ago tried by a court martial & sentenced to be dismissed, for precisely the same thing as this. Are Major Genls less bound by the law & Regulations than their subordinate" ALS, DNA, RG 108, Letters Sent (Press). On Aug. 25, Halleck telegraphed to USG. "Genl J. A. McClernand will repair to Springfield, Ill & assist the Governor in organizing volunteers." ALS (telegram sent), *ibid.*, RG 107, Telegrams Collected (Bound); copies, *ibid.*, RG 393, Dept. of the Tenn., Telegrams Received; *ibid.*, USG Hd. Qrs. Correspondence; DLC-USG, V, 4, 5, 7, 8, 9, 88. *O.R.*, I, xvii, part 2, 187. On Aug. 27, 1st Lt. Theodore S. Bowers issued Special Orders No. 174 ordering McClernand to Springfield, "to assist in organizing Vols." DS, DNA, RG 94, Special Orders, District of West Tenn.; copies, *ibid.*, RG 393, USG Special Orders; DLC-USG, V, 15, 16, 82, 87; McClernand Papers, IHi.

1. On Aug. 26, McClernand telegraphed to USG. "I send the above communication from Genl Logan. Gen Ross could return if Telegraphed by you by the time I get ready to leave—" The telegram from Brig. Gen. John A. Logan was undated. "I recd a telegraph from Corinth yesterday with leave of absence for six days. I have been compelled to ask this on account of family troubles that are of serious nature I leave this morning on the up train having turned over the command of this post to Col Lawler. Will return at the earliest practible moment" Telegram received, DNA, RG 393, Dept. of the Mo., Telegrams Received; copy, McClernand Papers, IHi. On Aug. 26, Col. Clark B. Lagow, Jackson, Tenn., telegraphed to USG. "Gen McClernand will leave here tomorrow. Gen Ross thought back from Corinth today Gen Logan had not left Will leave tomorrow. Had not better Genl Ross be the commdr in his absence. Col Crocker is commdr at Bolivar" Telegram received, DNA, RG 393, Dept. of the Mo., Telegrams Received. On Aug. 28, Brig. Gen. Leonard F. Ross, Jackson, telegraphed to USG. "Having assumed command of this district I await your orders—" Telegram received, *ibid.* On Aug. 30, Logan, Carbondale, Ill., telegraphed to USG. "My family & affairs generally are now in such a situation that if an extension of my leave is not granted deletirious result will follow if I am compelled to make a sacrifice by returning on monday an injustice will be done

me   I therefore beg of you to grant me an extension of at least a week or ten (10) days longer or have it done—" Telegram received, *ibid.*, RG 94, Generals' Papers and Books, John A. Logan. On Aug. 31, USG telegraphed to Logan. "you can remain a week longer, but your services are much needed—" Copy, *ibid.*

To Maj. Gen. Henry W. Halleck

Gen Grants Hd Qrs
Aug 26th 11 30 A M 1862

MAJ GEN H. W. HALLECK
GEN IN CHIEF.

Your dispatch about Cotton has been so mutulated in transmission that it is not understood—All Cotton seized by Gov.t is sold by Qr Master for the concern—Names of claimants & amount received kept so that claims can hereafter be settled by proper Tribunal

U. S. GRANT
Maj Genl

Telegram received, DNA, RG 94, Generals' Papers and Books, Telegrams Received by Gen. Halleck; copies, *ibid.*, RG 107, Telegrams Collected (Bound); *ibid.*, Telegrams Received in Cipher; *ibid.*, RG 393, USG Hd. Qrs. Correspondence; DLC-USG, V, 4, 5, 7, 8, 9, 88. *O.R.*, I, xvii, part 2, 188. On Aug. 25, 1862, Maj. Gen. Henry W. Halleck telegraphed to USG. "The secretary of war directs that you sieze in the name of the united states all cotton purchased or shipped by officers or men in the military service of the united states, and turn the same over to the Quartermaster's Dept to be sold on account of whomsoever it may concern" ALS (telegram sent), DNA, RG 107, Telegrams Collected (Bound); copies, *ibid.*, RG 94, Generals' Papers and Books, Telegrams Received by Gen. Buell; *ibid.*, RG 393, USG Hd. Qrs. Correspondence; DLC-USG, V, 4, 5, 7, 8, 9, 88. *O.R.*, I, xvii, part 2, 185; *ibid.*, III, ii, 453–54. On Aug. 27, Halleck telegraphed to USG. "My dispatch of the 25th is repeated   its object is to prevent officers & men in the Gov't service from trading in cotton on their private account   the Seccy of War directs that you seize in the name of the United States all cotton purchased & shipped by Officers or men in the military service of the U.S. & turn the same over to the Q M dep't to be sold on account of whom soever it may concern—" Telegram received, DNA, RG 393, Dept. of the Tenn., Telegrams Received; copies, *ibid.*, USG Hd. Qrs. Correspondence; DLC-USG, V, 4, 5, 7, 8, 9, 88. *O.R.*, I, xvii, part 2, 189.

On Aug. 30, 1st Lt. Theodore S. Bowers issued General Orders No. 79. "In future, all Officers and Soldiers of the Army, and all persons in any way connected with the Military Service of the United States, are positively prohibited from engaging in the purchase of Cotton or other products of Southern States, with the view of shipping the same to market. Where such purchases are made, it is the duty of the Commanding officer of the Post or troops to seize the same in the name of the United States and turn it over to the Quartermaster's Department, to be sold for the benefit of whom it may concern. All Officers and Soldiers are enjoined to report every case where there is reasonable grounds to suppose that the provisions of this Order, are being violated, to the end that an investigation may be had to establish the guilt or innocence of suspected parties." Copies, DLC-USG, V, 12, 13, 14, 95; DNA, RG 393, USG General Orders.

On Aug. 25, Halleck telegraphed to Maj. Gen. William T. Sherman. "While it is our object at present to get possession of as much cotton as possible, such contraband articles as salt, military stores, medicines, &c., must be excluded. The interior trade must be under the entire control of the military commander. I will write you more fully to-day." ALS (telegram sent), *ibid.*, RG 107, Telegrams Collected (Bound). *O.R.*, III, ii, 454.

On Aug. 29, L. M. Flourney, Paducah, telegraphed to Maj. John A. Rawlins. "Myself & several other citizens of this place have large amounts of Cotton at sevaral landings on Tenn River we desire to have permission for Steamer Collonna to go up for it" Telegram received, DNA, RG 393, Dept. of the Mo., Telegrams Received. On Aug. 29, Brig. Gen. William S. Rosecrans telegraphed to USG. "I have rec'd an important letter from Maj Miner Gov Sprauges agt saying that he is informed that Persons are moving his cotton at Iuka & Tuscumbia I did not know he had any cotton in particular I understood that when in compliance with your orders the cotton being collected at Iuka & other points was shipped to Capt Reynolds the captain would permit maj Miner as Gov Spragues Agt to have between three & four hundred bales delivered at Columbus at thirty cents per pound—All cotton belonging to the Govt has been shipped from this place & others on the line or is now on hand except fifty three (53) bales left here in a damaged condition & sold by your permission at thirty 30 cts per pound here—It appears that this man miner has got from Reynolds & others some 6 or 7 hundred bales & yet is talking of his cotton & specifing a lot taken from mann that he says was the first brough[t] into Iuka & probably the first sent forward—after his coming to my head Quarters & saying he would give for all cotton the government would have for sale as much as any other party & after my intercession for him that he might have the cotton we had been led to estimate at from three (3) hundred (300) to four hundred (400) bales at 30 cts his attempt to lengthen out the Qantity by claiming partiular lots dont look well—" Telegram received, *ibid.*; copy, *ibid.*, Army of the Miss., Telegrams Sent. On Aug. 25, Halleck wrote to Governor William Sprague of R.I. that orders had been issued to give cotton traders all facilities "consistent with military police and operations." *O.R.*, III, ii, 460.

To Maj. Gen. Henry W. Halleck

———

Cairo Ill [*Corinth, Aug.*] 28 [*1862*]

MAJ GENL H W HALLECK.

GEN.

Two divisions have gone to Buell & two more are expected to guard the line of Railroad[1]   without sending these I do not see how I am to further reinforce him[2]

U. S. GRANT
Maj Genl

Telegram received, DNA, RG 94, Generals' Papers and Books, Telegrams Received by Gen. Halleck; copies, *ibid.*, RG 393, USG Hd. Qrs. Correspondence; DLC-USG, V, 4, 5, 7, 8, 9, 88. *O.R.*, I, xvii, part 2, 189. On Aug. 28, 1862, Maj. Gen. Henry W. Halleck telegraphed to USG. "Genl Buell asks for reinforcements   you will give him all the assistance you can spare." ALS (telegram sent), DNA, RG 107, Telegrams Collected (Bound); telegram received, *ibid.*, RG 393, Dept. of the Tenn., Telegrams Received. *O.R.*, I, xvii, part 2, 189.

1. On Aug. 24, Brig. Gen. William S. Rosecrans telegraphed to USG. "Report from Col Roberts give details of destruction of train day before yesterday at one mile from Trinity   Eleven (11) companies of Rodds rebel cavalry appeared at that point where they had placed a rail across the track to throw the train off   They suceeded in this   the guard accompanying under Lieut Granger who fought them bravely killed and wounded 25 of them & come off having lost 8 men   Reinforcements from Courtland hurried the Rebels & killed 4 more of them but before those reinforcements came the Rebels burned the train   no further news except that I am seeking routes & information to strike Columbus. it works well so far"   Telegram received, DNA, RG 393, Dept. of the Mo., Telegrams Received; copy, *ibid.*, RG 94, War Records Office, Union Battle Reports. *O.R.*, I, xvii, part 1, 36–37. On Aug. 27, Rosecrans telegraphed to USG. "Col Sheridan sends tonight one regt Cavalry to Hatchie crossing to dash onto Ripley at day light & then strikes the ripley & Fulton road 12 miles south of Ripley   the third (3d) with the battery & 2 Cos. infantry goes to Blackland & the cavalry advance on the rebel pickets towards Carrollville & Ellistown while ords Cavalry goes via Kossuth & Breckensville on the ripley & Pocohonta road & attacks Ripley from the north. The whole ~~river~~ ripley force then moves south and joins sheridan at Blackland. nothing espeial from Morgan except a Terribly grumbling letter at the misbehavior of Thomas troops at Courtland   Three Cos of our Cavalry had a skirmish with rebel Cavalry south west of Courtland in which we lost 23 killed wounded & missing   no further particulars except all safe"   Telegram received, DNA, RG 393, Dept. of the Mo., Telegrams Received. On Aug. 28, Maj. Gen. Edward O. C. Ord wrote to Maj. John A. Rawlins. "The Col 15th Michigan commanding at chewalla reports a force of from one to three hundred cavalry hovering around within three miles of his

post—and he asks for cavalry having nown—On account of the enemies Cavalry being in bodies from 150 to 1000 (by reports) on our flank and working around to the north—I have Videtted all roads leading from here—this leaves me just ~~enough~~ about Seventy five cavalry for the duty of scouting—as far as an attemp to send after the Enemys cavalry it is with this contemptable force simply absurd —and I beg beg leave to report to the Genl that if we aim to protect the Rail Road from Columbus from beig cut by the enemys cavalry now in its Vicinity it is absolutely necessary to have some cavalry force held ready at this place to meet or send after parties of the enemy reported by by Genl Granger and others to be about one thousand strong and making demonstrations, to capture our traines from the North" Copy, *ibid.*, 16th Army Corps, Post of Corinth, Letters Sent. On Aug. 29, Rosecrans telegraphed to USG. "With your approval I propose to cover the road to Decatur by the following dispositions. Eight (8) co's Infantry six (6) cavalry & a section of Artillery at Moulton the same five (5) at Russell-ville Four (4) co's Infantry & four (4) of Cavalry at Frankfort one Reg't from Tuscumbia to Decatur Two (2) at Tuscumbia that will require the lines— from here to be stretched a little towards Decatur—*Reasons*: The Valley in which these troops will be placed covers all the approaches to the Tennessee River the troops can hold it against all Guerrillas & they will be driven into the Mountains where corn is scarce—To attack a force will only give the better chance to retreat or concentrate a surprise would be no worse there than elsewhere—" Telegram received, *ibid.*, Dept. of the Mo., Telegrams Received; copy, *ibid.*, Army of the Miss., Telegrams Sent. *O.R.*, I, xvii, part 2, 191.

2. On Aug. 25, Halleck wrote to Maj. Gen. Horatio G. Wright that President Abraham Lincoln and Secretary of War Edwin M. Stanton were dissatisfied with the slowness of Maj. Gen. Don Carlos Buell. Copy, DNA, RG 108, Letters Sent. *O.R.*, I, xvi, part 2, 421. On Aug. 24, Buell telegraphed to Halleck inform-ing him of his situation and asking for more troops. Copy, Buell Papers, TxHR. *O.R.*, I, xvi, part 2, 406–7. On Aug. 25, Buell telegraphed to Halleck, asking again for more troops, and suggesting that some of the railroad line ought to be abandoned. Copy, DNA, RG 393, Dept. of the Ohio, Telegrams Sent. *O.R.*, I, xvi, part 2, 416–17. On the same day, Buell telegraphed to USG. "Bragg has crossed the River at Chattanooga & two other points above with a very heavy force can you do any thing to help us it should be done quickly can you not at least throw a division across into North Alabama I attach so much impor-tance to keeping up the occupancy there that I have left small force at I confess great risk to it notwithstanding the urgent necessity for concentrating ~~my~~ (every) man I have. By that means also our communications with each other are kept up —otherwise they cannot be. I have given up the line from Nashville to Decatur. In fact as my main force is getting further to the East it is not necessary for us. I am trying as I say to to hold the line from Decatur to Stevinson & thence to Nashville" Telegram received (mutilated), DNA, RG 393, Dept. of the Mo., Telegrams Received; copy, *ibid.*, Dept. of the Ohio, Telegrams Sent. *O.R.*, I, xvi, part 2, 417–18. On Aug. 27, Halleck telegraphed to Buell. "Yours of the 25th just received. Two divisions of Grants army were directed to report to you some time ago, & two more placed at Tuscumbia & Decatur as a reserve, if required. He has also sent troops to reoccupy clarksville & the Cumberland. I doubt if he can spare more, but will try. For want of cavalry, take all the horses you can find in the country & mount infantry." ALS (telegram sent), DNA, RG 107, Telegrams Collected (Bound).

To Maj. Gen. Henry W. Halleck

Gen Grants Hd. Qrs
Aug 29th 7. P.M 1862

Maj Gen H. W. Halleck
Gen in Chief.

Independent forces can be organized here & from here east to Decatur—Shall they be accepted & received into the service? I am only in favor of it when they go into our old organizations

U. S. Grant
Maj Genl

Telegram received, DNA, RG 94, Generals' Papers and Books, Telegrams Received by Gen. Halleck; copies, *ibid.*, RG 107, Telegrams Collected (Bound); *ibid.*, Telegrams Received in Cipher; *ibid.*, RG 393, USG Hd. Qrs. Correspondence; DLC-USG, V, 4, 5, 7, 8, 9, 88. *O.R.*, I, xvii, part 2, 191; *ibid.*, III, ii, 487. On Sept. 1, 1862, Maj. Gen. Henry W. Halleck telegraphed to USG. "You are authorized to enlist in Tenn. into old regiments"   ALS (telegram sent), DNA, RG 107, Telegrams Collected (Bound); telegram received (dated Sept. 6), *ibid.*, RG 393, Dept. of the Tenn., Telegrams Received. *O.R.*, III, ii, 496.

On July 30, Thomas Maxwell, William H. Cherry and three other citizens of Savannah, Tenn., wrote to USG asking for military protection of their neighborhood until troops could be raised in the area. ALS, DNA, RG 108, Letters Received. On Aug. 5, USG forwarded the letter to hd. qrs., Dept. of the Miss. "Respectfully forwarded to Head Quarters of the Dept. Savannah is not Geographically within my command. I think however these people should have protection at least until they are ready and able to defend themselvs." AES, *ibid.* On Aug. 20, Maj. Gen. John A. McClernand telegraphed to Governor Andrew Johnson that Fielding Hurst had raised one company of cav., and McClernand believed that more could be raised. Telegram received, DLC-Andrew Johnson. On Aug. 29, Col. Isham N. Haynie, Bethel, telegraphed to USG. "I have here in my command nearly 2 hunded men able for duty who are without arms   this includes fifty (50) tennessee troops here   I have tried for weeks to get them cannot I have them ordered to me at once"   Telegram received, DNA, RG 393, Dept. of the Tenn., Telegrams Received. On the same day, Brig. Gen. Leonard F. Ross, Jackson, telegraphed to USG. "We have on hand here a large number of arms taken from citizens   with some repairs they will answer very well to arm our Tenn troops   where shall I send them for repairs"   Telegram received, *ibid.*, Dept. of the Mo., Telegrams Received.

Also on Aug. 29, Brig. Gen. William S. Rosecrans telegraphed to Maj. John A. Rawlins. "I have no doubt that the poverty & destuticn of the mountaineers in Northern alabama is such that we could raise a large force for border service   They appear to desire an organization as alabama troops—I have suggested to them the possibility of being at once organizend as Tenn troops   it is the opinion of Col Misener that this will not effect the purpose—Could you not obtain authority from War Dept to organize ala & miss. regts—I think the mesure should be promptly taken in hand or the people will be driven by want into brigandage" Telegram received, *ibid.*; copy, *ibid.*, Army of the Miss., Telegrams Sent. *O.R.*, I, xvii, part 2, 191. On the same day, Rosecrans telegraphed again to USG. "Nothing from Buell—Will give these mississippi & alabama boys an opportunity to go into the cavalry—there is no doubt but what on 23d the troops in Jackson were in a great state of excitement & Van Dorn under orders for Vicksburg where they had learned that there was a federal fleet of 8 Gun Bots & forty 40 transports landing at the mouth of the yazoo" Telegram received, DNA, RG 393, Dept. of the Mo., Telegrams Received; copy, *ibid.*, Army of the Miss., Telegrams Sent. *O.R.*, I, xvii, part 2, 191.

On Sept. 9, Rosecrans telegraphed to USG. "Have between two & three hundred Alabamans and Mississippians who have fled or been run off from their homes. They wish to enter the Union Army. Some have gone into the old Regiments but these remain and more are coming. Buell has four companies of the 1st alabama. Cant you have others of the same or of the 2nd Ala organized under my direction? If not what do you say to the Col. of the 1st Miss. Col. Shannon shall we organize them under him. We must have arms for our regular recruits and these new men. Cant some spare muskets be picked up among your troops. Please do all you can for us and that soon." Copy, DNA, RG 393, Army of the Miss., Telegrams Sent. On Sept. 10, Rosecrans telegraphed to USG. "What do you say as to the gentlemen who have come to you to raise the Mississippi troops. Will they answer?" Copy, *ibid.* On Sept. 11, Halleck telegraphed to USG. "West Tenn volunteers can be mustered in for one year. Gov. Johnson was instructed to raise twelve months men." ALS (telegram sent), *ibid.*, RG 107, Telegrams Collected (Bound); copies (dated Sept. 10), *ibid.*, RG 393, Dept. of the Tenn., Telegrams Received; (dated Sept. 12) *ibid.*, USG Hd. Qrs. Correspondence; DLC-USG, V, 4, 5, 7, 8, 9, 88.

On Sept. 18, Rawlins issued Special Orders No. 198. "Capt. F. E. Prime, U. S. Army, chief of Engineer Dept. Dist of West Tenn. is hereby appointed Mustering Officer during the absence of the Commanding General from Corinth, and will muster into the service of the United States for twelve months, three years, or during the War all companies of Alabama Vols. presenting themselves for Muster, who would be received into the service elsewhere giving them the privilege of joining such Regts as they may select." DS, DNA, RG 94, Special Orders, District of West Tenn.; copies, *ibid.*, RG 393, USG Special Orders; DLC-USG, V, 15, 16, 82, 87. On Sept. 29, Rosecrans telegraphed to USG. "Captain Prime was authorized to muster in the Mississippians and Alabamians He considers his authority was limited to the time you were absent. Please order Captain Farrand U. S. A. to muster in all such levies as are willing to go in for twelve (12) months three (3) years or during the war." Copy, DNA, RG 393, Army of the Miss., Telegrams Sent.

On Sept. 13, USG wrote to Maj. Gen. Edward O. C. Ord. "Ordering rations to be issued to all Mississippians who swear into the new regiment being organized by Genl. Boswell." Stan. V. Henkels, Catalogue No. 1210, March 21, 1918. For the efforts made by Daniel K. Boswell, Corinth, Miss., to recruit a U.S. brigade in his home state, see Lincoln, *Works*, V, 456–57. On April 19, Boswell had written to Johnson about his concern for his family in Corinth, mentioning that he had written to USG, among others, on this subject. ALS, DLC-Andrew Johnson.

To Maj. Gen. Henry W. Halleck

———

Grants Head Quarters [*Aug.*] 31 [*1862*]

GENL HALLECK.

GENL.

The following dispatch is received from Bolivar, Tenn. Col Hogg[1] in command of twentieth. Twenty ninth Ohio infantry & some cavalry were attacked by about four thousand Rebels yesterday   our troops behaved well driving the enemy whose loss was over one hundred. Ours twenty five men killed & wounded Col Hogg being one of the number

U. S. GRANT.

Telegram received, DNA, RG 94, Generals' Papers and Books, Telegrams Received by Gen. Halleck; copies, *ibid.*, RG 393, USG Hd. Qrs. Correspondence; DLC-USG, V, 4, 5, 7, 8, 9, 88.

To create a diversion which would make it possible to link his forces with those of Maj. Gen. Earl Van Dorn for a major attack on USG's left, Maj. Gen. Sterling Price sent Act. Brig. Gen. Frank C. Armstrong north from Guntown, Miss., on Aug. 22, 1862. On Aug. 26, Armstrong reached the Coldwater River, where he was reinforced by troops under the command of Col. William H. Jackson. Armstrong then had a total of about 3,500 troops. On Aug. 29, they crossed the Memphis and Charleston Railroad at La Grange, Tenn., and spent the night within nine miles of Bolivar, Tenn. On Aug. 30, Armstrong's superior force contacted units under the command of Col. Mortimer D. Leggett. Leggett called for reinforcements, with whose help his troops were able to retreat behind the fortifications at Bolivar. Leggett stated that he had fewer than 900 men, and that his losses were 5 killed, 18 wounded, and 64 missing. *O.R.*, I, xvii, part 1, 46–49; Harbert L. Rice Alexander, "The Armstrong Raid Including the Battles of Bolivar, Medon Station and Britton Lane," *Tennessee Historical Quarterly*, XXI, 1 (March, 1962), 31–37; Albert Castel, *General Sterling Price and the Civil War in the West* (Baton Rouge, 1968), pp. 94–96. For reports of the engagement, see *O.R.*, I, xvii, part 1, 43–51.

On Aug. 27, Brig. Gen. William S. Rosecrans telegraphed to USG. "Your dispatch rcd.   can that be Prices movement   you remember his cannon went west of Tupelo" Telegram received, DNA, RG 393, Dept. of the Mo., Telegrams Received. On Aug. 27, Rosecrans telegraphed to USG. "Granger telegraphs: 'My impression is that Genl Armstrong is march in on Humboldt Tenn. or some point in that vacinity. He left Gun Town with seven to nine regiments with ten days rations and a small wagon train on last Friday   He is marching on a road some distance West of here, and that attack yesterday was intended to cover his movements. The Companies belonging to Arkansas, Tenn. and Miss regts after arriving at Ripley marched West to a point between Salem and Holly Springs, then turned about, joined Falkner, and came here. Lookout for the R.R.'

I have forwarded the dispatches to Buell and Paine, and thence they will go by carrier" Copy, *ibid.*, Army of the Miss., Telegrams Sent. On Aug. 28, Brig. Gen. Gordon Granger, Rienzi, telegraphed to USG. "Information recd from prisoner yesterday & today confirms the report that armstrong is moving on Humboldt or vicinty with 6 thousand (6000) cavalry—" Telegram received, *ibid.*, Dept. of the Mo., Telegrams Received. On Aug. 27, Col. Isham N. Haynie, Bethel, Tenn., telegraphed to Maj. John A. Rawlins. "At What point & When did the cavalry pass north of Memphis & Charleston R.R. Will look after them" Telegram received, *ibid.* On Aug. 28, USG telegraphed to 1st Lt. James Wilson, Bolivar. "It is reported that a rebel force of 6,000 cavalry have been sent to attack our lines. Keep a sharp lookout." *O.R.*, I, xvii, part 2, 190. On Aug. 30, Haynie telegraphed to Rawlins. "one cavalry co in addition to those we have here it is absolutely necessary—Please send them immediately we have co here but their horses are poor & used up & they are poorly equipped" Telegram received, DNA, RG 393, Dept. of the Tenn., Telegrams Received. On Aug. 30, Brig. Gen. Leonard F. Ross, Jackson, Tenn., wrote to USG. "All is quiet within this command so far as I can learn. You will observe, however, from the communication addressed by Col. Dennis to Col. Lawler (a copy of which is herewith enclosed) that the Enemy is reported to be advancing towards LaGrange. If they advance within striking distance of Bolivar, with a force not larger than ours, had I not better send out and attack them? The arms I telegraphed you about are all unfit for use and I have ordered them sent forward to St. Louis for repairs. A large number of troops reported 'absent without leave' at the muster of the 18th Inst. are returning to their commands.—What shall be done with them? How shall they be reported on the next Muster-Rolls. There are is at Bolivar quite a number of soldiers, who have, at different times, been taken prisoners and paroled by the Enemy—can they be exchanged here, or should they be forwarded to Benton Barracks? Since I came here I have met many of the Citizens of Brownsville. They are all quite anxious that a force should be stationed there, to aid them until they can organize for their own defence. I have thought it bad policy to send a force there, unless it can *stay there* until an organization of the citizens can be perfected, and I do not feel that we have the force to spare at present. We have two Regiments at Estinaula, eight miles South East from Brownsville. If the new troops could come forward and guard the Rail-Road and occupy our fortifications, we could then, if thought advisable, send our old troops out to assist those unprotected points. I have promised to station a force at Brownsville, within the next ten days, if practicable—Is it probable that the number of troops in this command will be increased within that time? Our fortifications at Bolivar are nearly completed—Can we have two or three pieces of heavy Ordnance to place in them when finished?" ALS, *ibid.*, District of West Tenn., Letters Received. On the same day, Ross telegraphed to USG. "A Dispatch just rec'd from Col Crocker comdg at Bolivar reports a large force of Infantry & Cavalry approaching that place on Grand Junction to Middlebury Road he has drawn their cavalry back from his picket lines & skirmishing is now going on—" Telegram received, *ibid.*, Dept. of the Mo., Telegrams Received. On the same day, Ross telegraphed to USG. "I have just rec'd the following from Col Crocker at Bolivar. Col Leggett was sent out this morning about 9 nine oclock with his brigade and Six 6 companies of cavalry and one Section of artilery has been Skirmishing ever since Several have been killed—Col Leggett has sent in for reinforcements I have sent him three 3 regiments—He is out about four 4 miles if hard pushed he will fall back to report—The force of rebels about 4,000 Cavalry'. . . I have no fears as to the result" Telegram received, *ibid.*

Also on Aug. 30, Ross wrote to USG. "Hearing by telegraph of the engagement with the Enemy below this place, I took the evening train and arrived here at 6 Oclock this evening. I have just had the following report of the days work, from Col. Crocker, of the 13th Iowa Vol., who was in command :—. . . I am proud of my command here;—the officers and men, from all accounts, acted most gallantly." ALS, *ibid.*, RG 94, War Records Office, Union Battle Reports. The telegram of Col. Marcellus M. Crocker is in *O.R.*, I, xvii, part 1, 45–46.

On Aug. 31, Ross telegraphed to USG. "I left Bolivar this a m at 7½ being satisfied that there is no desire on the part of the Rebels to renew the fight. Their Genl supposed to be Armstrong is reported killed—Col Hogg fell leading his men in a gallant Sabre charge & is supposed to be killed   my impression is that their force have divided for the purpose of scouring the country south on the Hatchee—" Telegram received, DNA, RG 393, Dept. of the Mo., Telegrams Received. On Aug. 31, Rosecrans telegraphed to USG. "Mizners men captured mail 25 miles south of Russellville. Carrier, son of Col Hughes 27th Alabama, left Chattanooga 24th 5 P. M. Bragg 2½ miles north of Chattanooga. Forces 70,000, intends moving on Nashville. His advance 8 miles from Buells moves without tents only one wagon for 100 men on short rations : Hardee second in command—Beauregard not there. Report of Buells repulse in Mobile papers of Tuesday not true. Your good news of the Bolivar fight received. Granger told to see what he can do, about as much surprised at the capture as the companies themselves—Hope they will be thoroughly smashed.—give me word if they attempt to run-back this side of Corinth. Have ordered remedy at Tuscumbia." Copy, *ibid.*, Army of the Miss., Telegrams Sent. On Sept. 7, Ross wrote to Rawlins giving a full report of the operation and others connected with the Armstrong raid. ALS, *ibid.*, RG 94, War Records Office, Union Battle Reports. *O.R.*, I, xvii, part 1, 44–45. On Sept. 13, USG forwarded Ross's report to hd. qrs. of the army. AES, DNA, RG 94, War Records Office, Union Battle Reports.

1. All of the copies of this telegram retained by USG read "Leggett" rather than "Hogg."

Report on Shiloh

———

[*Aug.–Sept., 1862?*]

I cannot close this report without paying particular attention to the report of Brig. Gen (now Maj. Gen.) Nelson, commanding the 4th Division of the Army of the Ohio. Not having seen the report until within a few days attention could not be paid it before.—The report is a tissue of unsupported romance from begining to end some of which I will point out.—Gen. Nelson says that "~~he~~ I left Savanna at 1.30 p.m. on Sunday the 6th by my order, reiterated by Gen. Buell." My order was given Gen. Nelson not later than 7 O'clock, must have reached him not later than that hour, and was accompanied by a guide to show him the road. If not much mistaken the most of his Division must have been on the march before the arrival of Gen. Buell at Savanna. To say the least he showed great want of promptness in not leaving Savanna until 1.30 p.m. after receiving my orders and they given at so early an hour.

In the second paragraph four days are mentioned as the time consumed in making the march over most dreadful roads resulting from previously overflowed bottoms. Four hours were probably intended. Taking this charitable view of the matter the head of his column had made the distance from Savanna to Pittsburg Landing, had made the difficult ferrage at that point and were marching up the bank in just 30 minuets less time than the Gen.'s own statements show, that through great exertion, and anxiety to participate in a battle which they heard raging, took to march up the East bank of the river.

The fire of the rebel artillery began to reach the landing after the head of Gen. Nelsons column had assended the hill at Pittsburg Landing.

The semicircle of artillery spoken of had been established at an early hour in the day and were not unsupported at any time. The left of the artillery spoken of was not turned at any time and the abrupt nature of the ground and depth of backwater in the slew immediately in front of the artillery would have completely checked any attempt at such a movement. The gunners never fled from their pieces.

The Gen. shows great fluancy in guessing at the large numbers he found cowering under the river bank when he crossed placing the number at from 7000 to 10,000. I cannot see that he was called on to make any report in this matte[r] but if he did he should have informed himself somewhat of the necessity of men taking that position. He should recollect that large armies had been engaged in a terrible conflict all day compared with which the second days fight was mere childs play, and that the wounded were habitually carried back to the bank of the river. With them necessarily had to come men as nurses and supports who were not injured. This made a very large number; nearly equal to the Generals speculation who were back there lagitimately. In this I do not wish to shield the conduct of many who behaved badly and left the field on the first fire. Some excuse is to be found for them however, in the fact that they were perfectly raw having reached the ground but a few days before and having received their arms for the first time on their way to that scene of conflict.

Gen. Nelson claims to have directed Capt. Guinn of the gunboat service to throw an 8-inch shell in to the enemies camp every ten minuets during the night. This was great presumption in him if true his command being limited to a single division. The fact is I directed the gunboats to fire a shot into where we supposed the enemies camps to be every fifteen minuets and this is the order which was obeyed.

These are some of the glaring misstatements I would call attention. There are others with regard to who gave orders simply personal to myself which I abstain from noticing.

The statement of the killing of Gen. Johnson in front of the 4th Division of the Army of the Ohio on the 7th and of his body being in possession of the Federal troops might be mentioned. Southern official reports show that he was killed at about ½ past 2 O'clock on the day previous and was buried by his own friends.[1]

ADf, USG 3. USG provides the best clue for the date of this fragment by his reference to William Nelson as "now Maj. Gen." Nelson was confirmed as maj. gen. on July 17, and was killed on Sept. 29, 1862.

In answer to a U.S. Senate resolution of May 9, Secretary of War Edwin M. Stanton on June 27 submitted 116 official reports of Shiloh, printed as *SED*, 37–2–66. Nelson's report is included (pp. 173–75), containing the misprint of "days" for "hours" noted by USG in his second paragraph.

1. See telegram to Maj. Gen. Henry W. Halleck, April 8, 1862, note 1.

Calendar

1862, APRIL 1.   USG General Orders No. 31. "All officers command-ing companies of light artillery in this district will forthwith report to these Hd. Quarters the exact Condition of their respective Commands setting forth the number of enlisted men present for duty and their Knowledge and efficiency as artillerists the number of absentees (in-cluding officers) the length of time and by whose authority absent, the number Kind and Caliber of pieces, the number of Caissons and their Capacity, the number of rounds of ammunition, and other ordnance stores on hand, the number of artillery Horses fit for service, and the Condition of the artillery Harness in their possession   For any defi-ciency in material for outfits Requisition will be made on the proper departments immediately   All division Commanders with whose Command artillery is serving will see this order strictly complied with, the reports and returns must be sent in by Friday the 4th inst"—DS (Capt. John A. Rawlins), McClernand Papers, IHi.

1862, APRIL 1.   USG endorsement. "Before a requisition for Cavalry horses can be approved those first furnished must be accounted for. If they are worn out in service a Board of Survey should be called to examine and report upon their condition."—AES, NjP.

1862, APRIL 1.   Maj. Gen. Charles F. Smith to USG. "Respectfully forwarded to H Qrs D. W. T."—AES, DNA, RG 393, District of West Tenn., Letters Received. Written on a letter from Maj. Elbridge G. Ricker, 5th Ohio Cav., to Col. William H. H. Taylor, 5th Ohio Cav. "In accordance with your order, of to day, I marched at 2½ oclock P. M. on the road to Monterey with Two hundred men. Our pickets at the outpost informed me that the enemies pickets had been in sight for some time, and they thought them near at that time   We moved forward quickly and cautiously to the first house, where we found they had left about one hour before; Force estimated at two or three hun-dred; On examination of the horse tracks, am of the opinion their force was not quite equal to ours; We followed them for about three miles on the road to Monterey; When we discovered their rear guard, on Six in number, on a point some two hundred yards in advanc; We advanced quickly and exchanged Shots with them at Seventy five to one hundred yards; They fled, folowed by our advance guard, for half a mile when I recalled our advance, and took the road leading to the road leading to Owl Creek—As we entered the above named road, a half mile from the scene of action A fine Sorrel mare fully equiped for Cavalry met us and we secured her and brought her in We then moved quickly on the road to Veals examining all the roads and paths; Making no discoveries of fresh horse tracks. I am fully satisfied that there has been no movement of Cavalry in the vicinity of Veals or Gen. Meeks, for the last three days. There has been quite a stir of Cavalry between this camp & Monterey from the horse marks within the last three days"—ALS, *ibid.*

1862, APRIL 1.   Maj. Gen. Lewis Wallace to Capt. John A. Rawlins. "I enclose a report of a skirmish between our picket at Adamsville and a small body of the rebels, which resulted unfortunately for us. As the General will see, the officer reporting attributes the misfortune to a deficiency of arms. My opinion is, however, it was partly from that cause and partly from his bad management. Having, according to his own showing, but few arms, and the enemy being superior in number and armed with shot-guns, he ought either to have avoided a fight or charged pell-mell. What he says about the deficiency of arms, and its effect upon his men, I think worthy attention, and with that opinion, I beg to call the General's notice to it."—ALS, DNA, RG 94, War Records Office, Union Battle Reports. *O.R.*, I, x, part 1, 78. On the same day, Col. Charles R. Woods, 76th Ohio, wrote to Capt. Fred Knefler. "I have the honor to report that just at dark last evening the mounted Picket on the Purdy road was driven in by a superior mounted force of the enemy. There are three men missing & several horses wounded. I immediately sent forward two companies of Infantry to strengthen the Pickets & occupy the Purdy road, & hold the Enemy in check should he advance The advanced pickets (Infantry) report that there is great activity on the Rail Road in the direction of Purdy, six or seven trains having been heard to pass within a few hours Citizens Report to the Pickets that the Enemy have torn up all the bridges, from a point about four miles in advance to Purdy Enclosed Please find Report of Lieut C. H. Murray 5th O.V. Cavalry"—ALS, DNA, RG 393, District of West Tenn., Letters Received. The detailed report of 1st Lt. Charles H. Murray, 5th Ohio Cav., dated the same day, is in *O.R.*, I, x, part 1, 78–79.

1862, APRIL 2.   USG General Orders No. 33. "The Artillery and Cavalry of this Command will hereafter form a part of Divisions and not be attached to Brigades. The following assignments are hereby made. To the 1st Division Maj Genl. J. A. McClernand Comdg. four independent companies of Cavalry, one battalion of the 4th Ill Cavalry, Schwartzs, McAllisters, Burrows & Dressers batteries. To the 2d Division Maj Genl. C. F. Smith Comdg., two companies regular cavalry, two comps of 2d Ills cavalry and first battalion of 5th Ohio cavalry, Willards battery and three Missouri batteries under Maj Cavender. To the 3d Division Maj Genl L. Wallace Comdg., Bullis', Thompsons, Stones and Margroffs batteries, and the third battalion of the 11th Ill cavalry. To the 4th Division Brig. Genl. S. A. Hurlbut Comdg— Manns, Meyers & Ross batteries and 1st and 2d battalions of 5th Ohio Cavalry. To the 5th Division, Brig Genl. W. T. Sherman Comdg., Taylors, Waterhouses, and Morton batteries, and two battalions of the 4th Ills cavalry. To the 6th Division, Brig Genl. B. M. Prentiss Comdg., the 5th Ohio, 'Powells and Munches' batteries, and two battalions of the 11th Ills Cavalry. All transfers and changes necessary to comply with this order will be immidiately made."—DS, McClernand Papers, IHi; copies, DLC-USG, V, 12, 13, 14, 95; DNA, RG 94, 9th Ill., Letterbook; *ibid.*, RG 393, USG General Orders. *O.R.*, I, x, part 2, 87–88.

1862, APRIL 2. USG Special Orders No. 43. "The following assignments of Brig Generals is hereby made. Brig Genl. R. J. Oglesby to Command the Third Brigade 1st Division. Brig Genl. W. H L Wallace is assigned to the 2d Division and will be assigned to a Brigade by Maj Genl. C. F. Smith comdg. the Division. Brig Genl. J McArthur, when for duty, will report to Maj Genl. L. Wallace who will assign him to a Brigade. Brig Genl. J G Lauman will report to Brig Genl. S. A. Hurlbut Comdg 4th ~~Ills~~ Div and be assigned by him to a Brigade. As a general rule Brigadier Generals should be assigned to Brigades Commanded by the Junior Commanders within the Division to which they are attached."—DS, McClernand Papers, IHi; copies, DLC-USG, V, 15, 16, 82, 87, 89; DNA, RG 393, USG Special Orders. *O.R.*, I, x, part 2, 88.

1862, APRIL 2. Capt. John C. Kelton to USG. "The Major General Commanding the Department directs that Colonel Turner, returns to his regiment forthwith, and accounts to these Headquarters for his absence from his regiment, giving dates of his departure and return"

—LS, DNA, RG 393, Dept. of the Miss., Letters Sent (Press). Col. Thomas J. Turner, 15th Ill., though he nominally commanded a regt. from May 14, 1861, until Nov. 2, 1862, was usually kept from active service by the state of his health.—*The Biographical Encyclopedia of Illinois of the Nineteenth Century* (Philadelphia, 1875), p. 175.

1862, APRIL 2. Surgeon Henry S. Hewit to Capt. John A. Rawlins. "I have the honor to enclose a document which I respectfully request may receive the early attention of the Commanding General"—LS, DNA, RG 393, District of West Tenn., Letters Received. Hewit submitted a lengthy letter outlining sanitary and dietary provisions for the army which he recommended for inclusion in general orders.—LS, *ibid.*

1862, APRIL 3. Ill. Governor Richard Yates to USG. "In reference to furnishing arms for the troops from his State."—DLC-USG, V, 10; DNA, RG 393, USG Register of Letters Received.

1862, APRIL 4. Lt. Col. Thomas H. Burgess, 18th Ill., to USG. "Statements in reference to his arrest by order of Genl. McClernand." —DLC-USG, V, 10; DNA, RG 393, USG Register of Letters Received.

1862, APRIL 4. Capt. William W. Leland to Capt. John A. Rawlins. "We have on hand this day in this Department one Million two hundred and fifty thousand rations in good order, stored principally upon Commissary Boats, and are issueing about sixty thousand rations daily, being upward of twenty days rations on hand. I have reported the number of rations to the Commissary in Chief at St Louis"—LS, DNA, RG 393, District of West Tenn., Letters Received.

1862, APRIL 5. USG endorsement. "Approved" Written on a letter of April 4 from Brig. Gen. William H. L. Wallace to Capt. John A. Rawlins. "I request permission to take with me as acting assistant Quarter master, Lieut. G. I. Davis, 11th Ill inftry. Lieut. Davis has been acting with me in that capacity while I had command of the 2nd Brig. 1st Division, and I have recommended him to the President for appointment as A. Q. M."—LS, Wallace-Dickey Papers, IHi.

1862, APRIL 5. Maj. Gen. John A. McClernand to USG. "I called your attention, the other day, to the comparative smallness of my

Division, in point of numbers; and requested the addition of other regiments in order to bring it up to the average standard. I inferred from your remarks that you thought well of the proposition; or at least did not reject it. In view of the causes producing the diminution of my command—the casualties of battle and field service—I trust you will assign four additional regiments to my Division, which might be organized in either of two ways—1st. By constituting them a Brigade to be commanded by Col Lawler, who deserves well of his country and superiors—2d. By assigning one of them, respectively, to the 1st. and 3d. Brigades, and two to the 2d. Brigade. I feel great solicitude, Genl. upon this subject, and trust and hope that you may view it in the same light I do."—LS, DNA, RG 393, District of West Tenn., Letters Received.

1862, APRIL 8. Capt. William S. Hillyer to Maj. Gen. Lewis Wallace. "I am instructed by Maj Gen Grant to say to you that your communication was received at dark last evening and a reply immediately written and sent by one of his aids Capt Rowley, but he regrets to say that Capt R was unable to find you or your head quarters or any one who could give any information of your whereabouts—Capt R. found every other Division Commander without difficulty—You will hold your present position or advance to a comfortable camping ground and await further orders—"—ALS, Wallace Papers, InHi.

1862, APRIL 8. Capt. William R. Rowley to Maj. Gen. Lewis Wallace. "I am instructed by Major. Gen. Grant to request you to send out a detachment of Cavalry on the road to Savanna, to a point opposite that place for the purpose of ascertaining the practicability of passing a train over the road."—Copies, DLC-USG, V, 1, 2, 3, 86; DNA, RG 393, USG Letters Sent.

1862, APRIL 8. 1st Lt. William S. Bosbyshell, 30th Ill., Fort Donelson, to USG. "I have the honor to apply for instructions in relation to the disposal of property, which has been used by the Secession forces, when at this post, and which I am from time to time recovering from citizens residing in the neighborhood—Many of the citizens here have claims against the government for damage, to, and property supplied for use of the U. S. troops—certified to by officers Knowing the facts —Being desirous of acting in settling these claims, in the most favor-

able manner to the United States, I have at good prices used a portion
of the property, thus obtained, in settling up these matters. Some of
the citizens here are desirous to purchase horses, to enable them to
work their farms & in some instances these are bought to replace those
taken forcibly from them by the Rebels or U. S. Soldiers. In some
instances, I have disposed of captured property, in this manner, but
being disposed always to act for the best interests of the United States,
and wishing at the same time to do nothing which could be deemed
worthy of censure, or reflect blame upon myself, I consider it right
and proper to refer the matter to you for your decision. A considerable quantity of property was shipped by me to Paducah, and I have
since been informed by the Quartermaster at that point, that it is
scarcely worth the cost of transportation—Horses shipped there have
I am informed been sold at from $10 00 to $15 00, but in the settlement of the claims above referred to, many of which are approved by
you. I have obtained from $20 00 to 65 00 for horses, $30 to 112 00
for Mules and $80 for Wagons—thus you see better prices can be
secured here, than by shipping. Most of the horses and mules are in
miserable condition and many of the wagons are without beds and
otherwise imperfect— . . . P. S. I omitted to ask the question whether
I would be justifiable in allowing company officers or Soldiers to purchase horses at an appraised valuation made by a Board of Survey,
as it would enable me to dispose of that kind of property at a much
better price."—LS, DNA, RG 393, District of West Tenn., Letters
Received.

1862, APRIL 9. USG endorsement. "The 1st Division will furnish a
squadron of Cavalry to go with the bearer in search of beef cattle
stampeded during the late battle."—AES, McClernand Papers, IHi.
Written on a letter of April 9 from Capt. Chester B. Hinsdill to USG.
"I have the honor to report to you that the bearer agent for A. Pearce
& Co. Gov. beef contractors, during the engagement of Sunday and
Monday, lost 100 head of cattle,—Any assistance that can be rendered
him in recovering the same will for the benefit of the Government, the
troops being much in neede of fresh beef."—ALS, *ibid.*

1862, APRIL 9. Maj. Gen. John A. McClernand to USG. "Col Julius
Raith, of the 43d Regt Ills. Vols. who was in command of the third
Brigade of my Division, was wounded on Sunday morning during the

first engagement, his leg being broken, and remained unattended upon the ground until monday night, when he was brought in. Being destitute of surgical aid, I sent him on Tuesday to the river for the attention of the Medical Director. His Surgeon Dr Starkloff, informs me this morning that he is now on the hurricane deck of the Steamer Hannibal in an exposed situation, with no means of receiving proper attention. I have to request in the most urgent manner, that he be transferred to Savanna or if that be impracticable, that he be carried to the Steamer Emerald, where it is to be hoped accommodations may be found   The eleven wounded prisoners who are in a tent near my Head Quarters, as you were advised last evening, have yet no relief. If it is impossible for the chief Medical officer to attend to these cases, please indicate a mode in which it can be done"—Copy, McClernand Papers, IHi. This letter was endorsed by USG. "Refered to Surgeon Hewitt, Medical Director"—AES, *ibid.* The letter was then endorsed by Surgeon Henry S. Hewit. "A competant Surgeon has been in charge of the wounded on the *Hanibal*   The Acting Senior Surgeon of Genl McClernand's divn *should have been notified* of the *condition* of the 11 wounded prisoners"—AES, *ibid.*

1862, [APRIL 11]. USG endorsement. "Forwarded to Hd Qrs of the Dept."—AES, DNA, RG 393, Dept. of the Miss., Letters Received. Written on a letter of April 11 from Maj. Gen. Lewis Wallace to Capt. John A. Rawlins. "I have the honor to inform the General that one of my Scouts John C. Carpenter of the 5th Ohio Cavalry has just returned from Purdy, Bethel and the country around, he brings the information, that Purdy was evacuated on last Saturday and has not been occupied since, he remained there the past night, and reports all quite in that neighborhood, and that on yesterday a Rebel Regiment passed Bethel on the R. Road to Corinth, he reports the condition of the road to Purdy fair except Owl Creek Bottom near our lines, the above were the only reinforcements passing to Corinth since the Battle"—LS, *ibid.*

1862, APRIL 11. Maj. Gen. John A. McClernand to USG. "My apology for this communication is the interest felt by me, in common with the army and loyal citizens in the success and glory of the Federal arms. My information and reasoning lead me to believe, that the enemy is still ~~continuing to~~ increaseing his force in our front; and that he may, and probably will abandon Virginia and other portions of the Field and concentrate here for a decisive battle, ~~with the hope of~~ in this vicinity, with the hope of ~~maintaining~~ preserving control over the Gulf or Cotton states. In this view of the case, it occurs to me that we should early press the enemy—or intrench and reinforce by increasing our numbers."—DfS, McClernand Papers, IHi.

1862, April 11. Brig. Gen. William T. Sherman to USG. "I have the honor of acknowledging the receipt of your note and have to reply that I have had a party of cavalry in front of my line out as far as the ridge & find no enemy but roaming parties of cavalry picking up such of their wounded as can ride on horses."—LS, DNA, RG 393, District of West Tenn., Letters Received.

1862, April 13. Capt. Robert W. Healy, 58th Ill., to USG reporting the battle of Shiloh.—ALS, DNA, RG 94, War Records Office, Union Battle Reports. *O.R.*, I, x, part 1, 164–65. The report was improperly addressed.

1862, April 14. USG endorsement. "Disapproved, and respectfully forwarded to Head Quarters Department of the Mississippi"—ES, Records of 17th Ill., I-ar. Written on a letter dated April from Lt. Col. Enos P. Wood, 17th Ill., to USG. "In consequence of my unfitness for duty I would most respectfully request leave of Absence for seven (7) Days; reasons for same being duly given in Surgeons Certificate date of April 11th 1862 by Acting Brigade Surgeon L. D. Kellogg 1st Division. Respectfully submitted for approval"—ALS, *ibid*. On April 12, Col. Leonard F. Ross and Maj. Gen. John A. McClernand endorsed the letter favorably. On April 16, Capt. Nathaniel H. McLean endorsed the letter. "At this time this leave of absence cannot be granted."—AES, *ibid*.

1862, April 14. USG endorsement. "Disapproved, and respectfully forwarded to Head Quarters Department of the Mississippi"—ES, McClernand Papers, IHi. Written on a certificate of April 9 of 1st Asst. Surgeon Orange B. Ormsby, 18th Ill., concerning Capt. Henry S. Wilson, 18th Ill., who suffered "a *very severe* strain of the knee joint occasioned by a fall from his horse while in the performance of his duty (attempting to rally Soldiers who were retreating without just cause)

on the morning of the 8th inst.—"—ADS, *ibid.* On April 16, the cer-
tificate was endorsed by Capt. Nathaniel H. McLean. "Not granted."
—ES, *ibid.* On April 16, Maj. Mason Brayman endorsed the certificate.
"This paper returned at 6 P. M—a mistake—the *application* of Capt
Wilson having been approved and he carried home on the 14th this
certificate having become separated from it, probably."—AES, *ibid.*

1862, APRIL 14. Brig. Gen. Andrew J. Smith, chief of cav., to USG.
"You will direct the cavalry under your command to assemble immediately in the rear of General Sherman's Division at 8 o'clock tomorrow
morning."—Copies, DLC-USG, V, 8; DNA, RG 393, Dept. of the
Miss., Letters Sent. *O.R.,* I, lii, part 1, 235. Misdated April 4, copies,
DLC-USG, V, 4, 5, 7, 8, 9; DNA, RG 393, USG Hd. Qrs. Correspondence. On April 17, Capt. Nathaniel H. McLean wrote to USG.
"The Major General Commanding desires that at the earliest possible
moment you will forward to the Chief of Cavalry at these Headquarters,
an accurate report of the regiments, battalions and companies of cavalry in your army. If a return cannot be furnished, send one that is
approximate, stating the brigade and division to which they are
attached."—Copies, DLC-USG, V, 4, 5, 7, 8, 9; DNA, RG 393, USG
Hd. Qrs. Correspondence; *ibid.,* Dept. of the Miss., Letters Sent.

1862, APRIL 15. To Maj. Gen. Henry W. Halleck concerning three
prisoners: John H. Bills, Bolivar, Tenn.; Dr. Jesse Barford and Thomas
Boyle, Hardeman, Tenn. This letter is mentioned in a letter of April 16
from C. S. A. Brig. Gen. Samuel B. Maxey to Maj. George William-
son.—*O.R.,* I, x, part 2, 423. On April 15, Halleck endorsed USG's
letter with a pass beyond the lines.—*Ibid.*

1862, APRIL 16. USG endorsement. "Respectfully referred to Hd.
Quarters Department of the Mississippi."—ES, The Filson Club,
Louisville, Ky. Written on a letter of April 14 from A. F. McKinney,
Savannah, to Maj. Gen. Charles F. Smith. "I was arested on the
battlefield more than a week ago while seeking the body of a beloved
son. I am a citizen—an old man diseased & frail—have never bourne
arms, nor never expected to do so I pray you to release me so that
I may yet seek my son ~~him~~ among the wounded, peradventure he may
yet live Oh! if you are a father do not deny this *sad boon*!! If this is
incompatable with views of duty, permit me to depart for my home,

where I am mourned as dead, by such a route as would place me with-out your lines."—ALS, *ibid*. On April 15, Smith endorsed this letter to USG. "Respectfully refered to Head Quarters U. S. Forces Pitts-burg."—ES, *ibid*.

1862, APRIL 16. Capt. Nathaniel H. McLean to USG. "The Major Genl Comdg desires that you will detail daily, three mounted Ordilies, to report to the Asst Adjt Genl at these Head Quarters, at 5½ A. M." —Copies, DLC-USG, V, 83; DNA, RG 393, Dept. of the Miss., Letters Sent.

1862, APRIL 16. Capt. Nathaniel H. McLean to USG. "The parole and countersign will be sent to your Headquarters daily, and the Major General Commanding desires that you will have same communicated to the proper officers of your Army."—Copy, DNA, RG 393, Dept. of the Miss., Letters Sent.

1862, APRIL 17. USG endorsement. "Respectfully forwarded to Hd. Qrs. of the Dept."—Typescript, Atwood Collection, InU. Written on a letter of April 17 from Brig. Gen. William T. Sherman to Maj. John A. Rawlins. "I paste on the top of this sheet samples of labels taken from cartridges used by the enemy during the late battle, thou-sands of which are strewed upon the ground. I think it well that this information viz: that the rebels procure their cartridges of E. & A. Ludlow, Birmingham, England, should be conveyed to the War Department and thence to the merchants of New York in order that this firm should suffer the consequences of their infamous traffic."— Typescript, *ibid*.

1862, APRIL 18. USG endorsement. "Respectfully forwarded to Maj. Gen. Halleck."—AES, DNA, RG 393, Dept. of the Miss., Letters Received. Written on a letter of April 18 from Brig. Gen. William T. Sherman to Maj. John A. Rawlins. "This morning in consequence of the advance of Genls McCooks & Wallace's Divisions to points in my immediate front, I have withdrawn my pickets & guard from the Corinth Road & shall establish them on the Purdy Road as prelimi-nary thereto, this morning I sent a Cavalry scout of twenty five men to a point six miles out with orders to take post at or near Veal's lane. The Officer in command has sent in word that he has been out to

Stantonville within seven miles of Purdy or two and a half beyond
Veal's without seeing any of the enemy's Cavalry Pickets, or hearing
of them since the wednesday after the battle. Veals is the point on the
Purdy Road, where a well travelled road from Savannah to Corinth
crosses, and I will continue to watch it. I also sent out this morning
under the guidance of McDaniel a Lieut and twenty five men from
Buckland's Brigade to proceed up Owl Creek by blind paths to Genl
Meeks' place, with instructions to bring him in, as I was convinced
that he has been playing us false. This party has also returned, and the
Officer reports no enemy's pickets along Owl Creek, or at Meaks' lane.
A Cavalry picket had been at Meaks' lane up to last monday. Genl
Meaks had cleared out for Mississippi. There is no enemy at the Long
Fields. I report these facts as bearing on any proposed demonstration
against whatever force the enemy now has on the Corinth Road near
Chambers' "—Copy, *ibid.*

1862, APRIL 18.   USG endorsement. "Turn such articles as were
taken from dead bodies of rebels over to the Provost Marshal General.
Where taken from our own troops give them to Comd.g Officers of
regiments or Detachments to which the owners belonged, to the end
that friends may get them."—AES, IHi. Written on a note of April 18
from Col. William H. W. Cushman, 53rd Ill., to Maj. John A. Rawlins.
"A Burial Party was detailed a few days since from this Regiment
some of the Bodys burried had upon them some articles such as memno.,
Pictures &c. What shall be done with them   please inform me."—
ANS, *ibid.*

1862, APRIL 18.   To Governor Richard Yates of Ill. "Respectfully
refered to Hon. R. Yates, Governor off Illinois, with the request that
the appointments recommended be made at his earlyest convenience."
—AES, Records of 53rd Ill., I-ar. Written on a letter of April 18 from
Col. William H. W. Cushman, 53rd Ill., to Yates requesting promotions and transfers for several men of his regt.—ALS, *ibid.*

1862, APRIL [19].   To Maj. James Simons. "Refered to Medical
Director."—AES, McClernand Papers, IHi. Written on a letter of
April 19 from Capt. Addison S. Norton to Maj. John A. Rawlins. "Maj
Genl McClernand requests Surgeon Williams may be assigned to the
Batallion of Artilley attached to his Division."—ALS, *ibid.* Simons

added an undated endorsement. "There is not an unassigned Medical officer her[e] at present. Dr. Williams has annulled his contract."— AES, *ibid.*

1862, April 19. USG pass. "Mr. Gibbs, a citizen of Tennesse who has given valuable aid to the Union cause, acting as guide and in giving information, will be permitted to pass free on any government steamer to St. Louis, and return."—ADS, DNA, RG 94, Letters Received. Theodore H. Gibbs of Grafton, Tenn., was then attempting to secure the release of his son, Gilbert C. Gibbs, captured at Clarksville and taken to Camp Chase, Columbus, Ohio. Other documents, *ibid.*, indicate his final success. He may be the person referred to by USG as "H. Gibbs of Clifton." See letter to Maj. Melancthon Smith, March 24, 1862.

1862, April 19. Maj. Gen. John A. McClernand to USG. "Doubtless Col Webster, chief of your staff has reported the result of our reconnoissance of our lines and their exterior relations. I only write to say, that we are agreed in our opinion as to the ground for a new camp, if you should think proper to direct us to make one"—LS, McClernand Papers, IHi. In an endorsement dated April 18 (an apparent error), Maj. John A. Rawlins approved the plans for a new camp. —ES, *ibid.*

1862, April 20. USG General Orders No. 41. "Companies and Regiments having a variety of Calibre of arms will exchange and transfer from one company to another so as to secure but one Calibre in a Company. This is highly essential to convenienc[e] in issueing ammunition. Where neccessary, arms may be returned to the Ordinance Officer, on the Steamer Rockett, and an exchange effected there. This matter should receive the immediate attention of Division Commanders."—DS, McClernand Papers, IHi; copy, DNA, RG 94, 48th Ill., Letterbook. Dated April 21, copies, *ibid.*, 9th Ill., Letterbook; *ibid.*, RG 393, USG General Orders; DLC-USG, V, 12, 13, 14, 95. *O.R.*, I, x, part 2, 116.

1862, April 20. Maj. Gen. John A. McClernand to USG. "I write to ask your opinion whether it will be competent to inflict fines as a disciplinary mode of punishment. My own opinion is, that the stoppage of pay for the lighter Military offences, if permissable, is the best mode of punishment which can be adopted. You are aware that Convening a Court Martial and executing the sentence is attended with so much inconvenience that the offender not unfrequently escapes the punishment necessary to ensure proper discipline. Although the mode of punishment suggested may not be in *strict* conformity to the Regulations, yet in some cases I think it might be adopted with good results."—Copies, McClernand Papers, IHi.

1862, APRIL 21.   USG endorsement. "Respectfully forwarded to Head Quarters Dept. of the Mississippi"—ES, DNA, RG 393, District of West Tenn., Letters Received. Written on a letter of April 17 from Col. Morgan L. Smith to Maj. Gen. Lewis Wallace. "The officers of this Brigade having been paid only to 31. Decr. 1861 their financial condition is in a very unsatisfactory state. If they could be paid for one month I think the public service would be promoted thereby—"—ALS, *ibid.* On April 21, Wallace endorsed the letter to USG.—AES, *ibid.*

1862, APRIL 21.   Maj. Gen. John A. McClernand to USG. "Enclosed you will find a commission and communication which explain themselves. As G. L. Fort is now Captain of Co. I. 11th Ill., having a commission of early date, and as by the acceptance of the accompanying commission he would not, ~~be~~ thereby, be promoted, and as, in my view, the order for his transfer should be made or approved ~~by~~ by you, I have deemed it proper to invoke your ~~consider~~ decision in the matter—adding my consent to the transfer, as a matter of personal accommodation to Capt. Fort, whose health is quite feeble and whose affairs, as late Post Quarter Master at Birds' need personal attention."—Copies, McClernand Papers, IHi.

1862, APRIL 21.   Col. David E. Wood, 14th Wis., to USG reporting the conduct of his regt. at the battle of Shiloh.—ALS, DNA, RG 94, War Records Office, Union Battle Reports. *O.R.,* I, x, part 1, 372–73.

1862, APRIL 22.   To Maj. Gen. John A. McClernand. "Make the consolidation asked provided no more commissioned officers are left to a company than is authorized by law."—AES, McClernand Papers, IHi. Written on a letter of April 19 from McClernand to USG. "I am informed that all of the 58th Ill Regt. were Captured in the Battle of the Tennessee at this place, except 150 men and one or two ~~Officers~~ Company Officers. This remnant consists of Irishmen who, together with their Officers, have applied to Col Lawler 18th Ill, for permission to join his Regiment. I hope you will be satisfied to make the order accordingly."—Copy, *ibid.* On April 26, Maj. William Larned wrote to USG. "There have been various applications here of late from soldiers of the 58th Ill Vols for pay, who have no descriptive rolls or discharge papers. As I understand that most of ~~all~~ the officers of this regiment have been taken prisoner, I would respectfully inquire whether there is any officer left who is duly authorized to furnish descriptive rolls or discharge papers for the men of this regiment not captured. Since the battles of Fort Donelson & Pittsburg, the large number of sick & wounded men on furlough are making urgent appeals upon this Dept for pay, many having had no pay for *four or five months.* They are often without descriptive rolls & I would suggest the importance of having the commanders of Comps. furnish all sick or wounded men on furlough with these rolls *at their departure.* If not provided them they might be forwarded to their respective residences. Although not *as yet* officially authorized to pay the sick & wounded volunteers in *this District* upon descriptive rolls, I anticipate that instructions will very soon be given to that effect, the great necessities of these men rendering such a course necessary for their relief"—ALS, DNA, RG 393, District of West Tenn., Letters Received.

1862, APRIL 22.   Col. James B. Fry to [USG]. "In reference to physical condition of his father and requesting that he be ordered to Illinois." —DLC-USG, V, 10; DNA, RG 393, USG Register of Letters Received.

1862, APRIL 23.   Maj. Gen. Henry W. Halleck to USG. "You will detail two (2) Regiments of Cavalry and two Regts. of Infantry to report to Brig. Gen. A. J. Smith at Shiloh Church to morrow morning at seven, (7) oclock, prepared to make a forced reconnoissance in advance."—Copy, DNA, RG 393, Dept. of the Miss., Letters Sent.

1862, APRIL 23.   Capt. Andrew C. Kemper to USG. "The Major General Commanding desires that you detail on special service, Private Charles G. Roberts of Bolton's Battery Second Regiment Illinois Volunteer Artillery, to report to Col F. D. Callender, Chief of Ordnance at these Head Quarters."—Copy, DNA, RG 393, Dept. of the Miss., Letters Sent.

1862, APRIL 25. USG endorsement. "Respectfully forwarded to Head Quarters of the Dept. I know of no way by which absent furloughed soldiers are to join their regiment except at their own expense unless brought back as deserters. In the present instance I would be glad however if these men could be restored to their regt."—AES, DNA, RG 393, Dept. of the Miss., Letters Received. Written on a letter of April 22 from Capt. Addison S. Norton to Maj. John A. Rawlins. "Herewith you will find two communications which persuasively and impressively explain themselves. I am directed by General M Clernand to respectfully urge that such prompt and favorable action will be taken by the General commanding the Army of the Tennessee as will secure the immediate return of the absentees referred to, as will enable the famous 11th to be early filled up An authority to issue papers, under such restrictions and regulations as the Genl may prescribe will doubtless answer the purpose"—ALS, *ibid.* Enclosed were letters of April 1 and 21 from Col. Thomas E. G. Ransom, 11th Ill., to Maj. Gen. John A. McClernand requesting passes for men on furlough and recruits to join his regt.—ALS, *ibid.*

1862, APRIL 26. To hd. qrs., Army of the Miss. "reports, that John Smith visits Corinth habitually, probably as a spy. &c"—DNA, RG 393, Dept. of the Miss., Register of Letters Received. A fragment which appears to have been the last thirteen lines and closing of this letter was sold by Parke-Bernet Galleries on April 27, 1954. "He learns that James Smith who has two brothers in the Southern Army . . . is in the habit of visiting Corinth probably acting as a spie. He also learned from Citizens that sixteen Southern Cavalry crossed the river . . . A man by the name of Fisher living opposite Eastport has a boat in which he is constantly crossing troops."—Robert F. Batchelder, Catalogue No 4 [1972].

1862, APRIL [26?]. USG endorsement. "Respectfully forwarded to Head Quarters of the Dept."—AES, DNA, RG 393, Dept. of the Miss., Letters Received. Written on a letter of April 24 from Lt. Col. Charles W. Smith, 14th Mo., to Capt. William C. Clark. "I desire to state for the information of Brig Genl. R. J. Oglesby, that after the organization of the Regt. 16 enlisted men of Capt. Michal Piggotts company were detached for the Regimental Band,—That subsequently another order of Major Genl. Halleck Comdg. Dept. of the Mississippi, the band was mustered out of service. This leaves the company with about 45 enlisted men. I am informed that a company of 40 recruits under a Lieut were at camp chase Ohio, and desire to be ordered here to join his company, and that no objection exists to their being ordered here. Can the proper order be obtained and transportation from Camp Chase to this point be given them? I would be gratified to obtain these recruits, and hope I may succeed in doing so."—LS, *ibid.*

1862, April 26. Capt. William S. Hillyer to Maj. Gen. John A. McClernand. "I am instructed by Maj Gen Grant to say to you that he has just received information that you have sent out a portion of your command to make a reconnoisance in force in some direction The Gen Grant does not know by what authority this is done. He would not make the order himself without the instructions of the commander in chief. If not made by the order of Gen Halleck you will have the force immediately returned."—ALS, McClernand Papers, IHi. On April 26, McClernand wrote to USG. "Your communication ordering the reconnoitering force sent out by me this morning to return is received, and will be immediately complied with. My authority for sending it out rests upon conversations with you that I would feel and ascertain my relations to the enemy's pickets and any out post he may have established in my front, and upon the distinct statements made by Col. McPherson, a member of your staff yesterday and to day, that it would be advisable to feel in my front and advance of my if it should be found safe to do so, with the view to rest my right on the bridge across Owl creek he is now constructing. I am not concious that I have erred, and think that I have not, yet, as already mentioned, the force referred to will be immediately returned to camp."—Copy, *ibid.*

1862, April 28. To hd. qrs., Dept. of the Miss. "recommends the dismissal of Sutler Bradford, for a violation of his order and for taking his claim before a member of Congress before calling upon Military Authority."—Copies, DNA, RG 107, Orders and Endorsements Sent; *ibid.*, RG 94, Register of Letters Received. Sutler George G. Bradford, 53rd Ohio, complained that he had purchased two barrels of coffee from privates of the 53rd Ohio at Pittsburg Landing which had been seized on April 3 by Capt. Algernon S. Baxter, by order of USG, at Savannah. On April 7, Bradford wrote to U.S. Representative Samuel S. Cox of Ohio about this matter, and, on April 15, Cox forwarded the letter to Secretary of War Edwin M. Stanton.—ALS, *ibid.*, Letters Received. The letter was forwarded through the AGO to hd. qrs., Dept. of the Miss., and, on April 26, by Capt. Andrew C. Kemper to USG.—*Ibid.* By Special Orders No. 82, Dept. of the Miss., June 1, Bradford was dismissed from U.S. service.

1862, APRIL 28. To Col. William W. Lowe. "You may release the Tobacco with held from Jordon Giles of Paducah, amounting to something over 20 Boxes."—Copies, DLC-USG, V, 2, 86; DNA, RG 393, USG Letters Sent.

1862, APRIL 29. USG General Orders No. 47. "Division Provost Marshalls will immediately collect and turn over to the Chief Qr Mast all horses which have been heretofore captured, and are now held by officers, soldiers, servants or other persons. No officer, not entitled to forage, will be allowed to keep a private horse on any account whatever   Where officers not entitled to forage have horses which they claim as their own, they will be required to make a certificate of the fact stating when and how they obtained them, and if the evidence is satisfactory that the horses are their property a permit will be granted to ship or dispose of them. No horse, or other property, once captured and afterwards sold, will be considered private property, and to avoid possible error, when property has been purchased south of the Ohio river, evidence must be adduced to show that it was not captured. Division Commanders will see that this order is promptly executed." —Copies, DLC-USG, V, 12, 13, 14, 95; DNA, RG 393, USG General Orders. *O.R.*, I, x, part 2, 141.

1862, APRIL 30. Capt. Andrew C. Kemper to USG. "The Major General Commanding directs that you order the Companies of the Fourth Regiment United States Cavalry in your command to report forthwith to Lieut. Col. Oakes at Major General Buell's Head Quarters, and that Co. "C." Second Regiment U. S. Cavalry report at once at these Hd. Quarters."—Copy, DNA, RG 393, Dept. of the Miss., Letters Sent.

1862, [APRIL ?].   Col. Benjamin Allen, 16th Wis., to USG reporting the part played by his regt. in the battle of Shiloh.—*O.R.*, I, x, part 1, 285–86.

1862, MAY 1.   Maj. Gen. John A. McClernand to USG. "Herewith you will find a dispatch which I hope you will cause to be telegraphed to its address   Canister of the description mentioned therein cannot be obtained here, and the Battery is entirely without it"—Copy, McClernand Papers, IHi.

1862, MAY 2.   Maj. Gen. John A. McClernand to USG explaining that it was not his fault, nor that of his officers or men, that Brig. Gen. Henry M. Judah, inspector gen., Dept. of the Miss., found the condition of the 1st Brigade of his division unsatisfactory on April 28.—LS, DNA, RG 393, Dept. of the Tenn., Letters Received from Reserve Corps, Jackson, Tenn.; copy, McClernand Papers, IHi.

1862, MAY 3.   Maj. Gen. John A. McClernand to USG discussing a proposal for transporting ammunition.—LS, DNA, RG 393, Dept. of the Tenn., Letters Received from Reserve Corps, Jackson, Tenn.; copy, McClernand Papers, IHi. On May 22, McClernand wrote an almost identical letter to USG.—Copies, *ibid*.

1862, MAY 6.   USG endorsement. "Approved."—AES, Brayman Papers, ICHi. Written on Special Orders No. 8 of Maj. Gen. John A. McClernand transferring a private soldier.—Copy, *ibid*.

1862, MAY 8.   Maj. Gen. John A. McClernand to USG. "Hearing yesterday (as I informed you orally) that mounted men of the enemys pickets had shown themselves, at the bridge across owl creek on the road from Pittsburg to Purdy—I directed Genl Wallace to cause the correctness of the information to be tested and if found true to drive back the enemys pickets, and take effectual neasures to secure his detachment guarding the line of Owl creek against surprise   In answer to this order I have the honor to report that Genl Wallace caused Capt S. C. Burbridge commanding a detachment of Cavalry, to proceed on the Purdy road to Stantonville, thence north to the Shun Pike road, thence along that road in the direction of of Purdy to the bridge which he found to be obstructed by felled trees   Genl Wallace further reports that Capt Burbridge learned that a considerable number of the enemys cavalry were at Adamsville   Returning to Stauntonville and thence south west to his encampment Capt B neither saw nor heard of the enemy in that direction   Capt B returned to his Camp at 2° Oclock A. M. this morning   I deduced from the information thus obtained, that the report of the enemys pickets being seen near or at the Purdy bridge is unfounded"—Copies, DNA, RG 393, Dept. of the Tenn., Letters Received from Reserve Corps, Jackson, Tenn.; McClernand Papers, IHi.

1862, MAY 8. Col. Lewis B. Parsons, St. Louis, to USG. "The Steamer Minnehaha was employed at Pittsburg Tenn, in March, under order of Capt Kountz, A Q M. The certificate of employment called for settlement here. I asked a certificate that she had been employed, all the time named, and that she should report all fuel used. The Captain had a bill made out at $275. per day for some 24 days. This boat should receive about $200. per day (when running, but if lying still a deduction of from 60 to 100$ a day should be made for fuel) as per a list I have sent Capt Chandler, A. Q. M, at Pittsburgh. I write you as the Captain says he will go to you for settlement as you had previously settled a small demurrage claim at $275. per day. It is proper to say this boat was offered to Government at $195. per day, furnishing fuel and paying all her own expenses, in January last."—LS (Press), Parsons Papers, IHi.

1862, MAY 9. USG endorsement. "Respectfully refered to Gen. Head Quarters with the request that the transfer asked be temporarily made."—AES, DNA, RG 393, Dept. of the Tenn., Letters Received from Reserve Corps, Jackson, Tenn. Written on a letter of May 9 from Capt. Fritz Anneke to Brig. Gen. Henry M. Judah. "As Capt. McAllister, hitherto commander of Company D 1st Illinois Light Artillery, has resigned, and as neither in that company, nor in any of the other 4 Batteries of your Division, all of whom are very short of officers, a suitable man can be found to take command over McAllister's 24 pound howitzer battery, I respectfully suggest, that senior first Lieutenant Henry Tons of the 24 pound rifled Indiana Battery No. 11, Capt. Sutermeister, now attached to Gen. Buell's Army, be detailed for taking command over McAllister's Battery, he being a competent experienced officer and his Battery being able to get along without him."—ALS, *ibid*. On the same day, Judah endorsed the letter favorably to Maj. Gen. John A. McClernand, and McClernand to USG. On May 10, Capt. John C. Kelton endorsed the letter to Col. John V. D. Du Bois, chief of art., Dept. of the Miss. Du Bois added an endorsement misdated April 9. "Disappd—The present officers of the battery although young fought it gallantly & well in the last battle. The enlisted men will not submit to German commanders willingly— If officers are wanted in McAllisters battery there are doubtless worthy non com officers capable of filling honorably the positions"—AES, *ibid*.

On May 13, McClernand resubmitted the letter to USG. "Herewith you will find a paper with endorsements thereon which explain themselves. I would respectfully suggest regarding Col Dubois' remarks, that I was personally a witness of the bearing of the young officers he refers to, they acted well, but that does not meet the case. Since Capt McAllister has resigned, and Lieut Wood has been assigned to the command of Dresser's and Schwartz' Batteries (consolidated) I would ask, who in McAllister's Battery is competent to command it. If Col Dubois will name the officer he will avert consequences for which I shall not hold myself responsible, if my efforts to control them are counteracted. Differing from Col. Dubois in another particular, I hold it to be the duty of enlisted men to submit to German or any other officers, properly set over them; and in my command it is the established rule, that if they do not do so willingly, they must unwillingly." —ALS, *ibid*. On May 19, USG endorsed McClernand's letter. "I deem it not advisable to go out of the Army of the Tennessee to find a commander for one of our batteries therefore decline forwarding this a second time to Gen. Head Quarters."—AES, *ibid*.

1862, MAY 9. Maj. Gen. John A. McClernand to USG discussing a plan to cut all railroads to Corinth, forcing the C. S. A. army there to attack U.S. forces or surrender.—LS, DNA, RG 393, Dept. of the Miss., Letters Received.

1862, MAY [10]. To Maj. Gen. John A. McClernand. "You will cause the command under Brig'r Genl. Judah to move to morrow to the position now occupied by Genl. W T Sherman. The position is to the right and slightly advanced of that indicated in the note of Maj Rawlins of this morning"—Register of Letters, McClernand Papers, IHi. On the same day, Maj. John A. Rawlins wrote to McClernand.

"I am instructed by Major Gen. U. S. Grant, to say that you will immediately send your Engineer Officer to our right, with the view of ascertaining the best road to Cogdil's house. It is expected to move Gen. Judah's Division to that position tomorrow, his left resting on Cogdil's house, the line of battle running parallel with the Purdy and Farmington roads."—Copies, DLC-USG, V, 1, 2, 3, 86; DNA, RG 393, USG Letters Sent. On May 11, McClernand wrote to USG. "The 1st Division of the Reserves (Genl Judah) is encamped upon the ground assigned to it, by your order. A Battalion of Infantry with proportionate detachments of Cavalry and Artillery have been sent forward on the 'State line' road a mile and a half to the crossing of Muddy creek the Cavalry being instructed to reconnoitre to and picket the crossing of said road with the Purdy and Corinth road, about a half mile in advance. Observations made since my arrival here prompt and, I think, justify me in suggesting the importance of strengthening and extending the right of my line by the addition of Genl Wallace's Division, now behind. If this suggestion should meet your approbation, upon notice of the fact, I will immediatly order up Genl Wallace's Division."—LS, *ibid.*, District of West Tenn., Letters Received; DfS, *ibid.*, Dept. of the Tenn., Letters Received from Reserve Corps, Jackson, Tenn. On May 11, Rawlins wrote to McClernand. "I am instructed by Major Gen. U. S. Grant to acknowledge the receipt of your communication suggesting the propriety of Ordering up Gen. Wallace's Division to strengthen your right. This cannot be done without orders from Gen. Halleck. Besides it would leave too much of our rear unprotected"—Copies, DLC-USG, V, 1, 2, 3, 86; DNA, RG 393, USG Letters Sent.

1862, MAY 10. USG pass. "The bearer of this W F. Harrison is on duty at these Head Quarters. Any officer in the U S Army will render him all aid in their power whenever called upon. Guards and Pickets will pass him at will   Military Rail Roads will pass him free"— Copy, Dodge Papers, IaHA.

1862, MAY 12. Maj. Gen. Henry W. Halleck to USG. "I wish to see you about six o'clock P. M., for consultation. I have sent an Aide to ask Major General Sherman to meet you."—Copies, DLC-USG, V, 7, 8; DNA, RG 393, USG Hd. Qrs. Correspondence; *ibid.*, District of West Tenn., Letters Received.

1862, MAY 12. Maj. Gen. John A. McClernand to USG. "Upon reaching the ground assigned by you for the encampment of the 1st Division of the Reserves, yesterday, a regiment of Infantry with a section of artillery, and a company of Cavalry was thrown forward to the crossing of the State line road with little muddy creek   This point is almost due west of the present encampment of the Division. The artillery is posted in a commanding position on this side of the creek, Supported by the Infantry, except so much of the same as has been thrown still further forward to guard the approaches to the creek   The Cavalry were advanced yesterday evening, to Easels house, finding and driving back some of the enemys pickets in that direction—Upon their return, mistaken for the enemy, they were fired upon by Genl Shermans pickets, but without harm. This morning the same Cavalry advanced Some half or three fourths of a mile beyond Easels on the road to Corinth, and were again fired upon by Genl Shermans picket, and again without harm. Since this casualty, measures have been taken to obviate its recurrence, and the line of Genl. Shermans and Judahs pickets are joined. Between 11 and 12 O.clock to day, Lieut. Col. McCullough reports that he advanced his Cavalry still further beyond Easels to a Camp of the enemy just evacuated. The Camp had had been a pretty Strong one, consisting of Infantry, Cavalry, and Artillery. He adds that upon the return of the Cavalry, one of our Scouts Snapped a carbine at Capt Townsend. The way being clear, Genl Sherman, I understand, is advancing a detachment to establish an out post at or beyond Easels."—LS, DNA, RG 393, District of West Tenn., Letters Received; copy, *ibid.*, Dept. of the Tenn., Letters Received from Reserve Corps, Jackson, Tenn.

1862, MAY 12. Maj. Gen. John A. McClernand to USG. "Herewith you will find a Mobile paper of the 8th inst. found by one of my mounted men, in the evacuated Camp of the Enemy, beyond Eazels'. I would, particularly, call your attention to the remarks of Col. Richards, commanding the detachment from the 1st Division of the reserves, to be found in pencil, on the margin of the paper. Col. Richards' reports that the Camp alluded to was about a half mile beyond Eazels', and that it consisted of some twelve or fifteen hundred of all arms— Infantry, Cavalry and Artillery. He further reports that my Cavalry have advanced a half mile beyond the evactuated Camp without finding the pickets of the enemy."—ALS, DNA, RG 393, Dept. of the Tenn., Letters Received from Reserve Corps, Jackson, Tenn.

1862, MAY 13. Maj. Gen. John A. McClernand to USG. "I am informed by Brig Genl. L. F. Ross. that he has a colored man, who will act as a scout & in whom he places entire confidence to execute successfully a mission to Corinth or to the. M. & C. R. R. west of Corinth to ascertain the movements of the enemy. He will send him out if leave is granted & desires permission to do so"—ADfS, DNA, RG 393, Dept. of the Tenn., Letters Received from Reserve Corps, Jackson, Tenn.; copy, McClernand Papers, IHi.

1862, MAY 14. Capt. John C. Kelton to USG. "Direct T. W. Sherman's, McKean's, and Davies' divisions to advance to-morrow to vicinity of seven mile creek the left resting on Corinth road. W. T. Sherman's division will not advance beyond Russell's or will remain near its present position. One Brigade of McClernand will occupy road from near 'the Locusts' to Easel's. The Cavalry of McKean's, Davies & W. T. Sherman's divisions will be in readiness at seven o'clock to report to Brig. Genl. A. J. Smith at Genl. W. T. Sherman's Head Qrs. Genl. Hurlbut's division will be ready to support the right in case of an attack. Genl. McClernand's Cavalry will make a reconnoissance on his right in the direction of Purdy. Genl. Wallace will push a reconnoissance in the direction of Purdy and also towards Veals and Stantonville."—LS, DNA, RG 393, District of West Tenn., Letters Received. *O.R.*, I, x, part 2, 189. On the same day, Maj. John A. Rawlins issued Special Orders No. 80 in which Kelton's letter was repeated virtually verbatim.—Copies, DLC-USG, V, 15, 16, 82, 87, 89; DNA, RG 393, USG Special Orders.

1862, [MAY 16]. To Maj. Gen. John A. McClernand. "Require both Divisions of the Reserve to keep on hand at all times two days cooked rations."—Misdated March 16, Register of Letters, McClernand Papers, IHi.

1862, MAY 16. Maj. Gen. John A. McClernand to USG. "Genl. Wallace com'g 3d Divn of the Reserves, reports, that, yesterday, Col Thayer, with three Regaments of this Brigade—1st Neb. 58th and 68th Ohio, accompanied by 4. pieces of Thompson's Battery under Lt.

Porter, and a squadron of the 11th Ills. Cavalry—Capt. Burbridge, proceeded from his camp on the Purdy road, to its junction with the Corinth road—thence, to a point two miles this side of the town of Purdy. Halting the Infantry and the artillery, Col. Thayer send forward the cavalry—which entering and passing through the town found none of the enemy there; and Col. Thayer, learned none of them had been there since last Sunday."—ALS, DNA, RG 393, District of West Tenn., Letters Received.

1862, MAY 18. To Maj. Gen. John A. McClernand. "Order up one Brigade of Maj Genl. Wallace's division to Cooks House."—Telegram, Register of Letters, McClernand Papers, IHi. On May 18, McClernand wrote to USG. "With your permission I will send a brigade, more or less, to the rail road, west of this place, to discover if the enemy ~~are~~ is there, and to break up the road."—ADfS, DNA, RG 393, Dept. of the Tenn., Letters Received from Reserve Corps, Jackson, Tenn.; copy, McClernand Papers, IHi. Also on May 18, McClernand wrote to USG. "I have ordered the expedition sanctioned by you. It will probable reach the intersection of the two roads refd. to by day light tomorrow morning."—Copies, *ibid.*

1862, MAY 18. Maj. Gen. John A. McClernand to USG. "The question is suggested by General Order No 27 Head Quarters Department of the Miss dated May 17th 1862 whether Commanders of of 'Army Corps' in the 'Army of the Tenn.' are authorized & expected to grant leaves of absence and furloughs as indicated in Par 3 General Order No 14 from same Head Quarters dated April 2d 1862 I would respectfully ask ~~your~~ your instructions"—LS, DNA, RG 393, Dept. of the Tenn., Letters Received from Reserve Corps, Jackson, Tenn. On May 19, Maj. John A. Rawlins endorsed this letter. "A similar question to the one within, was yesterday referred to Maj. Gen. Halleck, Commanding, who dicided that they had not."—ES, *ibid.*

1862, MAY 19. To Brig. Gen. Lorenzo Thomas. "My commission as Major General has not yet reached me."—Telegram received, DNA, RG 94, Letters Received; *ibid.*, RG 107, Telegrams Received (Press). On May 22, Maj. Julius P. Garesché telegraphed to USG. "A. ~~Copp~~ copy of your commission was sent today"—Telegram received, *ibid.*, RG 393, Dept. of the Mo., Telegrams Received; copies, *ibid.*, USG Hd. Qrs. Correspondence; DLC-USG, V, 7.

1862, MAY 19. Maj. Gen. Henry W. Halleck to USG. "I return herewith the papers relating to Mr. Chapman, a Reporter of the N. Y. Herald. I have told Mr. Chapman that the matter of police of each Army Corps and Division will be left to its appropriate commander and that if he returned within your lines with a proper pass, you would take such measures in the premises as you might deem proper. It is impossible for me to examine into each individual case of these newspaper reporters and it is needless to attempt it."—Copy, DNA, RG 393, Dept. of the Miss., Letters Sent. For an account of Halleck's efforts to rid his army of newspaper reporters as "unauthorized hangers on," see J. Cutler Andrews, *The North Reports the Civil War* (Pittsburgh, 1955), pp. 184–86. Andrews has gathered evidence that reporters of major New York newspapers, Frank Chapman among them, expected to remain after their competitors were expelled.—*Ibid.*, p. 186.

1862, MAY 20. Maj. Gen. Henry W. Halleck to USG. "Major Genl. W. T. Sherman will advance to-morrow morning from his present position to Russell's House, his left extending South-East to the creek which crosses the road North of that point and his right extending north to near his present entrenchments. He will entrench himself in that position and move up and establish in batterey a part of his heavy Artillery. One Brigade of Genl. Judah's Division will advance and occupy Maj. Gen. Sherman's present entrenchments, connecting by detachments with the Locusts, and keeping up a strong reconnoissance in front towards the Rail Road. Genl. Hurlbut's Division will take position on the left of Major Genl. Sherman extending towards Brig. Genl. T. W. Sherman's present position. Brig. Genl. Davies will advance and occupy the same line, a Brigade of Brig. Gen. McKean's Division filling up the space if necessary. The main body of this latter Division will occupy its present position as a Reserve or second line of the right wing."—LS, DNA, RG 393, District of West Tenn., Letters Received. *O.R.*, I, x, part 2, 205. On the same day, Capt. John C. Kelton added a note at the bottom of Halleck's letter. "This order has been telegraphed to Maj Genl Sherman. I enclose copies for Maj Genls Thomas and McClernand. It will be soon enough to forward the order to Genl

McClernand early in the morning."—AES, DNA, RG 393, District of West Tenn., Letters Received. *O.R.*, I, x, part 2, 205.

1862, MAY 21. To Maj. Gen. George H. Thomas. "Send one Company of Cavalry to report here for Picket duty, on the road back towards Monterey. This guard will be kept up and relieved daily until otherwise directed."—Copies, DLC-USG, V, 1, 2, 3, 86; DNA, RG 393, USG Letters Sent.

1862, MAY 21. Maj. Gen. John A. McClernand to USG. "I have the honor to report that one Brigade (Genl Logan) of Genl Judah's Division was moved up to Genl Sherman's camp of this morning— arriving there at an early hour, before Genl Sherman's command had left. Another Brigade (Genl. Ross') as you are advised is encamped about half way between Genl. Logan's present position and this place. A Regiment of another Brigade (Col. Lawler's) forms an out post— covering, in part, the portions of both Genl. Ross and Col. Lawler, and in addition a picket line covers the three Brigades of the Division. If it is desired that other intermediate posts Should be established please advise me. In concluding this communication permit me to add that but little remains of either of these Brigades after their guards, pickets and out posts are subtracted—particularly is this true in regard to Col Lawlers Brigade. If other troops are arriving might not some of them take the places of Gen Wallace's, troops, in rear and enable them to join the advance of the Reserve Corps"—Copies, DNA, RG 393, Dept. of the Tenn., Letters Received from Reserve Corps, Jackson, Tenn.; McClernand Papers, IHi.

1862, MAY 21. Maj. Gen. John A. McClernand to USG requesting the assignment of Lt. Col. Ferdinand F. Rempel, 58th Ohio, as provost marshal, Pittsburg Landing, and Capt. Charles A. Barker, 58th Ohio, as asst. provost marshal, Pittsburg Landing. McClernand discussed this matter in two letters of the same date.—Copies, DNA, RG 393, Dept. of the Tenn., Letters Received from Reserve Corps, Jackson, Tenn.; McClernand Papers, IHi.

1862, MAY 22. USG endorsement. "Respectfully forwarded to Gen. Head Quarters."—AES, DNA, RG 393, 16th Army Corps, Miscellaneous Papers. Written on a letter of May 20 from Maj. Gen. John A.

McClernand to USG. "I enclose herewith a report made by the Forage Master relating to short issues of Forage; which unmistakably explains the cause of the numerous complaints upon that subject—and which at the same time accounts for the poverty and unservicableness of many of the public animals. This imposition (calling it by the mildest name) needs to be corrected—It is dishonoring to the Government, unjust to individuals and injurious to the public service. The explanation sometimes offered, that the Forage is turned over at the weight at which it was purchased is a pretext and affords. no justification whatever. Besides, if such a practice was permitted it would encourage negligence by indemnifying it against partial loss or waste of Corn, Oats or Hay. In addition to the above mentioned abuse, I feel it to be my imperative duty to call your attention to another which, while depriving the soldier of his lawful right, is sapping his health and destroying his usefulness, I refer to the unsound food issued to the men. In illustration of the character of evils alluded to and the extent to which they are carried— I beg leave to call your attention to the accompanying papers—Nos. A. B. & C. In view of the alleged facts, I respectfully ask and urge your interference to arrest and punish the continuance of this grievious abuse."—LS, *ibid.* On May 23, Capt. John C. Kelton endorsed this letter to Maj. Osborne Cross, who added an undated endorsement. "My attention has long since been drawn to the complaint of the weights of grain and have ordered that it be weighed when received from contractors and issued in like way—If the officers wishes it to be weighed on its being issued to him so far as time is allowed the officer in charge of the Forage it will be attended to—In relation to the food of the men I have to report that it belongs to the Commissary department—I here enclose Capt Lymans report and list of weights" —AES, *ibid.* Kelton then endorsed the letter to McClernand.—AES, *ibid.*

1862, MAY 22. Maj. Gen. Henry W. Halleck to USG. "I noticed to-day that the ammunition left in Genl McKeans old camp, to which I called your attention two days ago, is still there without any guard. You will have the matter investigated immediately, and arrest the officer who abandonned it."—ALS, DNA, RG 393, District of West Tenn., Letters Received.

1862, MAY 22. Maj. Gen. John A. McClernand to USG. "By 8. O.clock this morning, I had the 3d Brigade of the 3d Division (Maj

Genl L. Wallace) moved up to the position, on the right of Genl Judah, and west of Monterey to which Maj. Mudd called your attention yesterday, at my instance   I am revising my pickets, to day, agreeably to the new disposition. The firing last night (if you heard it) was commenced by some four or five men in charge of some Qr. Mrs.' stores, encamped some three fourths of a mile west of Monterey. The disturbance thus occasioned, while without real cause, extended all along the right of my picket line   I will order thess men away from their present camp"—Copies, DNA, RG 393, Dept. of the Tenn., Letters Received from Reserve Corps, Jackson, Tenn.; McClernand Papers, IHi.

1862, MAY 22.   Maj. Gen. John A. McClernand to USG. "Although, as I am informed by Genl. Wallace Comg 3d Division of the Reserves, the 14th Wis. was detached by him, simply under instructions to guard one of the passes of Owl Creek, the officer commanding the Regiment refuses to report to him: and has disregarded my order, as I am further informed, to do so—pleading an order from Hd. Qs. Dept. Miss. directing him to report to the commandant of the Post of Pittsburg Landing, as his justification. Neither Genl. Wallace, nor myself know any thing of such an order. I speak positively as to myself and inferentially as to Genl. Wallace. Please advise me as to the true relation of this Regiment to Genl Wallace's command, that I may deal with the Officer commanding the Regiment accordingly"—Copies, DNA, RG 393, Dept. of the Tenn., Letters Received from Reserve Corps, Jackson, Tenn.; McClernand Papers, IHi.

On May 27, USG wrote to McClernand. "In reply to yours, relative to the 14th Wisc Vol. That the Regiment remain's in charge of Pittsburg Landing in pusuance of Maj Genl Hallecks Special order, and cannot take possession in Genl. Wallace's Division, until relieved from present duty, by same authority. Col. Woods has been ordered to make returns of his forces ~~to~~ as required by existing orders to Genl Wallace."—Register of Letters, *ibid*. On the same day, Maj. John A. Rawlins wrote to Col. David E. Wood, 14th Wis. "I am directed by Major Gen. Grant to say to you that you will make daily reports ~~to these Head Quarters your~~ Re. of your Regt to Major Gen. L. Wallace instead of to these HeadQuarters, your Regt. having been assigned to his Division of the Army by Special Orders No 78, a copy of which is herewith enclosed. You will, however, remain where you are until further orders from these or General Head Quarters."—Copies, DLC-USG, V, 1, 2, 3, 86; DNA, RG 393, USG Letters Sent.

1862, MAY 23. Brig. Gen. Thomas A. Davies to [USG]. "Statement in regard to beeves butchered in his Division."—DLC-USG, V, 10; DNA, RG 393, USG Register of Letters Received.

1862, MAY 24. Maj. Gen. John A. McClernand to USG. "Enclosed please find copy of a communication from Col Brayman Commanding 29th Regt Ills Infy. respecting the want in his Regt of Quarter Master & Ordnance Stores. I would add that I regret the necessity of again alluding to this subject, but, as yet Quarter Masters & Ordnance officers have failed to respond to the many requisitions made upon them for the supply of these moste pressing wants of the troops, as indicated in Col Braymans. Communication"—Copy, DNA, RG 393, District of West Tenn., Letters Received; *ibid.*, Dept. of the Tenn., Letters Received from Reserve Corps, Jackson, Tenn. A copy of a letter of May 22 from Col. Mason Brayman to Lt. A. H. Ryan is *ibid.* On May 24, Maj. John A. Rawlins wrote to McClernand. "I am directed by Major Gen. U. S. Grant, to say in reply to your communication of this date, that the Quartermasters Department has now on hand all Articles of Camp and Garrison Equipage necessary to supply the Army. The General therefore directs that you will cause requisitions to be made out at once, and teams sent to the landing for such Articles as your command may require, leaving blank the name of the Quartermaster in the requisition, and present them to Major Cross personally who will see that they are promptly filled."—Copies, DLC-USG, V, 1, 2, 3, 86; DNA, RG 393, USG Letters Sent.

1862, MAY 24. Col. Rodney Mason, 71st Ohio, Clarksville, to USG. "Have prisoner at Donelson charged with persuading & assisting deserters from garrison, & a clear case, Can be proved. What shall have done with him."—Telegram received, DNA, RG 393, Dept. of the Mo., Telegrams Received.

1862, MAY 26. Maj. Gen. John A. McClernand to USG. "Dr. Gordon, surgeon of the 30th Ill, who was taken prisoner at Belmont reported to me to day. He says he left Memphis on the 15th inst.— that while at that place he met some of some of his professional classmates there, in the rebel service, who informed him that, on that date, the enemy's force at Corinth numbered 146.000—including 10.000 men from Va. He says these forces were brought from Ark. Mo. La. Ala. and Fld. among other places, and that details were given which I cannot now recount, prospectively increasing the number to 200.000. He adds, however, that a considerable portion of the force at Corinth consists of new levies—being in large part boys or old men. He says that his acquaintances giving him that information had, notwithstanding the preparations mentioned, despaired of the rebel cause; and that a majority of the inhabitants of Memphis are favorably inclined to our side. Having given you this statement, I forbear any comments upon it, except to repeat an opinion some time since communicated—that the enemy will show himself in large force at Corinth, if he should show himself, there, at all. Dr. Gordon says Memphis is ŧ almost, tottally devoid of permanent fortifications; and that large quantities of sugar and cotton have been concealed near Fort Pickering, in anticipation of the capture of the city."—ALS, DNA, RG 393, District of West Tenn., Letters Received; ADfS, *ibid.*, Dept. of the Tenn., Letters Received from Reserve Corps, Jackson, Tenn. *O.R.*, I, x, part 2, 214.

1862, MAY 26.   Maj. Gen. John A. McClernand to USG. "The following is a copy of a telegram just received from Genl. Sherman. 'My Cavalry reports an Infantry camp of the enemy one mile west of Sam Chamber's, who is two and a half miles west of the Locusts, and where the state Line Road crosses the Mobile and Ohio Rail Road. They also report the roads and creeks obstructed by fallen timber' &c. Doubtless this information is already possessed by you. The fallen timber is, probably, the same discovered by you some days since, and the camp the same spoken of by Genl Logan, to day."—Copies, DNA, RG 393, Dept. of the Tenn., Letters Received from Reserve Corps, Jackson, Tenn.; McClernand Papers, IHi.

1862, MAY 26.   Maj. Gen. John A. McClernand to USG. "I avail myself of the opportunity afforded by Col. Adams to advise you of what is passing on this part of our lines. A negro came into camp the other day who reported that he had been employed for some time at Chewalla, some eight or ten miles west of Corinth, on the Memphis and Charleston road. He says that on last Wednesday three trains laden with troops passed on the road to Corinth. The troops, according to his statement, consisted of raw levies, being boys and old grey headed men. He further says that there is a mixed force of Cavalry and Infantry at Chewalla, numbering, in all, some six hundred men. Genl ~~Col~~ Logan, also, reports a camp of Cavalry and ~~artillery~~ Infantry on the same road—estimating the Infantry at about a Brigade. Yesterday, some eighty bales of cotton were brought into this camp, and will be forwarded to the Quarter Master at the Landing. Col. Marsh is returned, but is not yet able for duty. Can't you arrange to give both him and Col. Lawler, respectively, command of a Brigade in the 1st Divn. of my corps? I hope you will be pleased to do so. Of the merit of these officers it is unnecessary, here, to speak, as you are fully acquainted with it. I learn indirectly this morning that Maj. Stolbrand, 2nd Ill. Art. is assigned to duty in the Artillery of the 1st Divn. The order making this assignment was not communicated through me, and from what I learn from Col. Adams, probably, not through you. . . . P. S. I am still hoping that Genl. Wallace's Division will be strengthened by the addition of other regiments, and that such arrangements will be made as will make it safe for him to bring up his command."— ALS, DNA, RG 393, District of West Tenn., Letters Received.

1862, MAY 29. Maj. Gen. John A. McClernand to USG. "After holding an exposed position from yesterday until late this evening on the extreme right of Genl. Sherman's Division and sustaining the casualty of three or four men being wounded, Genl. Logan's Brigade returned to its camp at Ezells. A detachment of the 2nd Brigade (Genl. Ross) holds a commanding position at the deep cut of the M. & O. Rail Road, and will continue to entrench it to night. I propose holding this position until otherwise ordered at all hazzards; with it in our possession the enemy can hardly flank our right at all without our knowing it."—Copies, DNA, RG 393, Dept. of the Tenn., Letters Received from Reserve Corps, Jackson, Tenn.; McClernand Papers, IHi.

1862, MAY 30. Maj. Gen. Henry W. Halleck to USG. "There is every indication that the enemy will attack our left this morning, as troops have been moving in that direction for some time. It will be well to make preperation to send as many of the Reserves as can be spared of the Right Wing in that direction as soon as an attack is made in force. At any rate be prepared for an order to that effect."—Copies, DLC-USG, V, 4, 5, 7, 8, 88; DNA, RG 393, USG Hd. Qrs. Correspondence; *ibid.*, Dept. of the Miss., Letters Sent. *O.R.*, I, x, part 2, 228. On the same day, Maj. John A. Rawlins wrote to Maj. Gen. John A. McClernand. "Make preperation to move as many of the Reserve Corps as can be spared of the Right Wing to the Left should an attack be made in force. in that direction"—Copies, DLC-USG, V, 1, 2, 3, 86; DNA, RG 393, USG Letters Sent.

1862, MAY 31. Maj. Gen. John A. McClernand to USG. "Transmitting a reconnoisance report made by Maj M K M Wallace, by Telegraphic order from Maj Genl. McHalleck."—Register of Letters, McClernand Papers, IHi.

1862, MAY 31. Iowa AG Nathaniel B. Baker to [USG]. "Requesting an extension of furlough in the case of Jerome Lucas Co. "A" 8th Iowa Inf Vols."—DLC-USG, V, 10; DNA, RG 393, USG Register of Letters Received.

1862, JUNE 1. Maj. Gen. John A. McClernand to USG presenting a plan for the capture of Memphis.—Copy, DNA, RG 393, Dept. of the Tenn., Letters Received from Reserve Corps, Jackson, Tenn.

1862, JUNE 1. Maj. Gen. John A. McClernand to USG reporting information from Mr. Jones that three regts. of C. S. A. inf. and one battalion of cav. were camped on the Tuscumbia River and outlining plans to capture them.—Copies, DNA, RG 393, Dept. of the Tenn., Letters Received from Reserve Corps, Jackson, Tenn.; McClernand Papers, IHi.

1862, JUNE 2. Maj. Gen. John A. McClernand to USG. "Recent changes in the commanding officers of the 1st Division of the Reserves making it proper that a reorganization of the Brigade composing it should be effected, I respectfully recommend the following plan for accomplishing the object, for your approval.
1st Brigade:—Col. M K Lawler, 18th 30th 31st and 49th Ills. Infty.
2nd Brigade—Col C. C. Marsh   8th 20th 45th 48th Ills. and 12th Mich
3rd Brigade—Col. T. E. G. Ransom   11th 17th 29th and 61st Ills.
I await your direction in the premises."—Copy, McClernand Papers, IHi.

1862, JUNE 3. Maj. Gen. John A. McClernand to USG. "As advised by Genl. L Wallace, of this date, I have the honor to report that with a regiment of his Division, he was arrived at Purdy this morning, momentarily expecting to be joined by other portions of the same   So soon as much as a Brigade shall have joined him he will push on and confirm the anticipated possession of the bridge across Hatchie by his cavalry which went forward last night at 10 o'clock under instructions to seize the bridge. He further advises me that he was invited last night to take possession of Bolivar, near the bridge, by two citizens from that place, who inform him that, that and the neighborhood of Grand Junction are infested by small marauding rebel cavalry parties, and by none other—the entire Army of Beauregard having gone Southward, leaving no considirable hostile body nearer than Holly Springs Miss. If I might venture a seggestion, would it not be advisable in view of this information, for Genl. Wallace to seize both the bridge mentioned and Grand Junction; or if only one of them, for me to send another Division forward to seize the other?"—Copies, DNA, RG 393, Dept. of the Tenn., Letters Received from Reserve Corps, Jackson, Tenn.; McClernand Papers, IHi.

1862, JUNE 3. Maj. Gen. John A. McClernand to USG requesting that the 7th Mo., then at Pittsburg Landing, be assigned to the 1st Division, Reserve Corps.—Copies, DNA, RG 393, Dept. of the Tenn., Letters Received from Reserve Corps, Jackson, Tenn.; McClernand Papers, IHi.

1862, JUNE 4. Col. T. Lyle Dickey, 4th Ill. Cav., to USG. "Requesting that his regiment be united"—DLC-USG, V, 10; DNA, RG 393, USG Register of Letters Received. On June 11, Maj. John A. Rawlins issued General Orders No. 54 consolidating all the cav. of USG's command (except the 1st Ohio Cav. of Maj. Gen. George H. Thomas's division) into a cav. brigade to be commanded by Dickey.—Copies, DLC-USG, V, 12, 95; DNA, RG 393, USG General Orders. *O.R.*, I, xvii, part 2, 4. On June 20, Rawlins issued General Orders No. 56 revoking General Orders No. 54.—Copies, DLC-USG, V, 12, 95; DNA, RG 393, USG General Orders. *O.R.*, I, xvii, part 2, 20.

1862, JUNE 5. Maj. Gen. John A. McClernand to USG. "Infantry, artillery and cavalry of the 1st Division encamped last night within

four miles of Purdy. The muddy bottom is almost impassible. I had
to corduroy a considerable part of it—build a bridge across the stream,
and cut new roads in some places. The consequence is that a considerable portion of the Brigade trains, and all the supply train is still
behind. Hence, my march to day will be considerably shortened. Genl
Halleck's order directed me to move the Division in the direction of
Bolivar, and that he expected me to report to him instrumentally if a
Telegraph line—to be extended to Bethel. He did not say that I
(personally) was to stop at Bethel or to go on to Bolivar. As both my
Divisions move forward to Bolivar, and as the matters to form the
subject of future reports must for the most part, transpire about Boli-
var, and information of the same be transmitted from that place, I will
(personally) go on to that place, unless otherwise ordered. Being there
I will be better enabled to hasten information forward to the office at
Bethel than I would be by remaining at the latter place."—Copies,
DNA, RG *393*, Dept. of the Tenn., Letters Received from Reserve
Corps, Jackson, Tenn.; McClernand Papers, IHi. On June *3*, Maj. Gen.
Henry W. Halleck ordered McClernand to move his former division
toward Bolivar, and a copy of the letter was sent to USG.—Copies,
DLC-USG, V, 7, 8; DNA, RG *393*, USG Hd. Qrs. Correspondence;
ibid., District of West Tenn., Letters Received. *O.R.*, I, x, part 2,
248. On June 4, McClernand wrote to Halleck and to USG. "In pursuance of orders, 1st Division moved from near Eazells, this morning
at 8 O'ck by the Stage Road, were detained several hours, by construction of a bridge across Muddy Cr'k & a road across the bottom.
Will bevouac here, 4 miles S of Purdy, & move to Bethel through
Purdy to-morrow"—Register of Letters, McClernand Papers, IHi.

1862, JUNE 5.   Col. Cyrus Hall, 14th Ill., to [USG]. "Requesting that
the band of his regiment be mustered out of the service."—DLC-USG,
V, 10; DNA, RG *393*, USG Register of Letters Received.

1862, JUNE 6.   Surgeon Nelson R. Derby, Monterey, Tenn., to USG.
"I beg leave to represent that at this hospital there are about eleven
hundred Sick—that a Chaplains appropriate work can be more effectually performed here than in a regiment moving in the field—and
would respectfully request that the Rev Mr Davis Chaplain of the 7 Ill
Reg be detailed to remain here so long as this hospital may be continued—Mr Davis has, with the consent of his Col remained for a few

days, but thinks he cannot remain longer without more certain authority—He is an earnest worker and has done much good—"—LS, DNA,
RG 393, District of West Tenn., Letters Received. On May 22, Derby
had written to Capt. John C. Kelton asking that forty men be detailed
to guard the hospital at Monterey.—LS, *ibid*. On May 24, Kelton
directed USG to send the guard.—ES, *ibid*.

1862, June 10. Maj. John A. Rawlins to Brig. Gen. Stephen A.
Hurlbut. "Respectfully referred to Brig. Gen. S. A. Hurlbut for investigation and report. Report to be accompanied by Statements of Officers,
as far as practicable to procure them, who know the facts."—Copy,
DLC-USG, V, 83. Written on a letter of May 15 from Lt. Governor
Benjamin Stanton of Ohio to Brig. Gen. Catharinus P. Buckingham
asking for an explanation concerning an enclosed newspaper article
defending the conduct of the 13th Ohio Battery at the battle of Shiloh
and accusing Hurlbut of incompetence and unfairness.—Copy, *ibid*. On
Aug. 18, Hurlbut wrote to Rawlins explaining and detailing his charges
of cowardice against the 13th Ohio Battery.—Copies, DNA, RG 94,
Generals' Papers and Books, William T. Sherman; *ibid*., War Records
Office, Union Battle Reports. *O.R.*, I, x, part 1, 208–11. On Aug. 29,
USG sent forward Hurlbut's report.—DNA, RG 94, Register of Letters Received. See John F. Marszalek, Jr., "William T. Sherman and
the Verbal Battle of Shiloh," *Northwest Ohio Quarterly*, 42 (Fall,
1970), 82–84.

1862, June 10. Maj. Gen. John A. McClernand, Camp Bethel, Tenn.,
to USG. "I am occupying the country, for the most part, from Bethel
to Humbolt, Boliver and the Memphis and Ohio R. Road beyond
Somerville. The demand for cavalry to reconnoiter R. Roads, guard
bridges, escort trains and establish pickets is necessarily very great.
Three companies of cavalry are now at Jackson, and a fourth starts for
that place, today. The two companies of Theildman's cavalry are badly
armed. What will be my strait if I send the three companies of Dickey's
cavalry away before they are replaced? Learning informally from Col
Dickey, some days since, that his cavalry would be taken from me;
not knowing that I could communicate with you upon the subject, I
telegraphed Genl. Halleck, who authorized me to suspend the transfer
until he could see you. Nevertheless, I will send the required companies so soon as they return from a reconnoisance, which will prob-

ably be to night, unless you direct otherwise. As I understand it to be the purpose to reconnoiter and re-open the Rail Road to Columbus: would it not be advisable to order all or a portion of the five companies of the 2nd Ill. cavalry at Hickman to explore the rail road from that place to Jackson, and at the same time disperse any lawless bands on the way? Including these five companies; eleven at Paducah and two at Columbus, there are eighteen companies in that district; besides two companies lately at Sikeston, Mo. If necessary the cavalry at Hickman could be replaced by a detachment from Paducah. I name the cavalry at Hickman for the proposed reconnoisance because it is well armed. Not so with that at Paducah. Our occupation of the country south of the Mississippi must have a quieting effect upon all the country between the Tennessee and Mississippi Rivers and north of the Memphis and Charleston Rail Road. The cavalry at Hickman and Paducah are fresh, while that with the army, in this field, is very much worn and wasted."—LS, DNA, RG 393, District of West Tenn., Letters Received.

1862, JUNE 11.   Maj. Gen. John A. McClernand, Camp Bethel, to USG. "We would consider it a great favor for you to visit this part of your command at this place. Can you come? We are getting along very well but have to use great diligence to supply the different Divns."—Telegram received, DNA, RG 393, Dept. of the Mo., Telegrams Received; copies, *ibid.*, Dept. of the Tenn., Letters Received from Reserve Corps, Jackson, Tenn.; McClernand Papers, IHi.

1862, JUNE 13.   USG [?] endorsement. "This Soldier will be dropped from the rolls as a deserter"—Copy, Oglesby Papers, IHi. Written on a letter of 1st Lt. John M. Duffield, 2nd Iowa, reporting a soldier absent for more than sixty days.—*Ibid.* This is the first of a large number of endorsements attributed to USG dealing with routine matters in June and July, 1862, entered in the endorsement records of Brig. Gen. Richard J. Oglesby. Entries for Aug. are attributed to USG's staff, but in Sept. the attribution returns to USG. Similar entries for other officers in these records, as well as the pattern of other endorsements from USG's hd. qrs., suggest that all, or almost all, were prepared by staff officers, and were recorded to indicate the officer in authority rather than the officer actually writing the endorsement. For these reasons, later endorsements from the same source will not be printed.

1862, JUNE 25. Medical Director John G. F. Holston to USG reporting the condition of hospital facilities at Memphis and recommending the use of the Overton House as a convalescent hospital.—ALS, DNA, RG 393, District of West Tenn., Letters Received. On June 27, Holston wrote to USG. "I have the honour to present for your inspection Ords No 2-N 2—which in my opinion should be published in the papers by authority. I regrett to state, that a case of *small pox* has made its appearance at this hospital which is the immediate cause of Ord. N 2. I had the patient at once removed to a remote room in the 5th story and made requisition on the Provost martia[l] for an isolated house to be used as a Lazaretto, which has not yet been given. The 50 fatigue men ordered yesterday, have not reported to day, only One story as yet is cleansed, they will be needed for a week more. The carpenters reported *without tools* and had therefore to be sent back. I would request a renewal of the order with the addition of the words till discharged or else a substitution of a fresh party dayly till the work is done. The size of the house is enormous and the water has to be carried, thence the slo[w] progress in the upper story"—ALS, *ibid.* On July 1, Holston wrote to USG reporting progress on the Overton House hospital.—ALS, *ibid.* On June 24, Maj. John A. Rawlins issued General Orders No. 57 assigning Holston, then senior medical officer of the District of West Tenn., as medical director.—Copies, DLC-USG, V, 12, 13, 95; DNA, RG 393, Dept. of the Tenn., Miscellaneous Letters Received; *ibid.*, USG General Orders. *O.R.*, I, xvii, part 2, 30.

1862, JUNE 27. USG pass. "The Guards will pass Mr. R. J. Lackland through ~~the~~ and back this evening on the road leading to the South East from the city."—ADS, The Boatmen's National Bank of St. Louis, St. Louis, Mo. Rufus J. Lackland, trustee of the Boatmen's Savings Institution in St. Louis, where USG once had an account, was then looking for some cotton on which his bank had loaned money.—W. G. Rule, *"The Means of Wealth, Peace, and Happiness": The Story of the Oldest Bank West of the Mississippi* (St. Louis, 1947), p. 59.

1862, JUNE 29. B. W. Sharp, Memphis, engineer and superintendent, Memphis and Ohio Railroad, to USG reporting the condition of the railroad.—*O.R.*, I, lii, part 1, 260. On July 8, Brig. Gen. Isaac F. Quinby, Columbus, Ky., who had appointed Sharp, telegraphed to USG questioning his loyalty.—Telegram received, DNA, RG 109, Union Provost Marshals' File of Papers Relating to Individual Civilians.

1862, JUNE 30. Flag Officer Charles H. Davis to USG. "I have the honor to submit to you the enclosed communication, and to say, that I should be very happy to have the transfer of Lieut. Morton, to the Naval flotilla, effected if possible. I am in want of a Pilot for those tributaries of the Mississippi, with which he professes to be acquainted."—Copy, DNA, RG 45, Letterbook of Charles H. Davis.

1862, JULY 2. Capt. Nathaniel H. McLean to USG. "Respectfully referred to Maj Genl Grant Comdg Dist West Tenn. Copies of all orders issued by Comdg. Officers should be forwarded to Dept Head Quarters for file."—AES, DNA, RG 393, District of West Tenn., Letters Received. Written on a letter of June 23 from Brig. Gen. William S. Ketchum to Brig. Gen. George W. Cullum asking whether USG had regularly sent copies of his orders.—LS, *ibid.* On Aug. 16, USG transmitted copies of Special Orders Nos. 150–161 to McLean and to Brig. Gen. Lorenzo Thomas.—Copies (of the covering letter), DLC-USG, V, 4, 5, 7, 8, 9, 88; DNA, RG 393, USG Hd. Qrs. Correspondence. On Aug. 19, USG transmitted copies of General Orders Nos. 67–74 to Thomas.—Copies (of the covering letter), *ibid.* On Aug. 31, USG transmitted General Orders No. 76 to Thomas.— Copies (of the covering letter), *ibid.*

1862, JULY 3. USG Special Orders No. 127. "~~The observance of~~ The birth day of our National Independence will be ~~kept~~ observed in this City by the firing of the National Salute at 12 O'clock, M. Brig. Gen. A. P. Hovey will direct the salute on the part of the Army, and Capt. W. M'Gunnigle U. S. N. on the part of his branch of service. Any further observance desired on the part of Brigade and Regimental commanders will not be objected to, but may be conducted under their supervision."—Copies, DLC-USG, V, 15, 16, 82, 87; DNA, RG 393, USG Special Orders. On July 3, Capt. J. Condit Smith, division q. m. at Moscow, Tenn., telegraphed to USG. "May we fire the National Salute tomorrow morning at Sunrise"—Telegram received, *ibid.*,

Dept. of the Mo., Telegrams Received. On July 4, Smith telegraphed to USG. "Col Worthington Commanding Post at Lafayette requests permission to fire National Salute at 12 M today when did my train leave Memphis"—Telegram received, *ibid.* On July 4, Col. William S. Hillyer, provost marshal, District of West Tenn., issued Special Orders No. 12. "If any proprietor or occupant of any building in any town or city within this District, in the occupancy of the Federal army, shall display or suffer to be displayed, from his or her ho[us]e any treasonable flag or other emblem intended to insult the Federal army or loyal citizens, it shall be the duty of the Local Provost Marshal to take immediate possession of such building and remove the occupants, and convert the same to hospital or other Government uses."— *Memphis Bulletin*, July 6, 1862. On July 4, Col. John M. Thayer, 1st Neb., sponsored the celebration to which various dignitaries were invited, including Charles A. Dana and Albert D. Richardson of the *New York Tribune*, and USG. Toasts were offered to various dignitaries, and Thayer proposed a toast to USG. "General Grant remarked that he dropped speech-making when he donned his uniform, and added that he would rather repeat the day of Donelson than talk, talked he ever so well." After several other toasts, USG proposed a toast to the *Union Appeal.*—*Memphis Union Appeal*, July 5, 1862. See also *Richardson*, p. 265.

1862, JULY 3. To Lt. Col. DeWitt C. Anthony, 23rd Ind., provost marshal at Memphis, "ordering the release of S. A. Meacham, 'who was confined this morning by my order . . .' "—*Charles Hamilton Auction No. 15*, Nov. 3, 1966, p. 24.

1862, JULY 3. Col. Peter E. Bland to [USG]. "Tenders his resignation and applies for leave of absence to await action."—DLC-USG, V, 10; DNA, RG 393, USG Register of Letters Received. On Oct. 26, Maj. John A. Rawlins issued Special Orders No. 233. "Col Peter E Bland of the 6th Regt Missouri Infantry Vols, having reported to these Head Qrs for duty pursuant to orders, will proceed to Memphis Tenn, and report to Maj Genl W T Sherman Commanding 'Disct of Memphis' for the purpose of assuming command of said Regiment." —Copies, DLC-USG, V, 15, 16, 82, 87; DNA, RG 393, USG Special Orders; *ibid.*, RG 94, District of West Tenn., Special Orders.

1862, July 4. USG General Orders No. 61. "Officers and Soldiers
are hereby prohibited, under severe penalties, from selling military
clothing, arms or ammunition whether the same be public or private
property, to Citizens. In cases where such sales have been heretofore
made, the citizens who purchased the same will at once return the
property so purchased to the Commanding Officer of the Company or
Regiment to which the Soldier belongs, of whom the articles were
obtained, or to the Post Quartermaster, under the penalty of being
arrested and placed in confinement. It is made the duty of all Officers
to see that this order is strictly enforced, and that all Officers, Soldiers
or Citizens violating the same by either selling or purchasing are
arrested."—Copies, DLC-USG, V, 12, 13, 14, 95; DNA, RG 393,
USG General Orders. *O.R.*, I, xvii, part 2, 70.

1862, July 4. To Maj. Gen. Henry W. Halleck. "There are 5 Co's
of the 6th Ill Cavalry at Germantown without a Surgeon. J N Niglas,
Surgeon to that Regt, is on duty in Hospital at Paducah. I would
respectfully request that he be ordered here for duty."—Copies, DLC-
USG, V, 4, 5, 7, 8, 88; DNA, RG 393, USG Hd. Qrs. Correspondence.
John N. Niglas of Peoria, Ill., had been mustered in to the 6th Ill.
Cav. as surgeon on Jan. 9, 1862.

1862, July 5. USG pass. "L Slicer will be permitted to pass North
to St. Louis, Mo."—ADS, DNA, RG 109, Union Provost Marshals'
File of Papers Relating to Individual Civilians. After Lawrence Slicer
reached St. Louis, S. V. Clark of that city swore out a complaint before
a notary public on July 22 alleging that Slicer had been a member of
C. S. A. Brig. Gen. Nathan B. Forrest's cav. and a U.S. prisoner.—
DS, *ibid.* On the same day, Slicer signed a loyalty oath to the U.S.
—DS, *ibid.*

1862, July 6. Capt. J. Condit Smith to USG. "When Genl Hurbuts
train leave Memphis"—Telegram received, DNA, RG 393, Dept. of
the Mo., Telegrams Received. On July 6, 1st Lt. Theodore S. Bowers
endorsed the telegram. "Referred to Comy of Subsistence to ascertain
time. Reply in accordance with accompanying note from Capt. Hindsdall
C. S."—AES, *ibid.* On the same day, Capt. Chester B. Hinsdill, commissary of subsistence, wrote to Maj. John A. Rawlins. "The Train
left yesterday morning about nine Oclock"—ALS, *ibid.* On July 7,

Brig. Gen. Stephen A. Hurlbut wrote to Rawlins. "In pursuance of par. 467 General Regulations, I have the honor to report the arrival of the fourth Division, Dist. of W. Tenn.e at LaGrange, Tenn., under orders from Maj. Gen'l W. T. Sherman."—ALS, *ibid.*, District of West Tenn., Letters Received.

1862, JULY 8. Maj. John A. Rawlins to Col. John M. Thayer, Memphis. "About 1 O'clock this morning some soldier of our Army fired some seven shots near these Head Quarters aimed at houses on the opposite side of the Street. The gun used was an Enfield Rifle of the Calibre of 58. Such unauthorized firing is not only dangerous, but is calculated to excite alarm among the citizens and troops. You will make diligent inquiries to learn if possible, whether the firing was done by any soldier of your command, and report the result of your investigation. Similar notes have been sent to other commanders."—LS, Ritzman Collection, Aurora College, Aurora, Ill.

1862, JULY 14. Brig. Gen. William S. Ketchum to USG. "Neither leaves of absence, nor extensions thereof, furloughs or resignations are acted upon at this office."—ALS, DNA, RG 393, Dept. of the Mo., Letters Sent (Press).

1862, JULY 17. Capt. Nathaniel H. McLean to USG. "It has been the custom at these Head Quarters to give out the Parole & Countersign every two days. Capt. McMichael A. A. G informs me that he furnished you with Parole & Countersign for yesterday and to day. Those entitled to the Parole & Countersign will of course, expect to receive the same from your Head Quarters, and not from Dept Hd. Quarters. any longer."—ALS, DNA, RG 393, District of West Tenn., Letters Received.

1862, JULY 17. Col. William S. Hillyer, Memphis, to USG. "Gen Hovey issued an order to the following effect—Is it not premature— All male citizens between the ages of Eighteen and forty-five capable of bearing arms must take the oath of allegiance or leave *lines* under penalty of being treated as spies also orders Provost Marshal to banish all uttering treason or sedition into Arkansas"—Telegram received, DNA, RG 393, Dept. of the Mo., Telegrams Received. On July 17, Brig. Gen. Alvin P. Hovey issued General Orders No. 1,

the substance of which Hillyer had telegraphed.—*Memphis Bulletin,*
July 18, 1862.

1862, JULY 18.   Medical Director John G. F. Holston, Memphis, to
USG. "To judge by the number of patients sent to the hospital in this
city, your army is in an extremely healthy condition. To day 350 sick
& wounded men were brought from Genrl. Curtis command & have
immediately been provided for. I have also commenced the establishment of a hospital Camp for convalescents, which will much shorten
the time for the sick to return to duty. I regrett however to have some
cause to complain. My predecessor left neither books, nor papers, nor
verbal explanations, so that I am totally ignorant *1st of the Geographical
limits of your command & my charge*   2dly I am entirely unacquainted
with *the names & posts of the medical officers thereof.* I beg for information
on the first and I request most respectfully that *an order to the Commanders of Divisions may issue, to see that the Medical Directors (Senior
surgeons)* of each Division forthwith make a report to me on form
N 17 Rev. Regul. Med. Departn as has been required of them by *my*
order. An abuse has crept into the service, to which I beg leave to
draw your attention, as it has been the source of endless confusion.
Medical men, particularly those connected with the regular army, have
arrogated th to themselves functions appertaining to commanding officers. E. G. Contracts have been made for the services of private prac-
titioners, by medical officers, whereas according to SS 1268 to 1272
Rev. Reg. this belongs only to the Commanding officer—thus a Surgeon Satterlee with no other official distinction than U S. A and as I
see, connected with the Bellevue hospital of N. York, engages 3 surgeons   directs them to report to Surg. McDougall U S A & he to
me—I stationed them in this hospital, a few days ago and now 2 are
down sick, with western fever; while if needed, we could have plenty
acclimated western men. Then the transfers of medical men, from different Divisions and even Districts to others, without the knowledge
·of their immediate superiors. Medical, like all other officers, so far *as
change of post is regarded* are under military orders, and a superior
medical officer desiring a change in this respect, ought to effect it by
report & advice to the military authorities. Steamboats are hired &
ordered in the same way. All those things are disorderly & contrary
to Regulation, unless recent laws have made a change. And it is to
those conflicting orders of men, having but little idea of military disci-

pline & government, that all the chaos of Confusion, in the Department is traceable. The medical Department, is simply advisory—though ordinarily, its advice ought to be & will be taken, the *military* (strictly) being *the Executive.* I could quickly organize this ~~Depar~~ District if these things were observed, and I do not despair of doing it as it is— I think the order asked for above & marked with red ink, would go a good piece toward effecting the object, for armed with the power of your names—I could bring the medical officers, straight up to the work, if I simply knew their whereabout . . . Additional July 19th 450 Additional men have just been thrust upon me from Genrl. Hurlbut & Shermans Divisions, coming by way of Columbus, of which not the slightest previous notice had been given—they are being provided for"—ALS, DNA, RG 393, District of West Tenn., Letters Received.

1862, July 19. USG endorsement. "Respectfully forwarded to Hd Qrs. Depart. of the Miss."—ES, DNA, RG 107, Letters Received. Written on a letter of July 16 of Lt. Joseph B. Dorr, 12th Iowa, to Brig. Gen. Pleasant A. Hackleman charging that C. S. A. guards had mistreated and murdered U. S. officers and men who had been captured at Shiloh. On July 17, Hackleman forwarded the letter to Brig. Gen. Richard J. Oglesby.—AES, *ibid.* On July 19, Oglesby forwarded the letter to Maj. Gen. Edward O. C. Ord. "I enclose for the notice of the commanding generals of the Post District and Department. The official statement of Lieut J B Dorr 12 Iow Inftry in regard to the treatment and punishment of union soldiers prisoners of war at Montgomery and Tuscaloosa by the rebel authorities   I have asked for the communication that it may be officially known as far as is possible to make it official—the barbarous and inhuman treatment our poor soldiers receive as prisoners of war from the Rebel army—"—AES, *ibid.* Ord forwarded the letter to USG.

1862, July 19. USG endorsement. "Respectfully forwarded to Head Quarters Department of the Mississippi."—ES, Records of 66th Ill., I-ar. Written on a list of men of the Western Sharpshooters recommended for commissions. The list was eventually forwarded to Governor Hamilton R. Gamble of Mo., who ordered the commissions issued.—AES, *ibid.*

1862, July 19. To Maj. Gen. William T. Sherman. On July 22, Sherman wrote to Col. William S. Hillyer, provost marshal. "I have a telegraph from Gen'l. Grant dated 19th inst. giving me instructions as to a Mrs. Connor of Memphis, whose husband is a surgeon in the Confederate Army, but the father in Memphis is a good man. Please find her out and notify her, that she is at liberty to go to her father-in-Law Mr. Connor of Nashville, via Cairo & Louisville; give her the necessary pass. Cannot you frame some Rules about the trade on the River, and into the country, that will obviate the necessity of passes. The are a nuisance, and don't interfere with the mischevious, but do with the honest man."—Copy, DNA, RG 94, Generals' Papers and Books, William T. Sherman, Letters Sent.

1862, JULY 19. Capt. Nathaniel H. McLean to USG. "Respectfully referred to Maj Genl Grant Comdg Dist West Tennessee."—AES, DNA, RG 393, Dept. of the Tenn., Miscellaneous Letters Received. Written on a telegram of July 17 from Maj. William S. Oliver, provost marshal at Pittsburg Landing, to Col. John C. Kelton asking advice as to the disposition of two cases, one involving Henry T. Newman, a rebel sympathizer charged with the murder of Robert Smith near Decaturville, Tenn., and the other involving Lt. Col. Francis C. Taylor, Tenn. state militia, charged with arresting Union men.—Telegram received, *ibid.*

1862, JULY 19. Maj. Gen. John A. McClernand to USG. "The officers of the 68th Ohio present reasons for sending Col Stedman Commanding before the Commission which has adjourned from here to Bolivar—the function of the commission is to inquire concerning the qualifications of officers and with your approbation he will be summoned before the commission"—Telegram received, DNA, RG 393, Dept. of the Mo., Telegrams Received; copy, McClernand Papers, IHi.

1862, JULY 20. Brig. Gen. William K. Strong to USG. "Acknowledging receipt of order assigning him to command of Dist. West Tenn."—DLC-USG, V, 10; DNA, RG 393, USG Register of Letters Received.

1862, JULY 20. George E. Flynt to [USG]. "Statements in reference to his nephew *James H. Flynt,* Co. B. 15th Iowa Inf. Vols."—DLC-USG, V, 10; DNA, RG 393, USG Register of Letters Received.

1862, July 21.   Col. Thomas J. Haines, St. Louis, to USG. "The General Comd'g the Department having ordered Captain B Du Barry, C. S. to Corinth as Chief Comsy of the Dist of West Tennessee, I would respectfully suggest that when absent from your Head Quarters, the Captain may be authorized (in your name) to issue such orders as may be necessary for the proper administration of the affairs of the Subst Dept in the District. As Corinth will I presume continue to be the important Depot, and it may be impracticable for the Captain to consult with you personally or by letter at times when prompt action may be required, I have taken the liberty to make the above suggestion."—LS, DNA, RG 94, Staff Papers.

1862, July 22.   To Col. William Hoffman, commissary gen. of prisoners. USG requested that an exchange be made of 1st Lt. Daniel T. Bowler, 7th Iowa, captured at the battle of Belmont, for C. S. A. 1st Lt. George T. Moorman, of the staff of Brig. Gen. Bushrod Johnson, captured at Fort Donelson, "held by us as a prisoner I believe at Chicago."—Theodore Sheldon collection, Mercury Stamp Company, Inc., catalogue, June 5, 1970, p. 10. See *O.R.*, I, vii, 363–64; *ibid.*, II, iii, 864. On July 29, Bowler wrote to Hoffman. "I arrived here this morning bearing a litter from Genl Grant. for the release of Lieut Geo T Moorman taken at Donelson and serving on Genl Johnsons staff at that time   I learned at Chicago that he probaby was at Johnsons Island near Sandusky   I was in hopes to find you here but in the uncertainty of the time your being here I leave Genl Grants litter and presume Moorman will be sent as directed in Exchange for me. I was Eight Months a prisoner in the South, and I desire to see my family much. I leave here for Keokuk Iowa where I shall await communication from you. please advise me as soon as possible that I may know that the exchange has been made and feel releived"—ALS, DNA, RG 249, Letters Received.

1862, July 22.   Maj. Gen. John A. McClernand, Jackson, Tenn., to USG. "If available please send a Paymaster here."—Register of letters, McClernand Papers, IHi.

1862, July 22.   Maj. Gen. George H. Thomas, Tuscumbia, Ala., to USG. "Lt Col Shepherd had a Dr Desprie living at Cheroke arrested some days since for carrying supplies to rebels or communicating with them—from all I can learn Col Shepherd was misinformed for I am assured by Mr Calvin Goodlae that he knows there were no rebel cavalry or infantry on cedar creek at that time. He is a man of veracity and promises to hold himself responsible that Dr Despries has not given aid or comfort to the enemy and asks that he be released"— Telegram received, DNA, RG 109, Union Provost Marshals' File of Papers Relating to Individual Civilians.

1862, July 22.   Col. William W. Lowe to USG. "The following dispatch has just been recd 'From Smithland 22d   Col W. W. Low comdg Ft Henry   can you spare a company of cavalry on Election day—we shall require more assistance here to inforce the laws   signed A. D. Daugherty Lt Comdg   From this it is to be seen that I am called upon from distant points for assistance   I now have a party scouting from and around Donelson"—Telegram received, DNA, RG 393, Dept. of the Mo., Telegrams Received.

1862, July 23.   USG endorsement. "Disapproved and respectfully forwarded to Hd. Qrs. Depart. of the Miss"—ES, USGA, gift of Dr. Donald R. Mackay, St. Paul, Minn. Written on a letter of July 19 from 1st Lt. Benjamin F. Butler, Co. D, 4th Minn., to Col. John B. Sanborn, 4th Minn., resigning his commission for reasons of health. —ALS, *ibid.* Butler's resignation was accepted as of Nov. 4.

1862, July 23.   USG endorsement. "Refered to the Act. provost Marshal who will report the facts and return this to these Head Quarters without delay."—AES, DNA, RG 393, District of West Tenn., Letters Received. Written on a letter of July 23 from Capt. John P. Hawkins to Maj. John A. Rawlins reporting that the wife of the owner of a contraband female slave had forcibly taken the slave from Hawkins's house with the help of the provost guard and act. provost marshal of Corinth.—ALS, *ibid.* On the same day, Lt. Thomas H. Hedrick, act. provost marshal, wrote that the statements of Hawkins were "*entirely* without truth."—AES, *ibid.* On July 24, Maj. Gen. Edward O. C. Ord wrote to Rawlins. "I have questioned Capt Duff of Genl. Judahs Staff—who with another officer (quite sick) are boarders at Mrs Boswells—who took the mulatto girl from Capt Dodds—the Capt states that in his presence Capt Dodd told Mrs. B. to go to his house and get the girl—that she did so—that he (Duff) did not do more than accompany her—that the boarders at the house pay the girl

—and that he thinks it highly unofficerlike for a brother officer to entice her from a sick officer whom he Duff now has to wait upon. In my opinion, with the enemy in our front in force, moving towards us— officers who occupy the time of Generals Commanding in efforts to procure mulatto girls—or retain them—should be summarily dealt with. In the last twenty four hours, I have been anxious to inspect the works now nearly completed for the defence of this place—but my time has been principally occupied in mulatto girl investigations—to the private gratification of official competitors this makes the third case of contests for mulatto girls which officers of Rank have endeavoured to intrude into my official archives. If the Genral Commanding will publish an order directing such people to be left where they now are, (generally in the hands of some officer)—and arresting all concerned in further squabbles over them—I will be able to attend to more of my duties—"—ALS, *ibid*.

1862, JULY 23.   Capt. Nathaniel H. McLean to USG. "Respectfully referred to Maj Genl Grant Comdg Dist West Tenn, with the request that he will give the orders to Comdg Officers in his district as requested within."—AES, DNA, RG 393, USG Letters Received. Written on a letter of July 23 from Surgeon Charles McDougall, medical director, Dept. of the Miss., to McLean requesting copies of all orders relating to the operation of the medical services.—ALS, *ibid*. On July 24, Maj. John A. Rawlins issued General Orders No. 63. "Copies of all orders heretofore given by Commanders of Army Corps, Division or smaller commands affecting the Govenment of Hospitals will be furnished, with as little delay as practicable, to the Medical Director of the Department. A copy of all hereafter published effecting the same will be furnished as indicated above at the time of their publication."—Copies, DLC-USG, V, 12, 13, 14, 95; DNA, RG 393, USG General Orders; (printed), *ibid*., RG 94, Special Orders, District of West Tenn.; *ibid*., 48th Ill., Letterbook.

1862, JULY 23.   Governor Richard Yates of Ill. to USG. "Being advised that Mrs. P. C. Yates Matron of one of your Hospitals, and who is a very benevolent lady, is desirous of being transferred to the Army of the Potomac, I respectfully request that you will comply with her request if possible, granting such facilities as are under your control."—Copy, Yates Papers, IHi.

1862, JULY 24.   USG endorsement. "Respectfully forwarded to Head Quarters Department of the Mississippi."—ES, DNA, RG 249, Letters Received. Written on a letter of July 19 of Col. Mason Brayman, 29th Ill., Jackson, Tenn. "When this Regiment left camp before Corinth, for this place, it became necessary to leave behind, the sick. among these was a Son of 2nd Lt Theodore Millspaugh. The Father had leave to remain with him. The Son died. The Father accompanied his remains to his home in Illinois for burial—*not having obtained leave of absence.* He had previously, tendered his resignation, in conseqence of wounds received in battle. He attempted to re-join his Regiment—*via* Mississippi River and by Rail from Memphis. Being on the train captured in June by Jackson's cavalry, on the Memphis & Charleston Road, he is now a *prisoner* and I am not advised *where* he is. By 'Special Field Order No 154,' issued from Department Head Quarters, at Corinth, July 13, 1862, the resignation of Lt. Millspaugh was accepted to take ~~place~~ effect from that date. It is desireable that he, and his captors, know the fact that he is out of the U. S. Service, so that he may be reclaimed : and I have deemed it proper to state all the circumstances of his absence, to enable the Department Commander, to dispose of the case advisedly—adding that he was a good man and faithful Officer, and doubtless impelled by great grief and anxiety on account of his Son, to depart in the manner stated."—LS, *ibid.*

1862, JULY 25.   Brig. Gen. William S. Rosecrans to Maj. John A. Rawlins. "Does 'paroled prisoners' in S. O. No 143. mean our soldiers put on their parole by the rebels ?"—Telegram, copy, DNA, RG 393, Army of the Miss., 16th Army Corps, Telegrams Sent. On July 15, Brig. Gen. Lorenzo Thomas telegraphed to Maj. Gen. Henry W. Halleck. "It is expected that as arrangements will soon be made for an exchange of prisoners of War—The point in the West at which the prisoners will be assembled will be near Vicksburg—The Secretary of War directs that the arms and ammunition be sent with the prisoners to be put in the hands of those returned to us from the rebels, that they may be at once put on duty."—Copy, *ibid.*, RG 94, Letters Sent. On July 24, Rawlins issued Special Orders No. 143. "Commanders of Divisions, Brigades, and detached commands in the vicinity of Corinth will send to Major Gen. Ord on Saturday the 26th inst. all paroled prisoners now with their respective commands. Gen. Ord will immediately after receiving these prisoners, forward them to Benton Bar-

racks, Mo. in accordance with General Orders from the War Dept."
—Copies, DLC-USG, V, 15, 16, 82, 87; DNA, RG 393, USG Special
Orders; *ibid.*, RG 94, Special Orders, District of West Tenn.; *ibid.*,
21st Ill., Order Book; *ibid.*, 48th Ill., Order Book. On July 25, Rawlins
issued Special Orders No. 144. "Hereafter all charge of Political prisoners will be left with the Provost Marshal, under direction of the
Provost Marshal General   All prisoners confined will have their cases
examined into with as little delay as practicable and the result of the
examination reported to these Hd. Qrs. Maj Gen Ord, Commdg. Post,
will furnish the Provost Marshal General with all orders heretofore
issued pertaining to the duties from which this order relieves him. The
Provost Marshal General will be charged with granting permits for
all persons not connected with the Army to pass over the railroads and
through the lines with such restrictions as are, or may be ordered."—
Copies, DLC-USG, V, 15, 16, 82, 87; DNA, RG 393, USG Special
Orders.

1862, JULY 26.   Brig. Gen. William K. Strong, Cairo, to USG. "Insane Soldier here—Paragraph one hundred sixty nine (169) army
regulations requires your order to send him to Washington or is there
any other place to which he can be sent   please reply"—Telegram
received, DNA, RG 393, Dept. of the Mo., Telegrams Received. Dept.
commanders could not discharge insane soldiers, but were required to
send them to Washington, D.C., for admission to the federal asylum.
—*Revised Regulations for the Army of the United States, 1861* (Philadelphia, 1861), p. 31.

1862, JULY 26.   Col. James M. Shackelford, 25th Ky., Camp Clark
near Fort Henry, to USG. "Mr. Wm Mills of Christian County Kenty
is a reliable truthful gentleman—He has been an active loyal citizen
and engaged for Some time past in recruiting for my Regiment   He
has lost a Slave and probably a horse taken from him by the rebels—
Any assistance you might give to [him] in recovering his Servant and
horse would be thankfully received by him—And properly appreciated
by your friends—"—ALS, DNA, RG 109, Union Provost Marshals'
File of Papers Relating to Individual Civilians.

1862, JULY 27.   Brig. Gen. Isaac F. Quinby, Columbus, Ky., to USG.
"The companies of infantry that I sent up the Ohio river to the point

said to have been taken by the rebels have returned but the Rob Roy with the section of artilery is detained by order, I am told of Maj Genl Love. The whole thing was a farce and the detention is unneccissary I am powerless to get the boat & artilery back. May I ask you to give the necessary order. They are supposed to be at Henderson Ky."— Telegram received, DNA, RG 393, Dept. of the Mo., Telegrams Received. On July 18, Brig. Gen. Jeremiah T. Boyle, Louisville, Ky., telegraphed to Brig. Gen. William K. Strong, Cairo, that Henderson, Ky., had been taken by C. S. A. troops and asked for a gunboat and troops to be sent.—Telegram received, *ibid.*; copy, *ibid.*, District of West Tenn., Letters Received. On July 19, Strong wrote to Quinby asking for troops.—Copy, *ibid.*

1862, JULY 27.   Capt. Beekman Du Barry, Cairo, to USG. "In obedience to S. O. No 289 Hd: Qrs: Dept: of the Miss: St: Louis Mo. July 20 1862. I have the honor to report that I have just returned from inspecting at Columbus, Hickman, Island No 10, and New Madrid, and will proceed to Helena, Ark: by the first opportunity and thence via Memphis & Columbus, Ky, to Corinth with as little delay as practicable. Should you have any instructions for me previous to my reaching Corinth will you please have them addressed to me at Columbus, Ky, so that I may receive them on my return to that place."— ALS, DNA, RG 393, District of West Tenn., Letters Received.

1862, JULY 29.   To hd. qrs., Dept. of the Miss. "Asks if the resignation of Col. W. W. Coler of 25 Ills. Vols. has not been forwarded not to do so &c."—DNA, RG 393, Dept. of the Miss., Register of Letters Received. On Aug. 4, Capt. Andrew C. Kemper wrote, probably to USG. "Application to resign was recd. 3d April 1862   Not granted —but instead thereof a leave of Absence expiring 28 April 1862. No application recd. since then."—*Ibid.*

1862, JULY 29.   To Brig. Gen. William S. Rosecrans. "I regard your Command as coming within the perview of paragraph 1023"—Telegram, copy, DNA, RG 393, Army of the Miss., Telegrams Received. On July 29, Rosecrans telegraphed to USG. "Please inform me if this Corps de Armie is an Army in the field within the perview of the paymaster or of paragraph 1023 Army regulations"—Telegram received, *ibid.*, Dept. of the Mo., Telegrams Received; copy, *ibid.*, Army of the Miss., 16th Army Corps, Telegrams Sent. Paragraph 1023, Revised Army Regulations, authorized an officer commanding a dept. or army in the field to dispose of condemned property except ordnance materiel unless the property was of great value, in which case he was to refer the question to the proper staff officer of the War Dept.— *Revised Regulations for the Army of the United States, 1861* (Philadelphia, 1861), p. 152.

1862, July 29. Capt. William McMichael to USG. "Major McLean has just received a telegraphic order from Maj. Genl. Halleck. to remove the archives &c of the Department to Saint Louis. He will leave as soon as possible, and desires me to advise you of the receipt of the above order and to ask whether you will need a further supply of blanks of which there is an abundance here."—ALS, DNA, RG 393, District of West Tenn., Letters Received.

1862, July 29. Col. John L. Doran, 17th Wis., to [USG]. "In reference to the reinstatement of certain officers of his regiment."—DLC-USG, V, 10; DNA, RG 393, USG Register of Letters Received.

1862, July 29. Col. John D. Stevenson, Pittsburg Landing, to USG. "Prisoner Boyd was discharged in accordance with your telegraph. I Shall Send to Genl Ord the prisoners of 2nd Ky Cavalry."—Telegram received, DNA, RG 393, Dept. of the Mo., Telegrams Received.

1862, July 29. Medical Director John G. F. Holston to USG. Holston asked USG to clarify his relationship to USG's new command, and about the status of a medical circular issued on July 12 by Medical Director Charles McDougall, Dept. of the Miss., and its relationship to General Medical Dept. Orders No. 3, issued by Holston at Memphis on June 25. Holston was particularly concerned that McDougall's order, which required brigade reports to the medical director, would entail a great deal more work than his order, which required reports from the division level only.—ALS, DNA, RG 393, District of West Tenn., Letters Received. A printed copy of General Medical Orders No. 3 is *ibid*. On July 27, Maj. John A. Rawlins issued Special Orders No. 146. "The senior or Division Surgeon of each Division will immediately make out and forward to Brigade Surgeon Jno G Holsten, Medical Director of the Disct, a return of the Medical Officers of their respective Divisions as required by revised Army Regulations, form

17. Medical Dept. Certificates of Disability for Discharge of enlisted men will be forwarded to the Medical Directors of the respective Army Corps to which they belong. From the Discts of Cairo & Miss, and the Army of the Tenn, except the forces at Memphis, they will be forwarded, for the present, to Brigade Surgeon H. Wardner, at Corinth, who is authorized to act until the arrival of surgeon Holsten, Medical Director."—DS, McClernand Papers, IHi; copies, DLC-USG, V, 15, 16, 82, 87; DNA, RG 393, USG Special Orders.

1862, JULY 29.   Maj. Richard H. Nodine to [USG]. "Requests that Lieut. and R. Q. M. C. P. Ford be ordered to Lebanon, Mo. to straighten up his affairs."—DLC-USG, V, 10; DNA, RG 393, USG Register of Letters Received.

1862, JULY 29.   Capt. Marcellus G. V. Strong, Cairo, to USG. "I have received a telegraph from you in words following—Keep the company you refer to until the work they are engaged in completed   I apprehend this dispatch to be missent, not understood here. Genl Strong I suppose to be with you"—Telegram received, DNA, RG 393, Dept. of the Mo., Telegrams Received. On the same day, Brig. Gen. Isaac F. Quinby, Columbus, telegraphed to USG. "The company of fifth Mo Vols at Columbus are at work on Magizines   there is here a very large amount of ammunition for which we have no Secure storage and in case of attack we Should be liable to distruction explosion; the more dangerous articles have been and are now being moved into the four Magizines already completed   When the larger one in the main work is finished upon which we are now at work our Storage for powder &c will be Sufficient for any amount likely to be Sent here   Am I right in the inference From your Despatch of the 28th that I can keep the company ~~that~~ refered to until the large Magizine is finished"—Telegram received, *ibid.*

1862, JULY 30.   To Brig. Gen. William S. Rosecrans. "Two deserters from the 56th Ills. Allen and William Jones have been apprehended, and confined at Cairo   Detail a suitable person to go after them and bring them here for Trial"—Telegram, copy, DNA, RG 393, Army of the Miss., Telegrams Received.

1862, JULY 30.   To Brig. Gen. William S. Rosecrans. "Permit such females as you may choose to remain in your Army Corps"—Telegram, copy, DNA, RG 393, Army of the Miss., Telegrams Received. On July 21, Maj. John A. Rawlins issued Special Orders No. 140. "No females will be allowed to leave Columbus, Ky, or any intermediate railway station by Railroad to join any part of the Army of this District without a Special written permit from Dept Hd. Qrs. or these Head Quarters. All females from abroad remaining within the camp lines after the 31st inst. not having such permit, shall be arrested and sent out of the District. Division, Brigade, Post, Regimental and Company Commanders will see to the faithful execution of this order throughout their respective commands"—Copies, DLC-USG, V, 15, 16, 82, 87; DNA, RG 393, USG Special Orders; *ibid.*, RG 94, 21st Ill., Order Book; (misdated and misnumbered) *ibid.*, Special Orders, District of West Tenn.

On July 21, Brig. Gen. Isaac F. Quinby telegraphed to USG. "Am I right in directing permits to be refused to laundresses hospital matrons nurses & soldiers wives except in cases approved by your. order Applications are innumerable"—Telegram received, *ibid.*, RG 393, Dept. of the Mo., Telegrams Received. On July 27, Capt. Daniel Howell, 12th Wis., Columbus, Ky., telegraphed to USG. "My wife matron of hospital returning to Regiment at Humboldt. Please send pass, answer"—Telegram received, *ibid.* On July 23, Col. Silas C. Toler, 60th Ill., Columbus, telegraphed to USG. "Mrs Marks wife of Capt Marks now commanding 18th Ills is here en route to Jackson Tenn—Will you give special permission for her and Servant to go on morning train"—Telegram received, *ibid.*, RG 109, Union Provost Marshals' File of Papers Relating to Individual Civilians.

USG received numerous other requests for permission to bring women into the District of West Tenn. On Aug. 1, William H. Willcox telegraphed to USG from Columbus asking for passes for his wife and servants to Jackson.—Telegram received, *ibid.*, RG 393, Dept. of the Mo., Telegrams Received. On Aug. 5, Asst. Surgeon Lyman Hall telegraphed to USG for passes for two female nurses.— Telegram received, *ibid.* On Aug. 6, Maj. Christian Thieleman telegraphed to USG asking for a permit for his wife.—Telegram received, *ibid.* On Aug. 9, Col. Thomas W. Harris telegraphed to Rawlins asking for permits for the wives of several officers.—Telegram received, *ibid.* On Aug. 14, G. W. Whitlock telegraphed to USG asking for a pass for Ruth Parsons.—Telegram received, *ibid.* On Aug. 24, Rosecrans telegraphed to USG asking whether he might pass the wife of C. S. A.

Maj. Gen. John C. Breckinridge.—Copy, *ibid.*, Army of the Miss.,
Telegrams Sent. On Sept. 5, Quinby telegraphed to USG asking about
a pass for a Mrs. Hamilton which USG had purportedly written.—
Telegram received, *ibid.*, RG 109, Union Provost Marshals' File of
Papers Relating to Individual Civilians. On Sept. 6, Brig. Gen. John
A. Logan telegraphed to USG asking for permits for two women to
visit their husbands.—Telegram received, *ibid.*

1862, JULY 30.   Col. John C. Kelton, Washington, D.C., to USG.
"Respectfully referred to Maj Genl Grant for, investigation and report. If Surgeon Derby has sent the officer away without proper
authority he will be arrested"—Copy, DLC-USG, V, 83. Written on
a letter of Col. Thomas T. Heath, 5th Ohio Cav., Memphis, July 23,
requesting to be reinstated. "Was sent Home by Surgeon Derby on
account of sickness, writing to if the Leave of Absence he had applied
for was granted. after being at Home three weeks was notified that
his application for leave was disapproved. Left his command on the
6th of May started back on the 18th of June, but having been mis-
directed did not reach his regiment till the 7th July—immediately forwarded to Dept Hd. Qrs a statement accounting for his absence,
accompanied by proper ~~authority~~ certificate. Was notofied on 23d July
that he was mustered out of service—Believing that injustice has been
done him asks to have the order mustering him out of service service,
revoked."—Copy, *ibid.*
   On Aug. 23, and again on Aug. 27, Maj. Gen. William T. Sherman
forwarded to Maj. John A. Rawlins statements of Surgeon Nelson R.
Derby explaining his actions.—DNA, RG 393, Army of the Tenn.,
5th Division, Endorsements. On Aug. 26, Sherman wrote to Rawlins
that Derby was under arrest, but still in charge of the Overton Hospital.—Copies, *ibid.*, RG 94, Generals' Papers and Books, William T.
Sherman, Letters Sent; DLC-William T. Sherman. *O.R.*, I, xvii,
part 2, 188. On Sept. 6, Sherman endorsed to Rawlins a statement by
Heath. "Genl. Hurlbuts Division to which the 5th Ohio Cavalry is
attached marches today for Brownsville. Col Taylor of the 5th Ohio
Cavalry is now in Cincinnati on Recruiting service   I have no official
or personal knowledge of the merits of this case. Except that Surgeon
Derby admitted that he had granted the leave for which Dr Derby is
now 'in arrest' and the papers sent to Gen Halleck thru Gen. Grant."
—DNA, RG 393, Army of the Tenn., 5th Division, Endorsements.

1862, July 30. 1st Master Jason Goudy, commanding gunboat *Alfred Robb*, Pittsburg Landing, to USG. "Have just returned from Perry County, took Seven (7) wealthy citizens as hostages for Stolen government property and released them on parole & gave them until Saturday to return the property   if it is not returned then I hold these seven men responsible—There is a Guerrilla Band in Perry County who threatened to defend the property at all hazard   I was assisted by the Scout Breckenridge & about forty Citizens   could have got enough to take the ~~property~~ party which they tell me amounts to about one hundred (100) But could not get arms and ammunition. Can I get a detachment from the 7th Regt. Mo. Vols. to go down   I will endevor to send these Recovered union citizens out to State the condition of the country"—Telegram received, DNA, RG 393, Dept. of the Mo., Telegrams Received. Later, Goudy telegraphed to USG. "I have issued two hundred (200) guns & accotrements with amunition to the loyal citizens of E. perryville & Canonville Tenn. About two hundred (200) more of the loyal citizens in those vicnties have requested to do what I could to arm them—If you will let me have two hundred more muskets & accoutrements with amunition I will supply the above named ~~u~~ upon the 13th inst I came upon a party of guerrillas on the bank of the river at the mouth of Cedar Creek & immediately opened fire upon them. They retired without reply ~~both~~ with the Tennessians I have already armed in ~~hot que~~ hot pursuit with scout Breckendge at their head. I will have to confine my self to a short ~~telegraph~~ length of river if the river continues to fall as it has within the last few days"—Telegram received (undated), *ibid.*

1862, July 31. USG pass for Maj. Thomas P. Robb. "Pass Maj. Robb, Sanitary Agent for the State of Illinois, through all parts of the Dist. of West Tennessee and over the Military roads *free of charge.*" —ADS, Robb Papers, IHi. On Aug. 28, Governor Richard Yates of Ill. wrote to USG. "I beg to return you my thanks for many courtesies and attentions paid to our state agent Maj. T. P. Robb. He is I think doing a very important, and noble work, and I am glad to hear that you sustain and assist him."—Copy, Yates Papers, *ibid.*

1862, July 31. Capt. Joseph B. Gilpin, commissary of subsistence, Columbus, Ky., to USG. "Capt Jno C. Cox of Columbus having written you on the subject of stores, I beg leave to state my reasons for not receipting to him to be the non arrival of the stores mentioned in Invoices. in one case there was to have been fifteen (15) car loads I got but nine (9)—In another Eighteen (18) Sacks of Coffee; I got *none* In fact the shipments never turn out right—Genl Logan & Capt Hawkins both told me I was right in not ~~going~~ giving a Receipt for more than I got."—Telegram received, DNA, RG 393, Dept. of the Mo., Telegrams Received.

1862, JULY 31.   Mark D. Crane, telegraph operator, Corinth, to USG. "Mr. Weir disolving connection with the Telegraph & Mr Parker being absent ~~at~~ north, we are left without any one to put your message in cypher I have telegraphed for the key to be sent me immediately, as it has been an over sight. I can send your message to Cairo in english & have it put in cypher there if you think proper"— Telegram received, DNA, RG 393, Dept. of the Mo., Telegrams Received.

1862, AUG.   USG endorsement. "Captain Heath will have to call on Colonel Hoffman, superintendent of prisoners of war, Detroit, Mich., to effect this exchange."—*O.R.*, II, iv, 320. Written on a letter of July 31 from Capt. Joshua W. Heath, Co. A, 46th Ohio, Memphis, to Maj. Gen. William T. Sherman explaining that he and five men were captured by cav. of Col. William H. Jackson. He was released on condition he would attempt to secure the exchange of his men and thirty-two others held at Grenada, Miss.—*Ibid.* On Aug. 27, Col. William Hoffman referred the letter to Brig. Gen. Lorenzo Thomas.—*Ibid.*

1862, AUG. 1.   To [Maj. Gen. John Love, Ind. Legion]. "Lieut. Col. Foster Twenty Fifth Indiana (25) can remain at Henderson, Ky. until his services can be dispensed with, or until he receives further orders." —Copy, Morton Papers, In. On July 31, Love telegraphed to Lt. Col. John W. Foster. "Applied to Gen. Grant to extend your fourlough, tell Col Gavin the two companies did not start this morning, but will at noon, they are over two hundred strong, are any more troops needed?"—Copy, *ibid.*

1862, AUG. 1.   Brig. Gen. John A. Logan, Jackson, Tenn., to USG. "There are two men here propose to tender two (2) or three (3) Companies of Cavalry if they can be mustered into the service Shall

I do it?''—Telegram received, DNA, RG 393, Dept. of the Mo., Telegrams Received.

1862, Aug. 1.   Brig. Gen. Isaac F. Quinby to USG. "There is some movement of the enemy in the rear of Reel foot Lake and I am apprehensive of an attack on I[s]land No 10   I have there but two (2) small companies of infantry one company of cavalry and a section of artillery—should the rebels get possession our fleet would be blockaded—Is it not possible to send there a regiment of Infantry from some point north''—Telegram received, DNA, RG 393, Dept. of the Mo., Telegrams Received. On July 31, Capt. Robert B. Jones, 34th Ind., commanding at New Madrid, Mo., wrote to Quinby emphasizing the need for more troops to guard the region of southeastern Mo. and northeastern Ark. On Aug. 2, Quinby referred a copy of this letter to USG.—ES, *ibid.*, District of West Tenn., Letters Received.

1862, Aug. 1.   Medical Director Charles McDougall to USG. "Respectfully referred to Hd. Qrs. Dist of West Tenn. with request that the detail be made''—AES, DNA, RG 393, Dept. of the Tenn., Miscellaneous Letters Received. Written on a letter of July 25 from Brigade Surgeon Alexander H. Hoff to McDougall requesting the detail of a list of men for service as nurses on the hospital ship *D. A. January.*—ALS, *ibid.* On Aug. 4, Maj. John A. Rawlins issued Special Orders No. 153 making the assignments. — DS, *ibid.*, RG 94, Special Orders, District of West Tenn.; copies, *ibid.*, RG 393, USG Special Orders; DLC-USG, V, 15, 16, 82, 87.

1862, Aug. 1.   Private Richard Ealey to [USG]. "Making complaint against his commanding officer.''—DLC-USG, V, 10; DNA, RG 393, USG Register of Letters Received.

1862, Aug. 3.   USG endorsement. "Order the buildings and grounds taken for Hospital purposes.''—AES, DNA, RG 393, District of West Tenn., Letters Received. Written on a letter of Aug. 3 from Medical Director Charles McDougall to USG transmitting a report by Brig. Surgeon James D. Strawbridge, Jackson, Tenn., recommending the occupation of a number of buildings in Jackson for use as hospitals.— ALS, *ibid.* USG also wrote on the report. "Forward with the order to comd.g officer at Jackson to procure certain houses & grounds for

Hospital purposes this report."—AES, *ibid.* On Aug. 5, Strawbridge
wrote to McDougall complaining of the encampment of troops near
the hospital at Jackson, which he anticipated would make it impossible
to use the grounds for hospital tents.—ALS, *ibid.* On Aug. 7, Act.
Medical Director Charles H. Rawson, Dept. of the Miss., endorsed
this letter to USG. "Respectfully refered to Maj Gen Grant, with the
request, 'if not already done' that the buildings, also ground occupied
by 20th regt. Ill Infty, be ordered vacated & turned over for Hospital
use & kept for that purpose"—AES, *ibid.*

1862, AUG. 3.   To Maj. Gen. Don Carlos Buell. "The foregoing
despatch just received   Col Walker & Regiment are not in my com-
mand   thinking that he may be in yours & important that the order
should reach him I transmit the same to you"—Telegram received,
DNA, RG 94, Generals' Papers and Books, Telegrams Received by
Gen. Buell; copies, *ibid.*, RG 393, Dept. of the Ohio, Telegrams
Received. On Aug. 3, Maj. Gen. Henry W. Halleck telegraphed to
USG to ask him to order Col. John C. Walker, 35th Ind., to St. Louis.
—ALS (telegram sent), *ibid.*, RG 107, Telegrams Collected (Bound);
telegram received, *ibid.*, RG 393, Dept. of the Tenn., Telegrams
Received. On the same day, USG forwarded Halleck's telegram to
Buell.—Telegram received, *ibid.*, RG 94, Generals' Papers and Books,
Telegrams Received by Gen. Buell; copy, *ibid.*, RG 393, Dept. of the
Ohio, Telegrams Received. On the same day, Maj. John A. Rawlins
telegraphed to Brig. Gen. William S. Rosecrans. "Is the 35th Inda
Regt, Col Jno. C Walker Comdg, in your command. Do you know
where it, or Col Walker is."—Copy, *ibid.*, Army of the Miss., Tele-
grams Received. On the same day, Rosecrans telegraphed to Rawlins.
"Lt Col Chandler commands the 35th Illinois, and it is stationed at
Jacinto"—Copy, *ibid.*, Telegrams Sent. On Aug. 4, Buell telegraphed
to Halleck that the 35th Ind. was in the command of Maj. Gen. William
Nelson near McMinnville, Tenn.—*O.R.*, I, xvi, part 2, 258.

1862, AUG. 4.   USG endorsement. "Approved and respectfully forwarded to Head Quarters of the Department."—AES, Parsons Papers,
IHi. Written on a letter of Aug. 3 from Medical Director Charles
McDougall to Maj. John A. Rawlins requesting the purchase of the
wharfboat *Nashville* at Evansville, Ind., for use at Columbus, Ky., as a
hospital boat for the District of West Tenn.—ALS, *ibid.* The letter

was eventually forwarded to Maj. Gen. Henry W. Halleck, who approved the purchase on Aug. 20.—AES, *ibid.*

1862, AUG. 4.   Brig. Gen. James B. McPherson to USG. "I have the honor to acknowledge the receipt of Telegram from Major Genl. McClernand to yourself and referred to me. I reply I can state that Genl. McClernand is mistaken when he says Private goods are shipped over the road to the exclusion of Gov't. Freight. Orders were issued at the commencement that Gov't. Freight should take precedence over all private goods, and these orders as near as I can ascertain have been very faithfully adhered to—Whenever Sutlers goods have been shipped over the road, it has been at the Special request of some Officer comdg. Div. or Brigade; and I have two of Genl. McClernand's own letters on file in the Office at Columbus making such request, besides many most from other officers to the same purport—The practice at Columbus is to take a memorandum of all the cars for the Train. The Qr Master comes in and says he wants so many for the commissary, so many for the ordnance and the balance for himself ~~reserving~~ and they are furnished—Reserving one for 'Adams Express Co' and one or two as the case may be for Vegetables in accordance with an arrangement made with Major Genl. Ord, by which the Troops at this Station can be supplied with fresh Vegetables at a fair price—It is not the business of the Freight Agent to run around and see what is to come—We take what is offerred by the Qr. Master and ship it as fast as rolling stock will admit. In some few instances boxes of Private Freight have been placed in cars reserved to carry soldiers, and made to answer the purpose of seats, and occasionally goods marked 'Hospital Stores' come through which upon examination prove to be private goods in one instance nearly a car load upon which the owner was made to pay a *heavy* freight. I am aware that goods in small quantities have been smuggled into the cars and brought through and I have been and am still doing my best to stop it—I have with my assistants labored diligently to promote the interests of the Government in running the road, and shall continue to do so as long as I remain in charge—I did not seek the position, and would most gladly give it up to anyone, who may be appointed to succeed me. But as long as I am in charge of the road I shall run it independently of Generals and Colonels along the line, Considering myself subject to your orders alone—And in future shall pay no attention to communications or complaints written by

Officers who know nothing about the circumstances and who misstate facts or attempt to convey false impressions—"—ALS, DNA, RG 393, District of West Tenn., Letters Received. On Aug. 4, Maj. Gen. John A. McClernand telegraphed to USG. "Genl. Ross telegraphs of this date from Bolivar as follows. 'Our Hospital Stores at Columbus cannot be brought through for want of transportation. I am informed that private property can get through without trouble.' I dislike to annoy you upon this old theme, but can see no remedy unless you take control of the road into your hands."—Copies, McClernand Papers, IHi. On Aug. 1, McClernand had telegraphed to USG reporting a complaint of Brig. Gen. Leonard F. Ross that railroad agents at Columbus, Ky., accepted bribes to give preference to private shipments over military stores. He also alleged that corn and hay were rotting, and asked that USG deal with the matter.—Copies, *ibid.*

1862, AUG. 4. Brig. Gen. William K. Strong to USG. "There is about fifteen (15) Wagon loads of ammunition at Paducah mostly blank cartridges, I understand   The; commander writes me it must be removed at once as it is right right in the middle of the Town Where shall it be sent to Columbus or St Louis?   please reply—"— Telegram received, DNA, RG 393, Dept. of the Mo., Telegrams Received.

1862, AUG. 5. Maj. Gen. Henry W. Halleck to USG. "Col Kahlman's Regt. of Missouri vols., called 2d Reserve corps, will be ordered to St. Louis to report to Genl Schofield."—ALS (telegram sent), DNA, RG 107, Telegrams Collected (Bound); telegram received, *ibid.*, RG 393, Dept. of the Tenn., Telegrams Received. On Aug. 11, Maj. John A. Rawlins issued Special Orders No. 160 ordering Col. Herman Kallman and the 2nd Mo. Reserve Corps to St. Louis.—DS, *ibid.*, RG 94, Special Orders, District of West Tenn.; copies, *ibid.*, RG 393, USG Special Orders; DLC-USG, V, 15, 16, 82, 87. *O.R.*, I, xvii, part 2, 164.

1862, AUG. 5. Col. Edward D. Townsend to USG. "The Genl in Chief directs the Brig Genl Elliott be releived from duty with the Army of the Mississippi and report in Person without delay to Maj Genl Pope in the Army of Verginia ~~Via Janesburg~~ near Fredricksburg"— Telegram received, DNA, RG 393, Dept. of the Tenn., Telegrams

Received; copies, *ibid.*, RG 94, Letters Sent; *ibid.*, RG 107, Telegrams Collected (Bound); *ibid.*, RG 393, USG Hd. Qrs. Correspondence; DLC-USG, V, 4, 5, 7, 8, 9, 88. On Aug. 11, Maj. John A. Rawlins issued Special Orders No. 160 relieving Brig. Gen. Washington L. Elliott from duty with the Army of the Miss., and ordering him to report to Maj. Gen. John Pope of the Army of Va.—DS, RG 94, Special Orders, District of West Tenn.; copies, *ibid.*, RG 393, USG Special Orders; DLC-USG, V, 15, 16, 82, 87. *O.R.*, I, xvii, part 2, 163.

1862, Aug. 5.   Medical Director Charles McDougall to USG. "Respectfully referred to Head Quarters Dist of West Tenne. The Order of Genl Ord is not warranted by the Regulations."—AES, DNA, RG 393, District of West Tenn., Letters Received. Written on a letter of Aug. 3 from Surgeon Archibald B. Campbell, General Hospital, Corinth, to McDougall asking whether the order of Maj. Gen. Edward O. C. Ord to turn over the effects of a dead soldier to his brother would relieve Campbell of responsibility.—ALS, *ibid.*

1862, Aug. 5.   Capt. James A. Ekin, Indianapolis, to USG. "Requisition is made by Col Spiely for clothing for twenty fourth 24th Regt. Indiana Vols now at Helena Ark—Shall they be supplied"—Telegram received, DNA, RG 393, Dept. of the Mo., Telegrams Received. Col. William T. Spicely then commanded the 24th Ind.

1862, Aug. [6?].   USG endorsement. "Respectfully forwarded to Hon. Richard Yates, Governor of Illinois."—AES, Records of 52nd Ill., I-ar. Written on a letter of Aug. 5 from Maj. Edwin A. Bowen, 52nd Ill., to 1st Lt. Edward Brainard pointing out that commissions granted to a number of officers and men after the battle of Shiloh and approved by the state of Ill. had not been received.—ALS, *ibid.*

1862, Aug. 6.   Maj. Gen. John A. McClernand to USG. "You Know how long I have been trying to arm our cavalry. Can you advise me where revolvers & carbines may be got"—Telegram received, DNA, RG 393, Dept. of the Mo., Telegrams Received; copies, McClernand Papers, IHi.

1862, Aug. 6.   Brig. Gen. Charles S. Hamilton to [USG]. "Applies for leave of absence for twenty days on important business."—DLC-

USG, V, 10; DNA, RG 393, USG Register of Letters Received. On
Aug. 6, Maj. John A. Rawlins issued Special Orders No. 155. "In
pursuance of Special Authority from the Secretary of War, leave of
absence, for twenty days is granted Brig. Gen. C. S. Hamilton,
Commdg. 3rd Division, Army of the Mississippi."—DS, DNA, RG 94,
Special Orders, District of West Tenn.; copies, *ibid.*, RG 393, USG
Special Orders; DLC-USG, V, 15, 16, 82, 87.

1862, AUG. 7. USG endorsement. "Refered to Col. Bissell for his
report which will be made through Gen. McPherson and this paper
returned."—AES, DNA, RG 393, District of West Tenn., Letters
Received. Written on an undated document signed by Col. Isham N.
Haynie, 48th Ill.; Col. John E. Smith, 45th Ill.; and Maj. Frederick A.
Bartleson, 20th Ill.; members of a commission ordered to investigate
the destruction by U.S. troops of property owned by J. D. Beadle and
his relatives, situated near a railroad trestle which C. S. A. troops
burned on July 28. The property had been burned after the owners
allegedly assisted the rebels in reaching the trestle. The commission
concluded that there had been insufficient evidence to warrant this
action. "We as officers of the United States Volunteer Army feel compelled to raise our voices   Such a course we regard as derogatory to
civilized Warfare & cruel in the extreme, and respectfully submit that
the tolerance of such conduct will while it can answer no good and
needlessly exasperate entire communities, against a rightious cause,
and array against us enemies where otherwise we should find friends"
—DS, *ibid*. On Aug. 4, Maj. Gen. John A. McClernand endorsed this
report to USG. "Respectfully refer.d to Maj. Genl. U. S. Grant for
~~the~~ his consideration and action. ~~on the case stated~~.   If Col Bissell
ever invades my district again and usurps authority which belongs to
me and not to him, he will be made to answer in a very exemplary way
for it."—AES, *ibid*. On Aug. 8, Col. Josiah W. Bissell, Bissell's Mo.
Engineers, wrote to USG defending the action of his unit in destroying
the property and blaming Capt. Stewart R. Trisilian, adjt. to Brig.
Gen. John A. Logan, whom Bissell thought was on the staff of McClernand.—ALS, *ibid*. On Aug. 10, Brig. Gen. James B. McPherson forwarded the letter to USG.—AES, *ibid*. See also W. A. Neal, *An
Illustrated History of the Missouri Engineer and the 25th Infantry Regiments* . . . (Chicago, 1889), pp. 64–66.

1862, Aug. 7. Maj. Gen. John A. McClernand to USG. "Enclosed please find statement of Col. Brayman 29th Ills. Infty. I wish you would refer the same to the Secretary of War for his decision & would be pleased if you would call his attention to the point that I make in the matter."—Copies, McClernand Papers, IHi.

1862, Aug. 8. USG endorsement. "I am clearly of opinion that this Chaplain should have found out much earlyer that he was not entitled to pay from Government . . ."—Paul C. Richards, Autographs, Catalogue No. 8 [1963]. Written on a letter of Aug. 8 from Chaplain Charles Caines, 1st Battalion, Yates Sharpshooters, who had served for nine months. Upon applying for his pay, Caines learned that a unit of this sort was not entitled to a chaplain. Caines wanted to know whether he was entitled to pay.—*Ibid.*

1862, Aug. 8. To Brig. Gen. William S. Rosecrans. "The permission you asked to send escort with the remains of Maj Matteson is granted I take it you do not want to send them out the Military district"—Telegram, copy, DNA, RG 393, Army of the Miss., Telegrams Received. On Aug. 8, Rosecrans telegraphed to USG. "Maj Mattison of the Yates Sharp Shooters, a young gallant and promising officer died of Typhoid fever in Camp to day. His friends are with his remains, and desires to go home by the morning train to Columbus Will you permit me to send with them Capt A H Payne of that command and four men"—Copy, *ibid.*, Telegrams Sent. Maj. Frederick W. Matteson of Springfield, Ill., son of former governor Joel A. Matteson, had commanded Yates Sharpshooters.—*Ill. AG Report*, IV, 315, 345; *O.R.*, I, xvii, part 2, 147; *Chicago Tribune*, Aug. 12, 1862.

1862, Aug. 8. Brig. Gen. William S. Rosecrans to USG. "I propose going on the line to Tuscumbia Start Seven 7 A.M. Will you go along"—Telegram received, DNA, RG 393, Dept. of the Mo., Telegrams Received; copy, *ibid.*, Army of the Miss., Telegrams Sent. On Aug. 8, Brig. Gen. James B. McPherson telegraphed to Rosecrans. "The train will leave here for Tuscumbia at seven A.M. and can be arranged so that you can return same day. Genl Grant thinks of going with you; be on hand, also I will try and accompany you"—Copy, *ibid.*, Telegrams Received.

1862, AUG. 8.   Brig. Gen. William S. Rosecrans to USG. "At present stationed as follows will be relieved in a day or two one Company at Eastport, three at Bear Creek, two at Buzzards Roost, two at Cherokee, & two at Cane Creek"—Telegram, copy, DNA, RG 393, Army of the Miss., Telegrams Sent.

1862, AUG. 8.   Brig. Gen. Stephen G. Burbridge, Georgetown, Ky., to USG. "I am ordered by the War Dept. to report to you for duty. Have been with Genl Buells Corps previous to my promotion in command of the twenty Sixth (26th) Regt Kentucky Vols."—Telegram received, DNA, RG 393, Dept. of the Mo., Telegrams Received. On Aug. 22, Burbridge, Louisville, telegraphed to USG. "Am advised that orders have been issued for me to report to Maj Gen Wright— My services being needed here I can await the result"—Telegram received, *ibid.* See telegram to Maj. Gen. Horatio G. Wright, Sept. 4, 1862. On Aug. 31, Maj. Nathaniel H. McLean ordered Burbridge to report by telegraph to Wright.—*O.R.*, I, xvi, part 2, 467. On Sept. 1, Burbridge, Louisville, telegraphed to USG. "Send orders here to report to Gen Wright"—Telegram received, DNA, RG 393, Dept. of the Mo., Telegrams Received.

1862, AUG. 9.   USG endorsement. "Respectfully forwarded to Head Quarters of the Army at Washington, and recommended"—ES, DNA, RG 94, Letters Received. Written on a letter of July 25 from Brig. Gen. Stephen A. Hurlbut to Maj. John A. Rawlins requesting a leave of absence.—ALS, *ibid.*

1862, AUG. 9.   USG endorsement. "Respectfully forwarded to Head Quarters of the Depart."—AES, DNA, RG 109, Union Provost Marshals' File of Papers Relating to Individual Civilians. Written on a letter of Aug. 6 from Brig. Gen. Isaac F. Quinby to Maj. John A. Rawlins enclosing a report of a claim by Jonathan Parks of Columbus, Ky., for property allegedly belonging to Parks which was seized by U.S. troops upon their occupation of Columbus.—LS and enclosed documents, *ibid.*

1862, AUG. 9.   To Brig. Gen. William S. Rosecrans. "There is no objections to firing the salute"—Telegram, copy, DNA, RG 393, Army of the Miss., Telegrams Received. On Aug. 9, Rosecrans had telegraphed to USG. "The Commander of Tottens battery applies for authority to fire a Salute tomorrow the anniversary of Battle of Wilsons Creek in which this battery was conspicuous. Is there any objection to this"—Telegram received, *ibid.*, Dept. of the Mo., Telegrams Received.

1862, AUG. 9. Brig. Gen. Lorenzo Thomas to commanding gen., Dept. of the Miss. Thomas ordered that all q.m.'s in excess of lawful numbers and all adjts. of vol. cav. battalions be mustered out of the service.—Telegram received, DNA, RG 393, Dept. of the Mo., Telegrams Received. *O.R.*, III, ii, 336. On Aug. 11, Maj. Thomas M. Vincent telegraphed to USG ordering all regt. bands mustered out and authorizing the establishment of brigade bands.—Copies, DLC-USG, V, 7; DNA, RG 393, USG Hd. Qrs. Correspondence. Dated Aug. 9 in *O.R.*, III, ii, 336. On Aug. 12, Maj. John A. Rawlins issued General Orders No. 73 directing corps commanders to implement the orders received from Thomas and Vincent.—Copies, DLC-USG, V, 13, 14, 95; (printed) DNA, RG 393, USG General Orders.

1862, AUG. 9. Maj. Gen. Henry W. Halleck to USG. "You will cause the conduct of Capt Silforrsparre, 1st Ill Light Artillery, as represented by Lieut Col Adams to your chief of Artillery on the 6th of June to be immediately investigated & the facts reported to these Head Qrs."—ALS (telegram sent), DNA, RG 107, Telegrams Collected (Bound); copies, *ibid.*, RG 393, USG Hd. Qrs. Correspondence; DLC-USG, V, 4, 5, 7, 8, 88. On Aug. 12, Col. Joseph D. Webster wrote to USG that Capt. Axel Silfversparre, Co. H, 1st Ill. Light Art., had been tried by court-martial and acquitted. Webster expressed surprise at the verdict and said he thought Silfversparre unfit for command. —ALS, DNA, RG 94, Generals' Papers and Books, Letters Received by Gen. Halleck. Silfversparre resigned on Feb. 22, 1863.

1862, AUG. 9. Brig. Gen. William S. Rosecrans to Maj. John A. Rawlins. "Say to the Genl Comdg that some men have been sentenced to long periods of hard Labor with ball & chain attached to their Legs for Misterious Conduct I wish instructions as to Garrison or post to which they should be sent for the proper execution of their sentence" —Telegram received, DNA, RG 393, Dept. of the Mo., Telegrams Received; copy, *ibid.*, Army of the Miss., Telegrams Sent.

1862, AUG. 9.   Col. Thomas E. G. Ransom, Cairo, to USG. "In per-
suance of your order we have removed five (5) Barges of Hay from
Smithland & am now loading what remains. Col. J. B. Fry & T. Sword
of Louisville telegraph that the stores at Smithland were intended for
Genl Buels forces & desire that they should not be disturbed. The hay
recd. here has already been sent down the river. I shall remove the
ballance at Smithland"—Telegram received, DNA, RG 393, Dept. of
the Mo., Telegrams Received.

1862, AUG. 10.   USG endorsement. "Respectfully forwarded to Head
Quarters of the Army."—AES, DNA, RG 94, Letters Received. Writ-
ten on a letter of Aug. 8 from Brig. Gen. John A. Logan to Maj.
John A. Rawlins requesting a leave of absence.—ALS, *ibid.*

1862, AUG. 10.   Maj. Gen. John A. McClernand to USG. "Col Smith
after the battle of Shiloh promoted certain Lieutenants to fill vacancies
caused by the battle   The Officer promoted entered upon duty & have
continued in its performance, the Gov't has issued commissions to them
of subsequent date giving them rank from the date of their promotion
Are they not entitled to pay from the date of their promotions   Please
answer"—Telegram received, DNA, RG 393, Dept. of the Mo.,
Telegrams Received; copies, McClernand Papers, IHi. On the same
day, McClernand telegraphed to USG asking whether AGO General
Orders No. 66, Aug. 26, 1861, did not cover the case.—Telegram
received, DNA, RG 393, Dept. of the Mo., Telegrams Received; copy,
McClernand Papers, IHi. AGO General Orders No. 66 provided that
commissioned officers of all vol. organizations were to be mustered
into the service and they were to take rank and receive pay from that
date.

1862, AUG. 10.   Maj. Gen. John A. McClernand to USG. "Having
advised you by telegraph of the activity of the rebels, in Fayette
County: of their purpose to organize a rebel force there and of the
indications of their success, I write now to suggest and urge the occupation, by federal troops, of some point between Bolivar and Memphis
for the purpose of overawing them and encouraging men who are loyal
to the Government. My preference, as previously expressed would be
the occupation of an advanced line running from Cold Water on the
west, to Rienzi on the east—a position near Holly Springs and Ripley
being on the line. But as, for reasons already explained by you, that line

may not soon, if at all be occupied, I would suggest and urge the occupation of a point in the rear of it, between Memphis & Bolivar. Probably the lofty hill immediately north of Somerville and the Loosahatchie river should be the point. It commands not only the town but the country for some distance south and west, and If I am correctly informed could be held by a small force against a large one   Two brigades of Infantry a battery of Artillery and battalion of Cavalry supported by the forces at Bolivar & Memphis would be able to repress disloyalty in the vicinity and prevent the enemy from passing north either to the Mississippi to the Hatchie or to the Miss Central or the Mobile and Ohio rail roads. They would relieve in part the consequences of the evacuation of Grand Junction, Lagrange and Moscow. If it be objected that the detachment of Infantry, Artillery and Cavalry could only be taken from our forces at or before Corinth, and could not be spared, I would answer, that in the event of an attack upon that place being threatened, reinforcements could be quickly sent from Bethel, here and Bolivar"—LS, DNA, RG 393, District of West Tenn., Letters Received.

1862, AUG. 11.   To Brig. Gen. Lorenzo Thomas. "Brig Genl J. B. Plummer died very suddenly in the Evening of the ninth at this place   disease congestion of the Brain."—Telegram received, DNA, RG 94, Letters Received; *ibid.*, RG 107, Telegrams Received (Bound, Press). On Aug. 9, Brig. Gen. Washington L. Elliott telegraphed to USG. "Genl J B Plummer U.S.V. arrived in this camp to day, from leave of absence, and died at 5 o.Clock P.M. of Congestive Chill   Genl Rosecrans absent at Tuscumbia"—Copy, *ibid.*, RG 393, Army of the Miss., Telegrams Sent. On Aug. 10, Brig. Gen. William S. Rosecrans telegraphed to USG. "Telegram ab announcing Genl Plummer death reached me at Iuka and I returned last evening. He came up from Hamburg yesterday & died of congestion of the brain at 5 PM   it being impossible to procure ice or a metalic coffin we shall inter it. The funeral will take place in the field south of Oglesbys camp at six (6) P M today"—Telegram received, *ibid.*, RG 94, Generals' Papers and Books, Joseph B. Plummer; copy, *ibid.*, RG 393, Army of the Miss., Telegrams Sent. On Aug. 10, Rosecrans telegraphed to USG. "A Salute is about to be fired over the grave of Genl Plummer."—Telegram received, *ibid.*, RG 94, Generals' Papers and Books, Joseph B. Plummer; copy, *ibid.*, RG 393, Army of the Miss., Telegrams Sent.

1862, AUG. 11.   Brig. Gen. William S. Rosecrans to USG. "I have the pleasure to inform you that an Expadition under Lt Col Miles captured Col Richard Mann, his Son Overseer and (7) Bales of Cotton & Several Horses and Mules—twelve (12) miles south of Iuka"— Telegram received, DNA, RG 393, Dept. of the Mo., Telegrams Received; copy, *ibid.*, Army of the Miss., Telegrams Sent.

1862, AUG. 11.   Ordnance sgt., Hamburg, Tenn., to USG reporting weapons and ammunition on hand.—Telegram received, DNA, RG 393, Dept. of the Mo., Telegrams Received.

1862, AUG. 12.   To Brig. Gen. William S. Rosecrans. "I wish you would come up here this morning   I want to see you on business of importance and can not go to your Camp"—Telegram, copy, DNA, RG 393, Army of the Miss., Telegrams Received.

1862, AUG. 12.   Maj. Gen. John A. McClernand to USG. "Your telegram of the 12th inst is recd. I hasten to correct the misapprehension it implies. Col Lawler's Brigade was sent from here to Bolivar persuant to your order to send most of the troops from here, there, to meet a threatoned attack. Before he swept the line of the Hatchie and took a position on that river, I had advised you of the reasons and purpose of the movement, and after he had executed it, I reported the fact by telegram from Bolivar, and afterwards, personally, in my interview with you at Corinth. For reasons deemed by me sufficient, I had before the receipt of your telegram ordered Col Dennis with the 20th and 30th Ill. to relieve Col Lawlers brigade by establishing a camp at or near Estenaula on the Hatchie. Col Dennis starts this evening for that purpose and will, at least for the present, continue the out-post there, unless you otherwise order. The forces forming this out-post are instructed to prevent the enemy from crossing or approaching to the Hatchie river between Bolivar and Brownsville, and ought to be able, particularly, if seconded by Cavalry, to cover the whole line of rail road from Bolivar to Humbolt from attack by any force having to cross the Hatchie between Bolivar and Brownsville. I should add, that in establishing this Out-post, I had in view the importance of securing speedy and certain communication between the officer commanding it, and the officer in command at Bolivar, and therefore directed it to be established at Estinaula, some twelve miles from Toon's Station, which is some eight miles, by rail from Bolivar. Moreover, looking to the importance of making occasional reconnoisances south of the river quite to Bolivar, I ordered Col Dennis to construct a foot way across the river capable of being easily and quickly distroyed. It is proper to state that the scission of the road within ten miles North and South of this place, by rebel Cavalry, was not owing to your order to send troops to Bolivar or my execution of that order, but, if avoidable at all, to the inadvertance of the Post commander to reinforce the guard at Meden Station, South, agreeably to my instruction, and to be warned by the attempt of Guerrillas, (probably,) the day before, at another place, North. At this point your second telegram of this date, (just received,) claims my attention. In communicating information concerning the reported advance of the enemy in the direction of Bolivar it was not my purpose to constrain your judgement ~~and~~ or action, but simply to do what you had required and duty dictates. Whether reinforced or not, I will hold Bolivar to the last, and beat the enemy if possible, if he attacks it.— Your telegrams seem to imply an improper withdrawal of forces from Jackson. How stands the case? You ordered all the forces here to Bolivar except one regiment. The next day, (perhaps,) you telegraphed me to leave or send back more. I had anticipated your last order by leaving four regiments here; besides which, Genl Logan kept back four companies of Col Lawler's brigade, which I had ordered to Bolivar. Since that time the 63d Ill. a stronger regiment has replaced the 11th Ill. which has gone to Cairo, and in addition, the 7th Mo has arrived. And when Col Lawler's four regiments have been relieved by Col Dennis' two, two more will be added making in all (7) seven regiments, which are here, exclusive of one ordered by Genl. Logan from Bethel while I was at Bolivar, which I have ordered back as being more needed there than here. With these regiments, and the two at Bethel, the local commander here ought to preserve the rail road under his jurisdiction from being seriously injured by local guerrillas; and with the out-post at Estinaula and the force at Bolivar ought to feel secure against any formidable attack from abroad. I infer that the medical officers to whom you refer in your first telegram of this date have complained. They have no cause for it. Before they had seen me they had ordered the Division Hospital and had required an Infantry Camp and the Female Seminary here to be vacated for their accommodation. After this had been done a Dr Strawbridge came to me to report, not what he wanted but what he had already required. He has so far as I know obtained every assistance asked. If it had been left to me, however, he should not have taken the Female Seminary which contains a library, labratory, and various valuable musical instruments, and which it had been the published purpose to reopen next month. Other large and commodious houses might have been obtained. Under the circumstances the diversion of the use of the building is gratuitous and impolitic. In conclusion, with all respect, I beg to say that I have neither done nor omitted anything which subsequent reflection condemns. If I have, I am ready, as ought to be held, to answer for it."— LS, DNA, RG 393, District of West Tenn., Letters Received.

1862, AUG. 12.   Maj. Gen. John A. McClernand to USG. "The small Cavalry Expadition from Bolivar under Capt Funk 11th Ills Cavalry of which I advised you yesterday has evidintly been most ~~been~~ successfully~~ Capt F. attacked a guerrilla party at Salsburg five ~~miles~~ or six miles east of Grand Junction. Captured the Rebels ~~with~~ ~~their~~ ~~equipments.~~ ~~The Boat above Bolivar~~ Captain and forty seven (47) Horses & Mules with their Equipments. The boat above Bolivar at Simons is distroyed. The one nearest Bolivar brought there. I am sending the 20th & 30th Ills to releive Genl Lawlers Brigade on the Hatchee. Move at large by train this Evening"—Telegram received, DNA, RG 393, Dept. of the Mo., Telegrams Received; copies, McClernand Papers, IHi.

1862, AUG. 12.   Capt. Levi W. Vaughn, provost marshal, Hamburg, Tenn., to USG. "I have many calls from the destitute families of this county who have called on me for Subsistance—What shall be done for them"—Telegram received, DNA, RG 393, Dept. of the Mo., Telegrams Received.

1862, AUG. 13.   To Flag Officer Charles H. Davis. "Respectfully refered to Flag Officer Davis U. S. N. off Memphis Ten."—AES, DNA, RG 45, Area 5. Written on a letter of May 16 from Daniel W. Lewis and others on detached service on the gunboat *St. Louis* to Col. John L. Riker, 62nd N. Y., requesting permission to return to their regiment.—ALS, *ibid.* Riker had been killed at Fair Oaks, Va., and Col. David J. Nevin then commanded the 62nd N. Y. The letter was sent to USG on Aug. 1 by Maj. Thomas M. Vincent with the request that he refer it "to the proper Naval Officers, for their action—"— AES, *ibid.*

1862, AUG. 13. Maj. Nathaniel H. McLean to USG. "Respectf. returned to Maj. Genl. Grant, Comdg. Dist. West Tenn., who is referred to remarks hereon of Act. Adjt Genl of Mo."—Copy, DNA, RG 393, Dept. of the West, Endorsements Sent. Written on a letter from Col. Chester Harding, 25th Mo., in regard to the mustering out of 1st Lt. James G. Allen, 18th Mo.—*Ibid.*

1862, AUG. 13. A. W. O'Neil, military telegrapher, to USG. "9 men who were detailed as repairers of Telegraph, have been releaved with orders to report to their regiments for duty. They say they cannot reach the regiments without money. Will you please send some one to muster them in."—Telegram received, DNA, RG 393, Dept. of the Mo., Telegrams Received.

1862, AUG. 14. To Brig. Gen. William S. Rosecrans. "All cotton seized by our troops have shipped to Corinth to Capt Reynolds Chief Q. M. to be sold by him when it is the property of local persons, They may sell it as they please The QM. at Tuscumbia Capt Howland reports that he can get one thousand bales"—Telegram, copy, DNA, RG 393, Army of the Miss., Telegrams Received.

1862, AUG. 14. 1st Master Jason Goudy, Hamburg, Tenn., gunboat *Alfred Robb*, to USG. "There are two (2) old fashioned guns six Inches on board the Transport Hamilton now ~~aground~~ lying aground at Beach Island & the Guerrillas have Examined them & threaten to make a battery on the bank Will I have them spiked or fetched away" —Telegram received, DNA, RG 393, Dept. of the Mo., Telegrams Received.

1862, AUG. 15. To Brig. Gen. Lorenzo Thomas. "Who pays additional regimental surgeons appointed by Governors under authority from the Secy of War of the thirtieth of April."—Telegram received, DNA, RG 94, Vol. Service Branch, Letters Received; copies, *ibid.*, RG 393, USG Hd. Qrs. Correspondence; *ibid.*, RG 107, Telegrams Received; DLC-USG, V, 4, 5, 7, 8, 88.

1862, AUG. 15. Col. John Bryner, 47th Ills., Rienzi, Miss., to [USG?]. "Applies for leave of absence to go to St. Louis to settle his accounts."—DLC-USG, V, 10; DNA, RG 393, USG Register of

Letters Received. On Aug. 18, Maj. John A. Rawlins issued Special
Orders No. 167. "Col. John Bryner, of the 47th Regt. Ills. Vols.,
having tendered his immediate and unconditional [*resignation*] has
leave of absence for twenty days for the purpose of proceeding to St
Louis to adjust unsettled business of the Regiment with the Ordnance
Officer at that City."—DS, *ibid.*, RG 94, Special Orders, District of
West Tenn.; copies, *ibid.*, RG 393, USG Special Orders; DLC-USG,
V, 15, 16, 82, 87.

1862, Aug. 15.   Col. William W. Lowe to USG. "The Provost
Marshall at Paducah takes fees for administering the oath of allegience
to citizens   proof is abundant"—Telegram received, DNA, RG 393,
Dept. of the Mo., Telegrams Received. On Aug. 24, Brig. Gen. James
M. Tuttle telegraphed to USG. "Adjt Hoislett Provost Marshall at
Paducah as reported here under arrest for charging fee for taking
oath   he charged 25 cts for those he visited in county & has duly
reported the money in his final report   says he was not aware of
orders against it. I am satisfied he did not intend to do wrong. has
been good officer   is Cavalry battallion Adjt & will be mustered out
as soon as released on Gen Order 71. What shall I do with him. No
new reg'ts here yet."—Telegram received, *ibid.*

1862, Aug. 15.   Surgeon Charles H. Rawson, act. medical director,
Dept. of the Miss., to USG. "I have the honor to state that Dr.
Warriner & myself having called upon you yesterday to see if Five
Hundred Dollars could not be advanced by the Commissary to pur-
chase vegetables to supply both General and Regimental Hospitals
You informed us of the following—viz—That according to army
Regulations the Commissary could not furnish the money from the
Hospl Fund but General Ord had a Post-Fund in his hands that might
be used for that purpose. As directed I applied to Genl. Ord & found
him absent and Genl Cadwalder in command   I applied to him this
PM & he replied it might possibly be so used but a Board of Administration would have to determine how it should be appropriated &c   I
presume he is correct but Dr. Warriner must return by the mornings
train to Columbus Ky. I beleive the project feasable & a good one &
will be faithfully executed by the Sanitary Commission & confer vast
benefit on the sick without any more risk of loosing the money than
anything else belonging to Government. If you sufficiently compre-

hended our wishes & explanation last eve to be willing to give the
money into the hands of the Sanitary Commission to be expended for
that purpose I would be pleased if you would give an order to Genl
Cadwalder to turn over the $500. of the money to Dr. Warriner and
he will receipt for the same. If you give the order please send it to
me"—ALS, DNA, RG 393, District of West Tenn., Letters Received.
On Aug. 15, Maj. John A. Rawlins issued Special Orders No. 164.
"Major Gen. E. O. C. Ord, Commdg. U.S. Forces, Corinth, Miss.
will direct that his Provost Marshal turn over to D̶r̶. Surg. Charles
H. Rawson, Acting Medical Director, Dept of the Miss., five hundred
dollars to enable him to create a Hospital Fund for this place and
Jackson."—Copies, DLC-USG, V, 15, 16, 82, 87; DNA, RG 393,
USG Special Orders.

1862, AUG. 15.   G. C. Spencer, Engineer Regt. of the West (Bissell's
Mo. Engineers), to USG asking redress of grievances. "let us have
at our head *men* in whom we can confide, and, if necessary, go up with
them to the very cannon's mouth, men who will not raise a revolver
to our heads and shoot us down like dogs for the most trivial affair,
nor bruise us with clubs whenever they feel inclined. All we ask is
Justice, and, in God's name, let us have it."—Joseph Rubinfine, Autographs, List 24 [1972]. On Aug. 18, Maj. John A. Rawlins referred
this letter to Brig. Gen. James B. McPherson.—*Ibid.*

1862, AUG. 16.   USG General Orders No. 74. "All non-residents of
this District, found within the same, who, if at home, would be subject
to draft, will at once be enrolled under the supervision of the local
commanders where they may be found, and in case of a draft being
made by their respective states, an̶d̶ equal proportion will be drawn
from persons thus enrolled. Persons so drawn will at once be assigned
to troops from the States to which they owe military service, and the
Executive thereof notified of such draft. All violations of trade by
Army followers may be punished by confiscation of stock in trade, and
the assignment of the offenders to do military duty as private soldiers."
—Copies, DLC-USG, V, 12, 13, 14, 95; DNA, RG 393, USG General
Orders; *ibid.*, RG 109, Union Provost Marshals' File of Papers Relating to Individual Civilians. *O.R.*, III, ii, 399. On Aug. 31, Brig. Gen.
James B. McPherson telegraphed to USG. "Will you please send me
a line exempting from draft Mr Thos Richardson one of my principal

Employees   he was enrolled at Trenton day before yesterday noth-withstanding he had letter from   he was engaged on Rail Road duty   I was coming out to see you this P M but the rain has pre-vented—"—Telegram received, DNA, RG 109, Union Provost Mar-shals' File of Papers Relating to Individual Civilians. On Aug. 31, 1st Lt. Theodore S. Bowers issued Special Orders No. 180. "Thomas E. Richardson a Citizen employed on the U. S. Military Railroad from Corinth, Miss. to Columbus, Ky. is hereby exempt from Draft in the Militia."—DS, *ibid.*, RG 94, Special Orders, District of West Tenn.; copies, *ibid.*, RG 393, USG Special Orders; DLC-USG, 15, 16, 82, 87.

1862, Aug. 16.   USG endorsement. "Approved and respectfully for-warded to Head Quarters of the Army"—ES, DNA, RG 94, Vol. Service Branch, W-720-1862. Written on a letter of Aug. 4 from Wis. AG Augustus Gaylord to Col. Robert C. Murphy, 8th Wis., request-ing the discharge of privates Levi J. Billings and James P. Corbin, appointed 2nd lts. in the 22nd and 23rd Wis. respectively.—LS, *ibid.*

1862, Aug. 16.   Brig. Gen. Stephen A. Hurlbut to [USG]. "Reports having arrested Capt. John M. Marble, Co. E. 46th Ills. Inf. Vols. for deserting his post."—DLC-USG, V, 10; DNA, RG 393, USG Regis-ter of Letters Received.

1862, Aug. 16.   Col. Lewis B. Parsons, St. Louis, to USG. "Relative to having chartered the Steamer 'Emilie' by order of Capt Cannon and she will report at Cairo on Wednesday noon"—Register of Letters, Parsons Papers, IHi.

1862, Aug. 17.   USG endorsement. "Respectfully forwarded to Head Quarters of the Department."—AES, DNA, RG 393, Dept. of the Mo., Letters Received. Written on a letter of Aug. 9 from Brig. Gen. James C. Veatch to Capt. Henry Binmore relating to pay for men of the 4th Mo. who had been prisoners at Benton Barracks, and who were allowed to enlist in the 25th Ind.—ALS, *ibid.* See letter to Brig. Gen. Eleazer A. Paine, Feb. 6, 1862.

1862, Aug. 17.   To Governor Richard Yates of Ill. "Respectfully forwarded to the Governer of the state of Illinois."—AES, Yates Papers, IHi. Written on a petition of Aug. 8 from officers of the 50th

Ill. to Ill. AG Allen C. Fuller requesting the promotion of Sgt. Charles W. Lyman to 2nd lt.—LS, *ibid.*

1862, AUG. 17.   Maj. Gen. William T. Sherman to USG. "I do not undertake to redress all past injuries, and must refer this to Gen'l. Grant. The fund arising from the sale of cotton, I do not understand to be under my control."—Copy, DNA, RG 393, Dept. of the Tenn., 5th Division, Endorsements Sent. Written on a letter of Lemuel Gilbert, Memphis, to Sherman complaining that he had been cheated by his partner and that the board of claims had confiscated his cotton and turned it over to Capt. Henry S. Fitch, q.m.—*Ibid.* On Sept. 5, Sherman's hd. qrs. received the reply.—*Ibid.*

1862, AUG. 17.   Brig. Gen. Leonard F. Ross, Bolivar, Tenn., to USG. "The 15th Regt. Mich Vols moved from here Early yesterday morning & ought now to be within twelve or fifteen miles of Corinth   it would be imposible for a Courier to overtake them & I have no Cavalry that I could send as an Escort."—Telegram received, DNA, RG 393, Dept. of the Mo., Telegrams Received.

1862, AUG. 17.   W. J. Stevens, railroad superintendent, Columbus, Ky., to USG. "Is Genl P. A. Hackleman at or about Corinth   I send tomorrow morning two (2) Cases marked Col Reggin"—Telegram received, DNA, RG 393, Dept. of the Mo., Telegrams Received. On June 24, Brig. Gen. Pleasant A. Hackleman had written to USG. "By a Special Field Order received by me this morning from the 'Head Quarters of the Department of the Mississippi,' I am assigned to duty with the Army under your command, and directed to report for orders in writing to you. I shall be pleased to receive them at your earliest convenience. . . . P.S. I sent a telegram to this effect, have received an answer to it & have reported for duty, but still I deem it proper to forward the above."—ALS, *ibid.*, RG 94, Generals' Papers and Books, Pleasant A. Hackleman.

1862, AUG. 18.   USG endorsement. "Knowing Col. Lawler to be a brave man and one ever ready to serve his country in any danger I endorse the within recommendation."—AES, DNA, RG 94, Letters Received. Written on a letter of Aug. 18 from Maj. Gen. John A. McClernand to President Abraham Lincoln recommending the pro-

motion of Col. Michael K. Lawler to brig. gen.—ALS, *ibid.* Lawler
was promoted on Nov. 29, 1862.

1862, AUG. 18. To Brig. Gen. Lorenzo Thomas. "I have the honor,
to transmit herewith a list of the names of the commissioned officers
detailed on recruiting service from my command to date. Where officers of higher rank than that of Lieutenant have been detailed it was
done because of their inability for active field service."—LS, DNA,
RG 94, Vol. Service Branch, Letters Received. Enclosed is an undated
document signed by Maj. John A. Rawlins containing a list of seventy-
three officers on recruiting details.—DS, *ibid.* On Aug. 17, Maj.
Thomas M. Vincent telegraphed to USG. "The Secy of War desires
at your Earliest convenience a list of Vol Commissioned Officers of
your command on Regl Recruiting Service"—Telegram received, *ibid.*,
RG 393, Dept. of the Tenn., Telegrams Received; copies, *ibid.*, USG
Hd. Qrs. Correspondence; DLC-USG, V, 4, 5, 7, 8, 88.

1862, AUG. 18.   USG endorsement. "Respectfully forwarded to Hd
Qrs. of the Army. I would recommend the acceptance of Capt. Gregory's resignation for the reason that, as he states verbally, he was
appointed at the instance of Gen. Todd to serve on his Staff, and the
Gen. now being out of service the position he was appointed to fill no
longer exists. Further, Capt. Gregory is evidertly in bad health and
could not properly fill a position occupying so much time as that of
Asst. Adj't. Gen."—AES, DNA, RG 94, Letters Received. Written
on a letter of Aug. 17 from Capt. J. Shaw Gregory to Maj. John A.
Rawlins submitting his resignation.—ALS, *ibid.* The resignation was
approved by Secretary of War Edwin M. Stanton, Aug. 23.—AES
(by Asst. Secretary Peter H. Watson), *ibid.* On July 20, Gregory had
been assigned by Special Orders No. 289, Dept. of the Miss., to duty
under USG at Corinth.—Copy, DLC-USG, V, 83.

1862, AUG. 18.   USG endorsement. "Respectfully forwarded to Surgeon General of the Army at Washington D.C."—AES, DNA, RG 94,
Letters Received. Written on a letter of Aug. 15 from Surgeon Charles
McDougall, Columbus, Ky., to Maj. John A. Rawlins asking for the
discharge of certain sick soldiers in the hospital at Memphis.—ALS,
ibid.

1862, AUG. 18.   USG permit. "Mr. J. Milner of Franklin County Alabama is hereby permitted to dispose of his cotton to go North and receive the proceeds in money, or to ship the cotton North for his own account."—ADS, DNA, RG 109, Union Provost Marshals' File of Papers Relating to Individual Civilians.

1862, AUG. 18.   Maj. Nathaniel H. McLean to USG. "Respy. refd. to Maj. Gl. Grant Comdg. Dist W. Tenn. It is not known at these Hd. Qrs. by whose order this Compy. was detached from its Regt., or on what duty it is serving. Genl. Grant will judge of the propriety of the Compy. being relieved & act accordingly."—DNA, RG 393, Dept. of the Miss., Register of Letters Received. Written on a letter of July 30 from Col. Robert A. Cameron, 34th Ind., Helena, Ark., requesting that Co. F, 34th Ind., at New Madrid, Mo., be ordered to join its regt.—*Ibid.*

1862, AUG. 18.   Col. Robert Allen, chief q.m., St. Louis, to USG. "Captain Jenkins regular Quartermaster has been ordered to Memphis."—Copies, DLC-USG, V, 7; DNA, RG 393, USG Hd. Qrs. Correspondence.

1862, AUG. 19.   To Brig. Gen. Lorenzo Thomas. "Gen L. F. Ross wishes to withdraw his resignation."—Telegram received, DNA, RG 94, ACP, Leonard F. Ross; *ibid.*, RG 107, Telegrams Received (Press). On Aug. 6, Brig. Gen. Leonard F. Ross wrote to Maj. Gen. John A. McClernand submitting his resignation for reasons of health and family difficulties.—ALS, *ibid.*, RG 94, Generals' Papers and Books, Leonard F. Ross. On the same day, McClernand forwarded the letter to USG. "I refer you this copy of an original letter from Genl. R. for your private information. Believing that Genl. Rs. feelings have misled him, both as to duty to the public and himself I have declined to approve his resignation and recommended him for leave of abscence."—AES, *ibid.* On Aug. 19, McClernand telegraphed to USG. "Genl L. F. Ross withdraws his resignation"—Telegram received, *ibid.*; copies, McClernand Papers, IHi. See *Calendar,* March 26, 1862.

1862, AUG. 19.   USG endorsement. "Respectfully forwarded to Hd Qrs. of the Dept."—AES, DNA, RG 393, Dept. of the Mo., Letters Received. Written on a letter of July 11 from Surgeon Alexander H.

Hoff to Medical Director Charles McDougall complaining that neither the q.m. nor the hospital in Memphis would take care of the burial of corpses from the hospital steamer *D. A. January.*—ALS, *ibid.* McDougall referred the letter to hd. qrs., Dept. of the Miss.—AES, *ibid.* On July 26, Maj. Nathaniel H. McLean forwarded the letter to USG for an investigation.—AES, *ibid.* On July 27, Maj. John A. Rawlins referred the letter to Maj. Gen. William T. Sherman, Memphis.— ES, *ibid.* Sherman referred the letter to Capt. Henry S. Fitch, asst. q.m.—AES, *ibid.* Fitch wrote to Sherman on Aug. 9 that he had no recollection of the case, but that procedures for handling such problems had been established.—ALS, *ibid.* Sherman returned the letters and endorsements to USG.—AES, *ibid.*

1862, AUG. 19. Capt. Simon M. Preston, St. Louis, to USG. "In obedience to orders received from Adjutant General's Office, you will please see that 'Descriptive lists and accounts of pay and clothing' of the following named Soldiers are made out and transmitted thru' these Hd. Qrs. to the 'Adjutant General of the Army' Washington, D. C. with as little delay as possible."—ALS, DNA, RG 393, Dept. of the Tenn., Miscellaneous Letters Received. Attached to the letter is a document listing men from the 8th, 12th, 14th, 16th, 17th, and 18th Wis.; the 1st Wis. Art.; and the 13th Iowa.

1862, AUG. 19. Brig. Gen. Isaac F. Quinby, Columbus, Ky., to USG. "I have at different times employed Citizens on Secret Service and just now it is more important than ever to do so. if you have at your disposal funds for this service will you direct a small amount to be placed in hands of Quarter Master here subject to my order"—Telegram received, DNA, RG 393, Dept. of the Mo., Telegrams Received. On the same day, Quinby telegraphed again to USG. "Two hundred Dollars will be Sufficient I think"—Telegram received, *ibid.*

1862, AUG. 19. Medical Director John G. F. Holston, Memphis, to USG. "I have the honour to report the medical state of your army in this region good. The hospitals are in fine working order and men are rapidly returned to duty. Deaths are few—If discharges for disability could be hastened or authority granted to send men home *while* their papers are being perfected, much would be gained, as a large percentage of death is in this class. I am fitting up an additional hospital, as

Genrl. Curtis, sends us new accessions almost dayly—"—ALS, DNA, RG 393, District of West Tenn., Letters Received.

1862, AUG. 20. USG endorsement. "Respectfully forwarded to Head Quarters of the Army at Washington D. C."—ES, DNA, RG 94, Vol. Service Branch, Letters Received. Written on the proceedings of a board of officers which recommended the discharge of 1st Lt. Ezra Bennett, 14th Ohio Battery.—DS, *ibid.*

1862, AUG. 20. Col. John C. Kelton to USG. "You will order the 25th Missouri Regiment to St. Louis to report to Genl Schofield to recruit and to dispose of the unexchanged prisoners still with the regiment. A list of those not exchanged will be furnished to Adjt. Genl Thomas. Commissioner now visiting the camps where the prisoners are confined arranging their exchange. This by order of Major Genl Halleck."—ALS, DNA, RG 108, Letters Sent (Press). On July 18, Col. Chester Harding, Jr., wrote to Maj. Nathaniel H. McLean transmitting a list of soldiers in the 25th Mo. captured at Lexington, Mo., Sept. 20, 1861, and recommending their exchange or discharge.— *O.R.*, II, i, 144. On July 24, 1862, Harding wrote to Maj. John A. Rawlins asserting that by War Dept. Special Orders No. 29, Feb., 1862, "the muster-out was cancelled and the officers and men were required to report to regimental headquarters for duty. Col. Everett Peabody who then commanded the regiment thereupon published his order to the effect that those who failed to report would be treated as deserters. Many of the men came back for no other reason than that they supposed these orders could and would be enforced against them. In a few instances men were taken from home by actual force and compelled to serve. Of both these classes there were those who had been and those who had not been exchanged. The ranks of the regiment were filled by recruiting and every company had more or less new recruits who then enlisted for the first time as well as more or less of the old regiment. At the battle of Shiloh (as was reported among and believed by the men) some of our wounded were recognized by the enemy as having been paroled and were bayoneted on the spot. This report the officers believe to be untrue but it has created uneasiness in the ranks."—*Ibid.*, p. 145. On June 25, Brig. Gen. Lorenzo Thomas wrote to Maj. Gen. Henry W. Halleck stating essentially the same thing.—*Ibid.*, p. 144. On Aug. 30, 1st Lt. Theodore S. Bowers issued

Special Orders No. 179. "The 25th Regt. Mo. Vol. Infy., Col. Chester Harding, Commdg, will proceed without delay to St Louis, Mo. and report to Brig. Gen. Schofield for the purpose of Recruiting and disposing of the unexchanged prisoners still with the Regiment. Two lists of these Prisoners will be made immediately and one copy furnished to Brig. Gen. Schofield upon the arrival of the Regiment at Saint Louis."—DS, DNA, RG 94, Special Orders, District of West Tenn.; copies, *ibid.*, RG 393, USG Special Orders; DLC-USG, V, 15, 16, 82, 87. *O.R.*, II, i, 146. On Sept. 7, Brig. Gen. John A. Logan telegraphed to USG. "At the suggestion of Surgeon here I have permitted the 25th Mo Regt to be ready to leave in the morning for St Louis   having no camp ~~Equipage~~ & Garrison Equipments they are much Exposed & one case small pox having appeared though no indications of more I thought best to allow them to proceed under their orders from you to St Louis & where if any more cases should occur it would not expose the Army to it—"—Telegram received, DNA, RG 393, Dept. of the Mo., Telegrams Received. On Sept. 11, Brig. Gen. Leonard F. Ross telegraphed to USG. "Were the prisoners taken with with Mulligan Lexington ever organized   some of them enlisted in other regts & now belong to this command & have reported here to be sent forward to Benton Barracks   should they be allowed to go—"—Telegram received, *ibid.*

1862, AUG. 20.   Brig. Gen. Isaac F. Quinby to USG. "Above just came by boat   there is some mistake in date of it has been carried by"—Telegram received, DNA, RG 393, Dept. of the Mo., Telegrams Received.

1862, AUG. 20.   Lt. Col. John Olney, 6th Ill. Cav., Paducah, to USG. "Will you appoint Frank B Smith Recruiting Officer Co C 2d Regt Ills Artillery   this Co. needs fifty (50) recruits—"—Telegram received, DNA, RG 393, Dept. of the Mo., Telegrams Received.

1862, AUG. 21.   Maj. Nathaniel H. McLean to hd. qrs. of the army. "Respectfully referred to the Head Quarters of the Army. The letters referred to were forwarded to Hd. Qrs Army, Augt 14, 62."—Copy, DNA, RG 393, Western Dept., Endorsements Sent. On Aug. 15, the office of Governor Edward Salomon of Wis. had written to McLean sending "letter to Genl Grant and his reply." Salomon asked that

papers referred to in the letters be forwarded to Washington, D.C.
—*Ibid.*

1862, AUG. 21. Maj. Gen. John A. McClernand to USG. "Is Capt
D Barry a mustering officer at Corinth"—Telegram received, DNA,
RG 393, Dept. of the Mo., Telegrams Received. On Aug. 16, Maj.
John A. Rawlins issued Special Orders No. 165 appointing Capt.
Beekman Du Barry mustering officer of the District of West Tenn.
—DS, *ibid.*, RG 94, Special Orders, District of West Tenn.; copies,
ibid., RG 393, USG Special Orders; DLC-USG, V, 15, 16, 82, 87;
McClernand Papers, IHi.

1862, AUG. 21. Brig. Gen. James M. Tuttle to USG. "Col. Dougherty 22d Ills Vols his leave expires 28th   He wishes to return to his
reg't & asks to have them at Birds point as he is not able to take the
field on account of his leg   if you can't consistently send his reg't
could you detach him so he can take command of a post in this district"
—Telegram received, DNA, RG 393, Dept. of the Mo., Telegrams
Received. See letter to Cols. Jacob G. Lauman and Henry Dougherty,
Nov. 6, 1861.

1862, AUG. 21. Col. Andrew J. Babcock, 7th Ill., to USG. "I send
for information with regard to the Guard now on duty at your Head
Quarters from this regiment, If the detail is still to be kept on until
tomorrow we would like to send a new detail."—Copy, DNA, RG 94,
7th Ill., Letterbook.

1862, AUG. 22. To Maj. Gen. William T. Sherman. "Within named
soldiers of Genl. Shermans Command are in Hospital at Corinth without Descriptive Rolls   Orders them sent on."—DNA, RG 393, 15th
Army Corps, Register of Letters Received. On Aug. 23, Sherman
endorsed this letter to Maj. John A. Rawlins. "These Regiments
belong to Genl. Hurlbuts Command. He will be instructed to send the
Descriptive Rolls.   but it is respectfully suggested that they be sent
here via Columbus. We have good hospitals"—Copy, *ibid.*, Dept. of
the Tenn., 5th Division, Endorsements Sent.

1862, AUG. 22. USG endorsement. "Respectfully forwarded to Head
Quarters of the Army at Washington, D.C."—ES, DNA, RG 94,

Vol. Service Branch, W-741-1862. Written on a letter of Aug. 7 from
Lt. Col. Lyman M. Ward, 14th Wis., to USG requesting the discharge
of 1st Lt. Chauncey Blakesley, 14th Wis., absent from service since
May 12.—Copy, *ibid.* Blakesley was discharged on Sept. 12, 1862.

1862, AUG. 23. USG Special Orders No. 172. "No Spiritous, Vinous,
or Malt Liquors, or any kind of intoxicating drinks whatever, will be
permitted to pass by Railroad or otherwise from Columbus South,
except for the Commissary or Medical Departments, or by special
written authority of Commanding Officers of Posts, which authority
will only be given for proper Medicinal or Sanitary purposes. In no
case will such authority be given to Sutlers, Traders or Citizens. Railroad employees will see that all shipments of liquors made under the
provisions of this order, are delivered to the parties to whom the are
consigned. Persons convicted of an attempt to evade this order will be
summarily punished.—The enforcement of this order is enjoined upon
all Commanders in this District, and especially upon the Commandant
at Columbus, Ky."—DS, DNA, RG 94, Special Orders, District of
West Tenn.; copies, *ibid.*, 48th Ill., Letterbook; *ibid.*, RG 393, USG
Special Orders; DLC-USG, V, 15, 16, 82, 87.

1862, AUG. 23. Brig. Gen. Grenville M. Dodge, Trenton, Tenn., to
USG. "Have nine hundred (900) shot guns—Five hundred (500)
rifles taken from guerrillas & citizens—"—Telegram received, DNA,
RG 393, Dept. of the Mo., Telegrams Received; copy, *ibid.*, Hd. Qrs.,
Central Division of the Miss., Letters and Telegrams Sent. *O.R.*, I,
xvii, part 2, 184.

1862, AUG. 23. Brig. Gen. Isaac F. Quinby, Columbus, Ky., to USG.
"Twenty-two guerrillas were captured on Monday night and Tuesday
morning 25 miles below here on the Missouri shore. It is the party
that fired into the Champion Sunday night. They were not duly
enlisted in the rebel service, but were on their way to Arkansas, armed
and mounted. I propose, with your sanction, to try them by a military
commission. They are now here. I have a list of prominent men in river
counties in Missouri, some of which are not within my district, who
are engaged in forwarding recruits to rebel army; proofs undoubted.
Shall I arrest all such, even though without my immediate command?"
—*O.R.*, I, xvii, part 2, 184.

1862, AUG. 25.   Medical Director John G. F. Holston to USG. "I have the honour to submitt the draft, of an order for the regulation of issues to hospitels. I also respectfully suggest the necessity of a general order, announcing & defining *my position*—as by your order Brig. surgeon Wardner was authorized to perform *a part* of my functions —till my arrival—which would seem to require an *official* announcement   Also Brig. Surg. Charles H Rawson, having an office in Corinth and acting under the style and title of *Acting* Medical Director, by authority unknown to me— . . . Additional—Another medical Director has just appeared on the stage—I enclose a document from him." —ALS, DNA, RG 94, Medical Officers and Physicians, Personal Papers, Dr. John G. F. Holston.

1862, AUG. 25.   Capt. Charles A. Reynolds, asst. q.m., Corinth, to USG. "It is nessary for me to go to Columbus in the morning. Major Mener Gov Sprauges ajt is very sick & wants me to come without fail.   answer"—Telegram received, DNA, RG 393, Dept. of the Mo., Telegrams Received.

1862, AUG. 25.   E. W. M. King, Memphis, to USG. "Will you be so good at your earliest convenience to transmit to the Provost Marshall of Memphis your action in the case of the U. S. versus Elijah Cheeck on a charge of murdering a man in Ark. I make this request as counsel of Mr. Cheeck. It is important to Cheeck to have this matter finally determined"—ALS, Parsons Papers, IHi. On Oct. 1, Maj. John A. Rawlins endorsed this letter. "Mr. Cheek, in the case referred to, was honorably acquitted. The proceedings of the Court Martial have been forwarded to the proper authorities, Washington D. C." —ES, *ibid.* Elijah Cheek, owner of the steamboats *Mark R. Cheek* and *Aid*, had been accused of the murder of John P. Beeman, but a military commission discharged him after finding no evidence for the charge. A handbill exonerating Cheek and numerous related papers are *ibid.* See also *O.R.*, II, ii, 1552–53.

1862, AUG. 27.   To Brig. Gen. Leonard F. Ross. "Yes"—Telegram, copy, DNA, RG 393, Dept. of the Mo., Telegrams Received. On Aug. 26, Ross telegraphed to USG. "one (1) company of 4th Infantry is here under orders to report to you   shall the two (2) companies a & c of 11th now here proceed directly to Corinth with it"—Telegram received, *ibid*. On Aug. 27, Ross telegraphed to USG asking permission to retain cos. A and C of the 11th Ill. Cav. because of their acquaintance with the area.—Telegram received, *ibid*. On the same day, Ross telegraphed to USG that one co. of the 4th Ill. Cav. would be sent to Corinth.—Telegram received, *ibid*.

1862, Aug. 29. To Maj. Nathaniel H. McLean. "I transmit herewith copy of the Tri-monthly return of the Forces under my command for the first 10 days of August 1862."—Copies, DLC-USG, V, 4, 5, 7, 8, 9, 88; DNA, RG 393, USG Hd. Qrs. Correspondence.

1862, Aug. 29. USG endorsement. "Respectfully refered to Brig. Gen. McPherson"—AES, WHi. Written on a letter of Aug. 23 from George R. Stuntz, sanitary agent for the state of Wis., to USG. "Permit me to call your attention to the condition of the Rail Road between Columbus and Corinth: the method of running it and the general treatment of soldiers on that rout, and to protest in the name of the State of Wisconsin against the future exposure of troops on that road. I left Columbus on Wednesday of last week on my way to Corinth. The train consisted of seven or eight heavily loaded freight Cars and one for Officers not loaded. Upon the tops of these Cars were crowded about one hundred and fifty convalecent soldiers returning to their various Regiments. It was a burning hot day. The thermometre which I carried indicated 90° in the shade and the temperature of the car tops was much greater   These men were kept upon the car tops from 7 A.M. until 11 P.M sixteen hours exposed to the burning heat of the day, greater than can be safely bourn by healthy men and then exhausted, to the damps of a chilly night   A Barrel of ice water kept in the officers Car was furnished by one of the R. R. employees to soldiers at the Moderate sum of five cents pr glass. Those who were lucky enough to have small change could get wholesome water   Others not so fortunate I saw drinking water from under the green covering out of the ditches by the road side   The quality of this water was such that a horse would have to be in a famishing condition to drink of it   This exposure is every day in the week and the amount of travel is of such magnitude and likely to increase that the remidies should be applied at once. The experience of the past four months has demonstrated that there are dangers more terrible than the bullets of rebels They can—will they be remided"—ALS, *ibid*. On Aug. 30, Brig. Gen.

James B. McPherson endorsed the letter to USG. "Respectfully returned to Maj. Genl. Grant. The Evils complained of are being remedied by putting on passenger cars as fast as they can be procured. The bad Effects of riding on top of the cars are very much exaggerated I think. I have been on the road to Columbus and back twice, and both times have ridden a good part of the way on top of the car from choice, because it was cooler than inside though the sun was shining brightly —We have never attempted to furnish ice water to the Soldiers— There has been a cask filled with water & ice put in it when we could get it, and any are allowed to help themselves—I think it must be a mistake about any Employee selling it at 5¢ pr glass, I have been over the Road several times several of my agents have been and I have a 'detective' on the road all the time who I am certain would report any such practice to me—The Evil can be remedied effectually in *one way*, and that is make the Troops *march* from Columbus to Corinth."— AES, *ibid.*

1862, Aug. 30. Maj. Thomas M. Vincent to USG. "I am instructed to acknowledge receipt of an endorsement by you upon a letter of Commanding Officer, 2nd Battalion 1st Regiment Missouri Light Artillery in reference to the supposed desertion of major Cavender and Surgeon Connya, and in reply to inform you that Major Cavender was discharged the service by Special Orders No 207 dated August 26th. from this office. There is nothing known here of the movements of the Surgeon. If you are satisfied that he is improperly absent and thereby a deserter, a stateme[nt] of the case, with your recommendation will secure his dismissal."—Copies, DNA, RG 94, Vol. Service Division, Letters Sent; *ibid.*, RG 393, USG Hd. Qrs. Correspondence; DLC-USG, V, 7.

1862, Aug. 30. Maj. Thomas M. Vincent to USG. "Respectfully returned to Major Gen. Grant, Commanding Dist of West. Tenn, who will please cause Major Bush to be mustered into Service, in accordance with the recommendations herein"—Copies, DNA, RG 94, Special Orders, District of West Tenn.; *ibid.*, RG 393, USG Special Orders; DLC-USG, V, 15, 16, 82, 87. On Sept. 12, Maj. John A. Rawlins issued Special Orders No. 192. "Brig Genl. Quinby, Commdg, Dist of Miss. will at once appoint a suitable Commissioned Officer of his command as Mustering Officer for the purpose of mustering into the service of the United States for Pay, Major Bush, of the 2nd Regt Ills. Cavalry Vols. to date from the time Major Bush entered upon duty with said Regiment as shown by Regimental Rolls."—DS, DNA, RG 94, Special Orders, District of West Tenn.; copies, *ibid.*, RG 393, USG Special Orders; DLC-USG, V, 15, 16, 82, 87. Daniel B. Bush, Jr., was appointed maj. to rank from Sept. 23, 1861.

1862, AUG. 31. Capt. Simon M. Preston to USG. "Respy. returned through Maj. Genl. Grant & attention called to endorsement made at Hd. Qrs. of the Army."—Copy, DNA, RG 393, Western Dept., Endorsements Sent. Written on a letter of Col. Chester Harding regarding the absence of two officers.—*Ibid.* On Aug. 25, Col. John C. Kelton, Washington, D.C., authorized Harding to relieve the officers from recruiting service.—*Ibid.*

1862, AUG. 31. Brig. Gen. John M. Schofield, St. Louis, to USG. "I am requested by Maj McLean to notify you that instructions from Head Qrs of the Army Dept, that all mail for Hd Qrs dept of the Miss will until further orders be sent to had qrs of the army"—Telegram received, DNA, RG 393, Dept. of the Mo., Telegrams Received; copies, *ibid.*, USG Hd. Qrs. Correspondence; DLC-USG, V, 4, 5, 7, 8, 9, 88.

Index

All letters written by USG of which the text was available for use in this volume are indexed under the names of the recipients. The dates of these letters are included in the index as an indication of the existence of text. Abbreviations used in the index are explained on pp. xvi–xx. Individual regts. are indexed under the names of the states in which they originated.